Just Desserts!

Beta Sigma Phi

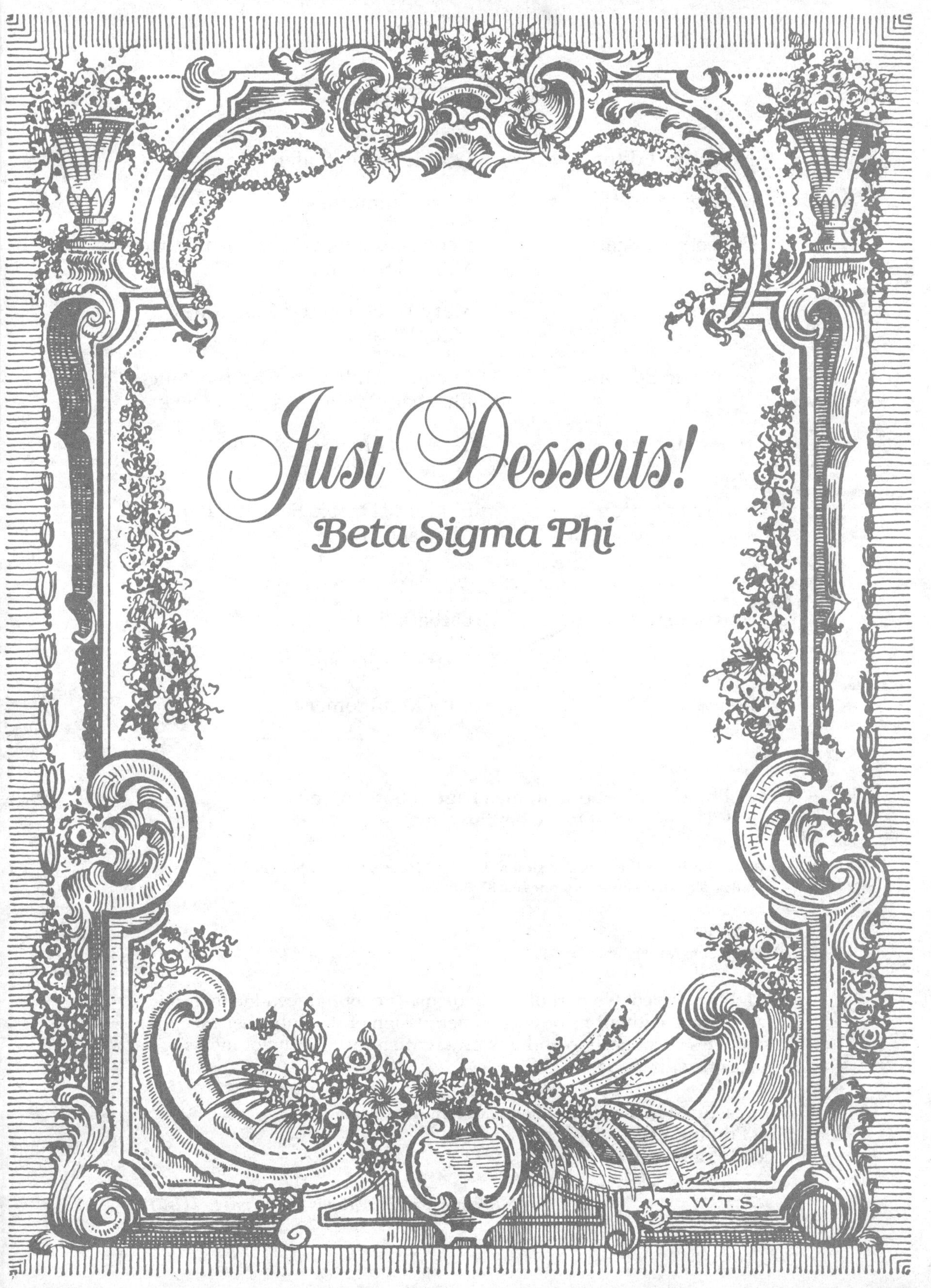

Just Desserts!

Beta Sigma Phi

EDITORIAL STAFF

Executive Editor	Debbie Seigenthaler
Managing Editor	Mary Cummings
Project Managers	Georgia Brazil, Shirley Edmondson Maribel S. Wood
Editors	Mary Jane Blount, Linda Jones Mary Wilson
Associate Editors	Lucinda Anderson, Carolyn King Elizabeth Miller, Judy Van Dyke
Typographers	Sara Anglin, Jessie Anglin Walter Muncaster
Award Selection Judges	Bill Ross, Debbie Seigenthaler Charlene Sproles
Art Director	Steve Newman
Illustrator	Barbara Ball
Test Kitchen	Charlene Sproles
Essayist	Lory Montgomery

Cover Photograph: Borden, Inc.; Page 1: Borden, Inc.;
Page 2: The Haagen-Dazs Company Inc.

P.O. Box 305141, Nashville, Tennessee 37230

ISBN: 0-87197-439-8
Library of Congress Number: 95-70535

Manufactured in the United States of America
First Printing 1995
Second Printing 1995

Recipes for photographs are on pages 212–213.

Contents

Beta Sigma Phi

Linda Rostenberg

Dear Beta Sigma Phi Sisters:

Every year, the staffs of Favorite Recipes® Press and Beta Sigma Phi International rack their brains to come up with a new cookbook concept that's a little bit different from all the others—something that will excite the cooks in our crowd! Well, we hit the Big Casino with this year's concept—thousands and thousands of recipes came piling in, resulting in not just one, but two fabulous cookbooks to enjoy this year.

Hearth to Heart: Hearty, Healthy Recipes for the Family on the Go and **Just Desserts** are just what you (and friends, and family) need. In the **Hearth to Heart** cookbook, you'll find favorite kitchen and family-tested recipes that can be prepared without much fuss. (You'll also see that we're helping you eat a little smarter and healthier, too.) As a special treat, we've got a section of recipes submitted by Beta Sigma Phi husbands and men friends, too.

For those who appreciate some frankly fattening goodies, you'll find wonderful sweet breads, punches, cakes, cookies, pies, tortes and more in **Just Desserts**. (Every Beta Sigma Phi seems to be equipped with a certified sweet tooth.)

And the fun doesn't stop there! We certainly hope you were a winner in our annual cooking contest. As usual, we've awarded prizes in various food categories; these "best-of-the-best" recipes are specially marked by a diamond symbol ✣ in the cookbooks.

Pages and pages of pure eating pleasure-that's what these new Beta Sigma Phi cookbooks are all about! This year and every year, we say thanks to you for making our cookbooks possible. By sharing your family's favorites, you help us create a Beta Sigma Phi heirloom of sorts. Think about that the next time you and your sorority sisters get together to nosh, to nibble . . . to think great thoughts and make dreams come true.

Yours in Beta Sigma Phi,

Linda Rostenberg
Beta Sigma Phi International
Executive Committee

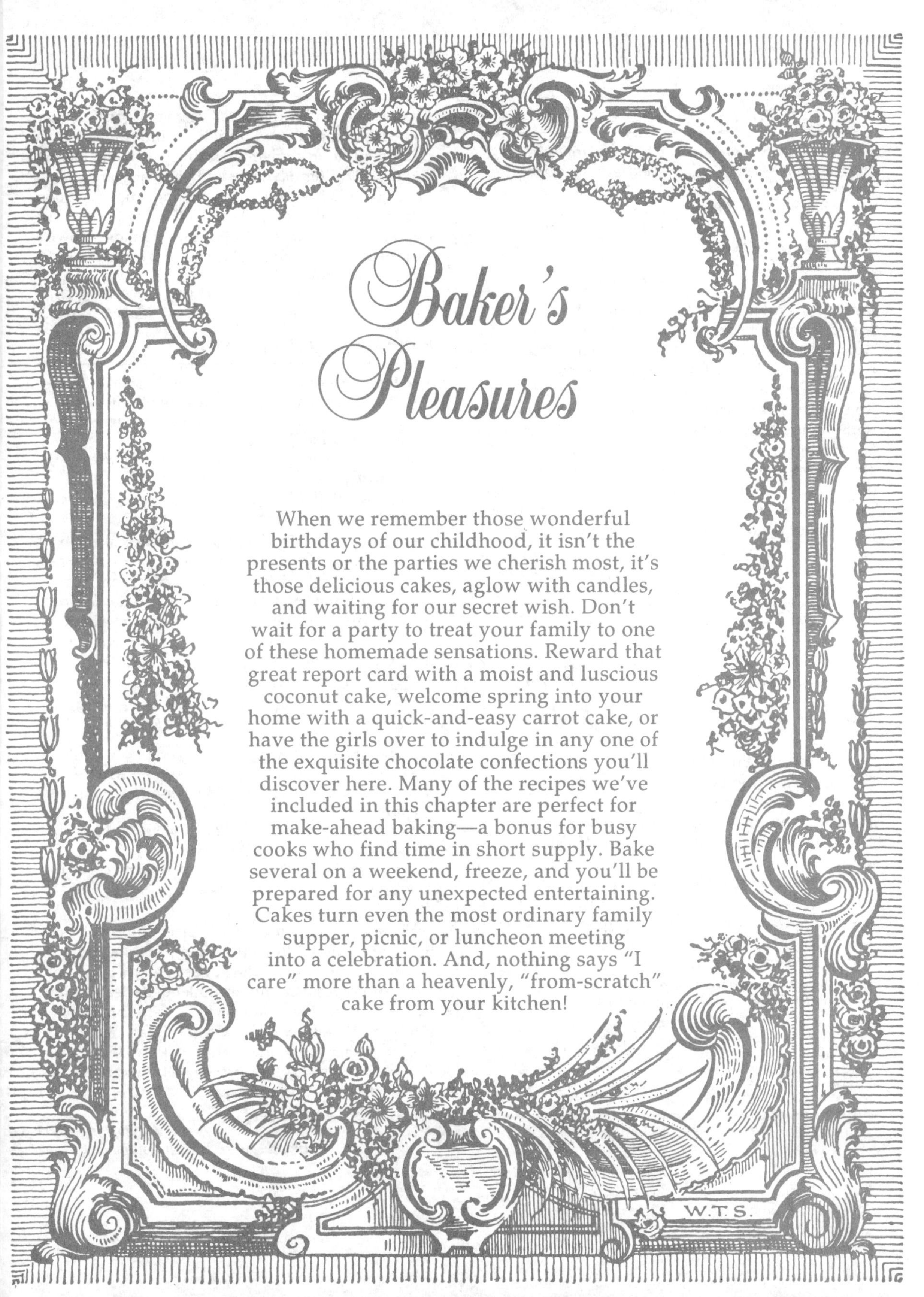

Baker's Pleasures

When we remember those wonderful birthdays of our childhood, it isn't the presents or the parties we cherish most, it's those delicious cakes, aglow with candles, and waiting for our secret wish. Don't wait for a party to treat your family to one of these homemade sensations. Reward that great report card with a moist and luscious coconut cake, welcome spring into your home with a quick-and-easy carrot cake, or have the girls over to indulge in any one of the exquisite chocolate confections you'll discover here. Many of the recipes we've included in this chapter are perfect for make-ahead baking—a bonus for busy cooks who find time in short supply. Bake several on a weekend, freeze, and you'll be prepared for any unexpected entertaining. Cakes turn even the most ordinary family supper, picnic, or luncheon meeting into a celebration. And, nothing says "I care" more than a heavenly, "from-scratch" cake from your kitchen!

ANGEL BERRY ROLL

1 (2-layer) package angel food cake mix
1 1/2 tablespoons baking cocoa
6 to 8 cups strawberry-banana frozen yogurt, softened
1 to 2 envelopes unflavored gelatin
2 to 4 tablespoons strawberry juice
1 (10-ounce) package frozen strawberries, thawed
1 ripe banana

Preheat oven to 350 degrees. Coat a 10-by-15-inch jelly roll pan with nonstick cooking spray; line with waxed paper. Prepare and bake cake in prepared pan using package instructions. Sprinkle cocoa on clean towel; invert cake onto towel. Remove waxed paper. Roll in towel as for jelly roll. Cool. Unroll and spread with yogurt. Reroll cake. Freeze until serving time. Soften gelatin in strawberry juice in bowl. Purée strawberries and banana with gelatin mixture in blender. Chill until serving time. Slice cake. Spoon purée over slices. Garnish with additional strawberries and/or banana slices. Yield: 8 to 10 servings.

Sandra Kellough, Preceptor Alpha Beta
Marrero, Louisiana

ANGEL SURPRISE

1 (16-ounce) can juice-pack fruit cocktail
1 (9-inch) angel food cake
1 teaspoon grated lemon rind
1 envelope unflavored gelatin
1 cup lemon nonfat yogurt
12 ounces low-fat whipped topping

Drain fruit cocktail, reserving 1/2 cup juice. Cut 1-inch slice from top of cake, reserving slice. Remove center of remaining cake with fork, leaving 1-inch shell. Combine reserved juice and lemon rind in saucepan. Sprinkle gelatin over juice. Let stand for 1 minute to soften. Bring to a boil over medium heat. Boil for 3 minutes, stirring constantly. Remove from heat. Cool. Stir in yogurt. Chill until slightly thickened. Mix half the whipped topping and fruit cocktail in medium bowl. Fold into gelatin mixture. Spoon into cake. Cover with reserved cake top. Spread side and top of cake with remaining whipped topping. Chill for 8 hours or longer. Yield: 12 servings.

Fran S. Davis, Laureate Beta Phi
Osage Beach, Missouri

APPLE CAKE

1 1/2 cups margarine, softened
2 cups sugar
3 eggs
3 cups all-purpose flour
1/2 teaspoon each cinnamon, nutmeg and salt
1 teaspoon baking soda
1 teaspoon butter flavoring
1 teaspoon vanilla extract
3 cups diced apples
1 cup chopped pecans
1 cup golden raisins

Preheat oven to 325 degrees. Cream margarine, sugar and eggs in mixer bowl until light and fluffy. Beat in mixture of flour, cinnamon, nutmeg, salt and baking soda. Add butter flavoring and vanilla, beating until blended. Stir in apples, pecans and raisins. Spoon into greased tube pan. Bake at 325 degrees for 1 1/2 hours. Cool in pan for 10 minutes. Remove to wire rack to cool completely. Place on serving plate. Yield: 16 servings.

Linda Wilkins, Xi Delta Delta
Suffolk, Virginia

APPLE COUNTRY CAKE

1 (2-layer) package yellow cake mix
1 egg
1/3 cup margarine
2 (21-ounce) cans apple pie filling
3/4 cup packed light brown sugar
1/2 cup chopped walnuts
2 teaspoons cinnamon
1 cup plain yogurt
1 egg
1 teaspoon vanilla extract

Preheat oven to 350 degrees. Combine cake mix, 1 egg and margarine in medium bowl; mix well. Press into lightly greased 9-by-13-inch cake pan. Spread with pie filling; sprinkle with brown sugar. Sprinkle with mixture of walnuts and cinnamon. Combine yogurt, 1 egg and vanilla in bowl; mix well. Swirl over top. Bake at 350 degrees for 30 minutes. Yield: 8 to 10 servings.

Julie O'Neal, Preceptor Mu Tau
Round Rock, Texas

EASY APPLE CAKE

3 peeled Granny Smith apples, sliced
Sugar to taste
1 cup butter or margarine, softened
1 cup sugar
3 eggs, beaten
1 3/4 cups all-purpose flour
2 teaspoons baking powder
Confectioners' sugar to taste

Preheat oven to 350 degrees. Place apple slices in bowl; sprinkle with a little sugar. Let stand for 15 minutes. Cream butter and sugar in mixer bowl until light. Add eggs, beating until blended. Beat in flour and baking powder; batter will be very thick. Spoon into greased 8-by-8-inch cake pan. Arrange apples close together; press into batter. Bake at 350 degrees for 1 hour or until golden brown. Let stand until cool. Dust with confectioners' sugar. Yield: 12 to 16 servings.

Judy Barton, Xi Psi
North Vancouver, British Columbia, Canada

FRESH APPLE CAKE

2 cups sugar
2 cups all-purpose flour
1 teaspoon salt
1 teaspoon baking soda
1 teaspoon cinnamon
1/2 cup margarine
4 cups chopped peeled apples
1 tablespoon lemon juice (optional)
2 eggs
1 teaspoon vanilla extract

Preheat oven to 350 degrees. Sift sugar, flour, salt, baking soda and cinnamon into bowl; mix well. Cut in margarine until crumbly. Stir in apples. Add lemon juice, mixing well. Beat eggs in mixer bowl until frothy. Add vanilla, mixing well. Add to apple mixture; mix well. Spoon into greased and floured 9-by-13-inch cake pan. Bake at 350 degrees for 45 to 55 minutes or until cake tests done. Let stand until cool. Store uncovered. Yield: 12 to 16 servings.

Dorothy Conway, Xi Chi Nu
San Marcos, California

FRESH APPLE BUNDT CAKE

1 cup vegetable oil
2 cups sugar
3 eggs
2 cups self-rising flour
2 teaspoons cinnamon
1/2 teaspoon nutmeg
1/2 teaspoon salt
1 teaspoon vanilla
1 cup chopped pecans (optional)
1 cup raisins
3 cups chopped peeled apples

Preheat oven to 350 degrees. Combine oil, sugar and eggs in mixer bowl; beat until blended. Combine flour, cinnamon, nutmeg and salt in bowl, mixing thoroughly. Add to sugar mixture; mix well. Add vanilla. Stir in pecans, raisins and apples. Turn into greased and floured bundt pan. Bake at 350 degrees for 1 hour. Cool on wire rack. Yield: 8 to 12 servings.

Pam Medcalf, Xi Theta
New Albany, Indiana

GERMAN APPLE CAKE

2 eggs
2 cups sifted all-purpose flour
2 teaspoons cinnamon
1 teaspoon baking soda
1/2 teaspoon salt
1 cup vegetable oil
1 teaspoon vanilla extract
2 cups sugar
4 cups sliced apples

Preheat oven to 350 degrees. Combine eggs, flour, cinnamon, baking soda, salt, oil, vanilla, sugar and apples in large bowl; mix well. Spread in floured 9-by-13-inch cake pan. Bake at 350 degrees for 45 to 60 minutes or until cake tests done. Cool on wire rack. Yield: 15 servings.

Linda Goeller, Zeta Eta
Roosevelt, Arizona

GLAZED APPLE CAKE

3/4 cup butter or margarine, softened
1 1/2 cups sugar
2 eggs
2 1/4 cups all-purpose flour
1 1/2 teaspoons baking soda
1/2 teaspoon salt
1 teaspoon vanilla extract
3/4 cup strong coffee, cooled
3 cups diced apples
1/2 cup packed light brown sugar
1 teaspoon cinnamon
1/2 cup pecans
1 cup sugar
1/3 cup butter or margarine
1/2 cup whipping cream
2 teaspoons vanilla extract

Preheat oven to 350 degrees. Cream 3/4 cup butter and 1 1/2 cups sugar in mixer bowl until light and fluffy. Add next 6 ingredients, beating well. Batter will be stiff. Fold in apples. Spread in greased 9-by-13-inch cake pan. Sprinkle with mixture of brown sugar, cinnamon and pecans. Bake at 350 degrees for 30 to 40 minutes or until cake tests done. Cool in pan. Turn onto serving plate. Combine 1 cup sugar, 1/3 cup butter and cream in saucepan. Bring to a boil over medium heat, stirring constantly; remove from heat. Stir in 2 teaspoons vanilla. Drizzle over cake. Yield: 24 servings.

Pat Morehart, Xi Alpha Iota
Eyota, Minnesota

LOW-FAT CARAMEL APPLE SPICE CAKE

2 large apples
2 1/2 cups all-purpose flour
1/2 teaspoon baking soda
1/2 teaspoon baking powder
2 teaspoons cinnamon
2 tablespoons butter substitute
1 1/2 cups sugar
1/2 cup egg substitute
1/2 cup fat-free sour cream
3/4 cup evaporated skim milk
1/4 cup caramel ice cream topping
1/4 cup rolled oats
1/3 cup packed light brown sugar
5 to 6 tablespoons caramel ice cream topping

Preheat oven to 350 degrees. Shred apples; set aside. Sift together flour, baking soda, baking powder, cinnamon and butter substitute. Combine sugar, egg substitute, sour cream and evaporated milk in food processor. Process until smooth. Pour over apples; mix well. Add flour mixture to apple mixture; mix well. Spoon into 9-by-12-inch cake pan sprayed with nonstick cooking spray. Drizzle with 1/4 cup topping. Sprinkle mixture of oats and brown sugar over cake batter. Drizzle with remaining ice cream topping. Bake at 350 degrees for 45 to 60 minutes or until cake tests done. Yield: 12 to 16 servings.

Janet Stockebrand, Xi Epsilon Psi
Iola, Kansas

ROCKY APPLE CAKE

3 tablespoons margarine, softened
1 teaspoon vanilla extract
1 cup sugar
1 egg, beaten
1 cup all-purpose flour
1 teaspoon baking soda
1/2 teaspoon salt
1/2 teaspoon cinnamon
1/2 teaspoon nutmeg
3 cups diced peeled apples
1/2 cup chopped pecans
1/2 cup packed light brown sugar
1/2 cup sugar
1/4 cup margarine
1/2 cup whipping cream
Salt to taste
1 teaspoon vanilla extract

Preheat oven to 350 degrees. Cream 3 tablespoons margarine, 1 teaspoon vanilla and 1 cup sugar in mixer bowl until light and fluffy. Add egg; mix well. Sift flour, baking soda, 1/2 teaspoon salt, cinnamon and nutmeg together. Add to creamed mixture; beat until blended. Stir in apples and pecans. Spread in greased 9-by-9-inch square cake pan. Bake at 350 degrees for 1 hour or until cake tests done. Let stand until cool. Combine brown sugar, 1/2 cup sugar, 1/4 cup margarine, cream and salt in saucepan. Bring to a boil over low heat, stirring constantly. Stir in 1 teaspoon vanilla. Drizzle warm sauce over cake slices just before serving. Yield: 9 servings.

Janice Roth, Xi Epsilon Xi
Dodge City, Kansas

APPLE SKILLET CAKE

1 1/2 cups all-purpose flour
1 teaspoon baking soda
1 teaspoon salt
1 cup sugar
1 teaspoon cinnamon
1/2 teaspoon allspice
3/4 cup vegetable oil
1/2 cup buttermilk
1 egg, slightly beaten
2 Granny Smith apples, peeled, sliced
1 teaspoon vanilla extract
1 cup chopped pecans

Preheat oven to 350 degrees. Sift flour, baking soda, salt, sugar, cinnamon and allspice into bowl. Add oil, buttermilk, egg, apples, vanilla and pecans; mix well. Spoon into greased 9- or 10-inch iron skillet. Bake at 350 degrees for 40 to 50 minutes or until cake tests done. Cool in skillet. Yield: 12 servings.

Marjorie Culpepper, Preceptor Mu Sigma
Houston, Texas

Robert (Jean) Holeczy, Exemplar Preceptor, Spring Hill, Kansas, makes Creamy Strawberry Angel Cake by splitting an angel food cake into 3 layers, preparing sugar-free strawberry gelatin with 1 cup boiling water, 1/2 cup cold water, 2 cups sliced strawberries and half of an 8-ounce carton of whipped topping, partially congealing and spreading between layers. Garnish with remaining whipped topping and additional strawberries.

APPLE WALNUT CAKE

3 eggs, beaten
2 cups sugar
1/2 cup vegetable oil
2 teaspoons vanilla extract
2 teaspoons cinnamon
1/4 teaspoon salt
2 teaspoons baking soda
1/2 teaspoon nutmeg
2 cups all-purpose flour
4 cups diced unpeeled apples
1/2 cup coarsely chopped walnuts
8 ounces cream cheese, softened
1/4 cup margarine, softened
1 1/2 cups confectioners' sugar
1/2 teaspoon vanilla extract

Preheat oven to 325 degrees. Combine eggs, sugar, oil and 2 teaspoons vanilla in large bowl; mix well. Add mixture of cinnamon, salt, baking soda, nutmeg and flour; mix well. Stir in apples and walnuts. Spread in greased 9-by-13-inch cake pan. Bake at 325 degrees for 50 to 60 minutes or until cake tests done. Let stand until cool. Combine cream cheese, margarine, confectioners' sugar and 1/2 teaspoon vanilla in bowl; beat until creamy and of spreading consistency. Spread over top of cooled cake.
Yield: 15 servings.

Elsie Lougheed
Phoenix, Arizona

WARM APPLE PUDDING CAKE

1/4 cup butter or margarine
6 cups sliced peeled apples
1 cup sugar
1 teaspoon ground cinnamon
2 cups water
2 cups all-purpose flour
1 cup sugar
1 tablespoon baking powder
1 teaspoon salt
1/2 cup melted butter or margarine
2/3 cup milk
2 eggs
2 teaspoons vanilla extract

Preheat oven to 375 degrees. Melt 1/4 cup butter in 9-by-13-inch cake pan. Add apples, tossing to coat. Sprinkle mixture of 1 cup sugar and cinnamon evenly over apples. Pour water over top. Combine flour, 1 cup sugar, baking powder and salt in a medium mixer bowl. Add melted butter, milk, eggs and vanilla, beating for 2 minutes or until smooth. Spread evenly over apple mixture. Bake at 375 degrees for 40 minutes. Let stand for 15 minutes. Cut into squares while warm. Place cake pieces on dessert plates. Spoon pan juices over cake. Serve warm with whipped cream or ice cream. Yield: 12 servings.

Judy Webster, Xi Gamma
Winnepeg, Manitoba, Canada

APPLESAUCE CAKE

This recipe is at least 70 years old. I have served it for over 65 years and it is always a huge success. Because it is so moist, the eggless cake does not require frosting or whipped cream.

1/2 cup shortening
1 cup sugar
1 cup packed light brown sugar
3 cups unsweetened applesauce
1 tablespoon plus 1 teaspoon baking soda
1 teaspoon salt
2 teaspoons cinnamon
1 teaspoon cloves
1 teaspoon nutmeg
2 3/4 cups (scant) all-purpose flour
1/2 teaspoon allspice
1/2 cup pecans
2 cups raisins

Preheat oven to 350 degrees. Cream shortening, sugar and brown sugar in mixer bowl until light and fluffy. Combine applesauce and baking soda in bowl; mix well. Add to creamed mixture, beating until blended. Add salt, cinnamon, cloves, nutmeg, flour and allspice; mix until smooth. Stir in pecans and raisins. Spoon into greased 9-by-13-inch cake pan. Bake for 45 minutes or until cake tests done. Yield: 15 servings.

Bernadine I. Kohler, Laureate Delta Alpha
Aurora, Colorado

APPLESAUCE CITRUS CAKE

I have baked this cake for over 40 years; my mother baked it when I was a little girl. It is best made at least a month before Christmas. You can use brandy or apple juice to drizzle over cake about once a week until serving time.

4 cups warm applesauce
1 1/2 cups sugar
1 tablespoon baking soda
1/2 cup butter or margarine, softened
1 teaspoon each allspice, cinnamon and nutmeg
1 (15-ounce) package seedless raisins
2 cups walnuts
4 cups all-purpose flour
Citrus fruit (any kind) to taste
1 (8-ounce) package dried mixed fruits (optional)

Preheat oven to 250 degrees. Combine applesauce, sugar, baking soda, butter and spices in bowl; mix well. Stir in raisins, walnuts, flour, citrus fruit and dried fruit. Spread in greased and floured tube pan lined with waxed paper. Bake at 250 degrees for 1 hour. Increase temperature to 350 degrees. Bake for 1 hour longer. Yield: 16 servings.

Louise Morris, Laureate Alpha Omicron
Roanoke, Virginia

MOM'S APPLESAUCE CAKE

This cake should be made at least a week in advance of serving. Mom used to make it at Thanksgiving to serve at Christmas.

2 cups sugar
1/2 cup butter, softened
1/2 cup margarine, softened
2 cups unsweetened applesauce
3 1/2 cups all-purpose flour
1/4 teaspoon salt
2 tablespoons baking cocoa
1 teaspoon each allspice, cloves, cinnamon and nutmeg
1 tablespoon baking soda
1 tablespoon hot water
1 cup raisins
1 cup pecans
1 cup chopped dates

Preheat oven to 325 degrees. Cream sugar, butter and margarine in mixer bowl until light and fluffy. Heat applesauce in saucepan until bubbly; add to creamed mixture. Sift flour, salt, cocoa and spices together. Reserve a small amount. Add remaining flour mixture to creamed mixture. Add mixture of baking soda and hot water; mix well. Dust reserved flour mixture over raisins, pecans and dates in separate bowl. Stir into creamed mixture. Spoon into greased and floured bundt pan. Bake at 325 degrees for 1 to 1 1/2 hours or until cake tests done. Let stand until cool. Remove from pan. Wrap in waxed paper. Insert small apple and wrap in foil. Store, covered, in cool place for 1 week or longer. Yield: 16 servings.

Lee (Norma J.) Boyer, Preceptor Beta Iota
Colorado Springs, Colorado

APPLESAUCE RAISIN CAKE

1 cup unsalted butter or margarine, softened
2 cups superfine sugar
2 cups applesauce
3 cups all-purpose flour
1 teaspoon each cinnamon, nutmeg and mace
1 3/4 teaspoons baking soda
1 teaspoon vanilla extract
1 cup coarsely chopped pecans
1 cup golden raisins

Preheat oven to 325 degrees. Line 9-inch tube pan with waxed paper; spray with nonstick baking spray. Cream butter and sugar in mixer bowl until light and fluffy. Add applesauce; mix well. Sift in flour, spices and baking soda; beat until blended. Add vanilla. Stir in pecans and raisins. Spoon into prepared pan. Bake at 325 degrees for 1 1/2 to 1 3/4 hours or until cake tests done; do not overbake. Let stand until cool. Remove from pan. Store, covered, for 1 day before serving. Yield: 16 servings.

LaNelle Denison, Texas Nu
Houston, Texas

APPLESAUCE SPICE CAKE

2 1/2 cups all-purpose flour
2 cups sugar
1 1/2 teaspoons baking soda
1 1/2 teaspoons salt
3/4 teaspoon ground cinnamon
1/2 teaspoon each ground allspice, nutmeg and baking powder
1 1/2 cups applesauce
1/2 cup water
1/2 cup shortening
2 eggs
1 cup raisins
1/2 cup chopped walnuts
1/3 cup margarine, softened
3 cups confectioners' sugar
2 teaspoons grated orange rind
2 tablespoons orange juice

Preheat oven to 350 degrees. Combine dry ingredients and next 4 ingredients in large mixer bowl; beat until blended, scraping bowl constantly. Beat at high speed until smooth, scraping bowl occasionally. Stir in raisins and walnuts. Spoon into 2 greased 8-by-8-inch round cake pans. Bake at 350 degrees for 50 to 55 minutes or until wooden pick inserted in center comes out clean. Cool in pans for 10 minutes. Cool on wire racks. Combine margarine, confectioners' sugar and orange rind in mixer bowl. Add orange juice a little at a time, beating until of spreading consistency. Spread between layers and over top and side of cake. Yield: 12 to 16 servings.

Sandy Whidden, Preceptor Theta Iota
Tampa, Florida

SPICY APPLESAUCE CAKE

The first time I made this special cake was in November, 1969. I mailed it to my son, Dennis, who was stationed in Cu Chi, Vietnam, in a Christmas box.

3/4 cup shortening
2 cups sugar
2 eggs
3 cups minus 2 tablespoons all-purpose flour
1 teaspoon baking powder
2 teaspoons baking soda
1/2 teaspoon each salt and cloves
1 teaspoon nutmeg
2 teaspoons cinnamon
2 cups applesauce
1/4 to 1/2 cup milk (optional)
1 cup raisins
1 1/2 cups chopped dates
2 cups chopped pecans

Preheat oven to 350 degrees. Cream shortening and sugar in mixer bowl until light and fluffy. Beat in eggs. Sift together flour, baking powder, baking soda, salt and spices; add to creamed mixture alternately with applesauce, beating after each addition. May add 1/4 to 1/2 cup milk if batter seems a little stiff. Stir in raisins, dates and pecans. Spoon into greased and floured 10-inch tube pan. Bake at 350 degrees for 1 1/2 hours or until cake tests done. Yield: 12 servings.

Bette Pitcock, Laureate Gamma Sigma
Abilene, Texas

APPLESAUCE-SPICE CAKE WITH RAISINS

This recipe came from my grandmother in Gering, Nebraska. She wouldn't have used Fuji apples, though, because they weren't available in the U.S. 40 years ago. I made the cake for a birthday cake one day when I couldn't find a box of cake mix on my shelf—and everyone, even my husband and sons, complimented me.

2 cups applesauce
1/2 teaspoon baking soda
1 cup raisins plumped, drained
1 cup pecans
1/2 cup shortening
1 1/4 cups sugar
1/2 teaspoon cloves
1/2 teaspoon cinnamon
1/2 teaspoon allspice
3 cups all-purpose flour

Preheat oven to 350 degrees. Combine first 9 ingredients in order listed in large bowl, mixing well after each addition. Add flour a little at a time, beating well after each addition until batter is stiff. Spoon into greased 8-by-12-inch cake pan. Bake at 350 degrees for 50 to 60 minutes or until cake tests done. Yield: 12 to 16 servings.

Joyce Faye Bladorn, Laureate Beta Upsilon
Chico, California

APRICOT CAKE

1 (2-layer) package lemon supreme cake mix
1/2 cup sugar
1 (12-ounce) can apricot nectar
3/4 cup vegetable oil
4 eggs
1 cup confectioners' sugar
2 to 3 tablespoons any flavor fruit juice

Preheat oven to 350 degrees. Combine cake mix, sugar, nectar, oil and eggs in large bowl; mix well. Spoon into greased 9-by-13-inch cake pan. Bake at 350 degrees for 40 to 45 minutes or until cake tests done. Blend confectioners' sugar and fruit juice in bowl; drizzle over warm cake. Yield: 15 servings.

Linda Clark, Beta Kappa
Whitesburg, Kentucky

APRICOT NECTAR CAKE

1 (2-layer) package yellow cake mix
3/4 cup vegetable oil
3/4 cup apricot nectar
3 tablespoons lemon extract
4 eggs
Juice of 3 lemons
2 cups confectioners' sugar

Preheat oven to 350 degrees. Combine cake mix, oil, nectar and lemon extract in mixer bowl. Beat for 6 minutes. Spoon into greased tube pan. Bake at 350 degrees for 55 minutes. Pour mixture of lemon juice and confectioners' sugar over warm cake.
Yield: 16 servings.

Maxine McGuire, Laureate Theta
Knoxville, Tennessee

APRICOT NUT CAKE

My sister, Nancy, gave me this recipe. It is a favorite of all who have tested it and a favorite of mine because it can be made up so quickly.

2 cups self-rising flour
2 cups sugar
3 eggs
1 teaspoon each ground cinnamon and allspice
1 cup vegetable oil
1 cup chopped pecans
1 (8-ounce) jar baby food apricots
Confectioners' sugar to taste

Preheat oven to 350 degrees. Combine flour, sugar, eggs, spices, oil, pecans and apricots in large bowl; mix well. Spoon into greased and floured 10-inch tube or bundt pan. Bake at 350 degrees for 1 hour. Let stand until cool. Invert onto serving plate. Sprinkle with confectioners' sugar. Yield: 16 servings.

Paula S. Franklin, Xi Gamma Epsilon
Columbus, Georgia

BANANA CAKE

This recipe was one used by my husband's mother when he was a child and is his favorite.

1 1/2 cups all-purpose flour
1/2 teaspoon baking soda
1/2 teaspoon salt
1/2 teaspoon nutmeg
1 teaspoon vanilla extract
1/2 cup margarine, softened
1 1/2 cups sugar
2 eggs
1 cup mashed bananas
3 tablespoons buttermilk

Preheat oven to 350 degrees. Sift flour, baking soda, salt and nutmeg together. Cream vanilla, margarine and sugar in mixer bowl until light and fluffy. Beat in eggs. Add flour mixture to creamed mixture, beating until blended. Stir in bananas and buttermilk. Spread evenly in greased and floured 9-by-9-inch square cake pan. Bake at 350 degrees for 45 minutes. May double all ingredients and increase baking time to 1 hour. Yield: 9 servings.

Deborah Selby, Xi Gamma Lambda
Gage, Oklahoma

Audrey Couzens, Laureate Psi, Ottawa, Ontario, Canada, makes Butterscotch Coconut Cake by beating 2 eggs, 1 cup sugar, 1 cup all-purpose flour, 1 teaspoon baking powder, pinch of salt and 1/2 teaspoon vanilla extract in mixer bowl and adding 1/2 cup scalded milk and 2 tablespoons butter or margarine. Bake in greased and floured 9-inch square cake pan in preheated 350-degree oven for 30 minutes. Boil 3 tablespoons butter or margarine, 5 tablespoons light brown sugar, 2 to 3 tablespoons cream and 1 cup coconut for 5 minutes, spread on cake and broil until brown.

THE BEST BANANA CAKE

1 (2-layer) package super moist yellow cake mix
1 1/2 cups mashed ripe bananas
1/2 cup water
1/4 cup vegetable oil
3 eggs
1/2 cup chopped pecans
8 ounces cream cheese, softened
1/2 cup butter or margarine, softened
2 cups confectioners' sugar
2 teaspoons vanilla extract

Preheat oven to 350 degrees. Combine cake mix, bananas, water, oil and eggs in large mixer bowl. Beat for 2 to 3 minutes. Stir in pecans. Spoon into greased and floured 9-by-13-inch cake pan. Bake at 350 degrees for 35 to 40 minutes or until cake tests done. Cool in pan for several minutes. Cool completely. Beat cream cheese, butter and confectioners' sugar in mixer bowl until light and fluffy. Stir in vanilla. Frost cake. Yield: 15 servings.

Sharon Billdt, Eta Theta
Arlington, Washington

BANANA BLACK WALNUT SHEET CAKE

1/2 cup shortening
2 cups sugar
1 egg
1 egg white, beaten
1 cup buttermilk
1 cup mashed ripe bananas
2 cups all-purpose flour
1 teaspoon baking soda
1 teaspoon salt
1 teaspoon vanilla extract
3/4 cup black walnuts
6 tablespoons butter or margarine
3/4 cup packed light brown sugar
1/3 cup all-purpose flour
Salt to taste
1 1/4 cups milk
1 egg yolk
1 1/2 teaspoons vanilla extract
3/4 cup chopped black walnuts

Preheat oven to 350 degrees. Cream shortening and sugar in mixer bowl until light and fluffy. Beat in 1 egg and egg white. Add buttermilk and bananas; mix well. Sift in 2 cups flour, baking soda and 1 teaspoon salt; mix well. Stir in 1 teaspoon vanilla and 3/4 cup walnuts. Spread in greased 11-by-17-inch sheet cake pan. Bake at 350 degrees for 35 minutes or until cake tests done. Combine butter and brown sugar in small saucepan. Cook over medium heat until butter is melted. Combine 1/3 cup flour and salt with 1/4 cup milk in small bowl, stirring until smooth. Add the remaining 1 cup milk gradually, stirring until smooth. Beat in 1 egg yolk. Stir into brown sugar mixture; mix well. Cook until very thick, stirring constantly. Stir in 1 1/2 teaspoons vanilla and remaining walnuts. Cool mixture. Spread over top of cake. Yield: 18 servings.

Darlene M. Gumfory, Laureate Alpha Sigma
Iola, Kansas

FAVORITE BANANA CAKE

I can remember this cake being served at family reunions when I was very young. I loved it then and it is still one of my very favorite recipes.

2 eggs
1/2 cup vegetable oil or butter
1/4 cup sour milk
1 1/2 cups sugar
2 cups all-purpose flour
1 teaspoon baking soda
1/2 teaspoon salt
1 teaspoon vanilla extract
1 cup mashed bananas

Preheat oven to 350 degrees. Combine eggs, oil, milk and sugar in large bowl, mixing well. Add flour, baking soda, salt and vanilla; mix until blended. Stir in bananas. Spoon into greased 9-by-13-inch cake pan. Bake at 350 degrees for 40 minutes. May top with icing—but cake is very good served plain. Yield: 12 servings.

Beverly J. Corning, Preceptor Beta Xi
Potwin, Kansas

BANANA NUT CAKE

This recipe is our family favorite. I make it every Thanksgiving and on other special occasions. It comes to us courtesy of my grandmother, who loved to teach her granddaughters special recipes!

1 cup shortening
1 1/2 cups sugar
3 eggs
1 egg yolk
1/2 cup buttermilk
1 teaspoon baking soda
2 1/2 cups all-purpose flour
1 cup chopped pecans
1 cup mashed bananas
1/2 cup margarine, softened
1 (1-pound) package confectioners' sugar
1 egg white
1 cup chopped pecans
1 teaspoon vanilla extract
3 to 4 tablespoons milk (optional)

Preheat oven to 350 degrees. Cream shortening and sugar in mixer bowl until light and fluffy. Add eggs and egg yolk 1 at a time, beating after each addition. Add mixture of buttermilk and baking soda alternately with flour; mix well. Fold in pecans and bananas. Spoon into 3 greased and floured 8-inch round cake pans. Bake at 350 degrees for 20 to 25 minutes or until baked layers test done. Cool on wire rack. Cream margarine and 4 tablespoons confectioners' sugar in mixer bowl until light and fluffy. Beat in egg white. Add remaining confectioners' sugar, mixing well. Stir in pecans and vanilla. Add 3 to 4 tablespoons milk if frosting seems a little dry, mixing until of desired consistency. Spread frosting between layers, allowing some frosting to drizzle down side. Yield: 18 to 24 servings.

Lou Ellen Smith, Xi Alpha Tau
Monroe, North Carolina

BANANA CAKE WITH ORANGE ICING

This is my husband's recipe. My sorority sister requests that he make this delicious cake when it is my turn to provide dessert for a sorority meeting.

3 bananas, mashed
2 eggs
1/2 cup melted margarine
1/2 cup sour milk
1 teaspoon vanilla extract
2 cups all-purpose flour
1 teaspoon baking soda
1 teaspoon baking powder
1 1/4 cups sugar
1 1/2 teaspoons grated orange rind
1 teaspoon orange juice
1/4 teaspoon lemon juice
1/4 cup margarine, softened
1 egg yolk
Salt to taste
2 cups confectioners' sugar

Preheat oven to 350 degrees. Combine bananas, eggs, melted margarine, milk and vanilla in bowl; mix well. Combine flour, baking soda, baking powder and sugar in large bowl; add banana mixture, beating until blended. Spoon into greased 9-by-13-inch cake pan. Bake at 350 degrees for 1 hour. Cool. Combine orange rind, orange juice and lemon juice in small bowl, mixing well. Cream 1/4 cup margarine in mixer bowl until light and fluffy. Beat in egg yolk and salt. Add confectioners' sugar alternately with juice mixture, beating well after each addition. Spread over top of cake. Yield: 8 to 12 servings.

Bert (Catherine) Hoad, Xi Zeta Nu
Renfrew, Ontario, Canada

BIRTHDAY CAKE

6 egg whites
1 cup sugar
6 egg yolks, beaten
1/3 cup water
2 teaspoons baking powder
1 1/3 cups cake flour
1/3 cup cornstarch
1/2 cup sugar
2 cups milk
1 egg yolk
1 teaspoon vanilla extract
1 cup butter or margarine, softened
1 cup confectioners' sugar

Preheat oven to 350 degrees. Beat egg whites in mixer bowl. Add 1 cup sugar; beat until fluffy. Beat egg yolks with water. Add to egg whites, beating until blended. Sift baking powder and flour 6 or 7 times. Fold gently into egg mixture. Spoon into 3 ungreased 8-inch or 9-inch round cake pans. Bake at 350 degrees for 15 minutes. Cool. Combine cornstarch, 1/2 cup sugar, milk, 1 egg yolk and vanilla in top of double boiler. Cook until of custard consistency, stirring constantly. Cool. Cream butter and confectioners' sugar in mixer bowl until light and fluffy. Fold into custard mixture. Spread between baked layers and over top and side of cake. Yield: 12 to 16 servings.

Kayce L. Weber, Xi Alpha Eta
Torrington, New York

BEST BLUEBERRY CAKE

1/2 cup butter or margarine, softened
2 cups sugar
2 eggs
3 1/4 cups all-purpose flour
1 teaspoon cream of tartar
1/2 teaspoon baking soda
1 cup milk
1 3/4 to 2 3/4 cups blueberries, rinsed
1/2 cup sugar
1 teaspoon cinnamon
1/2 cup melted margarine

Preheat oven to 350 degrees. Cream butter and 2 cups sugar in mixer bowl until light and fluffy. Add eggs, beating until blended. Add mixture of flour, cream of tartar and baking soda alternately with milk, beating until smooth. Stir in blueberries. Spoon into greased and floured 9-by-13-inch cake pan. Sprinkle with mixture of 1/2 cup sugar and cinnamon. Bake at 350 degrees for 40 to 50 minutes or until cake tests done. Brush with melted margarine. Let stand for 15 minutes. Serve warm or cold with whipped cream or vanilla ice cream. Yield: 12 servings.

Nancy E. Hutchinson, Beta Chi
Ocala, Florida

BLUEBERRY SOUR CREAM CAKE

This recipe was given to me by a dear friend in Canada. We used to pick the blueberries together on fruit farms.

1/2 cup sugar
1/2 cup butter or margarine, softened
1 egg
1 teaspoon vanilla extract
1 1/2 cups all-purpose flour
1 1/2 teaspoons baking powder
3 cups fresh or frozen blueberries
2 cups sour cream
2 egg yolks
1/2 cup sugar
1 teaspoon vanilla extract

Preheat oven to 350 degrees. Cream 1/2 cup sugar and butter in mixer bowl until light and fluffy. Stir in egg and 1 teaspoon vanilla. Stir mixture of flour and baking powder gradually into creamed mixture, beating until smooth. Spread in buttered 9- or 10-inch springform pan. Sprinkle blueberries on top. Combine sour cream, egg yolks, 1/2 cup sugar and 1 teaspoon vanilla in mixer bowl; mix well. Pour over berries. Bake at 350 degrees for 60 minutes. If using frozen blueberries; do not thaw. Yield: 8 servings.

Lyn Massey, Xi Gamma Nu
Dallas, Texas

BUTTER BRICKLE CAKE

1 (4-ounce) package butterscotch pudding and pie filling mix
2 cups milk
1 (2-layer) package butter brickle cake mix
1 cup butterscotch chips
1/2 to 1 cup walnuts

Preheat oven to 350 degrees. Combine pudding mix and milk in saucepan; bring to a boil over medium heat, stirring constantly. Remove from heat. Add cake mix; mix well. Spoon into greased 11-by-13-inch cake pan. Sprinkle with butterscotch chips and walnuts. Bake at 350 degrees for 30 minutes. Yield: 8 to 10 servings.

Doneen M. Clark, Beta Theta
Hulett, Wyoming

BUTTERNUT CAKE AND FROSTING

1 cup shortening
1 cup milk
2 cups sugar
2 cups self-rising flour
4 eggs
1 tablespoon butternut flavoring
1/2 cup margarine, softened
8 ounces cream cheese, softened
1 (1-pound) package confectioners' sugar
1 tablespoon butternut flavoring
1 cup chopped pecans

Preheat oven to 350 degrees. Combine shortening, milk, sugar, flour, eggs and 1 tablespoon butternut flavoring in large mixer bowl; mix well. Spoon into 3 greased and floured 9-inch round cake pans. Bake at 350 degrees for 30 to 35 minutes or until baked layers are brown on top. Cool on wire rack. Cream margarine, cream cheese and confectioners' sugar in mixer bowl until light and fluffy. Stir in remaining 1 tablespoon butternut flavoring. Spread between layers and over top and side of cake, sprinkling pecans between layers. Yield: 8 to 12 servings.

Carole Tatum, Florida Preceptor Epsilon Theta
St. Petersburg, Florida

BUTTERSCOTCH DELIGHT

A very elderly lady brought this cake to my husband's place of business some years ago. It was so popular that I asked for the recipe. The cake has gotten rave reviews at every dinner meeting I have taken it for the past several years.

1 (4-ounce) package butterscotch pudding and pie filling mix
2 cups milk
1 egg
3/4 cup vegetable oil
1 (2-layer) package yellow cake mix
2 cups butterscotch chips
1/2 cup pecans

Preheat oven to 300 degrees. Cook pudding mix with milk using package directions. Cool. Beat egg and oil. Add to pudding; mix well. Combine pudding mixture and cake mix in mixer bowl; beat until smooth and thick. Spread in greased and floured 11-by-14-inch cake pan. Sprinkle with butterscotch chips and pecans. Bake at 300 degrees for 35 to 40 minutes or until cake tests done. May substitute white cake mix for yellow cake mix. Yield: 12 servings.

Molly A. Patterson, Preceptor
Seminole, Oklahoma

CARROT CAKE

3 cups all-purpose flour
1 tablespoon baking soda
1½ teaspoons baking powder
1 teaspoon salt
1 tablespoon cinnamon
1½ cups packed light brown sugar
1½ cups applesauce
1 cup egg substitute
3 cups shredded carrots
1½ cups crushed pineapple
1 cup seedless raisins
1 cup chopped pecans

Preheat oven to 350 degrees. Combine flour, baking soda, baking powder, salt, cinnamon, brown sugar, applesauce, egg substitute, carrots, pineapple, raisins and pecans in large bowl, mixing well after each addition. Spoon into greased and floured bundt pan. Bake at 350 degrees for 45 to 60 minutes or until cake tests done. Yield: 16 servings.

Ora (Mary) Burke, Xi Delta Upsilon
Bloomington, Illinois

CARROT-WALNUT CAKE

1 cup corn oil
2 cups sugar
4 eggs
2 cups all-purpose flour
2 teaspoons baking powder
1 teaspoon each baking soda and salt
2 teaspoons cinnamon
3 cups grated carrots
1 cup chopped walnuts (optional)

Preheat oven to 325 degrees. Combine corn oil and sugar in mixer bowl; mix well. Beat eggs in small mixer bowl until light; add to corn oil mixture, beating until smooth. Sift in mixture of flour, baking powder, baking soda, salt and cinnamon; mix well. Add carrots and walnuts; mix well. Spoon into greased and floured tube or bundt pan. Bake at 325 degrees for 65 minutes. May substitute vegetable oil for corn oil. Yield: 16 servings.

Gloria Gonie, Xi Alpha Gamma
Saskatoon, Saskatchewan

HAWAIIAN CARROT CAKE

2 cups sugar
1½ cups vegetable oil
3 eggs
2 teaspoons vanilla extract
2¼ cups all-purpose flour
1½ teaspoons cinnamon
2 teaspoons baking soda
1 teaspoon salt
2 cups shredded carrots
2 cups coconut
1 cup crushed pineapple, drained
1 cup raisins
1 cup walnuts
3 ounces cream cheese, softened
¼ cup melted butter or margarine
2 tablespoons milk
1 teaspoon vanilla extract
⅛ teaspoon salt
3½ cups (about) confectioners' sugar

Preheat oven to 350 degrees. Combine sugar, vegetable oil, eggs and vanilla in bowl; mix well. Sift flour, cinnamon, baking soda and salt into large bowl. Add to egg mixture, stirring until smooth. Fold in carrots, coconut, pineapple, raisins and walnuts. Spoon into greased 9-by-13-inch cake pan. Bake at 350 degrees for 40 to 45 minutes or until wooden pick inserted in center comes out clean. Let stand until cool. Combine cream cheese, butter, milk, vanilla and salt in mixer bowl; beat until blended. Beat in confectioners' sugar until of spreading consistency. Spread over top of cake. Yield: 12 servings.

Denise M. Pointer, Iota Chi
St. Louis, Missouri

CHERRY GELATIN CAKE

My son always wants this cake for his birthday.

1 (2-layer) package white cake mix
1 (3-ounce) package cherry gelatin
1 (21-ounce) can cherry pie filling
8 ounces whipped topping

Preheat oven to 350 degrees. Prepare cake mix using package instructions; spoon into greased 9-by-13-inch cake pan. Bake at 350 degrees for 30 minutes or until cake tests done. Let stand until cooled to room temperature. Prepare gelatin using package instructions. Punch holes in cake; pour gelatin over top. Chill for 1 to 2 hours or until firm. Spread pie filling over top. Top with whipped topping. Yield: 12 servings.

Pat Kirkbride, Zeta Epsilon
Wheeling, West Virginia

CHERRY NUT CAKE

This recipe was given to my mother in the 1940s and has been our family's favorite birthday cake ever since.

1½ cups sugar
½ cup butter or margarine, softened
2 cups sifted cake flour
2½ teaspoons baking powder
¼ cup cherry juice
¾ cup water
15 large maraschino cherries, chopped
½ cup chopped pecans
3 egg whites, stiffly beaten
4 to 5 drops red food coloring

Preheat oven to 350 degrees. Cream sugar and butter in mixer bowl until light and fluffy. Sift in cake flour and baking powder alternately with mixture of cherry juice and water, mixing well after each addition. Stir in cherries and pecans. Fold in egg whites gently. Add red food coloring. Spoon into 2 greased 8- or 9-inch round cake pans. Bake at 350 degrees for 25 to 30 minutes or until layers test done. Cherries and pecans will sink to bottom of layers. Frost with 7-minute frosting, placing bottoms of layers together. Yield: 12 servings.

Nancy J. Middleton, Laureate Gamma Alpha
Liberty, Missouri

CREAM CAKE WITH CHERRIES

1 (2-layer) package cherry chip cake mix
1/3 cup all-purpose flour
3 eggs
1 1/4 cups milk
1/3 cup olive oil
1 cup sour cream
1 (16-ounce) can ready-to-spread white frosting
1 (21-ounce) can cherry pie filling

Preheat oven to 350 degrees. Combine cake mix, flour, eggs, milk and olive oil in mixer bowl; mix well on medium speed. Spoon into greased 9-by-13-inch cake pan. Bake at 350 for 37 minutes. Let stand until cool. Combine sour cream and frosting in mixer bowl; mix well. Frost top and sides of cake. Top with cherry pie filling. Yield: 12 servings.

Rita W. Bennet, Xi Alpha
Bozeman, Montana

CHOCOLATE ALMOND CAKE WITH ICING

2 (1-ounce) squares baking chocolate
1/2 cup butter or margarine, softened
1/3 cup olive oil
1 cup water
2 cups sugar
2 cups all-purpose flour
1/2 teaspoon salt
1 teaspoon baking soda
2 eggs
1 teaspoon vanilla extract
1/2 teaspoon almond extract
2 (1-ounce) squares baking chocolate
1/4 cup plus 2 tablespoons milk
1/4 cup butter or margarine
3 cups confectioners' sugar
1 1/2 cups sliced almonds
1 teaspoon almond extract

Preheat oven to 375 degrees. Combine 2 squares chocolate, 1/2 cup butter, olive oil and water in saucepan; bring to a boil over medium heat. Sift sugar, flour, salt and baking soda into bowl; mix well. Blend in chocolate mixture. Stir in eggs, vanilla and 1/2 teaspoon almond extract; batter will be thin. Pour into greased 9-by-13-inch baking pan. Bake at 375 degrees for 25 minutes. Combine 2 squares chocolate, milk and 1/4 cup butter in saucepan; bring to a boil over medium heat. Add confectioners' sugar, almonds and 1 teaspoon almond extract, mixing until blended. Pour over hot cake. Sprinkle with additional almonds. Yield: 14 to 16 servings.

Harriette S. Bland, Laureate Delta Delta
Arlington, Texas

COCOA APPLESAUCE CAKE

1/2 cup shortening
1 1/2 cups sugar
2 eggs
3 tablespoons baking cocoa
2 cups all-purpose flour
1/2 teaspoon cinnamon
1/2 teaspoon salt
1 1/2 teaspoons baking soda
2 cups applesauce
1 cup chocolate semisweet chips
2 tablespoons sugar
1/2 cup walnuts

Preheat oven to 350 degrees. Cream shortening, 1 1/2 cups sugar and eggs in mixer bowl until light and fluffy. Sift in cocoa, flour, cinnamon, salt and baking soda alternately with applesauce, mixing well after each addition. Spoon into greased 9-by-13-inch cake pan. Sprinkle with mixture of chocolate chips, 2 tablespoons sugar and walnuts. Bake at 350 degrees for 30 minutes. Yield: 15 to 20 servings.

Denise Jahay, Mu Kappa
Ellinwood, Kansas

CHOCOLATE BANANA CAKE

This is my husband's grandmother's recipe and has been the birthday cake recipe for the Atkinson family for 3 generations.

2 1/2 cups all-purpose flour
1/2 cup baking cocoa
2 teaspoons baking soda
1/4 teaspoon salt
1 cup butter or margarine
2 cups sugar
2 eggs, beaten
2 ripe bananas, mashed
1/2 cup sour milk
1 cup boiling water

Preheat oven to 375 degrees. Combine flour, cocoa, baking soda and salt in bowl; set aside. Cream butter and sugar in mixer bowl until light and fluffy. Add eggs; mix well. Stir in flour mixture, bananas and sour milk; beat until smooth. Add boiling water; mix well. Spoon into 3 greased 8- or 9-inch round cake pans or one 9-by-13-inch cake pan. Bake at 375 degrees for 30 minutes or until cake tests done. Frost as desired. Yield: 12 to 16 servings.

Donna Atkinson, Phi
Moscow, Idaho

BLACK FOREST CHERRY CAKE

This cake is quick and easy and always gets rave reviews.

1 (2-layer) package chocolate cake mix
1 (21-ounce) can cherry pie filling
2 eggs or equivalent egg substitute
1/2 teaspoon almond extract
1/3 cup all-purpose flour
1 cup chopped walnuts
Whipped topping (optional)

Preheat oven to 350 degrees. Combine cake mix, pie filling, eggs, almond extract and flour in large bowl; mix well. Spoon into greased 9-by-13-inch cake pan. Sprinkle with walnuts. Bake at 350 degrees for 35 to 40 minutes or until cake tests done. Cool. Top with whipped topping. May substitute strawberry or cherry cake mix for chocolate cake mix for a pink cake. Yield: 12 to 16 servings.

Esther Halsall, Preceptor Beta
Honolulu, Hawaii

MOCK BLACK FOREST CAKE

1 (21-ounce) can cherry pie filling
1/4 cup brandy (optional)
1 (2-layer) package chocolate cake mix
2 (4-ounce) packages chocolate pudding and pie filling mix
Whipped topping to taste

Preheat oven to 350 degrees. Combine pie filling with brandy. Prepare and bake cake mix using package instructions for 8- or 9-inch cake pans. Let stand until cool. Cook pudding using package instructions. Split cake layers horizontally. Alternate layers of cake, pudding and pie filling mixture in punch bowl, ending with pie filling. Top with whipped topping. Yield: 12 to 16 servings.

Darlene Snowdon, Zeta Gamma
Port Hardy, British Columbia, Canada

CHOCOLATE CHERRY ANGEL DELIGHT

1/3 cup baking cocoa
1 package two-step angel food cake mix
1 envelope whipped topping mix
1/2 cup cold skim milk
1/2 teaspoon vanilla extract
1 (21-ounce) can reduced-calorie cherry pie filling, chilled

Preheat oven to 350 degrees. Sift cocoa over flour packet of cake mix in bowl; stir to mix. Prepare cake mix using package instructions. Spoon into ungreased 10-inch tube pan. Bake at 350 degrees for 35 to 40 minutes or until cake tests done. Let stand until cool. Run serrated knife along edges of pan to loosen cake; remove from pan. Slice horizontally into 3 layers. Prepare whipped topping mix with skim milk and vanilla using package instructions. Fold 1/2 of pie filling into whipped topping. Layer cake and whipped topping mixture 1/3 at a time on a serving plate, ending with whipped topping mixture. Top with remaining cherry pie filling. Serve immediately. Store cake, covered, in refrigerator.
Yield: 14 servings.

Teddy Van Stolk, Laureate Eta
Prince George, British Columbia, Canada

CHOCOLATE CHERRY CAKE

This recipe is quick and easy. I got it from my neighbor in Gregory, Michigan when my son was a toddler. He's now 26 years old.

1 (2-layer) package chocolate cake mix
2 eggs, beaten
1 (21-ounce) can cherry pie filling
1 teaspoon almond extract (optional)
1 cup sugar
1/3 cup milk
5 tablespoons butter or margarine
1 cup semisweet chocolate chips

Preheat oven to 350 degrees. Prepare cake mix with 2 eggs using package instructions and adding cherry pie filling and almond extract. Spoon into greased and floured 9-by-13-inch cake pan. Bake at 350 degrees for 35 to 40 minutes or until cake tests done. Bring sugar, milk and butter to a boil in saucepan; stir in chocolate chips. Cook until chocolate chips melt, stirring constantly. Pour over hot cake.
Yield: 12 servings.

Darline Austin, Preceptor Mu Tau
Austin, Texas

CHERRY MILK CHOCOLATE CAKE

1 (2-layer) package extra-moist milk chocolate cake mix
2 eggs
1 (21-ounce) can cherry pie filling
1 teaspoon almond extract

Preheat oven to 350 degrees. Place cake mix in bowl, making well in center. Beat eggs in mixer bowl until light. Pour into well with pie filling and almond extract; mix until well blended. Spoon into greased 9-by-13-inch cake pan. Bake at 350 degrees for 30 to 35 minutes or until cake tests done. Let stand until cool. Frost with favorite milk chocolate frosting.
Yield: 15 servings.

Patricia L. Winter, Theta Phi
Cairo, Illinois

CHOCOLATE-CHERRY RING

This cake is especially good to share with friends and relatives during the month of February.

2 cups all-purpose flour
3/4 cup sugar
1 teaspoon baking soda
1 teaspoon cinnamon
1/8 teaspoon salt
2 eggs, beaten
1/2 cup vegetable oil
2 teaspoons vanilla extract
1 (21-ounce) can cherry pie filling
1 cup semisweet chocolate chips
1 cup chopped walnuts
Confectioners' sugar to taste

Preheat oven to 350 degrees. Sift flour, sugar, baking soda, cinnamon and salt into large mixer bowl. Combine eggs, oil and vanilla in bowl; beat until blended. Add to flour mixture; mix well. Stir in pie filling, chocolate chips and walnuts. Turn into greased and floured 10-inch fluted tube pan. Bake at 350 degrees for 1 hour. Let cool in pan for 10 minutes; turn onto wire rack to cool completely. Sprinkle with confectioners' sugar before serving. Yield: 12 to 14 servings.

Edna Irene Piper, Alpha Beta
Bedford, Indiana

✣ SWISS CHOCOLATE CHERRY CAKE

1 (2-layer) package Swiss chocolate cake mix
16 ounces cream cheese, softened
1 (16-ounce) can ready-to-spread French Vanilla frosting
2 (21-ounce) cans cherry pie filling

Preheat oven to 350 degrees. Prepare and bake cake mix using package instructions for bundt pan. Cool completely. Combine cream cheese and frosting in bowl; mix well. Slice cake horizontally into 3 layers. Layer cake, cream cheese mixture and pie filling 1/3 at a time on cake plate. Yield: 16 servings.

Sharon K. Hackbarth, Preceptor Eta Omega
El Sobrante, California

CHOCOLATE CAKE

My husband Alex first made this cake as a cook during World War II.

2 tablespoons white vinegar
1 3/4 cups milk
2 eggs
1 1/4 cups sugar
1/2 cup shortening
2 cups all-purpose flour
2 teaspoons each baking powder and baking soda
1 teaspoon salt
3 tablespoons baking cocoa
2 teaspoons vanilla extract

Preheat oven to 350 degrees. Combine vinegar and milk in small bowl; set aside. Beat eggs in mixer bowl until light. Add sugar and shortening; cream until light and fluffy. Combine flour, baking powder, baking soda and salt in bowl. Add dry ingredients and milk mixture alternately 1/2 at a time, mixing well after each addition. Add cocoa and vanilla, beating until smooth. Spoon into greased 9-by-13-inch cake pan. Bake at 350 degrees for 40 minutes or until cake tests done. Let stand until cool. Frost as desired. Yield: 15 servings.

Jadelle Stokes, Preceptor Kappa Psi
Sebastopol, California

CHOCOLATE-CHOCOLATE CAKE

This cake is not sinfully rich, but sinfully good!

3/4 cup baking cocoa
2 1/4 cups all-purpose flour
1 3/4 cups sugar
1 1/2 cups buttermilk
1 cup vegetable oil
2 teaspoons baking soda
3 eggs
1 1/2 teaspoons vanilla extract
1 1/4 teaspoons salt
3/4 cup baking cocoa
1 teaspoon vanilla extract
1/4 teaspoon salt
6 tablespoons margarine or butter
2 2/3 cups confectioners' sugar
1/3 cup milk
2 tablespoons light corn syrup

Preheat oven to 350 degrees. Combine 3/4 cup cocoa, flour, sugar, buttermilk, oil, baking soda, eggs, 1 1/2 teaspoons vanilla and 1 1/4 teaspoons salt in large mixer bowl; beat at low speed until blended, scraping bowl constantly. Beat at medium speed for 3 minutes, scraping bowl occasionally. Dust greased tube pan with additional cocoa. Spoon batter into prepared pan. Bake at 350 degrees for 50 minutes or until wooden pick inserted in center comes out clean. Cool in pan for 10 minutes. Remove to wire rack to cool completely. Beat 3/4 cup baking cocoa, 1 teaspoon vanilla, 1/4 teaspoon salt, margarine, confectioners' sugar, milk and corn syrup in large mixer bowl until smooth and glossy, adding additional milk if necessary to make frosting of spreading consistency. Yield: 16 servings.

Colleen Gilks, Beta Preceptor
Fredericton, New Brunswick, Canada

CHOCOLATE CINNAMON CAKE WITH FROSTING

2 cups sugar
2 cups all-purpose flour
1/2 cup margarine
1/2 cup shortening
1/4 cup baking cocoa
1 cup water
1 teaspoon salt
1 teaspoon baking soda
1 teaspoon cinnamon
2 eggs, slightly beaten
1 teaspoon vanilla extract
1/2 cup sour milk
1/2 cup margarine
1/4 cup baking cocoa
6 tablespoons milk
1/4 teaspoon salt
1 (1-pound) package confectioners' sugar, sifted
1 teaspoon vanilla extract
1 cup chopped pecans

Preheat oven to 400 degrees. Sift sugar and flour into large bowl. Combine 1/2 cup margarine, shortening, 1/4 cup cocoa and water in saucepan; bring to a rapid boil. Add to sugar mixture, mixing well. Stir in 1 teaspoon salt, baking soda, 1 teaspoon cinnamon, eggs, 1 teaspoon vanilla and sour milk. Spoon into greased 9-by-13-inch cake pan. Bake at 400 degrees for 30 minutes. Combine 1/2 cup margarine, 1/4 cup cocoa and milk in saucepan. Bring to a boil; remove from heat. Stir in salt, confectioners' sugar, 1 teaspoon vanilla and pecans. Spread over hot cake. Yield: 15 servings.

Becky Bradley, Xi Alpha Kappa
Clarksville, Arkansas

Bonnie Pomasko, Phi, Peterborough, New Hampshire, makes Chocolate Crunch Cake by preparing a devil's food cake mix and baking in layer cake pans after sprinkling with 1 cup graham cracker crumbs mixed with 1/4 cup melted butter, 1/2 cup chopped pecans and 1/4 cup semisweet chocolate chips. Frost with chocolate buttercream frosting.

COLD WATER CHOCOLATE CAKE

Our children always wanted this cake for special occasions. My husband always asks for it when he serves lunch to his Masonic Lodge.

3 cups all-purpose flour
2 cups sugar
2 teaspoons baking soda
1/2 teaspoon salt
1/2 cup baking cocoa
3/4 cup vegetable oil
2 cups water
3 tablespoons white vinegar
1/4 cup shortening
1/4 cup milk
1 cup sugar
1/2 cup semisweet chocolate chips

Preheat oven to 350 degrees. Combine flour, 2 cups sugar, baking soda, salt, cocoa, oil, water and vinegar in large bowl; mix thoroughly. Spread into greased and floured 9-by-13-inch cake pan. Bake at 350 degrees for 30 minutes. Combine shortening, milk and 1 cup sugar in saucepan. Bring to a boil over low heat. Cook for 1 minute, stirring constantly. Add chocolate chips; beat until of spreading consistency. Frost top of cake. Yield: 15 servings.

Gladys Pullins, Laureate Rho
Hot Springs, South Dakota

CRAZY CHOCOLATE CAKE

I was given this recipe by my high school home economics teacher and have been using it for over 35 years.

1 cup sugar
1 egg
1/2 cup milk
1/2 cup margarine
1/2 teaspoon salt
1 teaspoon baking soda
1 teaspoon vanilla extract
11/2 cups all-purpose flour
1/2 cup baking cocoa
1/2 cup boiling water

Preheat oven to 375 degrees. Place sugar, egg, milk, margarine, salt, baking soda, vanilla, flour and cocoa in order listed in large mixer bowl; do not mix. Add boiling water; beat until smooth. Spoon into greased 9-inch square or round cake pan. Bake at 375 degrees for 35 to 40 minutes or until cake tests done.
Yield: 16 servings.

Donna Clapton, Xi Delta Alpha
Revelstoke, British Columbia, Canada

DEEP DARK CHOCOLATE CAKE

I always make this delicious cake for all the birthday celebrations in my home.

13/4 cups all-purpose flour
2 cups sugar
3/4 cup baking cocoa
11/2 teaspoons each baking powder and baking soda
1 teaspoon salt
2 eggs
1 cup milk
1/2 cup vegetable oil
2 teaspoons vanilla extract
1 cup boiling water

Preheat oven to 350 degrees. Combine flour, sugar, cocoa, baking powder, baking soda and salt in large mixer bowl. Add eggs, milk, oil and vanilla; beat for 2 minutes. Stir in boiling water; batter will be thin. Spoon into greased tube pan or 9-by-13-inch cake pan. Bake at 350 degrees for 1 hour and 10 minutes for tube pan; 35 to 40 minutes for 9-by-13-inch pan or until cake tests done. Cool in tube pan for 10 minutes. Invert onto serving plate. Frost with favorite icing. Yield: 15 to 16 servings.

Janine Waldner, Beta
Estevan, Saskatchewan, Canada

DOUBLE CHOCOLATE CAKE

This recipe was given to me by a special friend; now I share it with friends. Everyone enjoys it and that makes me happy.

1 (2-layer) package yellow cake mix
1 (6-ounce) package chocolate instant pudding mix
1/2 cup sugar
3/4 cup vegetable oil
3/4 cup water
4 eggs
1 cup sour cream
2 cups semisweet chocolate chips

Preheat oven to 350 degrees. Combine cake mix, pudding mix and sugar in large bowl; mix well with wooden spoon. Add oil, water and eggs; mix until smooth. Add sour cream; mix well. Stir in chocolate chips. Spoon into greased bundt pan. Bake at 350 degrees for 45 to 50 minutes or until cake tests done. Freezes well. Yield: 16 servings.

Deanna Stansell, Alpha Pi Mu
Mt. Pleasant, Texas

CHOCOLATE DREAM CAKE

This recipe is a favorite of a Beta Sigma Phi sister who is on a leave of absence.

2 cups sugar
2 cups all-purpose flour
1/2 cup margarine
1 cup water
1/2 cup shortening
1/4 cup baking cocoa
1/2 cup buttermilk
2 eggs, slightly beaten
1 teaspoon each baking soda, cinnamon and vanilla extract
1/2 cup margarine
1/4 cup baking cocoa
6 tablespoons milk
1 (1-pound) package confectioners' sugar
1 teaspoon vanilla extract
1/2 to 3/4 cup chopped pecans

Preheat oven to 350 degrees. Combine sugar and flour; set aside. Combine 1/2 cup margarine, water, shortening and 1/4 cup cocoa in saucepan. Bring to a boil over medium heat, stirring frequently. Combine buttermilk, eggs, baking soda, cinnamon and 1 teaspoon vanilla in bowl; mix well. Add cocoa mixture; beat until blended. Fold in sugar mixture. Spoon into greased 9-by-13-inch cake pan. Bake at 350 degrees

for 35 to 40 minutes or until cake tests done. Combine 1/2 cup margarine, 1/4 cup cocoa and milk in saucepan. Bring to a boil, stirring constantly. Stir in confectioners' sugar and 1 teaspoon vanilla; beat until smooth. Stir in pecans. Spread over hot cake. Sprinkle with additional pecans.
Yield: 10 to 12 servings.

Frances Hounsell, Xi Kappa Chi
Refugio, Texas

FROSTED CHOCOLATE CAKE

As kids, my brother and sister and would love it when Mom sent Dad to the store for a "few" things because he always brought home a "Van de Kamp" chocolate cake. A slice of this cake with a cold glass of milk brings back those pleasant memories!

1/2 cup baking cocoa
2 teaspoons instant coffee granules
1 cup boiling water
2 teaspoons vanilla extract
3/4 cup unsalted butter or margarine, softened
11/4 cups sugar
2 eggs, at room temperature
11/4 cups all-purpose flour
1/2 teaspoon baking soda
1/2 teaspoon salt
1 tablespoon instant coffee granules
1 tablespoon vanilla extract
1 cup butter or margarine, softened
2 cups confectioners' sugar
1 egg yolk, beaten or 2 tablespoons egg substitute

Preheat oven to 350 degrees. Dust 2 greased 9-inch cake pans with flour and line with waxed paper. Combine 1/2 cup cocoa, 2 teaspoons coffee granules and water in bowl; mix well. Cool to room temperature. Add 2 teaspoons vanilla, mixing well. Beat 3/4 cup butter until light. Add sugar, beating until fluffy. Mix in 2 eggs 1 at a time, beating well after each addition. Combine flour, baking soda and salt in bowl. Add cocoa mixture and flour mixture alternately 1/3 at a time to butter mixture, mixing well after each addition. Spoon into prepared pans. Bake at 350 degrees for 25 to 30 minutes or until firm in center when lightly pressed. Cool in pans for 10 minutes; remove to wire rack to cool completely. Combine 1 tablespoon coffee granules and 1 tablespoon vanilla in small bowl, mixing until granules dissolve. Beat 1 cup butter in mixer bowl until light. Add confectioners' sugar. Beat for 3 minutes. Add coffee mixture and egg yolk; beat until fluffy. Spread between layers and over top and side of cake.
Yield: 12 to 16 servings.

Vickie L. Beaver, Xi Beta Beta
Lincoln, Nebraska

CHOCOLATE FUDGE CAKE

1 cup butter or margarine
1 cup water
1/2 cup vegetable oil
1 teaspoon vanilla extract
5 tablespoons baking cocoa
2 cups all-purpose flour
2 cups sugar
2 eggs
1/2 cup buttermilk
1 teaspoon baking soda
1/4 cup butter or margarine
6 tablespoons baking cocoa
2 tablespoons vegetable oil
1/2 cup minus 1 tablespoon milk
Confectioners' sugar to taste

Preheat oven to 350 degrees. Combine 1 cup butter, water, 1/2 cup oil, vanilla and 5 tablespoons cocoa in medium saucepan; mix well. Bring to a boil over medium heat. Add to mixture of flour and sugar in large bowl, stirring until blended. Add eggs 1 at a time, mixing after each addition. Add mixture of buttermilk and baking soda. Spoon into greased and floured 9-by-9-inch square cake pan. Bake at 350 degrees for 35 minutes; do not overbake. Combine 1/4 cup butter, 6 tablespoons baking cocoa, 2 tablespoons oil and milk in saucepan; mix well. Cook over low heat until butter melts, stirring constantly. Add enough confectioners' sugar to make of spreading consistency. Frost top of cake. Yield: 9 servings.

Debi Kent, Eta Mu
Bay City, Texas

HOT FUDGE SUNDAE CAKE

1 cup all-purpose flour
3/4 cup sugar
2 tablespoons baking cocoa
2 teaspoons baking powder
1/4 teaspoon salt
1/2 cup milk
2 tablespoons vegetable oil
1 teaspoon vanilla extract
1 cup chopped pecans (optional)
1 cup packed light brown sugar
1/4 cup baking cocoa
13/4 cups hot water
Favorite ice cream

Preheat oven to 350 degrees. Combine flour, sugar, 2 tablespoons cocoa, baking powder and salt in ungreased 9-by-9-inch square cake pan. Mix in milk, oil and vanilla with fork, stirring until smooth. Add pecans; mix well. Sprinkle with mixture of brown sugar and 1/4 cup cocoa. Pour hot water over batter. Bake at 350 degrees for 40 minutes. Let stand for 15 minutes. Spoon into dessert dishes. Top with ice cream and spoon sauce from pan over servings.
Yield: 9 servings.

Joyce Seger, Xi Epsilon Lambda
Coffeyville, Kansas

INSIDE-OUT CHOCOLATE BUNDT CAKE

1 (4-ounce) package chocolate instant pudding mix
1 (2-layer) package devil's food or chocolate cake mix
2 cups semisweet chocolate chips
1 3/4 cups milk
2 eggs
2 tablespoons baking cocoa
1 tablespoon plus 2 teaspoons hot water
1 tablespoon vegetable oil (optional)
1 cup confectioners' sugar

Preheat oven to 350 degrees. Combine pudding mix, cake mix, chocolate chips, milk and eggs in large bowl; mix well with spoon. Spoon into greased and floured 12-cup tube or bundt pan. Bake at 350 degrees for 50 to 55 minutes or until cake springs back when center is lightly pressed; do not overbake. Cool in pan for 15 minutes; remove to wire rack to cool completely. Combine cocoa, hot water, oil and confectioners' sugar in bowl; mix well. Add additional confectioners' sugar to thicken, or additional water to thin mixture. Spoon over cake. Yield: 8 to 10 servings.

Mary C. Henchon, Laureate Beta
Trenton, New Jersey

CHOCOLATE KAHLUA CAKE

1 (2-layer) package light chocolate cake mix
1 (4-ounce) package vanilla instant pudding mix
2 cups plain low-fat yogurt
3 egg whites or 2 whole eggs
1/3 cup Kahlúa
1/4 cup vegetable oil
1 cup semisweet chocolate chips
Confectioners' sugar to taste

Preheat oven to 350 degrees. Combine cake mix, pudding mix, yogurt, egg whites, Kahlúa and oil in bowl; mix well. Add chocolate chips; mix thoroughly. Spoon into greased bundt pan. Bake at 350 degrees for 45 minutes; do not overbake. Cool in pan for 10 minutes. Remove from pan. Let stand for 20 minutes. Sprinkle with confectioners' sugar. May make cake using regular instead of low-fat products.
Yield: 10 to 12 servings.

Sheri Brewer, Gamma Rho
Show Low, Arizona

CHOCOLATE LOVER'S CAKE

4 eggs
1 cup shortening
2 cups sugar
1 1/2 cups all-purpose flour
1 1/2 cups chopped pecans
1/3 cup baking cocoa
Salt to taste
1 (7-ounce) jar marshmallow creme
1/2 cup shortening
1/3 cup baking cocoa
1/3 cup milk
1 teaspoon vanilla extract
1 (1-pound) package confectioners' sugar

Preheat oven to 350 degrees. Combine eggs, 1 cup shortening, sugar, flour, pecans, 1/3 cup cocoa and salt in large bowl, mixing well. Spread in greased and floured 9-by-13-inch cake pan. Bake at 350 degrees for 40 to 45 minutes or until cake tests done. Spread marshmallow creme over hot cake. Combine 1/2 cup shortening, 1/3 cup cocoa, milk, 1 teaspoon vanilla and confectioners' sugar in large mixer bowl; mix until smooth. Spread over top of cake.
Yield: 15 servings.

Lucy Hillestad, Epsilon Gamma
Woodruff, Wisconsin

CHOCOLATE MAYONNAISE CAKE

My mother-in-law gave me this recipe and I make this cake for all family members' birthdays.

1 cup lukewarm water
3/4 cup mayonnaise-type salad dressing
2 cups all-purpose flour
1 cup sugar
1/2 cup baking cocoa
1 1/2 teaspoons baking soda
1/2 teaspoon salt
1 teaspoon vanilla extract

Preheat oven to 325 degrees. Combine water and salad dressing in mixer bowl, stirring until blended. Add flour, sugar, cocoa, baking soda, salt and vanilla, mixing well. Beat for 2 minutes. Spoon into greased 9-by-9-inch cake pan. Bake at 325 degrees for 45 minutes or until wooden pick inserted in center comes out clean. Yield: 9 servings.

Bette Brailey, Preceptor Gamma Beta
Grand Rapids, Michigan

MOIST CHOCOLATE CAKE

I always get compliments on the moistness of this cake. It goes well with any frosting, but I prefer cream cheese frosting.

3 cups all-purpose flour
2 cups sugar
1 teaspoon salt
5 tablespoons baking cocoa
2 teaspoons baking soda
2/3 cup vegetable oil
2 tablespoons white vinegar
1 tablespoon vanilla extract
2 cups cold water

Preheat oven to 350 degrees. Combine flour, sugar, salt, cocoa and baking soda in bowl; mix well. Add oil, vinegar, vanilla and water; beat until blended. Spoon into greased and floured 9-by-13-inch cake pan. Bake at 350 degrees for 35 to 40 minutes or until wooden pick inserted in center comes out clean.
Yield: 15 servings.

Mary McKinney, Preceptor Beta Psi
Huntington, Oregon

MINT CHOCOLATE CAKE

1 (2-layer) package white cake mix
3 tablespoons crème de menthe
1 (16-ounce) can chocolate syrup
8 ounces whipped topping
1/4 cup crème de menthe

Preheat oven to 350 degrees. Prepare cake mix using package instructions, substituting 3 tablespoons crème de menthe for water. Spoon into greased 9-by-13-inch cake pan. Bake at 350 degrees for 25 to 35 minutes or until cake tests done. Let stand until cool. Punch holes in cake. Pour chocolate syrup over cake. Frost with mixture of whipped topping and 1/4 cup crème de menthe. Yield: 15 servings.

Cheryl Short, Xi Zeta
Billings, Montana

MOM'S CHOCOLATE CHIP CAKE

My mom made this when I was growing up. It is a family favorite that all daughters-in-law are required to learn to make—and sons-in-law love!

1/2 cup margarine, softened
2 cups all-purpose flour
2 cups packed light brown sugar
1 cup milk
1 teaspoon each salt and baking soda
1 teaspoon vanilla extract
2 eggs
2 cups semisweet chocolate chips

Preheat oven to 350 degrees. Combine margarine, flour and brown sugar in large bowl; reserve 1 cup of mixture. Add milk, salt, baking soda, vanilla and eggs to remaining margarine mixture; mix well. Batter will be thin and slightly lumpy. Pour into greased 9-by-13-inch cake pan. Sprinkle reserved mixture over top. Add chocolate chips. Bake at 350 degrees for 25 to 30 minutes or until cake tests done.
Yield: 24 servings.

Angela Ahlberg
Urbandale, Iowa

CHOCOLATE NUT CAKE

1 1/4 cups butter or margarine
1/2 cup baking cocoa
1 cup water
2 cups all-purpose flour
1 1/2 cups packed light brown sugar
1 teaspoon baking soda
1 teaspoon cinnamon
1/2 teaspoon salt
1 (14-ounce) can sweetened condensed milk
2 eggs
1 teaspoon vanilla extract
1 cup confectioners' sugar
1 cup chopped pecans

Preheat oven to 350 degrees. Melt 1 cup butter in small saucepan. Stir in 1/4 cup cocoa and water. Heat just to boiling; remove from heat. Combine flour, brown sugar, baking soda, cinnamon and salt in large mixer bowl. Beat in cocoa mixture. Add 1/3 cup condensed milk, eggs and vanilla; mix well. Spoon into greased 10-by-15-inch cake pan. Bake at 350 degrees for 15 minutes. Melt remaining 1/4 cup butter in saucepan. Stir in remaining 1/4 cup cocoa and remaining condensed milk. Add confectioners' sugar and pecans; mix well. Spread over warm cake.
Yield: 8 to 12 servings.

Donna Betts, Alpha Alpha Rho
Grain Valley, Missouri

CHOCOLATE POUND CAKE WITH ICING

2 (1-ounce) squares chocolate
3 cups all-purpose flour
1/4 teaspoon baking powder
1/2 teaspoon salt
1 cup butter or margarine, softened
1/2 cup shortening
3 cups sugar
5 eggs
1 1/4 cups milk
1 tablespoon vanilla extract
1/4 cup margarine, softened
8 ounces cream cheese, softened
1 (1-ounce) square chocolate, melted
1 (1-pound) package confectioners' sugar
1 teaspoon vanilla extract
1/4 cup (or more) evaporated milk

Preheat oven to 300 degrees. Melt two 1-ounce squares of chocolate in double boiler over hot water; set aside. Combine flour, baking powder and salt in bowl. Cream butter and shortening in mixer bowl. Beat in sugar until light and fluffy. Add eggs 1 at a time, beating after each addition. Add flour mixture alternately with milk, mixing well after each addition. Stir in melted chocolate and 1 tablespoon vanilla. Spoon into greased tube pan. Bake at 300 degrees for 1 hour and 30 minutes or until cake tests done. Cool in pan for 10 minutes. Invert onto cake plate. Cream margarine and cream cheese in mixer bowl until light. Melt 1 square chocolate in double boiler over hot water. Blend melted chocolate, confectioners' sugar and vanilla into cream cheese mixture. Add enough evaporated milk gradually to make of spreading consistency, beating until smooth. Frost top and side of cake. Yield: 16 servings.

Marilyn Brown, Preceptor Alpha Nu
Dublin, Georgia

Julaine Zavalney, Laureate Zeta, Williston, North Dakota, makes Black Russian Cake with a yellow cake mix, small chocolate instant pudding mix, 4 eggs, 1 cup oil, 3/4 cup water and 1/4 cup each Kahlúa and vodka. Bake in greased and floured bundt pan in preheated 350-degree oven for 50 minutes.

KENTUCKY CHOCOLATE POUND CAKE

3 cups all-purpose flour
1/4 teaspoon baking powder
1/2 cup baking cocoa
3 cups sugar
1/2 cup butter or margarine
1/2 cup shortening
1 teaspoon vanilla extract
5 egg yolks, beaten
1 1/4 cups milk
5 egg whites

Preheat oven to 300 degrees. Sift flour, baking powder and cocoa. Cream sugar, butter and shortening in mixer bowl until light and fluffy. Beat in vanilla and egg yolks. Add flour mixture alternately with milk, beating well after each addition. Beat egg whites in mixer bowl until stiff. Fold into cocoa mixture. Spoon into greased and floured tube pan. Bake at 300 degrees for 1 hour and 25 minutes. Frost with chocolate buttercream icing. Yield: 16 servings.

Carolyn Lotz, Theta Xi
Crescent, Oklahoma

LOUISIANA CHOCOLATE POUND CAKE

1 cup margarine, softened
1/2 cup shortening
3 cups sugar
5 eggs
1/2 cup baking cocoa
1/2 teaspoon baking powder
3 cups all-purpose flour
1 cup milk
2 teaspoons vanilla extract
1 cup pecan halves

Preheat oven to 325 degrees. Cream margarine, shortening and sugar in large mixer bowl until light and fluffy. Beat in eggs 1 at a time, mixing well after each addition. Add sifted mixture of cocoa, baking powder and flour alternately with milk and vanilla, mixing well after each addition. Stir in pecan halves. Spoon into greased bundt pan. Bake at 325 degrees for 1 hour. Yield: 16 servings.

Tommie May, Laureate Zeta Gamma
Houston, Texas

BIRTHDAY CHOCOLATE PUDDING CAKE

My husband's mother used to make this cake for his birthday every year. After we married, she gave me the recipe. He says I make the cake as well as his Mom.

3/4 cup sugar
1 cup sifted self-rising flour
1/4 teaspoon baking powder
2 tablespoons baking cocoa
1/2 cup milk
3 tablespoons melted margarine, cooled
1 teaspoon vanilla extract
1/2 cup sugar
1/2 cup packed light brown sugar
1/4 cup baking cocoa
1 1/2 cups water

Preheat oven to 325 degrees. Sift 3/4 cup sugar, flour, baking powder and 2 tablespoons cocoa into greased 9-by-9-inch square cake pan. Stir in milk, margarine and vanilla. Sprinkle with mixture of 1/2 cup sugar, brown sugar and 1/4 cup cocoa. Pour water over top. Bake at 325 degrees for 45 minutes or until top of cake springs back when lightly touched.
Yield: 6 servings.

Karen Singley, Zeta Gamma
Delhi, Louisiana

CHOCOLATE CHIP PUDDING CAKE

3/4 cup all-purpose flour
1/2 teaspoon salt
1 1/2 teaspoons baking powder
1/4 cup baking cocoa
2/3 cup sugar
1/2 cup milk
3 tablespoons vegetable oil
2/3 cup packed light brown sugar
1/4 cup baking cocoa
1/4 cup semisweet chocolate chips
1 teaspoon vanilla extract
1 1/4 cups hot water

Preheat oven to 350 degrees. Combine flour, salt, baking powder, 1/4 cup cocoa and sugar in ungreased 8-inch cake pan. Add milk and oil; mix well. Sprinkle with mixture of brown sugar, 1/4 cup cocoa and chocolate chips. Pour mixture of vanilla and hot water over top. Bake at 350 degrees for 30 to 35 minutes or until cake surface is brown and dry in appearance. Yield: 9 servings.

Georgie McCann
Balmertown, Ontario, Canada

RICH MOIST CHOCOLATE CAKE

1/2 cup shortening
1 cup sugar
1/8 teaspoon salt
1 teaspoon vanilla extract
1/2 cup baking cocoa
1/3 cup water
2 1/2 cups all-purpose flour
1 cup water
3 egg whites
3/4 cup sugar
1 1/3 teaspoons baking soda
2 tablespoons boiling water

Preheat oven to 350 degrees. Cream shortening, 1 cup sugar, salt and vanilla in mixer bowl until light and fluffy. Mix cocoa and 1/3 cup water in bowl. Add to creamed mixture alternately with flour and 1 cup water, beating until blended. Beat egg whites until foamy. Add 3/4 cup sugar; beat until stiff. Fold into creamed mixture. Combine baking soda and boiling water, mixing well. Stir into batter. Spoon into greased and floured 9-by-13-inch cake pan. Bake at 350 degrees for 35 to 40 minutes or until cake tests done. Yield: 12 to 16 servings.

Annette Myers, Tau Beta
Newtown, Missouri

CHOCOLATE ROLL (BUCHE DE NOEL)

We served this cake at our "Christmas in Paris" social last December. Everyone enjoyed it. The recipe is a long one but does not take long to make.

1/3 cup sifted flour
1/2 teaspoon baking powder
1/4 cup baking cocoa
1/4 teaspoon salt
4 eggs, separated
3/4 cup sugar
1 teaspoon vanilla extract
Confectioners' sugar to taste
1/4 cup sugar
3 tablespoons cornstarch
1/4 teaspoon salt
1 (20-ounce) can crushed pineapple
1 egg, beaten
1/2 cup whipping cream, whipped
2 (1-ounce) squares semisweet chocolate
2 tablespoons shortening
2 teaspoons light corn syrup

Preheat oven to 400 degrees. Sift flour, baking powder, cocoa and 1/4 teaspoon salt together. Beat 4 egg whites in mixer bowl until stiff. Beat in 3/4 cup sugar gradually until stiff peaks form. Beat 4 egg yolks with vanilla until thick and light. Fold into egg white mixture. Fold in flour mixture. Spoon into greased 10-by-15-inch cake pan lined with greased waxed paper. Bake at 400 degrees for 10 to 13 minutes or until cake springs back when lightly touched in center. Invert onto clean cloth sprinkled with confectioners' sugar; remove waxed paper. Roll as for jelly roll in towel. Cool on wire rack. Unroll; remove cloth. Combine 1/4 cup sugar, cornstarch and 1/4 teaspoon salt in saucepan; stir in pineapple and juice. Cook over medium heat until clear and thickened, stirring constantly. Stir a small amount of hot mixture into 1 beaten egg; stir egg into hot mixture. Cook for 1 minute longer, stirring constantly. Cool, covered. Fold in whipped cream. Unroll cake. Spread with pineapple filling; reroll. Place on serving plate. Melt chocolate with shortening in double boiler over hot water. Stir in corn syrup. Spread at once over cake. Yield: 8 to 10 servings.

Lynne Prevost, Xi Alpha Beta
Rose Valley, Saskatchewan, Canada

CHOCOLATE SAUERKRAUT CAKE

2/3 cup margarine, softened
1 1/2 cups sugar
3 eggs
1 teaspoon vanilla extract
1 teaspoon baking soda
1/4 teaspoon salt
1/2 cup baking cocoa
2 1/4 cups all-purpose flour
1 teaspoon baking powder
1 cup water
2/3 cup chopped sauerkraut, rinsed, drained

Preheat oven to 350 degrees. Cream margarine and sugar in mixer bowl until light and fluffy. Beat in eggs and vanilla. Sift in baking soda, salt, cocoa, flour and baking powder alternately with water, mixing well after each addition. Stir in sauerkraut. Spoon into greased 9-by-13-inch cake pan. Bake at 350 degrees for 30 minutes. Yield: 15 servings.

Tangie Granzella, Alpha Eta
Salida, Colorado

SAUERKRAUT CHOCOLATE CAKE

I have a daughter who still refuses to taste this because of the sauerkraut!

2 1/4 cups all-purpose flour
1/2 cup baking cocoa
1 teaspoon baking powder
1 teaspoon baking soda
1/4 teaspoon salt
2/3 cup butter or margarine, softened
1 1/2 cups sugar
3 eggs
1 teaspoon vanilla extract
1 cup water or strong coffee
2/3 cup sauerkraut, coarsely chopped, rinsed, drained

Preheat oven to 350 degrees. Stir flour, cocoa, baking powder, baking soda and salt into bowl. Cream butter in large mixer bowl until light and fluffy. Add sugar gradually, mixing well. Add eggs 1 at a time, beating well after each addition. Beat in mixture of dry ingredients. Add vanilla, water and sauerkraut, beating after each addition. Spoon into 2 greased and floured 8-inch round or 8-inch square cake pans. Bake at 350 degrees for 25 to 30 minutes or until cakes test done. Frost as desired. Yield: 12 to 16 servings.

Carol Stade, Saskatchewan Laureate Theta
Estevan, Saskatchewan, Canada

CHOCOLATE SHEET CAKE

2 cups sugar
2 cups all-purpose flour
1/4 teaspoon salt
1/4 cup baking cocoa
1 cup margarine
1 cup water
1/2 cup vegetable oil
2 eggs, beaten
1 teaspoon baking soda
1/2 cup buttermilk
1/2 cup margarine
1/4 cup milk
1/4 cup baking cocoa
3 cups sifted confectioners' sugar
1 teaspoon vanilla extract
1/2 cup pecans

Preheat oven to 375 degrees. Combine sugar, flour, salt and baking cocoa in bowl. Bring 1 cup margarine, water and oil to a boil in saucepan. Pour over flour mixture; mix well. Add eggs, stirring until smooth. Dissolve baking soda in buttermilk; stir into flour mixture. Spoon into greased and floured 10-by-15-inch cake pan. Bake at 375 degrees for 20 to 25 minutes or until cake tests done. Melt 1/2 cup margarine in saucepan with 1/4 cup milk. Add mixture of 1/4 cup cocoa and 3 cups confectioners' sugar. Add vanilla; mix well. Frost cake. Top with pecans. Yield: 16 servings.

Joyce Risse, Xi Alpha Tau
Martin, South Dakota

SOUR CREAM CHOCOLATE CAKE

I've always kept whipping cream on hand in the refrigerator to sour for this cake. This was my grandma's recipe. She died when my mother was 13 years old. My images of her come through stories told by my mother and aunt. My grandmother would skim the cream off their cows' milk and let it sour for the cake. Since they didn't have electric mixers, they had to beat the cake for 10 minutes by hand, making their arms tired.

2 tablespoons baking cocoa
1/2 cup boiling water
1 1/2 cups sifted all-purpose flour
1 1/4 cups sugar
1/2 teaspoon salt
2 eggs
1 cup whipping cream, soured
1 teaspoon vanilla extract
1 teaspoon baking soda
2 tablespoons hot water
2 tablespoons butter or margarine, softened
1/2 teaspoon salt
2 1/2 cups confectioners' sugar
1 egg white
Milk to taste
1 teaspoon vanilla extract

Preheat oven to 350 degrees. Dissolve cocoa in boiling water in saucepan. Cook until thickened; set aside to cool. Sift flour, 1 1/4 cups sugar and 1/2 teaspoon salt together 3 times into mixer bowl. Add eggs and whipping cream; mix well. Add cocoa mixture and vanilla. Beat for 4 to 5 minutes. Add baking soda dissolved in hot water; mix well. Spoon into greased and floured 9-by-13-inch cake pan. Bake at 350 degrees for 25 to 30 minutes or until cake tests done. Let stand until cool. Cream butter and 1/2 teaspoon salt in mixer bowl until light. Add confectioners' sugar, egg white and milk, beating after each addition. Mix in 1 teaspoon vanilla; beat until creamy. Frost cooled cake. Yield: 15 servings.

Tammy Dighero, Xi Zeta Rho
Lamar, Missouri

CHOCOLATE UPSIDE-DOWN CAKE

This cake is always a winner at sorority meetings; men love it, too.

1 cup packed light brown sugar
1/2 cup baking cocoa
2 cups water
12 to 14 marshmallows, quartered
1 (2-layer) package chocolate cake mix
1/2 cup chopped walnuts

Preheat oven to 350 degrees. Combine brown sugar, cocoa, water and marshmallows in greased 9-by-13-inch cake pan; mix well. Prepare cake mix using package instructions. Spoon over brown sugar mixture. Sprinkle with walnuts. Bake at 350 degrees for 25 to 35 minutes or until cake tests done. Cool in pan. Invert to serve. Serve with whipped cream or ice cream. Yield: 12 servings.

Shirley Gatzke, Preceptor Mu Lambda
McKinleyville, California

CHOCOLATE ZUCCHINI CAKE

1/2 cup margarine, softened
1/2 cup vegetable oil
1 1/2 cups sugar
2 eggs
1 teaspoon vanilla extract
1/2 cup sour milk
2 1/2 cups all-purpose flour
1/2 teaspoon baking powder
1 teaspoon each baking soda and cinnamon
1/2 teaspoon cloves
2 cups grated zucchini
1/2 cup semisweet miniature chocolate chips

Preheat oven to 325 degrees. Combine margarine, oil, sugar, eggs and vanilla in bowl; mix well. Add sour milk, flour, baking powder, baking soda, cinnamon and cloves, stirring until blended. Stir in zucchini and chocolate chips. Spoon into greased 9-by-13-inch cake pan. Bake at 325 degrees for 40 to 45 minutes or until cake tests done. Do not frost.
Yield: 12 to 14 servings.

Leona Seever, Preceptor Beta Psi
Huntington, Oregon

CHOCOLATE ZUCCHINI BUNDT CAKE

2 cups shredded zucchini
3 eggs
3/4 cup vegetable oil
1/2 cup milk
1 cup sugar
1 cup packed light brown sugar
1 cup chopped walnuts
2 1/2 cups all-purpose flour
2 1/2 teaspoons baking powder
1 1/2 teaspoons baking soda
1 teaspoon salt
1/2 cup baking cocoa

Preheat oven to 350 degrees. Combine zucchini, eggs, oil, milk, sugar, brown sugar and walnuts in large bowl; mix well. Add flour, baking powder, baking soda, salt and cocoa; mix well. Spoon into greased bundt pan. Bake at 350 degrees for 1 hour. Cool in pan for 15 minutes. Remove to wire rack to cool completely. Yield: 16 servings.

June Bean, Beta Master
Courtenay, British Columbia, Canada

Eileen Balch, Zeta Eta, Derby, Kansas, makes a Light Gelatin Cake by preparing and baking a white cake mix by the light recipe instructions, poking holes in cake, pouring any flavor prepared gelatin over cake, chilling and serving with whipped topping.

CHOCOLATE DELUXE ZUCCHINI CAKE

This recipe is a family favorite, since we are gardeners and have an abundance of zucchini each summer.

3 cups all-purpose flour
1 1/4 teaspoons each baking powder and baking soda
1 teaspoon salt
1/4 teaspoon cinnamon
4 eggs
3 cups sugar
3 (1-ounce) squares unsweetened chocolate, melted
1 1/2 cups vegetable oil
1 1/2 teaspoons vanilla extract
1/2 teaspoon almond extract
3 cups coarsely chopped zucchini
1 cup chopped pecans
1/2 cup chopped dates
Confectioners' sugar to taste

Preheat oven to 350 degrees. Sift flour, baking powder, baking soda, salt and cinnamon in bowl. Beat eggs in mixer bowl. Add sugar, melted chocolate, oil, vanilla and almond flavorings gradually, mixing well. Fold in flour mixture. Squeeze zucchini dry. Stir in zucchini, pecans and dates into batter. Spoon into 2 greased loaf pans or 1 greased tube pan. Bake at 350 degrees for 1 1/4 hours. Sprinkle with confectioners' sugar before serving. Yield: 12 to 16 servings.

Kirsten Ousey, Xi Upsilon Kappa
San Marcos, Texas

COCA-COLA CAKE

2 cups all-purpose flour
2 cups sugar
1 cup margarine
3 tablespoons baking cocoa
1 cup Coca-Cola
1/2 cup buttermilk
1 teaspoon baking soda
1 tablespoon vanilla extract
1 1/2 cups miniature marshmallows
2 eggs, beaten
1/2 cup margarine
3 tablespoons baking cocoa
6 tablespoons Coca-Cola
1 (1-pound) package confectioners' sugar
1 teaspoon vanilla extract
1 cup chopped walnuts

Preheat oven to 350 degrees. Mix flour and sugar in large bowl. Combine 1 cup margarine, 3 tablespoons cocoa and 1 cup Coca-Cola in saucepan; heat just to boiling. Add to flour mixture, mixing well. Stir in buttermilk, baking soda, 1 tablespoon vanilla, marshmallows and eggs; do not beat. Spoon into greased and floured 9-by-13-inch cake pan. Bake at 350 degrees for 35 to 40 minutes or until cake tests done. Bring 1/2 cup margarine, 3 tablespoons cocoa and 6 tablespoons Coca-Cola to a boil in saucepan. Cook for 1 minute. Pour over confectioners' sugar in mixer bowl; beat until blended. Add 1 teaspoon vanilla and walnuts, mixing well. Spread over warm cake. Yield: 15 servings.

Nancy Krebeck, Xi Alpha Delta
Henderson, Nevada

COOKIES-AND-CREAM CAKE

8 cups cookies and cream ice cream, softened
1 (2-layer) package chocolate cake mix
3 eggs
1 1/3 cups water
1/2 cup vegetable oil
8 ounces whipped topping

Spread ice cream evenly in two 9-inch round cake pans lined with plastic wrap. Freeze for 1 hour or longer. Remove from pans; return ice cream layers to freezer. Preheat oven to 350 degrees. Combine cake mix, eggs, water and oil in large mixer bowl; beat until smooth. Spoon into 3 greased 9-inch round cake pans. Bake at 350 degrees for 20 to 23 minutes or until layers test done. Cool in pans on wire racks for 10 minutes. Remove to wire racks to cool completely. Remove plastic wrap from ice cream. Stack cake and ice cream layers alternately on cake plate. Frost with whipped topping. Store in freezer.
Yield: 12 to 16 servings.

Barbara Stoltenberg, Alpha Tau Master
Garden Grove, California

CRUNCHY PECAN DEVIL'S FOOD CAKE

This recipe was given to me 42 years ago by my aunt, who is now 87 years old. The combination of chocolate and spices makes a very different and delicious cake.

1/2 cup baking cocoa
1/2 cup hot water
1 teaspoon baking soda
1 cup buttermilk
2 cups all-purpose flour
1/2 teaspoon each cloves, cinnamon and nutmeg
2 cups sugar
1/2 cup margarine, softened
2 eggs
2 teaspoons vanilla extract
2 tablespoons each shortening and margarine
1/2 cup packed light brown sugar
2 tablespoons milk
1 cup chopped pecans

Preheat oven to 350 degrees. Stir cocoa into hot water in bowl; set aside. Stir baking soda into buttermilk; set aside. Mix flour and spices in bowl. Cream sugar and margarine in mixer bowl until light and fluffy. Beat in eggs 1 at a time. Beat in cocoa mixture gradually. Beat in flour mixture alternately with buttermilk mixture. Mix in vanilla. Spoon into greased and floured 9-by-13-inch cake pan. Bake at 350 degrees for 30 to 35 minutes or until cake tests done. Bring mixture of shortening, margarine, brown sugar and milk to a boil in saucepan. Cook for 1 to 2 minutes, stirring constantly. Stir in pecans. Cool slightly. Pour over warm cake, spreading evenly. Place cake under broiler. Broil until pecans are lightly toasted.
Yield: 18 to 24 servings.

Ila S. Hood, Theta Gamma
Ruston, Louisiana

EARTHQUAKE CAKE

I served this at our potluck Christmas party, and even though it looks like #7 on the Richter scale, it is delicious. It got rave reviews.

1 cup chopped pecans
1 cup coconut
1 (2-layer) package German sweet chocolate cake mix
8 ounces cream cheese, softened
1/2 cup margarine
1 (1-pound) package confectioners' sugar

Preheat oven to 350 degrees. Sprinkle pecans and coconut in greased 9-by-13-inch baking pan. Prepare cake mix using package instructions. Spoon into pan. Combine cream cheese, margarine and confectioners' sugar in mixer bowl; mix well. Spoon over batter. Bake at 350 degrees for 1 hour or until brown.
Yield: 15 servings.

Mika Maples, Xi Alpha Epsilon
Manitowoc, Wisconsin

FUDGE CAKE

This batter is so good that I sometimes eat three to four spoonfuls before it leaves the pan.

3/4 cup butter or margarine, softened
2 1/4 cups sugar
1 1/2 teaspoons vanilla extract
3 eggs
3 (1-ounce) squares semisweet chocolate, melted
1 1/2 teaspoons baking soda
3/4 teaspoon salt
3 cups all-purpose flour
1 1/2 cups cold water
1/4 cup shortening
1/4 cup baking cocoa or carob powder
1/4 cup milk
1 cup sugar
Salt to taste
1/2 teaspoon vanilla extract

Preheat oven to 350 degrees. Cream butter and 2 1/4 cups sugar in mixer bowl until light and fluffy. Add 1 1/2 teaspoons vanilla, eggs, chocolate, baking soda and 3/4 teaspoon salt; beat until blended. Add flour alternately with water, beating constantly. Spoon into greased and floured 9-by-13-inch cake pan. Bake at 350 degrees for 30 to 35 minutes or until cake tests done. Cool completely. Combine shortening, 1/4 cup baking cocoa, milk, 1 cup sugar and salt in saucepan. Bring to a boil. Cook for 1 minute. Cool slightly. Add 1/2 teaspoon vanilla; beat until of spreading consistency. Spread over top of cake. May use nondairy creamer substitute for milk if allergic to dairy products. May substitute 5 tablespoons baking cocoa or carob powder for semisweet chocolate.
Yield: 12 to 16 servings.

Crystal Marker, Xi Alpha Eta
Torrington, Wyoming

FUDGE PUDDING CAKE

3/4 cup sugar
1 tablespoon butter or margarine, softened
1/2 cup milk
1 cup all-purpose flour
2 tablespoons baking cocoa
1 teaspoon baking powder
1/4 teaspoon salt
1/2 cup chopped walnuts
1/2 cup sugar
1/2 cup packed light brown sugar
1/4 cup baking cocoa
1 1/4 cups boiling water
Ice cream (optional)

Preheat oven to 350 degrees. Beat 3/4 cup sugar, butter and milk in mixer bowl until blended. Beat in mixture of flour, 2 tablespoons cocoa, baking powder and salt. Stir in walnuts. Spoon into greased 9-by-9-inch square cake pan. Combine 1/2 cup sugar, brown sugar and 1/4 cup cocoa in bowl; mix well. Sprinkle over batter. Pour water over top; do not stir. Bake at 350 degrees for 30 minutes. Cool for 10 minutes before serving. Spoon ice cream over top.
Yield: 9 servings.

Neldalea Dotray, Preceptor Delta Tau
Greenville, Illinois

GATEAU AU CHOCOLAT

4 (1-ounce) squares sweet chocolate
1/2 cup butter, softened
4 egg whites, room temperature
4 egg yolks
4 teaspoons sugar
4 teaspoons flour
Confectioners' sugar (optional)
Chocolate curls (optional)

Preheat oven to 425 degrees. Melt chocolate in double boiler over hot water, stirring occasionally. Remove from heat. Stir in butter. Beat egg whites in mixer bowl until stiff peaks form; set aside. Beat egg yolks until thick and light yellow. Add 4 teaspoons sugar gradually, beating constantly. Add flour gradually; mix well. Blend into chocolate mixture. Fold into stiffly beaten egg whites gently. Spoon into lightly greased 5-by-9-inch loaf pan lined with waxed paper. Place pan in oven. Reduce oven tempersature to 350 degrees. Bake at 350 degrees for 25 minutes. Cool on wire rack. Chill for 4 hours or longer. Loosen from sides of pan. Invert onto serving plate. Dust with confectioners' sugar or garnish with chocolate curls. Cut into 3/4-inch slices.
Yield: 16 servings.

S. Marlene Gawley, Preceptor Sigma
Penticton, British Columbia, Canada

Marilyn Vogt, Epsilon Beta, Truman, Minnesota, spreads a hot, freshly baked yellow cake with mixture of 1 cup apricot preserves, 1 tablespoon lemon juice, 1 1/3 cups flaked coconut and 1 1/2 cups miniature marshmallows and broiling until brown for a Broiled Party Cake.

GOOD BAPTIST CAKE

This recipe was a finalist in the "overall recipe" division of a local contest sponsored by our newspaper. It won for "overall dessert".

1 (2-layer) package German chocolate cake mix
1 (14-ounce) can sweetened condensed milk
1 (5-ounce) jar caramel topping
8 ounces whipped topping
6 Heath or Skor candy bars, crushed
Roasted almonds (optional)
1 (4-ounce) jar maraschino cherries

Preheat oven to 350 degrees. Prepare cake mix using package instructions. Spread into greased 9-by-13-inch cake pan. Bake at 350 degrees for 25 to 35 minutes or until cake tests done. Poke holes in cake. Top with condensed milk, caramel topping, whipped topping and crushed Heath bars. Arrange almonds and cherries on top. Chill for 4 hours or longer. Yield: 15 servings.

Paula Crook, Alpha Beta
McComb, Mississippi

KRAZY CAKE

My mother told me that this recipe comes from the Depression era.

1 1/2 cups all-purpose flour
1 cup sugar
1 teaspoon salt
1 teaspoon baking soda
3 tablespoons baking cocoa
1 teaspoon vanilla extract
1 tablespoon vinegar
3 tablespoons vegetable oil
1 cup water
1 tablespoon confectioners' sugar

Preheat oven to 350 degrees. Sift flour, sugar, salt, baking soda and cocoa into bowl. Make 3 wells in mixture. Add vanilla, vinegar and oil. Pour in water; mix well. Spoon into greased 8-by-8-inch square cake pan. Bake at 350 degrees for 35 minutes. Sprinkle hot cake with confectioners' sugar. Let stand until cool. Yield: 16 servings.

Jeanne L. Phillips, Preceptor Lambda Phi
Garland, Texas

LOVER'S CAKE

1 (2-layer) package chocolate cake mix
1/2 (14-ounce) can sweetened condensed milk
3/4 cup caramel topping
16 ounces whipped topping
3 Skor candy bars, crushed

Preheat oven to 350 degrees. Prepare cake mix using package instructions. Spoon into greased 9-by-13-inch cake pan. Bake at 350 degrees for 25 to 35 minutes or until cake tests done. Poke holes in cake. Pour condensed milk over cake. Cool to lukewarm. Drizzle caramel topping. Add whipped topping and sprinkle with crushed candy bars.
Yield: 12 to 16 servings.

Pat Potyka, Xi Chi
Butler, Pennsylvania

MAYONNAISE CAKE

I have been making this cake for over 27 years. It has a mild chocolate taste with a flair.

2 cups all-purpose flour
1 1/2 teaspoons baking soda
1 cup sugar
1/8 teaspoon salt
4 teaspoons baking cocoa
1 cup mayonnaise
1 cup boiling water
1 teaspoon vanilla extract

Preheat oven to 375 degrees. Sift flour, baking soda, sugar, salt and cocoa into large bowl. Stir in mayonnaise. Add boiling water and vanilla; mix well. Spoon into greased and floured 9-by-13-inch cake pan or two 9-inch round pans. Bake at 375 degrees for 30 minutes. Frost with any favorite chocolate, vanilla or butter frosting. Yield: 12 to 16 servings.

Debbie Wood, Xi Beta Upsilon
Edmond, Oklahoma

MOUND CAKE

1 (2-layer) package devil's food cake mix
1 cup sugar
24 large marshmallows
1 cup milk
1 (14-ounce) package flaked coconut
1/2 cup margarine
1 cup sugar
1/2 cup milk
1 1/2 cups semisweet chocolate chips

Preheat oven to 350 degrees. Prepare cake mix using package instructions. Spread into greased 9-by-13-inch cake pans. Bake at 350 degrees for 25 to 30 minutes or until cake tests done. Combine sugar, marshmallows and 1 cup milk in saucepan. Cook over low heat until marshmallows melt, stirring constantly. Stir in coconut. Spread over warm cake. Combine margarine, 1 cup sugar and 1/2 cup milk in heavy saucepan. Bring to a boil over medium heat. Add chocolate chips; mix until melted. Spread over top of cake. Yield: 15 servings.

Lynne Stahl, Preceptor Xi
Baxter Springs, Kansas

Martha Thomas, Omega Lambda, Fort White, Florida, makes Easy Coconut Cake by adding 3 1/2 ounces coconut to a prepared white cake mix and baking. Poke holes in cake and drizzle with 4 ounces cream of coconut. Top cake with 6 ounces whipped topping and sprinkle with additional coconut. Store in refrigerator.

RAVE REVIEWS COCONUT CAKE

1 (2-layer) package yellow cake mix
1 (4-ounce) package vanilla instant pudding mix
1 1/3 cups water
4 eggs
1/4 cup vegetable oil
2 cups flaked coconut
1 cup chopped pecans
4 tablespoons butter or margarine
2 cups flaked coconut
8 ounces cream cheese, softened
2 teaspoons milk
3 1/2 cups sifted confectioners' sugar
1/2 teaspoon vanilla extract

Preheat oven to 350 degrees. Combine cake mix, pudding mix, water, eggs and oil in large mixer bowl. Beat at medium speed for 4 minutes, scraping bowl occasionally. Stir in 2 cups coconut and pecans. Spoon into 3 greased and floured 8-inch cake pans. Bake at 350 degrees for 35 minutes or until cake tests done. Cool in pan for 15 minutes. Remove to wire rack to cool completely. Melt 2 tablespoons of the butter in skillet. Add 2 cups coconut. Cook over low heat until golden brown, stirring constantly. Spread on paper towel to cool. Cream remaining 2 tablespoons butter and cream cheese in medium mixer bowl. Add milk and confectioners' sugar; beat until creamy. Add vanilla. Stir in 1 3/4 cups of the coconut. Spread icing between layers and over top and side of cake. Sprinkle with remaining coconut.
Yield: 12 servings.

Polly A. Patton, Xi Epsilon Beta
Woodstock, Virginia

CRUMB CAKE

2 cups all-purpose flour
1 cup sugar
1 teaspoon cinnamon
1 teaspoon nutmeg
1 teaspoon cloves
1/2 cup shortening
1 cup sour milk or buttermilk
1 teaspoon baking soda
1/4 teaspoon salt

Preheat oven to 350 degrees. Mix flour, sugar, cinnamon, nutmeg, cloves and shortening in medium bowl with fork until crumbly. Reserve 1 cup crumb mixture. Stir sour cream, baking soda and salt into remaining crumb mixture. Spoon into greased and floured 5-by-9-inch loaf pan. Sprinkle with reserved crumb mixture. Bake at 350 degrees for 1 hour or until cake tests done. Yield: 12 servings.

Kathy Beauchamp, Preceptor Alpha Theta
Jackson, Michigan

Debbie Benge, Beta Kappa, Whitesburg, Kentucky, makes Dreamsicle Cake by preparing and baking orange supreme cake mix substituting water for milk and adding 1 tablespoon orange extract. Frost cooled cake with mixture of 2 cups whipped topping, 2 cups sour cream and 2 cups confectioners' sugar.

DREAM CAKE

I am allergic to whipped topping and it's difficult to find recipes of this type that do not use it. My sorority sisters and I enjoy this very rich tasting, but fairly low-fat dessert.

1 (2-layer) package yellow cake mix
1 egg
1/2 cup margarine, softened
1/2 cup chopped pecans
8 ounces nonfat cream cheese, softened
2 eggs
1 teaspoon vanilla extract
1 (1-pound) package confectioners' sugar

Preheat oven to 350 degrees. Combine cake mix, 1 egg and margarine in medium mixer bowl; mix well. Stir in pecans. Press into ungreased 9-by-13-inch cake pan; set aside. Beat cream cheese, 2 eggs, vanilla and confectioners' sugar in medium mixer bowl. Spread evenly over prepared layer. Bake at 350 degrees for 30 minutes. Cut into squares.
Yield: 24 servings.

Shiela Davis-Sweat, Laureate Lambda
Stuart, Florida

EGG-BUTTER-MILK-LESS CAKE

My Grandmother McGregor baked this cake for all family occasions. The recipe is about 100 years old.

2 cups sugar
1 cup shortening
2 teaspoons cinnamon
1/2 teaspoon ground cloves
1 teaspoon allspice
2 teaspoons nutmeg
2 cups hot water
2 cups raisins
4 cups all-purpose flour
2 teaspoons baking soda
2 teaspoons vanilla extract
Salt to taste
1 cup coarsely chopped English walnuts
3 cups packed light brown sugar
1 1/2 cups cream
3 tablespoons butter or margarine

Preheat oven to 350 degrees. Bring sugar, shortening, cinnamon, cloves, allspice, nutmeg, hot water and raisins to a boil in large saucepan; remove from heat. Let stand until cool. Add flour, baking soda, vanilla and salt, mixing well after each addition. Stir in walnuts. Spoon into 3 greased and floured 9-inch cake pans. Bake at 350 degrees for 35 to 40 minutes or until layers test done. Cool. Combine brown sugar, cream and butter in medium saucepan. Cook over medium heat to 280 degrees on candy thermometer, soft-ball stage. Spread between layers and over top and side of cake. May substitute 9-by-13-inch cake pan for round cake pans. Yield: 15 servings.

Catherine Maulsby, Xi Epsilon Omicron
Claremore, Oklahoma

QUEEN ELIZABETH CAKE

This is my husband's favorite recipe.

1 cup rolled oats
1 1/2 cups boiling water
1/2 cup butter or margarine, softened
1 cup packed dark brown sugar or 1 1/2 cups brownulated sugar
1 cup sugar
2 eggs
1 1/2 cups all-purpose flour
1/2 teaspoon salt
1 teaspoon cinnamon
1 teaspoon baking soda
1/2 cup melted butter or margarine
1 cup flaked coconut
2 tablespoons cream
1 cup packed dark brown sugar
1 cup chopped pecans

Mix oats and boiling water in small bowl. Let stand for 20 minutes. Preheat oven to 350 degrees. Cream butter, brown sugar and sugar in large mixer bowl until light and fluffy. Add eggs; mix well. Add sifted mixture of flour, salt, cinnamon and baking soda. Stir in oats mixture. Pour into nonstick 9-by-13-inch cake pan. Bake at 350 degrees for 40 minutes or until cake tests done. Combine melted butter, coconut, cream and brown sugar in small bowl; mix well. Stir in pecans. Spread over cake. Broil 4 inches from heat source until brown and bubbly. Yield: 24 squares.

Susie Anand, Xi Epsilon Zeta
Sikeston, Missouri

ENGLISH CAKE

This recipe belonged to my husband's Grandma Walton. Brought from England in the early 1900s, it's a family favorite, served at special occasions.

4 cups all-purpose flour
1 (1-pound) package raisins
2 cups sugar
1 teaspoon salt
2 teaspoons nutmeg
1 cup shortening
4 eggs, beaten
2 teaspoons lemon extract
1 cup sour milk
2 teaspoons baking soda

Preheat oven to 350 degrees. Combine 1/2 cup of the flour and raisins in small bowl; set aside. Combine remaining 3 1/2 cups flour, sugar, salt and nutmeg in large bowl. Cut shortening into flour mixture with pastry blender. Add eggs and lemon extract; stirring just until moistened. Add raisin mixture; mix well. Stir in mixture of sour milk and baking soda just until moistened; batter will be stiff. Spoon into greased and floured tube pan. Bake at 350 degrees for 1 hour or until cake tests done. Cool in pan. Invert onto serving plate. Store tightly covered.
Yield: 16 to 20 servings.

Brenda Walton, Preceptor Omicron
Niagara Falls, New York

FRENCH CAKE

This cake contains no milk or fat, which is good for some restricted diets. My children loved it, and now it's a favorite of my grandchildren.

1 cup all-purpose flour
1 cup sugar
1 teaspoon baking powder
3 eggs
1 teaspoon vanilla extract

Preheat oven to 350 degrees. Sift flour, sugar and baking powder into medium bowl. Add eggs and beat well. Stir in vanilla. Pour into greased and floured 8-by-8-inch square cake pan. Bake at 350 degrees for 25 minutes or until light brown. Cool in pan. Cut into squares. Yield: 8 servings.

Bobbe Pollak, Preceptor Alpha Beta
New Orleans, Louisiana

FRUITCAKE

2 eggs, lightly beaten
1 (14-ounce) jar mincemeat
1/2 cup rum
1 (14-ounce) can sweetened condensed milk
2 1/2 cups all-purpose flour
1 teaspoon baking soda
1 cup coarsely chopped pecans
2 cups mixed candied fruit

Preheat oven to 300 degrees. Mix eggs, mincemeat, rum and condensed milk in large mixer bowl until well mixed. Add mixture of flour and baking soda; mix well. Stir in pecans and fruit. Spoon into greased and floured 9-by-9-inch cake pans. Bake at 300 degrees for 1 hour and 45 to 1 hour and 50 minutes. Cool in pans for 15 minutes. Invert onto wire rack to cool completely. Yield: 12 servings.

Sister in Beta Sigma Phi

ICEBOX FRUITCAKE

1 (1-pound) package graham crackers, crushed
1 (1-pound) package candied cherries, cut into small pieces
1 (15-ounce) can pineapple tidbits, drained
1 cup chopped dates
1 cup raisins
1 (3-ounce) can flaked coconut
4 cups chopped pecans
1 (14-ounce) can sweetened condensed milk

Combine graham cracker crumbs, cherries, pineapple, dates, raisins, coconut and pecans in large bowl; mix well. Stir in condensed milk. Spoon into greased and floured tube pan. Chill, covered, in pan until serving time; will keep in refrigerator for 3 to 4 days.
Yield: 16 servings.

Willie L. White, Beta Chi
Ocala, Florida

SPICY DARK FRUITCAKES

I make this fruitcake every year the Friday after Thanksgiving to give as Christmas presents.

3 1/2 cups mixed dried fruit
1 1/4 cups dark seedless raisins
1 1/4 cups golden seedless raisins or 1 1/4 cups additional dark seedless raisins
1 cup chopped walnuts
1 cup chopped pecans
3 cups sifted all-purpose flour
1 teaspoon each baking powder, salt, cinnamon and allspice
1/2 teaspoon nutmeg
1/2 teaspoon ground cloves
1 cup shortening
2 cups packed dark brown sugar
4 eggs
1 to 3 cups grape juice

Preheat oven to 275 degrees. Place a large baking pan full of water on bottom oven rack for moisture during baking time. Combine dried fruit, dark raisins, golden raisins, walnuts and pecans in medium bowl. Mix flour, baking powder, salt and spices together in small bowl. Sprinkle 1/4 cup flour mixture over fruit mixture. Cream shortening and brown sugar together in large mixer bowl. Add eggs 1 at a time, beating well after each addition. Stir dry ingredients into creamed mixture alternately with grape juice until very moist. Stir in fruit mixture. Fill two 5-by-9-inch or five 3-by-5-inch greased and floured loaf pans lined with waxed paper 3/4 full. Bake at 275 degrees for 2 1/2 hours or until wooden pick comes out clean. Cool in pans. Yield: 24 servings.

Elizabeth Petrunak, Xi Omicron Upsilon
Bridgeport, California

YUM YUM FRUITCAKE

This recipe has been handed down in my family for many generations.

2 cups cold water
2 cups sugar
2 tablespoons shortening
2 tablespoons cinnamon
1/2 cup baking cocoa
1 (1-pound) package raisins
3 cups all-purpose flour
1/2 teaspoon baking soda
1 1/2 teaspoon baking powder
1/2 teaspoon salt
1 teaspoon vanilla extract
1 apple, sliced

Preheat oven to 350 degrees. Bring cold water, sugar, shortening, cinnamon, baking cocoa and raisins to a boil in medium saucepan. Boil for 5 minutes; remove from heat. Let stand until cool. Combine flour, baking soda, baking powder and salt in large bowl. Stir in raisin mixture; mix well. Add vanilla. Spoon into greased and floured tube pan or two loaf pans. Bake at 350 degrees until firm to touch. Store in airtight container with sliced apple. Yield: 16 servings.

Diane Olsen, Xi Rho
New Minas, Nova Scotia, Canada

TWELFTH-NIGHT CAKE

Special ingredients baked in the cake represent the gifts of the wise men. The dried apricot is gold. A clove is frankincense, and a raisin myrrh. To enhance a festive occasion, let the one who finds the cherry in his or her cake be the king or queen of the evening or "Twelfth Night." As in England or France, this ruler can lead the games for the party.

1 cup butter or margarine, softened
3 cups sugar
6 egg yolks
3 cups sifted all-purpose flour
1/4 teaspoon baking soda
1 cup sour cream
6 egg whites
1 dried apricot
1 whole clove
1 raisin
1 cherry

Preheat oven to 300 degrees. Cream butter and sugar in large mixer bowl until light and fluffy. Beat in egg yolks 1 at a time, mixing well after each addition. Sift flour and baking soda together 2 times. Add alternately with sour cream to sugar mixture, beating well after each addition. Beat egg whites in small mixer bowl until stiff peaks form; fold into the creamed mixture. Spoon into greased and floured bundt pan. Hide the apricot, clove, raisin and cherry in batter. Bake at 300 degrees for 1 1/2 hours or until cake tests done. Cool in pan. Invert onto cake plate. Yield: 10 to 12 servings.

Brenda Hubbell, Delta Theta
Hendersonville, Tennessee

NO-BAKE CHRISTMAS SURPRISE CAKE

1 cup sugar
1 cup butter or margarine, softened
2 eggs, beaten
1/4 cup shredded coconut
1/8 teaspoon salt
34 arrowroot biscuits, crushed
1/4 cup whole red glacéed cherries
1/4 cup halved red glacéed cherries
1/4 cup whole green glacéed cherries
1/4 cup halved green glacéed cherries
1 cup white miniature marshmallows
1 recipe butter icing

Combine sugar, butter and eggs in top of double boiler; mix well. Stir in coconut and salt. Cook over boiling water for 15 minutes or until mixture is of custard consistency and coats the back of spoon, stirring occasionally. Remove from heat and let stand until cool. Stir in biscuit crumbs, cherries and marshmallows. Spread in buttered 9-by-12-inch cake pan. Top with icing. Chill, covered, in refrigerator until serving time. Yield: 15 servings.

Norma Patterson, Laureate Beta
Winnipeg, Manitoba, Canada

FRUIT COCKTAIL CAKE

2 cups all-purpose flour
1 1/2 cups sugar
2 teaspoons baking soda
1/4 teaspoon salt
2 eggs, beaten
1 (28-ounce) can fruit cocktail
1/2 cup margarine
2 cups packed light brown sugar
1 cup evaporated milk
2 teaspoons vanilla extract
1/2 cup pecans or coconut

Preheat oven to 325 degrees. Combine flour, sugar, baking soda, salt, eggs and fruit cocktail in large mixer bowl; beat until well mixed. Pour into 9-by-13-inch greased and floured cake pan or bundt pan. Bake at 325 degrees for 55 to 60 minutes or until cake tests done. Combine margarine, brown sugar and evaporated milk in small saucepan. Cook over medium heat until thickened, stirring constantly. Remove from heat. Stir in vanilla and pecans. Pour half the glaze over warm cake. Slice cake and place on individual serving plates. Spoon remaining glaze over cake slices to serve. Yield: 12 to 15 servings.

Betty Lou Menard, Xi Alpha Theta
Sudbury, Ontario, Canada

GINGERBREAD

This recipe has been passed down through my family for more than 100 years.

1/2 cup shortening
1/2 cup sugar
1 egg, beaten
2 1/2 cups sifted all-purpose flour
1 1/2 teaspoons baking soda
1 teaspoon cinnamon
1 teaspoon ginger
1/2 teaspoon ground cloves
1/2 teaspoon salt
1 cup molasses
1 cup hot water

Preheat oven to 350 degrees. Cream shortening and sugar in large mixer bowl. Beat in egg. Sift flour, baking soda, cinnamon, ginger, cloves and salt together. Mix molasses with hot water in small bowl. Add dry ingredients alternately with molasses mixture to creamed mixture; beating well after each addition. Spoon into 9-by-9-inch cake pan lined with waxed paper. Bake at 350 degrees for 45 minutes or until gingerbread tests done. Yield: 12 to 16 servings.

Jo Schenck, Xi Gamma Iota
Old Forge, New York

Cheryl Weadon, Xi Omicron Upsilon, San Angelo, Texas, makes Spring Delight Cake by preparing a yellow cake mix with 4 eggs, 1/2 cup oil, 1 can apricot nectar and a package of mixed fruit gelatin. Bake in greased bundt pan in preheated 300-degree oven for 1 1/2 hours.

HOT MILK CAKE

1 cup milk
1/2 cup butter or margarine
4 eggs
2 cups sugar
2 teaspoons vanilla extract
2 cups all-purpose flour
Salt to taste
2 teaspoons baking powder
1 cup butter or margarine, softened
1 teaspoon vanilla extract
1 (1-pound) package confectioners' sugar
3 tablespoons milk

Preheat oven to 350 degrees. Heat 1 cup milk and 1/2 cup butter in small saucepan over low heat. Beat eggs in large mixer bowl. Add sugar, 2 teaspoons vanilla, flour, milk mixture, salt and baking powder, mixing well after each addition. Pour into greased and floured 9-by-13-inch cake pan or two 9-inch round cake pans. Bake at 350 degrees for 30 to 35 minutes. Cool in pan for 10 minutes. Invert onto wire rack to cool completely. Place on serving plate. Cream 1 cup butter and 1 teaspoon vanilla in small mixer bowl. Add confectioners' sugar; mix well. Add enough milk to make of desired consistency. Spread over cake. Yield: 10 to 12 servings.

Carla Hargett, Beta Gamma
Pasadena, Maryland

HUSBAND'S NO-EGG CAKE

3/4 cup shortening
1 1/2 cups sugar
1 cup tomato soup
3/4 cup water
1 teaspoon baking soda
3 cups all-purpose flour
3/4 teaspoon salt
1 tablespoon baking powder
1 1/2 teaspoons cinnamon
1 teaspoon ground cloves
1 teaspoon nutmeg
1 1/2 cups raisins
1 cup chopped pecans
1 cup packed light brown sugar
1/2 cup sugar
1/3 cup milk
2 tablespoons shortening
2 tablespoons butter
1 tablespoon light corn syrup
1/4 teaspoon salt
1 teaspoon vanilla extract

Preheat oven to 350 degrees. Cream 3/4 cup shortening and 1 1/2 cups sugar in large mixer bowl. Add mixture of tomato soup, water and baking soda; mix well. Add mixture of flour, 3/4 teaspoon salt, baking powder, cinnamon, cloves and nutmeg. Stir in raisins and pecans. Spoon into greased and floured 9-by-13-inch cake pan. Bake at 350 degrees for 1 hour or until cake tests done. Bring brown sugar, 1/2 cup sugar, milk, 2 tablespoons shortening, butter, corn syrup and salt to a rolling boil in saucepan. Boil for 1 minute, stirring constantly. Remove from heat. Cool to lukewarm. Stir in vanilla. Beat until of spreading consistency. Spread over cake. Yield: 15 servings.

Cordelia M. Holst
Miles City, Montana

ITALIAN CREAM CAKE

2 cups sugar
1/2 cup margarine
1/2 cup shortening
5 egg yolks
2 cups sifted all-purpose flour
1 teaspoon baking soda
1/2 teaspoon salt
1 cup buttermilk
2 cups flaked coconut
1 cup chopped pecans
1 teaspoon vanilla extract
5 egg whites, stiffly beaten
8 ounces cream cheese, softened
1/2 cup margarine, softened
1 (1-pound) package confectioners' sugar
2 teaspoons vanilla extract
1 cup chopped pecans

Preheat oven to 350 degrees. Cream sugar, 1/2 cup margarine and shortening in large mixer bowl. Add egg yolks 1 at a time, mixing well after each addition. Add mixture of flour, baking soda and salt alternately with buttermilk, mixing well after each addition. Stir in coconut, 1 cup pecans and 1 teaspoon vanilla; mix well. Fold in egg whites gently. Pour into three 8-inch round cake pans lined with waxed paper. Bake at 350 degrees for 20 to 30 minutes or until wooden pick inserted in center comes out clean. Cool in pans for 10 minutes. Invert onto wire racks to cool completely. Beat cream cheese and 1/2 cup margarine in medium mixer bowl until creamy. Add confectioners' sugar and 2 teaspoons vanilla; beat until smooth and of spreading consistency. Stir in 1 cup pecans. Spread between layers and over top and side of cake.
Yield: 12 to 16 servings.

Jeri Lynn Henderson, Eta Mu
Bay City, Texas

OLD-FASHIONED JAM CAKE

1 cup sugar
3/4 cup shortening
1/2 cup sour milk
3 eggs
2 cups all-purpose flour
1 teaspoon baking soda
1 teaspoon cinnamon
1 teaspoon nutmeg
1 teaspoon ground cloves
1 teaspoon allspice
1 cup apricot or pineapple jam

Preheat oven to 350 degrees. Cream sugar and shortening in large mixer bowl until light and fluffy. Add milk and eggs; mix well. Add mixture of flour, baking soda, cinnamon, nutmeg, cloves and allspice; mix well. Stir in jam just until blended. Spoon into greased and floured 9-by-13-inch cake pan. Bake at 350 degrees for 25 to 30 minutes or until cake tests done. Yield: 15 servings.

Sharon Kenefick, Laureate Rho
Hot Springs, South Dakota

LEMON CAKE

1 (2-layer) package lemon cake mix
1 (4-ounce) package lemon instant pudding mix
1 cup water
4 eggs
1/2 cup vegetable oil
1 cup confectioners' sugar
Juice of 1 lemon

Preheat oven to 350 degrees. Spray bundt pan with nonstick cooking spray; dust with flour. Combine cake mix, pudding mix, water, eggs and oil in large mixer bowl. Beat at medium speed for 2 minutes, scraping bowl occasionally. Spoon into prepared bundt pan. Bake at 350 degrees for 45 to 55 minutes or until cake tests done. Cool in pan on wire rack for 25 minutes. Invert onto serving plate. Beat confectioners' sugar and lemon juice in small mixer bowl until smooth. Drizzle over warm cake.
Yield: 16 servings.

Betty Kastashuk, Laureate Phi
Canada

LEMON DELUXE CAKE

My mother likes to serve this dessert at parties. It makes a pretty Easter cake.

1 (2-layer) package lemon cake mix
2 tablespoons vegetable oil
2 (4-ounce) packages lemon instant pudding mix
2 envelopes whipped topping mix
2 1/2 cups milk
Coconut to taste

Preheat oven to 350 degrees. Prepare cake mix using package directions and adding 2 tablespoons oil. Bake cake using package directions in three greased and floured 9-inch round cake pans. Cool in pans for 10 minutes. Invert onto wire racks to cool completely. Combine pudding mix, whipped topping mix and milk in medium mixer bowl; mix well. Spread between layers and over top of cake. Sprinkle with coconut. Chill until serving time. Store in refrigerator. May substitute chocolate cake mix and chocolate instant pudding mix for the lemon cake mix and lemon pudding mix. Yield: 10 servings.

Ruth A. Harper, Laureate Alpha Alpha
Charleston, West Virginia

GLAZED LEMON CAKE

4 eggs, separated
1 (3-ounce) package lemon gelatin
3/4 cup boiling water
1 (2-layer) package yellow cake mix
3/4 cup vegetable oil
1/2 cup fresh lemon juice
1/4 cup plus 2 tablespoons margarine
1 cup sugar

Preheat oven to 325 degrees. Beat egg yolks in bowl with fork until light. Beat egg whites in mixer bowl until stiff peaks form. Dissolve gelatin in boiling water in large mixer bowl. Add cake mix, oil and egg yolks; beat at medium speed until smooth. Fold in egg whites gently. Spoon into greased and floured tube pan. Bake at 325 degrees for 1 1/4 hours or until cake tests done. Combine lemon juice, margarine and sugar in small saucepan over low heat. Heat until well blended, stirring constantly; do not boil. Drizzle over hot cake. Yield: 16 servings.

Debbie White, Xi Beta Kappa
Deatsville, Alabama

LEMON PUDDING CAKE

My mother chose this recipe for my entry into the amazing world of baking when I was 10 years old. That was 60 years ago.

1 cup sugar
3 tablespoons all-purpose flour
2 egg yolks
1 cup milk
Juice of 1 lemon
Grated rind of 1 lemon
2 egg whites, stiffly beaten

Preheat oven to 325 degrees. Combine sugar and flour in large mixer bowl. Add egg yolks, milk, lemon juice and lemon rind; mix well. Fold stiffly beaten egg whites into sugar mixture gently. Spoon into ungreased 1 3/4-quart ovenproof bowl. Set bowl in pan of water. Bake at 325 degrees for 1 hour. Yield: 6 to 8 servings.

Dolores Crosby, Preceptor Alpha Upsilon
Orange, California

LEMON SPONGE CAKE

This recipe has been in my husband's family for several years.

1 (2-layer) package lemon cake mix
1/2 cup sugar
3/4 cup vegetable oil
1 cup apricot nectar
4 eggs
Lemon juice to taste
2 cups confectioners' sugar

Preheat oven to 350 degrees. Combine cake mix, sugar, oil and apricot nectar in large mixer bowl. Add eggs 1 at a time, beating well after each addition. Beat for 10 minutes, scraping bowl occasionally. Spoon into greased and floured bundt pan. Bake at 350 degrees for 45 minutes. Reduce oven temperature to 325 degrees. Bake for 10 minutes longer. Cool slightly in pan. Invert onto wire rack to cool completely. Place on serving plate. Add enough lemon juice to confectioners' sugar to make of glaze consistency. Drizzle over cooled cake. Yield: 10 to 12 servings.

Lisa Collins, Xi Alpha Lambda
Whitesburg, Kentucky

GOLDEN LOAF CAKE WITH LEMON SAUCE

2 cups all-purpose flour
1 1/4 cups sugar
2 1/4 teaspoons baking powder
2/3 cup corn oil margarine, softened
2 egg whites
3/4 cup skim milk
1 teaspoon vanilla extract
3 or 4 drops yellow food coloring
1 cup sugar
2 tablespoons cornstarch
2 cups water
2 tablespoons corn oil margarine
2 tablespoons lemon juice
2 tablespoons grated lemon rind

Preheat oven to 325 degrees. Combine flour, 1 1/4 cups sugar and baking powder in large mixer bowl. Add 2/3 cup margarine, egg whites and 1/4 cup milk. Beat at medium speed for 2 minutes. Add remaining 1/2 cup milk, vanilla and food coloring. Beat at medium speed for 2 minutes longer. Spoon into oiled and floured 5-by-9-inch loaf pan. Bake at 325 degrees for 1 hour or until cake tests done and top is cracked. Bring 1 cup sugar, cornstarch and water to a boil in medium saucepan, stirring constantly. Boil for 1 minute, stirring constantly. Remove from heat. Stir in 2 tablespoons margarine, lemon juice and lemon rind. Serve spooned over cake. May serve sauce with pound cake or other dessert. Yield: 14 servings.

Myrna McNeely, Laureate Sigma
Tempe, Arizona

MORNING GLORY CUPCAKES

This rich and moist cupcake recipe is a variation I created from my carrot cake recipe. My grandchildren love them.

3 cups grated carrots
2 cups all-purpose flour
1 cup plus 2 tablespoons sugar
1 cup packed light brown sugar
2 teaspoons baking soda
1 teaspoon baking powder
1/2 teaspoon salt
1 teaspoon cinnamon
4 eggs, beaten
1 1/4 cups vegetable oil
2 teaspoons vanilla extract
1 (7-ounce) can flaked coconut
1 cup chopped pecans

Preheat oven to 350 degrees. Combine carrots, flour, sugar, brown sugar, baking soda, baking powder, salt and cinnamon in large bowl. Add eggs, oil and vanilla; mix well. Add coconut and pecans; mix well. Fill paper-lined muffin cups with 1/2 cup batter. Bake at 350 degrees for 25 to 30 minutes or until cupcakes test done. Yield: 24 cupcakes.

Geneva Rawlings, Alpha Phi
Charlestown, Indiana

OATMEAL CAKE

1 1/4 cups boiling water
1 cup quick-cooking oats
1/2 cup margarine, cut in pieces
3/4 cup sugar
3/4 cup packed light brown sugar
2 eggs
1 1/3 cups sifted all-purpose flour
1 teaspoon baking soda
1 teaspoon baking powder
1 teaspoon cinnamon
1 teaspoon salt
6 tablespoons melted butter or margarine
1 cup packed light brown sugar
1/4 cup cream or milk
1 cup flaked coconut
1 cup chopped pecans

Preheat oven to 350 degrees. Combine boiling water, oats and margarine in small bowl; set aside. Mix sugar, brown sugar and eggs in medium mixer bowl. Add mixture of flour, baking soda, baking powder, cinnamon and salt; mix until well blended. Add oats mixture; mix well. Spoon into greased and floured 9-by-13-inch cake pan. Bake at 350 degrees for 30 minutes or until cake tests done. Combine butter, brown sugar and cream in small mixer bowl; beat until blended. Stir in coconut and pecans. Spread over hot cake. Broil 4 inches from heat source until brown and bubbly. Yield: 15 servings.

Phyllis Hodge, Laureate Alpha Tau
Sanford, Florida

OATMEAL AND CHOCOLATE CHIP CAKE

1 cup rolled oats
1 1/2 cups boiling water
2 eggs, beaten
1 cup sugar
1 cup packed light brown sugar
1 teaspoon salt
1 teaspoon cinnamon
1 teaspoon baking soda
1 1/2 cups all-purpose flour
1 teaspoon vanilla extract
3/4 cup semisweet chocolate chips
3/4 cup packed light brown sugar

Preheat oven to 350 degrees. Mix oats and boiling water in small bowl. Let stand for 15 minutes. Beat eggs, sugar and 1 cup brown sugar in large mixer bowl until smooth. Add oats mixture; beat until well mixed. Add mixture of salt, cinnamon, baking soda and flour; mix well. Add vanilla. Spoon into greased and floured 9-by-13-inch cake pan. Sprinkle mixture of chocolate chips and 3/4 cup brown sugar over top. Bake at 350 degrees for 45 minutes or until cake tests done. Let stand until cool. May substitute raisins for chocolate chips. Yield: 15 servings.

Lois Croisier, Gamma Zeta
Kirkland Lake, Ontario, Canada

OATMEAL CAKE WITH COCONUT GLAZE

1 cup rolled oats
1/2 cup butter or margarine, softened
1 1/4 cups boiling water
2 eggs
1 cup sugar
1 cup packed light brown sugar
1 1/3 cups all-purpose flour
1 teaspoon baking soda
1/2 teaspoon salt
1 teaspoon baking powder
1/2 teaspoon cinnamon
1/2 cup butter or margarine, softened
1/2 cup packed light brown sugar
6 tablespoons milk
1 1/2 cups flaked coconut

Preheat oven to 350 degrees. Combine oats, 1/2 cup butter and boiling water in large bowl. Let stand for 20 minutes. Add eggs; mix well. Stir in a mixture of sugar, 1 cup brown sugar, flour, baking soda, salt, baking powder and cinnamon; mix well. Spoon into a greased 9-by-13-inch cake pan. Bake at 350 degrees for 40 to 50 minutes or until cake tests done. Combine 1/2 cup butter, 1/2 cup brown sugar, milk and coconut in small mixer bowl. Spread over hot cake. Broil 4 inches from heat source until golden brown and bubbly. Yield: 12 to 15 servings.

Merilee Bacon, Xi Rho
Kentville, Nova Scotia, Canada

ORANGE CHIFFON CAKE

My dear mother acquired this cake recipe from a baker especially for me on my 8th birthday. I have never seen this recipe in any cookbook. I hope to give this special cake to my daughter on her birthdays.

2/3 cup sugar
1 cup all-purpose flour
1 teaspoon orange zest
1/2 cup orange juice
8 egg yolks
8 egg whites
1 teaspoon cream of tartar
2/3 cup sugar
1 cup confectioners' sugar
1 teaspoon orange zest
2 tablespoons orange juice
2 drops yellow food coloring
1 drop red food coloring

Preheat oven to 325 degrees. Combine 2/3 cup sugar, flour, 1 teaspoon orange zest, 1/2 cup orange juice and egg yolks in medium mixer bowl; mix well. Beat egg whites and cream of tartar in small mixer bowl until soft peaks form. Beat in 2/3 cup sugar gradually, beating until stiff peaks form. Fold into creamed mixture. Spoon into 10-inch nonstick tube pan. Bake at 325 degrees for 1 hour and 10 minutes. Invert onto funnel to cool completely. Loosen cake from side of pan; invert onto a cake plate. Combine confectioners' sugar, 1 teaspoon orange zest, 2 tablespoons orange juice and food coloring in small bowl. Drizzle over top and side of cake. Yield: 12 servings.

Laura Hannan, Xi Delta Iota
Hays, Kansas

ORANGE POPPY SEED CAKE

1 (2-layer) package French vanilla white cake mix
1 (6-ounce) package vanilla instant pudding mix
1 cup orange juice
1/2 cup vegetable oil
5 eggs
1 tablespoon almond extract
2 tablespoons poppy seeds

Preheat oven to 350 degrees. Combine cake mix, pudding mix, orange juice and oil in large mixer bowl. Add eggs 1 at a time, mixing well after each addition. Stir in almond extract and poppy seeds. Spoon into greased bundt pan. Bake at 350 degrees for 45 minutes. Invert onto serving plate. May glaze top if desired. Yield: 16 servings.

Sister in Beta Sigma Phi

✣ ORANGE RING CAKE

I have been serving this cake for Christmas and Thanksgiving for more than 30 years.

1 cup butter or margarine, softened
1 cup sugar
3 egg yolks
1 cup sour cream
Grated rind of 1 orange
2 cups sifted cake flour
1 teaspoon baking soda
1 teaspoon baking powder
3 egg whites
Juice of 2 oranges
Juice of 1 lemon
3/4 cup sugar
Salt to taste

Preheat oven to 325 degrees. Cream butter and 1 cup sugar in large mixer bowl until light and fluffy. Add egg yolks 1 at a time, mixing well after each addition. Add sour cream and orange rind; mix well. Add mixture of cake flour, baking soda and baking powder; mix until well blended. Beat egg whites until stiff peaks form; fold into creamed mixture. Spoon into oiled and floured 9-inch tube pan. Bake at 325 degrees for 1 hour or until cake tests done. Cool in pan for 10 minutes. Loosen cake from side of pan. Invert onto serving plate with rim. Bring orange juice, lemon juice, 3/4 cup sugar and salt to a boil in medium saucepan. Boil gently for 3 to 4 minutes, stirring constantly. Pour slowly over top of baked layer. Yield: 8 to 10 servings.

Katherine Voss, Xi Omicron Sigma
Lakehead, California

SUNSHINE CAKE

1 (2-layer) package yellow butter recipe cake mix
1/2 cup vegetable oil
4 eggs
1 (11-ounce) can mandarin oranges
1 (6-ounce) package vanilla instant pudding mix
1 (8-ounce) can crushed pineapple
8 ounces whipped topping

Preheat oven to 350 degrees. Combine cake mix and oil in medium mixer bowl. Add eggs 1 at a time, mixing well after each addition. Stir in mandarin oranges. Spoon into greased and floured 9-by-13-inch cake pan. Bake at 350 degrees for 30 minutes or until cake tests done. Combine pudding mix, pineapple and whipped topping in medium bowl; mix well. Spread over cake. Yield: 15 servings.

Nancy Tillette, Preceptor Gamma
Beckley, West Virginia

OUT OF THIS WORLD CAKE

1 cup melted butter or margarine
2 cups sugar
4 eggs
1 tablespoon baking powder
4 cups graham cracker crumbs
1 cup sweetened condensed milk
1 tablespoon vanilla extract
1 cup flaked coconut
1 cup chopped pecans
1 cup sugar
1/4 cup all-purpose flour
1 (16-ounce) can crushed pineapple

Preheat oven to 350 degrees. Cream butter and 2 cups sugar in large mixer bowl. Add eggs 1 at a time, mixing well after each addition. Add mixture of baking powder and graham cracker crumbs alternately with mixture of condensed milk and vanilla, stirring until blended. Fold in coconut and pecans. Spoon into greased and floured 9-by-13-inch cake pan. Bake at 350 degrees for 35 to 40 minutes or until cake tests done. Blend 1 cup sugar and flour in medium saucepan. Stir in undrained pineapple. Cook over low heat until thickened, stirring constantly. Spread over top of hot cake. Yield: 15 servings.

Martha Collier, Laureate Alpha Alpha
South Charleston, West Virginia

CRUNCHY PEANUT BUTTER CAKE

2/3 cup crunchy peanut butter
1/3 cup shortening
1 cup sugar
2 eggs
1 cup milk
1 1/2 cups sifted all-purpose flour
1 tablespoon baking powder
1 teaspoon salt
1 teaspoon vanilla extract

Preheat oven to 350 degrees. Beat peanut butter, shortening and sugar in large mixer bowl until blended. Add eggs and milk, beating well after each addition. Stir in sifted mixture of flour, baking powder and salt. Add vanilla. Spoon into 2 greased and floured 8-inch cake pans. Bake at 350 degrees for 30 minutes or until cake tests done. Frost with favorite peanut butter frosting. Yield: 12 servings.

Janet Hansen, Preceptor Alpha Phi
Harvard, Nebraska

PINEAPPLE CAKE

1/4 cup butter or margarine, softened
1 (20-ounce) can crushed pineapple
2 cups all-purpose flour
2 cups sugar
2 eggs
2 teaspoons baking soda
1 cup chopped pecans
4 ounces cream cheese, softened
1 teaspoon vanilla extract
1 cup confectioners' sugar
1/4 cup butter or margarine, softened

Preheat oven to 350 degrees. Combine 1/4 cup butter and undrained pineapple in large bowl, stirring with a spoon. Add flour, sugar, eggs, baking soda and pecans, stirring well after each addition. Spoon into greased 9-by-13-inch cake pan. Bake at 350 degrees for 35 minutes. Combine cream cheese, vanilla, confectioners' sugar and 1/4 cup butter in small mixer bowl; beat until smooth. Spread over warm cake. Yield: 15 servings.

Gail Wylie, Phi
Moscow, Idaho

PINEAPPLE CARROT CAKE

11/2 cups vegetable oil
2 cups sugar
4 eggs, beaten
2 cups all-purpose flour
1/2 teaspoon baking powder
2 teaspoons baking soda
1/2 teaspoon salt
1 cup walnuts
2 cups grated carrots
1 (14-ounce) can crushed pineapple, drained
4 ounces cream cheese, softened
2 teaspoons vanilla extract
1/2 cup butter or margarine, softened
2 cups confectioners' sugar

Preheat oven to 325 degrees. Mix oil and sugar in large mixer bowl. Add eggs and mixture of flour, baking powder, baking soda and salt; mix well. Stir in walnuts, carrots and pineapple. Spoon into greased 9-by-13-inch cake pan. Bake at 325 degrees for 11/4 hours or until springy to the touch. Let stand until cool. Beat cream cheese, vanilla, butter and confectioners' sugar in medium mixer bowl until smooth and creamy. Spread over cooled cake. Yield: 24 servings.

Caryl Wylie, Xi Alpha Theta
Prince George, British Columbia, Canada

PINEAPPLE-FILLED CAKE

1 (2-layer) package yellow cake mix
1 (8-ounce) can crushed pineapple
1 tablespoon cornstarch
3 tablespoons sugar
4 cups whipping cream
1/4 cup sugar
2 teaspoons vanilla extract

Preheat oven to 350 degrees. Prepare and bake cake mix in 2 round 9-inch cake pans using package directions. Combine pineapple, cornstarch and 3 tablespoons sugar in small saucepan over medium heat. Cook until thick and clear, stirring constantly. Remove from heat. Let stand until cool. Beat whipping cream, 1/4 cup sugar and vanilla in medium mixer bowl until stiff peaks form. Fold 1/4 of the whipped cream mixture into the pineapple mixture. Spread between layers. Spread remaining whipped cream mixture over top and side of cake. Yield: 8 to 10 servings.

Kristen Dalpiaz, Alpha Eta
Tucson, Arizona

PINEAPPLE SHEET CAKE

2 cups sugar
2 eggs, beaten
1 (20-ounce) can crushed pineapple
1 teaspoon vanilla extract
2 cups all-purpose flour
2 teaspoons baking soda
3/4 cup pecans (optional)
13/4 cups confectioners' sugar
8 ounces cream cheese, softened
1/4 cup butter or margarine
1 teaspoon vanilla extract
1/2 cup pecans

Preheat oven to 350 degrees. Combine sugar, eggs, pineapple, 1 teaspoon vanilla, flour and baking soda in large mixer bowl, mixing well after each addition. Stir in 3/4 cup pecans. Spread in greased and floured 12-by-18-inch baking pan. Bake at 350 degrees for 25 minutes. Cool. Beat confectioners' sugar, cream cheese, butter and vanilla in medium mixer bowl until smooth and creamy. Stir in 1/2 cup pecans. Spread over cooled cake. Yield: 10 to 12 servings.

Kim Emmendorfer, Alpha Alpha Mu
Lee's Summit, Missouri

PINEAPPLE UPSIDE-DOWN CAKE

1/2 cup butter or margarine
1 cup packed dark brown sugar
1 (20-ounce) can sliced pineapple
2 tablespoons whole pecans
3 egg yolks
1 cup sugar
5 tablespoons pineapple juice
1 cup cake flour
1 tablespoon baking powder
1/8 teaspoon salt
3 egg whites

Preheat oven to 375 degrees. Melt butter in cast-iron skillet or large cake pan. Sprinkle brown sugar over butter. Drain pineapple, reserving 5 tablespoons juice. Arrange pineapple slices over brown sugar, filling spaces with pecans. Beat egg yolks in medium mixer bowl until thick and pale yellow, adding sugar gradually. Add pineapple juice and sifted cake flour, baking powder and salt; mix well. Fold in stiffly beaten egg whites. Pour over pineapple. Bake at 375 degrees for 30 minutes or until cake tests done. Invert onto serving plate while hot. Yield: 12 servings.

Rita M. Horn, Preceptor Xi Epsilon

EASY PINA COLADA CAKE

1 (2-layer) package yellow cake mix
1 (4-ounce) package vanilla instant pudding mix
1 (15-ounce) can cream of coconut
1/2 cup plus 2 tablespoons rum
1/3 cup vegetable oil
4 eggs
1 (8-ounce) can crushed pineapple, drained
Whipped cream
Pineapple chunks
Maraschino cherries
Toasted coconut

Preheat oven to 350 degrees. Combine cake mix, pudding mix, 1/2 can cream of coconut, 1/2 cup rum, oil and eggs in large mixer bowl. Beat at medium speed for 2 minutes. Stir in pineapple. Spoon into greased and floured 10-inch tube pan. Bake at 350 degrees for 50 to 55 minutes. Cool in pan for 5 minutes. Invert onto serving plate. Pierce holes 1 inch apart in cake almost to the bottom with a table knife or skewer. Combine remaining cream of coconut and rum in bowl. Pour over cake. Chill for 2 to 4 hours. Garnish with whipped cream, pineapple chunks, maraschino cherries and toasted coconut. Yield: 16 servings.

Linda R. Cole, Laureate Beta Omega
Port Orchard, Washington

HUMMINGBIRD CAKE

3 cups all-purpose flour
2 cups sugar
1 teaspoon baking soda
1 teaspoon salt
1 teaspoon cinnamon
3 eggs, beaten
1 cup vegetable oil
1 1/2 teaspoons vanilla extract
1 teaspoon butter flavoring
1 (8-ounce) can crushed pineapple
1 cup chopped pecans
2 cups chopped bananas
8 ounces cream cheese, softened
1/2 cup butter or margarine, softened
1 (1-pound) package confectioners' sugar, sifted
1/2 cup chopped pecans

Preheat oven to 350 degrees. Combine flour, sugar, baking soda, salt and cinnamon in large bowl. Add eggs and oil, stirring just until moistened. Add vanilla, butter flavoring, pineapple, 1 cup pecans and bananas; mix well. Spoon into 3 greased and floured 9-inch round cake pans. Bake at 350 degrees for 25 to 30 minutes or until wooden pick inserted in center comes out clean. Cool in pan for 10 minutes. Remove to wire rack to cool completely. Beat cream cheese, butter and confectioners' sugar in medium mixer bowl until smooth and creamy. Spread between layers and over top and side of cake. Sprinkle pecans over top of cake. Chill, covered, for 2 to 24 hours before serving. Yield: 12 to 16 servings.

Margaret R. Trujillo, Xi Beta Lambda
Los Ojos, New Mexico

CHINESE WEDDING CAKE

1 (1-layer) package white cake mix
2 cups milk
1 (6-ounce) package vanilla instant pudding mix
8 ounces cream cheese, softened
1 (20-ounce) can crushed pineapple, drained
8 ounces whipped topping
1 cup flaked coconut

Prepare and bake cake mix using package directions for greased and floured 9-by-13-inch cake pan. Let stand until cool. Combine milk, pudding mix and cream cheese in medium mixer bowl. Beat for 2 minutes or until smooth. Layer cream cheese mixture, pineapple and whipped topping over cooled baked layer. Sprinkle with coconut. May substitute bananas for pineapple. Yield: 12 servings.

Shirley Morris, Laureate Alpha Phi
Paris, Ontario, Canada

SWEDISH CAKE

This is a favorite cake to take, to give or to eat. It's also low-fat, is made with no oil and can be made with low-cholesterol cream cheese and margarine.

2 cups all-purpose flour
2 teaspoons baking soda
2 cups sugar
2 eggs
1 (20-ounce) can crushed pineapple
2 teaspoons vanilla extract
1/2 cup chopped walnuts
8 ounces light cream cheese, softened
1/2 cup light margarine, softened
1 teaspoon vanilla extract
2 cups (or more) confectioners' sugar

Preheat oven to 350 degrees. Combine flour, baking soda, sugar, eggs, undrained pineapple and 2 teaspoons vanilla in large mixer bowl, mixing well after each addition. Stir in walnuts. Spoon into ungreased 9-by-13-inch cake pan. Bake at 350 degrees for 35 to 40 minutes or until cake tests done. Beat cream cheese, margarine and 1 teaspoon vanilla in medium mixer bowl, blending until smooth. Add enough confectioners' sugar to make of frosting consistency. Spread over cooled cake. Yield: 15 to 20 servings.

Sherry Kelly, Preceptor Beta Omega
Emporia, Kansas

Cindy Emond, Psi, Alouette, Quebec, Canada, makes Peaches and Cream Cake by layering vanilla cake, whipped cream, well-drained canned peach slices and cake, then blending 1/2 cup whipped cream with seven-minute icing to frost top and side of cake and decorating with peach slices.

PLUM CAKE

1½ cups all-purpose flour
1 cup sugar
1 teaspoon baking soda
½ teaspoon salt
1 teaspoon baking powder
1 tablespoon vinegar
1 egg
½ cup cold water
⅓ cup vegetable oil
⅓ cup raisins
1 (4-ounce) jar baby food plums
2 cups confectioners' sugar
¼ cup margarine
½ teaspoon vanilla extract
1 tablespoon baby food plums

Preheat oven to 350 degrees. Combine flour, sugar, baking soda, salt and baking powder in large mixer bowl; mix well. Add vinegar, egg, cold water, oil, raisins and 4 ounces plums, mixing well. Spoon into ungreased 9-by-9-inch cake pan. Bake at 350 degrees for 30 minutes or until cake tests done. Spread with mixture of confectioners sugar, margarine, vanilla and 1 tablespoon baby food plums.
Yield: 12 servings.

Louise Lynn, Xi Gamma Omega
Quesnel, British Columbia, Canada

BABY FOOD CAKE

This is my daughter's favorite recipe.

2 cups self-rising flour
2 cups sugar
1 teaspoon cinnamon
2 (8-ounce) jars baby food plums
3 eggs
1 cup vegetable oil

Preheat oven to 350 degrees. Combine self-rising flour, sugar and cinnamon in medium mixer bowl. Stir in plums, eggs and oil, beating well. Spoon into nonstick 9-by-13-inch cake pan. Bake at 350 degrees for 45 to 60 minutes, or until knife inserted in center comes out clean. Yield: 15 servings.

Monnie Conaway, Xi Gamma Nu
Garland, Texas

POUND CAKE

This cake freezes well.

1 cup butter or margarine, softened
½ cup shortening
3 cups sugar
5 eggs
3 cups cake flour
1 cup milk
1 teaspoon vanilla extract
½ teaspoon baking powder

Cream butter and shortening in large mixer bowl. Beat in sugar gradually. Beat for 10 minutes or until smooth, scraping bowl occasionally. Add eggs 1 at a time, beating well after each addition. Add cake flour gradually; mix well. Add milk and vanilla gradually; mix well. Stir in baking powder. Spoon into greased and floured bundt pan. Place in cold oven. Bake at 325 degrees for 1¼ hours. Cool in pan slightly. Invert onto serving plate. Yield: 15 servings.

Judy Moore, Xi Kappa Chi
Refugio, Texas

1-2-3-4 POUND CAKE

This is my dad's favorite cake. My family (even my husband) bakes this cake not only for his birthday, but for any occasion. It is so moist that it does not need toppings.

4 eggs
1 cup vegetable shortening
2 cups sugar
3 cups all-purpose flour
1 tablespoon baking powder
½ teaspoon salt
2 teaspoons vanilla extract
1 cup milk
¼ cup sugar

Preheat oven to 350 degrees. Beat 4 eggs in a 1 cup measure to lubricate cup for shortening. Pour eggs into large mixer bowl. Fill 1 cup measure with shortening; add to eggs. Stir in 2 cups sugar. Beat until creamy. Add mixture of flour, baking powder and salt; mix well. Stir in vanilla and milk. Beat at medium speed for 5 minutes or longer, scraping the bowl occasionally (the longer the beating time, the lighter and higher the cake). Spoon batter into greased and floured tube pan. Sprinkle with ¼ cup sugar. Bake at 350 degrees for 1 hour.
Yield: 16 servings.

Joy Steely, Lambda Eta
Lamar, Missouri

BUTTER AND SOUR CREAM POUND CAKE

1 cup butter or margarine, softened
3 cups sugar
6 eggs
3 cups all-purpose flour
1 cup sour cream
1 tablespoon vanilla extract

Cream butter and sugar in large mixer bowl until light and fluffy. Add eggs 1 at a time, mixing well after each addition. Add flour and sour cream alternately, blending well after each addition. Stir in vanilla. Spoon into greased and floured tube pan. Place in cold oven. Bake at 300 degrees for 1½ hours.
Yield: 16 servings.

Sharlene Brantley, Preceptor Alpha Nu
Dubbin, Georgia

CREAM CHEESE POUND CAKE

1 cup margarine, softened
½ cup butter or margarine, softened
8 ounces cream cheese, softened
2½ cups sugar
6 eggs
3 cups all-purpose flour
2 teaspoons baking powder
2 teaspoons vanilla extract

Preheat oven to 325 degrees. Beat margarine and butter in large mixer bowl until well blended. Add cream cheese and beat until light and fluffy. Add sugar gradually, blending well. Add eggs 1 at a time, beating well after each addition. Add sifted mixture of flour and baking powder gradually to creamed mixture; mix well. Stir in vanilla. Spoon into greased and floured 10-inch tube pan. Bake at 325 degrees for 1¼ hours. Cool in pan for 10 minutes. Remove to wire rack to cool completely. Store in airtight container. Yield: 12 servings.

Jean Kyle, Preceptor Delta
Montgomery, Alabama

HEARTY POUND CAKE

10 to 12 egg yolks
10 to 12 egg whites
2 cups butter or margarine
2½ cups sugar
4 cups all-purpose flour
1 teaspoon baking powder
1 teaspoon vanilla extract

Preheat oven to 350 degrees. Beat egg yolks until pale yellow color; set aside. Beat egg whites in mixer bowl until stiff peaks form; set aside. Cream butter and sugar in large mixer bowl until smooth. Add egg yolks; mix well. Add mixture of flour and baking powder alternately with egg whites, mixing well after each addition. Stir in vanilla. Spoon into greased and floured tube pan. Bake at 350 degrees for 1 hour. Yield: 16 servings.

Becky Starring, Eta Sigma
Copperhill, Tennessee

HOMEMADE POUND CAKE

This cake is good hot, and even better the next day.

6 egg yolks
¼ cup shortening
1 cup margarine, softened
3 cups sugar
3 cups sifted all-purpose flour
¾ teaspoon salt
¼ teaspoon baking soda
1 cup buttermilk
2 teaspoons vanilla extract
6 egg whites

Preheat oven to 325 degrees. Beat egg yolks in large mixer bowl until pale yellow. Add shortening and margarine; beat well. Add sugar gradually, beating constantly. Add sifted mixture of flour and salt alternately with mixture of baking soda and buttermilk, mixing well after each addition. Stir in vanilla. Beat egg whites in small mixer bowl until stiff peaks form. Fold into buttermilk mixture. Spoon into greased and floured tube pan. Bake at 325 degrees for 70 to 75 minutes. Yield: 12 to 16 servings.

Blanche H. Wilks, Zeta Gamma
Delhi, Louisiana

LEMON POUND CAKE

1 (2-layer) package lemon cake mix
4 eggs, at room temperature
½ cup sugar
½ cup vegetable oil
1 cup apricot nectar
1 cup confectioners' sugar
3 tablespoons lemon juice

Preheat oven to 350 degrees. Combine cake mix, eggs, sugar, oil and apricot nectar in large mixer bowl. Beat at medium speed for 4 minutes. Spoon into greased and floured tube or bundt pan. Bake at 350 degrees for 40 to 45 minutes or until cake tests done. Invert onto cake plate. Combine confectioners' sugar and lemon juice in small bowl; blend well. Pour over hot cake. Yield: 16 servings.

Cindy Dempsey, Omega Lambda
Lake City, Florida

LEMON AND ORANGE POUND CAKE

I won a blue ribbon at the county fair with this recipe.

1 cup shortening
2½ cups sugar
4 egg yolks
4 egg whites, stiffly beaten
3 cups plus 2 tablespoons sifted all-purpose flour
1 teaspoon baking powder
1 cup milk
1 tablespoon lemon juice
1 tablespoon orange juice
¼ teaspoon vanilla extract
1 tablespoon grated orange rind
1 tablespoon grated lemon rind
1 cup chopped pecans
⅔ cup sugar
3 tablespoons lemon juice
½ cup orange juice

Preheat oven to 350 degrees. Cream shortening and 2½ cups sugar in large mixer bowl until fluffy. Add egg yolks 1 at a time, beating well after each addition. Fold in egg whites. Add mixture of flour and baking powder alternately with milk, blending well after each addition. Stir in 1 tablespoon lemon juice, 1 tablespoon orange juice and vanilla; mix well. Stir in orange and lemon rinds and pecans. Spoon into greased and floured 10-inch tube pan. Bake at 350 degrees for 1 hour. Cool in pan for 10 minutes. Invert onto cake plate. Combine ⅔ cup sugar, 3 tablespoons lemon juice and ½ cup orange juice in small bowl; mix well. Spoon over warm cake.
Yield: 16 servings.

Joyce Sparks, Laureate Gamma Pi
LaVernia, Texas

MOTHER'S POUND CAKE

This has been my favorite cake for a long time. When my mother was living in Mississippi, she would bake it and ship it to me by UPS.

1 cup butter or margarine, softened or 1 cup shortening plus 1/2 teaspoon salt
3 cups sugar
5 egg yolks, room temperature
3 cups (heaping) cake flour
1/8 teaspoon baking soda
1 cup buttermilk
1 teaspoon each lemon extract, orange extract and vanilla extract
5 egg whites, room temperature

Preheat oven to 325 degrees. Cream butter and 2 1/4 cups sugar in large mixer bowl until light and fluffy. Add egg yolks 1 at a time, mixing well after each addition. Add 1 cup flour; mix well. Add mixture of 2 cups cake flour and baking soda alternately with buttermilk, blending well after each addition. Stir in lemon, orange and vanilla extracts; mix well. Beat egg whites with remaining 3/4 cup sugar in small mixer bowl until stiff peaks form. Fold into creamed mixture. Spoon into greased and floured tube pan. Bake at 325 degrees for 1 hour; do not overbake. Yield: 16 servings.

Marianna Bond, Laureate Zeta Eta
Bryan, Texas

MY FAVORITE AUNT'S POUND CAKE

When I was young back in the 50s and 60s, my Aunt Eula baked this cake, and always made an extra one for our family. When I'd visit her, she almost always served this cake.

1 cup butter or margarine, softened
3 cups sugar
1/2 cup shortening
6 eggs
3 cups cake flour, sifted
1 cup milk
1 teaspoon vanilla extract
1 teaspoon lemon extract
1/2 teaspoon baking powder

Cream butter and sugar in a large mixer bowl until light and fluffy. Add shortening; mix well. Add eggs 1 at a time, mixing well after each addition. Combine cake flour and milk in small bowl; mix well. Add vanilla and lemon flavorings. Sprinkle with baking powder; mix well. Pour into sugar mixture; mix well. Spoon into greased and floured tube pan. Place in cold oven. Bake at 350 degrees for 1 hour to 1 hour and 15 minutes. Yield: 16 servings.

Linda M. Griffith, Laureate Mu
West Columbia, South Carolina

PINEAPPLE POUND SURPRISE

1 pound cake
8 ounces whipped topping
1 (4-ounce) package vanilla instant pudding mix
1 (20-ounce) can crushed pineapple
1 teaspoon almond extract
2 cups slivered almonds

Slice pound cake horizontally into 3 layers. Combine whipped topping and pudding mix in medium bowl. Drain pineapple, reserving half the juice. Add pineapple to whipped topping mixture. Mix reserved juice with almond extract in small bowl. Drizzle over the 3 layers of cake. Alternate layers of cake and pineapple mixture on cake plate. Sprinkle almonds on top. Chill until serving time.
Yield: 8 to 10 servings.

Celeste Fulk, Zeta Omega
Weston, Missouri

PIXY POUND CAKE

This recipe is great used as shortcake and served with fresh strawberries and whipped cream.

1 cup shortening
1/2 cup butter or margarine, softened
3 cups sugar
6 eggs
3 1/4 cups all-purpose flour
1 teaspoon baking powder
1/2 teaspoon salt
1 cup milk
1 teaspoon vanilla extract
1/2 teaspoon almond extract

Preheat oven to 350 degrees. Cream shortening, butter and sugar in large mixer bowl until smooth and creamy. Add eggs 1 at a time, beating well after each addition. Add sifted mixture of flour, baking powder and salt alternately with milk, mixing well after each addition. Stir in vanilla and almond flavorings. Spoon into greased and floured 10-inch tube pan. Bake at 350 degrees for 1 1/2 hours or until cake tests done. Yield: 24 servings.

Donna Sjogren, Preceptor Lambda
Ely, Nevada

SOUR CREAM POUND CAKE

This cake is always a special treat served with a cup of coffee for a good visit with a friend or family member.

1 cup sour cream
1 cup margarine, softened
3 cups sugar
6 eggs
3 cups all-purpose flour
1/4 teaspoon baking soda
1 teaspoon vanilla extract

Preheat oven to 325 degrees. Beat sour cream, margarine and sugar in large mixer bowl until smooth. Add eggs 1 at a time, mixing well after each addition.

Add flour and baking soda. Stir in vanilla; mix well. Spoon into greased and floured bundt or tube pan. Bake at 325 degrees for 1 hour and 10 minutes. Yield: 16 servings.

Diana Ashe, Epsilon Rho
Pelham, Alabama

SOUR CREAM AND LEMON POUND CAKE

2/3 cup margarine, softened
2 2/3 cups sugar
1 1/4 cups frozen egg substitute, thawed
1 1/2 cups low-fat sour cream
1 teaspoon baking soda
4 1/2 cups sifted cake flour
1/4 teaspoon salt
2 teaspoons vanilla extract
1/2 cup sifted confectioners' sugar
1 teaspoon grated lemon rind
1 tablespoon fresh lemon juice
Lemon slices (optional)
Lemon rind curls (optional)

Preheat oven to 325 degrees. Cream the margarine and sugar in large mixer bowl at medium speed until light and fluffy. Add egg substitute; mix well. Add mixture of sour cream and baking soda alternately with mixture of cake flour and salt, mixing well after each addition. Stir in vanilla. Spoon into 10-inch tube pan coated with nonstick cooking spray. Bake at 325 degrees for 1 hour and 20 minutes or until wooden pick inserted in center comes out clean. Cool in pan for 10 minutes. Invert onto wire rack to cool completely. Combine confectioners' sugar, lemon rind and lemon juice in small bowl. Place cake on serving plate. Drizzle lemon glaze over top of cake. Garnish with lemon slices and lemon rind curls. Yield: 24 servings.

Mickey Hughey, Preceptor Omicron Epsilon
Kilgore, Texas

NORMA'S SPECIAL POUND CAKE

Norma was a cousin from Valdosta, Georgia who was well known since 1945 for her pound cakes. The secret of this cake is to have eggs at room temperature and place the cake in a cold oven before baking.

2 cups cake flour
1 cup butter or margarine, softened
2 cups sugar
6 eggs
Salt to taste
1 teaspoon vanilla extract

Sift cake flour 2 times into bowl. Cream butter and sugar in large mixer bowl until light and fluffy. Add cake flour and eggs alternately, mixing well after each addition. Stir in salt and vanilla; mix well. Spoon into greased and floured tube pan. Place in cold oven. Bake at 325 degrees for 1 hour. Yield: 16 servings.

Lillian B. Stephens, Georgia Alpha Nu
Dublin, Georgia

YOGURT POUND CAKE

1/2 cup butter, softened
1/2 cup margarine, softened
1 1/2 cups sugar
4 eggs
3 cups all-purpose flour
1/2 teaspoon baking soda
1 teaspoon baking powder
1/4 teaspoon salt
1 cup coffee yogurt
2 teaspoons vanilla extract

Preheat oven to 300 degrees. Combine butter, margarine and sugar in food processor container; process until smooth. Add eggs; process until mixed. Add mixture of flour, baking soda, baking powder and salt 1/3 at a time, processing after each addition. Add yogurt and vanilla. Process for 10 to 15 seconds; batter will be thick. Spoon into greased and floured springform or bundt pan. Bake at 300 degrees for 1 hour to 1 hour and 10 minutes or until cake tests done. Yield: 18 to 24 servings.

Irene Weir, Xi Gamma Iota
Old Forge, New York

GLAZED PRUNE CAKE

1 cup prunes
2 cups all-purpose flour
1 teaspoon baking soda
1 teaspoon salt
1 teaspoon ground cloves
1 teaspoon cinnamon
1 teaspoon ginger
1 teaspoon nutmeg
2 cups sugar
1 cup vegetable oil
3 eggs
1 teaspoon vanilla extract
1 cup pecans
1 cup sugar
1/2 teaspoon baking soda
1/4 cup butter
1/2 cup buttermilk
1 teaspoon vanilla extract

Cook prunes in water to cover until plump and tender. Let stand until cool. Drain. Discard pits; cut prunes into small pieces; set aside. Preheat oven to 325 degrees. Combine flour, baking soda, salt, cloves, cinnamon, ginger, nutmeg and sugar in large mixer bowl. Add oil, eggs and 1 teaspoon vanilla; mix well. Stir in prunes and pecans. Spoon into greased and floured 9-by-13-inch cake pan. Bake at 325 degrees for 45 minutes. Combine sugar and baking soda in small bowl. Melt butter in medium saucepan. Add sugar mixture; mix well. Add buttermilk and 1 teaspoon vanilla gradually. Bring to a boil, stirring constantly. Boil for 1 minute, stirring constantly. Pour over hot cake. Yield: 15 servings.

Mary Ellen Thomas, Laureate Beta Kappa
Middletown, Ohio

PRUNE CAKE

Don't let the name fool you. It tastes better than you think. No person living today has ever died from eating prune cake.

2 cups all-purpose flour
1 teaspoon baking soda
1 teaspoon nutmeg
1 teaspoon cinnamon
3/4 teaspoon allspice
1/2 cup shortening
1 cup sugar
1 egg
1 cup sour milk
1 cup stewed prunes, drained, cut into small pieces

Preheat oven to 350 degrees. Combine flour, baking soda, nutmeg, cinnamon and allspice in large mixer bowl. Add shortening and sugar; beat until smooth. Add egg and milk; mix well. Stir in prunes. Pour into greased and floured cake pan. Bake in moderate oven until cake tests done. Yield: 10 servings.

Patricia Johannes, Xi Zeta Epsilon
Vicksburg, Michigan

THANKSGIVING PUMPKIN CAKE

This recipe was handed down to me by my mother.

1 1/2 cups canned pumpkin
1 1/2 teaspoons baking soda
1 1/2 cups vegetable oil
4 eggs
2 cups all-purpose flour
2 1/2 teaspoons cinnamon
1 teaspoon salt
2 cups sugar
1 cup chopped walnuts (optional)
8 ounces cream cheese, softened
1/4 cup butter or margarine
2 1/2 cups confectioners' sugar
1 teaspoon black walnut flavoring

Preheat oven to 350 degrees. Combine pumpkin, baking soda and oil in large mixer bowl; blend until smooth. Add eggs 1 at a time, mixing well after each addition. Add flour, cinnamon, salt and sugar; mix well. Stir in walnuts. Spoon into greased and floured tube pan. Bake at 350 degrees for 1 hour. Invert onto wire rack to cool. Remove to serving plate. Beat cream cheese, butter and confectioners' sugar in small mixer bowl until smooth. Add black walnut flavoring; mix well. Spread over baked cake.
Yield: 16 servings.

Robin Throm, Xi Zeta Phi
Marysville, Kansas

PUMPKIN CHOCOLATE CHIP CAKE

3 cups all-purpose flour
2 teaspoons baking powder
2 teaspoons baking soda
1/2 teaspoon salt
2 cups sugar
4 eggs
1 teaspoon cinnamon
2 cups canned pumpkin
1 cup semisweet chocolate chips
1 cup crushed walnuts

Preheat oven to 350 degrees. Combine flour, baking powder, baking soda, salt and sugar in large mixer bowl. Add eggs 1 at a time, mixing well after each addition. Add cinnamon and pumpkin; mix well. Stir in chocolate chips and walnuts. Spoon into greased and floured bundt or tube pan. Bake at 350 degrees for 1 hour to 1 1/4 hours or until cake tests done. Cool in pan for 10 minutes. Invert onto cake plate. Yield: 12 servings.

Claudette Y. Foucault, Laureate Beta Gamma
Hanmer, Ontario, Canada

PUMPKIN CAKE BARS

4 eggs
1 (16-ounce) can pumpkin
1 2/3 cups sugar
1 cup vegetable oil
2 cups all-purpose flour
2 teaspoons baking powder
2 teaspoons ground cinnamon
1 teaspoon baking soda
1 cup chopped pecans
6 ounces cream cheese, softened
1/2 cup butter or margarine, softened
2 teaspoons vanilla extract
2 cups confectioners' sugar
1/4 cup chopped pecans

Preheat oven to 350 degrees. Combine eggs, pumpkin, sugar and oil in large mixer bowl, blending until smooth. Add mixture of flour, baking powder, cinnamon and baking soda; mix well. Stir in 1 cup pecans. Spread in greased and floured 10-by-15-inch cake pan. Bake at 350 degrees for 25 to 30 minutes or until cake tests done. Cool. Combine cream cheese, butter and vanilla in small mixer bowl; beat until fluffy. Stir in confectioners' sugar gradually, beating until smooth. Spread over cake. Sprinkle with 1/4 cup pecans. Cut into bars. Yield: 12 to 18 servings.

Gwyn Hicks, Xi Chi Delta
Corcoran, California

PUMPKIN ROLL

When chapter parties are planned, the menu planning begins with this dessert. There's never a shortage of volunteers to host a party because they know I always bring an extra dessert for the hostess.

3 eggs, chilled
2 cups sugar
2/3 cup pumpkin
1 teaspoon lemon juice
3/4 cup all-purpose flour
1 teaspoon baking powder
2 teaspoons cinnamon
1 teaspoon salt
1/2 teaspoon nutmeg
1 cup chopped pecans
1/2 cup confectioners' sugar
1 teaspoon vanilla extract
6 ounces regular or light cream cheese, softened
1/4 cup butter, margarine or light margarine, softened
1 cup confectioners' sugar

Preheat oven to 375 degrees. Beat eggs in large mixer bowl at high speed for 5 minutes. Add sugar gradually; mix well. Stir in pumpkin and lemon juice. Add mixture of flour, baking powder, cinnamon, salt and nutmeg; mix well. Spread in greased and floured

10-by-15-inch jelly roll pan. Top with pecans. Bake at 375 degrees for 15 minutes. Invert onto towel sprinkled with 1/2 cup confectioners' sugar. Roll up cake and towel as for jelly roll, beginning at narrow end. Let stand until cool. Unroll cake onto work surface; remove towel. Cream vanilla, cream cheese and butter in small mixer bowl until smooth. Add 1 cup confectioners' sugar; beat until creamy. Spread over cake. Roll up as for jelly roll. Chill, covered, for 2 to 3 hours or freeze. Cut into slices before serving. Yield: 16 servings.

Avon Crocker, Xi Alpha Sigma
Cape Girardeau, Missouri

PUMPKIN CHEESE ROLL

I made this dessert for my new mother-in-law, who is a wonderful cook. She was greatly impressed with her new daughter-in-law.

3 eggs
1 cup sugar
2/3 cup canned pumpkin
3/4 cup minus 2 tablespoons all-purpose flour
1 teaspoon baking soda
1/2 teaspoon cinnamon
2 cups chopped pecans
1/2 cup (about) confectioner's sugar
8 ounces cream cheese, softened
1 cup confectioners' sugar
2 tablespoons margarine, softened

Preheat oven to 375 degrees. Combine eggs, sugar and pumpkin in bowl; mix well. Add sifted mixture of flour, baking soda and cinnamon; mix until blended. Spoon into greased 10-by-15-inch sheet cake pan lined with waxed paper. Sprinkle with pecans. Bake at 375 degrees for 15 minutes. Turn onto clean towel sprinkled with 1/2 cup confectioners' sugar. Remove waxed paper. Roll in towel as for jelly roll. Cool. Unroll cake slowly onto work surface; remove towel. Combine cream cheese, 1 cup confectioners' sugar and margarine in bowl; mix until smooth. Spread over cake. Roll as for jelly roll. Wrap in foil. Freeze until serving time. Slice and serve while frozen. Yield: 8 to 10 servings.

Donna L. Coffin, Preceptor Eta Phi
Satellite Beach, Florida

LEMON-GLAZED PUMPKIN SPICE CAKE

This cake is good for serving during Thanksgiving or Christmas.

1 (2-layer) package spice cake mix
1 (16-ounce) can pumpkin
1/4 cup vegetable oil
2 eggs
1/2 cup golden raisins
1/2 cup chopped walnuts
11/2 cups confectioners' sugar
1 teaspoon grated lemon rind
2 to 3 tablespoons lemon juice
Walnut halves to taste

Preheat oven to 350 degrees. Combine cake mix, pumpkin, oil and eggs in mixer bowl; mix well. Stir in raisins and walnuts. Turn into greased 2- or 3-quart fluted tube pan. Bake at 350 degrees for 40 to 50 minutes or until cake tests done. Cool in pan for 10 minutes. Loosen edges with knife and invert onto wire rack to cool completely. Combine confectioners' sugar, lemon rind and lemon juice in bowl; mix well. Drizzle over cake. Garnish with walnut halves. Yield: 22 servings.

Connie Leetsch, Laureate Delta Eta
Abilene, Texas

PUMPKIN UPSIDE DOWN CAKE

I have used this recipe, always a great hit, at Thanksgiving and Christmas.

3 eggs
2 (16-ounce) cans pumpkin
11/4 cups sugar
1 (12-ounce) can evaporated milk
2 teaspoons cinnamon
1 teaspoon nutmeg
1/2 teaspoon ginger
1 (2-layer) package cake mix (any flavor)
3/4 cup melted butter or margarine
1 cup chopped walnuts

Preheat oven to 350 degrees. Combine eggs, pumpkin, sugar, evaporated milk, cinnamon, nutmeg and ginger in mixer bowl; beat until well blended. Spread into greased 9-by-13-inch cake pan. Sprinkle cake mix evenly over top. Drizzle with melted butter. Bake at 350 degrees for 30 minutes. Top with walnuts. Bake for 30 minutes longer. Let stand until cool. Serve with whipped cream. Yield: 15 servings.

Roberta Cunningham, Laureate Beta Zeta
Bremerton, Washington

RHUBARB CAKE

4 cups (or more) chopped rhubarb
1 cup sugar
1 (3-ounce) package strawberry gelatin
4 cups miniature marshmallows
1 (2-layer) package golden yellow cake mix

Preheat oven to 350 degrees. Layer rhubarb in greased 9-by-13-inch cake pan. Sprinkle with mixture of sugar and gelatin. Top with marshmallows. Prepare cake mix using package instructions. Spread over marshmallow layer. Bake at 350 degrees for 25 to 30 minutes or until cake tests done. Let stand until cool. Invert onto serving platter. Serve with whipped cream. Yield: 15 servings.

Lynda Russell, Laureate Alpha Alpha
Kingston, Ontario, Canada

RHUBARB CANDY CAKE

1/2 cup shortening
1 1/2 cups sugar
1/2 teaspoon salt
1 egg
1 teaspoon baking soda
2 cups plus 1 tablespoon all-purpose flour
1 cup sour milk
3 cups 1/2-inch rhubarb pieces
1/4 cup multi-colored candy sprinkles
1/3 cup sugar
1/3 cup chopped pecans
1 teaspoon cinnamon

Preheat oven to 350 degrees. Cream shortening, 1 1/2 cups sugar, salt and egg in bowl. Add baking soda and flour alternately with sour milk, mixing well after each addition. Stir in rhubarb and candy sprinkles. Spoon into greased and floured 9-by-13-inch baking pan. Sprinkle with mixture of 1/3 cup sugar, pecans and cinnamon. Bake at 350 degrees for 45 minutes. Yield: 12 to 15 servings.

Debbie Austin, Laureate Beta Omega
Port Orchard, Washington

KNOBBY RHUBARB CAKE

1 cup sugar
1/4 cup butter or margarine, softened
1 egg
1 teaspoon vanilla extract
1 cup all-purpose flour
1/2 teaspoon baking powder
1/2 teaspoon baking soda
1/4 teaspoon cinnamon
1/4 teaspoon nutmeg
Salt to taste
3 cups diced rhubarb
1/4 cup chopped pecans

Preheat oven to 350 degrees. Cream sugar and butter in mixer bowl until light and fluffy. Add egg and vanilla; mix well. Add mixture of flour, baking powder, baking soda, cinnamon, nutmeg and salt; mix until blended. Stir in rhubarb and pecans; batter will be very thick. Spoon into greased 8-by-8-inch square cake pan. Bake at 350 degrees for 45 minutes. Yield: 9 servings.

Diane Price, Kappa Epsilon
Millerton, New York

RHUBARB MARSHMALLOW CAKE

My sister shared this fun and easy recipe with me. As the cake bakes, the marshmallows rise to the top and the rhubarb sinks to the bottom of the pan.

2 to 2 1/2 cups miniature marshmallows
1 (2-layer) package white or yellow cake mix
3 cups fresh or frozen chopped rhubarb
1/2 cup water
1 cup sugar
1 (3-ounce) package strawberry gelatin
Whipped topping (optional)

Preheat oven to 350 degrees. Sprinkle marshmallows over bottom of 9-by-13-inch cake pan. Prepare cake mix using package instructions. Spread over marshmallows. Combine rhubarb, water, sugar and gelatin in saucepan. Cook over low heat until sugar and gelatin dissolve, stirring constantly. Cool to room temperature. Pour over batter. Bake at 350 degrees for 40 minutes. Serve with whipped topping. Store, covered, in refrigerator. Yield: 15 servings.

Angela Black
Adrian, Michigan

✣ RICOTTA CAKE

2 (16-ounce) cartons ricotta cheese
3/4 cup sugar
3 eggs, lightly beaten
1 (2-layer) package pudding-recipe yellow or lemon cake mix
Confectioners' sugar to taste

Preheat oven to 350 degrees. Combine ricotta cheese, sugar and eggs in mixer bowl; mix well. Prepare cake mix using package instructions. Spoon into greased and floured 9-by-13-inch cake pan. Spread ricotta cheese mixture over top. Bake at 350 degrees for 60 to 65 minutes or until cake tests done. Cool in pan on wire rack. Sprinkle with confectioners' sugar. Yield: 12 servings.

Mary Miller, Xi Delta Eta
Los Angeles, California

RUM CAKE

This cake has been a family favorite, especially for birthdays and for our Canadian visitors.

1/2 cup sliced almonds
1 (2-layer) package pudding-recipe yellow cake mix
4 eggs
1/2 cup vegetable oil
1/2 cup cold water
1/2 cup rum
1/2 cup margarine
1 cup sugar
1/4 cup rum
1/4 cup water

Preheat oven to 325 degrees. Sprinkle almonds into greased large bundt pan. Prepare cake mix following package instructions, using eggs, oil, 1/2 cup water and 1/2 cup rum. Spoon over almonds. Bake at 325 degrees for 55 to 60 minutes or until wooden pick inserted in center comes out clean. Combine margarine, sugar, 1/4 cup rum and 1/4 cup water in saucepan. Bring to a boil over low heat. Cook for 2 minutes, stirring constantly. Pour over hot cake. Let stand for 20 to 30 minutes or until sauce is absorbed. Invert onto cake plate. Yield: 12 to 16 servings.

Evelyn Ciolfe, Preceptor Phi Epsilon
Lemon Grove, California

RUM NUT CAKE

This cake is submitted by my husband because at Christmastime he takes it to his office so that all those who work for him know they are appreciated.

1 cup chopped pecans or walnuts
1 (2-layer) package yellow cake mix
1 (4-ounce) package vanilla instant pudding mix
4 eggs
1/2 cup cold water
1/2 cup vegetable oil
1/2 cup dark rum
1/2 cup butter or margarine
1/4 cup water
1 cup sugar
1/2 cup dark rum
Whipped cream
Chocolate shavings

Preheat oven to 325 degrees. Sprinkle pecans in greased and floured 10-inch tube or 12-inch bundt pan. Combine cake mix, pudding mix, eggs, 1/2 cup water and oil in large bowl; mix well. Mix in 1/2 cup rum. Spoon into prepared pan. Bake at 325 degrees for 1 hour. Cool completely. Invert onto serving plate. Prick holes in top. Melt butter in saucepan over low heat. Add 1/4 cup water and sugar. Bring to a boil. Boil for 5 minutes, stirring constantly. Remove from heat. Stir in 1/2 cup rum. Spoon over cake gradually to allow glaze to be absorbed. Garnish with whipped cream and chocolate shavings. Yield: 8 to 10 servings.

Jay (Carol) Lanctot, Mu Sigma
Mt. Pleasant, Michigan

SHERRY CAKE

1 (2-layer) package yellow cake mix
1 (4-ounce) package vanilla instant pudding mix
1/2 teaspoon nutmeg
4 eggs
3/4 cup cream sherry
3/4 cup vegetable oil

Preheat oven to 350 degrees. Combine cake mix, pudding mix, nutmeg, eggs, sherry and oil in large mixer bowl. Beat at low speed until moistened. Beat at high speed for 3 minutes. Spoon into greased and floured bundt pan. Bake at 350 degrees for 45 to 50 minutes or until cake tests done. May frost with confectioners' sugar frosting, if desired. Yield: 10 to 12 servings.

Ruth Krusell, Laureate Alpha Beta
Oregon City, Oregon

SOUR CREAM CAKE

1 cup margarine, softened
2 cups sugar
4 eggs
1 teaspoon vanilla extract
1 cup sour cream
1 teaspoon baking soda
3 cups sifted all-purpose flour

Preheat oven to 350 degrees. Cream margarine and sugar in mixer bowl until light and fluffy. Add eggs 1 at a time, beating after each addition. Add vanilla and sour cream; mix well. Add sifted mixture of baking soda and flour; mix until blended. Spoon into greased tube or bundt pan. Bake at 350 degrees for 1 hour. Yield: 16 servings.

Alice Luetger, Chi Epsilon
Downers Grove, Illinois

SOUR CREAM SPICE CAKE

2 cups all-purpose flour
1 1/2 cups packed light brown sugar
1 cup sour cream
1/2 cup margarine
1/2 cup shortening
2 eggs
1/2 cup water
2 teaspoons cinnamon
1 1/4 teaspoons baking soda
1 teaspoon baking powder
3/4 teaspoons ground cloves
1/2 teaspoon salt
1/2 teaspoon nutmeg
1 cup raisins soaked in warm water, drained
1/2 cup walnuts

Preheat oven to 350 degrees. Combine first 13 ingredients in large mixer bowl. Beat at high speed for 2 minutes. Stir in raisins and walnuts. Spoon into greased and floured bundt pan. Bake at 350 degrees for 45 to 55 minutes or until cake springs back when lightly touched in center. Yield: 12 to 15 servings.

Robin Jones, Theta Chi
Chesapeake, Virginia

STRAWBERRY CAKE

This recipe was handed down to me by my aunt, who is a 50-year member of Beta Sigma Phi.

1 (2-layer) package white cake mix
1 (3-ounce) package strawberry gelatin
2 tablespoons all-purpose flour
3/4 cup vegetable oil
1/2 cup water
4 eggs
1 (10-ounce) package frozen sliced sweet strawberries, thawed, drained
3 tablespoons all-purpose flour
1 cup milk
1/2 cup margarine
1 cup sugar
3/4 cup shortening

Preheat oven to 350 degrees. Combine cake mix, gelatin and 2 tablespoons flour in large bowl; mix well. Add oil and water; mix until blended. Add eggs 1 at a time, mixing after each addition. Stir in half the strawberries. Spoon into greased and floured 9-by-13-inch cake pan. Bake at 350 degrees for 40 minutes. Combine 3 tablespoons flour and milk in saucepan. Cook over low heat until thickened, stirring constantly. Remove from heat; cool. Beat in margarine and sugar gradually. Add shortening gradually, beating until thickened. Stir in remaining strawberries. Spread over top of cake. Yield: 8 to 12 servings.

Kathleen Harpel, Laureate Gamma Epsilon
Toledo, Ohio

HOLIDAY STRAWBERRY CAKE

1 (3-ounce) package strawberry gelatin
1 cup boiling water
1 (2-layer) package white cake mix
3/4 cup corn oil
4 eggs
1 (10-ounce) package frozen strawberries, thawed
2 cups confectioners' sugar

Preheat oven to 350 degrees. Dissolve gelatin in boiling water in bowl. Let stand until cool. Combine cake mix, gelatin mixture and corn oil in mixer bowl; mix well. Beat in eggs 1 at a time. Drain strawberries, reserving juice. Stir strawberries into batter. Spoon into 9-by-13-inch cake pan. Bake at 350 degrees for 35 to 40 minutes or until cake tests done. Blend confectioners' sugar and enough reserved strawberry juice to make glaze in bowl. Punch holes in hot cake; pour strawberry glaze over cake. Serve with whipped topping or ice cream, if desired.
Yield: 12 servings.

Donna Pierson, Laureate Gamma
Spencer, Iowa

FRESH STRAWBERRY CAKE

1 (2-layer) package white cake mix
1 (3-ounce) package strawberry gelatin
1 cup crushed fresh strawberries
1/3 cup vegetable oil
4 eggs
1/2 cup melted margarine
1 (1-pound) package confectioners' sugar, sifted
1 cup crushed fresh strawberries

Preheat oven to 350 degrees. Combine cake mix, gelatin, strawberries and oil in mixer bowl; mix well. Add eggs 1 at a time, beating after each addition. Spoon into greased 9-by-13-inch baking pan. Bake at 350 degrees for 30 minutes. Let stand until cool. Combine margarine and confectioners' sugar in bowl; mix well. Stir in strawberries. Spread over cake. Yield: 12 to 15 servings.

Shirley Spears, Epsilon Gamma
Gallatin, Tennessee

STRAWBERRY SPARKLE CAKE

1 package angel food cake mix
1 (3-ounce) package strawberry gelatin
1 cup boiling water
1 (16-ounce) package frozen strawberries
Whipped topping

Preheat oven to 350 degrees. Prepare and bake cake mix using package instructions. Dissolve gelatin in boiling water in bowl. Add strawberries, stirring to mix. Invert cake onto serving plate. Cut 1-inch slice horizontally off top of cake; set aside. Carve out inside of cake, leaving 1-inch shell at sides and bottom. Slice carved-out cake into small pieces; mix with gelatin mixture in bowl. Pour gelatin mixture evenly into hollowed cake. Place top slice on cake. Top with whipped topping. Chill until firm.
Yield: 16 servings.

Danielle Head, Theta Omega
Salisbury, Missouri

SWEET POTATO CAKE

2 cups sugar
4 eggs
1 cup vegetable oil
1 teaspoon vanilla extract
2 cups all-purpose flour
2 teaspoons each baking soda and cinnamon
1 (16-ounce) can yams, undrained
8 ounces cream cheese, softened
1/2 cup butter or margarine, softened
1 (1-pound) package confectioners' sugar

Preheat oven to 350 degrees. Combine sugar and eggs in mixer bowl; mix well. Mix in oil and vanilla. Add mixture of flour, baking soda and cinnamon; mix until blended. Add yams and syrup. Beat for 2 minutes. Spoon into greased and floured tube pan. Bake at 350 degrees for 1 hour. Combine cream cheese, butter and confectioners' sugar in mixer bowl; beat until smooth and creamy. Frost cake.
Yield: 8 to 10 servings.

Sharon Lee Combs, Alpha Xi
Hazard, Kentucky

EASY FUDGE FROSTING

1 cup sugar
1/4 cup milk
1/4 cup margarine
1/2 cup semisweet chocolate chips

Combine sugar, milk and margarine in saucepan. Bring to a boil over medium heat. Cook for 1 minute, stirring constantly. Add chocolate chips, stirring until melted and of spreadable consistency.
Yield: frosting for 24 cupcakes.

Kay Benson, Laureate Rho
Oral, South Dakota

SPECIAL FROSTING

5 tablespoons all-purpose flour
1 cup milk
1 cup sugar
1/2 cup butter or margarine, softened
1/2 cup shortening
Flavoring of choice

Combine flour and milk in small saucepan. Cook over low heat until very thick, stirring constantly. Cream sugar, butter and shortening in mixer bowl until light and fluffy. Beat for 10 minutes on highest speed. Beat in milk mixture. Add flavoring. Store, loosely covered, in refrigerator.
Yield: 8 to 12 servings.

June Ferries, Preceptor, Xi Epsilon
San Diego, California

Quick Pick-Me-Ups

It's three o'clock and the afternoon blahs hit. It's time to take a break. But instead of soda and a bag of chips, why not recharge your batteries with something truly tasty! If cookies are your passion, we have recipes galore. From the ultimate chocolate chip to some updated versions of your old favorites, you'll find lots of recipes to tempt you. Or try your hand at some homemade fudge or caramel chewies. If you've never made candy before, if you'll pardon the expression, you're in for a treat! Get the kids involved and let them help make something yummy to take to their friends at school. Everyone has a sweet tooth, and a tin of your homemade confections will brighten anyone's day. And after a long, hard day at work or volunteering, why not end your day with a tasty morsel that's sure to guarantee some very sweet dreams!

ALMOND ROCA

2 cups melted butter or margarine
2 cups sugar
1 (2 1/2-pound) chocolate bar
Paraffin wax, cut up
Sliced almonds to taste

Combine butter and sugar in saucepan. Bring to a boil, stirring until sugar is light brown. Spoon onto waxed paper with waxed side down on 12-by-18-inch baking sheet. Chill until cooled. Melt chocolate in saucepan over low heat. Remove from heat; add paraffin. Mix until of spreadable consistency. Spread over sugar layer. Sprinkle with almonds. Break into bite-size pieces to serve. Yield: 12 to 16 servings.

Lisa Richardson, Alpha Epsilon
If, Idaho

APLETS

1/2 cup peeled grated tart apples
2 tablespoons unflavored gelatin
3/4 cup grated apples
2 cups sugar
1 teaspoon vanilla extract (optional)
1/2 to 1 cup chopped walnuts
1/2 cup confectioners' sugar
1 tablespoon cornstarch

Sprinkle 1/2 cup apples over gelatin in medium bowl. Let stand for 10 minutes. Combine 3/4 cup apples and sugar in saucepan. Bring to a boil over low heat. Add gelatin mixture; mix well. Cook for 15 minutes longer. Let stand until cool. Add vanilla. Stir in walnuts. Spoon into greased 8-by-8-inch square pan. Let stand for 24 hours. Cut into pieces; roll in mixture of confectioners' sugar and cornstarch. Roll in confectioners' sugar mixture a second time if sugar mixture soaks into candies. Yield: 8 to 10 servings.

Marlyce Gholston, Laureate Alpha Beta
Portland, Oregon

BUTTERSCOTCH BARS

1/2 cup butter or margarine
1 1/2 cups graham cracker crumbs
1 cup milk chocolate chips
1 cup butterscotch chips
1/2 cup coconut
1 cup crisp rice cereal
1 (14-ounce) can sweetened condensed milk

Preheat oven to 350 degrees. Melt butter in 9-by-13-inch baking pan; spread evenly. Layer graham cracker crumbs, chocolate chips, butterscotch chips, coconut, cereal and condensed milk in pan in order listed; do not mix. Bake at 350 degrees for 15 to 20 minutes or until lightly browned. Cut into squares when cool. Yield: 32 servings.

Shawne Wilton, Beta Nu
Chatham, Ontario, Canada

EASY MICROWAVE CARAMELS

1 cup butter or margarine
2 1/3 cups packed light brown sugar
1 cup light corn syrup
1/8 teaspoon salt
1 teaspoon vanilla extract
1/2 cup chopped nuts

Combine butter, brown sugar, corn syrup and salt in microwave-safe bowl. Microwave on High for 3 to 4 minutes or until mixture is bubbly, stirring once. Microwave for 14 minutes longer; do not stir. Mix in vanilla and nuts. Let stand for 10 minutes, stirring frequently. Spoon into greased 9-by-13-inch dish. Chill until set. Invert pan onto serving plate and tap out whole block of candy. Cut into squares. Wrap individually with waxed paper. Yield: 3 to 4 dozen.

Stacy Freese, Xi Epsilon
Plymouth, Nebraska

EASY CHOCOLATE-COVERED CHERRIES

I have treasured sharing this holiday tradition for many years with friends near and far.

1 (14-ounce) can sweetened condensed milk
1/2 cup butter or margarine, softened
8 cups confectioners' sugar
120 to 130 maraschino cherries with stems, drained, frozen
1 pound chocolate almond bark candy
1 pound white almond bark
2 cups milk chocolate chips
2 to 3 tablespoons shredded paraffin

Combine condensed milk and butter in large bowl. Stir in confectioners' sugar. Knead until smooth. Transfer to small bowl. Cover with waxed paper. Let stand for 15 minutes. Pinch off small portions; roll into dime-sized balls. Place on serving trays lined with waxed paper, spacing so that 30 fit on each tray. Chill for 5 minutes. Flatten each ball into disc large enough to wrap around a cherry. Wrap individually around frozen cherries. Roll by hand to make smooth balls; replace on tray. Freeze to set. Combine 2 pieces chocolate almond bark, 1 piece white almond bark, 1/4 cup chocolate chips, and 1 tablespoon paraffin in microwave-safe bowl. Microwave on High until melted, stirring once per minute; do not burn. Set bowl on warming plate on low heat. Dip frozen cherries into chocolate mixture, twirling by stems to remove excess. Replace on waxed paper-lined trays. Repeat process until all cherries are covered. Store in semi-cool area. Editor's Note: Place cherries in miniature paper bonbon cups and arrange in an attractive container to use as gifts or a special party presentation. Yield: 6 to 7 dozen.

Tamela A. Jones, Xi Beta Phi
Urbandale, Iowa

CHOCOLATE-COVERED PEANUT BUTTER HEARTS

Our sorority has made 25 batches of these hearts each Februrary for the last 10 years.

8 ounces cream cheese, softened
1/2 cup margarine, softened
1 (18-ounce) jar peanut butter
2 (1-pound) packages confectioners' sugar
1 tablespoon vanilla extract
Dash of salt
Melted chocolate for dipping

Mix first 3 ingredients in bowl. Add confectioners' sugar gradually, mixing well after each addition. Stir in vanilla and salt. Roll on waxed paper. Cut with cookie cutter. Dip in chocolate; return to waxed paper. Yield: 25 servings.

Mary Kaufman, Xi Beta Sigma
Paxtonville, Pennsylvania

CHOCOLATE DROP CANDY

1/2 cup melted butter or margarine
4 cups chopped pecans
2 (1-pound) packages confectioners' sugar
1 teaspoon vanilla extract
1 (14-ounce) can sweetened condensed milk
1 cup flaked coconut
2 cups milk chocolate chips
1/4 pound paraffin

Pour butter over pecans in large bowl. Sift confectioners' sugar into bowl. Stir in vanilla, condensed milk and coconut. Knead until firm. Shape into small balls; arrange on waxed paper-lined 12-by-18-inch baking sheets. Place wooden pick in each ball. Chill for 15 minutes. Melt chocolate chips and paraffin in top of double boiler over hot water; mix well. Dip each coconut ball into chocolate; return to waxed paper. Store covered. Yield: 100 (1-ball) servings.

Roberta Griffith, Xi Upsilon Rho
Oxnard, California

COCONUT BALLS

1 (14-ounce) package flaked coconut
3 cups chopped pecans
1 (14-ounce) can sweetened condensed milk
2 1/2 cups semisweet chocolate chips
1/4 pound paraffin

Combine first 3 ingredients in large bowl. Chill for 30 minutes. Shape into balls. Chill until set. Melt chocolate chips and paraffin in double boiler over hot water. Remove from heat; stir until blended. Dip chilled coconut balls in chocolate. Arrange on waxed paper on serving tray. Yield: 2 to 3 dozen.

Nena Kirkhart, Xi Epsilon Omega
Rosston, Oklahoma

CRACKER CANDY

2 cups sugar
2/3 cup milk
1 teaspoon vanilla extract
6 tablespoons peanut butter
1/4 pound soda crackers, crumbled

Bring sugar and milk to a boil in saucepan. Cook for 3 minutes, stirring occasionally. Remove from heat. Add vanilla and peanut butter; mix well. Stir in cracker crumbs. Add additional milk to thin or confectioners' sugar to thicken if needed. Drop by spoonfuls or pat into greased 8-by-8-inch pan. Cut into squares. Yield: 1 to 2 dozen.

Jalayne Ewing, Mu Kappa
Ellinwood, Kansas

WHITE DIVINITY CANDY

4 cups sugar
2/3 cup light corn syrup
1 cup water
2 egg whites
2 teaspoons vanilla extract
2 cups chopped walnuts

Combine sugar, corn syrup and water in large saucepan. Bring to a boil over low heat. Cook until mixture registers 250 to 268 degrees on candy thermometer, hard-ball stage. Do not stir while cooking. Beat egg whites in mixer bowl until stiff. Add sugar mixture; beat until blended. Stir in vanilla. Beat until thick. Stir in walnuts. Spoon into greased 9-by-13-inch dish. Yield: 3 to 4 dozen.

Carole T. Fryover, Preceptor Lambda
Gorham, Maine

COOKIES AND MINT FUDGE

This recipe is one I developed after deciding, along with my daughter Julie, to experiment with cookies and mint candy bars when they first became available.

2 1/2 cups semisweet chocolate chips
5 cookies and mint candy bars, broken into small pieces
2 ounces unsweetened chocolate
1 cup butter or margarine, softened
2 cups miniature marshmallows
1 (12-ounce) can evaporated milk
4 cups sugar

Combine first 5 ingredients in large mixer bowl; mix well. Combine evaporated milk and sugar in saucepan. Bring to a boil over medium heat; reduce heat to low. Simmer for 10 minutes, stirring constantly. Spoon chocolate mixture into sugar mixture. Cook over low heat until marshmallows are melted, stirring constantly. Spoon into 9-by-13-inch pan lined with waxed paper. Chill for 8 hours or longer.
Yield: 6 to 7 dozen.

Darlene K. Lannholm, Preceptor Mu Tau
Galesburg, Illinois

FAMOUS FUDGE

3 cups semisweet chocolate chips
1 cup butter or margarine
1 teaspoon vanilla extract
2 cups chopped walnuts (optional)
4 1/2 cups sugar
1 (12-ounce) can evaporated milk

Combine chocolate chips, butter, vanilla and walnuts in large bowl. Combine sugar and evaporated milk in large saucepan. Bring to a boil over low heat. Cook for 6 minutes, stirring constantly. Add to chocolate chip mixture; stir until chips and butter are melted and mixture is smooth. Spoon into buttered 9-by-13-inch pan. Yield: 6 to 7 dozen.

Donna Wertz, Alpha Tau Master
Cypress, California

FOUR-MINUTE VELVET MARBLE FUDGE

1 1/2 cups semisweet chocolate chips
1 (8-ounce) can sweetened condensed milk
1 1/2 cups peanut butter chips
5 tablespoons confectioners' sugar
2 teaspoons vanilla extract

Combine chocolate chips and half the condensed milk in microwave-safe container. Microwave, uncovered, on High for 2 minutes; do not stir. Combine peanut butter chips and remaining condensed milk in second microwave-safe container. Microwave, uncovered, on High for 2 minutes; do not stir. Stir 2 1/2 tablespoons confectioners' sugar and 1 teaspoon vanilla into chocolate mixture. Stir 2 1/2 tablespoons confectioners' sugar and 1 teaspoon vanilla into peanut butter mixture. Stir each mixture until smooth. Add peanut butter mixture to chocolate mixture, stirring 2 or 3 times to marbleized. Spread evenly in buttered 8-by-8-inch pan. Chill until firm. Store, tightly covered, for up to 2 weeks.
Yield: 64 (1-inch) squares.

Jeannie Mason
Asheville, North Carolina

LAZY WOMAN'S FUDGE

1 2/3 cups packed light brown sugar
2/3 cup evaporated milk or heavy cream
1 cup finely chopped marshmallows
1 cup chopped pecans
1 teaspoon vanilla extract

Combine brown sugar and evaporated milk in medium saucepan. Bring to a boil. Cook for exactly 5 minutes, stirring constantly. Remove from heat. Add marshmallows, pecans and vanilla, mixing until marshmallows are melted. Spoon into buttered pie plate. Let stand until cool. Yield: 32 servings.

Linda Gillette, Preceptor Iota Psi
San Gabriel, California

PEANUT BUTTER FUDGE

3 1/2 cups peanut butter
1 cup packed light brown sugar
6 cups confectioners' sugar
1 teaspoon vanilla extract
1 cup melted margarine
2 cups semisweet chocolate chips
5 tablespoons margarine

Mix peanut butter, brown sugar, confectioners' sugar and vanilla in large bowl. Blend in melted margarine. Pat into greased 9-by-13-inch pan or two 8-by-8-inch square pans. Melt chocolate chips and margarine in saucepan, stirring until blended. Spread over fudge mixture. Chill until set. Yield: 4 to 5 dozen.

Ann Joy Matison, Xi Zeta Iota
Winter Haven, Florida

EASY PEANUT BUTTER FUDGE

1 cup crunchy peanut butter
1 cup butterscotch chips
1 (14-ounce) can sweetened condensed milk

Combine peanut butter, chips and condensed milk in microwave-safe container. Microwave on High for 2 minutes, stirring once. Press mixture into greased 9-by-13-inch pan. Chill until set. Yield: 1 to 2 dozen.

Joyce Ruppel-Rada, Laureate Beta Omega
Port Orchard, Washington

CRUNCHY PEANUT BUTTER FUDGE

2 cups butter or margarine
3 cups extra-crunchy peanut butter
2 (1-pound) packages confectioners' sugar

Combine butter and peanut butter in medium saucepan. Cook until butter is melted and mixture is smooth, stirring constantly. Remove from heat. Stir in confectioners' sugar gradually. Spread on greased 12-by-18-inch baking sheet. Let stand for 30 minutes or until cool. Cut into squares. Yield: 4 to 5 dozen.

Pauline Scherschel, Alpha Beta
Bedford, Indiana

Chris Jeter, Preceptor Theta, Chesapeake, Virginia, makes Heavenly Crackers by melting 2/3 pound milk chocolate, 2/3 pound white chocolate and 1 tablespoon shortening in microwave, blending well and dipping mini peanut butter Ritz crackers in the mixture. Place on waxed paper to set up.

PEANUT BUTTER MARSHMALLOW FUDGE

This is a family favorite at Christmas.

5 cups sugar
1 (12-ounce) can evaporated milk
1/2 cup butter or margarine
1 (13-ounce) jar marshmallow creme
1 1/2 cups peanut butter
1 cup chopped pecans

Combine sugar, evaporated milk and butter in saucepan. Bring to a boil over low heat, stirring frequently. Cook until mixture registers 234 to 240 degrees on candy thermometer, soft-ball stage. Remove from heat. Add marshmallow creme and peanut butter, stirring until smooth. Stir in pecans. Spoon into buttered 9-by-13-inch pan. Let stand until cool. Cut into 1-inch squares. Yield: 6 dozen.

Shirley Roth, Preceptor Tau
Cocoa, Florida

PEANUT BUTTER CHOCOLATE FUDGE

3 cups semisweet chocolate chips
1 (14-ounce) can sweetened condensed milk
Dash of salt
1 1/2 teaspoons vanilla extract
1/2 cup crunchy peanut butter

Combine chocolate chips and condensed milk in heavy medium saucepan. Cook over low heat until chips melt, stirring until blended. Remove from heat. Add salt, vanilla and peanut butter; mix well. Spread in 9-by-13-inch pan lined with waxed paper. Chill until firm. Yield: 1 dozen.

Marlene Markey, Preceptor Epsilon Theta
St. Petersburg, Florida

PINEAPPLE FUDGE

I make this candy at Christmas, when Pi Chapter delivers about 100 boxes of homemade candy to shut-ins, as it has been doing for about 35 years.

3 cups sugar
1 tablespoon light corn syrup
1/2 cup heavy cream
1/2 cup drained crushed pineapple
2 tablespoons butter
1/2 teaspoon vanilla extract
1/2 cup chopped walnuts (optional)

Combine sugar, corn syrup, cream and pineapple in well-buttered heavy saucepan. Bring to a rolling boil over low heat. Cook until mixture registers 234 to 240 degrees on candy thermometer, soft-ball stage, stirring constantly. Remove from heat. Add butter; do not stir. Cool in pan until lukewarm. Add vanilla; beat until candy begins to thicken. Stir in walnuts. Spoon into greased 9-by-9-inch pan. Chill until set. Cut into squares. May freeze. Yield: 2 to 3 dozen.

Evelyn Smith, Pi
Brunswick, Missouri

QUICK FUDGE

Wait until the candy has set to have a chocolate attack! You can speed up the process by placing the candy in the freezer for 5 to 10 minutes.

1 (1-pound) package confectioners' sugar
1/3 cup baking cocoa
1/2 cup butter or margarine
1/4 cup half-and-half
1 tablespoon vanilla extract
1 cup chopped nuts

Combine sugar and cocoa in microwave-safe container. Add butter; do not mix. Microwave on High for 1 1/2 minutes. Remove from oven; stir until blended. Add half-and-half, vanilla and nuts; mix well. Spoon into greased 8-by-8-inch pan. Chill for 30 minutes. Yield: 2 dozen.

Jackie Engle, Mu Kappa
Ellinwood, Kansas

ROYAL PEANUT BUTTER FUDGE

This is a secret recipe from a candy company, broken down for individual use. It's fit for a king!

2/3 cup milk
2 cups sugar
1 1/2 cups creamy peanut butter
1 tablespoon vanilla extract

Combine milk and sugar in buttered heavy saucepan. Bring to a rolling boil; reduce heat to medium. Cook for 8 to 10 minutes or until mixture registers 234 to 240 degrees on candy thermometer, soft-ball stage. Remove from heat. Stir in peanut butter and vanilla. Spoon into buttered 5-by-9-inch bread pan. Let stand for 25 to 30 minutes or until set.
Yield: 3 to 4 dozen.

Kathleen Molloy, Delta Master
Muskegon, Michigan

GRAHAM GOODIES

12 graham crackers, separated into 4 sections
1/2 cup butter
1/2 cup margarine
1/2 cup sugar
1 cup chopped walnuts

Preheat oven to 375 degrees. Arrange graham crackers in foil-lined 10-by-15-inch baking pan. Combine butter, margarine and sugar in saucepan. Bring to a boil over low heat. Cook for 2 minutes, stirring constantly. Spread over crackers. Sprinkle with walnuts. Bake at 375 degrees for 10 minutes. Break into individual pieces. Yield: 12 servings.

Eleanor Tucker, Preceptor Alpha Beta
Lawndale, California

LECHE QUEMADA (SWEET TREAT)

2 cups pecans
1/2 cup margarine
2/3 cup packed light brown sugar
1 cup sweetened condensed milk
1 teaspoon vanilla extract

Arrange pecans on glass plate. Microwave on High for 8 minutes, stirring every 2 minutes; set aside. Place margarine in 8-cup microwave-safe container. Microwave on High for 1 minute or until melted. Stir in brown sugar and condensed milk. Microwave on High for 7 minutes, stirring every minute. Beat until stiff. Add vanilla and pecans; mix well. Pour into greased 8-by-8-inch dish. Chill until set. Cut into squares. Yield: 64 servings.

Deelyn Evans, Xi Gamma Lambda
Shattuck, Oklahoma

MARSHMALLOW ROLL

1 (10-ounce) package miniature marshmallows
1/4 cup water
1/2 cup sweetened condensed milk
1/2 cup walnuts
1/2 cup finely chopped dates
2 1/2 cups graham cracker crumbs
Whipped cream
Cherries

Combine marshmallows and water in mixer bowl. Add condensed milk, walnuts and dates; mix well. Add crumbs; mix until blended. Shape into 3-by-6-inch roll. Wrap in waxed paper. Chill for 12 hours or longer. Slice and add whipped cream and cherries to individual servings. May use graham cracker crumbs to prevent mixture from sticking to your hands. Yield: 10 servings.

Lela Breger, Epsilon Master
Phoenix, Arizona

PEANUT BUTTER BARS

2 cups sugar
2/3 cup milk
1 teaspoon vanilla extract
2/3 cup flaked coconut
6 tablespoons peanut butter
32 soda crackers, crushed

Combine sugar and milk in saucepan. Bring to a boil over low heat. Cook for 3 minutes, stirring constantly. Add vanilla, coconut, peanut butter and cracker crumbs; mix well. Stir until cool. Spoon into buttered 6-by-10-inch pan. Cool and cut into bite-size bars. May substitute skim milk for whole milk and chopped pecans for coconut. May line pan with waxed paper or spray with nonstick cooking spray instead of using butter. Yield: 1 to 2 dozen.

Evelyn F. Whitely, Beta Epsilon Omicron
Brackettville, Texas

PEANUT BUTTER SNOWBALLS

1 cup confectioners' sugar
1/2 cup creamy peanut butter
3 tablespoons butter or margarine, softened
1 pound white almond bark

Combine confectioners' sugar, peanut butter and butter in mixer bowl; mix well. Shape into 1-inch balls. Arrange on waxed paper-lined 10-by-15-inch sheet pan. Chill for 30 minutes or until firm. Melt almond bark in double boiler over hot water. Dip peanut butter balls into almond bark. Place on waxed paper. Let stand until cool. Yield: 2 dozen.

Joan Sittel, Nu Master
Amarillo, Texas

PEANUT BRITTLE

1 cup raw peanuts
1 cup sugar
1/2 cup plus 1 tablespoon light corn syrup
1/8 teaspoon salt
1 tablespoon margarine
1 teaspoon vanilla extract
1 teaspoon baking soda

Combine peanuts, sugar, corn syrup and salt in microwave-safe container. Microwave on High for 2 minutes. Mix well. Microwave on High for 6 minutes longer. Add margarine and vanilla; mix well. Microwave on High for 1 1/2 minutes. Add baking soda; mix until blended. Spoon onto greased 12-by-18-inch sheet pan. Let stand until cool. Break into pieces. Yield: 1 dozen.

Peggy Rudolph, Kappa Theta
Lees Summit, Missouri

PEANUT CLUSTERS

2 cups semisweet chocolate chips
8 squares white almond bark
1 pound Spanish peanuts

Melt chocolate chips and almond bark in double boiler over hot water. Add peanuts; mix well. Drop by teaspoonfuls onto waxed paper. Let stand until cool. Yield: 4 dozen.

Chanelle M. Carlin, Preceptor Psi
Vancouver, Washington

PEANUT PATTIES

2 cups sugar
1/2 cup light corn syrup
1/4 cup water
1/2 cup milk
1/4 teaspoon salt
3 drops of red food coloring
1 teaspoon vanilla extract
1 cup confectioners' sugar
2 cups roasted peanuts

Combine sugar, corn syrup, water, milk, salt and food coloring in saucepan. Bring to a rolling boil over low heat. Cook for 7 to 10 minutes or until mixture registers 234 to 240 degrees on candy thermometer, soft-ball stage. Remove from heat. Add vanilla, confectioners' sugar and peanuts; beat until thickened. Drop by teaspoonfuls onto waxed paper. Yield: 3 to 4 dozen.

Sue Altimore, Preceptor Beta Phi
Anderson, Texas

PECAN JERKY (PRALINES)

My mother-in-law gave me this recipe more than 30 years ago.

Whole cinnamon graham crackers
1/2 cup margarine
1 cup packed light brown sugar
1 cup chopped pecans

Preheat oven to 350 degrees. Line 9-by-13-inch baking pan with graham crackers. Bring margarine, brown sugar and pecans to a boil in medium saucepan, stirring constantly. Pour over crackers. Bake at 350 degrees for 8 to 10 minutes or until golden brown. Cool in pan for 5 minutes. Remove warm candy to smooth surface to cool. Cut into pieces. Yield: 24 small servings.

Ella G. (Trudy) Phillips, Laureate Pi
Highland Village, Texas

POTATO CANDY

1 small potato, cooked, drained
1 teaspoon vanilla extract
2 (1-pound) packages confectioners' sugar
1 (12-ounce) jar peanut butter

Mash potato in bowl with fork. Add vanilla; mix well. Add confectioners' sugar gradually until dough is firm. Roll dough to thickness of pie crust on flat surface sprinkled with additional confectioners' sugar. Spread with peanut butter. Roll as for jelly roll; slice. Chill for 1 hour. Store in refrigerator. Yield: 2 to 3 dozen.

Alice Nichols, Preceptor Alpha Nu
Dublin, Georgia

PRALINES

1 teaspoon baking soda
1 cup buttermilk
2 cups sugar
1 teaspoon vanilla extract
1 tablespoon margarine
2 cups chopped pecans

Dissolve baking soda in mixture of buttermilk and sugar in saucepan. Cook over medium heat until bubbly or until mixture reaches soft-ball stage, stirring constantly. Remove from heat. Add vanilla, margarine and pecans. Beat until glossy. Drop by spoonfuls onto waxed paper, shaping into 2-inch candies. Yield: 25 to 30 servings.

Nita Henderson, Xi Alpha Mu
Midland, Texas

PRALINE GRAHAMS

1/3 (16-ounce) package graham crackers
3/4 cup butter or margarine
1/2 cup sugar
1 cup chopped pecans

Preheat oven to 300 degrees. Separate graham crackers into 4 sections. Arrange in 9-by-13-inch baking pan with edges touching. Melt butter in saucepan over low heat. Add sugar and pecans; mix well. Bring to a boil. Cook for 3 minutes, stirring frequently. Spread evenly over graham crackers. Bake at 300 degrees for 12 minutes. Remove to waxed paper to cool. Yield: 3 to 4 dozen.

Meredith Crews, Preceptor Alpha Rho
Brunswick, Georgia

SALTED NUT ROLL

2 1/2 tablespoons margarine
1 (14-ounce) can sweetened condensed milk
2 cups peanut butter chips
1 cup miniature marshmallows
1 (16-ounce) jar dry roasted peanuts

Combine margarine, condensed milk and peanut butter chips in microwave-safe container. Microwave on High until chips are melted; mix well. Add marshmallows; stir until marshmallows melt and mixture is smooth. Layer half the peanuts, cooked mixture and remaining peanuts in 9-by-13-inch baking pan. Let stand for 2 to 3 hours or until firm. Cut into squares. Yield: 4 to 5 dozen.

Ruth King, Laureate Alpha Rho
Leon, Kansas

"HOMEMADE" SKOR

1 cup shaved almonds
1 cup semisweet chocolate chips
2 cups sugar
2 cups butter or margarine
6 tablespoons water
2 tablespoons light corn syrup

Sprinkle half the almonds and half the chocolate chips evenly in greased 12-by-18-inch baking pan. Combine sugar, butter, water and corn syrup in deep fryer or nonstick saucepan. Bring to a boil. Cook until mixture registers 280 degrees on candy thermometer, soft-crack stage. Pour evenly over almonds and chocolate chips in prepared pan. Sprinkle with remaining almonds and chocolate chips. May spread evenly as chocolate chips melt. Let stand until cool. Yield: 3 to 4 dozen.

Marilyn Mercer, Alpha Xi
Spruce Grove, Alberta, Canada

SODA CRACKER CHOCOLATE CANDY

This is a special treat when served at family Christmas get-togethers.

35 to 40 soda crackers
1 cup butter or margarine
1 cup packed light brown sugar
$1^1/_2$ cups semisweet chocolate chips
$1^1/_2$ cups coarsely chopped walnuts

Preheat oven to 350 degrees. Line 10-by-15-inch baking sheet with foil; spray with nonstick cooking spray. Arrange crackers in rows on prepared pan. Melt butter in saucepan. Add brown sugar. Bring to a boil. Cook for 3 minutes, stirring frequently. Spread evenly over crackers. Bake at 350 degrees for 5 minutes; crackers will float. Remove from oven. Sprinkle with chocolate chips and walnuts. Bake for 5 minutes longer or until chocolate is melted. Press walnuts into chocolate with greased spatula. Cut into 1-inch squares while warm. Yield: 5 dozen.

Claudia Blumer, Preceptor Epsilon
Kalispell, Montana

STRAWBERRY POPCORN

2 cups sugar
$1^1/_2$ cups water
1/2 cup light corn syrup
1 teaspoon vinegar
1 teaspoon vanilla extract
1/2 teaspoon salt
1 (3-ounce) package strawberry gelatin
8 cups popping corn, popped

Combine sugar, water, corn syrup, vinegar, vanilla and salt in heavy saucepan. Bring to a boil over medium-high heat. Cook until mixture registers 250 to 268 degrees, hard-ball stage. Mix in gelatin. Pour over popped corn in bowl; toss to coat. Spread onto greased 10-by-15-inch sheet pan. Let stand until cool. Break into bite-size pieces. Store in airtight container. May substitute sugar-free gelatin. May substitute any flavor gelatin. Yield: 5 to 6 dozen.

Nikki Stricklin, Xi Beta Upsilon
Edmond, Oklahoma

TIPSY TIDBITS

2 (1-pound) packages confectioners' sugar
8 ounces cream cheese, softened
1 to 2 teaspoons crème de menthe
1 cup chopped walnuts

Cream confectioners' sugar and cream cheese in mixer bowl until light and fluffy. Add crème de menthe; mix well. Shape into log. Roll in walnuts. Transfer to serving plate. May substitute crème de cacao, sloe gin or vanilla or peppermint extract for crème de menthe. Yield: 2 to 3 dozen.

Lynn Lester, Preceptor Gamma Xi
Wauna, Washington

TOFFEE

8 milk chocolate bars
1/4 cup chopped pecans
1 cup butter or margarine
1 cup sugar
3 tablespoons water
1 teaspoon vanilla extract

Arrange 4 chocolate bars and half the pecans in greased 8-by-8-inch dish. Cook butter, sugar, water and vanilla in saucepan until thickened, stirring frequently. Pour over chocolate-pecan layer. Top with remaining chocolate bars and pecans. Let stand until cool. Break into pieces. Yield: 1 to 2 dozen.

Addie Heck, Laureate Gamma Psi
Westcliffe, Colorado

EASY "TOFFEE" CANDY

This recipe is submitted by my husband, Jerry.

$1^1/_4$ cups butter
35 to 40 soda crackers
1 cup packed dark brown sugar
$1^1/_4$ cups sweetened condensed milk
$1^1/_2$ cups semisweet chocolate chips
3/4 cup finely chopped walnuts

Preheat oven to 425 degrees. Melt 1/4 cup butter in saucepan over low heat. Pour into foil-lined 10-by-15-inch jelly roll pan. Arrange crackers in pan. Melt remaining butter in saucepan over low heat. Add brown sugar. Bring to a boil over medium heat; reduce heat. Cook for 2 minutes, stirring occasionally. Remove from heat. Add condensed milk; mix well. Spread over crackers. Bake at 425 degrees for 10 to 12 minutes or until bubbly and slightly darkened. Cool for 1 minute. Sprinkle with chocolate chips. Let stand for 5 minutes or until chips melt. Spread chocolate evenly. Sprinkle with walnuts; press walnuts into chocolate. Chill until set. Remove foil. Cut into $1^1/_2$-by-2-inch pieces. Yield: 1 dozen.

Susan Keen, Zeta
Hendersonville, Tennessee

ENGLISH TOFFEE

Everyone loved this candy when I made it for a sorority meeting.

1/2 cup walnuts, chopped
1 cup butter or margarine
1 cup packed light brown sugar
1/2 cup walnuts, chopped
4 milk chocolate bars, broken into pieces

Sprinkle 1/2 cup walnuts in greased 9-by-13-inch pan. Melt butter in saucepan over low heat. Add brown sugar. Bring to a boil. Cook for 12 minutes, stirring constantly. Remove from heat; stir in remaining walnuts. Pour into prepared pan. Top with chocolate pieces. Spread chocolate evenly as it melts. Yield: 2 dozen.

Julie Whitacre, Preceptor Zeta
Winchester, Virginia

TOFFEE HEATH BARS

35 to 40 crackers
1 cup butter
1 cup packed light brown sugar
2 cups chocolate chips
1 cup chopped nuts (optional)

Preheat oven to 350 degrees. Arrange crackers 5 across and 7 to 8 down in foil-lined 10-by-15-inch baking pan. Combine butter and brown sugar in microwave-safe dish. Microwave on High for 4 minutes. Mix until thickened. Pour over crackers. Bake at 350 degrees for 15 to 20 minutes or until bubbly. Sprinkle with chocolate chips. Spread chocolate evenly as it melts. Sprinkle with nuts. Chill for 30 minutes. Break into pieces. Yield: 1 to 2 dozen.

Nancy Taflan, Preceptor Chi
Myrtle Beach, South Carolina

TURTLES

2 cups semisweet chocolate chips
2 cups butterscotch chips
Vanilla extract to taste
2 cups peanuts
1 (5-ounce) can chow mein noodles

Melt chocolate and butterscotch chips in saucepan over low heat; mix well. Remove from heat. Add vanilla; mix thoroughly. Cool slightly. Stir in peanuts and noodles. Drop by teaspoonfuls onto waxed paper. Let stand until cool. Yield: 2 1/2 dozen.

Wendie Beynon, Laureate Beta Gamma
Sudbury, Ontario, Canada

TURTLES OR MILLIONAIRES

All my friends wait at Christmas time for this special treat.

1 (14-ounce) package caramels
2 1/2 tablespoons evaporated milk
2 cups chopped pecans
1 cup semisweet chocolate chips
6 to 7 plain milk chocolate bars
1 bar paraffin

Combine caramels and evaporated milk in microwave-safe container. Microwave on Medium for 2 minutes and 25 seconds or until caramels melt. Mix well. Stir in pecans. Drop by teaspoonfuls onto buttered 10-by-15-inch baking sheet. Freeze for 1 hour or longer. Melt chocolate chips, candy bars and paraffin in double boiler over hot water, stirring constantly. Dip caramels in chocolate mixture. Let stand until cool. Yield: 36 servings.

Deanna Lege, Xi Beta Xi
Kaplan, Louisiana

SUGARY TURTLES

4 (14-ounce) packages toffee candy
2 to 4 tablespoons water
2 cups pecan halves
1 cup packed light brown sugar
1/2 cup margarine
2 cups confectioners' sugar
1 cup semisweet chocolate chips
2 to 4 tablespoons coffee

Combine toffee and water in microwave-safe bowl. Microwave on High for 1 to 3 minutes or until toffee melts. Stir in pecans. Drop by teaspoonfuls onto greased 10-by-15-inch baking pans. Freeze for 1 hour or longer. Combine brown sugar and margarine in mixer bowl. Beat in confectioners' sugar until light and fluffy. Spread over one side of pecan candies. Return to freezer. Combine chocolate chips and coffee in microwave-safe bowl. Microwave on High for 1 to 3 minutes or until chips melt; mix well. Dip other side of pecan candies in chocolate mixture. Store in freezer. Yield: 50 to 100 servings.

Wendy Lunge, Gamma Omega
Lozo, British Columbia, Canada

JANUARY GOODIES

1/2 cup sugar
1/3 cup molasses
1/3 cup butter
1/3 cup water
Salt to taste
1/2 teaspoon vanilla extract

Combine sugar, molasses, butter, water and salt in heavy saucepan. Bring to a boil over low heat. Cook until mixture registers 270 to 290 degrees on candy thermometer, soft-crack stage. Add vanilla; mix well. Spoon onto greased serving plate. Let stand until cool. Cut into squares. Yield: 1 to 2 dozen.

Vanetto Nagamori, Laureate Gamma
Great Falls, Montana

NAN-NAN'S VINEGAR CANDY

This recipe is over 75 years old. It was given to my mother when I was a toddler. Pulling and eating this candy have enriched many evenings during my lifetime.

1 1/2 tablespoons butter
2 cups sugar
1/2 cup vinegar

Melt butter in saucepan over low heat. Add sugar and vinegar; mix well. Cook until mixture registers 300 to 310 degrees on candy thermometer, hard-crack stage. Pour into buttered 9-by-13-inch pan. Let stand until candy is cool enough to touch. Pull candy into strips until hard. Yield: 2 dozen.

Dorothy C. Ellis, Xi Alpha Upsilon
Independence, Missouri

ELEGANT SPICED NUTS

This recipe always brings back memories of past Christmases in New Jersey. My neighbor there shared this recipe with me; this last Christmas, she shared it again, as she is now my neighbor in Florida.

3 cups whole pecans or walnuts
1 cup sugar
1/3 cup water
1 tablespoon cinnamon
1/2 teaspoon cloves
1/2 teaspoon salt
1 1/2 teaspoons vanilla extract

Preheat oven to 275 degrees. Spread pecans evenly over greased 12-by-18-inch baking sheet. Bake at 275 degrees for 10 minutes. Combine next 5 ingredients in saucepan. Bring to a boil over low heat. Cook for 2 minutes, stirring occasionally. Stir in vanilla and nuts; mix well. Remove with slotted spoon to foil-lined plate. Separate with fork. Let stand until cool. Store tightly covered. Yield: 8 servings.

Mary Ann Chaddon, Laureate Lambda
Port St. Lucie, Florida

SUGARED PECANS

1 egg white
1 tablespoon water
1 cup sugar
1 teaspoon salt
1 tablespoon cinnamon
3 cups pecan halves

Preheat oven to 300 degrees. Combine egg white and water in mixer bowl; beat until frothy but not stiff. Beat in mixture of sugar, salt and cinnamon. Add pecans, tossing to coat. Spread on greased 12-by-18-inch baking sheet. Bake at 300 degrees for 45 minutes, stirring every 15 minutes. Cool in pan. Yield: 1 to 2 dozen.

Janet Johnson, Alpha Beta
St. Louis, Missouri

BROWNIES

2/3 cup margarine
1/4 cup water
1 1/2 cups sugar
2 cups chocolate chips
4 eggs
1/2 teaspoon baking soda
2 teaspoons vanilla extract
1 1/2 cups all-purpose flour

Preheat oven to 350 degrees. Combine margarine, water and sugar in microwave-safe container. Microwave on High until margarine melts. Add chocolate chips. Microwave on High just until chips begin to melt; mix well. Add eggs, baking soda, vanilla and flour; mix until blended. Spoon into greased 9-by-13-inch baking pan. Bake at 350 degrees for 20 to 25 minutes or until firm; do not overbake.
Yield: 15 servings.

Linda Gatzke, Xi Alpha Phi
Madison, Wisconsin

BEST-EVER BROWNIES

My husband and I make these and take them to farmers as a thank-you gift for allowing my husband to hunt on their land. Compliments are numerous.

1/2 cup melted butter or margarine
1 cup sugar
1 teaspoon vanilla extract
2 eggs
1/2 cup unsifted all-purpose flour
1/3 cup baking cocoa
1/4 teaspoon each baking powder and salt
1/2 cup chopped nuts (optional)
3 tablespoons butter or margarine, softened
3 tablespoons baking cocoa
1 tablespoon light corn syrup or honey
1/2 teaspoon vanilla extract
1 cup confectioners' sugar
1 to 2 tablespoons milk

Preheat oven to 350 degrees. Combine 1/2 cup butter, sugar and 1 teaspoon vanilla in large bowl. Add eggs; beat well with wooden spoon. Add mixture of flour, 1/2 cup cocoa, baking powder and salt gradually; mix until blended. Stir in nuts. Spoon into greased 9-by-9-inch baking pan. Bake at 350 degrees for 20 to 25 minutes or until brownies pull away from edges of pan. Cool completely. Cream 3 tablespoons butter, 3 tablespoons cocoa, corn syrup and 1/2 teaspoon vanilla in small mixer bowl. Add confectioners' sugar and milk; beat until of spreadable consistency. Frost tops of brownies. May double both brownies and frosting and bake brownies in 9-by-13-inch pan. Yield: 16 servings.

Teresa Rickabaugh, Alpha Chi
Chanute, Kansas

BLONDE BROWNIES

2 cups all-purpose flour
2 teaspoons baking powder
1/4 teaspoon salt
1/2 cup melted butter or margarine
2 cups packed light brown sugar
2 eggs
1 teaspoon vanilla extract
1 cup chopped walnuts (optional)

Preheat oven to 350 degrees. Sift flour, baking powder and salt into bowl; set aside. Combine butter and brown sugar in large bowl; mix well. Add eggs and vanilla; mix until blended. Stir in flour mixture and walnuts. Spread in greased 9-by-13-inch baking pan. Bake at 350 degrees for 30 minutes. Cut into squares while warm. Yield: 2 dozen.

Claudia Crager, Preceptor Eta Delta
Ormond Beach, Florida

BUTTERMILK BROWNIES

1/2 cup margarine
1 cup water
1/2 cup vegetable oil
2 eggs, beaten
1/2 cup buttermilk
1 1/2 teaspoons baking soda
1 teaspoon vanilla extract
1/4 cup baking cocoa
2 cups sugar
2 cups all-purpose flour
1 1/3 cups sugar
1/3 cup milk
1/3 cup margarine
1/2 cup chocolate chips

Preheat oven to 350 degrees. Combine 1/2 cup margarine, water and oil in saucepan. Bring to a boil; remove from heat. Let stand until cool. Combine eggs, buttermilk, baking soda and vanilla in bowl; mix well. Add cocoa, 2 cups sugar and flour; mix thoroughly. Stir in margarine mixture. Spread onto greased 12-by-18-inch baking pan. Bake at 350 degrees for 20 minutes. Cool completely. Combine 1 1/3 cups sugar, milk and 1/3 cup margarine in saucepan. Bring to a boil. Cook for 1 1/2 minutes, stirring constantly. Add chocolate chips; mix until of spreadable consistency. May add a small amount of cream if mixture becomes too thick. Spread over brownies. Yield: 2 to 3 dozen.

Bonnie DeLange, Beta Epsilon
Oregon, Wisconsin

CELEBRATION BROWNIES

1 cup margarine
1 cup water
1/4 cup baking cocoa
2 cups sugar
2 cups all-purpose flour
1 egg
1 egg white
1/2 cup sour skim milk
1 teaspoon vanilla extract
1 teaspoon baking soda
1/2 cup margarine
1/4 cup baking cocoa
6 tablespoons skim milk
4 cups confectioners' sugar
1 teaspoon vanilla extract

Preheat oven to 350 degrees. Combine 1 cup margarine, water and 1/4 cup cocoa in saucepan. Bring to a boil over low heat. Pour over mixture of sugar and flour in bowl; mix well. Add egg, egg white, sour milk, 1 teaspoon vanilla and baking soda; mix until blended. Spoon into greased 11-by-15-inch baking pan. Bake at 350 degrees for 20 minutes. Cool for 10 minutes. Combine 1/2 cup margarine, 1/4 cup cocoa and 6 tablespoons skim milk in saucepan. Heat just to boiling. Remove from heat. Add confectioners' sugar and 1 teaspoon vanilla; mix until smooth. Spread over brownies. Cut into squares.
Yield: 18 to 20 servings.

Audrey Becker, Epsilon Beta
Truman, Minnesota

CHERRY-CHEESE BROWNIE BARS

These brownies have been served at numerous Valentine's teas. The red and white colors are very festive for Christmas and other holidays as well.

1 (22-ounce) package fudge brownie mix
2 teaspoons vanilla extract
1 egg
1 (14-ounce) can sweetened condensed milk
8 ounces cream cheese, softened
1 (21-ounce) can cherry pie filling

Preheat oven to 350 degrees. Prepare brownie mix using package directions. Spoon into greased 9-by-13-inch baking pan. Bake at 350 degrees for 15 minutes. Combine vanilla, egg, condensed milk and cream cheese in mixer bowl; beat until thickened and smooth. Spread over brownie layer. Bake for 20 to 25 minutes longer or until topping is set. Cool for 2 hours. Top with pie filling. Cut into 1 1/2 - to 2-inch squares. Yield: 24 large or 48 small servings.

Charlotte McLemore, Xi Phi
Panama City, Florida

CHOCOLATE-ALMOND BROWNIES

1/3 cup shortening
2 (1-ounce) squares semisweet chocolate
1 cup sugar
3/4 cup all-purpose flour
1/2 teaspoon each baking powder and salt
2 eggs
1/2 cup chopped almonds
1/2 cup finely chopped almond paste or semisweet chocolate chips

Combine shortening and chocolate in 8-by-8-inch microwave-safe dish. Microwave, uncovered, on Medium-High for 3 to 4 minutes or until melted. Stir in sugar, flour, baking powder, salt, eggs and almonds. Mix in almond paste. Spread batter evenly. Elevate baking dish on inverted dinner plate in microwave oven. Microwave, uncovered, on Medium heat for 4 minutes; rotate dish 1/4 turn. Microwave on Medium for 4 to 8 minutes longer or until wooden pick inserted in center comes out clean, rotating dish 1/4 turn every 2 minutes. Cool completely on heat-proof surface; do not use rack. Cut into bars.
Yield: 9 to 12 servings.

Marie Faulhaber, Xi Eta
Omaha, Nebraska

Lorine Sweat, Eta Alpha, Powell, Tennessee, makes Chinese Fudge by melting 2 cups semisweet chocolate chips and 1 cup butterscotch chips in double boiler, blending well and then stirring in chow mein noodles until coated. Drop by teaspoonfuls onto waxed paper.

HEALTH-SMART BROWNIES

3/4 cup melted low-fat, low-cholesterol margarine
4 teaspoons canola oil
3/4 cup baking cocoa
2 cups sugar
6 egg whites
1 teaspoon vanilla extract
1 cup all-purpose flour
1 cup chopped walnuts (optional)

Preheat oven to 350 degrees. Mix margarine, oil and cocoa in bowl. Add sugar, egg whites and vanilla; mix until blended. Stir in flour and walnuts. Spread in greased 9-by-13-inch baking pan. Bake at 350 degrees for 30 to 35 minutes or until wooden pick inserted in center comes out clean; do not overbake. Cool and cut into squares. Yield: 15 servings.

Margaret Hoppough, Preceptor Beta
Grand Rapids, Michigan

MAJESTIC BROWNIES

1 (2-layer) package chocolate cake mix
1/3 cup vegetable oil
1 egg
1 (14-ounce) can sweetened condensed milk
1 cup semisweet chocolate chips
1 cup chopped pecans
1 teaspoon vanilla extract
Dash of salt

Preheat oven to 350 degrees. Combine cake mix, oil and egg in blender container; process until crumbly. Press half the mixture into greased 9-by-13-inch baking pan. Combine condensed milk, chocolate chips, pecans, vanilla and salt in bowl. Spread into prepared pan. Top with remaining crumbly mixture. Bake at 350 degrees for 30 to 45 minutes or until brownies test done. Cool completely. Cut into squares. Yield: 12 to 15 servings.

Beverly J. Haas, Xi Kappa
Sapalpa, Oklahoma

MARSHMALLOW KRISPIE BROWNIES

1 (22-ounce) package fudge brownie mix
1 (10-ounce) package miniature marshmallows
1 1/2 cups semisweet chocolate chips
1 cup creamy peanut butter
1 tablespoon butter or margarine
1 1/2 cups crispy rice cereal

Preheat oven to 350 degrees. Prepare brownie mix using package directions. Spoon into greased 9-by-13-inch baking pan. Bake at 350 degrees for 25 to 30 minutes or until brownies test done. Sprinkle with marshmallows. Bake for 5 minutes longer or until marshmallows are golden brown. Cool on wire rack. Combine chocolate chips, peanut butter and butter in saucepan. Cook over low heat until chocolate chips melt, stirring frequently. Remove from heat. Stir in cereal. Spoon over brownies. Chill. Cut into bars. Serve at room temperature. Yield: 36 servings.

Carolyn Smith, Laureate Beta Psi
Springfield, Ohio

MICROWAVE BROWNIES

1/2 cup butter or margarine, softened
1 cup sugar or packed light brown sugar
2 eggs
1 teaspoon vanilla extract
1/2 cup baking cocoa
1/2 cup all-purpose flour
1 cup chopped nuts (optional)

Cream butter and sugar in mixer bowl until light and fluffy. Add eggs 1 at a time, beating after each addition. Add vanilla; mix well. Add mixture of cocoa and flour; mix until blended. Stir in nuts. Spread into greased and sugared round microwave-safe glass baking dish. Microwave on Medium for 8 to 9 minutes or on High for 4 1/2 minutes or until brownies test done. Frost when cooled if desired.
Yield: 15 to 20 servings.

Dorothy Hillmann, Beta Mu
Thornhill, Ontario, Canada

FRESH APPLE BROWNIES

1 cup vegetable oil
1 3/4 cups sugar
3 eggs, beaten
1 teaspoon each salt, baking soda and cinnamon
2 cups chopped apples
1/2 cup chopped walnuts (optional)

Preheat oven to 350 degrees. Combine oil and sugar in bowl; mix well. Add eggs, salt, baking soda, cinnamon, apples and walnuts; mix well. Spoon into greased 9-by-13-inch baking pan. Bake at 350 degrees for 45 minutes. Yield: 15 servings.

Jean Haynes, Laureate Alpha Alpha
Charleston, West Virginia

WALNUT BROWNIES

1 cup margarine
3 tablespoons (heaping) baking cocoa
3 eggs
2 cups sugar
2 cups self-rising flour, sifted
2 teaspoons vanilla extract
1 cup chopped walnuts

Preheat oven to 350 degrees. Melt margarine in saucepan over low heat. Stir in cocoa; set aside to cool. Beat eggs in large mixer bowl. Add sugar alternately with cocoa mixture; mix until blended. Add flour, vanilla and nuts; mix well. Spoon into greased 9-by-13-inch baking pan. Bake at 350 degrees for 27 minutes. Yield: 12 to 15 servings.

Mahala R. Craft, Xi Alpha Lambda
Whitesburg, Kentucky

WHITE BROWNIES

1 (2-layer) package yellow cake mix
1/2 cup melted margarine
2 eggs
1 (1-pound) package confectioners' sugar
8 ounces cream cheese, softened
2 eggs

Preheat oven to 350 degrees. Mix cake mix, margarine and 2 eggs in large bowl. Spoon into greased 9-by-13-inch baking pan. Cream confectioners' sugar, cream cheese and 2 eggs in mixer bowl until light and fluffy. Spread over cake batter. Bake at 350 degrees for 40 to 45 minutes or until cake tests done. Cool completely. Cut into squares. Yield: 4 dozen.

Sally Summers, Preceptor Gamma Gamma
Tulsa, Oklahoma

ZEBRA BROWNIES

1 cup butter or margarine, softened
2 cups sugar
1 cup baking cocoa
4 eggs
1 cup all-purpose flour
1 teaspoon vanilla extract
1 1/2 cups sugar
24 ounces cream cheese, softened
5 eggs
1 1/2 teaspoons vanilla extract
1/2 cup all-purpose flour
Sugar to taste
Sliced almonds to taste

Preheat oven to 350 degrees. Cream butter and 2 cups sugar in mixer bowl until light and fluffy. Beat in cocoa and 4 eggs. Add 1 cup flour and 1 teaspoon vanilla; mix until blended. Spoon into 9-by-13-inch baking pan sprayed with nonstick cooking spray. Cream 1 1/2 cups sugar and cream cheese in mixer bowl until light and fluffy. Add 5 eggs 1 at a time, beating after each addition. Stir in 1 1/2 teaspoons vanilla and 1/2 cup flour. Spoon over chocolate batter. Swirl with knife for marbled effect. Sprinkle with sugar and almonds. Bake at 350 degrees for 45 minutes. Serve warm or chilled. Yield: 15 servings.

Doreen Nelson, Xi Eta
Omaha, Nebraska

ZUCCHINI BROWNIES

3 cups grated peeled zucchini
1 1/2 cups sugar
2/3 cup vegetable oil
3 cups all-purpose flour
1/2 teaspoon salt
2 teaspoons baking soda
1/3 cup baking cocoa
3 teaspoons vanilla extract
1/3 cup flaked coconut
1/2 cup chopped almonds
Confectioners' sugar to taste

Preheat oven to 350 degrees. Combine zucchini, sugar, oil, flour, salt, baking soda, cocoa, vanilla and coconut in large mixer bowl; mix until blended. Stir in almonds. Spread in 9-by-13-inch baking pan sprayed with nonstick cooking spray. Bake at 350 degrees for 25 minutes or until brownies test done. Cool. Dust with confectioners' sugar. Cut into 2-inch squares. Yield: 30 servings.

Mary LaVerne Boston, Alpha Beta
Paoli, Indiana

ALMOND OATMEAL BARS

1/2 cup all-purpose flour
1/4 teaspoon salt
1/2 cup chocolate milk mix
1/2 cup margarine
1 cup sugar
2 eggs
1 teaspoon almond extract
3/4 cup quick-cooking oats
1/2 cup slivered almonds

Preheat oven to 350 degrees. Sift flour, salt and chocolate milk mix together. Cream margarine and sugar in mixer bowl until light and fluffy. Add eggs and almond extract; mix well. Add flour mixture; mix well. Stir in oats and almonds. Spread in greased 9-by-9-inch baking pan. Bake at 350 degrees for 35 minutes. Yield: 2 dozen.

Anne Clement, Alpha Theta
Ripples, New Brunswick, Canada

ALMOND SQUARES

Graham crackers
1 cup butter or margarine
1 cup packed light brown sugar
1/4 teaspoon cream of tartar
1 tablespoon milk
3/4 cup almond slivers

Preheat oven to 350 degrees. Arrange graham crackers in greased 10-by-15-inch baking pan. Melt butter in saucepan over low heat. Add brown sugar, cream of tartar and milk. Cook over medium-low heat for 5 minutes, stirring constantly. Pour over crackers. Sprinkle with almond slivers. Bake at 350 degrees for 5 minutes. Cool in pan for 10 minutes. Remove to wire rack to cool completely. Yield: 18 to 24 servings.

Jocelyne Hutchison, Alpha
Calgary, Alberta, Canada

APRICOT BARS

1 1/2 cups sifted all-purpose flour
1 teaspoon baking powder
1 1/2 cups quick-cooking oats
1 cup packed light brown sugar
3/4 cup butter or margarine
1 cup apricot jam

Preheat oven to 350 degrees. Combine first 4 ingredients in bowl. Cut in butter until crumbly. Pat 2/3 of flour mixture into greased 9-by-13-inch baking pan. Spread with jam. Cover with remaining flour mixture. Bake at 350 for 25 minutes. Yield: 15 servings.

Florence Christensen, Laureate Gamma
Great Falls, Montana

GOLDEN APRICOT SQUARES

2/3 cup dried apricots, chopped
1 cup all-purpose flour
1/4 cup confectioners' sugar
1/2 cup butter or margarine
2 eggs
1 cup sugar
1/4 cup lemon juice
1/2 teaspoon grated lemon rind
2 tablespoons all-purpose flour
1/2 teaspoon baking powder
1/2 cup coconut (optional)

Preheat oven to 350 degrees. Place apricots in saucepan with water to cover. Simmer over low heat for 10 minutes; drain. Combine 1 cup flour and confectioners' sugar in bowl. Cut in butter until crumbly. Press into greased 9-by-9-inch baking pan. Bake at 350 degrees for 20 to 25 minutes or until lightly browned. Beat eggs in mixer bowl until creamy. Beat in sugar, lemon juice and lemon rind. Add mixture of 2 tablespoons flour and baking powder; mix well. Stir in apricots and coconut. Spread over baked layer. Bake for 25 minutes. Cool. Cut into bars. Sprinkle with confectioners' sugar. Yield: 30 servings.

Irene Oian, Laureate Zeta Zeta
Palmdale, California

APRICOT-OAT BARS

1 1/2 cups all-purpose flour
1 teaspoon baking powder
1/4 teaspoon salt
1 1/2 cups oats
1 cup packed light brown sugar
3/4 cup butter or margarine
1 cup apricot preserves
Chopped pecans to taste

Preheat oven to 375 degrees. Combine flour, baking powder, salt, oats, brown sugar and butter in bowl; mix well. Pat 2/3 of flour mixture into greased 9-by-13-inch baking pan. Spread with preserves. Cover with remaining flour mixture. Sprinkle with pecans. Bake at 375 degrees for 35 minutes.
Yield: 18 to 24 servings.

Christine Berry, Xi Iota Alpha
Adrian, Missouri

BABY FOOD BARS

1 teaspoon cinnamon
2 cups sugar
2 cups all-purpose flour
2 teaspoons baking soda
1 teaspoon salt
3 eggs, beaten
1 1/2 cups vegetable oil
1 (4-ounce) jar each strained carrots, apricots and applesauce
1/2 cup butter or margarine, softened
8 ounces cream cheese, softened
1 (1-pound) package confectioners' sugar
1 teaspoon vanilla extract

Preheat oven to 350 degrees. Sift cinnamon, sugar, flour, baking soda and salt together. Combine eggs and oil in mixer bowl; mix until smooth. Blend in flour mixture. Beat in baby food until smooth and creamy. Spoon mixture into 2 greased 9-by-13-inch baking pans. Bake at 350 degrees for 20 to 25 minutes or until bars test done. Cool completely. Cream butter, cream cheese and confectioners' sugar in mixer bowl until light and fluffy. Stir in vanilla. Frost top and sides of bars. Yield: 36 to 40 servings.

Mia Knoll, Pi Nu
Hays, Kansas

BANANA SQUARES

1/2 cup butter or margarine, softened
1 1/2 cups sugar
2 eggs
3/4 cup sour cream
1 teaspoon baking soda
1 teaspoon salt
1 teaspoon vanilla extract
2 cups all-purpose flour
2 ripe bananas, mashed

Preheat oven to 350 degrees. Cream butter, sugar and eggs in mixer bowl until light and fluffy. Add sour cream, baking soda, salt and vanilla; beat until smooth. Mix in flour. Fold in bananas gently. Spread in greased jelly roll pan. Bake at 350 degrees for 30 minutes or until done. Frost with favorite confectioners' sugar icing. Yield: 8 to 12 servings.

Penny Smith, Nu Psi
Lexington, Missouri

BLACK FOREST SQUARES

1 (2-layer) package chocolate cake mix
1 (21-ounce) can cherry pie filling
2 eggs, beaten
2 1/2 cups confectioners' sugar
1/2 cup baking cocoa
1/2 cup margarine
1/4 cup water

Preheat oven to 350 degrees. Combine cake mix, pie filling and eggs in bowl; mix well. Spoon into greased 11-by-17-inch baking pan. Bake at 350 degrees for 35 minutes. Cool completely. Sift confectioners' sugar and cocoa into bowl. Combine margarine and water in microwave-safe bowl. Microwave on High for 30 seconds. Add cocoa mixture; mix well. Spread over cake. Cut into squares.
Yield: 12 to 16 servings.

Ivy Barber, Eta Zeta
Simcoe, Ontario, Canada

BLARNEY STONES

2 egg whites
1/4 teaspoon salt
1/4 teaspoon cream of tartar
1 cup sugar
1 cup all-purpose flour
2 teaspoons baking powder
1/2 cup boiling water
1 teaspoon vanilla extract
2 egg yolks, beaten
1 cup margarine, softened
2 cups confectioners' sugar
Ground peanuts

Preheat oven to 350 degrees. Combine egg whites, salt and cream of tartar in mixer bowl; beat until stiff. Set aside. Sift sugar, flour and baking powder into mixer bowl. Add boiling water, vanilla and egg yolks; mix well. Fold in egg white mixture. Spoon into ungreased 9-by-9-inch baking pan. Bake at 350 degrees for 25 to 30 minutes or until brown. Cool in pan for 10 minutes. Loosen from sides of pan. Turn onto serving plate. Cut into squares. Combine margarine and confectioners' sugar; mix until of spreadable consistency. Frost top and sides. Roll in ground peanuts. May freeze before frosting to make frosting easier. Yield: 12 to 15 servings.

Vicki Haydock, Xi Gamma Lambda
Shattuck, Oklahoma

✣ BUTTERSCOTCH CHEESECAKE BARS

2 cups butterscotch chips
1/2 cup margarine
2 cups graham cracker crumbs
1 cup chopped pecans
8 ounces cream cheese, softened
1 (14-ounce) can sweetened condensed milk
1 egg
1 teaspoon vanilla extract

Preheat oven to 350 degrees. Combine butterscotch chips and margarine in double boiler over hot water. Cook until melted. Add graham cracker crumbs and pecans; mix well. Press half the graham cracker mixture into greased 9-by-13-inch baking pan. Combine cream cheese, condensed milk, egg and vanilla in bowl; mix well. Spread over graham cracker layer. Sprinkle with remaining graham cracker crumb mixture. Bake at 350 degrees for 20 to 30 minutes or until top is firm. Cut into 1-by-2-inch bars.
Yield: 15 servings.

Phyllis Wolfe, Xi Omicron
Bluefield, West Virginia

CANDY BAR SQUARES

1 cup margarine, softened
1 cup sugar
1 1/2 cups all-purpose flour
2 eggs
3 tablespoons baking cocoa
1 cup margarine
2 tablespoons light corn syrup
1 (14-ounce) can sweetened condensed milk
1 1/2 cups packed light brown sugar
1/4 cup all-purpose flour

Preheat oven to 350 degrees. Combine 1 cup margarine, sugar, 1 1/2 cups flour, eggs and cocoa in bowl; mix well. Press into greased 10-by-15-inch baking pan. Bake at 350 degrees for 15 minutes. Combine 1 cup margarine, corn syrup, condensed milk, brown sugar and 1/4 cup flour in saucepan; mix well. Bring to a boil over low heat. Cook until thickened, stirring constantly. Spread over baked layer. Cool completely. Frost with chocolate icing, if desired. Cut into squares. Yield: 15 servings.

Ida McLeod, Sigma
Estevan, Saskatchewan, Canada

CARAMEL SQUARES

1/2 cup butter or margarine, softened
1/2 cup sugar
2 egg yolks
1 1/2 cups all-purpose flour
1 teaspoon baking powder
1/4 teaspoon salt
1 teaspoon vanilla extract
2 egg whites
1 cup packed light brown sugar
1 teaspoon vanilla extract

Preheat oven to 350 degrees. Cream butter in mixer bowl until light. Add sugar and egg yolks; beat until fluffy. Add flour, baking powder, salt and 1 teaspoon vanilla; mix well. Press into greased 9-by-9-inch baking pan. Beat egg whites in mixer bowl until soft peaks form. Add brown sugar and 1 teaspoon vanilla gradually, beating until stiff peaks form. Spread over flour mixture. Bake at 350 degrees for 25 to 30 minutes or until light brown. Yield: 2 dozen.

Vicki Lynn Boutilier, Gamma
Riverview, New Brunswick, Canada

CHERRY FUDGE BARS

1 package chocolate fudge frosting mix
2 cups all-purpose flour
1 1/2 teaspoons baking soda
1/4 teaspoon salt
1 (21-ounce) can cherry pie filling
2 eggs
1 cup flaked coconut
1 tablespoon all-purpose flour
1/2 cup evaporated milk
1/2 cup margarine
1/2 cup chopped walnuts
1/2 teaspoon almond extract

Preheat oven to 375 degrees. Combine 2 1/2 cups of the frosting mix with 2 cups flour, baking soda, salt, pie filling and eggs in mixer bowl; mix well. Batter will be very thick. Spread into large greased 10-by-15-inch baking pan. Sprinkle with coconut. Bake at 375 degrees for 15 to 20 minutes or until firm. Cool for 15 minutes. Combine remaining frosting mix, 1 tablespoon flour, evaporated milk and margarine in saucepan. Bring to a boil, stirring constantly. Remove from heat. Stir in walnuts and almond extract. Cool slightly. Spread over baked layer. Let stand until firm. Cut into bars. Yield: 24 servings.

Suzanne M. Badstibner, Xi Theta Rho
Knob Noster, Missouri

CHOCOLATE CHIP SQUARES

1/2 cup butter or margarine, softened
1 cup sugar
2 eggs
1 teaspoon vanilla extract
3/4 cup all-purpose flour
1/2 teaspoon salt
1/2 teaspoon baking powder
1 cup chocolate chips
1 cup chopped walnuts (optional)

Preheat oven to 350 degrees. Cream butter and sugar in mixer bowl until light and fluffy. Add eggs and vanilla; mix well. Add sifted mixture of flour, salt and baking powder; mix until blended. Stir in chocolate chips and walnuts. Spread in greased 8-by-8-inch baking pan or layer pan. Bake at 350 degrees for 35 minutes; do not overbake. Cool completely. Cut into squares. May double recipe and bake in 9-by-13-inch baking pan. May freeze for later use. Yield: 9 servings.

Chris Pisauro, Xi Zeta
Billings, Montana

DOUBLE CHOCOLATE LAYER BARS

My mom is an excellent baker. We have always traded recipes for cookies and sweets. This is a favorite I passed on to her from my husband's side of the family.

1 (2-layer) package German chocolate cake mix
1 egg
1/2 cup melted margarine
2 cups flaked coconut
3/4 cup milk chocolate chips
3/4 cup butterscotch chips
1/2 cup chopped pecans
1 (14-ounce) can sweetened condensed milk

Preheat oven to 350 degrees. Combine cake mix, egg and margarine in bowl; mix well. Press firmly into 9-by-13-inch baking pan. Sprinkle with coconut, chocolate chips, butterscotch chips and pecans. Spread condensed milk evenly over top to edges of pan. Bake at 350 degrees for 30 minutes. Cool completely. Cut into bars. Yield: 20 to 24 servings.

Delinda Pinson, Gamma Delta
Aurora, Colorado

CHOCOLATE-OAT BARS

1 cup all-purpose flour
1 cup quick-cooking oats
1/2 cup butter or margarine, softened
3/4 cup packed light brown sugar
1 (14-ounce) can sweetened condensed milk
1 cup chopped walnuts
1 cup semisweet chocolate chips

Preheat oven to 350 degrees. Combine flour, oats, butter and brown sugar in bowl; mix well. Reserve 1/2 cup of oat mixture; set aside. Press remaining oat mixture into greased 9-by-13-inch baking pan. Bake at 350 degrees for 10 minutes. Spread condensed milk evenly over baked layer. Sprinkle with walnuts and chocolate chips. Press reserved oat mixture firmly over top. Bake for 25 to 30 minutes longer or until slightly brown. Cool completely. Cut into bars. Store, covered, at room temperature.
Yield: 36 servings.

Jan Angotti, Laureate Lambda
Walla Walla, Washington

CHOCOLATE CARAMEL OAT SQUARES

64 caramels
1 cup evaporated milk
2 cups all-purpose flour
2 cups rolled oats
11/2 cups packed light brown sugar
1 teaspoon baking soda
1/2 teaspoon salt
11/2 cups margarine
1 cup semisweet chocolate chips
1 cup chopped walnuts

Preheat oven to 350 degrees. Melt caramels with evaporated milk in double boiler over low heat, stirring constantly until smooth. Combine flour, oats, brown sugar, baking soda and salt in bowl. Cut in margarine until crumbly. Pat half the oat mixture into greased 10-by-15-inch baking pan. Bake at 350 degrees for 5 minutes. Sprinkle evenly with chocolate chips and nuts. Spoon caramel mixture evenly over top. Top with remaining oat mixture. Pat lightly. Bake for 25 to 30 minutes or until light brown. Cool. Cut into squares. Yield: 15 servings.

Marie Sproule, Alpha Beta Master
Sault Ste. Marie, Ontario, Canada

FUDGE BARS

1 cup sugar
1 cup packed light brown sugar
1 cup margarine, softened
2 cups all-purpose flour
3 cups rolled oats
2 eggs
1 teaspoon baking soda
1 cup semisweeet chocolate chips
1 (14-ounce) can sweetened condensed milk
1/2 cup margarine

Preheat oven to 350 degrees. Cream sugar, brown sugar and 1 cup margarine in mixer bowl until light and fluffy. Add flour, oats, eggs and baking soda; mix well. Spread half the flour mixture in greased 9-by-13-inch baking pan. Combine chocolate chips, condensed milk and 1/2 cup margarine in saucepan. Cook over low heat until chocolate chips and margarine are melted, stirring constantly. Spread into prepared pan. Cover with remaining flour mixture. Bake at 350 degrees for 30 minutes. Let stand until cool. Cut into bars. Yield: 15 servings.

Elizabeth Brennan, Beta
Clive, Iowa

FUDGY OATMEAL BARS

2 cups packed light brown sugar
1 cup margarine
2 eggs
1 teaspoon vanilla extract
2 1/2 cups all-purpose flour
1 teaspoon baking soda
1/2 teaspoon salt
3 cups oats
2 cups semisweet chocolate chips
1 (14-ounce) can sweetened condensed milk
2 tablespoons margarine
1 cup chopped walnuts
1 teaspoon vanilla extract
1/2 teaspoon salt

Preheat oven to 350 degrees. Combine brown sugar, 1 cup margarine, eggs, 1 teaspoon vanilla, flour, baking soda, 1/2 teaspoon salt and oats in bowl; mix well. Press 2/3 of the brown sugar mixture into greased 10-by-15-inch baking pan. Combine chocolate chips, condensed milk and 2 tablespoons margarine in medium saucepan. Cook over medium heat until chocolate chips and margarine are melted, stirring frequently. Stir in walnuts, 1 teaspoon vanilla and 1/2 teaspoon salt. Spread over brown sugar mixture. Crumble remaining brown sugar mixture over top. Bake at 350 degrees for 25 to 30 minutes or until browned. Cool slightly. Cut into bars while warm. Yield: 1 dozen.

Barbara Motes, Xi Delta Tau
Stillwater, Oklahoma

CHOCOLATE PECAN BARS

My secretary gave me this recipe from England. I especially like to make it for Christmas.

2 cups all-purpose flour
1 cup packed light brown sugar
1/2 cup margarine
1 cup pecan halves
2/3 cup margarine
1/2 cup packed light brown sugar
1 cup semisweet chocolate chips

Preheat oven to 350 degrees. Combine flour and 1 cup brown sugar in bowl. Cut in 1/2 cup margarine until crumbly. Press firmly into ungreased 9-by-13-inch baking pan. Sprinkle with pecans. Combine 2/3 cup margarine and 1/2 cup brown sugar in small saucepan. Bring to a boil over low heat, stirring constantly. Cook for 1 minute, stirring constantly. Pour over pecan layer; spread evenly. Bake at 350 degrees for 20 minutes or until brown sugar mixture is bubbly and light brown. Remove from oven. Sprinkle with chocolate chips. Let stand until chocolate chips are softened. Spread evenly or swirl over top. Let stand until cool. Cut into bars.
Yield: 16 to 20 servings.

Irene Gracey, Laureate Alpha Pi
Barrie, Ontario, Canada

CHOCOLATE PEPPERMINT BARS

These attractive bars have been a favorite at sorority Christmas parties.

2 (1-ounce) squares chocolate
1/2 cup margarine
1 cup sugar
2 eggs
1/2 cup all-purpose flour
1/2 cup chopped walnuts
1 1/2 cups confectioners' sugar
3 tablespoons margarine, softened
1 1/2 tablespoons milk
1 teaspoon peppermint extract
Green food coloring
1 1/2 (1-ounce) squares chocolate
1 1/2 tablespoons margarine

Preheat oven to 350 degrees. Melt 2 squares chocolate with 1/2 cup margarine in medium saucepan over low heat, stirring frequently. Add sugar, eggs, flour and walnuts; mix well. Spoon into greased 8-by-8-inch baking pan. Bake at 350 degrees for 25 minutes. Cool completely. Combine confectioners' sugar, 3 tablespoons margarine, milk, peppermint extract and food coloring in bowl; mix well. Spread over brownies. Chill for 2 hours or until hardened. Melt 1 1/2 squares chocolate and 1 1/2 tablespoons margarine in saucepan over low heat; stir until blended. Spread over second layer. Chill until set. Warm to room temperature. Cut into small squares.
Yield: 25 servings.

Shirley J. Wells, Preceptor Alpha Rho
Fairfield Bay, Arkansas

CHOCOLATE STREUSEL BARS

This dessert is always the first to go at cookie exchanges.

1 3/4 cups all-purpose flour
1 1/2 cups confectioners' sugar
1/2 cup baking cocoa
1 cup cold margarine
8 ounces cream cheese, softened
1 (14-ounce) can sweetened condensed milk
1 egg
2 teaspoons vanilla extract
1/2 cup chopped walnuts

Preheat oven to 350 degrees. Combine flour, confectioners' sugar and cocoa in bowl; mix well. Cut in margarine until crumbly. Reserve 2 cups of mixture; set aside. Press remaining flour mixture firmly into lightly greased 9-by-13-inch baking pan. Bake at 350 degrees for 15 minutes. Beat cream cheese in mixer bowl until light and fluffy. Add condensed milk gradually; mix until smooth. Mix in egg and vanilla. Spoon into prepared crust. Sprinkle with mixture of reserved flour mixture and walnuts. Bake for 25 minutes. Let stand until cool. Cut into bite-size pieces. Store in refrigerator. Yield: 24 servings.

Nancy Hathaway, Xi Phi
Bowie, Maryland

CHOCOLATE WAFER BARS

13 (2-inch) graham crackers
1/2 cup chopped walnuts
1/3 cup flaked or shredded coconut
1/2 cup butter or margarine
1/2 cup sugar
2 tablespoons baking cocoa
1 egg, beaten
2 tablespoons baking cocoa
3 tablespoons butter or margarine, softened
1 1/2 cups sifted confectioners' sugar
1 1/2 tablespoons milk

Break crackers into bowl. Add walnuts and coconut; toss to mix. Melt 1/2 cup butter in saucepan over low heat. Add sugar and 2 tablespoons cocoa; mix well. Add egg. Bring to a boil, stirring constantly. Spoon over crackers; mix well. Pour into greased 8-by-8-inch baking pan. Press gently into pan. Chill until set. Combine 2 tablespoons cocoa, 3 tablespoons butter, confectioners' sugar and milk in bowl; mix until smooth. Spread evenly over chilled layer. Cut into squares. Yield: 24 to 30 servings.

Diana Manuel, Omega
North Vancouver, British Columbia, Canada

CREAM CHEESE DELIGHT BARS

I received this recipe from a friend in my many travels.

1 (2-layer) package white cake mix
1 egg
1/2 cup melted butter or margarine
1 cup chopped pecans
8 ounces cream cheese, softened
2 eggs
1 (1-pound) package confectioners' sugar

Preheat oven to 300 degrees. Combine cake mix, 1 egg and 1/2 cup butter in bowl; mix well. Spoon into greased 9-by-13-inch baking pan. Bake at 300 degrees for 40 minutes. Let stand until cool. Sprinkle with pecans. Combine cream cheese, 2 eggs and confectioners' sugar in bowl; mix well. Spread over top. Yield: 21 servings.

Patti Kruse, Xi Tau Chi
San Diego, California

FROSTED COFFEE CREAMS

1/2 cup shortening
1 cup packed light brown sugar
1 egg
1/2 teaspoon salt
1 1/2 cups all-purpose flour
1/2 teaspoon each baking powder and baking soda
1 teaspoon cinnamon
1/2 cup hot coffee
1/2 cup raisins
Chopped nuts to taste
1 cup confectioners' sugar
1/4 teaspoon salt
1 tablespoon butter or margarine, softened
Hot coffee to taste

Preheat oven to 350 degrees. Combine shortening, brown sugar, egg and 1/2 teaspoon salt in bowl; mix well. Add flour, baking powder, baking soda, cinnamon, 1/2 cup coffee, raisins and nuts; mix well. Spoon into greased 12-by-18-inch baking sheet with rim. Bake at 350 degrees for 25 to 30 minutes or until light brown. Let stand until cool. Combine confectioners' sugar, 1/4 teaspoon salt and butter in mixer bowl; beat until light and fluffy. Add coffee as needed to make of spreadable consistency. Spread lightly over bars. Yield: 18 to 24 servings.

Joan Labrecque, Preceptor Lambda
Westbrook, Maine

CROWD PLEASERS

2 cups semisweet chocolate chips
8 ounces cream cheese
1 (5-ounce) can evaporated milk
1 cup chopped walnuts
1/2 teaspoon almond extract
3 cups all-purpose flour
1 1/2 cups sugar
2 teaspoons baking powder
1 cup margarine, softened
2 eggs

Preheat oven to 325 degrees. Combine chocolate chips, cream cheese and evaporated milk in microwave-safe container. Microwave on High until chips are melted. Add walnuts and almond extract; mix until blended. Cool for several minutes. Combine flour, sugar, baking powder, margarine and eggs in mixer bowl; mix until blended. Press 1/2 of flour mixture into greased 9-by-13-inch baking pan. Spread with chocolate mixture. Crumble remaining flour mixture over top. Bake at 325 degrees for 35 minutes. Cool in pan. Cut into squares.
Yield: 18 to 24 servings.

Elaine Swallow, Laureate Delta Delta
Fort Worth, Texas

DATE NUT BARS

1/2 cup melted butter or margarine
1 cup sugar
2 eggs, beaten
1/4 teaspoon baking powder
1/2 teaspoon salt
3/4 cup all-purpose flour
1 cup each finely chopped nuts and dates
Confectioners' sugar

Preheat oven to 350 degrees. Combine butter, sugar, eggs, baking powder and salt in mixer bowl; beat until light and fluffy. Stir in flour, nuts and dates. Spread in greased 9-by-9-inch baking pan. Bake at 350 degrees for 20 minutes. Cut into bars while warm; roll in confectioners' sugar. Yield: 16 servings.

Helen Bolt, Xi Beta Phi
Kingman, Arizona

DATE SQUARES

2 cups chopped dates
1 cup boiling water
1 tablespoon light brown sugar
1/4 teaspoon lemon juice
3/4 cup butter or margarine, softened
1/2 cup packed light brown sugar
11/4 cups each all-purpose flour and rolled oats
1 teaspoon baking soda

Preheat oven to 350 degrees. Cook dates, water and 1 tablespoon brown sugar over medium heat in saucepan until thickened, stirring occasionally. Remove from heat. Stir in lemon juice; set aside. Cream butter and 1/2 cup brown sugar in mixer bowl until light and fluffy. Add flour, oats and baking soda, mixing just until crumbly. Spread 1/2 of oat mixture in greased 9-by-13-inch baking pan. Spread date mixture on top. Cover with remaining oat mixture. Smooth with back of spoon. Bake at 350 degrees for 25 minutes. Yield: 20 squares.

Brenda Legge, Lambda Alpha
Welland, Ontario, Canada

SUGARLESS DATE NUT SQUARES

These squares were a favorite of my late husband, a diabetic. Whenever he had a sweet tooth, he could thaw a couple of them.

1/2 cup each chopped dates, raisins and apricots
1 cup water
1/4 cup margarine
1 teaspoon baking soda
1 teaspoon vanilla extract
1 cup all-purpose flour
1/4 teaspoon salt
1/2 teaspoon cinnamon
1/4 teaspoon nutmeg
2 eggs
3 tablespoons frozen unsweetened apple juice, undiluted
1/4 cup chopped pecans

Preheat oven to 350 degrees. Simmer dates, raisins, apricots and water in saucepan for 5 minutes. Stir in margarine. Cool for several minutes. Combine baking soda, vanilla, flour, salt, cinnamon, nutmeg, eggs, apple juice and pecans in large bowl; mix well. Stir in date mixture. Press into greased 9-by-13-inch baking pan. Bake at 350 degrees for 15 to 20 minutes or until brown on top. Cool completely. Cut into bars. Yield: 24 servings.

Alice McBride, Preceptor Theta Omega
McKinney, Texas

DATE OATMEAL COOKIES

1 cup butter or margarine, softened
1 cup packed light brown sugar
21/2 cups oats
2 cups all-purpose flour
1 teaspoon baking soda
1/2 teaspoon salt
1 (8-ounce) package dates
1 cup sugar
1/2 cup water

Preheat oven to 350 degrees. Combine butter, brown sugar, oats, flour, baking soda and salt in bowl; mix well. Spread 1/2 of oat mixture into greased 10-by-15-inch baking pan. Combine dates, sugar and water in saucepan. Cook over low heat until thickened, stirring frequently. Cool to room temperature. Spread over oat mixture in pan. Top with remaining oat mixture. Bake at 350 degrees for 25 minutes. Yield: 30 servings.

Marjorie Dent, Laureate Gamma
Pocatello, Idaho

DESSERT BARS

This recipe was given to me at my wedding shower.

1/3 cup melted butter or margarine
1 cup packed dark brown sugar
1 egg
1 cup all-purpose flour
1 teaspoon baking powder
1/4 teaspoon salt
1 teaspoon vanilla extract
1/4 cup chopped walnuts

Preheat oven to 400 degrees. Mix butter, brown sugar and egg in bowl. Stir in mixture of flour, baking powder and salt. Stir in vanilla and walnuts. Turn into greased 8-by-8-inch baking pan. Bake at 400 degrees for 15 to 20 minutes or until bars test done. May double recipe and bake in 9-by-13-inch baking pan. Yield: 1 dozen.

Pam Siminske, Xi Eta
Omaha, Nebraska

HELLO DOLLY SQUARES

My mother gave me this recipe. She makes it for me on holidays and birthdays.

1/4 cup margarine
1 cup graham cracker crumbs
1 cup flaked coconut
1 cup chopped pecans
1 cup semisweet chocolate chips
1 (14-ounce) can sweetened condensed milk

Preheat oven to 350 degrees. Melt margarine in 9-by-9-inch baking pan; spread evenly. Sprinkle with 1 layer each of crumbs, coconut, pecans and chocolate chips. Pour condensed milk over top. Bake at 350 degrees for 30 minutes. Yield: 25 servings.

Claudia Staton, Eta Sigma
Blue Ridge, Georgia

Alice Rush, Mu Kappa, Ellinwood, Kansas, makes Peanut Butter Krispies by bringing 1 cup light corn syrup and 1 cup packed light brown sugar to a boil, blending in 1 cup peanut butter and 8 cups crisp rice cereal. Mix well, press into buttered 9-by-13-inch pan with buttered spoon and cut into squares when firm.

✣ EASY LEMON BARS

1 (2-layer) package pudding-recipe lemon cake mix
1/3 cup melted butter or margarine
1 egg
1 (16-ounce) can ready-to-spread lemon frosting
1 egg
8 ounces cream cheese, softened
1/2 cup chopped pecans (optional)

Preheat oven to 350 degrees. Combine cake mix, butter and egg in bowl; mix well. Press into greased and floured 9-by-13-inch baking pan. Combine frosting, egg and cream cheese in bowl; mix until blended. Spread over batter. Bake at 350 degrees for 40 to 50 minutes or until firm. Sprinkle with pecans. Chill for 2 hours to overnight. Cut into bars.
Yield: 24 servings.

Faith Carey-Spark, Laureate Beta Eta
Urbandale, Iowa

LEMON BARS

This recipe was given to me by my daughter's first grade teacher. At the time she was young and single and this was the only thing she could cook.

1/2 cup margarine
1/4 cup confectioners' sugar
1 cup all-purpose flour
Dash of salt
2 eggs
1 cup sugar
2 tablespoons all-purpose flour
2 tablespoons lemon juice
Grated rind of 1 lemon

Preheat oven to 350 degrees. Combine margarine, confectioners' sugar, 1 cup flour and salt in bowl; mix until crumbly. Pat into greased 9-by-9-inch baking pan. Bake at 350 degrees for 15 minutes. Combine eggs, sugar, 2 tablespoons flour, lemon juice and lemon rind in bowl; mix well. Spoon over prepared crust. Bake for 20 minutes. Sprinkle with additional confectioners' sugar. Yield: 9 servings.

Claudia Weese, Xi Gamma Lambda
Shattuck, Oklahoma

BUTTERY LEMON BARS

1 cup butter or margarine
1/2 cup confectioners' sugar
2 cups all-purpose flour
2 cups sugar
1/4 cup all-purpose flour
1 teaspoon baking powder
4 eggs, beaten
6 tablespoons lemon juice

Preheat oven to 350 degrees. Combine butter, confectioners' sugar and 2 cups flour in large bowl; mix until crumbly. Pat into greased 9-by-13-inch baking pan. Bake at 350 degrees for 15 minutes. Combine sugar, 1/4 cup flour, baking powder, eggs and lemon juice in large bowl; mix well. Spread over prepared crust. Bake for 25 minutes. Cut into small squares. Dust with additional confectioners' sugar.
Yield: 2 to 3 dozen.

Becky Guilliams, Preceptor Mu Kappa
Shaver Lake, California

LEMON CHEESE BARS

1 (2-layer) package pudding-recipe yellow cake mix
1 egg
1/3 cup vegetable oil
8 ounces cream cheese, softened
1/2 cup sugar
1 teaspoon lemon juice
1 egg

Preheat oven to 350 degrees. Combine cake mix, 1 egg and oil in bowl; mix until crumbly. Reserve 1 cup cake mix mixture. Pat remaining mixture into ungreased 9-by-13-inch baking dish. Bake at 350 degrees for 15 minutes. Beat cream cheese, sugar, lemon juice and 1 egg in mixer bowl until light and smooth. Spread over prepared crust. Sprinkle reserved cake mix mixture over top. Bake for 15 minutes. Cool completely. Cut into bars.
Yield: 2 dozen.

Melissa Cantrell, Iota Beta
Shelbyville, Tennessee

LEMON-ICED AMBROSIA BARS

1 1/2 cups unsifted all-purpose flour
1/3 cup confectioners' sugar
3/4 cup cold margarine or butter
2 cups packed light brown sugar
4 eggs, beaten
1 cup flaked coconut
1 cup finely chopped pecans
3 tablespoons all-purpose flour
1/2 teaspoon baking powder
2 cups confectioners' sugar
3 tablespoons lemon juice from concentrate
2 tablespoons margarine, softened

Preheat oven to 350 degrees. Combine 1 1/2 cups flour and 1/3 cup confectioners' sugar in medium bowl. Cut in 3/4 cup margarine until crumbly. Press into lightly greased 9-by-13-inch baking pan. Bake at 350 degrees for 15 minutes. Combine brown sugar, eggs, coconut, pecans, 3 tablespoons flour and baking powder in large bowl; mix well. Spread over prepared crust. Bake for 20 to 25 minutes or until firm. Cool completely. Combine 2 cups confectioners' sugar, lemon juice and 2 tablespoons margarine in bowl; mix until smooth. Spread over topping. Cut into squares. Yield: 15 servings.

Margaret Leoty, Zeta Gamma
Delhi, Louisiana

LEMON SQUARES

1 cup sifted all-purpose flour
1/2 cup margarine, softened
1 cup confectioners' sugar
2 eggs, beaten
2 tablespoons all-purpose flour
2 tablespoons lemon juice
1 cup sugar
1 teaspoon baking powder
1 teaspoon grated lemon rind

Preheat oven to 350 degrees. Combine 1 cup flour, margarine and confectioners' sugar in bowl; mix until crumbly. Press into greased 8-by-8-inch baking pan. Bake at 350 degrees for 20 minutes. Combine eggs, 2 tablespoons flour, lemon juice, sugar, baking powder and lemon rind in large bowl; mix until smooth. Spread over prepared crust. Bake for 20 to 25 minutes or until firm. Bake for a shorter time if a moister dessert is desired; a longer baking time will yield a drier, crispier result. Yield: 16 servings.

Patricia Lewis, Preceptor Alpha Upsilon
Rowland Heights, California

BUTTERY LEMON SQUARES

1 cup butter or margarine, softened
2 cups all-purpose flour
1/2 cup confectioners' sugar
1/2 cup lemon juice
4 eggs
2 cups all-purpose flour
1 teaspoon baking powder

Preheat oven to 350 degrees; 325 degrees if using glass baking dish. Combine butter, 2 cups flour and confectioners' sugar in mixer bowl. Mix until crumbly. Pat into greased 9-by-13-inch baking pan. Bake at 350 degrees for 10 minutes. Combine lemon juice, eggs, 2 cups flour and baking powder in mixer bowl; beat until blended. Spread over hot crust. Bake for 30 minutes. Loosen edges from pan. Sprinkle with confectioners' sugar. Cool completely. Cut into squares. Yield: 12 to 15 servings.

Sandi Meyer, Beta Gamma
Pasadena, Maryland

MAGIC LEMON SQUARES

1 cup quick-cooking oats
1 cup all-purpose flour
1/2 cup each flaked coconut and chopped pecans or walnuts
1/2 cup packed light brown sugar
1 teaspoon baking powder
1/2 cup melted butter or margarine
1 (14-ounce) can sweetened condensed milk
1/2 cup lemon juice

Preheat oven to 350 degrees. Combine oats, flour, coconut, pecans, brown sugar, baking powder and butter in large bowl; mix until crumbly. Set aside. Combine condensed milk and lemon juice in bowl; mix thoroughly. Pat 1/2 of oat mixture into greased 9-by-9-inch baking pan. Spread condensed milk mixture on top. Press remaining 1/2 of oat mixture lightly over top. Bake at 350 degrees for 30 minutes. Cool completely. Cut into squares. Yield: 4 dozen.

Maida Gaiser, Laureate Alpha Tau
Dashwood, Ontario, Canada

MINCEMEAT SQUARES

1 cup rolled oats
1 cup all-purpose flour
1/4 teaspoon baking soda
1/4 teaspoon salt
1/2 cup packed light brown sugar
1/2 cup butter or margarine
1 1/4 cups mincemeat
1 tablespoon rum or brandy (optional)

Preheat oven to 350 degrees. Combine oats, flour, baking soda, salt and brown sugar in bowl. Cut in butter until crumbly. Press 1/2 of oat mixture into greased 8-by-8-inch baking pan. Top with mixture of mincemeat and rum. Spread with remaining oat mixture. Pack firmly. Bake at 350 degrees for 25 to 30 minutes or until browned. Yield: 3 dozen.

Betty Larkworthy, Tau Master
Stratford, Ontario, Canada

MIXED NUT SQUARES

These squares are a hit at our annual luncheon during our craft show. My sorority sisters won't let me make any other recipe!

2 cups all-purpose flour
1 cup packed light brown sugar
1 cup margarine, softened
1 teaspoon vanilla extract
1/4 teaspoon salt
1 egg yolk
1 cup butterscotch chips
1/2 cup light corn syrup
2 tablespoons margarine
1 tablespoon water
3 cups mixed nuts

Preheat oven to 350 degrees. Combine flour, brown sugar, 1 cup margarine, vanilla, salt and egg yolk in bowl; mix until crumbly. Press into ungreased 9-by-13-inch baking pan. Bake at 350 degrees for 20 to 25 minutes or until light brown. Cool. Combine butterscotch chips, corn syrup, 2 tablespoons margarine and water in saucepan. Cook over low heat until chips melt; mix well. Spread cooled sauce over crust. Press nuts into top. Chill for 1 hour or until firm. Yield: 2 to 3 dozen.

Sue Parker, Xi Zeta Eta
Cherokee, Iowa

MYSTERY SQUARES OR COCONUT-WALNUT SQUARES

2 tablespoons sugar
1/2 cup butter or margarine, softened
1 cup all-purpose flour
2 eggs
1 1/2 cups packed light brown sugar
1/2 cup finely flaked coconut
1 cup walnuts, whole or chopped
1 tablespoon all-purpose flour
1 teaspoon baking powder
1 teaspoon vanilla extract
Salt to taste

Preheat oven to 375 degrees. Cream sugar and butter in mixer bowl until light and fluffy. Add 1 cup flour; mix well. Press into greased 8-by-8-inch baking pan. Bake at 375 degrees for 5 minutes. Remove from oven. Increase oven temperature to 400 degrees. Combine remaining ingredients in mixer bowl; mix until blended. Spread over baked layer. Bake at 400 degrees for 25 minutes. Yield: 1 dozen.

Dorothy Range, Laureate Eta
Prince George, British Columbia, Canada

NANAIMO BARS

1/2 cup melted butter or margarine
1/4 cup sugar
1/3 cup baking cocoa
1 egg
2 cups graham cracker crumbs
1 cup flaked coconut
1/2 cup chopped walnuts
1/4 cup butter or margarine, softened
2 tablespoons custard powder
1 teaspoon vanilla extract
3 tablespoons milk
2 cups confectioners' sugar
1/2 cup semisweet chocolate chips
1 tablespoon butter or margarine

Mix 1/2 cup butter, sugar, cocoa, egg, crumbs, coconut and walnuts in bowl until crumbly. Press into 9-by-9-inch pan. Chill for 1/2 hour. Cream 1/4 cup butter, custard powder and vanilla in mixer bowl until light and fluffy. Blend in milk and confectioners' sugar gradually. Spread over chilled layer. Melt chips and 1 tablespoon butter in saucepan. Drizzle over top. Chill until set. Yield: 1 to 2 dozen.

Linda Blanchet, Theta Iota
Marietta, Georgia

NEIMAN MARCUS CAKE

This is our son's favorite recipe and the one he wants made for his birthday cake.

1 (2-layer) package yellow cake mix
2 eggs
1/4 cup vegetable oil
1/2 cup chopped pecans
8 ounces cream cheese, softened
4 1/2 cups confectioners' sugar
2 eggs, beaten
1/2 cup chopped pecans

Preheat oven to 300 degrees. Combine cake mix, 2 eggs, oil and 1/2 cup pecans in bowl; mix well. Pat into ungreased 9-by-13-inch baking pan. Combine cream cheese, confectioners' sugar, 2 eggs and 1/2 cup pecans in bowl; mix until blended. Spread over batter. Bake at 300 degrees for 1 1/4 hours.
Yield: 15 servings.

Linda Heise, Xi Theta Gamma
Mt. Pleasant, Iowa

OATMEAL CARROT BARS

1/2 cup raisins
1 cup boiling water
1/3 cup margarine, softened
1/2 cup packed light brown sugar
1 egg
1 1/4 cups grated carrots
1/2 teaspoon cinnamon
1/4 teaspoon nutmeg
1/2 teaspoon freshly grated lemon rind
1 cup whole wheat flour
1/2 cup quick-cooking oats
1 teaspoon baking powder
1/2 teaspoon vanilla extract
1 tablespoon confectioners' sugar

Preheat oven to 350 degrees. Cover raisins with boiling water in bowl. Soak for 15 minutes; drain and set aside. Cream margarine and brown sugar in large mixer bowl until light and fluffy. Beat in egg. Stir in carrots. Add spices and lemon rind; mix well. Add mixture of flour, oats and baking powder; beat until blended. Add vanilla; mix well. Stir in raisins. Spoon into greased 9-by-13-inch baking pan. Bake at 350 degrees for 20 to 25 minutes or until browned. Cool completely. Sprinkle with confectioners' sugar. Cut into bars. Yield: 24 servings.

Billie K. Lowe, Preceptor Omicron Epsilon
Kilgore, Texas

PEANUT CHEWS

1 1/2 cups all-purpose flour
2/3 cup packed light brown sugar
1/2 teaspoon each baking powder and salt
1/4 teaspoon baking soda
1/2 cup margarine, softened
1 teaspoon vanilla extract
2 egg yolks
3 cups miniature marshmallows
2/3 cup light corn syrup
1/4 cup margarine
2 teaspoons vanilla extract
2 cups peanut butter chips
2 cups crisp rice cereal
2 cups salted peanuts

Preheat oven to 350 degrees. Combine flour, brown sugar, baking powder, salt, baking soda, 1/2 cup margarine, 1 teaspoon vanilla and egg yolks in large bowl; mix until crumbly. Press into greased 9-by-13-inch baking pan. Bake at 350 degrees for 12 to 15 minutes or until brown. Remove from oven. Sprinkle with marshmallows. Return to oven. Bake for 2 minutes longer or until marshmallows begin to puff. Cool completely. Combine corn syrup, 1/4 cup margarine, 2 teaspoons vanilla and peanut butter chips in large saucepan. Cook over low heat until peanut butter chips melt and mixture is smooth, stirring constantly. Remove from heat. Stir in cereal and peanuts. Spoon evenly over crust mixture. Chill until set. Cut into squares. Yield: 15 servings.

Karen Massingham, Zeta Gamma
Port Hardy, British Columbia, Canada

PECAN PIE SQUARES

3 cups all-purpose flour
6 tablespoons sugar
3/4 cup margarine
1/2 teaspoon salt
4 eggs, beaten
1 1/2 cups sugar
1 1/2 cups light corn syrup
3 tablespoons melted margarine
1 1/2 teaspoons vanilla extract
2 1/2 cups chopped pecans

Preheat oven to 350 degrees. Combine flour, 6 tablespoons sugar, 3/4 cup margarine and salt in large bowl; mix until crumbly. Press firmly into greased 9-by-13-inch baking pan. Bake at 350 degrees for 20 minutes or until light golden brown. Combine eggs, 1 1/2 cups sugar, corn syrup, 3 tablespoons margarine and vanilla in mixer bowl; mix well. Stir in pecans. Spread evenly over baked layer. Bake for 25 minutes or until set. Cool completely. Cut into 1 1/2-inch squares. Yield: 5 to 6 dozen.

Lyn Sizelove, Xi Epsilon Omega
Laverne, Oklahoma

PRALINE PECAN CRUNCH

1 (16-ounce) package oat squares cereal
2 cups pecan pieces
1/2 cup light corn syrup
1/2 cup packed light brown sugar
1/4 cup margarine
1 tablespoon vanilla extract
1/2 teaspoon baking soda

Preheat oven to 250 degrees. Combine cereal and pecans in greased 9-by-13-inch baking pan; mix well and spread evenly in pan. Set aside. Combine corn syrup, brown sugar and margarine in large saucepan; mix well. Bring to a rolling boil, stirring constantly. Remove from heat. Stir in vanilla and baking soda. Spoon over cereal mixture, tossing to coat. Bake at 250 degrees for 1 hour, stirring every 20 minutes. Spread on greased 12-by-18-inch baking sheet to cool. Break into pieces. Store in airtight container. Yield: 12 to 15 servings.

Jean Plunkett, Laureate Alpha Delta
Columbus, Kansas

✣ STREUSEL PECAN PIE SQUARES

3 cups unbleached flour
3/4 cup packed light brown sugar
1 1/2 cups chilled margarine
3/4 cup packed light brown sugar
1 1/2 cups light corn syrup or maple syrup
1 cup milk
1/3 cup melted margarine or butter
1 teaspoon vanilla extract
4 eggs
1 1/2 cups chopped pecans

Preheat oven to 400 degrees. Combine flour, 3/4 cup brown sugar and 1 1/2 cups margarine in large bowl; mix until crumbly. Reserve 2 cups of crumb mixture. Press remaining crumb mixture into bottom and 3/4 inch up sides of ungreased 10-by-15-inch baking pan. Bake at 400 degrees for 10 minutes. Combine 1/4 cup reserved crumb mixture, 3/4 cup brown sugar, corn syrup, milk, 1/3 cup margarine, vanilla and eggs in large bowl; mix well. Stir in pecans. Spread over baked layer. Bake for 10 minutes. Reduce oven temperature to 350 degrees. Sprinkle remaining 1 3/4 cups reserved crumb mixture over filling. Bake at 350 degrees for 20 to 25 minutes or until filling is set and crumbs are golden brown. Yield: 15 servings.

Marilyn Fitch, Preceptor Xi Epsilon
San Diego, California

PERSIMMON BARS

1 3/4 cups all-purpose flour
1 teaspoon each salt, cinnamon and nutmeg
1/4 teaspoon ground cloves
2 to 3 medium pointed-tip, ripe persimmons
1 1/2 teaspoons lemon juice
1 teaspoon baking soda
1 egg
1 cup sugar
1/2 cup vegetable oil
1 (8-ounce) package pitted dates, chopped
1 cup chopped walnuts
1 cup confectioners' sugar
2 tablespoons lemon juice

Preheat oven to 350 degrees. Sift flour, salt, cinnamon, nutmeg and cloves together. Cut persimmons in half; scoop out pulp, discarding skin, seeds and stems. Purée in food processor container a portion at a time until smooth. Stir in 1 1/2 teaspoons lemon juice and baking soda; set aside. Beat egg in large bowl. Stir in sugar, oil and dates. Add flour mixture and persimmon mixture alternately to date mixture, stirring just until blended. Stir in walnuts. Spread in lightly greased and floured 10-by-15-inch baking pan. Bake at 350 degrees for 25 minutes or until lightly browned and wooden pick inserted near center comes out clean. Cool in pan on wire rack for 5 minutes. Spread with mixture of confectioners' sugar and 2 tablespoons lemon juice. Cool completely. Cut into bars. Yield: 30 servings.

Carol Tyrrell, Xi Upsilon Omicron
Altaville, California

RAISIN BARS

1 cup raisins
1 cup water
1/2 cup shortening
1/2 teaspoon baking soda
Salt to taste
2 cups all-purpose flour
3/4 cup sugar
1 teaspoon cinnamon
1/2 teaspoon cloves
1/2 cup chopped pecans

Preheat oven to 375 degrees. Cover raisins with water in saucepan; bring to a boil over medium heat. Remove from heat. Add shortening and baking soda; mix well. Add salt, flour, sugar, spices and pecans; mix well. Spread into greased 9-by-13-inch baking pan. Bake at 375 degrees for 20 minutes. Cool completely. Spread with favorite confectioners' sugar frosting. Cut into bars. Yield: 2 to 3 dozen.

Ellen Cotten, Preceptor Alpha Epsilon
Carbondale, Illinois

RASPBERRY BARS

1 (2-layer) package raspberry cake mix
2 eggs
3/4 cup water
1/4 cup packed light brown sugar
1/4 cup margarine, softened
1 cup vanilla chips
2 tablespoons milk
2 tablespoons melted margarine
3/4 teaspoon vanilla extract
Confectioners' sugar to taste

Preheat oven to 375 degrees. Combine cake mix, eggs, water, brown sugar and 1/4 cup margarine in large bowl; mix well. Stir in vanilla chips. Spoon into greased 9-by-13-inch baking pan. Bake at 375 degrees for 24 to 27 minutes or until light brown. Cool completely. Combine remaining ingredients in bowl; mix until of spreadable consistency. Spread over tops of bars. Cut into bars. Yield: 15 servings.

Wanda Wantiez, Xi Alpha Tau
Dandridge, Tennessee

RASPBERRY COCONUT BARS

1 cup all-purpose flour
1 teaspoon baking powder
1/2 cup margarine
1 egg
1 teaspoon milk
Raspberry jam to taste
1/2 cup sugar
2 cups flaked coconut
2 tablespoons margarine
1 teaspoon vanilla extract
1 egg, beaten

Preheat oven to 350 degrees. Combine first 5 ingredients in bowl; mix well. Spread in greased 9-by-13-inch baking pan. Top with jam. Combine sugar, coconut, 2 tablespoons margarine, vanilla and egg in bowl; mix until blended. Spoon over jam. Bake at 350 degrees for 35 minutes. Yield: 15 servings.

Josie Ferguson, Theta Alpha
Cache Creek, British Columbia, Canada

RASPBERRY OAT BARS

3/4 cup margarine, softened
1 cup packed light brown sugar
11/2 cups rolled or quick-cooking oats
11/2 cups all-purpose flour
1 teaspoon salt
1/2 teaspoon baking soda
1 (10-ounce) jar red raspberry preserves

Preheat oven to 400 degrees. Cream margarine and brown sugar in mixer bowl until light and fluffy. Add oats, flour, salt and baking soda; mix until crumbly. Press half the mixture into greased 9-by-13-inch baking pan. Spread with preserves. Top with remaining crumb mixture. Bake at 400 degrees for 20 to 25 minutes or until light brown. Cool completely. Cut into bars. Yield: 2 dozen.

Sharon Grogan, Xi Beta Xi
Manhattan, Kansas

SHORTBREAD

2 cups all-purpose flour
1 cup confectioners' sugar
1 cup cornstarch
1 cup butter
Confectioners' sugar

Preheat oven to 325 degrees. Combine flour, sugar and cornstarch in large bowl; mix well. Melt butter in saucepan over low heat. Pour over flour mixture; mix until blended. Press firmly into 2 greased 8-by-8-inch baking pans. Press with fork around edges and centers. Bake at 325 degrees on lower shelf of oven for 50 minutes or until brown. Remove from oven. Cut into squares immediately. Sprinkle with confectioners' sugar. Cool in pan for 15 minutes. Remove to wire rack to finish cooling. Store in airtight container. Yield: 16 servings.

Marilyn Silva, Preceptor, Xi Epsilon

TOFFEE BARS

13/4 cups all-purpose flour
1 cup sugar
1 cup butter or margarine, softened
1 egg yolk
1 teaspoon vanilla extract
1 egg white, beaten
1/2 cup chopped walnuts

Preheat oven to 275 degrees. Combine flour, sugar, butter, egg yolk and vanilla in large mixer bowl; beat at low speed just until blended, scraping bowl occasionally. Beat at medium speed until well mixed. Pat evenly into greased 10-by-15-inch baking pan. Brush with egg white. Sprinkle with walnuts. Bake at 275 degrees for 1 hour and 10 minutes or until golden. Cut crosswise immediately into 12 strips; cut each strip into 4 pieces. Remove to wire racks to cool. Store in tightly covered container. Yield: 4 dozen.

Jennifer Yarnell, Alpha Delta Lambda
Cameron, Missouri

BUCKEYES

1 cup margarine, softened
2 cups crunchy peanut butter
1 (1-pound) package confectioners' sugar
3 cups crisp rice cereal
2 cups milk chocolate chips
1/2 bar paraffin, shaved

Combine margarine, peanut butter, confectioners' sugar and cereal in large bowl; mix with hands. Chill, covered, for 30 minutes. Shape into walnut-sized balls. Melt chocolate chips and paraffin in top of double boiler. Dip balls into chocolate mixture. Cool on waxed paper. Yield: 80 buckeyes.

Jean Howe, Preceptor Laureate Chi
Salem, Oregon

BUTTERFINGER BARS

2/3 cup sugar
2/3 cup light corn syrup
1 (18-ounce) jar chunky peanut butter
3 cups cornflakes
2 cups milk chocolate chips

Bring sugar and corn syrup to a boil in medium saucepan. Remove from heat. Stir in peanut butter; mix well. Add cornflakes, stirring until coated. Press into ungreased 9-by-13-inch dish. Melt chocolate chips in small saucepan. Spread over peanut butter mixture. Chill, covered, for 20 to 30 minutes or until chocolate is almost firm. Cut into squares.
Yield: 12 servings.

Lucille DeLauriea, Laureate Beta Epsilon
Woodridge, Illinois

BUTTERSCOTCH CRUNCHIES

This is an easy-to-prepare treat for sorority meetings or for the kids after school.

2 cups butterscotch chips
1 cup peanut butter
5 cups cornflakes
1 cup semisweet chocolate chips
1 cup miniature marshmallows

Melt butterscotch chips and peanut butter in small saucepan over low heat. Remove from heat. Stir in cornflakes, chocolate chips and marshmallows, mixing well after each addition. Spread on waxed paper. Let stand until cool. Break into bite-size pieces.
Yield: 2 dozen.

Maria Terkelsen, Delta Gamma Psi
San Jose, California

Vicky Osmundson, Beta Delta, Calmar, Iowa, makes Butterscotch Quickies by melting 2 cups butterscotch chips with 1/4 cup peanut butter and mixing in 4 to 5 cups Special-K cereal. Drop by teaspoonfuls onto waxed paper.

CHOCOLATE BLOBS

2 (1-ounce) squares unsweetened chocolate
2 cups sugar
1/2 cup milk
1/2 cup butter or margarine, softened
1 teaspoon vanilla extract
1/2 cup peanut butter
3 cups oats

Melt chocolate in large saucepan. Add sugar, milk, butter and vanilla, mixing well after each addition. Bring to a boil. Reduce heat to medium. Add peanut butter; mix well. Remove from heat. Stir in oats. Drop by tablespoonfuls onto baking sheet. Chill, covered, for 2 hours or longer. Yield: 4 dozen.

Peggy Beach, Xi Delta Gamma
Nokesville, Virginia

CHOCOLATE FROSTIES

1/3 cup packed light brown sugar
1/4 cup light corn syrup
1/4 cup peanut butter
2 tablespoons melted butter or margarine
1 teaspoon vanilla extract
3 cups frosted cornflakes
4 (1-ounce) squares semisweet chocolate
1/4 cup peanut butter

Combine brown sugar, corn syrup, 1/4 cup peanut butter, butter and vanilla in medium bowl, mixing well after each addition. Stir in frosted cornflakes. Press into buttered 8-by-8-inch dish. Melt chocolate in small saucepan. Stir in 1/4 cup peanut butter, mixing until smooth. Spread over cornflake mixture. Chill in refrigerator until firm. Cut into squares.
Yield: 16 squares.

Donna McBride, Theta
Moose Jaw, Saskatchewan, Canada

CHOCOLATE MARBLE BALLS

This 40-year-old recipe was my mother's favorite.

1 cup butter or margarine
1 cup peanut butter
1 cup graham cracker crumbs
1 (1-pound) package confectioners' sugar
1 cup flaked coconut
1 cup chopped pecans
1/2 bar paraffin, chopped
2 cups milk chocolate chips

Melt butter and peanut butter in medium saucepan. Stir in crumbs. Remove from heat. Add confectioners' sugar, coconut and pecans, mixing well after each addition; batter will be stiff. Shape by teaspoonfuls into balls. Melt paraffin and chocolate chips in small saucepan. Dip balls into chocolate mixture. Cool on waxed paper. Yield: 5 dozen.

Virginia Kesner, Gamma Nu
Romney, West Virginia

CHOCOLATE SCOTCHAROOS

1 cup light corn syrup
1 cup sugar
1 cup peanut butter
7 cups crisp rice cereal
1 cup semisweet chocolate chips
1 cup butterscotch chips

Bring corn syrup and sugar to a boil in large heavy saucepan. Remove from heat. Add peanut butter, stirring until well blended. Stir in cereal. Press into buttered 9-by-13-inch dish. Melt chocolate chips and butterscotch chips in top of small double boiler over low heat. Spread over cereal mixture. Let stand until cool. Cut into squares. Yield: 15 servings.

Angie Steger, Zeta Upsilon
Independence, Missouri

CREAMY CRISPY TREATS

24 caramels
1 (14-ounce) can sweetened condensed milk
1/2 cup melted margarine
1 cup miniature marshmallows
2 cups crisp rice cereal

Melt caramels in medium saucepan. Add condensed milk, margarine and marshmallows; mix well. Stir in cereal. Spread into 9-by-13-inch glass baking dish sprayed with nonstick cooking spray. Let stand until cool. Cut into squares. Yield: 8 servings.

Donetta Bantle, Xi Delta Tau
Stillwater, Oklahoma

CRUNCHY NO-BAKE COOKIES

1 cup light corn syrup
1 cup sugar
6 cups crushed Special-K cereal
1 1/3 cups crunchy peanut butter
2 cups melted semisweet chocolate chips

Bring corn syrup and sugar to a boil in large saucepan. Remove from heat. Add crushed cereal and peanut butter, mixing well after each addition. Spread in greased 9-by-13-inch dish. Spread melted chocolate chips over top. Chill in refrigerator. Cut into squares. Yield: 15 servings.

Carol Frye, Beta Gamma
Linthicum, Maryland

NO-BAKE DATE BALLS

2 eggs
1 cup sugar
Salt to taste
2 tablespoons butter or margarine
2 cups dates
2 1/2 to 2 3/4 cups crisp rice cereal
1/2 cup flaked coconut

Combine eggs, sugar, salt, butter and dates in medium saucepan. Cook until thickened, stirring constantly. Remove from heat. Stir in cereal. Cool. Shape into balls. Roll in coconut. Yield: 3 dozen.

Dorothy Kaiser, Laureate Rho
Hot Springs, South Dakota

FUN FUDGE SANDWICHES

1 cup butterscotch chips
1/2 cup peanut butter
4 cups crisp rice cereal
1 cup semisweet chocolate chips
2 tablespoons butter or margarine
1 tablespoon water
1/2 cup confectioners' sugar

Melt butterscotch chips and peanut butter in medium saucepan over low heat, stirring constantly; remove from heat. Stir in cereal; mix until coated. Press half the mixture into buttered 8-by-8-inch square dish. Chill in refrigerator. Combine chocolate chips, butter and water in small saucepan. Cook until chocolate melts, stirring constantly. Remove from heat. Stir in confectioners' sugar. Spread over chilled layer. Press remaining cereal mixture over top. Chill until serving time. Cut into bars. Yield: 16 servings.

Sue Rine-Steagall, Alpha Alpha Epsilon
Jacksonville, Florida

CRISPY CRUNCH BARS

3 cups peanut butter
3 3/4 cups confectioners' sugar
1/2 cup margarine, softened
5 cups crisp rice cereal
2 cups semisweet chocolate chips
2 tablespoons margarine

Place peanut butter in large microwave-safe bowl. Microwave until softened. Blend in confectioners' sugar and 1/2 cup margarine. Add cereal; mix well. Press into greased 9-by-13-inch dish. Microwave chocolate chips in small microwave-safe bowl until melted, stirring several times. Add 2 tablespoons margarine, stirring until smooth and glossy. Spread over peanut butter mixture. Chill until firm. Cut into bars. Yield: 6 dozen.

Dawn Malasky, Alpha Beta
Saskatoon, Saskatchewan, Canada

CRISPY PEANUT BUTTER AND CHOCOLATE BARS

1 cup sugar
1 cup light corn syrup
2 cups chunky peanut butter
2 tablespoons margarine
5 cups crisp rice cereal
2 cups semisweet chocolate chips

Cook sugar and corn syrup in large saucepan over medium heat for 5 minutes or until sugar dissolves, stirring constantly. Remove from heat. Blend in peanut butter and margarine. Stir in cereal. Press into buttered 9-by-13-inch dish. Melt chocolate chips in small saucepan, stirring constantly. Spread over cereal mixture. Chill, covered, for 1 hour. Cut into bars. Yield: 2 dozen.

Irene Freiberg, Laureate Epsilon
North Platte, Nebraska

CRISPY RICE CEREAL SQUARES

1 cup packed light brown sugar
1/2 cup butter or margarine
1/2 cup light corn syrup
1 tablespoon baking cocoa
Salt to taste
1 teaspoon vanilla extract
5 cups crisp rice cereal

Bring brown sugar, butter, corn syrup, cocoa and salt to a boil in small saucepan. Boil for 2 minutes. Stir in vanilla. Remove from heat. Pour over rice cereal in large bowl; mix well. Press into 9-by-13-inch dish. Chill for 1 hour or until firm. Cut into squares. Yield: 2 dozen.

Annette McKenzie, Nu
Richmond, British Columbia, Canada

SIX-MINUTE MARSHMALLOW CRISPS

I tint these orange, put then in plastic food storage bags with my name, and give them to trick or treaters.

1/2 cup margarine
8 ounces marshmallows or 2 cups marshmallow creme
5 cups crisp rice cereal or 5 cups popped popcorn

Melt margarine and marshmallows in small double boiler over low heat, stirring constantly. Stir in cereal. Press into lightly greased 9-by-13-inch dish. Let stand until cool. Cut into squares. Yield: 2 dozen.

Mary Patricia Shorey, Xi Alpha Xi
Bridgton, Maine

NO-BAKE CHOCOLATE COOKIES

2 cups sugar
1/4 cup margarine, softened
Salt to taste
1/2 cup milk
1/4 cup baking cocoa
1 teaspoon vanilla extract
1/2 cup peanut butter
3 cups oats

Bring sugar, margarine, salt, milk and cocoa to a boil in large saucepan. Boil for 1 minute. Remove from heat. Stir in vanilla, peanut butter and oats; mix well. Drop by spoonfuls onto waxed paper. Let stand until cool. Yield: 3 dozen.

Elizabeth Smith, Preceptor Gamma Lambda
Sedalia, Colorado

O'HENRY BARS

1/2 cup melted margarine
1 cup sugar
1 cup light corn syrup
1 cup peanut butter
8 cups crisp rice cereal
2 cups milk chocolate chips
2 cups butterscotch chips

Bring margarine, sugar and corn syrup to a boil in small saucepan. Remove from heat. Add peanut butter; mix well. Pour over rice cereal in large bowl; stir until coated. Press into 9-by-13-inch nonstick dish. Melt chocolate chips and butterscotch chips in small saucepan. Pour over cereal mixture. Let stand until cool. Cut into squares. Yield: 1 dozen.

Julie Hebberd, Pi Sigma
Overland Park, Kansas

O'HENRY SQUARES

16 whole graham crackers
1 cup packed light brown sugar
1/2 cup milk
1/2 cup butter or margarine
1 teaspoon vanilla extract
1 cup graham cracker crumbs
1 cup finely grated unsweetened coconut
1 cup chopped walnuts

Line an 8-by-8-inch or 9-by-9-inch nonstick dish with whole graham crackers, cutting to fit. Bring brown sugar, milk and butter to a boil in a small saucepan. Boil for 1 minute. Remove from heat. Add vanilla. Stir in mixture of crumbs, coconut and walnuts; mix well. Spread over graham crackers in dish. Top with remaining whole graham crackers. Spread with butter icing or canned frosting. Chill until set. Cut into small squares. Yield: 16 servings.

Alicia Wylie, Laureate Alpha Alpha
Amherstview, Ontario, Canada

ORANGE NO-BAKE COOKIES

I've used this recipe many times for children in church school classes and Girl Scouts to make and share with others.

1 (12-ounce) package vanilla wafers, finely crumbled
1/4 cup margarine, softened
1 (6-ounce) can frozen orange juice concentrate
3/4 cup chopped walnuts or pecans
1/4 cup confectioners' sugar

Combine crumbs, margarine, orange juice concentrate and walnuts in large bowl; mix well. Shape into balls. Roll in confectioners' sugar. Chill thoroughly. Store in covered container in refrigerator.
Yield: 3 to 4 dozen.

Myrna Schroder, Beta Omega
Savannah, Missouri

Evanell J. Truszkowski, Laureate Pi, Farmers Branch, Texas, makes Orange Balls by combining 4 cups vanilla wafer crumbs with 6 ounces orange juice concentrate and 1/4 cup melted butter. Shape into balls and roll in confectioners' sugar, then in finely chopped walnuts or pecans and chill until firm.

PEANUT BUTTER BALLS

1 cup margarine, softened
1 cup peanut butter
1 cup flaked coconut
1 cup graham cracker crumbs
2 cups confectioners' sugar
1 cup semisweet chocolate chips
1 cup milk chocolate chips
1/2 bar paraffin, chopped

Combine margarine, peanut butter, coconut, graham cracker crumbs and confectioners' sugar in large bowl, mixing well after each addition. Shape into quarter-sized balls. Melt chocolate chips and paraffin in small saucepan. Dip balls in chocolate mixture. Place on waxed paper to cool. Yield: 4 dozen.

Melissa J. Roos, Omega Upsilon
Appleton City, Missouri

PEANUT BUTTER CEREAL BARS

1 1/2 cups sugar
1 1/2 cups light corn syrup
3 1/2 cups peanut butter
3 cups Cheerios
3 1/2 cups crisp rice cereal

Bring the sugar and corn syrup to a full boil in large saucepan. Remove from heat. Stir in peanut butter. Stir in Cheerios and rice cereal. Press into ungreased 12-by-18-inch dish. Let stand until cool. Cut into squares. Yield: 4 dozen.

Rita Kae Mann, Preceptor Sigma
Brookfield, Connecticut

PEANUT BUTTER CUPS

1 cup melted margarine
1 cup graham cracker crumbs
1 cup crunchy peanut butter
1 (1-pound) package confectioners' sugar
1 cup milk chocolate chips

Combine first 4 ingredients in large bowl; mix well. Press into greased 9-by-13-inch dish. Melt chocolate chips in small saucepan. Spread over peanut butter mixture. Cut into squares. Chill until firm.
Yield: 2 dozen.

Darlene Hobbs, Preceptor Mu Kappa
Armona, California

PEANUT BUTTER GOODIES

2 pounds white almond bark
1 cup peanut butter
2 cups salted dry roasted peanuts
3 cups crisp rice cereal
2 cups miniature marshmallows

Line two 12-by-18-inch baking sheets with waxed paper. Microwave almond bark on High in small microwave-safe bowl for 5 to 7 minutes or until melted. Stir in peanut butter. Pour over mixture of peanuts, cereal and marshmallows in large bowl. Stir gently until mixed. Drop by spoonfuls onto waxed paper. Yield: 5 dozen.

Mary Nita Wing, Xi Master
Lake Jackson, Texas

PEANUT BUTTER SQUARES

1/2 cup packed light brown sugar
1/4 cup light corn syrup
1/2 cup margarine
1 cup peanut butter
1 teaspoon vanilla extract
2 cups cornflakes
1 cup crisp rice cereal
1/4 cup evaporated milk
1 cup packed light brown sugar
2 tablespoons margarine
2 tablespoons light corn syrup
1 1/4 cups confectioners' sugar

Bring 1/2 cup brown sugar, 1/4 cup corn syrup and 1/2 cup margarine to a boil in large saucepan. Boil for 1 minute. Add peanut butter, vanilla, cornflakes and rice cereal, mixing well after each addition. Press into buttered 8-by-8-inch dish. Chill in refrigerator. Bring evaporated milk, 1 cup brown sugar, 2 tablespoons margarine and 2 tablespoons corn syrup to a boil in small saucepan. Boil for 2 minutes. Remove from heat. Let stand until cool. Add confectioners' sugar to thicken. Spread over cereal mixture. Cut into squares to serve. Yield: 2 dozen.

Gisela Karrer, Preceptor Beta Lambda
Britannia Beach, British Columbia, Canada

PEANUT BUTTER GRAHAM SQUARES

1/2 cup margarine, softened
1 cup confectioners' sugar
1 cup peanut butter
12 double graham crackers, crushed
2 cups milk chocolate chips

Combine margarine, confectioners' sugar, peanut butter and crumbs in large bowl; mix well. Press firmly into 12-by-18-inch baking sheet. Melt chocolate chips in small saucepan. Spread over peanut butter mixture. Let stand until cool. Cut into 1-inch squares. Yield: 100 squares.

Audrey M. Sasse, Xi Gamma
Miles City, Montana

POPCORN TOPPING OR "GOOP"

My children love this as a treat. Cook the topping a little longer for easy-to-make popcorn balls.

1/2 cup light corn syrup
1 1/3 cups sugar
1 cup margarine
1 teaspoon vanilla extract
2 quarts popped popcorn

Microwave corn syrup, sugar and margarine in medium microwave-safe bowl on High until boiling; stir until mixture reaches soft-ball stage and is light caramel colored. Stir in vanilla. Pour over popcorn in large serving bowl; mix gently. May add nuts to popcorn. Yield: 8 to 10 servings.

Kay Weakland, Preceptor Alpha Pi
Beatrice, Nebraska

RUM BALLS

1 cup semisweet chocolate chips
3 tablespoons dark corn syrup
3/4 cup dark rum
2 1/4 cups chocolate wafer crumbs
1/2 cup confectioners' sugar
1 cup finely chopped pecans
1/4 cup chopped candied cherries
1/4 cup sugar

Melt chocolate chips in large saucepan. Remove from heat. Stir in corn syrup and rum. Combine next 4 ingredients in medium bowl. Add chocolate mixture; mix well. Let stand for 30 minutes. Shape into 1-inch balls. Roll in sugar. Chill in sealable plastic container lined with waxed paper. Yield: 4 dozen.

Julie Shipston, Alpha Epsilon
Thunder Bay, Ontario, Canada

SCOTCHEROOS

1 cup sugar
1 cup light corn syrup
1 cup peanut butter
6 cups crisp rice cereal
1 cup semisweet chocolate chips
1 cup butterscotch chips

Bring sugar and corn syrup to a boil in 3-quart saucepan, stirring frequently. Remove from heat. Add peanut butter; mix well. Stir in rice cereal. Press into buttered 9-by-13-inch dish. Melt chocolate chips and butterscotch chips in double boiler over hot water, stirring until smooth. Remove from heat. Spread evenly over cereal mixture. Cool until firm. Cut into bars. Yield: 4 dozen.

Rae Ann Boyett, Delta Iota Xi
Corcoran, California

SOCCER SQUARES

1 cup sugar
1 cup light corn syrup
1 cup peanut butter
6 cups crisp rice cereal
1 cup semisweet chocolate chips
1 cup butterscotch chips

Cook sugar and corn syrup in saucepan over medium heat until bubbly, stirring frequently. Remove from heat. Stir in peanut butter and rice cereal. Press into 9-by-13-inch dish. Melt chocolate chips and butterscotch chips in small saucepan over medium heat, stirring frequently. Spread over cereal mixture. Chill for 1 hour. Cut into squares. Yield: 2 dozen.

Reta Waldrop, Epsilon Rho
Helena, Alabama

SPECIAL-K TREATS

1 1/2 cups sugar
1 1/2 cups light corn syrup
1 (18-ounce) jar peanut butter
1 teaspoon margarine
1 teaspoon vanilla extract
6 cups Special-K cereal

Bring sugar and corn syrup to a boil in large saucepan. Remove from heat immediately. Add peanut butter, margarine and vanilla; mix well. Add cereal, stirring until coated. Drop by spoonfuls onto waxed paper. Let stand until cool. Store in tightly covered containers. Yield: 6 dozen.

Pearl E. Cave, Preceptor Theta Omega
McKinney, Texas

STRAWBERRY CONFECTION

5 tablespoons butter
1 cup sugar
2 eggs, beaten
1 1/2 cups chopped dates
Salt to taste
1 teaspoon vanilla extract
2 1/2 cups crisp rice cereal
1 cup chopped pecans
Red sugar crystals to taste

Combine butter and sugar in large saucepan. Stir in eggs and dates. Cook over low heat for 10 minutes, stirring constantly. Turn off heat. Add salt, vanilla, cereal and pecans; mix well. Let stand until cool. Form into strawberry shapes. Roll in red sugar crystals. May use green decorator icing to make leaves and stems if desired. Yield: 2 dozen.

Allie T. Archer, Preceptor Zeta Gamma
Tampa, Florida

SWEET MARIE BARS

1/2 cup packed light brown sugar
1/2 cup light corn syrup
1/2 cup peanut butter
1 tablespoon butter or margarine
1/2 cup salted peanut halves
2 1/2 to 3 cups crisp rice cereal
1 2/3 cups milk chocolate chips
1 tablespoon butter or margarine

Cook brown sugar, corn syrup, peanut butter and 1 tablespoon butter in large saucepan over low heat until butter is melted. Remove from heat. Stir in peanuts and cereal. Press into 8-by-8-inch dish. Chill in refrigerator. Melt chocolate chips and 1 tablespoon butter in small saucepan over low heat. Spread over chilled layer. Let stand until firm. Cut into bars. Yield: 16 servings.

Sylvie Hills, Delta Omicron Roster
Campbell River, British Columbia, Canada

TRUFFLES

These are great for Valentine's Day, Easter and Christmas to make and give as gifts. Put them in a candy gift box and they look store-bought.

1 (14-ounce) can sweetened condensed milk
2/3 cup baking cocoa
1/2 cup semisweet chocolate chips
1/4 cup all-purpose flour
1 tablespoon vanilla extract
1 cup miniature marshmallows
13/4 cups cinnamon graham cracker crumbs

Combine condensed milk, cocoa and chocolate chips in 1-quart microwave-proof measuring cup. Microwave on High until chocolate chips melt, stirring frequently. Add flour, vanilla and marshmallows, mixing well after each addition. Chill for 2 hours or until firm. Shape by teaspoonfuls into balls. Roll in graham cracker crumbs. Place in small paper candy cups. Yield: 50 truffles.

Debbie Gwynn, Xi Delta Rho
Miami, Florida

TWIX BARS DELIGHT

1 (16-ounce) package club crackers
1/2 cup sugar
1/2 cup packed light brown sugar
1/4 cup milk
1/2 cup margarine
1 cup crushed vanilla wafers
2/3 cup crunchy peanut butter
1/2 cup milk chocolate chips
1/2 cup butterscotch chips

Place layer of crackers in 9-by-13-inch dish. Bring sugar, brown sugar, milk, margarine and crumbs to a boil in small saucepan. Boil 3 to 4 minutes, stirring frequently. Pour over crackers in dish. Add a second layer of crackers. Melt peanut butter, chocolate chips and butterscotch chips in small saucepan. Pour peanut butter mixture over crackers. Yield: 3 dozen.

Kerri Ness, Omicron Omega
Shawnee, Kansas

ICEBOX BUTTERSCOTCH COOKIES

Every time my family would visit Aunt Bertha and Uncle Ben, Aunt Bertha would bake these cookies for us. This kept us all very quiet.

5 cups packed light brown sugar
11/2 cups butter or margarine, softened
6 eggs, beaten
8 cups all-purpose flour
11/2 tablespoons baking soda
1 tablespoon cream of tartar
8 teaspoons vanilla extract

Cream brown sugar and butter in mixer bowl until light and fluffy. Add eggs 1 at a time, beating after each addition. Add flour, baking soda, cream of tartar and vanilla; mix until blended. Shape into 3 to 4 logs; wrap in waxed paper. Chill overnight. Preheat oven to 400 degrees. Cut dough into slices. Place on greased 12-by-18-inch cookie sheet. Bake at 400 degrees for 8 minutes. Yield: 3 to 4 dozen.

Tanya Morris, Eta Upsilon
Madera, California

ICEBOX CINNAMON COOKIES

1 cup sugar
1 cup packed light brown sugar
1 cup shortening
3 eggs
31/2 cups all-purpose flour
2 teaspoons cinnamon
2 teaspoons baking soda
1 cup chopped pecans

Cream sugar, brown sugar and shortening in bowl. Beat in eggs. Add flour, cinnamon and baking soda; mix well. Stir in pecans. Press into greased bread pan. Chill for 2 hours or overnight. Preheat oven to 350 degrees. Slice dough 1/4 inch thick. Place on cookie sheet. Bake at 350 degrees for 10 minutes. Yield: 3 to 4 dozen.

Delsa Cline, Laureate Beta Omega
Bremerton, Washington

ICEBOX PECAN COOKIES

This was one of my mother's favorite recipes. She baked these cookies every Thanksgiving and Christmas. Whenever I bake these cookies now, I remember my mother and feel I am honoring her memory.

11/2 cups butter or margarine
1 cup packed light brown sugar
1/2 cup sugar
3 eggs
1 teaspoon baking soda
1 teaspoon salt
2 teaspoons cinnamon
4 cups sifted all-purpose flour
1 cup chopped pecans

Cream butter, brown sugar and sugar in mixer bowl until light and fluffy. Add eggs 1 at a time, beating well after each addition. Add sifted mixture of baking soda, salt, cinnamon and flour; mix until blended. Stir in pecans. Shape into logs. Wrap in waxed paper. Chill until ready to bake. Cut into slices. Place on nonstick cookie sheet. Preheat oven to 400 degrees. Bake at 400 degrees for 5 to 8 minutes or until golden brown. Remove to wire rack to cool. Yield: 4 dozen.

Mary Alice White, Beta Zeta Phi
Archer City, Texas

REFRIGERATOR COOKIES

1/2 cup shortening
1/2 cup packed light brown sugar
1/2 cup sugar
1 egg
1/2 teaspoon vanilla extract
1 3/4 cups all-purpose flour
1/2 teaspoon baking soda
1/4 teaspoon salt
1 cup chopped black walnuts

Preheat oven to 400 degrees. Combine shortening, brown sugar, sugar, egg and vanilla in bowl; mix well. Mix in flour, baking soda, salt and walnuts. Shape into logs. Wrap in waxed paper. Chill until firm. Slice 1/8 inch thick. Place on ungreased 12-by-18-inch cookie sheet. Bake at 400 degrees for 8 to 10 minutes or until golden brown. Yield: 6 dozen.

Susan Mancuso, Preceptor Mu Pi
Missouri City, Texas

DATE-FILLED COOKIES

1 cup shortening
1/2 cup each sugar and packed light brown sugar
1 egg, beaten
1 cup all-purpose flour
1 teaspoon baking soda
2 1/2 cups rolled oats
1 1/2 cups finely chopped dates
1/2 cup packed light brown sugar
1 cup water

Preheat oven to 350 degrees. Cream shortening, sugar and 1/2 cup brown sugar in mixer bowl until light and fluffy. Add egg; mix well. Add sifted mixture of flour, baking soda and oats; mix until blended. Roll dough into sheet on floured surface. Cut into thin rounds. Place on greased 12-by-18-inch cookie sheet. Bake at 350 degrees for 10 minutes. Cool completely. Combine dates, 1/2 cup brown sugar and water in saucepan. Bring to a boil. Cook until thickened. Frost tops of half the cookies. Top each with unfrosted cookie. Yield: 1 to 2 dozen.

Kim White, Kappa
Bathurst, New Brunswick, Canada

GINGERBREAD COOKIES

Every year, my family and friends look forward to my gingerbread men cookies!

2/3 cup each packed light brown sugar and molasses
1 teaspoon each ginger and cinnamon
1/2 teaspoon cloves
3/4 tablespoon baking soda
2/3 cup butter or margarine
1 egg
4 cups all-purpose flour

Preheat oven to 325 degrees. Combine brown sugar, molasses, ginger, cinnamon and cloves in saucepan; mix well. Heat just to boiling. Remove from heat. Add baking soda; mix until blended. Pour over butter in large mixer bowl; beat until butter melts. Stir in egg and flour. Knead dough and shape into ball. Chill until firm enough to roll easily. Roll on lightly floured board. Cut into desired shapes. Place on greased 12-by-18-inch cookie sheet. Bake at 325 degrees for 8 minutes. Bake for 10 minutes for crispier cookies. Yield: 2 to 4 dozen.

Anna D. Worrell, Iota Nu
Chesapeake, Virginia

GINGERSNAPS

3/4 cup sugar
3/4 cup margarine, softened
1 egg
1 cup molasses
1 tablespoon vinegar
2 tablespoons cold water
4 cups all-purpose flour
1 tablespoon ginger
1 tablespoon baking soda

Preheat oven to 350 degrees. Combine sugar, margarine and egg in mixer bowl; beat until light and fluffy. Stir in molasses, vinegar and water. Add mixture of flour, ginger and baking soda. Chill for 1 hour. Roll out and cut into desired shapes. Arrange on greased 12-by-18-inch cookie sheet. Bake at 350 degrees for 8 minutes. Yield: 4 to 5 dozen.

Donna Young, Xi Gamma
Winnipeg, Manitoba, Canada

HEARTS

This recipe, handed down from generation to generation for years, has been modified from its original high-fat content, using butter, to a reduced-fat version, using regular cottage cheese, to its present low-fat version, using light cottage cheese.

2 cups margarine
2 cups light or 1% milkfat cottage cheese
1 tablespoon vanilla extract
4 cups all-purpose flour

Preheat oven to 400 degrees. Combine margarine, cottage cheese, vanilla and flour in bowl; mix until crumbly. Shape into ball. Divide into 4 parts. Chill for 1 hour. Roll on floured board, 1 part at a time, to 1/4-inch thickness. Cut into heart shapes with heart cookie cutter. Arrange on ungreased 12-by-18-inch cookie sheet. Bake at 400 degrees for 15 to 20 minutes or until light brown; do not overbake. Cool completely. Frost, if desired, with mixture of confectioners' sugar, milk and vanilla. Yield: 4 dozen.

Janice Waryk, Xi Zeta Zeta
Strongsville, Ohio

Jerry Abshire, Xi Beta Xi, Kaplan, Louisiana, makes German Chocolate Cookies by combining a German chocolate cake mix, 1 cup coconut, 1 cup chopped pecans, 1/4 cup vegetable oil, 1/4 cup water and 1 egg in bowl and mixing well. Drop by tablespoonfuls onto cookie sheet and bake in preheated 350-degree oven for 9 to 11 minutes.

MEXICAN WEDDING COOKIES

1 cup sugar
2 cups shortening
1 teaspoon anise seeds
2 eggs
6 cups sifted all-purpose flour
1 tablespoon baking powder
1 teaspoon salt
1/4 cup water
1 teaspoon cinnamon
1/2 cup sugar

Preheat oven to 350 degrees. Cream 1 cup sugar, shortening and anise seeds in mixer bowl until light and fluffy. Add eggs; beat until blended. Add sifted mixture of next 3 ingredients; mix well. Stir in water. Roll to 1/2-inch thickness on floured surface. Cut into desired shapes. Place on ungreased 12-by-18-inch cookie sheet. Bake at 350 degrees for 10 minutes or until light brown. Roll in mixture of cinnamon and 1/2 cup sugar while warm. Yield: 6 dozen.

Minnie McDonnell, Xi Iota Sigma
Archie, Missouri

OATCAKES

3 cups each all-purpose flour and rolled oats
1 cup sugar
2 teaspoons salt
1 teaspoon baking soda
1 1/4 cups shortening
1 cup cold water

Preheat oven to 350 degrees. Combine flour, oats, sugar, salt, baking soda, shortening and water in large bowl in order listed; mix well. Shape into ball. Sprinkle additional flour and rolled oats on board. Cut dough into 4 sections on board. Roll each to 1/8-inch thickness. Cut into shapes with cookie cutter or knife. Place on nonstick cookie sheet. Bake at 350 degrees for 10 to 15 minutes or until light brown. Serve alone or with date and cheese filling, or top with cream cheese flavored with lemon butter. Yield: 8 dozen.

Marie Gordon, Beta Master
Comox, British Columbia, Canada

FESTIVE SHORTBREAD

My sister gave me this recipe for Christmas shortbread about 23 years ago. I make this shortbread every Christmas and always share it with my sister and mother. I have made as many as 40 dozen of this recipe for one holiday season!

2 cups butter or margarine, softened
1 3/4 cups sifted confectioners' sugar
4 1/2 cups sifted all-purpose flour

Preheat oven to 350 degrees. Cream butter in mixer bowl. Beat in confectioners' sugar gradually until light and fluffy. Add flour a small amount at a time, beating after each addition. Wrap dough in waxed paper and chill. Warm dough slightly; knead for 1 minute. Roll on lightly floured board to 1/4-inch thickness. Cut into shapes with cookie cutter. Arrange on ungreased 12-by-18-inch cookie sheet. Bake at 350 degrees for 15 to 20 minutes or until light brown. Yield: 5 dozen.

Linda Facey, Xi Rho
Kentville, Nova Scotia, Canada

SPRINGERLE

Springerle cookies taste best if kept tightly covered for a few days before serving. I took these cookies to a Valentine's Day cookie exchange by Alpha Omicron. The girls were surprised and delighted at the taste of these cookies; not many had eaten them before.

4 eggs
4 cups sifted confectioners' sugar
20 drops of anise oil
1 teaspoon baking soda
3 1/2 to 4 cups sifted all-purpose flour
Crushed anise seeds to taste

Beat eggs in mixer bowl until light. Add confectioners' sugar gradually; beat until of consistency of soft meringue. Add anise oil; mix well. Add sifted mixture of baking soda and flour; mix until blended. Let stand, tightly covered, for 15 minutes. Divide into thirds. Roll each into 1/4-inch-thick (8-inch) square on floured board. Let stand for 1 minute. Roll or press hard enough to make clear design with floured rolling pin or mold. Cut into cookie shapes with sharp knife. Let stand, covered, on lightly floured surface for 8 hours or longer. Preheat oven to 300 degrees. Sprinkle greased 12-by-18-inch cookie sheets with 1 1/2 to 2 teaspoons crushed anise seeds. Brush excess flour from dough. Rub cold water on undersides of dough. Bake at 350 degrees for 20 minutes or until light straw color. Yield: 6 dozen.

Virginia Ayers, Master Alpha Omicron
Findlay, Ohio

SUGAR COOKIES

1 cup butter or margarine, softened
1 1/2 cups sugar
3 eggs
1 teaspoon vanilla extract
3 1/2 cups sifted all-purpose flour
2 teaspoons cream of tartar
1 teaspoon baking soda
1/2 teaspoon salt

Preheat oven to 375 degrees. Cream butter in mixer bowl until light. Add sugar gradually, beating until fluffy. Beat in eggs 1 at a time. Stir in vanilla. Add sifted mixture of flour, cream of tartar, baking soda and salt; beat until blended. Chill for 3 hours or until firm. Roll on floured surface to 1/8- to 1/4-inch thickness. Cut into desired shapes. Arrange on ungreased 12-by-18-inch cookie sheets. Bake at 375 degrees for 6 to 8 minutes or until light brown. Cool slightly on baking sheets. Remove to wire rack to cool completely. May decorate with red cinnamon candies, candy decorettes or colored sugar while warm or frost with ornamental frosting or confectioners' sugar when cool. Yield: 8 dozen thin cookies.

LeAnna Mullins, Beta Kappa
Whitesburg, Kentucky

BEST SUGAR COOKIES

1/2 cup sour cream
1 cup margarine, softened
1 cup sugar
2 eggs
1 teaspoon vanilla extract
1/2 teaspoon each baking soda and salt
1 teaspoon baking powder
3 cups all-purpose flour
2 (1-pound) packages confectioners' sugar
1/2 cup margarine
1 teaspoon vanilla extract
Milk to taste

Preheat oven to 375 degrees. Cream sour cream, 1 cup margarine, sugar, eggs and 1 teaspoon vanilla in mixer bowl until smooth. Add mixture of baking soda, salt, baking powder and flour; beat until blended. Dough will be sticky. Chill for 1 hour or longer. Cut into desired shapes about 1/4-inch thick on floured board. Arrange on greased 12-by-18-inch cookie sheet. Bake at 375 degrees for 8 minutes. Do not overbake; underbaking will yield better results. Cool completely. Combine confectioners' sugar, 1/2 cup margarine and 1 teaspoon vanilla in bowl; mix until blended. Add milk to make of spreading consistency. Spread thickly over cookies. Yield: 3 to 4 dozen.

Jolene Whear, Xi Alpha Zeta
Price, Utah

MOM'S BROWN SUGAR COOKIES

1/4 cup (or more) hot water
1 cup packed light brown sugar
1 teaspoon baking soda
1/2 cup shortening
1 teaspoon cinnamon
11/2 cups all-purpose flour

Preheat oven to 350 degrees. Add enough hot water to brown sugar in large bowl to moisten sugar. Add baking soda and shortening; mix well. Stir in mixture of cinnamon and flour. Roll out dough; cut into desired shapes. Arrange on greased 12-by-18-inch cookie sheet. Bake at 350 degrees for 5 to 8 minutes or until browned. Yield: 1 to 2 dozen.

Ruth Kirk, Beta Master
Comox, British Columbia, Canada

CONFECTIONERS' SUGAR COOKIES

1 cup vegetable oil
1 cup margarine, softened
1 cup sugar
1 cup confectioners' sugar
2 eggs
2 teaspoons vanilla extract
5 cups all-purpose flour
1 teaspoon baking soda
1 teaspoon cream of tartar

Preheat oven to 350 degrees. Combine oil, margarine, sugar, confectioners' sugar and eggs in large bowl; mix well. Stir in vanilla. Sift flour, baking soda and cream of tartar together. Add to creamed mixture; mix well. Shape into walnut-size balls Place on nonstick cookie sheet. Flatten each ball with bottom of glass dipped in sugar. Bake at 350 degrees for 7 to 8 minutes or until light brown. Yield: 41/2 to 5 dozen.

Lori Henry, Gamma Xi
Fulton, Missouri

GRANDMA'S SUGAR COOKIES

1/2 cup butter-flavored shortening
11/2 cups sugar
3 egg yolks or 2 eggs
3 tablespoons milk
1 teaspoon vanilla extract
1/2 teaspoon almond extract
4 cups all-purpose flour
1 teaspoon baking soda
1 teaspoon cream of tartar
1/2 teaspoon salt

Preheat oven to 375 degrees. Combine shortening, sugar, egg yolks, milk, vanilla and almond extract in bowl; beat until light and fluffy. Add flour, baking soda, cream of tartar and salt; mix until blended. Chill for 1 hour or longer. Roll dough on floured surface. Cut into desired shapes. Arrange on greased 12-by-18-inch cookie sheet. Bake at 375 degrees for 8 to 10 minutes or until light brown.
Yield: 4 to 5 dozen.

Patricia Varga, Xi Beta Beta
Lincoln, Nebraska

GUILT-LESS SUGAR COOKIES

1/4 to 1/2 cup butter or margarine, softened
1/2 to 3/4 cup applesauce
1 cup sugar
2 egg whites
1 teaspoon vanilla extract
2 teaspoons baking powder
3 cups all-purpose flour
1/2 cup melted semisweet chocolate chips
Cookie decorations

Preheat oven to 400 degrees. Combine butter, applesauce and sugar in mixer bowl; mix well. Add egg whites and vanilla; beat until blended. Add baking powder and flour, 1 cup at a time; beat until blended. Do not chill dough. Divide into 2 balls. Roll each to about 1/8-inch thickness on floured board. Cut into heart shapes with cookie cutters. Place on lightly greased cookie sheet. Bake at 400 degrees for 6 to 7 minutes or until light brown. Dip 1/2 of each heart in melted chocolate. Sprinkle chocolate side with cookie decorations. Yield: 3 to 4 dozen.

Linda Knox, Epsilon Xi
Page, Arizona

OLD-FASHIONED SUGAR COOKIES

My married daughter still loves these cookies served at the end of a home-cooked meal. She says they are the best she ever tasted.

1/2 cup butter or margarine, softened
3/4 cup sugar
1 egg
1/2 teaspoon vanilla extract
1 teaspoon grated orange rind
2 cups all-purpose flour
1/4 teaspoon salt
1/2 teaspoon baking powder
2 to 3 tablespoons milk

Preheat oven to 375 degrees. Cream butter and sugar in mixer bowl until light and fluffy. Add egg; beat until blended. Mix in vanilla and orange rind. Add sifted mixture of flour, salt and baking powder alternately with milk; mix well. Chill dough until firm. Roll to 1/8-inch thickness on floured surface. Cut with 4- to 5-inch cookie cutter. Arrange on greased 12-by-18-inch cookie sheet. Sprinkle with additional sugar. Bake at 375 degrees for 12 minutes. Yield: 1 1/2 dozen.

Phyllis Kraich, Preceptor Beta Psi
Akron, Colorado

ROLL-OUT SUGAR COOKIES

I used special cookie cutters for these cookies every holiday season for my children, and now do the same for my grandson.

1/2 cup melted shortening
3/4 cup sugar
2 eggs, beaten
1 teaspoon vanilla extract
2 cups all-purpose flour
2 teaspoons baking powder
1/2 teaspoon salt

Mix shortening and sugar in bowl until blended. Add eggs and vanilla; mix well. Stir in flour, baking powder and salt. Chill for 8 hours or longer. Preheat oven to 350 degrees. Roll dough on floured surface; cut into desired shapes with cookie cutter. Arrange on greased 12-by-18-inch cookie sheet. Bake at 350 degrees for 8 minutes. Cool completely. Ice with confectioners' sugar icing. Yield: 2 dozen.

Dorothy B. Redpath, Alpha Omicron Master
Findlay, Ohio

SPICY SUGAR COOKIES

1 teaspoon baking soda
1 cup sour milk or buttermilk
2 cups sugar
1/2 cup butter or margarine, softened
1/2 cup shortening
2 eggs
1 teaspoon vanilla or lemon extract
1 teaspoon nutmeg
2 teaspoons baking powder
1 teaspoon salt
5 to 6 cups all-purpose flour

Preheat oven to 350 degrees. Dissolve baking soda in sour milk. Combine with sugar, butter, shortening, eggs, vanilla, nutmeg, baking powder, salt and flour in bowl in order listed; mix until well blended. Roll out dough. Cut into desired shapes. Arrange on greased 12-by-18-inch cookie sheets. Bake at 350 degrees for 10 to 12 minutes or until light brown at edges and bottoms. Frost with favorite frosting. Yield: 3 dozen.

Teresa Keele, Beta Sigma Phi
Show Low, Arizona

TEA BISCUITS

Tea biscuits are a Newfoundlander's favorite—especially with a bit of homemade jam.

1 egg or 2 egg whites
Skim milk to taste
2 cups all-purpose flour
4 teaspoons baking powder
1/4 cup sugar or 6 to 8 packets artificial sweetener
1/2 cup diet butter or margarine, softened
1/2 cup raisins

Preheat oven to 375 degrees. Beat egg in mixer bowl with enough skim milk to make 3/4 cup. Combine flour, baking powder and sugar in bowl. Cut in butter until crumbly. Stir in raisins. Add egg mixture; beat until blended. Add small amount of skim milk if mixture is too dry. Roll dough on lightly floured surface to 1/2-inch thickness. Cut into rounds. Place on lightly greased 12-by-18-inch cookie sheet. Bake at 375 degrees for 15 minutes. Yield: 2 to 3 dozen.

Helen Pollock, Preceptor Eta
Lewisporte, Newfoundland, Canada

ALMOND BISCOTTI

2 cups all-purpose flour
1 cup sugar
1 teaspoon baking powder
1/8 teaspoon salt
2 eggs, lightly beaten
1/4 cup melted butter or margarine
1 teaspoon vanilla extract
3/4 cup chopped toasted almonds

Preheat oven to 350 degrees. Combine flour, sugar, baking powder and salt in bowl. Add eggs, butter and vanilla; mix until crumbly. Stir in almonds. Knead until smooth. Divide dough in half. Roll into 1 1/2-by-13-inch logs. Place on 12-by-18-inch cookie sheet. Bake at 350 degrees for 30 minutes or until firm. Cool on wire rack for 10 minutes. Slice logs diagonally 1/2 inch thick with serrated knife. Arrange cut-side down on greased 12-by-18-inch cookie sheet. Bake for 5 to 6 minutes per side or until golden brown. Yield: 4 dozen.

Amy Beth Blue, Chi Psi
Marseilles, Illinois

ALMOND PUFFS

1/2 cup margarine
1 cup all-purpose flour
2 tablespoons water
1/2 cup margarine
1 cup water
1 teaspoon almond extract
1 cup all-purpose flour
3 eggs
1 1/2 cups confectioners' sugar
2 tablespoons margarine, softened
1 to 1 1/2 teaspoons almond extract or 1/2 teaspoon vanilla extract
1 to 2 tablespoons warm water
Almonds to taste

Preheat oven to 350 degrees. Cut 1/2 cup margarine into 1 cup flour in bowl until crumbly. Sprinkle 2 tablespoons water over mixture; mix well. Shape into ball and divide in half. Pat each half into 3-by-12-inch strip on ungreased 12-by-18-inch cookie sheet; arrange strips about 3 inches apart. Combine 1/2 cup margarine and 1 cup water in saucepan. Bring to a rolling boil over medium heat. Remove from heat. Stir in 1 teaspoon almond extract and 1 cup flour. Return to heat. Cook over low heat until mixture forms ball, stirring vigorously. Remove from heat. Add eggs all at one time; beat until smooth. Spread evenly over strips. Bake at 350 degrees for 1 hour or until topping is crisp and brown. Cool completely. Combine confectioners' sugar, 2 tablespoons margarine and 1 teaspoon almond extract in bowl. Add enough warm water to make of spreading consistency; mix until smooth. Spread over cookies. Sprinkle generously with almonds.
Yield: 1 to 2 dozen.

Betty Snowadzki, Alpha Xi
Spruce Grove, Alberta, Canada

AMISH WHITE COOKIES

1 cup sugar
1 cup confectioners' sugar
1 cup margarine, softened
1 cup vegetable oil
2 eggs
1 teaspoon vanilla extract
1/4 teaspoon almond extract
4 1/2 cups sifted all-purpose flour
1 teaspoon baking soda
1 teaspoon cream of tartar
1/2 teaspoon salt

Preheat oven to 350 degrees. Combine sugar, confectioners' sugar, margarine and oil in bowl; mix well. Mix in eggs. Add vanilla, almond extract, flour, baking soda, cream of tartar and salt; mix until blended. Shape dough into small balls. Place on ungreased 12-by-18-inch cookie sheet. Flatten with fork. Bake at 350 degrees for 15 minutes. Yield: 6 dozen.

Cheryl Crouch, Alpha Alpha Mu
Lee's Summit, Missouri

BUTTER DREAM COOKIES

1/2 cup butter or margarine, softened
1/2 cup shortening
1/2 cup sugar
1 teaspoon almond extract
2 1/2 cups all-purpose flour
48 maraschino cherries

Preheat oven to 350 degrees. Cream butter and shortening in mixer bowl until light and fluffy. Add sugar gradually; mix well. Blend in almond extract. Add flour gradually; beat until blended. Shape into balls, using 1 level tablespoon for each ball. Press a cherry into each ball. Place on ungreased 12-by-18-inch cookie sheet. Bake at 350 degrees for 8 to 10 minutes or until browned. Yield: 4 dozen.

Barbara Hall, Preceptor Xi
Baxter Springs, Kansas

CHOCOLATE BUTTER SWEETS

1/2 cup butter or margarine, softened
1/2 cup confectioners' sugar
1/4 teaspoon salt
1 teaspoon vanilla extract
1 cup all-purpose flour
1 cup confectioners' sugar
3 ounces cream cheese, softened
1 teaspoon vanilla extract
2 tablespoons all-purpose flour
1/2 cup chopped walnuts
1/2 cup flaked coconut
1/2 cup semisweet chocolate chips
2 tablespoons water
2 tablespoons butter or margarine
1/2 cup confectioners' sugar

Preheat oven to 350 degrees. Cream 1/2 cup butter and 1/2 cup confectioners' sugar in mixer bowl until light and fluffy. Add salt and 1 teaspoon vanilla; mix well. Stir in 1 cup flour. Shape into balls. Place on ungreased 12-by-18-inch cookie sheet. Press hole in each. Bake at 350 degrees for 12 to 15 minutes or until light brown. Cream 1 cup confectioners' sugar, cream cheese and 1 teaspoon vanilla in mixer bowl until light and fluffy. Add 2 tablespoons flour gradually; mix well. Stir in walnuts and coconut. Fill holes in cookies with coconut mixture. Combine chocolate chips, 2 tablespoons water, 2 tablespoons butter and 1/2 cup confectioners' sugar in saucepan. Cook over low heat until chips melt and mixture thickens, stirring constantly. Drizzle over cookies. Yield: 2 dozen.

Lesa Speyer, Nu
Lovelock, Nevada

CHOCOLATE CHIP COOKIES

2 cups vegetable oil
1 cup sugar
2 cups packed light brown sugar
4 eggs
1/2 teaspoon salt
2 teaspoons vanilla extract
2 teaspoons baking soda
5 cups all-purpose flour
4 cups semisweet chocolate chips
2 cups chopped walnuts

Preheat oven to 350 degrees. Cream oil, sugar, brown sugar and eggs in mixer bowl until light and fluffy. Stir in salt, vanilla and baking soda. Add flour 1/2 cup at a time, mixing well after each addition. Stir in chocolate chips and walnuts. Shape into walnut-sized balls. Place on greased 12-by-18-inch cookie sheet. Bake at 350 degrees for 12 to 15 minutes or until light brown. Yield: 6 dozen.

Violet Salles, Laureate Rho
Hot Springs, South Dakota

BEST-EVER CHOCOLATE CHIP COOKIES

2 cups butter or margarine, softened
2 cups sugar
2 cups packed light brown sugar
4 eggs
2 teaspoons vanilla extract
1 (7-ounce) milk chocolate bar, grated
4 cups semisweet chocolate chips
3 cups chopped walnuts
5 cups rolled oats, finely crushed
1 teaspoon salt
2 teaspoons baking soda
4 cups all-purpose flour
2 tablespoons baking powder

Cream butter, sugar and brown sugar in large mixer bowl until light and fluffy. Beat in eggs 1 at a time. Add vanilla, grated chocolate, chocolate chips and walnuts; beat well. Add mixture of oats, salt, baking soda, flour and baking powder; mix well. Chill overnight. Preheat oven to 375 degrees. Shape dough into 1-inch balls and place 2 inches apart on ungreased 12-by-18-inch cookie sheet. Bake at 375 degrees for 10 minutes. Cool completely. Store in airtight container. Recipe may be halved. Yield: 9 to 10 dozen.

Norma Archibald, Laureate Sigma
Brookings, Oregon

OATMEAL PEANUT BUTTER CHOCOLATE CHIP COOKIES

1 1/2 cups packed light brown sugar
1 cup creamy peanut butter
3/4 cup margarine, softened
1/3 cup water
1 egg
1 teaspoon vanilla extract
3 cups quick-cooking oats
1 1/2 cups all-purpose flour
1/2 teaspoon baking soda
2 cups semisweet chocolate chips
Sugar to taste

Preheat oven to 350 degrees. Cream brown sugar, peanut butter and margarine in large mixer bowl until light and fluffy. Add water, egg and vanilla; mix well. Mix in oats, flour and baking soda. Stir in chocolate chips. Chill for 1/2 hour or until firm. Shape into 1-inch balls. Place on ungreased 12-by-18-inch cookie sheet. Flatten balls. Sprinkle with sugar. Bake at 350 degrees for 8 to 10 minutes or until light brown. Yield: 5 dozen.

Kay Black, Zeta Nu
Sherman, Texas

PASTEL CREAM CHEESE COOKIES

1 cup margarine, softened
3 ounces cream cheese, softened
1 cup sugar
1 egg yolk
1 teaspoon vanilla extract
2 1/4 cups all-purpose flour
Food coloring

Preheat oven to 375 degrees. Cream margarine, cream cheese, sugar, egg yolk and vanilla in mixer bowl until light and fluffy. Beat in flour. Divide into 2 equal parts. Add a different food coloring to each; mix well. Roll into balls with tablespoon; flatten into rounds 2 inches apart on greased 12-by-18-inch cookie sheet. Bake at 375 degrees for 8 to 10 minutes or until golden at edges. Remove to wire rack to cool. Yield: 5 dozen.

Virginia Leclair, Preceptor Alpha Phi
Kinston, North Carolina

DANISH KRINGLA

This is one of my grandmother's favorites and ours, too.

1 cup buttermilk
1/2 cup margarine, softened
1 cup sugar
1 egg, beaten
3 1/2 cups all-purpose flour
1 teaspoon baking soda
2 teaspoons baking powder
1 teaspoon vanilla extract
1/2 teaspoon salt

Preheat oven to 400 degrees. Combine buttermilk, margarine, sugar, egg, flour, baking soda, baking powder, vanilla and salt in large bowl; mix well. Add additional 1/2 cup flour if dough is not stiff. Cover with waxed paper. Chill until firm. Roll dough into walnut-sized balls. Shape into figure 8's on greased 12-by-18-inch cookie sheet. Bake at 400 degrees for 10 minutes. Yield: 4 dozen.

Susan Rundlett, Preceptor Epsilon Phi
Miami, Florida

"FRENCH LOVE" COOKIES

1 cup butter, softened
1/4 cup sugar
1 teaspoon vanilla extract
1/2 teaspoon salt
2 cups all-purpose flour
1 cup finely chopped pecans
1/2 cup confectioners' sugar

Preheat oven to 325 degrees. Combine butter, sugar, vanilla and salt in bowl; mix well. Stir in flour and pecans. Shape into walnut-sized balls. Flatten tops with glass dipped in sugar. Place on ungreased 12-by-18-inch cookie sheet. Bake at 325 degrees for 20 to 30 minutes or until light brown; do not overbake. Remove to wire rack to cool. Sprinkle with confectioners' sugar. Do not use margarine in this recipe. Store in airtight container. Yield: 30 servings.

Shirley Jones, Laureate Beta Mu
Shingletown, California

FROSTED PARTY COOKIES

1 cup butter or margarine, softened
5 tablespoons confectioners' sugar
2 cups all-purpose flour
1/2 teaspoon vanilla extract
1 cup ground pecans
1 teaspoon water
1 cup (or more) confectioners' sugar
3 tablespoons shortening
1 egg white

Preheat oven to 350 degrees. Combine butter, 5 tablespoons confectioners' sugar, flour, vanilla, pecans and water in large bowl; mix well. Chill for at least 1/2 hour. Roll into 3/4- to 1-inch balls. Flatten slightly. Place on lightly greased 12-by-18-inch cookie sheet. Bake at 350 degrees for 10 minutes or until light brown. Remove to wire rack to cool. Combine 1 cup confectioners' sugar, shortening and egg white in bowl; mix well. Frost cookie tops. May tint frosting with food coloring. Yield: 30 servings.

Linda Kennedy, Laureate Alpha Alpha
South Charleston, West Virginia

GINGERSNAP COOKIES

3/4 cup butter or margarine, softened
1 cup sugar
1/4 cup light molasses
1 egg, beaten
2 cups all-purpose flour
2 teaspoons baking soda
1/4 teaspoon salt
1 teaspoon cinnamon
1/2 teaspoon each cloves and ginger

Preheat oven to 375 degrees. Combine butter, sugar, molasses, egg, flour, baking soda, salt and spices in large bowl; mix until blended. Shape into small balls. Roll in additional sugar. Place on greased 12-by-18-inch cookie sheet. Bake at 375 degrees for 10 minutes. Yield: 2 to 3 dozen.

Sue Jack, Xi Chi
Butler, Pennsylvania

GINGER SPARKLERS

2 cups all-purpose flour
2 teaspoons baking soda
1/2 teaspoon salt
1 teaspoon each cinnamon and ginger
1/2 teaspoon cloves
1 cup packed light brown sugar
3/4 cup butter or margarine, softened
1/4 cup molasses
1 egg
Sugar to taste

Preheat oven to 375 degrees. Combine flour, baking soda, salt and spices in bowl; mix well. Cream brown sugar, butter, molasses and egg in mixer bowl until light and fluffy. Stir in flour mixture. Shape dough into 1-inch balls. Roll in sugar. Place 2 inches apart on greased 12-by-18-inch cookie sheet. Bake at 375 degrees for 8 to 10 minutes or until light brown. Cool slightly before removing from cookie sheet.
Yield: 5 dozen.

Cathy Markovic, Eta Omicron
Ajax, Ontario, Canada

GUMDROP COOKIES

When I was a child, my mother used to make these cookies as a special treat.

1/2 cup shortening
1/2 cup packed light brown sugar
1/2 cup sugar
1 teaspoon vanilla extract
1 cup sifted all-purpose flour
1/2 teaspoon baking soda
1/2 teaspoon baking powder
1/4 teaspoon salt
1 egg, beaten
1/2 cup each grated coconut, chopped nuts and small gumdrops
1 cup quick-cooking oats

Preheat oven to 350 degrees. Combine shortening, brown sugar, sugar and vanilla in mixer bowl; beat until light and fluffy. Add sifted mixture of flour, baking soda, baking powder and salt alternately with egg. Stir in coconut, nuts, gumdrops and oats. Pinch off small pieces of dough; roll into 1-inch balls. Flatten with bottom of cup dipped in milk. Bake at 350 degrees for 10 minutes. Yield: 3 to 4 dozen.

Theresa Darst
Ennis, Texas

Peggy Matrone, Delta Masters, North Muskegon, Michigan makes Ginger Cookies by creaming 1/2 cup margarine, 1 cup sugar, 1 egg and 1/4 cup molasses, adding 2 cups all-purpose flour, 1 teaspoon cinnamon, 2 teaspoons baking soda, 1/4 teaspoon salt and 3/4 teaspoon each cloves and ginger and mixing well. Add 1/2 cup raisins or nuts if desired, shape into balls and bake in preheated 350-degree oven for 10 to 14 minutes.

KOURAMBIATHES (GREEK COOKIES)

1 cup butter or margarine, softened
1 egg yolk
2 tablespoons anise flavoring
1/4 cup confectioners' sugar
2 1/2 cups all-purpose flour
Confectioners' sugar to taste

Preheat oven to 350 degrees. Combine butter, egg yolk and anise in bowl; mix until frothy. Add 1/4 cup confectioners' sugar and flour; mix until blended. Shape dough into crescents. Place on greased 12-by-18-inch cookie sheet. Bake at 350 degrees for 20 minutes; do not overbake. Sprinkle heavily with confectioners' sugar. Yield: 2 to 3 dozen.

Sophia McMillon, Preceptor Alpha Gamma
Horseshoe Bend, Arkansas

LADY LOCKS COOKIES

I first tasted these wonderful cookies when I was in a friend's wedding many years ago. It has taken 25 years of searching to find the recipe for them. This is a "must" recipe for our Christmas Cookie Exchange each year.

4 cups all-purpose flour
1 1/4 cups shortening
1 tablespoon sugar
2 teaspoons baking powder
2 eggs
2 teaspoons vanilla extract
1 package dry yeast
1 cup lukewarm milk
1/2 cup each all-purpose flour and sugar
1 cup milk
2 tablespoons cornstarch
1/2 cup margarine, softened
1/2 cup shortening
3/4 cup sugar
1 teaspoon vanilla extract

Preheat oven to 350 degrees. Combine 4 cups flour, 1 1/4 cups shortening, 1 tablespoon sugar and baking powder in bowl; cut with pastry blender until crumbly. Add eggs and 2 teaspoons vanilla; mix well. Dissolve yeast in 1/2 cup milk. Add to flour mixture alternately with remaining 1/2 cup milk; mix well. Roll small portions of dough at a time in mixture of 1/2 cup flour and 1/2 cup sugar. Cut into 1/2-inch strips about 6 inches long. Roll around foil-wrapped clothespins. Arrange on greased 12-by-18-inch cookie sheet. Bake at 350 degrees for 15 minutes or until light brown. Remove from oven. Remove clothespins. Cool. Combine 1 cup milk and cornstarch in saucepan. Cook over low heat until thickened. Cool. Cream margarine and 1/2 cup shortening in mixer bowl until light and fluffy. Add 3/4 cup sugar and 1 teaspoon vanilla; mix thoroughly. Beat in cornstarch mixture. Use cookie press with fill tip or pastry bag with large tip to fill each cookie shell. Sprinkle with additional confectioners' sugar. Yield: 5 dozen.

R. Sue Chase, Laureate Lambda
Port St. Lucie, Florida

MOCK COCONUT MACAROONS

This is a great recipe for those who aren't able to eat coconut but like its flavor.

1 1/3 cups buttermilk baking mix
1 1/4 cups instant potato flakes
1/2 cup melted margarine
1 cup sugar
1 egg
1 to 2 teaspoons coconut extract

Combine baking mix, potato flakes, margarine, sugar, egg and coconut extract in large bowl; mix well. Chill for 1 hour to overnight. Shape into small balls. Place on ungreased 12-by-18-inch cookie sheet. Preheat oven to 350 degrees. Bake at 350 degrees for 8 to 10 minutes or until light brown. Cool on cookie sheet. Yield: 4 to 5 dozen.

Dorothy Amedee, Preceptor Alpha Beta
Terrytown, Louisiana

NUT ROLLS

My grandma Liz taught me how to make these cookies. We now make them at Christmas; my husband and grandmother roll them out and I fill them.

2 cups butter or margarine, softened
4 cups all-purpose flour
16 ounces cream cheese, softened
2 cups finely chopped walnuts
1/2 cup sugar
2 egg whites, beaten

Cream butter, flour and cream cheese in mixer bowl until light and fluffy. Shape into 1/2-inch balls. Stack on waxed paper; place waxed paper between layers. Chill overnight. Preheat oven to 350 degrees. Mix walnuts, sugar and egg whites in bowl. Roll out balls on surface sprinkled with confectioners' sugar. Spread with walnut mixture. Roll into logs; pinch ends together. Place on nonstick cookie sheet. Bake at 350 degrees for 15 minutes. Yield: 4 to 5 dozen.

Kathleen Creamer, Delta Sigma
Louisville, Colorado

ONE HUNDRED BEST COOKIES

1 cup vegetable oil
1 cup sugar
1 egg
3 1/2 cups all-purpose flour
1 teaspoon cream of tartar
1 cup crisp rice cereal
1 cup flaked coconut
1 cup butter or margarine, softened
1 cup packed light brown sugar
1 teaspoon each salt and baking soda
1 cup oats
1 cup chopped walnuts

Preheat oven to 325 degrees. Combine oil, sugar, egg, flour, cream of tartar, cereal, coconut, butter, brown sugar, salt, baking soda, oats and walnuts in large bowl; mix well. Shape into balls. Place on greased 12-by-18-inch cookie sheet. Flatten with fork. Bake at

325 degrees for 15 to 20 minutes or until light brown. Yield: 7 to 8 dozen.

Sandra Badini, Theta Chi
Grand Rapids, Michigan

HOMEMADE OREO COOKIES

My sorority sisters look forward to meetings at my home because I make these delicious cookies for them.

2 (2-layer) packages devil's food cake mix
4 eggs
1 1/2 cups shortening
8 ounces cream cheese, softened
1/2 cup margarine, softened
3 1/2 cups confectioners' sugar
1 teaspoon vanilla extract

Preheat oven to 350 degrees. Combine cake mixes and eggs in large bowl; mix well. Cut in shortening until crumbly. Shape into balls. Place on ungreased 12-by-18- inch cookie sheet. Bake at 350 degrees for 9 minutes or until tops are cracked. Cool completely. Combine cream cheese, margarine, confectioners' sugar and vanilla in bowl; mix well. Spread between 2 cookies. Yield: 5 to 6 dozen.

Rhonda Breuer, Alpha Sigma
Devil's Lake, North Dakota

MY SPECIAL NEIGHBORS' PEANUT BUTTER COOKIES

1 cup shortening
1 cup packed light brown sugar
1 cup sugar
1 cup peanut butter
2 eggs, beaten
1 teaspoon vanilla extract
2 teaspoons baking soda
2 cups sifted all-purpose flour

Preheat oven to 325 degrees. Cream shortening, brown sugar, sugar, peanut butter, eggs and vanilla in large mixer bowl until light and fluffy. Add baking soda and flour 1/2 cup at a time, beating after each addition. Shape into small balls. Place on greased 12-by-18-inch cookie sheet. Flatten slightly with fork. Bake at 325 degrees for 8 to 12 minutes or until light brown. Yield: 5 to 6 dozen.

Sandra G. Burison, Preceptor Theta
Virginia Beach, Virginia

PEANUT BUTTER CHOCOLATE COOKIES

1/2 cup butter or margarine, softened
1/2 cup each sugar and packed light brown sugar
1/4 cup creamy peanut butter
1 egg, lightly beaten
1 teaspoon vanilla extract
1 1/2 cups all-purpose flour
1/2 cup baking cocoa
1/2 teaspoon baking soda
3/4 cup confectioners' sugar
3/4 cup creamy peanut butter

Preheat oven to 375 degrees. Cream butter, sugar, brown sugar and 1/4 cup peanut butter in mixer bowl until light and fluffy. Add egg and vanilla; mix well. Add mixture of flour, cocoa and baking soda; mix well and set aside. Combine confectioners' sugar and 3/4 cup peanut butter in small bowl; mix until blended. Shape into 1-inch balls; flatten. Shape brown sugar mixture into 1-inch balls. Place on peanut butter circles; shape peanut butter circles around brown sugar balls to enclose completely. Place on ungreased 12-by-18-inch cookie sheet. Bake at 375 degrees for 7 to 9 minutes or until golden brown. Let stand for 1 to 2 minutes. Remove to wire rack to cool completely. Yield: 2 dozen.

Patricia Johnson, Laureate Alpha Tau
Sanford, Florida

CHRISTMAS PECAN COOKIES

1 cup butter or margarine, softened
1/2 cup sugar
1 teaspoon vanilla extract
1/4 cup water
2 cups self-rising flour
1 cup chopped pecans
Confectioners' sugar to taste

Preheat oven to 300 degrees. Cream butter and sugar in mixer bowl until light and fluffy. Add vanilla and water; mix well. Add flour and pecans; mix well. Shape into walnut-sized balls. Roll in confectioners' sugar. Place on greased 12-by-18-inch cookie sheet. Bake at 300 degrees for 25 minutes. Let stand until cool. Roll again in confectioners' sugar to coat well. Yield: 3 dozen.

Carolyn J. Southard, Iota Iota
Blairsville, Georgia

POTATO CHIP COOKIES

1 cup butter or margarine, softened
1 teaspoon vanilla extract
1/2 cup sugar
1/2 cup crushed potato chips
1/2 cup finely chopped walnuts
2 cups sifted all-purpose flour
Sugar to taste

Preheat oven to 350 degrees. Cream butter, vanilla and sugar in mixer bowl until light and fluffy. Stir in potato chips and walnuts. Add flour; mix well. Shape into 1-inch balls. Place on ungreased 12-by-18-inch cookie sheet. Flatten with bottom of glass dipped in sugar. Bake at 350 degrees for 12 to 15 minutes or until light brown. Yield: 4 dozen.

Roberta Summers, Delta Omicron
Columbia, South Carolina

PRINCESS GEMS OR COCONUT COOKIES

My aunt, Iris Gerhart, always made these cookies at Christmas. They are so flavorful, unusual and such pretty "white" cookies—they always create conversation!

1 1/2 cups margarine, softened
2 cups sugar
2 teaspoons powdered ammonium carbonate
2 1/2 cups all-purpose flour
1 cup shredded coconut
2 cups confectioners' sugar

Preheat oven to 325 degrees. Cream margarine in mixer bowl until light and fluffy. Add sugar and ammonium carbonate gradually; mix well. Crush ammonium carbonate, if necessary, to blend; avoid breathing fumes. Add flour a little at a time; beat until blended. Stir in coconut. Shape into 3/4-inch balls. Place 1 inch apart on greased 12-by-18-inch cookie sheet. Bake at 325 degrees for 15 minutes or until light brown. Cool slightly. Roll in confectioners' sugar. Yield: 4 dozen.

Nancy D. Zeliff, Mu Lambda
Skidmore, Missouri

THE BEST SUGAR COOKIES

1 cup confectioners' sugar
1 cup sugar
1 cup margarine, softened
1 cup vegetable oil
2 eggs
1 teaspoon each vanilla and almond extracts
1 teaspoon salt
1 teaspoon each baking soda and cream of tartar
4 cups plus 4 tablespoons all-purpose flour
Sugar to taste

Preheat oven to 375 degrees. Cream confectioners' sugar, 1 cup sugar, margarine, oil and eggs in large mixer bowl until light and fluffy. Add vanilla and almond extracts; mix well. Add sifted mixture of next 4 ingredients gradually; mix until blended. Shape into walnut-sized balls. Roll in sugar. Place on ungreased 12-by-18-inch cookie sheet. Flatten to 1/4-inch thickness. Bake at 375 degrees for 10 to 12 minutes or until light brown. Yield: 5 to 6 dozen.

Teresa Braswell, Beta Sigma Phi
Laverne, Oklahoma

WEDDING COOKIES

1 cup butter or margarine, softened
2 cups all-purpose flour
3 tablespoons (heaping) confectioners' sugar
1 1/8 teaspoons vanilla extract
1 cup chopped pecans

Preheat oven to 350 degrees. Cream butter in mixer bowl until light and fluffy. Add flour, confectioners' sugar, vanilla and pecans gradually; mix well. Shape into small balls. Place on ungreased 12-by-18-inch cookie sheet. Bake at 350 degrees for 10 to 15 minutes or until light brown. Roll warm cookies in additional confectioners' sugar. Yield: 3 1/2 to 4 dozen.

Lana Marler, Xi Kappa Kappa
Bismarck, Missouri

APPLE BUTTER COOKIES

1 cup margarine, softened
1 cup packed light brown sugar
1 egg
1/2 cup oats
1/2 cup apple butter
1 cup all-purpose flour
1/2 teaspoon salt
1/2 teaspoon baking powder
1/2 teaspoon baking soda
2 tablespoons milk
1/2 cup chopped walnuts
1/2 cup raisins

Preheat oven to 350 degrees. Cream margarine and brown sugar in large mixer bowl. Add egg, oats and apple butter, mixing well after each addition. Stir in mixture of flour, salt, baking powder and baking soda alternately with milk; beat until blended. Stir in walnuts and raisins. Drop by teaspoonfuls onto nonstick cookie sheet. Bake at 350 degrees for 15 minutes. Yield: 2 1/2 dozen.

Marsha Paris, Mu Psi
Waterford, Pennsylvania

APPLESAUCE COOKIES

1/2 cup low-calorie margarine
Liquid artificial sweetener equal to 1/2 cup sugar
1 teaspoon vanilla extract
1 egg
1 3/4 cups cake flour
1/2 teaspoon salt
1 teaspoon cinnamon
1/2 teaspoon nutmeg
1/2 teaspoon cloves
1 teaspoon baking soda
1 cup unsweetened applesauce
1/3 cup raisins
1 cup bran cereal

Preheat oven to 375 degrees. Cream margarine, artificial sweetener, vanilla and egg in large mixer bowl until light and fluffy. Add sifted mixture of cake flour, salt, cinnamon, nutmeg, cloves and baking soda alternately with applesauce, mixing well after each addition. Stir in raisins and cereal. Drop by teaspoonfuls 1 inch apart onto nonstick cookie sheet. Bake at 375 degrees for 15 to 20 minutes or until browned. Yield: 4 dozen.

LaJuana Saathoff, Xi Sigma Mu
Sierra Blanca, Texas

Angela Ramsey, Nu Kappa, Guthrie, Oklahoma, makes Butterscotch Haystacks by heating 2 cups butterscotch chips and 1 cup crunchy peanut butter in the microwave for 30 seconds at a time until melted and smooth, stirring in a package of chow mein noodles until coated and dropping by spoonfuls onto waxed paper.

SUGAR-FREE APPLESAUCE COOKIES

1 1/2 cups boiling water
1 cup raisins
1 cup all-purpose flour
2 teaspoons cinnamon
1 teaspoon baking soda
1/2 teaspoon salt
1/2 teaspoon nutmeg
1/4 teaspoon ground cloves
1/4 teaspoon allspice
1 cup quick-cooking oats
1 cup unsweetened applesauce
1/2 cup margarine, softened
2 eggs or egg substitute
2 teaspoons vanilla extract
1/2 cup artificial sweetener

Preheat oven to 375 degrees. Pour boiling water over raisins in small bowl. Let stand for 5 minutes. Combine flour, cinnamon, baking soda, salt, nutmeg, cloves and allspice in large mixer bowl. Add oats, applesauce, margarine, eggs, vanilla and artificial sweetener, mixing well after each addition. Drain raisins and add to applesauce mixture. Drop by teaspoonfuls onto lightly greased cookie sheet. Bake at 375 degrees for 10 to 12 minutes or until brown. Store in refrigerator. Yield: 3 dozen.

Joan M. Peterson, Preceptor Beta Theta
Redmond, Washington

APPLESAUCE-OATMEAL-RAISIN COOKIES

1 cup unsweetened applesauce
1 cup packed light brown sugar
1/2 cup sugar
1 (4-ounce) package egg substitute
1 teaspoon vanilla extract
1 1/2 cups all-purpose flour
1 teaspoon baking soda
1 teaspoon ground cinnamon
1/2 teaspoon salt (optional)
3 cups quick-cooking oats
1 cup raisins

Preheat oven to 350 degrees. Beat applesauce, brown sugar and sugar together in large mixer bowl. Add egg substitute and vanilla; mix well. Add mixture of flour, baking soda, cinnamon and salt; mix well. Stir in oats and raisins; mix well. Drop by rounded tablespoonfuls onto 12-by-18-inch cookie sheet sprayed with nonstick cooking spray. Bake at 350 degrees for 12 minutes or until light golden brown.
Yield: 4 dozen.

Sharla Jean White, Gamma
Columbus, Ohio

Dale Holt, Preceptor Theta Omega, Allen, Texas, makes Easy No-Bake Butter Pecan cookies using a 16-ounce tub of butter pecan frosting mixed with 16 ounces sugar cookie crumbs, shaped into balls and rolled in coconut.

BILLY GOAT COOKIES

This recipe has been a Christmas tradition in my family for more than 25 years. When my mother, a former Beta Sigma Phi, made them every year, my job was to "do the raisins." Now my daughter, Shannon, a legacy member, helps me make these Christmas treats.

1 (15-ounce) package raisins
1 cup water
1 teaspoon baking soda
1 cup butter or margarine, softened
3 eggs
4 cups all-purpose flour
2 cups sugar
1 teaspoon cinnamon
1 teaspoon nutmeg
1 teaspoon baking powder
1 teaspoon vanilla extract

Preheat oven to 400 degrees. Bring raisins and water to a boil in small saucepan; reduce heat. Simmer for 5 minutes. Remove from heat. Let stand until cool. Dissolve baking soda in raisin mixture. Beat butter and eggs in large mixer bowl until smooth. Add mixture of flour, sugar, cinnamon, nutmeg and baking powder; mix well. Stir in vanilla and raisin mixture; mix well. Drop by spoonfuls onto ungreased cookie sheet. Bake at 400 degrees for 15 minutes or until light brown. Yield: 3 to 4 dozen.

Barbie Stombock, Xi Alpha Eta
Luray, Virginia

BUFFALO COOKIES

1 cup butter-flavored shortening
1 cup sugar
1 cup firmly packed light brown sugar
2 tablespoons milk
1 teaspoon vanilla extract
2 eggs
2 cups all-purpose flour
1 teaspoon baking soda
1 teaspoon baking powder
1/2 teaspoon salt
1 cup quick-cooking oats or rolled oats
1/2 cup crushed cornflakes
1 cup semisweet chocolate chips
1/2 cup chopped pecans
1/2 cup flaked coconut

Preheat oven to 350 degrees. Mix shortening, sugar, brown sugar, milk and vanilla in large mixer bowl. Beat on low speed until blended. Add eggs and beat at medium speed until blended. Add mixture of flour, baking soda, baking powder and salt; mix at low speed. Stir in oats, cornflakes, chocolate chips, pecans and coconut with spoon. Fill 1/4 cup ice cream scoop or 1/4 cup measure with dough. Level off with knife. Drop 3 inches apart onto cookie sheet greased with butter-flavored shortening. Bake at 350 degrees for 13 to 15 minutes or until light brown on edges and slightly soft in center. Cool on cookie sheet for 3 minutes; remove to wire rack to cool completely. Yield: 2 to 2 1/2 dozen.

Cynthia K. Finleyson, Preceptor Alpha Rho
Brunswick, Georgia

BUTTER CRUNCH COOKIES

1 cup all-purpose flour
1/4 teaspoon baking powder
1/2 teaspoon baking soda
2/3 cup butter or margarine, softened
1 cup packed light brown sugar
1 egg
1 teaspoon vanilla extract
3/4 cup oats
1 cup flaked coconut
1 cup cornflakes

Preheat oven to 350 degrees. Sift flour, baking powder and baking soda together. Cream butter, brown sugar, egg and vanilla in mixer bowl. Stir in flour mixture. Stir in oats, coconut and cornflakes. Drop by rounded spoonfuls 2 inches apart onto ungreased cookie sheet. Bake at 350 degrees for 10 to 12 minutes or until browned. Yield: 3 1/2 dozen.

Irene Hess, Beta Mu
Scarborough, Ontario, Canada

CARROT COOKIES

1 cup shortening
3/4 cup sugar
1 egg
1/2 teaspoon lemon extract
1 (16-ounce) can diced carrots, drained
1/2 teaspoon salt
2 teaspoons baking powder
2 cups all-purpose flour
1/2 cup chopped pecans
1 (1-pound) package confectioners' sugar
1 tablespoon margarine, softened
Juice and grated rind of 1 orange
1/2 teaspoon lemon extract

Preheat oven to 350 degrees. Cream shortening and sugar in large mixer bowl until light and fluffy. Add egg, lemon extract and carrots, mixing well after each addition. Add mixture of salt, baking powder and flour; mix well. Stir in pecans. Drop by spoonfuls onto greased cookie sheet. Bake at 350 degrees for 15 minutes. Combine remaining ingredients in small mixer bowl; mix well. Spread over warm cookies. Yield: 5 dozen.

Charlotte McReynolds, Nu Epsilon
Boise City, Oklahoma

CARROT RAISIN COOKIES

1 cup all-purpose flour
1 cup natural bran
1/4 cup packed light brown sugar
2 teaspoons baking powder
1 teaspoon ground cinnamon
1/2 teaspoon salt
1/2 cup grated carrot
1/4 cup chopped raisins
2/3 cup 2% milk
1 egg
2 tablespoons melted margarine
1 teaspoon vanilla extract
1 tablespoon molasses

Preheat oven to 400 degrees. Combine dry ingredients in large bowl. Stir in carrot and raisins. Beat milk, egg, margarine, vanilla and molasses in small mixer bowl. Pour into a well made in flour mixture. Mix just until moistened; batter will be rough and lumpy. Drop by rounded tablespoonfuls 2 inches apart onto lightly greased cookie sheet. Bake at 400 degrees for 18 minutes. Yield: 2 dozen.

Anne Fleming, Alpha Eta
Nanton, Alberta, Canada

CREATE-A-COOKIE

1 cup butter or margarine, softened
1 1/4 cups packed light brown sugar
2 eggs
1/2 teaspoon vanilla extract
1 1/2 cups all-purpose flour
1 teaspoon baking soda
1/2 teaspoon salt
1/2 teaspoon cinnamon
3 cups oats

Preheat oven to 350 degrees. Beat butter and brown sugar in mixer bowl until light and fluffy. Blend in eggs and vanilla. Add mixture of flour, baking soda, salt and cinnamon; mix well. Stir in oats. Drop by rounded teaspoonfuls onto greased cookie sheet. Bake at 350 degrees for 10 to 12 minutes or until brown. Create a **Spicy Cookie:** Add 1/4 teaspoon each of nutmeg and cloves. Create a **Raisin Cookie:** Add 1 cup raisins. Create a **Nutty Cookie:** Add 1 cup chopped peanuts or cashews. Create a **Chocolate Cookie:** Add 1 cup semisweet chocolate chips. Create a **Fruity Cookie:** Add 1/2 cup chopped dried apricots, dates or mixed dried candied fruit. Create a **Coconut Cookie:** Add 1 cup shredded or flaked coconut. Create a **Sunflower Cookie:** Add 1/2 cup sunflower seeds. Create a **Hermit Cookie:** Add 1 cup raisins, 1/2 cup coconut, 1 teaspoon cinnamon, 1/2 teaspoon cloves, 1/2 teaspoon nutmeg and 1 cup chopped nuts. Yield: 5 1/2 dozen.

Maralyne Roberts, Preceptor Delta Epsilon

CHERRY COOKIES

1 cup butter or margarine, softened
2 cups sugar
3 eggs
1 teaspoon vanilla extract
1 teaspoon almond extract (optional)
3 cups all-purpose flour
2 teaspoons cream of tartar
1 teaspoon baking soda
1 teaspoon salt
2 3/4 cups raisins
1 cup chopped glacé cherries

Preheat oven to 350 degrees. Cream butter and sugar in large mixer bowl until light and fluffy. Add eggs, vanilla and almond extract; mix well. Add sifted mixture of flour, cream of tartar, baking soda and salt; mix well. Stir in raisins and cherries. Drop by spoonfuls onto nonstick cookie sheet. Bake at 350 degrees for 15 minutes. Yield: 3 dozen.

Kelly Carty Meghezi, Theta
Moose Jaw, Saskatchewan, Canada

BROWNIE-OAT COOKIES

2/3 cup all-purpose flour
1/3 cup sugar
1/3 cup artificial sweetener
1 cup quick-cooking oats
1/4 cup baking cocoa
1 teaspoon baking powder
2 egg whites
1/3 cup light corn syrup
1 teaspoon vanilla extract

Preheat oven to 350 degrees. Combine flour, sugar, artificial sweetener, oats, cocoa and baking powder in large mixer bowl; mix well. Stir in egg whites, corn syrup and vanilla, mixing just until moistened. Drop by teaspoonfuls onto cookie sheet sprayed with nonstick cooking spray. Bake at 350 degrees for 10 minutes or until set. Cool on cookie sheet for 2 minutes; remove to wire rack to cool completely. Yield: 2 dozen.

Constance J. Verity, Preceptor Eta Phi
Melbourne, Florida

CHOCOLATE CHIP COOKIES

2 cups butter or margarine, softened
2 1/4 cups packed dark brown sugar
1 1/2 cups sugar
2 tablespoons vanilla extract
3 eggs
6 cups all-purpose flour
1 1/2 teaspoons baking soda
4 cups semisweet chocolate chips
2 cups chopped walnuts (optional)

Preheat oven to 350 degrees. Cream butter, brown sugar and sugar in large mixer bowl until light and fluffy. Add vanilla and eggs; beat for 3 minutes. Add mixture of flour and baking soda gradually; mix well. Stir in chocolate chips and walnuts. Drop by spoonfuls onto foil-covered cookie sheet. Bake at 350 degrees for 10 to 15 minutes or until browned. Yield: 6 to 7 dozen.

Cassandra Deras, Preceptor Lambda Tau
Bakersfield, California

CRUNCHY CHOCOLATE CHIP COOKIES

1 cup butter or margarine, softened
1 cup sugar
1 cup packed light brown sugar
2 eggs
2 teaspoons vanilla extract
1 1/2 cups all-purpose flour
1 teaspoon baking powder
1 teaspoon baking soda
2 cups rolled oats
1 cup flaked coconut
2 cups crisp rice cereal
1 cup semisweet chocolate chips

Preheat oven to 325 degrees. Cream butter, sugar, brown sugar, eggs and vanilla in large mixer bowl until smooth. Add sifted mixture of flour, baking powder and baking soda; mix well. Stir in oats, coconut, cereal and chocolate chips. Drop by spoonfuls onto greased cookie sheet. Bake at 325 degrees for 12 to 15 minutes or until brown. Yield: 2 to 3 dozen.

Joanne Eek, Xi Delta Theta
Rock Creek, British Columbia, Canada

DOUBLE CHOCOLATE CHIP COOKIES

1 cup margarine, softened
3/4 cup packed light brown sugar
1 cup sugar
2 eggs
2 teaspoons vanilla extract
1 1/2 cups rolled oats
1 teaspoon baking soda
1 teaspoon baking powder
1 1/2 cups semisweet chocolate chips
4 ounces white chocolate

Preheat oven to 370 degrees. Cream margarine, brown sugar and sugar in large mixer bowl until light and fluffy. Beat in eggs and vanilla. Process oats in blender until of powder consistency; add to sugar mixture. Mix in baking soda, baking powder and chocolate chips. Drop by large spoonfuls onto greased cookie sheet. Soften white chocolate slightly in microwave. Cut into small chunks. Place chunk in center of each cookie. Bake at 370 degrees for 9 to 12 minutes. Yield: 4 dozen.

Jean Flintoft, Xi Gamma Omega
Quesnel, British Columbia, Canada

DOUBLE CHOCOLATE DELIGHTS

1 1/4 cups margarine, softened
2 cups sugar
2 eggs
2 teaspoons vanilla extract
2 cups all-purpose flour
3/4 cup baking cocoa
1 teaspoon baking soda
1/2 teaspoon salt
2 cups semisweet chocolate chips

Preheat oven to 350 degrees. Cream margarine, sugar, eggs and vanilla in large mixer bowl. Add mixture of flour, cocoa, baking soda and salt; mix well. Stir in chocolate chips. Drop by spoonfuls onto ungreased cookie sheet. Bake at 350 degrees for 8 to 9 minutes or until soft and puffy; do not overbake. Yield: 5 dozen.

Rose Snyder, Theta Alpha
Cache Creek, British Columbia, Canada

Evelyn Butker, Laureate Alpha Alpha, Charleston, West Virginia, makes Iowa Brownies by creaming 1/2 cup margarine, 1 cup sugar, adding one 16-ounce can chocolate syrup, 4 eggs one at a time, 1 cup all-purpose flour and 1 1/2 cups chopped walnuts. Bake in well-greased 9-by-13-inch pan in preheated 350-degree oven for 25 minutes. Frost with mixture of 1/2 cup margarine, 1 1/2 cups sugar and 1/2 cup evaporated milk boiled for 3 minutes and 1/3 cup semisweet chocolate chips and 1 teaspoon vanilla beaten in until smooth.

NO-GUILT CHOCOLATE CHIP COOKIES

This recipe was made for high-altitude baking; you may need to adjust the flour and oatmeal portions. These are very moist and delicious cookies.

- ***3/4 cup packed light brown sugar***
- ***1/2 cup sugar***
- ***3/4 cup applesauce***
- ***2 eggs or 1/2 cup egg substitute***
- ***2 1/4 cups all-purpose flour***
- ***1 teaspoon baking soda***
- ***1 cup oats***
- ***1/2 teaspoon salt (optional)***
- ***1 1/2 cups semisweet chocolate chips***

Preheat oven to 375 degrees. Beat the brown sugar, sugar and applesauce in large mixer bowl until well blended. Add eggs; mix well. Stir in mixture of flour, baking soda, oats and salt; mix well. Stir in chocolate chips by hand. Drop by spoonfuls onto cookie sheets sprayed with nonstick cooking spray. Bake at 375 degrees for 6 1/2 minutes. Yield: 45 cookies.

Hrefna Valdis Boyd, Alpha Iota
Gardnerville, Nevada

TEXAS GIANT CHOCOLATE CHIP COOKIES

These cookies are a big hit with everyone—especially my 5 grandsons.

- ***2/3 cup butter or margarine***
- ***1 1/4 cups packed light brown sugar***
- ***3/4 cup sugar***
- ***3 eggs, beaten***
- ***1 1/2 cups chunky peanut butter***
- ***6 cups rolled oats***
- ***2 teaspoons baking soda***
- ***1 1/2 cups raisins***
- ***2 cups semisweet chocolate chips***

Preheat oven to 350 degrees. Melt butter in large saucepan over low heat. Add brown sugar, sugar, eggs and peanut butter, blending after each addition until smooth. Add oats, baking soda, raisins and chocolate chips, stirring by hand. Drop onto greased cookie sheet using ice cream scoop or large spoon. Flatten cookies slightly. Bake at 350 degrees for 15 minutes or until browned. Yield: 2 to 3 dozen.

Maureen B. Staller, Alpha Pi Master
El Campo, Texas

WALNUT CHOCOLATE CHIP COOKIES

- ***1 cup margarine, softened***
- ***1 cup sugar***
- ***1 cup packed light brown sugar***
- ***2 eggs***
- ***1 teaspoon vanilla extract***
- ***2 1/2 cups rolled oats***
- ***2 cups all-purpose flour***
- ***1/2 teaspoon salt***
- ***1 teaspoon baking powder***
- ***1 teaspoon baking soda***
- ***2 cups semisweet chocolate chips***
- ***1 1/2 cups chopped walnuts***

Preheat oven to 375 degrees. Cream margarine, sugar and brown sugar in large mixer bowl until smooth. Blend in eggs and vanilla. Process oats in blender until of powder consistency. Add mixture of flour, oats, salt, baking powder and baking soda to sugar mixture; mix well. Stir in chocolate chips and walnuts. Drop by tablespoonfuls onto ungreased cookie sheet. Bake at 375 degrees for 8 to 10 minutes or until browned; do not overbake. Yield: 3 to 4 dozen.

Cheri Nieshe-Miller, Xi Beta Beta
Mt. Vernon, Washington

CHOCOLATE MARSHMALLOW COOKIES

This recipe was given to me by Frances Kuhns, who always gave so unselfishly of herself. She died of cancer in 1994.

- ***1 cup sugar***
- ***1/2 cup shortening***
- ***1 egg***
- ***1 teaspoon vanilla extract***
- ***1 3/4 cups all-purpose flour***
- ***1/2 teaspoon salt***
- ***1/2 teaspoon baking soda***
- ***1/2 cup baking cocoa***
- ***1/4 cup milk***
- ***20 large marshmallows, halved***
- ***1 (16-ounce) can milk chocolate frosting***

Preheat oven to 350 degrees. Cream sugar, shortening, egg and vanilla in large mixer bowl until light and fluffy. Add mixture of flour, salt, baking soda and cocoa alternately with milk, mixing well after each addition. Drop by teaspoonfuls onto greased cookie sheet. Bake at 350 degrees for 8 minutes. Remove from oven. Press marshmallow piece into top of each cookie. Bake 2 minutes longer. Let stand until cool. Spread each cookie with frosting.
Yield: 3 dozen.

Marilyn S. Manion, Xi Eta Eta
Greensburg, Pennsylvania

FIVE-HOUR CHOCOLATE MINT COOKIES

- ***2 egg whites***
- ***Salt to taste***
- ***1/2 teaspoon cream of tartar***
- ***3/4 cup sugar***
- ***1/2 teaspoon vanilla extract***
- ***1 1/2 cups mint chocolate chips***
- ***4 or 5 drops of green food coloring***

Preheat oven to 375 degrees. Beat egg whites and salt in large mixer bowl until foamy. Add cream of tartar and sugar; beat until stiff peaks form. Fold in vanilla, mint chocolate chips and food coloring. Drop by teaspoonfuls onto nonstick cookie sheet. Place in oven. Turn off oven. Let stand for 5 hours or longer; do not open oven door. Yield: 2 1/2 dozen.

Myrtle Nye, Preceptor Laureate
Plymouth, Indiana

DATE NUT COOKIES

1½ cups packed light brown sugar
1 cup butter or margarine, softened
2 eggs
3 cups all-purpose flour
1 teaspoon baking soda
1 teaspoon hot water
½ teaspoon cinnamon
1 cup raisins
1 cup chopped pecans
1 cup chopped dates

Preheat oven to 400 degrees. Cream brown sugar and butter in large mixer bowl until smooth. Add eggs; mix well. Add flour gradually, mixing well after each addition. Dissolve baking soda in hot water. Add to sugar mixture. Stir in cinnamon, raisins, pecans and dates; mix well. Drop by spoonfuls onto cookie sheet. Bake at 400 degrees for 8 minutes or until browned. Yield: 4 dozen.

Linda Nelson, Beta Pi
Lakeview, Oregon

DROP FRUIT COOKIES

These cookies freeze well, and are always a favorite when I have sorority meetings in my home.

½ cup butter or margarine, softened
1 cup packed light brown sugar
½ cup sugar
2 eggs, beaten
1 cup sour cream
1 teaspoon vanilla extract
2½ cups sifted all-purpose flour
½ teaspoon baking soda
1 teaspoon salt
1 teaspoon cinnamon
¼ teaspoon ground cloves
1 cup chopped pecans
1 cup glazed cherries
2 cups raisins
1 cup chopped dates
1 tablespoon grated orange rind

Preheat oven to 375 degrees. Cream butter, brown sugar and sugar in large mixer bowl until light and fluffy. Add eggs, sour cream and vanilla; mix well. Add sifted mixture of flour, baking soda, salt, cinnamon and cloves. Stir in pecans, cherries, raisins, dates and orange rind. Drop by tablespoonfuls onto nonstick cookie sheet. Bake at 375 degrees for 10 to 12 minutes or until browned. Yield: 4 dozen.

E. Audrey Styles, Laureate Phi
Ottawa, Ontario, Canada

FRUIT AND PECAN COOKIES

1 cup margarine, softened
1½ cups sugar
2 eggs
1½ cups self-rising flour
1 teaspoon baking soda
1 teaspoon salt
1 teaspoon cinnamon
1 cup self-rising flour
2 pounds dates, chopped
½ pound candied cherries, chopped
½ pound candied pineapple, chopped
4 cups chopped pecans

Preheat oven to 325 to 350 degrees. Cream margarine and sugar in large mixer bowl until light and fluffy. Add eggs; mix well. Stir in mixture of 1½ cups flour, baking soda, salt and cinnamon; mix well. Mix remaining 1 cup flour with dates, cherries and pineapples, stirring until fruit is coated. Add to creamed mixture. Stir in pecans. Drop by teaspoonfuls onto ungreased cookie sheet. Bake at 325 to 350 degrees for 10 to 12 minutes. Yield: 10 to 12 dozen.

Charlie E. Ross, Iota Iota
Blairsville, Georgia

EVERYDAY COOKIES

1 cup butter or margarine, softened
1 cup vegetable oil
1 cup sugar
1 cup packed light brown sugar
2 eggs
1 teaspoon vanilla extract
3½ cups all-purpose flour
1 teaspoon salt
1 teaspoon cream of tartar
1 teaspoon baking soda
1 cup crisp rice cereal
1 cup quick-cooking oats
1 cup unsweetened coconut
1 cup chopped pecans

Preheat oven to 350 degrees. Cream butter, oil, sugar and brown sugar in large mixer bowl. Add eggs and vanilla; mix well. Add mixture of flour, salt, cream of tartar and baking soda; mix well. Stir in cereal, oats, coconut and pecans. Drop by teaspoonfuls onto ungreased cookie sheet. Flatten slightly. Bake at 350 degrees on bottom oven rack for 5 minutes. Move to middle oven rack. Bake 5 minutes longer or until light brown. Remove to wire rack to cool.
Yield: 6 dozen.

Lori Hayes, Preceptor Beta Lambda
Squamish, British Columbia, Canada

FORGOTTEN COOKIES

Everyone is always surprised that this is not candy because of how light it is. Easy to make the night before serving.

2 egg whites
Salt to taste
⅔ to ¾ cup sugar
1 teaspoon vanilla extract
1 cup semisweet chocolate chips
1 cup chopped pecans

Preheat oven to 350 degrees. Beat egg whites in large mixer bowl until foamy. Stir in salt. Add sugar 1 tablespoon at a time, beating until stiff peaks form. Stir in vanilla, chocolate chips and pecans. Drop by teaspoonfuls onto foil-lined cookie sheet. Place in oven. Turn off oven. Let stand for 4 to 12 hours; do not open oven door. Store in airtight container.
Yield: 2 to 3 dozen.

Bonnie Brewster, Xi Epsilon Psi
Port Lavaca, Texas

JUBILEE JUMBLES

This recipe belonged to my grandmom who would have been 112 years old now.

- *1/2 cup shortening*
- *1 cup packed light brown sugar*
- *1/2 cup sugar*
- *2 eggs*
- *1 cup evaporated milk*
- *1 teaspoon vanilla extract*
- *2 3/4 cups sifted all-purpose flour*
- *1/2 teaspoon baking soda*
- *1 teaspoon salt*
- *1 cup chopped walnuts*
- *2 tablespoons butter or margarine*
- *2 cups sifted confectioners' sugar*
- *1/4 cup evaporated milk*

Preheat oven to 375 degrees. Combine shortening, brown sugar, sugar and eggs in large mixer bowl until smooth. Add 1 cup evaporated milk and vanilla; mix well. Add sifted mixture of flour, baking soda and salt. Stir in walnuts. Chill, covered, for 1 hour. Drop by rounded tablespoonfuls 2 inches apart on greased cookie sheet. Bake at 375 degrees for 10 minutes or until light brown. Heat butter in small saucepan until golden brown. Beat confectioners' sugar, 1/4 cup evaporated milk and butter in small mixer bowl until smooth. Spread over cookies. May substitute 1 cup coconut, dates, raisins or semisweet chocolate chips for walnuts. Yield: 4 dozen.

Joan Connor, Laureate Lambda
Salem, New Jersey

MACAROONS

This recipe was passed down to me from my grandmother. I make these for family gatherings.

- *2 egg whites*
- *1 cup sugar*
- *2 cups cornflakes*
- *1 cup coconut*
- *1 teaspoon vanilla extract*
- *1 cup chopped walnuts*

Preheat oven to 375 degrees. Beat egg whites in large mixer bowl until soft peaks form. Add sugar gradually, beating until stiff peaks form. Stir in cornflakes, coconut, vanilla and walnuts. Drop by spoonfuls onto ungreased cookie sheet. Bake at 375 degrees for 10 minutes or until golden brown. Yield: 3 dozen.

Beth Sturdivan, Xi Gamma Lambda
Port Orchard, Washington

SURPRISE MERINGUE COOKIES

- *2 egg whites*
- *1/8 teaspoon cream of tartar*
- *1/4 teaspoon peppermint extract*
- *1/8 teaspoon salt*
- *3/4 cup sugar*
- *1/2 cup semisweet chocolate chips*

Preheat oven to 300 degrees. Beat egg whites in mixer bowl until foamy. Add cream of tartar, peppermint extract and salt gradually, beating until soft peaks form. Add sugar gradually, beating until stiff peaks form. Stir in chocolate chips, reserving 24 chips. Drop by spoonfuls onto cookie sheet lined with baking parchment. Place 1 chocolate chip on top of each cookie. Bake at 300 degrees for 20 to 25 minutes or until browned. Cool on cookie sheet for 2 minutes; remove to wire rack to cool completely.
Yield: 1 1/2 to 2 dozen cookies.

Mary Ann Getzinger, Xi Omicron Sigma
Lakehead, California

CHRISTMAS MINCEMEAT COOKIES

This recipe was passed down from my husband's great-grandmother. It's a Christmas favorite. Kids love finding the gumdrops in them.

- *1 1/2 cups packed light brown sugar*
- *2/3 cup margarine, softened*
- *3 eggs*
- *1 teaspoon baking soda*
- *1 teaspoon ground cinnamon*
- *1 teaspoon ground nutmeg*
- *1/2 teaspoon salt*
- *1 cup mincemeat*
- *1 cup chopped dates*
- *1 cup chopped walnuts*
- *1 cup chopped gumdrops*
- *3 cups all-purpose flour*
- *Maraschino cherries to taste, chopped*

Preheat oven to 375 degrees. Cream brown sugar and margarine together in large mixer bowl until smooth. Add eggs; mix well. Add mixture of baking soda, cinnamon, nutmeg and salt; mix well. Stir in mincemeat, dates, walnuts, gumdrops and flour with a spoon. Drop by teaspoonfuls onto nonstick cookie sheet. Put a piece of cherry on top of each cookie. Bake at 375 degrees for 15 minutes. Yield: 6 dozen.

Val Rhodes, Xi Epsilon
Aberdeen, Washington

NUTTY BROWNIE DROPS

- *1/2 cup melted butter or margarine*
- *3 ounces unsweetened chocolate, melted*
- *1 1/2 cups sugar*
- *3 eggs*
- *1 1/2 cups all-purpose flour*
- *1 cup chopped pecans*

Preheat oven to 350 degrees. Mix melted butter and chocolate with sugar in large mixer bowl. Add eggs 1 at a time; mix well. Blend in flour gradually, mixing well after each addition. Stir in pecans. Chill, covered, for 2 hours or overnight. Drop by rounded teaspoonfuls onto greased cookie sheet. Bake at 350 degrees for 12 to 16 minutes or until browned.
Yield: 6 dozen.

Margie Debault, Xi Kappa Chi
Refugio, Texas

OATMEAL COOKIES

My sister developed this recipe for her husband, who has diabetes.

1 cup raisins
3 eggs, beaten
1 teaspoon vanilla extract
1/2 cup margarine
1/2 cup peanut butter
1/2 cup packed light brown sugar
1/2 cup sugar
2 1/2 cups all-purpose flour
1 teaspoon cinnamon
1 teaspoon baking powder
1/2 teaspoon salt
2 cups oats

Preheat oven to 425 degrees. Combine raisins, eggs and vanilla in bowl; mix well. Let stand for 10 minutes. Add margarine, peanut butter, brown sugar and sugar; mix well. Add mixture of flour, cinnamon, baking powder, salt and oats; mix well. Drop by teaspoonfuls onto greased cookie sheet. Bake at 425 degrees for 10 to 15 minutes or until browned. May add 1 cup semisweet chocolate chips and 1 cup pecans. Yield: 6 dozen.

Dorothy Falls, Laureate Zeta Zeta
California

FAMILY FAVORITE OATMEAL COOKIES

2 cups shortening
2 cups sugar
2 cups packed light brown sugar
4 eggs
2 teaspoons vanilla extract
3 cups all-purpose flour
2 teaspoons salt
2 teaspoons baking soda
6 cups rolled oats
2 cups chopped walnuts (optional)
2 cups semisweet chocolate chips

Preheat oven to 350 degrees. Cream shortening, sugar and brown sugar in large mixer bowl until light and fluffy. Blend in eggs 1 at a time, mixing well after each addition. Stir in vanilla. Add mixture of flour, salt and baking soda; mix well. Stir in oats, walnuts and chocolate chips. Drop by tablespoonfuls onto greased cookie sheet. Bake at 350 degrees for 12 to 15 minutes or until browned. Yield: 6 to 7 dozen.

Peggy Aagenes, Preceptor Epsilon
Kalespell, Montana

OATMEAL AND COCONUT COOKIES

1/4 cup margarine, softened
1/2 cup butter-flavored shortening
3/4 cup packed light brown sugar
3/4 cup sugar
1 teaspoon vanilla extract
2 eggs
1 1/2 cups all-purpose flour
1 teaspoon baking soda
1 teaspoon baking powder
1 teaspoon salt
3/4 cup shredded coconut
2 cups oats
1 1/2 cups raisins

Preheat oven to 350 degrees. Cream margarine, shortening, brown sugar and sugar in large mixer bowl until light and fluffy. Add vanilla and eggs; mix well. Add mixture of flour, baking soda, baking powder and salt; mix well. Stir in coconut, oats and raisins. Drop by rounded tablespoonfuls onto nonstick cookie sheet. Bake at 350 degrees for 9 minutes or until browned. Yield: 3 dozen.

Beth O'Brien, Delta Sigma
Louisville, Colorado

FAT-FREE OATMEAL RAISIN COOKIES

1 cup all-purpose flour
1/2 cup sugar
1/2 teaspoon salt
1/2 teaspoon baking powder
1/2 teaspoon baking soda
1/2 teaspoon cinnamon
2 egg whites
1/3 cup light corn syrup
1 teaspoon vanilla extract
1 cup quick-cooking oats
1/2 cup raisins

Preheat oven to 375 degrees. Combine flour, sugar, salt, baking powder, baking soda and cinnamon in large mixer bowl; mix well. Stir in egg whites, corn syrup and vanilla; mix well. Add oats and raisins. Drop by rounded teaspoonfuls onto cookie sheet sprayed with nonstick cooking spray. Bake at 375 degrees for 10 minutes or until firm; do not overbake. Remove to wire rack to cool. Yield: 2 1/2 dozen.

Lucy Brushaber, Preceptor Epsilon Theta
Pinellas Park, Florida

RAISIN OATMEAL COOKIES

These are delicious spicy-flavored oatmeal cookies that are not too sweet. My mother-in-law gave me this recipe.

1 cup raisins
1/2 cup boiling water
1 cup margarine, softened
1 cup sugar
2 eggs
2 cups all-purpose flour
1/2 teaspoon salt
1 teaspoon baking soda
1 teaspoon cinnamon
1 teaspoon vanilla extract
2 cups oats
1 cup chopped pecans (optional)

Preheat oven to 350 degrees. Soak raisins in boiling water; set aside to cool. Cream margarine and sugar in large mixer bowl until smooth. Beat in eggs 1 at a time. Add sifted mixture of flour, salt, baking soda and cinnamon alternately with raisin mixture, mixing well after each addition. Stir in vanilla, oats and pecans. Drop by tablespoonfuls onto lightly greased cookie sheet. Bake at 350 degrees for 10 to 12 minutes or until brown. Yield: 5 dozen.

Deborah Knight, Laureate Gamma
Wausau, Wisconsin

ORANGE SLICE COOKIES

3 eggs
2 cups packed light brown sugar
1 tablespoon cold water
1 teaspoon vanilla extract
2 cups all-purpose flour
1 cup chopped orange slice candy
1/2 cup chopped pitted dates
1 cup chopped pecans

Preheat oven to 350 degrees. Beat eggs in large mixer bowl until thick and pale yellow. Add brown sugar, water and vanilla; mix well. Sift flour over candy, dates and pecans; toss to coat. Stir candy mixture gently into egg mixture. Chill, covered, for 2 hours. Drop by spoonfuls onto lightly greased cookie sheet. Bake at 350 degrees for 8 to 10 minutes or until light brown. Let cookies stand 8 to 12 hours before serving. Yield: 3 dozen.

Jeannette Wilson, Theta Lambda
Colorado Springs, Colorado

ORANGE COOKIES

1 1/2 cups sugar
1 cup shortening
2 eggs, beaten
3 1/2 cups all-purpose flour
1/2 teaspoon salt
1 tablespoon baking powder
1 teaspoon baking soda
Juice of 2 oranges
1 teaspoon grated orange rind
1/2 cup buttermilk
1/2 cup butter or margarine, softened
1/8 teaspoon salt
3 1/2 cups confectioners' sugar
1 teaspoon grated orange rind
2 to 3 tablespoons orange juice

Preheat oven to 350 degrees. Cream sugar and shortening in large mixer bowl until light and fluffy. Add eggs; mix well. Add mixture of flour, 1/2 teaspoon salt, baking powder and baking soda. Stir in juice of 2 oranges and 1 teaspoon orange rind; mix well. Add buttermilk; mix well. Drop by spoonfuls onto lightly greased cookie sheet. Bake at 350 degrees for 10 minutes or until light brown on edges. Combine butter, 1/8 teaspoon salt, confectioners' sugar, 1 teaspoon orange rind and enough orange juice to make of spreading consistency in mixer bowl. Spread over cookies. Store in airtight container. Yield: 4 dozen.

Gretchen Childs, Xi Theta
Wellsville, New York

WHITE CHIP ORANGE DREAM COOKIES

1 cup butter or margarine, softened
1/2 cup sugar
1/2 cup packed light brown sugar
1 egg
2 to 3 teaspoons grated orange rind
2 1/4 cups all-purpose flour
3/4 teaspoon baking soda
1/2 teaspoon salt
2 cups white chocolate chips

Preheat oven to 350 degrees. Cream butter, sugar and brown sugar in large mixer bowl until creamy. Add egg and orange rind; mix well. Add mixture of flour, baking soda and salt gradually, mixing well after each addition. Stir in white chocolate chips. Drop by rounded tablespoonfuls onto ungreased baking sheet. Bake at 350 degrees for 10 to 12 minutes or until light brown. Cool on cookie sheet for 2 minutes; remove to wire rack to cool completely.
Yield: 3 dozen.

Marie Robinson, Xi Omega Nu
Sugarland, Texas

HEDIBLES (HEATHER'S EDIBLE COOKIES)

1 cup butter or margarine, softened
1 cup packed light brown sugar
1 cup sugar
2 eggs
1 cup peanut butter
3 cups all-purpose flour
2 teaspoons baking soda
1/4 teaspoon salt
1 cup (or more) semisweet chocolate chips
1 cup crisp rice cereal

Preheat oven to 375 degrees. Cream butter, brown sugar and sugar in mixer bowl together until creamy. Beat in eggs 1 at a time. Add peanut butter; mix well. Add mixture of flour, baking soda and salt; mix well. Stir in chocolate chips and cereal. Drop by spoonfuls onto ungreased cookie sheet; dip spoon in flour first to prevent dough from sticking. Bake at 375 degrees for 12 to 15 minutes or until brown. Yield: 6 dozen.

Heather George, Alpha Chi
Richmond, British Columbia, Canada

NO-FLOUR PEANUT BUTTER COOKIES

1 cup peanut butter
1 cup sugar
1 egg
1 teaspoon vanilla extract

Preheat oven to 350 degrees. Combine peanut butter, sugar, egg and vanilla in medium bowl, stirring to blend. Drop by spoonfuls onto ungreased cookie sheet. Flatten with fork in criss-cross pattern. Bake at 350 degrees for 8 to 12 minutes or until golden brown. Yield: 2 dozen.

Patti Boone, Alpha Psi Kappa
Humble, Texas

Carolyn MacPherson, Laureate Alpha Alpha, Kingston, Ontario, Canada, makes Lemon Bars by mixing 2 cups sifted all-purpose flour and 1/2 cup sugar, cutting in 1 cup butter or margarine and pressing into 9-by-13-inch pan and baking in preheated 350-degree oven for 15 minutes. Pour a mixture of 4 lightly beaten eggs, 2 tablespoons lemon juice, grated lemon rind and sifted mixture of 2 cups sugar, 1/4 cup all-purpose flour and 1 teaspoon baking powder over crust and bake for 25 minutes longer.

PEANUT BUTTER COOKIES

This recipe was handed down from my Irish-German grandmother.

1 cup butter or margarine, softened
2 eggs, beaten
1 cup packed light brown sugar
1 cup sugar
1 cup peanut butter
1 teaspoon vanilla extract
2 cups all-purpose flour
1 teaspoon baking soda
Salt to taste
1/2 cup wheat germ
1 teaspoon honey

Preheat oven to 350 degrees. Beat butter, eggs, brown sugar and sugar in large mixer bowl until creamy. Add peanut butter and vanilla; mix well. Add sifted mixture of flour, baking soda, salt and wheat germ; mix well. Stir in honey. Drop by teaspoonfuls onto nonstick cookie sheet. Flatten with fork in criss-cross pattern. Bake at 350 degrees for 10 to 13 minutes or until browned. May sprinkle with additional sugar before baking Yield: 4 dozen.

Pat Wolthausen, Laureate Kappa
Vancouver, Washington

GRANDMA'S PERSIMMON COOKIES

1/2 cup shortening
1 cup sugar
1 egg
1 cup persimmon pulp
1 teaspoon baking soda
2 cups all-purpose flour
1/2 teaspoon cloves
1/2 teaspoon nutmeg
1 teaspoon cinnamon
1 cup seedless raisins
1 cup ground walnuts

Preheat oven to 350 degrees. Cream shortening and sugar in large mixer bowl until light and fluffy. Add egg; mix well. Stir in mixture of persimmon pulp and baking soda. Add mixture of flour, cloves, nutmeg and cinnamon; mix well. Stir in raisins and walnuts. Drop by teaspoonfuls onto greased and floured cookie sheet. Bake at 350 degrees for 10 minutes or until browned. Yield: 3 dozen.

Linda Sharp, Xi Chi Delta
Corcoran, California

PINEAPPLE COOKIES

1 cup shortening
1 cup sugar
1 cup packed light brown sugar
2 eggs
4 cups all-purpose flour
1/2 teaspoon salt
1 1/2 teaspoons baking soda
1/2 teaspoon baking powder
1 (20-ounce) can crushed pineapple, drained
1 1/2 teaspoons vanilla extract
2 cups butterscotch chips
1 1/2 to 2 cups coconut flakes

Preheat oven to 375 degrees. Cream shortening, sugar and brown sugar in large mixer bowl until light and fluffy. Add eggs; mix well. Add mixture of flour, salt, baking soda and baking powder; mix well. Stir in pineapple and vanilla. Stir in butterscotch chips and coconut. Drop by rounded spoonfuls onto ungreased cookie sheet. Bake at 375 degrees for 12 to 15 minutes or until light brown; do not overbake. Store in airtight container. The cookies soften upon standing; they are moister after a few days.
Yield: 4 to 5 dozen.

Susan Theodore, Delta Alpha
Lima, Ohio

PUMPKIN COOKIES

2 eggs
1 (16-ounce) can pumpkin
2 teaspoons milk
1 cup vegetable oil
2 teaspoons vanilla extract
4 cups all-purpose flour
2 cups sugar
4 teaspoons baking powder
2 teaspoons cinnamon
1 teaspoon salt
2 teaspoons baking soda
1 cup chopped walnuts
2 cups semisweet chocolate chips

Preheat oven to 350 to 375 degrees. Combine eggs, pumpkin, milk, oil and vanilla in large mixer bowl; mix well. Add mixture of flour, sugar, baking powder, cinnamon, salt and baking soda; mix well. Stir in walnuts and chocolate chips. Drop by teaspoonfuls onto greased cookie sheet. Bake at 350 to 375 degrees for 10 to 15 minutes or until browned.
Yield: 5 dozen.

Margaret A. Belisle, Preceptor Lambda
Westbrook, Maine

JUMBO RAISIN COOKIES

2 cups raisins
2 cups water
1 cup butter or margarine, softened
1 3/4 cups sugar
2 eggs
1 teaspoon vanilla extract
3 1/2 cups all-purpose flour
1 teaspoon baking powder
1 teaspoon baking soda
1 teaspoon salt
1 teaspoon cinnamon
1/2 teaspoon nutmeg
1/2 cup chopped pecans

Preheat oven to 350 degrees. Bring raisins and water to a boil in small saucepan. Boil for 3 minutes; set aside to cool. Beat butter and sugar in large mixer bowl until creamy. Add eggs and vanilla; mix well. Stir in raisin mixture. Add mixture of flour, baking powder, baking soda, salt, cinnamon and nutmeg; mix well. Stir in pecans. Drop by tablespoonfuls 2 inches apart onto greased cookie sheet. Bake at 350 degrees for 12 to 15 minutes or until browned. Separate layers of cookies with waxed paper to store.
Yield: 2 1/2 dozen.

Sue Wartella, Laureate Chi
Pottsville, Pennsylvania

SUGAR COOKIES WITH ALMOND ICING

1/2 cup margarine, softened
1 egg
1 cup sugar
1/2 teaspoon vanilla extract
1/2 cup vegetable oil
2 1/2 cups all-purpose flour
Salt to taste
1 teaspoon cream of tartar
1 teaspoon baking soda
Sugar to taste
5 tablespoons margarine, softened
3 3/4 cups sifted confectioners' sugar
3/4 teaspoon almond extract
Food coloring (optional)
5 tablespoons (or less) milk

Preheat oven to 350 degrees. Beat 1/2 cup margarine, egg and 1 cup sugar in large mixer bowl until creamy. Add vanilla and oil; mix well. Add mixture of flour, salt, cream of tartar and baking soda; mix well. Drop by teaspoonfuls onto ungreased cookie sheet. Flatten with bottom of glass dipped in sugar. Bake at 350 degrees for 9 to 10 minutes or until browned. Combine 5 tablespoons margarine, confectioners' sugar, almond extract and food coloring in small mixer bowl; mix well. Add milk until of spreading consistency. Spread over cookies. Yield: 3 dozen.

Rebecca A. Scholes, Laureate Beta Eta
Waukee, Iowa

TEA CAKES

1 cup shortening
2 cups sugar
4 eggs
3 cups sifted all-purpose flour
2 teaspoons baking powder
Salt to taste
2 teaspoons vanilla extract

Preheat oven to 400 degrees. Cream shortening and sugar in large mixer bowl until light and fluffy. Add eggs 1 at a time; mix well. Add flour, baking powder and salt; mix well. Stir in vanilla. Drop by teaspoonfuls onto nonstick cookie sheet. Bake at 400 degrees for 12 minutes or until browned. Cool on baking sheet for 1 minute; remove to wire rack to cool completely. Yield: 3 dozen.

Terry L. Hollub, Eta Mu
Bay City, Texas

HEAVENLY TEA CAKES

1 cup margarine, softened
1 1/2 cups sugar
2 eggs
2 1/2 to 3 cups all-purpose flour
1/2 teaspoon baking soda
1 teaspoon baking powder

Preheat oven to 375 degrees. Beat margarine and sugar in large mixer bowl until light and fluffy. Add eggs; mix well. Mix flour, baking soda and baking powder together. Add to creamed mixture; mix well. Add enough additional flour to make stiff dough. Drop by teaspoonfuls onto greased cookie sheet. Bake at 375 degrees for 10 minutes; do not overbake. Let stand until cool. Store in airtight container. Yield: 3 dozen.

Angelia Simmons, Xi Sigma
Dodge City, Kansas

WAFFLE COOKIES

1/2 cup margarine
2 tablespoons baking cocoa
2 eggs
3/4 cup sugar
1 teaspoon vanilla extract
1 cup all-purpose flour
1/2 (16-ounce) can favorite frosting
Candy sprinkles to taste

Preheat nonstick waffle iron to Medium. Melt margarine in small saucepan over low heat. Add cocoa; blend well. Beat eggs and sugar in large mixer bowl until smooth. Stir in cocoa mixture and vanilla; blend well. Add flour; mix well. Drop by teaspoonfuls onto preheated waffle iron. Close iron. Bake for 1 to 2 minutes or until steaming stops. Remove to wire rack to cool. Spread with frosting and decorate with sprinkles. May serve without frosting.
Yield: 1 1/2 dozen.

Donita Balfour, Theta
Oklahoma City, Oklahoma

WHOOPIE PIES

2 eggs
1 cup melted shortening
2 teaspoons vanilla extract
1 cup sour milk
1 cup hot water
4 cups all-purpose flour
2 cups sugar
3/4 cup baking cocoa
2 teaspoons baking soda
1/2 teaspoon salt
4 teaspoons milk
2 eggs
4 teaspoons all-purpose flour
1 cup vegetable oil
Confectioners' sugar to taste

Preheat oven to 410 degrees. Beat 2 eggs in large mixer bowl. Add shortening, vanilla, sour milk and hot water; mix well. Mix 4 cups flour, sugar, cocoa, baking soda and salt together. Add to egg mixture gradually, mixing well after each addition. Drop by teaspoonfuls onto nonstick cookie sheet. Bake at 410 degrees for 10 to 15 minutes or until firm. Cool on cookie sheet for 1 to 2 minutes. Remove to wire rack to cool completely. Combine 4 teaspoons milk, 2 eggs, 4 teaspoons flour and oil in small mixer bowl. Add confectioners' sugar gradually, beating until of spreading consistency. Spread over half the cooled cookies; top with remaining cookies. Store in refrigerator. Yield: 4 dozen.

Joan Cherié Jordan, Xi Epsilon Rho
La Grange, Indiana

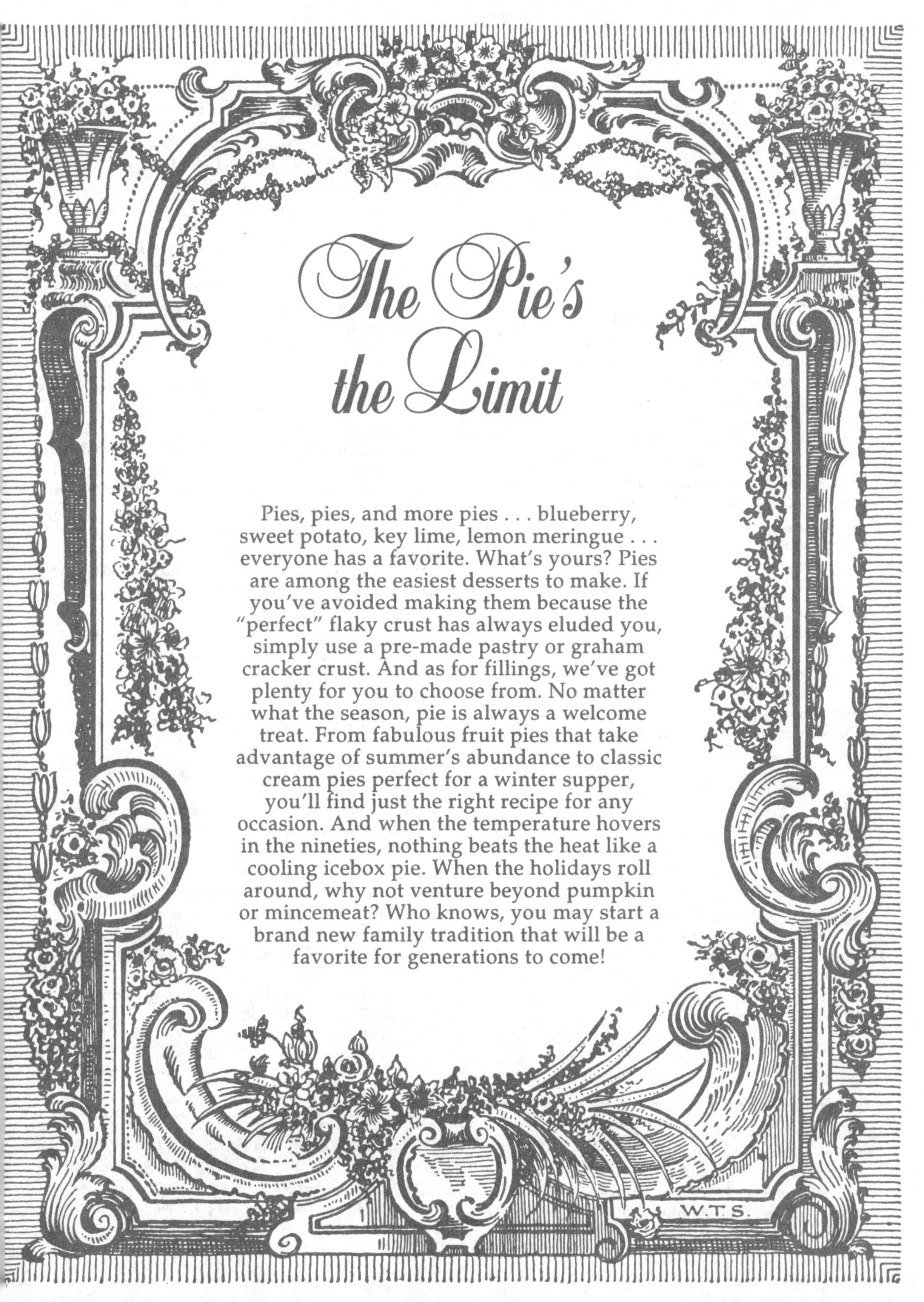

The Pie's the Limit

Pies, pies, and more pies . . . blueberry, sweet potato, key lime, lemon meringue . . . everyone has a favorite. What's yours? Pies are among the easiest desserts to make. If you've avoided making them because the "perfect" flaky crust has always eluded you, simply use a pre-made pastry or graham cracker crust. And as for fillings, we've got plenty for you to choose from. No matter what the season, pie is always a welcome treat. From fabulous fruit pies that take advantage of summer's abundance to classic cream pies perfect for a winter supper, you'll find just the right recipe for any occasion. And when the temperature hovers in the nineties, nothing beats the heat like a cooling icebox pie. When the holidays roll around, why not venture beyond pumpkin or mincemeat? Who knows, you may start a brand new family tradition that will be a favorite for generations to come!

ALMOND CREAM PIE

3 egg yolks
3/4 cup sugar
3 tablespoons cornstarch
2 cups milk
1/2 cup butter or margarine, softened
1 teaspoon almond extract
1 baked (9-inch) pie shell
12 ounces whipped topping
1/2 cup toasted sliced almonds

Beat egg yolks in mixer bowl until light; set aside. Combine sugar and cornstarch in bowl; mix well. Scald milk in saucepan over medium heat. Add sugar mixture. Place in double boiler over hot water. Cook until hot but not thickened, stirring constantly. Stir a small amount of hot milk mixture into egg yolks; stir egg yolks into milk mixture. Cook until thickened, stirring constantly. Remove from heat. Add butter and almond extract; mix well. Spoon into pie shell. Cool. Spread with whipped topping. Sprinkle with almonds. Chill for 4 to 6 hours.
Yield: 6 to 8 servings.

Beverly Flynn, Preceptor Delta Delta
Overland Park, Kansas

DELUXE APPLE PIE

6 cups sliced apples
6 tablespoons sugar
6 tablespoons packed light brown sugar
1/3 cup all-purpose flour
1 teaspoon cinnamon
1/4 teaspoon salt
1 recipe (2-crust) pie pastry
1/4 cup butter or margarine
3 tablespoons grated lemon rind
1/2 tablespoon whipping cream

Preheat oven to 450 degrees. Place apples in large bowl. Combine sugar, brown sugar, flour, cinnamon and salt in bowl; mix well. Add to apples; toss to coat. Place in pastry-lined pie plate. Dot with butter. Sprinkle with lemon rind. Top with whipping cream. Cover with remaining pastry, sealing edge and cutting vents for steam. Bake at 450 degrees for 10 minutes. Reduce heat to 350 degrees. Bake for 20 to 30 minutes longer or until golden brown.
Yield: 6 to 8 servings.

Maureen Vondrische, Theta Alpha
Cache Creek, British Columbia, Canada

Connie Reed, Tau Beta, Newtown, Missouri, makes Sugar-Free Banana Pie by preparing sugar-free vanilla instant pudding with 1 3/4 cups milk and beating 1 cup whipping cream with 3 teaspoons Equal and 4 tablespoons light cream cheese, folding into the pudding and adding 2 bananas, sliced. Pour into baked pie shell and chill.

NUMBER ONE APPLE PIES

While making my first apple pie, I discovered I did not have all the ingredients, so I left them out. The pie turned out great.

8 large cooking apples
1/2 cup water
2 recipes (2-crust) pie pastry
2 tablespoons all-purpose flour
1/2 cup sugar
1/2 cup packed light brown sugar
3/4 teaspoon ground cinnamon
1/4 teaspoon ground nutmeg
1/8 teaspoon salt
1 tablespoon lemon juice
3 tablespoons margarine, softened

Preheat oven to 450 degrees. Peel and slice apples into quarters; cut quarters into 3 pieces. Place in saucepan. Cover with 1/2 cup cold water. Heat to simmering. Cook for 3 to 4 minutes. Let stand until cool. Fill 2 pastry-lined pie plates with apples. Mix flour, sugar, brown sugar, spices, salt, lemon juice and margarine in mixer bowl. Spread over apples. Moisten edge of pastry shells. Top pie plates with remaining pastry, sealing edge and cutting vents. Bake at 450 degrees for 10 to 12 minutes. Reduce heat to 350 degrees. Bake for 45 minutes longer.
Yield: 12 to 16 servings.

Christian Burison, Preceptor Theta
Virginia Beach, Virginia

OLD-FASHIONED APPLE PIE

This is a favorite with my family and is made for all special occasions.

1 1/2 cups sugar
1/4 cup all-purpose flour
1 tablespoon cinnamon
5 to 6 Granny Smith apples, sliced
1 recipe (2-crust) pie pastry
2 tablespoons butter or margarine

Preheat oven to 350 degrees. Combine sugar, flour and cinnamon in large bowl; mix well. Reserve 4 tablespoons mixture. Add apples to remaining sugar mixture; mix well. Spoon into pastry-lined pie plate. Dot with butter. Top with remaining pastry, sealing edge and cutting vents. Sprinkle with reserved sugar mixture. Bake at 350 degrees for 30 to 45 minutes or until brown. Serve hot with ice cream.
Yield: 6 to 8 servings.

Kathy Evans, Xi Beta Iota
Weatherford, Texas

Piret Brown, Eta Lambda, Stouffville, Ontario, Canada, makes Easy Cherry Cheese Pie with prepared whipped topping, 8 ounces cream cheese and 1/2 cup sugar blended and poured into graham cracker pie shell. Top with cherry pie filling and chill.

OZARK APPLE PIE

1 egg
3/4 cup sugar
3/4 cup all-purpose flour
1/2 cup walnuts
1 1/2 teaspoons baking powder
Salt to taste
1 cup chopped apples
1 teaspoon each vanilla and lemon extracts
Almond extract to taste

Preheat oven to 350 degrees. Combine egg and sugar in bowl; mix well. Add flour, walnuts, baking powder, salt, apples, vanilla, lemon and almond extracts; mix well. Spoon into pie plate. Bake at 350 degrees for 20 minutes or until knife inserted near center comes out clean. Yield: 6 to 8 servings.

Mary Elizabeth Grice, Preceptor, Alpha Phi
Kinston, North Carolina

PAPER-BAG APPLE PIE

1/2 cup sugar
2 tablespoons all-purpose flour
1/2 teaspoon nutmeg
7 cups apples chunks
1 unbaked (9-inch) pie shell
2 tablespoons lemon juice (optional)
1/2 cup sugar
1/2 cup all-purpose flour
1/4 cup margarine

Preheat oven to 425 degrees. Sprinkle mixture of 1/2 cup sugar, 2 tablespoons flour and nutmeg over apples in bowl; toss to coat. Spoon apple mixture into pie shell. Drizzle lemon juice over top. Combine 1/2 cup sugar and 1/2 cup flour in small bowl. Cut in 1/4 cup margarine until crumbly. Sprinkle over apple mixture. Place pie shell in heavy brown paper bag; fold over and secure with paper clips. Bake at 425 degrees for 1 hour. Split bag and remove pie. Place on wire rack to cool. Editor's Note: Be sure bag is *not* made from recycled paper. Yield: 6 to 8 servings.

Helen Cichantek, Xi Alpha Epsilon
Manitowoc, Wisconsin

SUGAR-FREE APPLE PIE

3 tablespoons quick-cooking tapioca
1 cup unsweetened apple juice
4 large apples, sliced
1 teaspoon cinnamon
1 teaspoon vanilla extract
1 recipe (2-crust) pie pastry

Preheat oven to 400 degrees. Combine tapioca, apple juice and apple slices in saucepan. Cook over medium heat until thickened, stirring constantly. Remove from heat. Add cinnamon and vanilla; mix well. Spoon into pastry-lined pie plate. Cut strips from remaining pie pastry; arrange lattice-fashion over pie. Bake at 400 degrees for 10 minutes. Reduce heat to 350 degrees. Bake for 45 minutes longer. Yield: 8 servings.

Lisa Duke, Alpha Alpha Eta
West Columbia, Texas

BLUEBERRY-RASPBERRY GLAZED PIE

When we built our first home 25 years ago, we planted 6 blueberry bushes. Our oldest son was 2 years old. During that time, we swapped blueberries for raspberries from our neighbor. When my neighbor's husband died, she gave us 25 raspberry bushes. Our son served 7 1/2 months in the Persian Gulf during Operation Desert Storm. When he came home, this dessert was the first thing I served him!

8 ounces cream cheese, softened
1 baked (10-inch) pie shell
3 cups blueberries
3 cups raspberries
3/4 cup water
3 tablespoons cornstarch
1 cup sugar
2 tablespoons lemon juice

Spread cream cheese in pie shell. Combine 1/2 cup blueberries and 1/2 cup raspberries with water in saucepan. Bring to a boil. Cook for 2 minutes. Combine cornstarch and sugar in bowl. Add to blueberry mixture; mix well. Cook until thickened and clear, stirring constantly. Stir in lemon juice. Add remaining blueberries and strawberries; mix gently. Spread over cream cheese in shell. Chill until firm. Serve plain or with vanilla ice cream or whipped cream. Yield: 8 to 10 servings.

Margaret W.S. Bressler, Xi Delta Rho
Williamsport, Pennsylvania

BUTTERMILK PIES

1/2 cup self-rising flour
2 cups sugar
1/2 cup melted margarine
3 eggs, beaten
1/2 cup buttermilk
1 teaspoon vanilla extract
2 unbaked (8-inch) pie shells or 1 unbaked (10-inch) pie shell

Preheat oven to 350 degrees. Combine flour and sugar in bowl; mix well. Cut in margarine until crumbly. Stir in eggs, buttermilk and vanilla. Spread in pie shells. Bake at 350 degrees for 30 minutes. Reduce heat to 250 degrees. Bake for 20 minutes longer or until golden brown. Yield: 12 servings.

Lynda Keener, Iota Iota
Blairsville, Georgia

Pamela G. Hurdle, Alpha Omicron, Suffolk, Virginia, makes S'More Pie by melting 15 large marshmallows and 6 milk chocolate bars with almonds with 2 tablespoons milk, blending with 8 ounces whipped topping and 1 tablespoon vanilla. Spread in graham cracker pie shell and freeze.

RICH BUTTERMILK PIES

I remember while I was growing up, my mom would always make this pie to take to a family when someone was sick or had passed away. I find myself now reaching for this recipe quite often. I'll bake one for the family or friend in need, one for my family and another to freeze for emergencies or when a friend needs some cheering up. This pie freezes well.

3 3/4 cups sugar
1/2 cup all-purpose flour
1/2 teaspoon salt
6 eggs
1 teaspoon vanilla extract
1 cup buttermilk
1 cup melted butter or margarine
1 teaspoon butter extract
3 unbaked (9-inch) pie shells

Preheat oven to 350 degrees. Combine sugar, flour and salt in bowl. Add eggs and vanilla; mix well. Add buttermilk; mix until blended. Stir in butter and butter extract. Spread in pie shells. Bake at 350 degrees for 40 to 60 minutes or until set and golden brown. Yield: 18 to 24 servings.

Shonda Judy, Gamma Chi
Cynthiana, Kentucky

BUTTERSCOTCH MERINGUE PIE

1 cup packed light brown sugar
3 tablespoons (heaping) all-purpose flour
1 1/4 cups milk
Salt to taste
2 egg yolks, beaten
1 teaspoon butter or margarine
1 teaspoon vanilla extract
1 baked (9-inch) pie shell
2 egg whites
3 tablespoons sugar

Preheat oven to 350 degrees. Combine brown sugar, flour, milk and salt in top of double boiler over hot water. Bring to a boil over medium heat, stirring constantly. Cook until thickened, stirring constantly. Cover and continue to cook for 10 minutes longer. Stir a small amount of hot mixture into egg yolks; stir egg yolks into hot mixture. Cook for 3 minutes longer, stirring frequently. Remove from heat. Add butter and vanilla; mix well. Cool slightly. Spoon into pie shell. Beat egg whites in mixer bowl until soft peaks form. Add sugar, 1 tablespoon at a time, beating after each addition until stiff peaks form. Spread meringue over filling, sealing to edge. Bake at 350 degrees until brown. Yield: 6 to 8 servings.

Frances Quinn, Xi Zeta Nu
Renfrew, Ontario, Canada

BUTTERSCOTCH CHIP PIES

1 tablespoon (rounded) shortening
1 cup all-purpose flour
3 tablespoons water
1/2 teaspoon salt
6 cups milk
2 cups sugar
1/2 cup cornstarch
1 teaspoon salt
12 egg yolks
2 teaspoons vanilla extract
1 cup margarine
1 cup butterscotch chips
12 egg whites
2 tablespoons cornstarch
6 tablespoons confectioners' sugar

Preheat oven to 375 degrees. Cut shortening into flour until crumbly. Mix water and 1/2 teaspoon salt in bowl. Pour into flour mixture; mix well. Roll dough to make 2 pie shells. Place in two 9-inch pie pans. Prick pie shells. Bake at 375 degrees until light brown. Combine milk, sugar, cornstarch, 1 teaspoon salt, egg yolks, vanilla and margarine in large saucepan; mix well. Cook over low heat until thickened, stirring constantly. Remove from heat. Add butterscotch chips; mix until melted. Spread equally in pie shells. Combine egg whites, 2 tablespoons cornstarch and confectioners' sugar in large mixer bowl; beat until stiff peaks form. Spread over filling, sealing to edge. Bake at 375 degrees until brown. May substitute peanut butter chips or semisweet chocolate chips for butterscotch chips. Add 1/2 cup more sugar if using chocolate chips. May omit chips and add 1 cup drained crushed pineapple.
Yield: 12 to 16 servings.

Nancy Eads, Omega Mu
Ridgeway, Missouri

FRUIT AND NUT CHERRY PIES

1 (21-ounce) can cherry pie filling
1 (20-ounce) can crushed pineapple, undrained
3/4 cup sugar
1 tablespoon cornstarch
1 teaspoon red food coloring
4 medium firm bananas, sliced
1/2 cup chopped pecans
2 baked (9-inch) pie shells
Whipped cream to taste

Combine pie filling, pineapple, sugar, cornstarch and food coloring in large saucepan. Bring to a boil over medium heat. Cook for 2 minutes, stirring constantly. Remove from heat. Let stand until cool. Fold in bananas and pecans. Spoon into pie shells. Chill for 2 to 3 hours. Top with whipped cream. Store in refrigerator. Yield: 12 to 16 servings.

Cheri Salley, Preceptor Alpha Psi
Midlothian, Virginia

SWEET CHERRY PIE

I served this pie to my sorority sisters during the month of February; they all loved the pie and wanted the recipe!

2 cups all-purpose flour
1 teaspoon salt
2/3 cup plus 2 tablespoons shortening
1/4 cup water
2 1/2 tablespoons all-purpose flour
1 cup sugar
1/4 teaspoon almond extract
1 (21-ounce) can cherry pie filling
Butter or margarine to taste

Preheat oven to 425 degrees. Combine 2 cups flour and salt in bowl; cut in shortening until crumbly. Add water gradually; mix well. Shape into 2 balls; roll out on waxed paper. Fit 1 pastry into 9-inch pie plate. Combine 2 1/2 tablespoons flour, sugar, almond extract and pie filling in bowl; mix well. Spoon into pie shell. Dot with butter. Cover with remaining pastry, sealing edge and cutting vents. Bake at 425 degrees for 35 to 45 minutes or until golden brown. Yield: 6 to 8 servings.

Deanna Carson, Mu Epsilon
Jefferson City, Missouri

CHOCOLATE CHIP WALNUT PIE

1 1/3 cups semisweet chocolate chips
1 unbaked (10-inch) pie shell
2/3 cup chopped walnuts
1 cup dark corn syrup
1/4 cup light corn syrup
2 eggs
2 tablespoons melted butter or margarine

Preheat oven to 350 degrees. Spread chocolate chips in pie shell. Top with layer of walnuts. Combine dark and light corn syrups, eggs and butter in bowl; mix well. Spread over walnuts. Bake at 350 degrees for 40 minutes. Yield: 8 to 12 servings.

Leslie Greer, Preceptor Mu Kappa
Fresno, California

CHRISTMAS PIES

1 (21-ounce) can cherry pie filling
1 (20-ounce) can crushed pineapple
1 cup sugar
2 tablespoons cornstarch
1 (6-ounce) package strawberry-banana gelatin
1 1/2 cups chopped pecans
2 bananas, sliced
2 baked (10-inch) deep-dish pie shells
Whipped cream to taste

Combine first 4 ingredients in saucepan. Cook until thickened, stirring constantly. Remove from heat. Stir in gelatin until dissolved. Cool. Stir in pecans and bananas. Spoon into pie shells. Chill. Garnish with whipped cream. Yield: 12 to 16 servings.

Virginia Leatherman, Zeta Kappa
Napoleon, Ohio

"FAT-FREE" CHOCOLATE CREAM CHEESE PIE

1/2 cup Grape Nuts cereal
4 teaspoons diet margarine
8 ounces fat-free cream cheese, softened
1 cup fat-free sour cream
1 (4-ounce) package chocolate instant pudding mix
Light whipped topping (optional)

Preheat oven to 350 degrees. Mix cereal and margarine in bowl. Pat into 9-inch pie pan. Bake at 350 degrees for 10 minutes. Cool. Combine cream cheese, sour cream and pudding mix in bowl; mix well. Spread into pie shell. Chill or freeze until set. Serve with whipped topping. Yield: 6 to 8 servings.

Eleanor M. Anderson, Preceptor, Gamma Theta
Arkansas City, Kansas

FRENCH SILK PIE

1 cup butter or margarine, softened
1 cup sugar
3 (1-ounce) squares unsweetened baking chocolate, melted
1 teaspoon vanilla extract
4 eggs
1 baked (9-inch) pie shell

Cream butter and sugar in mixer bowl until light and fluffy. Add chocolate and vanilla; beat until blended. Add 2 eggs. Beat at high speed for 5 minutes. Add remaining eggs. Beat for 5 minutes. Spoon into pie shell. Chill for 1 hour or longer. Yield: 6 to 8 servings.

Gail Gengler, Preceptor Beta Eta
Monmouth, Oregon

SILK CHOCOLATE PIE WITH MERINGUE

2 cups milk
1 cup sugar
1/4 cup baking cocoa
1/4 cup cornstarch
1 cup milk
3 egg yolks
1 1/4 teaspoons vanilla extract
1 baked (9-inch) pie shell
3 egg whites
1/4 teaspoon cream of tartar
6 tablespoons sugar

Preheat oven to 300 degrees. Heat 2 cups milk in saucepan until warm. Remove from heat. Combine sugar, cocoa and cornstarch in bowl; mix well. Add remaining 1 cup milk and egg yolks; mix until blended. Stir into warm milk. Cook over medium heat until mixture thickens and begins to boil, stirring constantly. Cook for 2 to 5 minutes, stirring constantly. Remove from heat. Stir in vanilla. Spread into pie shell. Beat egg whites and cream of tartar in mixer bowl until frothy. Beat in sugar gradually; beat until peaks are stiff and glossy. Spread over pie mixture, sealing to edge. Bake at 300 degrees until browned. Yield: 6 to 8 servings.

Sarah Byerly, Preceptor Psi
Salisbury, North Carolina

FUDGE PIE

1 cup melted butter or margarine
1 cup sugar
1/4 cup baking cocoa
1/4 cup all-purpose flour
2 eggs, beaten
1 teaspoon vanilla extract
1/4 cup chopped pecans (optional)
1 unbaked (9-inch) pie shell

Preheat oven to 375 degrees. Combine butter, sugar, cocoa and flour in bowl; mix well. Add eggs, vanilla and pecans; mix until blended. Spoon into pie shell. Bake at 375 degrees for 25 to 30 minutes or until set. Do not overbake. Will make pie of custard consistency. Yield: 6 to 8 servings.

Mimi Smith, Eta Sigma
Blue Ridge, Georgia

LIGHT MOCHA FUDGE PIE

This is a wonderful dessert to serve at sorority meetings. Everyone loves it, especially since it's light!

1 (22-ounce) package light fudge brownie mix
2 teaspoons instant coffee granules
1 teaspoon vanilla extract
1 1/2 cups 1% milk
4 tablespoons Kahlúa or other coffee-flavored liqueur
2 teaspoons instant coffee granules
1 teaspoon vanilla extract
2 (4-ounce) packages chocolate instant pudding mix
16 ounces light whipped topping
2 tablespoons Kahlúa
2 teaspoons instant coffee granules
1 (1-ounce) square semisweet chocolate (optional)

Prepare brownie mix using package instructions, adding 2 teaspoons coffee granules dissolved in the water and 1 teaspoon vanilla. Spoon into greased 9-by-13-inch baking pan. Bake at 350 degrees for 30 to 45 minutes or until brownies test done. Combine milk, 4 tablespoons of the Kahlúa, 2 teaspoons of the coffee granules and remaining vanilla with pudding mix in large mixer bowl; beat until blended. Fold in half the whipped topping. Spread evenly over baked layer. Combine remaining 2 tablespoons Kahlúa and remaining 2 teaspoons coffee granules in bowl; mix well. Add remaining whipped topping; mix well. Spread over pudding mixture. Pull vegetable peeler across square of semisweet chocolate. Sprinkle chocolate curls over whipped topping. Serve immediately or store, loosely covered, in refrigerator. Yield: 16 servings.

Colleen Bixenman, Omicron Upsilon
Colby, Kansas

MILKY WAY PIE

1/2 cup milk
1 1/8 cups miniature marshmallows
7 milk chocolate candy bars
8 ounces extra-creamy whipped topping
Chocolate syrup to taste (optional)
1 (9-inch) chocolate crumb pie shell

Combine milk and marshmallows in saucepan. Cook over low heat until marshmallows melt, stirring constantly. Add chocolate bars. Stir until chocolate melts. Cool completely. Stir in whipped topping and chocolate syrup. Spoon into pie shell. Chill until set. Yield: 8 to 10 servings.

Valerie Rankin, Preceptor Epsilon Theta
Pinellas Park, Florida

CHOCOLATE MINT PIE

18 chocolate sandwich cookies, finely crushed
3 tablespoons melted butter or margarine
4 cups mint chocolate chip ice cream, softened
1 cup whipped cream
8 chocolate-covered mint candies

Combine cookie crumbs and butter in bowl; mix until crumbly. Press into 9-inch pie plate. Freeze for 1 hour. Spread ice cream in even layer in shell. Freeze for 8 hours. Spoon whipped cream over top. Garnish with candies. Serve immediately. Yield: 8 servings.

Sister in Beta Sigma Phi

NO-MILK CHOCOLATE PIE

1 1/4 cups sugar
1/2 cup all-purpose flour
3 tablespoons baking cocoa
2 cups water
3 egg yolks
1/4 cup butter or margarine
Salt to taste
1 teaspoon vanilla extract
1 baked (9-inch) pie shell
3 egg whites
3 tablespoons sugar

Preheat oven to 350 degrees. Combine sugar, flour and cocoa in bowl; mix well. Add enough of the water to make paste. Add egg yolks; mix well. Heat remaining water with butter and salt in saucepan until butter melts. Stir in sugar mixture. Cook until thickened, stirring constantly. Remove from heat. Add vanilla; mix until blended. Cool. Spoon into pie shell. Beat egg whites in mixer bowl until soft peaks form. Beat in 3 tablespoons sugar gradually, beating until stiff peaks form. Spread over filling, sealing to edge. Bake at 350 degrees until brown.
Yield: 6 to 8 servings.

Debbie Vieregge, Beta Zeta Mu
Malakoff, Texas

CARAMEL-COCONUT PIES

1/4 cup butter or margarine
1 (7-ounce) can flaked coconut
1 cup chopped pecans
1 (14-ounce) can sweetened condensed milk
8 ounces cream cheese, softened
16 ounces whipped topping
3 (9-inch) graham cracker pie shells
1 (12-ounce) jar caramel ice cream topping

Melt butter in large skillet over low heat. Add coconut and pecans. Sauté until golden brown, stirring frequently; set aside. Combine condensed milk and cream cheese in bowl; beat until smooth. Fold in whipped topping. Spoon into pie shells. Drizzle with caramel topping. Sprinkle with coconut mixture. Freeze, covered, until ready to serve. Thaw for 5 minutes before serving. Yield: 18 to 24 servings.

Tatia D. Randolph, Alpha Theta
Fallon, Nevada

MY COCONUT CUSTARD PIE

2 cups 2% milk
4 eggs
3/4 cup sugar
1/2 cup biscuit mix
1/4 cup melted margarine
1 teaspoon vanilla extract
1 (7-ounce) can shredded coconut

Preheat oven to 350 degrees. Combine first 6 ingredients in large mixer bowl; beat until blended. Pour into greased 10-inch deep-dish pie pan. Sprinkle with coconut. Bake at 350 degrees for 40 minutes. Yield: 6 servings.

Effie McVey, Eta Master
Beckley, West Virginia

COTTAGE CHEESE PIE

1 cup cottage cheese
1 cup sugar
1 egg
2 tablespoons cornstarch
1/2 cup milk
Nutmeg to taste
1 unbaked (9-inch) pie shell

Preheat oven to 350 degrees. Press cottage cheese through sieve or ricer. Combine cottage cheese with sugar, egg, cornstarch and milk; mix until blended. Sprinkle with nutmeg. Spoon into pie shell. Bake at 350 degrees for 30 minutes or until brown on top. Yield: 6 to 8 servings.

JoAnne Elling, Iota Kappa
Enid, Oklahoma

CRACKER PIE

3 egg whites
1/2 teaspoon baking powder
1 cup sugar
14 saltine crackers, crushed
2/3 cup chopped walnuts
1 envelope whipped topping mix
Food coloring (optional)

Preheat oven to 350 degrees. Beat egg whites in mixer bowl until stiff peaks form. Beat in baking powder and sugar. Fold in crackers and walnuts. Spread egg white mixture in greased 9-inch pie pan. Bake at 350 degrees for 30 minutes. Cool. Prepare topping mix using package instructions. Tint with food coloring of choice. Spread over baked layer. Chill for 2 hours before serving. Yield: 6 servings.

Linda Walker, Xi Beta Mu
Edmonds, Washington

✣ CRANBERRY PIE

1 (6-ounce) package raspberry gelatin
1/3 cup sugar
1 1/4 cups cranberry juice
3 ounces cream cheese
1/4 cup sugar
1 tablespoon milk
1 teaspoon vanilla extract
1/2 cup whipped topping
1 baked (9-inch) pie shell
1 (16-ounce) can jellied cranberry sauce
Whipped topping to taste

Combine gelatin and sugar in bowl. Bring cranberry juice to a boil in saucepan over medium heat. Remove from heat. Stir into gelatin mixture until gelatin dissolves. Chill until thickened. Combine cream cheese, sugar, milk and vanilla in mixer bowl; beat until light and fluffy. Fold in whipped topping. Spread in pie shell. Spoon cranberry sauce on top. Chill for 8 hours or longer. Top with additional whipped topping when ready to serve.
Yield: 6 servings.

Nancy Swingley, Delta Delta
Portland, Indiana

CREAM CHEESE PIE

1 cup graham cracker crumbs
1/3 cup margarine, softened
2 eggs
3/4 cup sugar
12 ounces cream cheese, softened
2 teaspoons vanilla extract
1 cup sour cream
3 1/2 teaspoons sugar
1 teaspoon vanilla extract

Preheat oven to 350 degrees. Combine graham cracker crumbs and margarine in bowl; mix until crumbly. Pat into 9-inch pie pan. Combine eggs, 3/4 cup sugar, cream cheese and 2 teaspoons vanilla in bowl; beat until fluffy. Spoon into pie shell. Bake at 350 degrees for 20 minutes. Remove from oven. Cool for 5 minutes. Combine sour cream, 3 1/2 teaspoons sugar and 1 teaspoon vanilla in bowl; mix well. Spoon over top of pie. Bake at 350 degrees for 10 minutes longer. Cool completely. Chill for 5 hours. Yield: 12 servings.

N. Marie Mchargue, Xi Iota Sigma
Archie, Missouri

COLD FRUIT PIE

3/4 to 1 cup sugar
2 tablespoons cornstarch
1 cup water
Food coloring (optional)
2 tablespoons flavored gelatin
1 tablespoon lemon juice
Favorite fruit
1 baked (9-inch) pie shell

Combine sugar, cornstarch and water in saucepan; mix well. Cook over low heat until thickened and clear, stirring constantly. Remove from heat; stir in food coloring, gelatin and lemon juice. Let stand until cool. Arrange fruit in pie shell. Spoon gelatin mixture over fruit. Chill until set. Serve cold. Yield: 6 to 8 servings.

Janet Taylor, Preceptor Epsilon Theta
St. Petersburg, Florida

FRUIT SALAD PIE

1 (8-ounce) can pineapple tidbits, drained
2 cups red seedless grapes
1 (8-ounce) can fruit cocktail, drained
1 orange, peeled, sectioned
3/4 cup sugar
1 recipe (2-crust) pie pastry
1 Red Delicious apple, peeled, sliced

Preheat oven to 350 degrees. Combine pineapple, grapes, fruit cocktail and orange in large bowl. Sprinkle sugar over fruit, tossing to coat. Spoon into pastry-lined pie shell. Top with apple slices. Cover with remaining pastry, sealing edge and cutting vents. Bake at 350 degrees for 45 minutes. Yield: 6 servings.

E. Fay Gellhaus, Gamma Delta
Charlestown, Indiana

GRASSHOPPER PIE

This was the first dessert that I served my family at Christmas dinner in my first home. The green color is very festive.

1 1/3 cups crushed chocolate wafers
3 tablespoons butter or margarine, melted
1/3 cup milk
25 large marshmallows
6 tablespoons crème de menthe
1 cup whipped cream

Combine chocolate wafers and butter in bowl; mix well. Press into greased 9-inch pie pan. Combine milk and marshmallows in double boiler over hot water. Cook over low to medium heat until marshmallows melt, stirring frequently. Let stand until cool. Stir in crème de menthe. Fold in whipped cream. Spread in pie shell. Chill for 3 to 4 hours. Yield: 6 to 8 servings.

Jennifer S. Dolson, Lambda Omega
Bolton, Ontario, Canada

RICH GRASSHOPPER PIE

1 cup chocolate wafer crumbs
1 cup milk
1 (10-ounce) package miniature marshmallows
1/4 teaspoon unflavored gelatin
1 tablespoon water
1/3 cup crème de menthe
2 cups whipped cream

Line bottom of greased 9-by-13-inch baking dish with chocolate wafer crumbs. Combine milk and marshmallows in saucepan. Cook over low to medium heat until marshmallows melt and mixture is smooth, stirring constantly. Soften gelatin in water; mix well. Stir into marshmallow mixture until dissolved. Blend in crème de menthe and whipped cream. Spoon into chocolate wafer crust. Chill until set. Yield: 12 servings.

Heather Abel, Lambda
Minnedosa, Manitoba, Canada

LEMON CHEESE PIE

2 tablespoons graham cracker crumbs
1 (4-ounce) package sugar-free lemon gelatin
2/3 cup boiling water
1 cup 1% cottage cheese
8 ounces cream cheese
2 cups light whipped topping

Sprinkle graham cracker crumbs evenly into 9-inch pie plate sprayed with nonstick cooking spray. Dissolve gelatin in boiling water. Place in blender container with cottage cheese and cream cheese. Process until smooth, scraping sides occasionally. Transfer to large bowl. Fold in whipped topping. Spread in prepared pie plate. Chill for 4 hours or until set. Yield: 6 to 8 servings.

Diane Beddinger, Xi Alpha Xi
Sykesville, Maryland

✤ LEMON YOGURT CHEESE PIE

1 (4-ounce) package lemon gelatin
1 cup boiling water
1/2 cup sugar
8 ounces cream cheese, softened
Juice of 1 lemon
8 ounces whipped topping
1 cup lemon yogurt
1 baked (9-inch) pie shell

Dissolve gelatin in boiling water in saucepan. Add sugar and cream cheese; mix well. Stir in lemon juice and half the whipped topping. Add yogurt; mix well. Spoon into pie shell. Chill until firm. Top with remaining whipped topping. Yield: 6 to 8 servings.

Esther Hobson, Laureate Alpha Theta
Lake Havasu, Arizona

EASY LEMON PIE

$1^1/3$ cups sugar
3 tablespoons (slightly rounded) cornstarch
$^1/3$ cup lemon juice
3 egg yolks, beaten
1 tablespoon butter or margarine
Dash of salt
$1^1/2$ cups boiling water
1 (baked) 9-inch pie shell
$^1/3$ cup sugar
3 egg whites, beaten

Preheat oven to 350 degrees. Combine first 6 ingredients in saucepan; mix well. Add boiling water. Cook until thickened, stirring constantly. Spoon into pie shell. Add sugar slowly to beaten egg whites in mixer bowl; beat until stiff and glossy. Spread over filling, sealing to edge. Bake at 350 degrees for 15 minutes or until brown on top. Yield: 6 servings.

Mary Ann Eisenmann, Laureate Alpha Chi
Mason City, Iowa

ENGLISH LEMON PIE

1 tablespoon butter or margarine, softened
1 cup sugar
2 eggs
1 medium lemon
$^1/2$ teaspoon lemon juice
2 large apples, grated
1 unbaked (9-inch) pie shell

Preheat oven to 350 degrees. Cream butter and sugar in mixer bowl until light and fluffy. Add eggs; beat until blended. Grate entire lemon. Add grated lemon and lemon juice to sugar mixture; mix well. Stir in apples. Spoon into pie shell. Bake at 350 degrees for 45 to 50 minutes or until crust is brown and filling is bubbly. Yield: 8 servings.

Barb Sherstone, Preceptor Gamma Lambda
Nanaimo, British Columbia, Canada

LEMON ICEBOX PIE

8 ounces cream cheese, softened
1 (14-ounce) can sweetened condensed milk
$^1/2$ cup lemon juice
$^1/3$ cup sugar
1 teaspoon vanilla extract
2 drops yellow food coloring
1 (9-inch) graham cracker pie shell

Beat cream cheese in mixer bowl until smooth. Add next 5 ingredients; mix until blended. Spoon into pie shell. Chill for 3 hours or until set. Yield: 8 servings.

Patsy Bowen, Beta Kappa
Whitesburg, Kentucky

LEMON JEWEL PIE

1 (16-ounce) can fruit cocktail
3 egg yolks
1 (6-ounce) package lemon instant pudding mix
2 tablespoons sugar
2 tablespoons butter or margarine
1 (9-inch) graham cracker pie shell
3 egg whites
2 tablespoons sugar

Preheat oven to 400 degrees. Drain fruit cocktail, reserving fruit. Add water to juice to measure $2^1/2$ cups of liquid; transfer to bowl. Add egg yolks; mix well. Combine pudding mix and 2 tablespoons sugar in saucepan. Stir juice mixture into pudding mixture. Bring to a boil, stirring constantly. Cook over medium heat until thickened, stirring constantly. Add butter; mix well. Remove from heat. Let stand until cool. Fold in reserved fruit. Spoon into pie shell. Beat egg whites in mixer bowl until foamy. Add sugar; beating until stiff peaks form. Spread over pie filling, sealing to edge. Bake at 400 degrees for 5 minutes. Yield: 8 servings.

Glenette Huckabay, Eta Upsilon
Madera, California

LEMON PIE PUDDING

1 cup all-purpose flour
$^1/2$ cup margarine
$^1/2$ cup pecans, finely chopped
8 ounces cream cheese, softened
1 cup confectioners' sugar
2 (4-ounce) packages lemon instant pudding mix
3 cups milk
Whipped topping to taste
Chopped pecans to taste

Preheat oven to 375 degrees. Combine flour, margarine and pecans in bowl; mix well. Press into greased 9-inch pie pan. Bake at 375 degrees for 15 minutes or until brown. Cool completely. Combine cream cheese, confectioners' sugar, pudding mix and milk in bowl; mix until blended. Spoon into prepared pie pan. Top with whipped topping and additional pecans. Yield: 6 to 8 servings.

Elisa F. Rose, Xi Sigma Mu
Sierra Blanca, Texas

EASY LEMON SPONGE PIE

I learned to make this pie as a very young teenager, as it was one of my very favorites.

2 egg whites
1 cup sugar
3 tablespoons butter or margarine, softened
2 egg yolks, beaten
Juice and grated rind of 1 lemon
3 tablespoons all-purpose flour
1 cup milk
1 unbaked (9-inch) pie shell

Preheat oven to 325 degrees. Beat egg whites in mixer bowl until stiff but not dry; set aside. Combine sugar, butter and egg yolks in mixer bowl; beat until light and fluffy. Add lemon juice and lemon rind; mix well. Beat in flour and milk. Fold in egg whites. Spoon into pie shell. Bake at 325 degrees for 45 minutes. Yield: 6 servings.

Estelle D. Seachrist, Laureate Beta
Claremont, New York

LEMON SPONGE PIE

This was my father's favorite dessert. My grandmother taught my mother to make it and we enjoyed it on his birthday, every February 6.

2 egg whites, stiffly beaten
1 cup sugar
2 tablespoons all-purpose flour
2 tablespoons melted butter or margarine
Salt to taste
2 egg yolks
Juice and grated rind of 1½ lemons
1 cup milk, scalded

Preheat oven to 375 degrees. Mix egg whites, sugar, flour, butter, salt, egg yolks, lemon juice, lemon rind and scalded milk in large bowl. Spoon into pie plate. Bake at 375 degrees for 30 to 35 minutes or until brown. Filling separates into pudding at bottom and cake-like top when baked. Yield: 8 servings.

Linda A. Gardrel, Xi Alpha Alpha
Derry, New Hampshire

PEACHES AND CREAM PIE

My husband and son won first place in a Cub Scout Father-Son Bake-Off with this recipe. It could be made lower in fat by using skim milk and fat-free cream cheese.

¾ cup all-purpose flour
1 teaspoon baking powder
½ teaspoon salt
1 egg
1 (4-ounce) package vanilla pudding and pie filling mix
3 tablespoons butter, softened
½ cup milk
1 (16-ounce) can sliced peaches
8 ounces cream cheese, softened
½ cup sugar
1 tablespoon sugar
½ teaspoon cinnamon

Preheat oven to 350 degrees. Combine first 7 ingredients in large mixer bowl; beat until blended. Pour into greased 10-inch pie plate. Drain peaches, reserving 3 tablespoons juice. Arrange peaches on batter. Beat cream cheese, ½ cup sugar and reserved peach juice until thickened and smooth. Spoon over top to within 1 inch of edge. Sprinkle mixture of 1 tablespoon sugar and cinnamon over top. Bake at 350 degrees for 30 minutes or until golden brown.
Yield: 8 servings.

Wilburn (Kathleen) Bolt, Preceptor Chi
Pineville, West Virginia

Amy Pieper, Xi Theta Phi, Beaman, Iowa, makes Dutch Peach Pie by arranging well drained peach slices from a 29-ounce can in pie shell and pouring mixture of ¼ flour and ½ cup sugar and 1 cup whipping cream over peaches. Bake in preheated 350-degree oven for 45 to 60 minutes or until firm.

GRANDMOTHER'S PEACHES AND CREAM PIE

6 large peaches, peeled
1 unbaked (9-inch) pie shell
1 cup sugar
¼ cup all-purpose flour
½ to ¾ cup heavy cream
Cinnamon to taste

Preheat oven to 400 degrees. Cut peaches into halves. Arrange peaches in pie shell as closely together as possible. Top with mixture of sugar and flour. Spoon cream on top. Sprinkle with cinnamon. Bake at 400 degrees for 10 minutes. Reduce heat to 350 degrees. Bake for 1 hour longer or until bubbly. May substitute half-and-half for heavy cream.
Yield: 6 to 8 servings.

Phyllis Reiter, Laureate Beta Eta
Clive, Iowa

PEANUT BUTTER PIES

2 cups all-purpose flour
1 teaspoon salt
⅔ cup shortening
5 to 7 tablespoons water
2 cups confectioners' sugar
1 cup peanut butter
4 cups milk
¾ cup butter or margarine
1 cup sugar
7 tablespoons cornstarch
½ cup water
6 egg yolks
Salt to taste
1 teaspoon yellow food coloring (optional)
2 tablespoons vanilla extract
2 cups whipping cream
¼ cup sugar
1 teaspoon vanilla extract (optional)

Preheat oven to 350 degrees. Combine flour and 1 teaspoon salt in bowl. Cut in shortening until crumbly. Add water 1 tablespoon at a time, mixing with fork until mixture forms ball. Shape into 2 balls. Chill, covered, for 30 minutes. Roll on lightly floured surface. Fit into pie plates. Bake at 350 degrees for 30 minutes or until golden brown. Combine confectioners' sugar and peanut butter in mixer bowl; mix until crumbly. Reserve 1 cup for topping. Sprinkle remaining mixture in pie shells. Combine milk, butter and 1 cup sugar in double boiler. Cook over medium heat until milk is hot and butter melts, stirring frequently. Combine cornstarch and ½ cup water in medium bowl. Add egg yolks, salt, food coloring and 2 tablespoons vanilla; beat until blended. Stir a small amount of hot mixture into egg yolk mixture; stir egg mixture into hot mixture. Cook until mixture thickens, stirring constantly. Spread over peanut butter mixture. Let stand until cool. Beat whipping cream in mixer bowl until thickened. Beat in ¼ cup sugar and 1 teaspoon vanilla; continue beating until thickened. Spread over pie tops. Sprinkle with reserved peanut butter mixture. Chill until set.
Yield: 12 to 16 servings.

Georgia Taylor, Preceptor Theta
Holly Hill, Florida

PEANUT BUTTER CREAM PIE

This pie is a favorite for serving on holidays or at family get-togethers.

1/3 cup peanut butter
3/4 cup confectioners' sugar
1 baked (9-inch) pie shell
1/3 cup all-purpose flour
1/2 cup sugar
1/8 teaspoon salt
2 cups milk
3 egg yolks
2 tablespoons margarine
1/2 teaspoon vanilla extract
3 egg whites
6 tablespoons sugar

Preheat oven to 350 degrees. Mix peanut butter and confectioners' sugar in bowl until mixture resembles coarse meal. Reserve 1/3 of the mixture. Sprinkle remaining mixture over pie shell. Combine flour, sugar, salt and milk in saucepan. Cook until bubbly, stirring frequently. Beat egg yolks in mixer bowl until light. Add a small amount of hot mixture to egg yolks; stir egg yolks into hot mixture. Cook until bubbly, stirring constantly. Remove from heat. Blend in margarine and vanilla. Spread over prepared layers. Beat egg whites and 6 tablespoons sugar in mixer bowl until stiff peaks form. Spread over filling, sealing to edge. Sprinkle with reserved peanut butter mixture. Bake at 350 degrees for 5 minutes or until brown. Yield: 6 to 8 servings.

Mary Johnson
Fredericktown, Missouri

PEANUT BUTTER CREAM CHEESE PIE

1/2 cup peanut butter
1 (1-pound) package confectioners' sugar
16 ounces cream cheese, softened
1/2 (14-ounce) can sweetened condensed milk
32 ounces whipped topping
1 (9-inch) chocolate crumb pie shell
Melted chocolate to taste

Combine peanut butter, confectioners' sugar, cream cheese and condensed milk in mixer bowl; beat until blended. Fold in half the whipped topping. Spoon into pie shell. Cover with remaining whipped topping. Freeze until serving time. Drizzle melted chocolate over top. Yield: 16 servings.

Dianne Wragg, Xi Alpha Epsilon
Louisville, Kentucky

CARAMEL PECAN PIE

36 caramels
1/4 cup margarine
1/4 cup water
3/4 cup sugar
3 eggs, beaten
1/2 teaspoon vanilla extract
1/4 teaspoon salt
1 cup pecans
1 unbaked (9-inch) pie shell

Preheat oven to 350 degrees. Melt caramels with margarine and water in saucepan over low heat, stirring constantly. Add sugar, eggs, vanilla and salt; mix well. Cook until thickened, stirring constantly. Stir in pecans. Spoon caramel mixture into pie shell. Bake at 350 degrees for 50 minutes. Yield: 6 to 8 servings.

Terrye Godfrey, Xi Delta Eta
Plainview, Texas

CHEESY PECAN PIE

8 ounces cream cheese, softened
1/4 cup sugar
1 teaspoon vanilla extract
1 egg
1 unbaked (9-inch) pie shell
1 1/4 cups pecans
1/4 cup sugar
1 teaspoon vanilla
3 eggs
1 cup light corn syrup
1/4 teaspoon salt

Preheat oven to 350 degrees. Combine cream cheese, 1/4 cup sugar, 1 teaspoon vanilla and 1 egg in mixer bowl; beat until blended. Spread in pie shell. Top with pecans. Combine 1/4 cup sugar, 1 teaspoon vanilla, 3 eggs, corn syrup and salt in mixer bowl; mix well. Spoon over pecans. Bake at 350 degrees for 35 to 40 minutes or until pie tests done.
Yield: 8 servings.

Kathy Cahill, Preceptor Nu Tau
Kilgore, Texas

CHOCOLATE CHIP BOURBON PECAN PIE

2 eggs
1 cup sugar
1/2 cup butter or margarine, softened
3 to 4 teaspoons bourbon
1 teaspoon vanilla extract
1/4 cup cornstarch
1 cup pecans
1 cup semisweet chocolate chips
1 unbaked (9-inch) pie shell
1/4 cup pecans

Preheat oven to 350 degrees. Beat eggs, sugar, butter, bourbon, vanilla and cornstarch in medium mixer bowl until well blended. Stir in 1 cup pecans and chocolate chips. Pour into pie shell. Arrange remaining pecans on top of pie. Bake at 350 degrees for 45 to 50 minutes. Let cool for 1 to 2 hours.
Yield: 8 servings.

Jo Feebeck, Xi Delta Kappa
Crescent Springs, Kentucky

Lorraine V. Cobble, Laureate Gamma Zeta, Rialto, California, makes Light Pineapple Pie with a mixture of 16-ounce can juice-pack pineapple, 1 cup nonfat sour cream and a small sugar-free vanilla instant pudding mix. Pour in baked pie shell and chill.

✣ PUMPKIN PECAN PIES

2 cups all-purpose flour
1/2 cup chopped pecans
1 teaspoon salt
2/3 cup plus 2 tablespoons shortening
4 to 5 tablespoons water
1 (30-ounce) can pumpkin pie filling
1 egg
1 (14-ounce) can sweetened condensed milk
1 cup packed light brown sugar
1/2 cup all-purpose flour
1/2 cup chopped pecans
1/2 cup butter or margarine, chopped
1 teaspoon cinnamon
Whipped cream

Preheat oven to 375 degrees. Combine 2 cups flour, 1/2 cup pecans and salt in medium bowl. Cut in shortening until crumbly. Add water 1 tablespoon at a time, mixing with fork until mixture forms a ball. Divide dough in half. Roll each on floured surface; fit into 2 pie plates. Pour mixture of pie filling, egg and condensed milk into pie shells. Sprinkle mixture of brown sugar, 1/2 cup flour, 1/2 cup pecans, butter and cinnamon over top of pie filling mixture. Bake at 375 degrees for 50 to 55 minutes. Garnish with whipped cream. Yield: 12 to 16 servings.

Michelle Graybeal, Iota Chi
Clayton, Missouri

SUPER EASY PECAN PIE

1 cup pecan halves
1 unbaked (9-inch) pie shell
1/4 cup butter or margarine, softened
1/2 cup sugar
1 cup light corn syrup
1/4 teaspoon salt
3 eggs

Preheat oven to 350 degrees. Arrange pecans in pie shell. Process butter, sugar, corn syrup, salt and eggs in blender until smooth. Pour over pecans. Bake at 350 degrees for 50 minutes. Yield: 8 servings.

Tina Jones, Xi Gamma Lambda
Shattuck, Oklahoma

PECAN PIE

4 eggs, beaten
1 tablespoon all-purpose flour
1 cup sugar
1 cup light corn syrup
2 tablespoons melted butter or margarine
1 teaspoon vanilla extract
1/2 teaspoon cinnamon
1/2 teaspoon nutmeg
1 unbaked (8-inch) pie shell
1/4 cup chopped pecans

Preheat oven to 325 degrees. Combine eggs and flour in large mixer bowl. Add sugar, corn syrup, butter, vanilla, cinnamon and nutmeg; mix well. Pour into pie shell. Sprinkle pecans on top. Bake at 325 degrees for 1 hour or until wooden pick inserted near center comes out clean. Yield: 8 servings.

Prissy Urban, Alpha Chi Chi
Pleasanton, Texas

CREAM CHEESE PINEAPPLE PIE

1/3 cup sugar
1 tablespoon cornstarch
1 (8-ounce) can crushed pineapple
8 ounces cream cheese, softened
1/2 cup sugar
1 teaspoon salt
2 eggs
1/2 cup milk
1/2 teaspoon vanilla extract
1 unbaked (9-inch) pie shell
1/4 cup chopped pecans

Preheat oven to 400 degrees. Combine 1/3 cup sugar, cornstarch and undrained pineapple in small saucepan. Cook over medium heat until mixture is thick and clear, stirring constantly. Let stand until cool. Beat cream cheese, 1/2 cup sugar and salt in small mixer bowl. Add eggs 1 at a time, mix well. Stir in milk and vanilla; mix well. Spread cooled pineapple mixture in bottom of pie shell. Top with cream cheese mixture. Sprinkle with pecans. Bake at 400 degrees for 10 minutes. Reduce oven temperature to 325 degrees. Bake for 50 minutes longer. Let stand until cool. Yield: 8 servings.

Rollande Danilovich, Gamma Zeta
Swastika, Ontario, Canada

CREAMY PINEAPPLE PIE

1 cup milk
1 (6-ounce) package vanilla instant pudding mix
1 pint vanilla ice cream, softened
1 (9-inch) graham cracker pie shell
2 1/2 cups crushed pineapple
1 teaspoon cornstarch

Beat milk, pudding mix and ice cream at low speed in large mixer bowl until blended. Pour into pie shell. Chill in refrigerator. Drain pineapple, reserving 1/2 cup syrup. Combine cornstarch and a small amount of reserved syrup in small saucepan, stirring until smooth. Add pineapple and remaining reserved syrup. Bring to a boil over medium heat. Cook until thick and clear, stirring constantly. Chill in refrigerator. Spread over ice cream layer. Chill, covered, for 1 hour. Yield: 8 servings.

Janet Williams, Xi Gamma Psi
St. Marys, Georgia

FANTASTIC PINEAPPLE PIE

1 (20-ounce) can crushed pineapple
1 (11-ounce) can mandarin oranges, drained
8 ounces whipped topping
1 (14-ounce) can sweetened condensed milk
1/4 cup lemon juice
1 (9-inch) graham cracker pie shell

Pour pineapple into colander. Press with spoon to drain thoroughly. Combine drained pineapple with drained mandarin oranges. Blend whipped topping, condensed milk and lemon juice in large bowl. Fold in pineapple and oranges. Pour into pie shell. Chill, covered, for 1 to 2 hours. Yield: 6 to 8 servings.

Lucille (Becky) Seipel, Lambda Master
Dayton, Ohio

GOLDEN TREASURE PINEAPPLE PIE

1/2 cup sugar
2 tablespoons cornstarch
2 (8-ounce) cans crushed pineapple
2 tablespoons water
2/3 cup sugar
1 tablespoon butter or margarine, softened
1/4 cup all-purpose flour
1 teaspoon vanilla extract
8 ounces cottage cheese
1/4 teaspoon almond flavoring
1/2 teaspoon salt
2 eggs, lightly beaten
1 1/4 cups milk (if using cream-style cottage cheese, do not add milk)
1 unbaked (10-inch) pie shell

Preheat oven to 450 degrees. Combine 1/2 cup sugar, cornstarch, pineapple and water in saucepan. Bring to a boil, stirring constantly. Cook for 1 minute, stirring constantly. Remove from heat; let stand until cool. Combine 2/3 cup sugar and butter in large mixer bowl. Add flour, vanilla, cottage cheese, almond flavoring and salt; mix well. Add eggs and milk; mix well. Spread pineapple mixture evenly in pie shell. Top with cottage cheese mixture; spread evenly. Bake at 450 degrees for 15 minutes. Reduce oven temperature to 325 degrees. Bake 45 minutes longer or until knife inserted near center comes out clean.
Yield: 8 to 10 servings.

Myrtle D. Grim, Laureate Rho
Hot Springs, South Dakota

GRANDMOTHER'S HEAVENLY PINEAPPLE PIES

1/4 cup lemon juice
1 (14-ounce) can sweetened condensed milk
1 cup chopped pecans
1 (20-ounce) can crushed pineapple, drained
16 ounces whipped topping
2 (8-inch) graham cracker pie shells

Combine lemon juice and condensed milk in large mixer bowl; beat until blended. Stir in pecans and pineapple. Fold in whipped topping. Pour into 2 pie shells. Chill for 2 hours or until serving time.
Yield: 12 servings.

Mary Richards, Preceptor Beta Zeta
Greensboro, North Carolina

MILLIONAIRE PINEAPPLE PIE

8 ounces cream cheese, softened
1 cup sugar
1 cup chopped pecans
1 (16-ounce) can crushed pineapple, drained
16 ounces whipped topping
2 (9-inch) graham cracker or chocolate cookie pie shells

Beat cream cheese with sugar in large mixer bowl. Add pecans, pineapple and whipped topping. Pour into 2 pie shells. Chill, covered, in refrigerator for 2 to 3 hours. Yield: 12 to 16 servings.

Cindy Mahanay, Xi Eta Delta
Salina, Kansas

MILLION DOLLAR PINEAPPLE PIE

18 graham crackers, crushed
2 tablespoons reduced-calorie margarine, softened
1 envelope artificial sweetener
1 small package sugar-free vanilla instant pudding mix
1 cup skim milk
2 cups crushed pineapple, drained
4 ounces cream cheese, softened
2 cups light whipped topping
1/2 cup chopped pecans

Preheat oven to 400 degrees. Press mixture of crumbs, margarine and artificial sweetener into 9-inch pie plate. Bake at 400 degrees for 8 minutes. Let stand until cool. Combine next 4 ingredients in medium mixer bowl; mix well. Pour into cooled crust. Top with whipped topping. Garnish with pecans. Chill until serving time. Yield: 8 servings.

Kellee Phillips, Eta Mu
Bay City, Texas

OUT-OF-THIS-WORLD PINEAPPLE PIE

1 (21-ounce) can cherry pie filling
3/4 cup sugar
1 (20-ounce) can crushed pineapple
1 tablespoon cornstarch
1 teaspoon red food coloring
1 (3-ounce) package red raspberry gelatin
6 bananas, sliced
1 cup chopped pecans
2 baked (9-inch) pie shells or 2 (9-inch) graham cracker pie shells
8 ounces whipped topping

Combine pie filling, sugar, pineapple, cornstarch and food coloring in large saucepan. Cook over medium heat until thickened, stirring constantly. Add gelatin; mix well. Let stand until cool. Stir in bananas and pecans. Pour into 2 pie shells. Top with whipped topping. Chill until serving time. Yield: 12 servings.

Marnell Comer, Omega Mu
Ridgeway, Missouri

PUMPKIN PIE

1 (16-ounce) can pumpkin
3/4 cup plus 2 tablespoons sugar
1/4 teaspoon nutmeg
1 teaspoon cinnamon
1/8 teaspoon ginger
1/4 teaspoon salt
1 tablespoon molasses
2 egg yolks, beaten
3/4 cup plus 2 tablespoons milk
2 egg whites, stiffly beaten
1 unbaked (9-inch) pie shell

Preheat oven to 425 degrees. Combine pumpkin, sugar, nutmeg, cinnamon, ginger, salt, molasses, egg yolks and milk in large mixer bowl; mix well. Fold in egg whites gently. Pour into pie shell. Bake at 425 degrees for 15 minutes. Reduce oven temperature to 375 degrees. Bake for 45 minutes longer. Yield: 6 to 8 servings.

Rhonda Stone, Beta Rho
Marianna, Florida

ALMOST LIKE REAL PUMPKIN PIE

Egg substitute equal to 3 eggs
1 cup 1% milk
2 cups pumpkin
1/2 teaspoon salt
1 cup sugar
1 teaspoon cinnamon
1/2 teaspoon nutmeg
1/4 teaspoon cloves
1 unbaked (9- or 10-inch) pie shell
8 ounces low-fat whipped topping

Preheat oven to 425 degrees. Beat egg substitute, milk and pumpkin in large mixer bowl until smooth. Stir in mixture of salt, sugar, cinnamon, nutmeg and cloves; mix well. Pour into pie shell. Bake at 425 degrees for 10 minutes. Reduce oven temperature to 375 degrees. Bake for 1 hour longer or until knife inserted near center comes out clean. Garnish with whipped topping. Yield: 6 to 8 servings.

Bonnie Shwaluk, Chi
Shoal Lake, Manitoba, Canada

EASY PUMPKIN AND ORANGE PIE

1 (16-ounce) can pumpkin or 2 cups puréed fresh pumpkin
1 (12-ounce) can evaporated skim milk
3 egg whites or 1/2 cup egg substitute
1/2 cup sugar
1/2 cup all-purpose flour
1 1/4 teaspoons cinnamon
1/2 teaspoon nutmeg
1/2 teaspoon ginger
1/4 teaspoon cloves
3/4 teaspoon baking powder
1/8 teaspoon salt
2 teaspoons grated orange rind (optional)
1/4 cup packed light brown sugar
1/4 cup quick-cooking oats
1 tablespoon margarine, softened
Whipped topping

Preheat oven to 350 degrees. Process pumpkin, evaporated milk and egg whites in blender until smooth. Add sugar, flour, cinnamon, nutmeg, ginger, cloves, baking powder, salt and orange rind, processing until smooth. Pour into 10-inch pie plate sprayed with nonstick cooking spray. Sprinkle with mixture of brown sugar, oats and margarine. Bake at 350 degrees for 50 to 55 minutes or until knife inserted near center comes out clean. Cool for 15 minutes. Chill in refrigerator for 4 hours. Garnish with whipped topping if desired. Yield: 8 servings.

Sharon L. Boling, Xi Zeta Zeta
Muskogee, Oklahoma

GOOD FOR YOU PUMPKIN PIE

1 (16-ounce) can pumpkin
1 (12-ounce) can evaporated skim milk
1/2 cup skim milk
3/4 cup packed light brown sugar
1/2 teaspoon ginger
1 teaspoon cinnamon
1/4 teaspoon cloves
1/4 teaspoon nutmeg
1/4 teaspoon allspice
1/2 cup light baking mix
2 teaspoons vanilla extract
3 egg whites

Preheat oven to 350 degrees. Combine pumpkin, evaporated milk and skim milk in large mixer bowl. Add brown sugar, ginger, cinnamon, cloves, nutmeg and allspice. Beat baking mix, vanilla and egg whites in bowl for 2 minutes or until well blended. Fold in vanilla and egg whites. Combine with pumpkin mixture, mixing well. Pour into pie pan sprayed with nonstick cooking spray. Bake at 350 degrees for 55 to 60 minutes. Yield: 8 servings.

Joyce Ann Smith, Preceptor Pi
Monclova, Ohio

FAMILY RECIPE PUMPKIN PIES

5 egg yolks, beaten
1 cup sugar
2 cups canned pumpkin
3 tablespoons butter or margarine, softened
1 teaspoon cinnamon
1 teaspoon cloves
1 teaspoon nutmeg
1 teaspoon allspice
1 teaspoon lemon extract
1 cup milk
5 egg whites
1 cup sugar
2 unbaked (9-inch) deep-dish pie shells

Preheat oven to 350 degrees. Combine egg yolks, 1 cup sugar, pumpkin and butter in large mixer bowl. Add cinnamon, cloves, nutmeg, allspice, lemon extract and milk; mix well. Beat egg whites until soft peaks form. Add remaining 1 cup sugar, beating until stiff peaks form. Fold beaten egg whites into pumpkin mixture. Pour into pie shells. Bake at 350 degrees for 45 to 50 minutes or until knife inserted near center comes out clean. Yield: 8 to 9 servings.

Mary Hansard, Beta Alpha Omega
Odessa, Texas

JACK-O'-LANTERN PUMPKIN PIE

Children never want to part with their jack-o'-lantern after Halloween. This is the perfect solution, especially if they help with the cooking and eating.

2 cups mashed cooked pumpkin
1 egg
1/2 cup dry milk powder
1 cup packed light brown sugar
1 teaspoon salt
1 tablespoon pumpkin pie spice
2 tablespoons all-purpose flour
1/4 cup (or less) water
1 unbaked (9-inch) pie shell

Preheat oven to 375 degrees. Process pumpkin, egg, milk powder and brown sugar in blender until smooth. Add salt, pumpkin pie spice and flour; process until smooth. Add enough water to make a thick purée. Pour into pie shell. Bake at 375 degrees for 50 to 60 minutes or until set. Yield: 8 servings.

Ruby Cheaney, Beta Epsilon Omicron
Brackettville, Texas

SENSATIONAL DOUBLE-LAYER PUMPKIN PIE

4 ounces cream cheese, softened
1 tablespoon milk or half-and-half
1 tablespoon sugar
1 1/2 cups whipped topping
1 (9-inch) graham cracker pie shell
1 cup milk or half-and-half
2 (4-ounce) packages vanilla instant pudding mix
1 (16-ounce) can pumpkin
1 teaspoon ground cinnamon
1/2 teaspoon ground ginger
1/4 teaspoon ground cloves
Whipped topping

Whisk cream cheese, 1 tablespoon milk and sugar with wire whisk in large bowl until smooth. Stir in 1 1/2 cups whipped topping gently. Spread over pie shell. Chill in refrigerator until firm. Combine 1 cup milk and pudding mix in large mixer bowl. Beat for 1 to 2 minutes or until blended and thick. Stir in pumpkin, cinnamon, ginger and cloves; mix well. Spread over cream cheese mixture. Chill, covered, for 2 hours or until serving time. Garnish with additional whipped topping. Yield: 6 to 8 servings.

Jennifer Bicking, Zeta Rho
Yucaipa, California

RAISIN PIE

1/4 cup orange juice
1 1/2 cups water
1/2 cup sugar
1 1/2 cups dark raisins
1/2 cup chopped pecans
Rind of 1/2 orange
2 tablespoons all-purpose flour
1/4 cup water
1 recipe (2-crust) pie pastry

Preheat oven to 425 degrees. Combine orange juice, 1 1/2 cups water, sugar, raisins, pecans and orange rind in large saucepan. Bring to a boil, stirring constantly; reduce heat. Cook for 15 minutes, stirring occasionally. Add mixture of flour and 1/4 cup water; mix well. Cook over low heat until thickened, stirring constantly. Remove from heat; let stand until cool. Pour into pastry-lined pie plate. Top with remaining pastry, sealing edge and cutting vents. Bake at 425 degrees for 15 minutes. Reduce oven temperature to 350 degrees. Bake for 15 minutes longer or until brown. Yield: 6 to 8 servings.

Ethel Peplowski, mother of Gwendolyn Puchalski
Manahawkin, New Jersey

SOUR CREAM RAISIN PIE

1 cup raisins
1 cup water
2 egg yolks, beaten
1 cup sugar
1 cup sour cream
1 teaspoon cinnamon
1/2 teaspoon cloves
3 tablespoons cornstarch
1 baked (8-inch) pie shell
2 egg whites
1/3 cup sugar

Preheat oven to 350 degrees. Boil raisins in water in large saucepan for 5 minutes. Combine egg yolks, 1 cup sugar and sour cream in large mixer bowl. Stir in cinnamon, cloves and cornstarch; mix well. Add to raisin mixture. Cook over low heat until thickened, stirring constantly. Pour into pie shell. Beat egg whites in mixer bowl until soft peaks form. Add 1/3 cup sugar gradually, beating until stiff peaks form. Spread over raisin mixture, sealing to edge. Bake at 350 degrees until golden. Yield: 8 servings.

Sharon Bittner, Xi Upsilon Omicron
Angels Camp, California

MOCK SOUR CREAM RAISIN PIE

1 cup skim milk
1 cup plain yogurt
1 large package sugar-free vanilla pudding mix
1/2 teaspoon ground allspice
3/4 cup raisins
1 baked (9-inch) pie shell
8 ounces light whipped topping

Bring milk, yogurt and pudding mix to a boil in medium saucepan, stirring constantly. Add allspice and raisins; mix well. Remove from heat. Cool for 10 minutes, stirring occasionally. Pour into pie shell. Chill, covered, for 2 hours or longer. Garnish with whipped topping. Yield: 8 servings.

Marion Olson, Preceptor Kappa
Havre, Montana

FAVORITE SOUR CREAM RAISIN PIE

2 cups raisins, rinsed, drained
1 unbaked (9-inch) pie shell
1 1/3 cups sugar
1/4 teaspoon cloves
1 teaspoon cinnamon
2 cups sour cream
3 egg yolks
Salt to taste
3 egg whites
1/3 cup sugar

Preheat oven to 350 degrees. Pour raisins into pie shell. Combine 1 1/3 cups sugar, cloves, cinnamon, sour cream, egg yolks and salt in medium mixer bowl; mix well. Pour over raisins. Bake at 350 degrees for 40 minutes. Beat egg whites with 1/3 cup sugar until stiff peaks form. Spread over filling, sealing to edge. Bake for 5 minutes longer or until meringue browns. Yield: 6 to 8 servings.

Margaret Gebhardt, Alpha Epsilon
Minneapolis, Minnesota

RED RASPBERRY PIE

1 1/2 cups all-purpose flour
1 tablespoon sugar
1/2 teaspoon salt
1/2 cup vegetable oil
1 tablespoon milk
1 cup water
1 cup sugar
2 tablespoons cornstarch
1 (3-ounce) package red raspberry gelatin
3 cups red raspberries
8 ounces whipped topping

Preheat oven to 400 degrees. Combine flour, 1 tablespoon sugar, salt, oil and milk in 9-inch pie plate, stirring with fork until mixture forms a ball. Press over bottom and side of pie plate. Bake at 400 degrees for 10 to 12 minutes or until light brown. Let stand until cool. Bring water, 1 cup sugar and cornstarch to a boil in small saucepan, stirring constantly. Boil for 1 minute or until thickened, stirring constantly. Dissolve gelatin in hot mixture. Remove from heat; let stand until cool. Arrange raspberries in baked pie shell. Pour gelatin mixture over the top. Chill until serving time. Top with whipped topping. May substitute strawberries or peaches for raspberries. Yield: 6 to 8 servings.

Eleanor DeVore, Preceptor Alpha
Cumberland, Maryland

STRAWBERRY PIE

1 cup plus 2 tablespoons sugar
1 cup water
1/8 teaspoon salt
3 tablespoons cornstarch
3 tablespoons water
2 tablespoons plus 2 teaspoons wild strawberry gelatin
1 teaspoon red food coloring
1 quart ripe fresh strawberries
1 baked (9-inch) pie shell
16 ounces low-fat whipped topping

Combine sugar, 1 cup water and salt in large saucepan. Boil until sugar is dissolved, stirring frequently. Add cornstarch dissolved in 3 tablespoons water. Cook until clear, stirring constantly. Remove from heat. Add gelatin and food coloring, stirring until gelatin is dissolved. Cool to lukewarm. Arrange strawberries in pie shell. Pour gelatin mixture evenly over the top. Top with whipped topping. Chill until serving time. Yield 6 to 8 servings.

Phyllis Putnam, Tau Beta
Harris, Missouri

STRAWBERRY-BANANA PIE

1 baked (10-inch) pie shell
3 bananas, sliced
2 cups whipping cream
3/4 cup confectioners' sugar
8 ounces cream cheese, softened
2 teaspoons vanilla extract
2 to 3 tablespoons cornstarch
1 (8-ounce) package frozen strawberries, thawed

Line bottom of pie shell with bananas. Beat whipping cream, confectioners' sugar, cream cheese and vanilla in medium mixer bowl until smooth. Pour over bananas. Combine cornstarch and strawberries in medium saucepan. Cook over low heat until thickened, stirring constantly. Remove from heat; let stand until cool. Spread over cream cheese mixture. Chill until serving time. Yield: 8 servings.

Nancy L. Fisher, Beta Alpha Omega
Odessa, Texas

STRAWBERRY LOVER'S PIE

2 (1-ounce) squares semisweet chocolate
1 tablespoon butter or margarine
1 baked (9-inch) pie shell
6 ounces cream cheese, softened
1/2 cup sour cream
Sugar to taste
3 tablespoons vanilla extract
3 to 4 cups fresh strawberries
1/3 cup strawberry jam, melted
1 (1-ounce) square semisweet chocolate

Melt 2 ounces chocolate and butter in small saucepan over low heat, stirring until blended. Spread over bottom and side of pie shell. Chill in refrigerator. Beat cream cheese, sour cream, sugar and vanilla in small mixer bowl until smooth. Spread over chocolate. Chill, covered, for 2 hours. Arrange strawberries stem end down over the filling. Brush jam over strawberries. Melt remaining 1 ounce chocolate. Drizzle over the top of strawberries.
Yield: 6 to 8 servings.

Kathy Loyd, Preceptor Alpha Mu
Deer Lodge, Tennessee

STRAWBERRY OR RASPBERRY CRACKER PIE

3 egg whites
1/4 teaspoon cream of tartar
1 teaspoon vanilla extract
1 cup sugar
16 crushed saltines
1/2 cup chopped pecans or walnuts
8 ounces whipped topping
1 quart fresh strawberries or 1 pound frozen strawberries, thawed, drained

Preheat oven to 325 degrees. Beat egg whites and cream of tartar in large mixer bowl until soft peaks form. Add vanilla and sugar gradually, beating until stiff peaks form. Fold in crumbs and pecans. Spread over bottom and side of 9-inch greased and floured pie pan. Bake at 325 degrees for 35 to 40 minutes or until light golden brown. Cool. Spoon mixture of whipped topping and strawberries into cooled crust. Chill until serving time. May substitute raspberries for strawberries. Yield: 6 to 8 servings.

Mary Hildebrand, Xi Lambda Mu
Sunrise Beach, Missouri

SUGAR-FREE STRAWBERRY PIE

1 small package sugar-free vanilla pudding mix
1 small package sugar-free strawberry gelatin
2 1/2 cups cold water
4 cups sliced or whole strawberries
1 baked (9-inch) pie shell or (9-inch) graham cracker pie shell
Whipped cream

Bring mixture of pudding mix, gelatin and water to a boil over medium heat, stirring constantly. Remove from heat. Cool in refrigerator until slightly thickened. Arrange strawberries in pie shell. Pour gelatin mixture over strawberries. Chill in refrigerator until set. Garnish with whipped cream.
Yield: 6 to 8 servings.

Margaret A. Dingess, Preceptor Chi
Tacoma, Washington

STRAWBERRY PIE SUPREME

4 cups fresh strawberries
1 cup sugar
1/4 teaspoon salt
3 tablespoons cornstarch
1 baked (9-inch) pie shell
1/2 cup whipping cream
Strawberry halves
Mint leaves

Mash 2 cups of strawberries. Mix with sugar, salt and cornstarch in medium saucepan. Cook over medium heat until mixture is thick, stirring constantly. Remove from heat. Let stand until cool. Add remaining 2 cups strawberries. Spoon into pie shell. Whip whipping cream in small mixer bowl until stiff; heap on top of strawberry mixture. Garnish with strawberry halves and mint leaves. Yield: 8 servings.

Wendy Pauzé, Xi Rho
Cambridge Station, Nova Scotia, Canada

SWEET POTATO PIE

3 cups mashed cooked sweet potatoes
1 cup applesauce
1/2 cup plain yogurt
1/4 cup honey
2 eggs, beaten
1/4 cup bran
2 teaspoons cinnamon
1/4 teaspoon ginger
1/4 teaspoon coriander
Nutmeg, allspice and cloves to taste
1 unbaked (9-inch) pie shell

Preheat oven to 350 degrees. Combine sweet potatoes, applesauce, yogurt, honey and eggs in large mixer bowl; mix well. Add bran, cinnamon, ginger, coriander, nutmeg, allspice and cloves; mix well. Pour into pie shell. Bake at 350 degrees for 25 minutes. Serve warm or chilled. Yield: 8 servings.

Lou Etta Cummins, Beta Alpha Omega
Odessa, Texas

OLD SOUTHERN RECIPE VINEGAR PIE

1 1/2 cups sugar
1 tablespoon all-purpose flour
1/2 cup melted margarine or butter, cooled
1 tablespoon vanilla extract
2 tablespoons apple cider vinegar
1 unbaked (9-inch) pie shell

Preheat oven to 300 degrees. Combine sugar, flour, margarine, vanilla and vinegar in medium mixer bowl; mix well. Pour into pie shell. Bake at 300 degrees for 45 minutes. Yield: 8 servings.

Linda D. Hinkle, Delta Sigma
Louisville, Colorado

ZUCCHINI PIE

People can't believe this pie is made with zucchini. It tastes and looks like apple pie.

3 cups sliced zucchini
3 tablespoons lemon juice
5 tablespoons (heaping) all-purpose flour
1 1/4 cups sugar
1/4 teaspoon salt
1/2 teaspoon cinnamon
1/2 teaspoon nutmeg
1 unbaked (9-inch) pie shell
3/4 cup margarine, softened
3/4 cup sugar
1 cup all-purpose flour

Preheat oven to 350 degrees. Combine zucchini and lemon juice in small bowl; set aside. Combine 5 tablespoons flour, 1 1/4 cups sugar, salt, cinnamon and nutmeg in medium bowl. Toss with zucchini. Pour into pie shell. Mix margarine, 3/4 cup sugar and 1 cup flour with fork until crumbly. Sprinkle over zucchini. Bake at 350 degrees for 1 hour. Yield: 8 servings.

Cathy Ross
Fremont, Nebraska

ZUCCHINI MOCK APPLE PIE

Zucchini
$1^1/_4$ cups sugar
2 tablespoons all-purpose flour
$1^1/_2$ teaspoons cream of tartar
$1^1/_2$ teaspoons cinnamon
2 tablespoons lemon juice
Salt and nutmeg to taste
1 recipe (2-crust) pie pastry
Butter or margarine to taste

Preheat oven to 400 degrees. Peel zucchini. Slice lengthwise; discard seeds and slice enough to yield 4 cups. Simmer zucchini in water to cover in small saucepan until tender; drain. Place in cold water for 5 minutes; drain. Combine next 7 ingredients in large bowl; mix well. Stir in zucchini. Spoon into pastry-lined pie plate. Dot with butter. Top with remaining pastry, sealing edge and cutting vents. Bake at 400 degrees for 40 to 50 minutes or until brown.
Yield: 6 to 8 servings.

Carol Brazeal, Beta Pi
Lakeview, Oregon

FOOLPROOF PIE CRUSTS

5 cups all-purpose flour
1 tablespoon sugar
2 teaspoons salt
$1^3/_4$ cups shortening
1/2 cup water
1 egg
1 tablespoon vinegar

Preheat oven to 450 degrees. Combine flour, sugar and salt in medium bowl. Cut in shortening until crumbly. Beat water, egg and vinegar together. Add to flour mixture; mix with fork until mixture forms a ball. Divide into 4 portions. Chill, wrapped in plastic wrap, for 30 minutes. Roll each portion into a 12-inch circle on lightly floured surface. Fit into pie plate. Prick in many places. Bake at 450 degrees for 12 to 15 minutes on lowest oven rack. Yield: 4 crusts.

Willy Felton, Beta Pi
Lakeview, Oregon

BLUEBERRY CRUMBLE TART

1 cup butter or margarine, softened
1/3 cup sugar
1 egg
$2^1/_2$ cups all-purpose flour
1 (21-ounce) can blueberry pie filling
Confectioners' sugar to taste

Preheat oven to 350 degrees. Cream butter, sugar and egg in small mixer bowl until light and fluffy. Stir in flour. Press half the dough into 10-inch springform pan. Spoon pie filling over the top. Grate remaining half of dough, using coarsest side of grater. Sprinkle over top of pie filling. Bake at 350 degrees for 50 to 60 minutes or until golden brown. Cool. Sprinkle with confectioners' sugar. Yield: 8 to 12 servings.

Nancy Fisher, Zeta Phi
Georgetown, Ontario, Canada

BUTTER TARTS

2 cups raisins
7 cups packed light brown sugar
2 cups margarine, softened
1/4 cup light corn syrup
1 teaspoon salt
4 teaspoons vanilla extract
1/4 cup all-purpose flour
8 eggs
4 dozen tart shells

Soak raisins in enough hot water to cover in small bowl for 10 to 15 minutes. Preheat oven to 350 degrees. Combine brown sugar, margarine, corn syrup, salt, vanilla and flour in large mixer bowl; mix well. Beat in eggs 1 at a time. Stir in raisin mixture. Fill pastry shells half full. Bake at 350 degrees for 15 to 20 minutes. Yield: 4 dozen.

Belinda Holliday, Xi Alpha Zeta
North Bay, Ontario, Canada

BEST-EVER BUTTER TARTS

2/3 cup butter or margarine, softened
1 cup all-purpose flour
$1^1/_2$ tablespoons confectioners' sugar
Salt to taste
Currants and chopped walnuts to taste
1/3 cup butter or margarine, softened
1 cup packed light brown sugar
1 egg
2 tablespoons evaporated milk
1 teaspoon vanilla extract

Preheat oven to 325 degrees. Cut 2/3 cup butter into flour with pastry blender in medium bowl. Stir in confectioners' sugar and salt; knead lightly. Roll on lightly floured surface. Cut with cookie cutter; fit into tart pans. Place currants and walnuts in tart shells. Beat 1/3 cup butter, brown sugar and egg in small mixer bowl. Add evaporated milk and vanilla; beat until thick. Spoon into tart shells. Bake at 325 degrees for 5 minutes or until golden brown. Serve warm. Yield: 1 dozen large or 2 dozen small tarts.

Laura Downey, Alpha Epsilon
Thunder Bay, Ontario, Canada

GREAT-GRANDMA'S BUTTER TARTS

1/2 cup raisins
1/4 cup butter or margarine, softened
1/2 cup packed light brown sugar
1/4 teaspoon salt
1/2 cup light corn syrup
1 egg, beaten
1 teaspoon vanilla extract
Lemon juice to taste
1 recipe pie pastry for 12 medium-size tarts

Preheat oven to 375 degrees. Combine raisins with boiling water to cover in small bowl. Soak until raisin edges turn white; drain. Combine butter and brown sugar in large mixer bowl, blending until smooth. Add salt, corn syrup, egg, vanilla and lemon juice; mix just until blended. Stir in raisins. Roll pastry to 1/8-inch thickness. Cut into 4-inch rounds; fit into tart pans. Fill half full with raisin mixture. Bake at 375 degrees for 20 to 25 minutes. Yield: 12 medium-size tarts.

Mary Ruth Noiles, Laureate Beta Tau
Waterford, Ontario, Canada

PECAN TARTS

3 ounces cream cheese, softened
1/2 cup butter or margarine, softened
1 cup sifted all-purpose flour
3/4 cup packed light brown sugar
1 tablespoon butter or margarine, softened
1 teaspoon vanilla extract
2/3 cup chopped pecans
1 egg

Preheat oven to 325 degrees. Beat cream cheese and 1/2 cup butter in small mixer bowl. Add flour gradually, mixing well. Chill, covered, in refrigerator for 1 hour. Shape dough into 24 one-inch balls. Press into ungreased small muffin cups. Combine brown sugar, 1 tablespoon butter, vanilla, pecans and egg in medium bowl; mix well. Spoon into tart shells. Bake at 325 degrees for 25 minutes. Let cool in pans. Yield: 24 small tarts.

Delores Kopec, Kappa Master
Bay City, Michigan

VANILLA FRUIT CHIP TART

3/4 cup butter or margarine, softened
1/2 cup confectioners' sugar
11/2 cups all-purpose flour
1 (10-ounce) package vanilla milk chips
1/4 cup whipping cream
8 ounces cream cheese, softened
1/4 cup sugar
1 tablespoon cornstarch
1/2 cup pineapple juice
1/2 teaspoon lemon juice
Assorted fresh fruit

Preheat oven to 300 degrees. Beat butter and confectioners' sugar in medium mixer bowl until light and fluffy. Blend in flour. Press over bottom and side of 12-inch round pizza pan. Bake at 300 degrees for 20 to 25 minutes or until light brown. Let stand until cool. Microwave vanilla chips and whipping cream in microwave-safe medium mixer bowl on High for 1 to 11/2 minutes or until chips are melted; stir until smooth. Beat in cream cheese. Spread over cooled crust. Combine sugar, cornstarch, pineapple juice and lemon juice in small saucepan. Cook over medium heat until thickened, stirring constantly. Remove from heat. Let stand until cool. Slice and arrange fruit over cream cheese mixture. Pour cooled juice mixture over the top. Yield: 10 to 12 servings.

Kathy Rand, Xi Alpha Pi
Madison, Wisconsin

APPLE PIZZAS

4 eggs
21/2 cups sugar
3 cups all-purpose flour
2 teaspoons baking powder
3/4 cup margarine
1 cup boiling water
4 apples, diced
1/4 cup sugar
1 teaspoon cinnamon

Preheat oven to 300 degrees. Combine first 4 ingredients in medium bowl. Melt margarine in boiling water. Add to egg mixture; mix well. Pour mixture into 2 large nonstick pizza pans. Top with apples. Sprinkle with mixture of sugar and cinnamon. Bake at 300 degrees for 25 to 30 minutes or until golden brown. Yield: 16 to 20 servings.

Nancy Burcsik, Laureate Beta Tau
Delhi, Ontario, Canada

BROWN SUGAR AND APPLE PIZZA

1 (20-ounce) package refrigerated sugar cookie dough
1/4 cup creamy peanut butter
8 ounces cream cheese, softened
1/2 cup packed light brown sugar
1/2 teaspoon vanilla extract
2 Yellow Delicious apples
Lemon-lime soda to taste
Cinnamon to taste
1/4 cup caramel ice cream topping
1/2 cup chopped peanuts

Preheat oven to 350 degrees. Press cookie dough into large pizza pan. Bake at 350 degrees for 11 to 14 minutes. Cool. Mix peanut butter, cream cheese and brown sugar in small mixer bowl until creamy. Add vanilla. Spread over cooled baked layer. Slice apples into small bowl; pour in enough lemon-lime soda to cover; drain. Arrange apples over peanut butter mixture. Sprinkle with cinnamon. Drizzle caramel topping over apples. Sprinkle peanuts over top. Yield: 10 to 12 servings.

Karen Brondel, Xi Chi
Jefferson City, Missouri

BROWNIE PIZZA

1 (22-ounce) package brownie mix
8 ounces cream cheese, softened
1/4 cup sugar
Sliced strawberries to taste
1/2 cup melted chocolate

Preheat oven to 350 degrees. Prepare brownie mix using package directions. Spread mixture onto 12-inch nonstick pizza pan. Bake using package directions. Cool. Blend cream cheese and sugar in small mixer bowl. Spread over brownie layer. Top with strawberries. Drizzle with melted chocolate. Yield: 8 to 10 servings.

Cindy Bentlage, Mu Epsilon
Jefferson City, Missouri

FRUIT PIZZA PIE

1/2 cup margarine, softened
1/2 cup shortening
1 cup sugar
1 egg
2 cups all-purpose flour
1 teaspoon baking soda
1 teaspoon cream of tartar
8 ounces cream cheese, softened
8 ounces whipped topping
Strawberry halves
Banana slices
Kiwifruit slices
1 (8-ounce) can pineapple chunks, drained
1/2 cup sugar
1/4 cup water
1/2 cup orange juice
1 tablespoon cornstarch
2 tablespoons lemon juice

Preheat oven to 350 degrees. Mix margarine, shortening, sugar and egg in large mixer bowl until light and fluffy. Add flour, baking soda and cream of tartar; mix well. Press over bottom and side of large pizza pan. Bake at 350 degrees until golden brown. Let stand until cool. Combine cream cheese and whipped topping in small mixer bowl; mix until smooth. Spread over baked layer. Arrange strawberries in circle around outer edge of pizza. Arrange circle of bananas, circle of kiwifruit and circle of pineapple. Place additional strawberries in center. Combine 1/2 cup sugar, water, orange juice, cornstarch and lemon juice in small saucepan. Bring to a boil, stirring constantly. Boil for 1 minute, stirring constantly. Remove from heat. Let stand until cool. Spread over fruit. Chill, covered, for 4 to 12 hours before serving. Yield: 10 to 12 servings.

Grace Hreno, Xi Eta Chi
Niles, Ohio

FRUIT AND CAKE PIZZA

1 (2-layer) package yellow cake mix
1/2 cup vegetable oil
1 tablespoon water
8 ounces cream cheese, softened
1 teaspoon lemon juice
11/2 cups confectioners' sugar
Bite-size assorted fruit

Preheat oven to 350 degrees. Combine cake mix, oil and water in bowl; mix well. Spread on ungreased pizza pan. Bake at 350 degrees for 6 to 10 minutes or until golden brown. Let stand until cool. Combine cream cheese, lemon juice and confectioners' sugar in small mixer bowl; beat until smooth. Spread over cooled baked layer. Chill in refrigerator. Top with assorted fruit just before serving.
Yield: 8 to 10 servings.

Lynda Kreklewich, Sigma
Estevan, Saskatchewan, Canada

FRUIT PIZZA WITH MARMALADE SAUCE

1 (20-ounce) package refrigerated sugar cookie dough
8 ounces cream cheese, softened
1 teaspoon vanilla extract
1/2 cup sugar
Strawberries, sliced
Grapes
Bananas, sliced
Kiwifruit, sliced
Cherries, pitted
Orange sections
Blueberries
1 cup orange marmalade

Preheat oven to 350 degrees. Press cookie dough into greased pizza pan. Bake at 350 degrees for 10 minutes or until golden brown. Combine cream cheese, vanilla and sugar in small mixer bowl; beat until smooth. Spread over cooled baked layer. Cut fruit into bite-size pieces. Arrange fruit in circular pattern on top. Microwave marmalade in small microwave-safe bowl on High for 1 minute. Spoon over top of fruit. Yield: 12 servings.

Gail Gunton, Eta Zeta
Simcoe, Ontario, Canada

FRUIT PIZZA WITH ORANGE SAUCE

1 (18-ounce) package refrigerated sugar cookie dough
41/2 ounces cream cheese, softened
41/2 ounces whipped topping
1 pint fresh strawberries, halved
2 to 3 bananas, sliced into rounds
1 (16-ounce) can sliced peaches, drained
1 (8-ounce) can pineapple chunks, drained
1/2 cup sugar
Salt to taste
1 tablespoon cornstarch
1/2 cup orange juice
2 tablespoons lemon juice
1/4 cup water
1/2 teaspoon grated orange rind

Slice cookie dough into 1/8-inch thick rounds. Arrange on lightly greased 14-inch pizza pan, beginning 1/4-inch from edge of pan in circular pattern and slightly overlapping. Press together lightly to seal. Bake according to package directions or until edges just begin to brown. Blend cream cheese and whipped topping in small mixer bowl until smooth. Spread over cooled baked layer. Arrange strawberries in circle around outer edge. Arrange circles of bananas, peaches and pineapple, placing additional strawberries in center. Combine sugar, salt and cornstarch in small saucepan. Add orange juice, lemon juice and water gradually, mixing well. Cook over medium heat until mixture thickens and comes to a boil, stirring constantly. Boil for 1 minute, stirring constantly. Remove from heat. Stir in orange rind. Let stand until cool. Spoon desired amount over fruit. Serve with remaining sauce. Yield: 12 servings.

Mary Christiansen, Preceptor Xi Xi
Norco, California

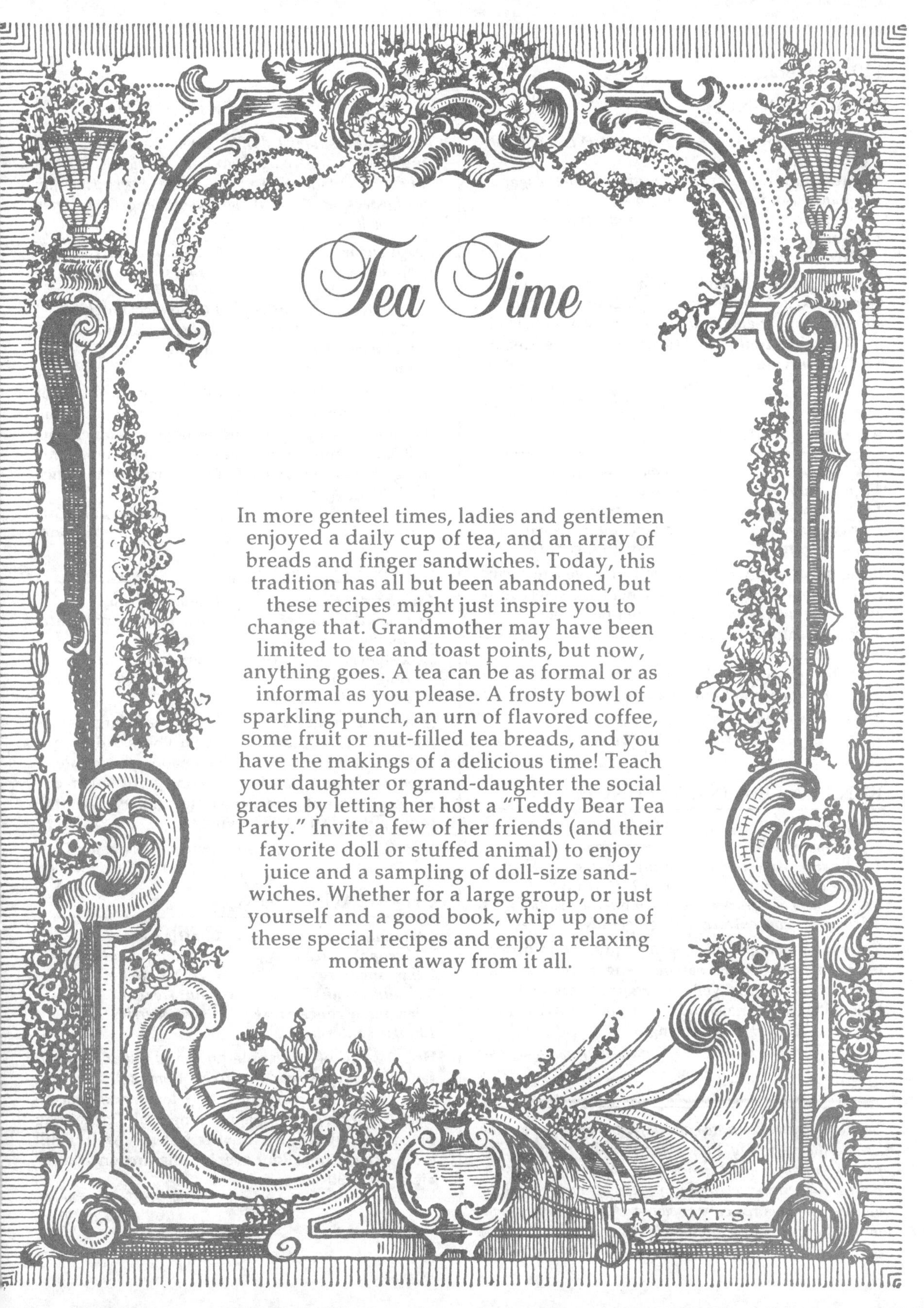

Tea Time

In more genteel times, ladies and gentlemen enjoyed a daily cup of tea, and an array of breads and finger sandwiches. Today, this tradition has all but been abandoned, but these recipes might just inspire you to change that. Grandmother may have been limited to tea and toast points, but now, anything goes. A tea can be as formal or as informal as you please. A frosty bowl of sparkling punch, an urn of flavored coffee, some fruit or nut-filled tea breads, and you have the makings of a delicious time! Teach your daughter or grand-daughter the social graces by letting her host a "Teddy Bear Tea Party." Invite a few of her friends (and their favorite doll or stuffed animal) to enjoy juice and a sampling of doll-size sandwiches. Whether for a large group, or just yourself and a good book, whip up one of these special recipes and enjoy a relaxing moment away from it all.

ALMOND PUNCH

1 (12-ounce) can frozen orange juice concentrate
1 (6-ounce) can frozen lemonade concentrate
1 (46-ounce) can pineapple juice
1 (12-ounce) can apricot nectar
1/2 cup (or more) sugar
1/2 to 3/4 small bottle almond extract

Prepare orange juice and lemonade in large container using package directions. Add pineapple juice, apricot nectar, sugar and almond extract; mix well. Chill until serving time. May freeze and serve slushy. Yield: 48 servings.

Judy Thornton, Xi Alpha Kappa
Clarksville, Arkansas

BANANA PUNCH

2 cups sugar
8 cups water
1 (12-ounce) can frozen orange juice concentrate
3 ounces lemon juice
1 (46-ounce) can pineapple juice
5 large bananas, mashed
2 quarts ginger ale

Bring sugar and water to a boil in large saucepan. Boil for 3 minutes. Remove from heat. Let stand until cool. Pour into large freezer container. Add orange juice concentrate, lemon juice, pineapple juice and bananas; mix well. Freeze completely. Let stand at room temperature until partially thawed. Spoon into punch bowl and add ginger ale to make a slush. Yield: 20 servings.

Danna Del McDermott, Xi Zeta Iota
Bartow, Florida

BANANA LEMONADE PUNCH

1 (46-ounce) can pineapple juice
1 (12-ounce) can orange juice concentrate
1 (12-ounce) can frozen lemonade concentrate
6 bananas, mashed
3 cups sugar
6 cups water
1 to 2 liters diet lemon-lime soda or ginger ale

Combine pineapple juice, orange juice concentrate, lemonade concentrate, bananas, sugar and water in large container; mix well. Freeze until serving time. Mix with lemon-lime soda in punch bowl before serving. Yield: 30 to 40 servings.

Sister in Beta Sigma Phi

June Lindbloom, Laureate Lambda, Jensen Beach, Florida, keeps Always-Ready Punch for drop-by friends. She freezes pineapple juice in ice cube trays and stores in plastic bags in freezer ready to place in punch bowl or glasses and adds red creme soda or tropical punch soda with a garnish of fresh mint and orange slices.

JAN'S BETA SIGMA PHI PUNCH

This recipe is submitted in loving memory of our sister, Jan Pearson who departed our circle of friends in 1989. This is an outstanding punch recipe. Every time Jan was hostess, we'd ask if she was serving Beta Sigma Phi Punch. She never let us down.

2 cups sugar
1 cup water
1 (46-ounce) can pineapple juice, chilled
3 (12-ounce) cans frozen pink lemonade concentrate, thawed
2 (25-ounce) bottles Tom Collins mix, chilled
1 (32-ounce) bottle ginger ale, chilled
Ice ring

Boil sugar and water in small saucepan until sugar dissolves. Combine pineapple juice, lemonade concentrate and sugar mixture in large container; mix well. Chill until serving time. Add Tom Collins mix and ginger ale; mix well. Pour over ice ring in punch bowl. Yield: 40 servings.

Bette Jalufka, Xi Psi Beta
Beeville, Texas

BOURBON SLUSH

4 tea bags
2 cups boiling water
2 cups sugar
1 (12-ounce) can frozen orange juice concentrate, thawed
1 (6-ounce) can lemonade concentrate, thawed
7 cups water
1 cup bourbon

Steep tea bags in 2 cups boiling water in large saucepan for 2 to 3 minutes. Remove tea bags. Add sugar, orange juice concentrate, lemonade concentrate, 7 cups water and bourbon, stirring until sugar dissolves. Pour into freezer containers. Freeze until serving time. Yield: 25 servings.

Leslie Verslues, Alpha Alpha Delta
Jefferson City, Missouri

CHAMPAGNE PUNCH

1 (46-ounce) can pineapple juice
2 cups sugar
3 (6-ounce) cans frozen lemonade concentrate
1 bottle sauterne
1 bottle Champagne
2 (28-ounce) bottles ginger ale
1 pint frozen strawberries

Heat 1/3 can of pineapple juice and sugar in small saucepan until sugar dissolves. Remove from heat. Pour into large container. Add lemonade concentrate, sauterne, Champagne, ginger ale, remaining pineapple juice and strawberries; mix well. Chill until serving time. Pour over ice rings in punch bowl. Yield: 20 to 30 servings.

Stephanie Cortez, Eta Mu
Bay City, Texas

CRANBERRY PUNCH

4 cups cranberry juice
$1^1/_2$ cups sugar
4 cups pineapple juice
1 tablespoon almond extract
2 liters ginger ale
Fresh fruit slices to taste
Rum to taste (optional)

Combine cranberry juice, sugar, pineapple juice and almond extract in large container, stirring constantly until sugar dissolves. Chill until serving time. Pour in punch bowl. Stir in ginger ale. Garnish with fruit slices. Rum may be added in desired amount. Yield: 30 servings.

Patti Stewart, Preceptor Mu Tau
Austin, Texas

LEMONADE SPECIAL

2 quartered unpeeled lemons
$1^1/_2$ cups sugar
2 cups milk
Ice and club soda to taste

Process lemons, sugar and milk in blender. Chill in refrigerator for 1 to 2 days. Fill serving glass $^1/_4$ full with lemon mixture. Add ice and club soda; mix well. Yield: 6 servings.

Patricia Shannon, Zeta Phi
St. Charles, Missouri

ORANGE MINT DRINK

2 cups sugar
$2^1/_2$ cups water
Mint leaves to taste
Juice of 3 oranges
Rind of 1 orange
Juice of 6 lemons
Ginger ale to taste
Chipped ice

Boil sugar and water in large saucepan for 10 minutes. Add mint leaves, orange juice, orange rind and lemon juice. Let stand until cool. Strain in sieve, reserving orange drink mixture. Serve half orange drink mixture-half ginger ale or to taste poured over chipped ice in serving glasses. Yield: 20 servings.

Ida M. Whitworth, Laureate Alpha
Albuquerque, New Mexico

PUNCH SUPREME

2 cups sugar
2 cups warm water
1 (12-ounce) can Five-Alive or frozen orange juice concentrate
1 (6-ounce) can frozen limeade concentrate
1 (46-ounce) can pineapple juice
1 liter lemon-lime soda
$^1/_4$ to $^1/_2$ bottle vodka

Dissolve sugar in warm water in punch bowl. Stir in Five-Alive concentrate, limeade concentrate, pineapple juice, lemon-lime soda and vodka. Chill until serving time. Yield: 30 servings.

Kathy Ward, Xi Eta Eta
Greensburg, Pennsylvania

QUICK AND EASY PARTY PUNCH

1 (6-ounce) can frozen lemonade concentrate
1 (6-ounce) can frozen pineapple juice concentrate
1 (6-ounce) can frozen orange juice concentrate
5 cups water
2 (29-ounce) bottles ginger ale, chilled
Ice ring
Orange and lemon slices
Halved strawberries
Sprigs of mint

Mix lemonade concentrate, pineapple concentrate and orange juice concentrate with water in large container. Chill until serving time. Pour in punch bowl. Add ginger ale and ice ring 5 minutes before serving. Garnish with orange and lemon slices, strawberries and mint. Frozen tangerine juice concentrate may be substituted for frozen orange juice concentrate. Yield: 20 servings.

Lynda Boland, Delta Pi
Everett, Washington

REFRESHING PUNCH

I obtained this recipe when I was a chapter member in El Paso in the early 70s. It is a delicious punch.

1 (46-ounce) can Hawaiian punch
1 (32-ounce) bottle grape juice
2 (6-ounce) cans frozen lemonade concentrate
$^1/_2$ cup sugar
Water to taste
1 (12-ounce) can ginger ale

Combine Hawaiian punch, grape juice, lemonade concentrate, sugar and water in large container; mix well. Chill until serving time. Pour into punch bowl. Add ginger ale just before serving. Yield: 20 servings.

Norma Smith, Preceptor Zeta Alpha
Hewitt, Texas

SLUSH PUNCH

3 cups sugar
2 quarts water
1 package unsweetened cherry drink mix
1 package unsweetened orange drink mix
$3^1/_4$ tablespoons lemon juice
1 (64-ounce) can pineapple juice
4 ripe bananas, mashed

Combine sugar, water, cherry drink mix, orange drink mix, lemon juice, pineapple juice and bananas in large freezer container; mix well. Freeze, covered, for 8 to 12 hours. Let stand at room temperature for 1 hour before serving. Crush with spoon to make slushy. Yield: 40 servings.

Carla Marquez, Xi Chi Delta
Corcoran, California

GOLDEN COLORED FRUIT PUNCH SLUSH

4 cups sugar
4 cups water
2 (3-ounce) packages lemon gelatin
1 (3-ounce) package orange-pineapple gelatin
9 cups hot water
1 (16-ounce) bottle lemon juice
2 (46-ounce) cans pineapple juice
2 large bottles ginger ale, at room temperature

Boil sugar and 4 cups water in small saucepan until a thin syrup consistency. Remove from heat. Mix lemon and orange-pineapple gelatin in 9 cups hot water in large container until gelatin dissolves. Add sugar mixture, lemon juice and pineapple juice; mix well. Freeze, covered in 2-quart freezer containers. Let stand at room temperature for 4 hours before serving. Place mixture in punch bowl. Chop with wooden spoon. Add ginger ale just before serving. Use silk or plastic yellow rosebuds in ice ring to float in punch bowl. Yield: 50 servings.

Pat Whitworth, Laureate Alpha Alpha
Charleston, West Virginia

MARGARITAS MUCHO GRANDE

1 (6-ounce) can frozen limeade concentrate
1 (6-ounce) can water
1 (6-ounce) can tequila
1/2 (6-ounce) can Triple Sec
Ice to fill blender

Combine limeade concentrate, water, tequila and Triple Sec in blender container. Add enough ice to fill blender container. Process until well blended and frothy. Yield: 6 servings.

Denise Bosch, Eta Sigma
Kamloops, British Columbia, Canada

ORANGE JULIE

1 (6-ounce) can orange juice concentrate
1/2 cup water
1 cup milk
1/2 teaspoon vanilla extract
1/4 cup sugar
Ice cubes

Process orange juice concentrate, water, milk, vanilla and sugar in blender until smooth. Add ice cubes 1 at a time until mixture reaches top of blender container. Yield: 8 servings.

Barbara Jueschke, Beta Upsilon
Warrensburg, Missouri

SPICED APPLE CIDER

1 gallon apple cider or apple juice
3/4 cup packed light brown sugar
1 tablespoon cinnamon
2 (1/2-inch thick) orange slices
2 (1/2-inch thick) apple slices studded with cloves
2 (1/4-inch thick) lemon slices

Combine apple cider, brown sugar and cinnamon in large saucepan. Add orange slices, apple slices with cloves and lemon slices. Simmer for 1 hour or longer. Yield: 32 servings.

Sandra K. PaskVan, Preceptor Gamma Gamma
Tulsa, Oklahoma

CHRISTMAS MULLED APPLE PUNCH

This punch will soon become a tradition, filling your house with a spicy, fruity aroma.

2 quarts apple juice
2 quarts cranberry juice cocktail
2 quarts orange juice
1 whole cinnamon stick
6 whole cloves
Sliced oranges or lemons

Combine apple juice, cranberry juice cocktail and orange juice in large saucepan. Add cinnamon stick and cloves. Bring to a slow simmer. Serve hot with slice of orange or lemon. Yield: 48 servings.

Susan Adams, Laureate Eta
Prince George, British Columbia, Canada

HOT CIDER PUNCH

2 (12-ounce) cans frozen apple juice concentrate
2 liters cranberry juice
6 cups water
1/3 cup packed light brown sugar
2 teaspoons whole cloves
4 cinnamon sticks
1 large orange, cut into pieces

Combine apple juice concentrate, cranberry juice and water in 30-cup percolator; mix well. Place brown sugar, cloves, cinnamon sticks and orange pieces in percolator basket. Percolate, covered, for 1 hour. Yield: 20 servings.

Marina Cram, Xi Zeta
Brandon, Manitoba, Canada

HOLIDAY HOT PUNCH

2 cups water
1 cup sugar
3 cinnamon sticks
2 cups pineapple juice
1 (6-ounce) can frozen lemonade concentrate
1 (6-ounce) can frozen orange juice concentrate
2 (36-ounce) bottles cranberry juice

Bring water, sugar and cinnamon sticks to a boil in large saucepan. Boil for 5 minutes. Add pineapple juice, lemonade concentrate, orange juice concentrate and cranberry juice; mix well. Heat through. Serve hot. Yield: 30 servings.

Diane K. Imlay, Xi Alpha Alpha
Havana, Illinois

CRANBERRY TEA

1 cup sugar
3 sticks cinnamon
1 cup water
1 1/2 tablespoons fresh lemon juice
1 cup orange juice
1 (32-ounce) bottle cranberry juice cocktail
2 cups water

Boil sugar, cinnamon and 1 cup water in large nonaluminum saucepan; mix well. Add lemon juice, orange juice, cranberry juice cocktail and 2 cups water. Simmer until serving time. Serve hot or cold. Yield: 16 servings.

Dee Gaston, Preceptor Theta Sigma
Brackettville, Texas

HOT SPICED TEA

1 tablespoon whole cloves
1 teaspoon allspice
3 or 4 cinnamon sticks
1 quart water
3 teaspoons leaf tea
1 (12-ounce) can frozen orange juice concentrate
1 (6-ounce) can frozen lemonade concentrate
1 cup sugar

Bring spices and water to a boil in large saucepan. Reduce heat. Simmer for 5 minutes. Add tea. Simmer 5 minutes longer. Stir in orange juice concentrate, lemonade concentrate, sugar and enough water to make 1 gallon of liquid. Cook until heated through. Strain and serve hot. Yield: 30 servings.

Arnalynn Kellner, Xi Kappa Chi
Refugio, Texas

FORGET-ME-NOT TEA

1 (15-ounce) jar orange instant breakfast drink mix
1 cup sugar
1 cup unsweetened instant tea mix
1/2 cup presweetened lemonade mix
1 package unsweetened cherry drink mix
2 teaspoons ground cinnamon
1 teaspoon ground nutmeg

Combine all ingredients in large airtight container; mix well. Stir 2 heaping tablespoons tea mix mixture into 1 cup hot or cold water, stirring until dissolved. Yield: 64 servings.

Shelly M. Rauzi, Alpha Beta Lambda
Lee's Summit, Missouri

INSTANT RUSSIAN TEA

2 cups orange instant breakfast drink mix
1 or 2 packages sweetened instant lemonade mix
1 cup instant tea mix
1 cup sugar
1 teaspoon ground cloves
1 teaspoon ground cinnamon

Combine all ingredients in large airtight container; mix well. Add 2 or 3 spoonfuls to 1 cup of boiling water to serve. Yield: 40 servings.

Sister in Beta Sigma Phi

SPICED TEA

3/4 cup instant tea
2 cups orange instant breakfast drink mix
1 (3-ounce) package mixed fruit gelatin
1 package instant lemonade mix
1 to 1 1/2 cups sugar
2 teaspoons ground cinnamon

Whisk all ingredients together in large airtight container. Mix 2 tablespoons tea mixture or to taste with 1 cup boiling water for each serving.
Yield: 40 servings.

Tammy Anspaugh, Mu Kappa
Great Bend, Kansas

ALMOND COFFEE CAKE

1 cup sour cream
1/2 cup sugar
1/2 cup butter or margarine, softened
1 teaspoon salt
2 packages dry yeast
1/2 cup warm water
2 eggs, beaten
4 cups all-purpose flour
16 ounces cream cheese, softened
3/4 cup sugar
1 egg, beaten
2 teaspoons vanilla extract
1/8 teaspoon salt
2 1/2 cups confectioners' sugar
1/4 cup milk
1 teaspoon vanilla extract
1/2 cup toasted sliced almonds

Cook mixture of sour cream, 1/2 cup sugar, butter and 1 teaspoon salt in medium saucepan over medium-low heat for 5 to 10 minutes or until well blended, stirring constantly. Cool to room temperature. Dissolve yeast in warm water in large mixer bowl. Add sour cream mixture and 2 eggs; mix well. Add flour gradually, mixing to form very soft dough. Chill, covered, 8 to 12 hours. Knead dough on floured surface 5 to 6 times. Divide dough into 4 portions. Roll each portion into 8-by-12-inch rectangle. Spread each with 1/4 blended mixture of cream cheese, 3/4 cup sugar, 1 egg, 2 teaspoons vanilla and 1/8 teaspoon salt to within 1 inch of edge. Roll as for jelly roll, sealing edge. Place seam side down on greased baking sheets. Cut 6 x's on top of each. Let rise, covered, for 1 hour or until doubled in bulk. Preheat oven to 375 degrees. Bake at 375 degrees for 20 to 25 minutes or until golden brown. Invert onto wire racks to cool. Drizzle mixture of confectioners' sugar, milk and 1 teaspoon vanilla over each loaf. Sprinkle with almonds. Store in refrigerator. Yield: 20 to 24 servings.

Ralph (Mildred E.) Carr, Iota Iota
Blairsville, Georgia

APPLE-TOPPED COFFEE CAKE

This recipe, given to me by my mother, is more than 50 years old.

2 cups all-purpose flour
3/4 cup sugar
1/4 teaspoon nutmeg
1/4 teaspoon cinnamon
1 teaspoon salt
4 teaspoons baking powder
1/4 cup vegetable shortening
3 eggs
1 cup milk
1 cup finely chopped apples
1/2 cup packed light brown sugar

Preheat oven to 350 degrees. Sift flour, sugar, nutmeg, cinnamon, salt and baking powder into large bowl. Cut in shortening until mixture resembles cornmeal. Add eggs and milk, stirring until smooth. Pour into greased 8-by-10-inch baking pan. Arrange apples on top. Sprinkle with brown sugar. Bake at 350 degrees for 30 minutes. Serve hot.
Yield: 8 servings.

Louise Summar, Alpha Master
Nashville, Tennessee

DUTCH APPLE COFFEE CAKE

1/2 cup packed light brown sugar
1 cup sugar
1/2 cup butter or margarine, softened
2 eggs
2 teaspoons grated orange rind
2 cups sifted all-purpose flour
11/2 teaspoons baking powder
1/2 teaspoon baking soda
1/2 teaspoon cinnamon
1 teaspoon salt
1 cup evaporated milk
2 cups finely chopped peeled apples
1/2 cup chopped pecans
2 tablespoons sugar

Preheat oven to 350 degrees. Cream brown sugar, 1 cup sugar and butter in large mixer bowl until light and fluffy. Add eggs and orange rind; mix well. Add sifted mixture of sifted flour, baking powder, baking soda, cinnamon and salt alternately with evaporated milk, mixing well after each addition. Stir in apples. Pour into greased 9-by-13-inch baking pan. Sprinkle with pecans and 2 tablespoons sugar. Bake at 350 degrees for 30 minutes or until cake tester inserted in center comes out clean. Yield: 12 servings.

Billie Burrus, Xi Gamma Lambda
Porter, Indiana

BROWN SUGAR COFFEE CAKE

1/2 cup sugar
1 cup margarine
1 (1 pound) package light brown sugar
4 eggs
2 cups all-purpose flour
1 cup pecans

Preheat oven to 350 degrees. Melt sugar and margarine in small saucepan over low heat. Pour over brown sugar in large mixer bowl; mix well. Add eggs 1 at a time, mixing well after each addition. Add flour gradually; mix well. Stir in pecans. Pour into greased 9-by-13-inch baking pan lined with waxed paper. Bake at 350 degrees for 30 to 40 minutes or until cake tests done. Let cool in pan 10 minutes; remove to wire rack. Remove waxed paper. Cut into squares. Yield: 15 servings.

Margaret Pringle, Preceptor Tau
Greenville, South Carolina

CHERRY COFFEE CAKE RINGS

41/2 cups all-purpose flour
1/2 cup sugar
1 teaspoon salt
1 envelope dry yeast
1 cup milk
1/4 cup water
1/2 cup butter or margarine
1 egg
2 cups pitted sour cherries, drained
1/2 cup all-purpose flour
1/2 cup packed light brown sugar
1/2 cup chopped walnuts
2 cups confectioners' sugar
2 tablespoons hot water or milk
1 teaspoon vanilla extract or almond extract

Combine 11/2 cups flour, sugar, salt and yeast in large mixer bowl; mix well. Heat milk, water and butter in small saucepan over low heat. Add to flour mixture. Beat at medium speed for 2 minutes. Add egg and 1 cup flour. Beat at high speed for 2 minutes. Add 2 cups flour; mix well. Chill, covered tightly with plastic wrap, for 3 to 12 hours. Divide dough into 2 portions. Roll each portion into 7-by-14-inch rectangle on lightly floured surface. Spread each with cherries and mixture of 1/2 cup flour, brown sugar and walnuts. Roll as for jelly roll, sealing edge. Place seam side down on greased baking sheet. Shape into ring; seal ends. Cut 2/3 through ring from outside edge at 1-inch intervals. Turn slices cut side down. Let rise, covered, for 1 hour or until doubled in bulk. Preheat oven to 375 degrees. Bake at 375 degrees for 20 to 25 minutes. Let stand until cool. Spread with mixture of confectioners' sugar, hot water and vanilla. Yield: 2 coffee cakes.

Carol Cyphery, Xi Delta Lambda
Windsor, Ontario, Canada

CHERRY COFFEE CAKE

11/2 cups sugar
1/2 cup margarine
1/2 cup vegetable shortening
11/2 teaspoons baking powder
1 teaspoon each vanilla and almond extract
4 eggs
3 cups all-purpose flour
1 (21-ounce) can cherry pie filling
1 cup confectioners' sugar
1 to 2 tablespoons milk

Preheat oven to 350 degrees. Beat sugar, margarine, shortening, baking powder, vanilla and almond extract in large mixer bowl at low speed; mix well.

Add eggs 1 at a time, mixing well after each addition. Beat at high speed for 3 minutes. Stir in flour. Spread 2/3 of the batter in 9-by-13-inch baking pan. Spread pie filling over the top. Drop remaining batter by tablespoonfuls over pie filling. Bake at 350 degrees for 40 to 45 minutes or until light brown. Mix confectioners' sugar and enough milk to make of desired consistency. Drizzle over cake. Yield: 15 servings.

Diane W. Cessna, Iota Chi
St. Louis, Missouri

CHEESECAKE COFFEE CAKE

1 1/4 cups baking mix
2 tablespoons sugar
2 tablespoons melted margarine
1/2 cup milk
1 tablespoon cinnamon
1/4 cup sugar
3 egg whites
1/2 teaspoon vanilla extract
8 ounces fat-free cream cheese, softened
1 teaspoon lemon extract
2 drops yellow food coloring

Preheat oven to 350 degrees. Combine baking mix, 2 tablespoons sugar, margarine, milk and cinnamon in large mixer bowl, beating until smooth. Press into bottom of round or 8-by-8-inch baking pan. Beat 1/4 cup sugar, egg whites, vanilla, cream cheese, lemon extract and food coloring in small mixer bowl until smooth. Spoon into prepared pan. Bake at 350 degrees for 15 to 20 minutes. Yield: 8 servings.

Joyce E. Hasson, Preceptor Alpha Theta
Jackson, Michigan

CHOCO COFFEE CAKE

1/2 cup butter or margarine, softened
1 cup sugar
2 eggs
1 teaspoon vanilla extract
2 cups all-purpose flour
1 teaspoon baking powder
1 teaspoon baking soda
1 teaspoon sour cream
1/2 cup semisweet chocolate chips
1/2 cup chopped pecans
1/2 cup packed light brown sugar
1/2 cup all-purpose flour
2 teaspoons baking cocoa
1/4 cup butter or margarine, softened

Preheat oven to 350 degrees. Cream 1/2 cup butter, sugar and 1 egg together in large mixer bowl until light and fluffy. Add remaining egg and vanilla; mix well. Add 2 cups flour, baking powder, baking soda and sour cream; mix well. Stir in chocolate chips and pecans. Pour into greased 9-by-13-inch baking pan. Sprinkle mixture of brown sugar, 1/2 cup flour, baking cocoa and 1/4 cup butter over the top. Bake at 350 degrees for 45 minutes or until wooden pick inserted near center comes out clean. Yield: 20 servings.

Gail Dodds, Sigma
Estevan, Saskatchewan, Canada

CINNAMON COFFEE CAKE

1 (2-layer) package yellow cake mix
3 eggs
1 (4-ounce) package vanilla pudding mix
3/4 cup vegetable oil
3/4 cup water
1 teaspoon vanilla extract
3/4 cup sugar
3 tablespoons cinnamon
Whipped topping

Preheat oven to 350 degrees. Mix first 6 ingredients in medium mixer bowl until creamy. Combine sugar and cinnamon in small bowl. Layer cake mix mixture and sugar mixture 1/2 at a time in greased 9-by-13-inch baking pan. Bake at 350 degrees for 25 to 30 minutes or until cake tests done. May top with whipped topping. Yield: 15 servings.

Sheila Brooks, Upsilon Omicron
Newton, Illinois

CINNAMON WALNUT COFFEE CAKE

1 (2-layer) package white or yellow cake mix
1 (4-ounce) package vanilla instant pudding mix
4 eggs
1 cup sour cream
1/2 cup vegetable oil
1/2 cup chopped walnuts
1/2 cup sugar
2 teaspoons cinnamon

Preheat oven to 350 degrees. Combine first 5 ingredients in large mixer bowl, beating until smooth. Combine walnuts, sugar and cinnamon in small bowl. Layer batter and sugar mixture 1/2 at a time in greased 10-inch tube pan. Bake at 350 degrees for 55 to 60 minutes. Yield: 10 servings.

Susan Lambert, Xi Mu
Londonderry, New Hampshire

MY AUNT'S FAVORITE CINNAMON COFFEE CAKE

1 cup butter or margarine, softened
1 3/4 cups sugar
2 teaspoons vanilla extract
4 eggs
2 cups sour cream
3 cups all-purpose flour
2 teaspoons baking powder
1 teaspoon baking soda
4 teaspoons (or more) cinnamon
3/4 cup sugar
1/2 cup chopped walnuts

Preheat oven to 350 degrees. Cream butter and 1 3/4 cups sugar in large mixer bowl. Add vanilla, eggs and sour cream; mix well. Add sifted mixture of flour, baking powder and baking soda. Beat at medium speed for at least 3 minutes. Combine cinnamon, 3/4 cup sugar and walnuts in small bowl. Layer batter and cinnamon mixture 1/3 at a time in nonstick tube pan. Marblelize batter with knife. Bake at 350 degrees for 1 hour. Yield: 16 servings.

Eleanor Harris, Xi Kappa Gamma
Cape Coral, Florida

COWBOY COFFEE CAKES

2 1/2 cups all-purpose flour
1/2 teaspoon salt
2 cups packed light brown sugar
2/3 cup vegetable shortening
2 teaspoons baking powder
1/2 teaspoon baking soda
1/2 teaspoon cinnamon
1/2 teaspoon nutmeg
1 cup sour milk
2 eggs, beaten

Preheat oven to 375 degrees. Combine flour, salt, brown sugar and shortening in large bowl; mix until crumbly. Reserve 1/2 cup flour mixture. Add baking powder, baking soda, cinnamon and nutmeg to remaining flour mixture; mix well. Beat in milk and eggs. Pour into 2 greased 8-by-8-inch baking pans. Sprinkle with reserved flour mixture. Bake at 375 degrees for 25 to 30 minutes. Yield: 8 servings.

Don (Mary) Stary, Alpha Xi Lambda
Cleveland, Texas

CREAM CHEESE COFFEE CAKE

2 packages crescent rolls
16 ounces cream cheese, softened
3/4 cup sugar
1 egg yolk
1/2 teaspoon vanilla extract
1 teaspoon lemon juice
1 egg white
1/4 cup chopped pecans
2 tablespoons confectioners' sugar

Preheat oven to 375 degrees. Press 1 package of rolls, sealing perforations, into bottom of lightly greased 9-by-13-inch baking pan. Combine cream cheese, sugar, egg yolk, vanilla and lemon juice in small mixer bowl. Spread over roll dough. Layer remaining package of rolls over the top. Beat egg white in small mixer bowl until foamy. Spread over top of roll dough. Sprinkle pecans over the top. Bake at 375 degrees for 20 minutes. Sprinkle wih confectioners' sugar. Yield: 12 servings.

Carol Weaver, Gamma Gamma
Duluth, Minnesota

DAD'S COFFEE CAKE

My dad died in 1993. This was his special coffee cake he made for us.

1 cup cold water
1 (4-ounce) package vanilla instant pudding mix
1 (4-ounce) package butterscotch instant pudding mix
1 (2-layer) package yellow cake mix
1/2 cup vegetable oil
4 eggs
3/4 cup packed light brown sugar
2 tablespoons cinnamon

Preheat oven to 350 degrees. Combine water, vanilla pudding mix, butterscotch pudding mix, cake mix and oil in large mixer bowl. Add eggs 1 at a time, mixing well after each addition. Pour into jelly roll pan or 9-by-13-inch nonstick baking pan. Sprinkle mixture of brown sugar and cinnamon over the top. Bake at 350 degrees for 45 minutes.
Yield: 15 servings.

Lisa Stirtz, Gamma #149
Omaha, Nebraska

GOLDEN COFFEE CAKE

1 (2-layer) package golden cake mix
2 tablespoons light brown sugar
2 teaspoons ground cinnamon
1 cup chopped walnuts
2 tablespoons plain low-fat yogurt
1/3 cup vegetable oil
1/4 cup water
1 (8-ounce) package frozen egg substitute, thawed

Preheat oven to 375 degrees. Combine 2 tablespoons of the cake mix, brown sugar, cinnamon and walnuts in small bowl; set aside. Mix remaining cake mix, yogurt, oil, water and egg substitute in large mixer bowl. Beat for 2 minutes at high speed. Spoon 2/3 of the batter into greased and floured tube pan. Sprinkle with brown sugar mixture. Layer remaining batter over the top. Bake at 375 degrees for 45 to 55 minutes. Yield: 10 to 12 servings.

Coeta Beaver, Laureate Zeta Gamma
Pasadena, Texas

LEMON CURD COFFEE CAKE

1 envelope dry yeast
1/4 cup warm water
1/3 cup sugar
1/2 cup sour cream
1/2 teaspoon grated lemon rind
1/4 teaspoon salt
2 eggs
2 1/2 to 2 3/4 cups all-purpose flour
1/3 cup butter or margarine, softened
3/4 cup lemon curd
1 egg, slightly beaten
1/4 cup chopped walnuts (optional)

Dissolve yeast in warm water in large mixer bowl. Add sugar; mix well. Heat sour cream in small saucepan over low heat until heated through. Add sour cream to yeast mixture with lemon rind and salt; mix well. Beat in 2 eggs and enough flour to make soft dough. Add butter; mix well. Turn out onto floured surface. Knead 6 to 7 minutes or until smooth. Place in lightly buttered bowl, turning to coat surface. Let rise, covered with plastic wrap, for 45 to 60 minutes or until doubled in bulk. Punch dough down. Roll into 12-by-18 inch rectangle. Spread lemon curd on dough, leaving 3/4-inch border on all sides. Roll to enclose filling, sealing edges. Slice into 3 1/2-inch rolls. Arrange in circle in greased 8- or 9-inch round baking pan. Let rise, covered, for 30 minutes. Preheat oven to 350 degrees. Brush dough with beaten egg. Sprinkle with walnuts. Bake at 350 degrees for 30 minutes. Yield: 6 to 8 servings.

Dolores Miller, Xi Alpha Alpha
Jacksonville, Florida

LIGHTNING CAKE

This cake was one of my mother's favorites. As the mother of six, she needed quick recipes.

1 cup all-purpose flour
1 cup sugar
1 teaspoon (heaping) baking powder
1 egg
1/4 cup melted butter or margarine
1/2 to 3/4 cup milk
1 teaspoon vanilla extract
3 tablespoons butter or margarine
5 tablespoons light brown sugar
2 tablespoons milk

Preheat oven to 350 degrees. Sift flour, sugar and baking powder into large mixer bowl. Drop egg into 1/4 cup melted butter in 1-cup measure. Add enough milk to measure 1 cup. Add to flour mixture; mix at low speed until blended. Stir in vanilla; mix well. Pour into 9-by-9-inch nonstick baking pan. Bake at 350 degrees until cake tests done. Heat 3 tablespoons butter, brown sugar and 2 tablespoons milk in small saucepan, stirring until blended. Spread over hot cake. Broil 4 inches from heat source for 5 minutes or until brown and bubbly. Yield: 9 to 12 servings.

Jeanette Deppisch, Laureate Tau
Pentecton, British Columbia, Canada

LUSCIOUS COFFEE CAKE

1 (2-layer) package yellow cake mix
1 (6-ounce) package vanilla instant pudding mix
1/2 cup vegetable oil
1 teaspoon vanilla extract
1 cup water
4 eggs
1/2 cup sugar
2 tablespoons cinnamon
1/2 cup chopped pecans
1/2 cup melted butter or margarine
1/4 cup water
1 cup dark rum or rum extract to taste

Preheat oven to 325 degrees. Combine cake mix, pudding mix, oil, vanilla and 1 cup water in large mixer bowl. Add eggs 1 at a time, mixing well after each addition. Combine sugar, cinnamon and pecans in small bowl. Alternate layers of cake mix mixture and sugar mixture in large nonstick bundt pan. Bake at 325 degrees for 65 minutes. Pierce holes in top of warm cake. Pour mixture of butter, 1/4 cup water and rum over the top. Yield: 16 servings.

Junella Coverdale, Laureate Gamma
Spencer, Iowa

MONKEY BREAD

3 (10-count) cans buttermilk biscuits
1/4 cup sugar
1 tablespoon cinnamon
1/2 cup sugar
1/2 cup packed light brown sugar
1/3 cup margarine
1/2 cup vanilla ice cream

Preheat oven to 350 degrees. Separate biscuits. Dip in mixture of 1/4 cup sugar and cinnamon. Stand on edge in nonstick bundt pan. Bring 1/2 cup sugar, brown sugar, margarine and ice cream to a boil in small saucepan. Pour over biscuit dough in pan. Bake at 350 degrees for 30 minutes. Let cool in pan for 1 minute; invert onto a serving plate. Serve warm. Yield: 16 servings.

Jean Martin, Beta Delta
Ossian, Iowa

OVERNIGHT COFFEE CAKE

1 cup sugar
1/2 cup packed light brown sugar
3/4 cup butter or margarine, softened
2 eggs, slightly beaten
2 cups all-purpose flour
1 teaspoon baking powder
1/2 teaspoon salt
1 teaspoon nutmeg
2 teaspoons baking soda
2 teaspoons cinnamon
1 cup sour cream
1/2 cup packed light brown sugar
1 teaspoon cinnamon

Cream sugar, 1/2 cup brown sugar and butter in large mixer bowl until light and fluffy. Add eggs; mix well. Add sifted mixture of flour, baking powder, salt, nutmeg, baking soda and 2 teaspoons cinnamon; mix well. Stir in sour cream with spoon. Pour into greased 9-by-13-inch baking pan. Top with mixture of 1/2 cup brown sugar and 1 teaspoon cinnamon. Chill, covered, for 8 to 12 hours. Preheat oven to 350 degrees. Bake, uncovered, at 350 degrees for 35 to 40 minutes. Yield: 15 servings.

Dayla Volkart, Pi Tau
California, Missouri

PINEAPPLE COFFEE CAKE

1 (8-ounce) can crushed pineapple
1 egg
1/4 cup sugar
2 cups baking mix
Cinnamon, brown sugar and nutmeg to taste

Preheat oven to 350 degrees. Drain pineapple, reserving 3/4 cup juice. Pour reserved juice into large mixer bowl. Add egg and sugar; mix well. Add baking mix; mix well. Pour into greased 9-by-9-inch baking pan. Spread pineapple over top. Sprinkle with cinnamon, brown sugar and nutmeg. Bake at 350 degrees for 20 minutes. Yield: 9 servings.

Marilyn Harkness, Preceptor Zeta Alpha
Waco, Texas

Sandy Teal-Schroller, Pi Beta Xi, Wichita, Kansas, keeps Cappuccino Mix on hand. Combine 1 cup instant coffee creamer, 1 cup hot chocolate mix and 2/3 cup instant coffee powder with 1/2 cup sugar, 1/2 teaspoon cinnamon and 1/2 teaspoon nutmeg; mix well and store in airtight container. Mix 3 tablespoons of the mix with 3/4 cup hot water.

QUICK AND EASY COFFEE CAKE

1 cup packed light brown sugar
1 cup sugar
2 1/2 cups all-purpose flour
1 cup vegetable oil
1 teaspoon salt
1 egg
1 cup buttermilk
1 teaspoon baking soda
1 teaspoon cinnamon
1 teaspoon nutmeg
1 teaspoon vanilla extract
1 cup chopped pecans (optional)

Preheat oven to 350 degrees. Combine brown sugar, sugar and flour in large mixer bowl. Beat in oil and salt, reserving 1 cup mixture. Add next 6 ingredients to remaining mixture; mix well. Stir in pecans. Pour into greased and floured 9-by-13-inch baking pan. Spread reserved sugar mixture over the top. Bake at 350 degrees for 45 minutes. Yield: 12 to 15 servings.

Sharon Bauer DeBerry, Theta Rho
Cuero, Texas

RHUBARB COFFEE CAKE

1/2 cup butter or margarine, softened
1/2 cup packed light brown sugar
1/4 cup sugar
1 egg
1 teaspoon vanilla extract
1 1/4 cups all-purpose flour
3/4 cup whole wheat flour
1 teaspoon baking powder
1/2 teaspoon baking soda
1/4 teaspoon salt
1/4 teaspoon cinnamon
1 cup buttermilk
2 cups chopped fresh or frozen rhubarb
1/4 cup packed light brown sugar
1 1/2 teaspoons cinnamon
1/2 cup walnuts

Preheat oven to 350 degrees. Cream butter, 1/2 cup brown sugar, sugar, egg and vanilla in large mixer bowl until light and fluffy. Add mixture of flour, whole wheat flour, baking powder, baking soda, salt and 1/4 teaspoon cinnamon alternately with buttermilk, mixing well after each addition. Stir in rhubarb; mix well. Pour into greased 9-by-13-inch baking pan. Sprinkle mixture of 1/4 cup brown sugar, 1 1/2 teaspoons cinnamon and walnuts over the top. Bake at 350 degrees for 35 minutes. Yield: 8 servings.

Lorraine Stripp, Xi Gamma Iota
Old Forge, New York

RISE AND SHINE COFFEE CAKE

3/4 cup margarine
1 1/2 cups sugar
3 eggs
1 1/2 teaspoons vanilla extract
3 cups all-purpose flour
1 1/2 teaspoons baking powder
1 1/2 teaspoons baking soda
1/4 teaspoon salt
1 1/2 cups sour cream
1/2 cup packed light brown sugar
1/2 cup chopped walnuts or pecans
1 1/2 teaspoons cinnamon

Preheat oven to 350 degrees. Beat margarine, sugar, eggs and vanilla in large mixer bowl for 2 minutes or until smooth. Add mixture of flour, baking powder, baking soda and salt alternately with sour cream, mixing well after each addition. Layer batter and mixture of brown sugar, walnuts and cinnamon 1/3 at a time in greased bundt pan. Bake at 350 degrees for 1 hour. Yield: 8 servings.

Mary Burton, Alpha Tau
Exeter, Ontario, Canada

BUTTER SOUR CREAM COFFEE CAKE

1/2 cup butter or margarine, softened
3/4 cup sugar
2 eggs, beaten
1 teaspoon vanilla extract
1 3/4 cups all-purpose flour
1/2 teaspoon salt
1 teaspoon baking powder
1 cup sour cream
1 teaspoon baking soda
1/4 cup packed light brown sugar
1 tablespoon cinnamon
2 tablespoon chopped pecans
Whipped cream to taste

Preheat oven to 350 degrees. Cream butter and sugar in large mixer bowl until light and fluffy. Add eggs and vanilla; mix well. Add sifted mixture of flour, salt and baking powder alternately with mixture of sour cream and baking soda, beginning and ending with flour mixture. Layer batter and mixture of brown sugar, cinnamon and pecans 1/2 at a time in greased and floured 8-inch square pan. Bake at 350 degrees for 45 to 50 minutes or until a tester inserted in middle comes out clean. Let stand until cool. May serve with whipped cream. Yield: 9 servings.

Margaret Franche, Xi Zeta Omicron
Carrying Place, Ontario, Canada

HEAVENLY SOUR CREAM COFFEE CAKE

1 1/2 cups baking mix
1/2 cup sugar
3 tablespoons butter or margarine, softened
3/4 cup sour cream
1 teaspoon vanilla extract
1/4 cup all-purpose flour
3 tablespoons butter or margarine, softened
3 tablespoons sugar
1/8 teaspoon cinnamon

Preheat oven to 350 degrees. Combine baking mix, 1/2 cup sugar, 3 tablespoons butter, sour cream and vanilla in medium mixer bowl, beating until smooth. Pour into greased 8-inch square baking pan. Sprinkle with mixture of flour, 3 tablespoons butter, 3 tablespoons sugar and cinnamon. Bake at 350 degrees for 35 to 45 minutes. Yield: 9 servings.

Audrey Forbes, Preceptor Beta Eta
Dallas, Oregon

SOUR CREAM COFFEE CAKE

1 cup sour cream
1 teaspoon baking soda
1/2 cup butter or margarine, softened
1 cup sugar
2 eggs, beaten
1 teaspoon vanilla extract
1 3/4 cups sifted cake flour
1/2 teaspoon baking powder
3/4 cup packed light brown sugar
1 teaspoon cinnamon

Preheat oven to 350 degrees. Combine sour cream and baking soda; set aside. Cream butter and sugar in large mixer bowl. Add eggs and vanilla; mix well. Add sifted mixture of sifted cake flour and baking powder alternately with sour cream mixture, mixing well after each addition. Layer batter and mixture of brown sugar and cinnamon 1/2 at a time in buttered and floured tube pan. Bake at 350 degrees for 45 to 50 minutes. Yield: 12 to 15 servings.

Helen Swindley, Preceptor Beta Zeta
Scarborough, Ontario, Canada

SPICE COFFEE CAKE

2 1/2 cups all-purpose flour
1 1/2 cups packed light brown sugar
1 tablespoon cinnamon
1 1/2 teaspoons baking powder
1/4 teaspoon nutmeg
3/4 teaspoon baking soda
1/2 teaspoon salt
1/8 teaspoon ground ginger
1/2 cup margarine or butter, softened
1 cup plain yogurt
1/2 teaspoon vanilla extract
3 eggs

Preheat oven to 350 degrees. Combine flour, brown sugar, cinnamon, baking powder, nutmeg, baking soda, salt and ginger in large mixer bowl. Add margarine, yogurt, vanilla and eggs, beating at low speed just until mixed, scraping bowl frequently with spatula. Beat on high for 2 minutes. Pour into greased and floured 10-inch tube pan. Bake at 350 degrees for 55 to 60 minutes. Cool in pan for 10 minutes. Remove to wire rack to cool completely. Yield: 16 servings.

Angie Peace, Xi Sigma Mu
Sierra Blanca, Texas

STREUSEL COFFEE CAKE

1 (2-layer) package yellow cake mix
1/4 cup margarine or butter, softened
1 cup chopped pecans
1 cup packed light brown sugar
3 eggs
1 1/2 cups sour cream

Preheat oven to 350 degrees. Combine 2/3 cup of the cake mix, margarine, pecans and brown sugar in medium mixer bowl. Beat eggs, sour cream and remaining cake mix in large mixer bowl until thick and smooth. Layer sour cream mixture and brown sugar mixture 1/2 at a time in greased and floured 9-by-13-inch baking pan. Bake at 350 degrees for 30 to 35 minutes. Yield: 15 to 20 servings.

Pam Speidel, Delta Omicron
Norfolk, Nebraska

SWEDISH TEA RING

2 cups all-purpose flour
2 tablespoons sugar
4 teaspoons baking powder
1/4 cup butter or margarine, chilled
3/4 cup (or more) milk
8 ounces cream cheese, softened
1/4 cup sugar
1/2 teaspoon vanilla extract
Chopped pecans, raisins and cherries to taste
Light corn syrup to taste
1/2 cup confectioners' sugar

Preheat oven to 425 degrees. Combine flour, 2 tablespoons sugar and baking powder in medium mixer bowl. Cut in butter until mixture is crumbly. Add enough milk to form soft dough. Roll into 8-by-12-inch rectangle on lightly floured surface. Spread with mixture of cream cheese, 1/4 cup sugar and vanilla. Sprinkle with pecans, raisins and cherries. Roll as for jelly roll, sealing edge. Place seam side down on greased baking sheet. Shape into ring; seal ends. Cut 1/2 of the way through ring from outside edge at 1-inch intervals. Turn each slice onto side. Bake at 425 degrees for 15 to 20 minutes or until browned. Brush hot tea ring with corn syrup to glaze. Drizzle cooled cake with mixture of confectioners' sugar and a small amount of water. Yield: 8 servings.

Diann Kellestine, Xi Gamma Theta
Kitchener, Ontario, Canada

PULL-APART COFFEE CAKE

Whoever gets out of bed first in the morning can pop this prepared recipe in the oven. It's wonderful to wake up to the aroma of this delicious coffee cake and the coffee brewing.

1 package frozen cloverleaf rolls
1/2 cup melted margarine
1 (4-ounce) package vanilla pudding and pie filling mix
4 teaspoons cinnamon
1/2 cup packed light brown sugar
1/2 cup chopped pecans

Generously butter a tube pan. Separate each frozen roll into 3 sections. Dip each section into melted margarine and arrange in pan. Combine remaining ingredients. Sprinkle over top of rolls. Let stand 8 to 12 hours, uncovered, at room temperature. Preheat oven to 375 degrees. Bake at 375 degrees for 20 minutes. Let cool in pan for 10 minutes. Invert onto serving plate. Yield: 8 servings.

Norma Deas, Beta Alpha Omega
Odessa, Texas

WALNUT COFFEE CAKE

1/2 cup margarine, softened
1 cup sugar
2 eggs, beaten
Salt to taste
1 1/2 cups all-purpose flour
1 1/2 teaspoons baking powder
1 cup sour cream
1 teaspoon baking soda
1 teaspoon vanilla extract
1/2 cup sugar
1/4 cup chopped walnuts
1 teaspoon cinnamon

Preheat oven to 350 degrees. Cream margarine and sugar in large mixer bowl until light and fluffy. Add eggs and salt; mix well. Add 3/4 cup of the flour and baking powder; mix well. Add mixture of sour cream and baking soda, remaining flour and vanilla; mix well. Combine sugar, walnuts and cinnamon in small bowl. Layer batter and cinnamon mixture 1/2 at a time in greased and floured 9-by-13-inch baking pan. Bake at 350 degrees for 45 minutes or until wooden pick inserted in center comes out clean. Yield: 15 servings.

Maryetta Dennis, Laureate Alpha Iota
Jefferson City, Missouri

YEAST SWEET DOUGH COFFEE CAKE

1 envelope dry yeast
1 teaspoon sugar
1/4 cup water
2 eggs, at room temperature
1 tablespoon water
2 cups milk
1/2 cup sugar
Salt to taste
1/4 cup butter or margarine, softened, or vegetable oil
6 cups all-purpose flour
Light brown sugar, pecans, raisins and cinnamon to taste
2 tablespoons confectioners' sugar

Dissolve yeast and 1 teaspoon sugar in 1/4 cup water. Beat eggs and 1 tablespoon water in small mixer bowl. Warm milk in small saucepan; do not boil. Cream 1/2 cup sugar, salt and butter in large mixer bowl. Add warm milk; mix well. Add egg mixture and yeast mixture; mix well. Add flour 1 cup at a time, mixing until a soft dough forms. Knead dough to smooth consistency, forming a large ball. Let rise, covered, for 2 hours or until doubled in bulk. Punch dough down. Let rise for 1 hour longer. Roll out dough on floured surface. Top with brown sugar, pecans, raisins and cinnamon. Roll as for jelly roll, sealing edge. Place seam side down in buttered cake pan. Let rise for 1 hour. Preheat oven to 350 degrees. Bake at 350 degrees for 45 minutes to 1 hour or until golden brown. Invert onto wire rack to cool. Sprinkle with confectioners' sugar before serving. Yield: 8 servings.

Barbara Kirk, Delta Kappa
Mississauga, Ontario, Canada

APPLE BREAD

This bread makes a great gift for holidays and additions to gift baskets.

1/2 cup margarine, softened
1 cup sugar
2 eggs
1 teaspoon vanilla extract
1 teaspoon baking soda
2 tablespoons plain yogurt
2 cups all-purpose flour
1/2 teaspoon salt
2 cups packed chopped peeled apples
2 tablespoons sugar
1 teaspoon cinnamon
2 tablespoons all-purpose flour
2 tablespoons margarine, softened

Preheat oven to 325 degrees. Cream 1/2 cup margarine and 1 cup sugar in large mixer bowl until light and fluffy. Add eggs and vanilla; mix well. Dissolve baking soda in yogurt in small bowl; add to mixture slowly. Add mixture of 2 cups flour and salt; mix well. Stir in apples. Pour into greased 5-by-9-inch loaf pan. Mix 2 tablespoons sugar, cinnamon and 2 tablespoons flour in small bowl. Cut in 2 tablespoons margarine until crumbly. Sprinkle over top of batter. Bake at 325 degrees for 1 hour and 10 minutes. For 4 miniature loaves, adjust baking time to 50 to 55 minutes. Yield: 1 loaf.

Rhonda Runge, Zeta Phi
St. Marys, Georgia

APPLESAUCE CINNAMON BREAD

This bread has a moist texture and wonderful aroma.

1/3 cup applesauce
1 cup milk
2 1/2 cups bread flour
1 teaspoon cinnamon
1 teaspoon salt
2 tablespoons light brown sugar
1 tablespoon butter or margarine, softened
1 1/2 teaspoons dry yeast

Pour applesauce, milk, flour, cinnamon, salt, brown sugar, butter and yeast into bread machine container. Set for white bread and prepare using manufacturer's directions. Yield: 1 loaf.

Shirley Heymann, Xi Delta Nu
Othello, Washington

JONATHAN APPLE BREAD

2 cups sugar
1 cup vegetable oil
4 eggs, beaten
2 teaspoons vanilla extract
4 cups chopped Jonathan apples
1 cup raisins
1 cup chopped pecans
2 2/3 cups all-purpose flour
1 1/2 teaspoons baking soda
1/2 teaspoon salt
2 teaspoons cinnamon
1 teaspoon ground cloves
3 teaspoons sugar

Preheat oven to 325 degrees. Mix 2 cups sugar and oil in large mixer bowl. Add eggs and vanilla; mix well. Stir in apples, raisins and pecans. Add mixture of flour, baking soda, salt, cinnamon and cloves; mix well. Pour into 5 greased 3-by-6-inch loaf pans. Tap to settle. Bake at 325 degrees for 20 minutes. Sprinkle 3 teaspoons sugar over top of loaves. Bake for 30 to 40 minutes longer. Cool in pans for 10 minutes. Remove to wire racks to cool. Yield: 5 loaves.

Lorrie A. Stickney, Phi Alpha Epsilon
Great Bend, Kansas

APPLESAUCE RAISIN BREAD

1 cup applesauce
1/2 cup vegetable oil
1/2 cup sugar
1 3/4 cups all-purpose flour, sifted
1 teaspoon baking soda
1/2 teaspoon salt
1 teaspoon cinnamon
1/2 teaspoon cloves
1/2 teaspoon nutmeg
1 egg, slightly beaten, or 2 egg whites
1 cup raisins

Preheat oven to 325 degrees. Combine applesauce, oil and sugar in large mixer bowl. Sift in sifted flour, baking soda, salt, cinnamon, cloves and nutmeg, mixing well after each addition. Add egg and raisins; mix well. Pour into greased and floured 5-by-9-inch loaf pan. Bake at 325 degrees for 1 hour and 20 minutes or until bread tests done. Yield: 16 servings.

Betty Hartman, Alpha Beta
St. Louis, Missouri

SPICY APPLE CINNAMON BREAD

This is one of my little boy's favorite recipes and he likes to help me make it.

6 eggs, lightly beaten
2 cups vegetable oil
4 cups sugar
4 teaspoons vanilla extract
4 cups chopped apples
6 cups all-purpose flour
2 teaspoons salt
2 teaspoons cinnamon
2 teaspoons baking soda
1 teaspoon baking powder

Preheat oven to 325 degrees. Beat eggs, oil, sugar and vanilla in large mixer bowl. Stir in apples. Add mixture of flour, salt, cinnamon, baking soda and baking powder; mix well. Pour batter into 4 greased and floured 5-by-9-inch loaf pans. Bake at 325 degrees for 1 hour or until wooden pick inserted in center comes out clean. Yield: 4 loaves.

DeAnn Adams, Alpha Delta Lambda
Cameron, Missouri

Debbie Lindeman, Xi Theta Phi, Marshalltown, Iowa, makes Gin Fizzies. Combine a 6-ounce can frozen limeade concentrate, 3/4 cup gin and 3/4 cup half-and-half in blender container. Fill with ice and process until slushy. Serve in frosted glasses garnished with lime slice.

APRICOT NIBBLE BREAD

1 egg, slightly beaten
1/2 cup orange juice
1/2 cup water
1 (17-ounce) package apricot nut quick bread mix
1/3 cup sugar
6 ounces cream cheese, softened
1 tablespoon all-purpose flour
1 egg
1 teaspoon grated orange peel

Preheat oven to 350 degrees. Combine 1 beaten egg, orange juice and water in small bowl. Add bread mix. Stir just until moistened. Pour 2/3 of mixture into nonstick 5-by-9-inch loaf pan. Combine remaining ingredients; mix well. Pour over top. Spoon remaining 1/3 bread mix mixture over the top. Bake at 350 degrees for 1 hour. Cool in pan 10 minutes. Remove to wire rack to cool. Wrap in foil. Chill in refrigerator. Yield: 1 loaf.

Glenda Rein, Preceptor Gamma Lambda
Sedalia, Colorado

APRICOT PECAN BREAD

1 cup sugar
1 tablespoon margarine, softened
1 egg, beaten
Juice of 1 orange
1 cup (or less) boiling water
2 cups all-purpose flour
1 teaspoon baking soda
1 teaspoon baking powder
1/4 teaspoon salt
1 cup ground apricots
1/2 cup chopped pecans

Preheat oven to 350 degrees. Cream sugar and margarine in large mixer bowl until light and fluffy. Add egg; mix well. Add orange juice to enough boiling water to measure 1 cup liquid. Add to sugar mixture alternately with mixture of flour, baking soda, baking powder and salt, mixing well after each addition. Stir in apricots and pecans. Pour into greased 5-by-9-inch loaf pan. Bake at 350 degrees for 35 minutes. Yield: 18 servings.

Cyndee Cox, Laureate Beta Eta
Clive, Iowa

BANANA BREAD

1 1/4 cups sifted all-purpose flour
1 cup minus 2 tablespoons sugar
1/2 teaspoon salt
1 teaspoon baking soda
1 cup mashed bananas
2 eggs, beaten
1/2 cup corn oil
1/2 cup chopped walnuts (optional)

Preheat oven to 350 degrees. Sift sifted flour, sugar, salt and baking soda into medium mixer bowl. Add bananas, eggs and oil; stir just until blended. Stir in walnuts. Pour into nonstick 5-by-9-inch loaf pan. Bake at 350 degrees for 40 to 45 minutes or until bread tests done. Yield: 1 loaf.

Joyce Foster, Laureate Sigma
Belleville, Ontario, Canada

BANANA BUTTER BREAD

3 ripe bananas, mashed
1 cup sugar
2 eggs
1/4 cup melted butter or margarine
1 1/2 cups all-purpose flour
1/4 teaspoon salt
1 teaspoon baking soda

Preheat oven to 375 degrees. Combine bananas, sugar, eggs and butter in large mixer bowl. Add sifted mixture of flour, salt and baking soda; mix well. Pour into greased 5-by-9-inch loaf pan. Bake at 375 degrees for 40 minutes. Yield: 1 loaf.

Pam Snow, Alpha Theta
Oromocto, New Brunswick, Canada

BUTTERMILK BANANA BREAD

1 cup sugar
1/2 cup vegetable shortening
1 egg
1/2 teaspoon vanilla extract
1/2 cup buttermilk
2 cups all-purpose flour
1 teaspoon baking soda
1/4 teaspoon salt
3 ripe bananas, mashed
1/2 cup chopped pecans (optional)

Preheat oven to 350 degrees. Beat sugar and shortening in large mixer bowl until light and fluffy. Add egg, vanilla and buttermilk; mix well. Add mixture of flour, baking soda and salt alternately with bananas, mixing well after each addition. Stir in pecans. Pour into lightly greased 5-by-9-inch loaf pan. Bake at 350 degrees for 1 hour. Yield: 1 loaf.

Janine Gustafson, Beta Sigma Phi
Spirit Lake, Iowa

BANANA CHIP BREAD

2 1/2 cups all-purpose flour
1 2/3 cups sugar
1 1/4 teaspoons each baking powder and baking soda
2/3 cup vegetable oil
2/3 cup milk
1 tablespoon vanilla extract
3 ripe bananas, mashed
3 eggs
1 cup semisweet chocolate chips

Preheat oven to 350 degrees. Mix first 4 ingredients in large bowl. Add oil, milk and vanilla. Stir 50 strokes with spoon. Add bananas and eggs; mix well. Stir in chocolate chips. Pour into greased bundt pan. Bake at 350 degrees for 50 to 55 minutes. Yield: 16 servings.

Kelly Kellerstrass, Alpha Delta Lambda
Cameron, Missouri

EASY BANANA BREAD

1/2 cup vegetable shortening
1 cup sugar
2 eggs
1/2 cup sour milk
2 cups all-purpose flour
1 teaspoon baking soda
Salt to taste
3 ripe bananas, mashed
3/4 cup chopped walnuts (optional)

Preheat oven to 350 degrees. Cream shortening and sugar in large mixer bowl until light and fluffy. Add eggs; mix well. Add sour milk alternately with mixture of flour, baking soda and salt, mixing well after each addition. Stir in bananas and walnuts. Pour into 1 greased and floured large loaf pan or 2 small loaf pans. Bake at 350 degrees for 55 to 60 minutes or until toothpick inserted in center comes out clean. Yield: 12 servings.

Beverly Jean Lockman, Preceptor Laureate Zeta
Cheyenne, Wyoming

QUICK BANANA FRUIT BREAD

1/3 cup vegetable shortening
2/3 cup sugar
3/4 teaspoon fresh or dried grated lemon rind
2 eggs or egg substitute equal to 2 eggs
1 to 1 1/4 cups mashed ripe bananas
1 3/4 cups all-purpose flour, sifted
2 1/4 teaspoons baking powder
1/2 teaspoon salt
1/2 cup chopped pecans
1 (8-ounce) package dried fruit bits

Preheat oven to 350 degrees. Cream shortening and sugar in large mixer bowl until light and fluffy. Add lemon rind, eggs and bananas, mixing well after each addition. Add mixture of sifted flour, baking powder and salt gradually, mixing well after each addition. Stir in pecans and dried fruit. Pour into greased 5-by-9-inch loaf pan. Bake at 350 degrees for 50 to 60 minutes or until wooden pick inserted in center comes out clean. Yield: 1 loaf.

Carolyn Hendrick, Xi Kappa Chi
Refugio, Texas

BANANA HAZELNUT BREAD

1/4 cup chopped hazelnuts
1/4 cup dates
2 1/4 cups self-rising flour
1/3 cup packed light brown sugar
1 cup mashed bananas
1/2 cup buttermilk
1/4 cup dry skim milk powder
2 tablespoons light corn syrup
2 egg whites

Preheat oven to 350 degrees. Combine hazelnuts, dates, self-rising flour and brown sugar in large bowl. Stir in bananas. Add buttermilk, milk powder, corn syrup and egg whites gradually, mixing well after each addition. Pour into lightly greased 5-by-9-inch loaf pan. Bake at 350 degrees for 45 minutes or until wooden pick inserted in center comes out clean. Yield: 12 servings.

Patricia Mather, Laureate Tau
Penticton, British Columbia, Canada

HEARTY BANANA BREAD

1/2 cup canola oil
2/3 cup honey
1 egg
1/4 cup buttermilk
1 teaspoon vanilla extract
1 teaspoon banana extract
1 cup whole wheat flour
1/2 cup unbleached flour
1 teaspoon baking soda
1 1/3 cups mashed bananas
1 cup English walnuts or 1/2 cup walnuts and 1/2 cup granola

Preheat oven to 350 degrees. Combine oil, honey and egg in large mixer bowl. Add mixture of buttermilk, vanilla and banana extract alternately with mixture of whole wheat flour, unbleached flour and baking soda, mixing well after each addition. Stir in bananas and walnuts. Pour into 5-by-9-inch loaf pan sprayed with nonstick cooking spray. Bake at 350 degrees for 50 to 60 minutes. Can use 3-by-5-inch loaf pans and bake for 40 minutes. Yield: 10 to 12 servings.

Jane Smirl, Epsilon Master
Kansas City, Missouri

LOW-FAT BANANA CHOCOLATE CHIP BREAD

1/2 cup baby food prunes
1 cup packed light brown sugar
4 egg whites, beaten
2 cups all-purpose flour
1/2 teaspoon salt
1/2 teaspoon baking powder
3/4 teaspoon baking soda
2 cups mashed bananas
1/2 cup miniature chocolate chips

Preheat oven to 350 degrees. Cream prunes and brown sugar in large mixer bowl. Add egg whites; mix well. Add mixture of flour, salt, baking powder and baking soda; mix well. Stir in bananas and chocolate chips. Pour into nonstick 5-by-9-inch loaf pan. Bake at 350 degrees for 45 minutes. Yield: 12 servings.

Juliette Lepine, Delta Sigma
Louisville, Colorado

BANANA PECAN BREAD

This bread is served to honeymoon couples for breakfast in a hotel in Montreal.

1 cup sugar
1/2 cup vegetable shortening or butter, softened
2 eggs
3 or 4 ripe bananas, mashed
1 3/4 cups all-purpose flour
1 teaspoon baking powder
1/3 teaspoon baking soda
Salt to taste
1 teaspoon vanilla extract
1/2 cup chopped pecans

Preheat oven to 350 degrees. Cream sugar and shortening in large mixer bowl until light and fluffy. Add eggs and bananas; mix well. Add sifted mixture of flour, baking powder, baking soda and salt. Stir in vanilla and pecans. Pour into greased 5-by-9-inch loaf pan. Bake at 350 degrees for 50 to 60 minutes. Serve warm with butter. May cut slices in half and spread with cream cheese or other filling for tea or brunch sandwiches. May crumble slices over fruit, pudding or ice cream. May serve with ice cream or fruit with chocolate syrup and whipped cream. Yield: 1 loaf.

Eva Welker, Xi Delta Eta
Torrance, California

BANANA NUT BREAD

1/2 cup vegetable oil
1 cup sugar
2 eggs
3 bananas, mashed
2 cups all-purpose flour
1 teaspoon baking soda
1/2 teaspoon baking powder
1/2 teaspoon salt
3 tablespoons milk
1/2 teaspoon vanilla extract
1/2 cup chopped pecans or walnuts

Preheat oven to 350 degrees. Beat oil and sugar in large mixer bowl. Add eggs and bananas; mix well. Add mixture of flour, baking soda, baking powder and salt alternately with mixture of milk and vanilla, mixing well after each addition. Stir in pecans. Pour into greased and floured 5-by-9-inch loaf pan. Bake at 350 degrees for 1 hour. Yield: 16 slices.

Teresa W. Penland, Theta Rho
Franklin, North Carolina

BANANA RAISIN BREAD

3/4 cup packed light brown sugar
1/4 cup sugar
1/2 cup butter or margarine, softened
4 small bananas, mashed
1/4 cup whipping cream
1 teaspoon vanilla extract
2 extra-large eggs
2 cups all-purpose flour
1 teaspoon baking soda
1/2 teaspoon cinnamon
1/2 teaspoon salt
1/2 cup chopped walnuts
1/2 cup raisins

Preheat oven to 350 degrees. Cream brown sugar, sugar and butter in large mixer bowl until light and fluffy. Stir in bananas, whipping cream and vanilla with spatula. Add eggs 1 at a time, mixing well after each addition. Add sifted mixture of flour, baking soda, cinnamon and salt. Stir in walnuts and raisins. Pour into nonstick 5-by-9-inch loaf pan. Bake at 350 degrees for 65 to 70 minutes. Yield: 1 loaf.

Debbie Yates, Xi Kappa Omega
Pickerington, Ohio

BANANA TEA BREAD

1/2 cup margarine, softened
11/3 cups sugar
1/2 cup egg substitute or 3 egg whites
1/4 cup nonfat sour cream
2 cups all-purpose flour
11/2 teaspoons baking powder
1/2 teaspoon baking soda
1/4 teaspoon salt
1 cup mashed bananas
2 tablespoons light rum
1 teaspoon almond extract
11/2 cups chopped pecans or walnuts

Preheat oven to 350 degrees. Cream margarine and sugar in large mixer bowl until light and fluffy. Add egg substitute and sour cream; mix well. Add mixture of flour, baking powder, baking soda and salt alternately with bananas, mixing well after each addition. Stir in rum and almond extract; mix well. Stir in pecans. Pour into nonstick 5-by-9-inch loaf pan. Bake at 350 degrees for 60 to 75 minutes or until wooden pick inserted in center comes out clean. Remove to wire rack to cool. Yield: 8 to 10 servings.

Susan Ernst, Xi Beta Beta
Amherst, Ohio

BANANA WALNUT BREAD

This recipe was given to me by a special friend and co-worker, Dona Smith, who died in November of 1994.

1 cup sugar
1/2 cup vegetable shortening
2 eggs
3 ripe bananas, mashed
11/3 cups all-purpose flour
1/2 teaspoon salt
1 teaspoon baking soda
1 cup chopped walnuts

Preheat oven to 350 degrees. Cream sugar and shortening in large mixer bowl until light and fluffy. Add eggs and bananas; mix well. Add mixture of flour, salt and baking soda; mix just until blended. Stir in walnuts. Pour into nonstick 5-by-9-inch loaf pan. Bake at 350 degrees for 1 hour or until wooden pick inserted in center comes out clean.
Yield: 12 to 15 servings.

Barbara Chavez, Xi Delta Lambda
Susanville, California

BLUEBERRY BREAD

2 eggs
1 cup sour milk
1/2 cup packed light brown sugar
1/2 cup rolled oats
1/2 cup vegetable oil
2 cups all-purpose flour
1 teaspoon baking powder
1 teaspoon baking soda
1 teaspoon salt
1/2 teaspoon nutmeg
11/2 cups blueberries
1 cup chopped pecans

Preheat oven to 350 degrees. Beat eggs in large mixer bowl. Add sour milk, brown sugar, oats and oil; mix well. Add sifted mixture of flour, baking powder, baking soda, salt and nutmeg; mix well. Stir in blueberries and pecans just until blended. Pour into 10-inch nonstick loaf pan. Bake at 350 degrees for 1 hour. Let stand until cool. Any type berries may be substituted for blueberries. Yield: 12 servings.

Rita Southcott, Laureate Delta
Grand Falls-Windsor, Newfoundland, Canada

CANNING JAR BREAD

This recipe originally came from my hometown newspaper and it really works. It makes nice gifts and sells well at bake sales.

2/3 cup vegetable shortening
22/3 cups sugar
4 eggs
2/3 cup water
2 cups mashed bananas
31/3 cups all-purpose flour
1/2 teaspoon baking powder
2 teaspoons baking soda
11/2 teaspoons salt
1 teaspoon cinnamon
1 teaspoon cloves
1 cup chopped pecans

Grease inside of 8 hot sterilized 1-pint widemouth jars. Preheat oven to 300 degrees. Cream shortening and sugar in large mixer bowl until light and fluffy. Add eggs; mix well. Add water and bananas; mix well. Stir in mixture of flour, baking powder, baking soda, salt, cinnamon and cloves with spoon; mix well. Stir in pecans. Fill jars 1/2 full of mixture. Bake at 300 degrees for 45 to 55 minutes. Remove jars from oven 1 at a time. Seal with 2-piece lids. May use as gifts using ribbons or ornaments to decorate jars.
Yield: 8 loaves.

Donna J. Myers, Preceptor Alpha Zeta
Flora, Illinois

CRANBERRY ORANGE BREAD

This is similar to a recipe for bread served for breakfast at an inn in Chatham, Massachusetts. The bread makes a wonderful gift.

2 cups all-purpose flour
1 cup sugar
11/2 teaspoons baking powder
1/2 teaspoon baking soda
1/2 teaspoon salt
1 egg
3/4 cup orange juice
1/3 cup melted margarine
1 teaspoon grated orange peel
11/2 cups fresh cranberries, chopped
1/4 cup orange juice
1/2 teaspoon almond extract
1/2 teaspoon butter extract
1/2 teaspoon vanilla extract
3/4 cup sugar

Preheat oven to 350 degrees. Combine flour, 1 cup sugar, baking powder, baking soda and salt in large mixer bowl. Add egg, 3/4 cup orange juice, margarine and orange peel, mixing well after each addition. Stir in cranberries. Pour into greased 5-by-9-inch loaf pan. Bake at 350 degrees for 1 hour. Remove to wire rack to cool. Combine 1/4 cup orange juice, almond extract, butter extract, vanilla and 3/4 cup sugar in small saucepan. Cook over low heat, stirring constantly until smooth. Spread glaze over hot bread with pastry brush. Yield: 1 loaf.

Becki Shrum, Xi Theta Gamma
Poplar Bluff, Missouri

LEMON BREAD

I am always asked for the recipe when serving this bread. It is one of the best lemon breads I've ever tasted and my family loves it.

3/4 cup butter or margarine, softened
1 1/2 cups sugar
3 eggs
3/4 cup milk
Grated rind of 1 1/2 lemons
Salt to taste
2 1/4 cups all-purpose flour
1 1/2 teaspoons baking powder
3/4 cup sugar
Juice of 1 1/2 lemons

Cream butter and 1 1/2 cups sugar in large mixer bowl until light and fluffy. Add eggs, milk and lemon rind; mix until smooth. Add salt, flour and baking powder; mix well. Pour into greased narrow loaf pan. Let rise for 20 minutes. Preheat oven to 350 degrees. Bake at 350 degrees for 50 minutes. Dissolve 3/4 cup sugar in lemon juice in small bowl. Pour over hot bread. Let cool in pan. Yield: 1 loaf.

Doreen Saunders, Laureate Alpha Alpha
Kingston, Ontario, Canada

LEMON LOAF

1/2 cup margarine, softened
1 cup sugar
2 eggs
Grated rind of 1 lemon
1 1/2 cups all-purpose flour
1 teaspoon baking powder
1/2 cup milk
1/2 cup chopped walnuts
Juice of 1 lemon
1 tablespoon sugar

Preheat oven to 350 degrees. Cream margarine and sugar in mixer bowl until light and fluffy. Add eggs and lemon rind; mix well. Add mixture of flour and baking powder alternately with milk. Stir in walnuts. Pour in greased 5-by-9-inch loaf pan. Bake at 350 degrees for 1 hour. Baste warm bread 2 times with mixture of lemon juice and 1 tablespoon sugar. Wrap cooled bread in waxed paper. Yield: 12 servings.

Shelli Manning, Xi Beta Gamma
Lenexa, Kansas

✣ QUICK LEMONADE BREAD

1/2 cup shortening
1 cup sugar
2 eggs
1 1/2 cups all-purpose flour
2 teaspoons baking powder
1/2 cup milk
1/3 cup plus 1 tablespoon frozen lemonade concentrate, thawed

Preheat oven to 350 degrees. Cream shortening and sugar in large mixer bowl until light and fluffy. Add eggs; mix well. Stir in flour, baking powder and milk. Beat at low speed for 3 minutes. Pour into greased and floured 5-by-9-inch loaf pan. Bake at 350 degrees for 50 to 60 minutes. Pierce holes in warm bread with wooden pick to bottom of pan. Pour lemonade concentrate over hot bread. Yield: 12 servings.

Donna Lundy, Preceptor Gamma Gamma
Tulsa, Oklahoma

ORANGE BREAD

2 (10-count) cans refrigerator buttermilk biscuits
3 ounces cream cheese, cut into 20 squares
1/2 cup melted margarine
3/4 cup sugar
1/2 cup chopped pecans
1 tablespoon grated orange rind
1 cup confectioners' sugar
2 tablespoons orange juice

Preheat oven to 350 degrees. Separate each biscuit into 2 layers. Place a cream cheese square between 2 layers and seal edges. Dip in margarine. Dredge in mixture of sugar, pecans and orange rind. Stand on edge, evenly spaced, in lightly greased 12-cup bundt pan. Drizzle with remaining margarine. Sprinkle with remaining pecan mixture. Bake at 350 degrees for 45 minutes or until golden brown. Invert onto serving plate immediately. Drizzle mixture of confectioners' sugar and orange juice over warm bread. Serve immediately. Yield: 16 servings.

Amie Brennan, Beta Sigma Phi
Kendallville, Indiana

PECAN BREAD

1 egg, beaten
1 1/4 cups milk
3 cups baking mix
1/2 cup sugar
1/2 cup pecans
1/2 cup dried mixed fruit

Preheat oven to 350 degrees. Combine egg, milk, baking mix and sugar in large mixer bowl; mix well. Stir in pecans and dried fruit. Pour into nonstick loaf pan. Bake at 350 degrees for 50 to 60 minutes. Yield: 1 loaf.

Johnny (Robbi) Callihan, Eta Sigma
Blue Ridge, Georgia

PISTACHIO NUT BREAD

1 (2-layer) package golden butter cake mix
1 small package pistachio instant pudding mix
1/4 cup vegetable oil
1/2 cup water
1 cup sour cream
4 eggs
1 cup packed light brown sugar
1 teaspoon cinnamon
1/2 cup chopped pecans

Preheat oven to 350 degrees. Combine cake mix, pudding mix, oil, water and sour cream in large mixer bowl. Add eggs 1 at a time, mixing well after each addition. Alternate layers of cake mix mixture and mixture of brown sugar, cinnamon and pecans in 2 greased and floured 5-by-9-inch loaf pans, ending with brown sugar mixture. Pull knife through batter to make swirl marbled effect. Bake at 350 degrees for 50 to 60 minutes. Yield: 2 loaves.

Pauline Jones, Missouri Omega Nu
Ridgeway, Missouri

POPPY SEED BREAD

3 cups all-purpose flour
2 cups sugar
3 eggs
1 1/2 teaspoons baking powder
1 1/2 teaspoons salt
1 1/2 tablespoons poppy seeds
1 1/2 cups milk
3/4 cup vegetable oil
1 1/2 teaspoons each vanilla and almond extract
1 1/2 teaspoons butter extract
1 cup confectioners' sugar
1/4 teaspoon vanilla extract
2 tablespoons orange juice
1/4 teaspoon almond extract
1/4 teaspoon butter extract

Preheat oven to 350 degrees. Combine flour, sugar, eggs, baking powder, salt, poppy seeds, milk, oil, 1 1/2 teaspoons vanilla, 1 1/2 teaspoons almond extract and 1 1/2 teaspoons butter extract in large mixer bowl; mix until smooth. Spoon into 2 greased and floured 5-by-9-inch loaf pans. Bake at 350 degrees for 1 hour. Pour mixture of confectioners' sugar, 1/4 teaspoon vanilla, orange juice, 1/4 teaspoon almond extract and 1/4 teaspoon butter extract over hot loaves. Cool in pans for 10 minutes. Remove to wire rack to cool completely. Yield: 2 loaves.

Georgia Bailey, Tau Delta
Lutz, Florida

ALMOND POPPY SEED BREAD

1 1/4 cups sugar
1 1/4 cups vegetable oil
1 cup evaporated milk
3 eggs
1/4 cup milk
2 1/2 cups all-purpose flour
2 1/4 teaspoons baking powder
1/8 teaspoon salt
1/4 cup poppy seeds
1 1/4 teaspoons almond extract

Preheat oven to 350 degrees. Combine sugar, oil, evaporated milk, eggs and milk in large mixer bowl; mix well. Add sifted mixture of flour, baking powder and salt, beating at low speed. Stir in poppy seeds and almond extract; mix well. Pour into 2 nonstick 5-by-9-inch loaf pans. Bake at 350 degrees for 60 to 70 minutes or until golden brown. Yield: 2 loaves.

Angela Timberlake, Preceptor Mu Kappa
Fresno, California

CRYSTAL-EDGED POPPY SEED BREAD

3 cups all-purpose flour
2 1/4 cups sugar
1/2 teaspoon salt
1 1/2 teaspoons baking powder
1 1/8 cups vegetable oil
3 eggs
1 1/2 cups milk
1 1/2 teaspoons vanilla extract
1 teaspoon butter extract
1 1/2 tablespoons poppy seeds
1/4 cup plus 2 tablespoons orange juice
1 cup plus 2 tablespoons sugar
3/4 teaspoon vanilla extract
3/4 teaspoon butter extract
3/4 teaspoon almond extract

Preheat oven to 350 degrees. Combine flour, 2 1/4 cups sugar, salt and baking powder in large mixer bowl. Add oil, eggs, milk, 1 1/2 teaspoons vanilla, 1 teaspoon butter extract and poppy seeds, mixing well after each addition. Pour into 2 nonstick 5-by-9-inch loaf pans. Bake at 350 degrees for 1 hour or until wooden pick inserted in center comes out clean. Bring orange juice, 1 cup plus 2 tablespoons sugar, 3/4 teaspoon vanilla, 3/4 teaspoon butter extract and almond extract to a boil in small saucepan. Remove from heat. Pour over hot loaves in pan. Let stand until sugar crystals form around edge. Remove to wire racks to cool. Yield: 2 loaves.

Kari Kimbro, Theta Sigma
Hays, Kansas

POPPY SEED BREAD WITH LEMON ALMOND GLAZE

1 1/8 cups vegetable oil
2 cups sugar
3 eggs
1 1/2 teaspoons vanilla extract
2 1/2 teaspoons almond extract
1 1/2 cups milk
2 tablespoons poppy seeds
3 cups all-purpose flour
1 1/2 teaspoons baking powder
1 1/2 teaspoons salt
2 tablespoons melted butter or margarine
1/2 teaspoon vanilla extract
3/4 cup confectioners' sugar
1/2 teaspoon almond extract
1/2 teaspoon lemon juice
2 tablespoons milk

Beat oil, sugar, eggs, 1 1/2 teaspoons vanilla, 2 1/2 teaspoons almond extract, 1 1/2 cups milk and poppy seeds together in large mixer bowl. Add sifted mixture of flour, baking powder and salt; mix well. Pour into 2 greased and floured 5-by-9-inch loaf pans. Bake at 350 degrees for 1 hour. Make slashes in warm bread with knife and loosen edges from sides of pans. Pour mixture of butter, 1/2 teaspoon vanilla, confectioners' sugar, 1/2 teaspoon almond extract, lemon juice and 2 tablespoons milk over the top. Remove to serving plate to cool. Yield: 2 loaves.

Kimberly Ann Hoendorf, Legacy Member
Gladstone, Missouri

POPPY SEED BREAD WITH ORANGE GLAZE

3 cups all-purpose flour
2 1/4 cups sugar
1 1/2 teaspoons salt
1 1/2 teaspoons baking powder
3 eggs
1 1/2 cups milk
1 1/8 cups vegetable oil
1 1/2 tablespoons poppy seeds
2 teaspoons vanilla extract
2 teaspoons almond extract
2 teaspoons butter extract
3/4 cup sugar
1/4 cup orange juice

Preheat oven to 350 degrees. Combine flour, 2 1/4 cups sugar, salt and baking powder in large mixer bowl. Add eggs, milk and oil, mixing well after each addition. Stir in poppy seeds, 1 1/2 teaspoons vanilla, 1 1/2 teaspoons almond extract and 1 1/2 teaspoons butter extract; mix well. Pour into 5 small nonstick loaf pans. Bake at 350 degrees for 35 to 40 minutes. Spread mixture of 3/4 cup sugar, orange juice and remaining 1/2 teaspoon vanilla, 1/2 teaspoon almond extract and 1/2 teaspoon butter extract over warm bread. Yield: 5 loaves.

Louise Stangl, Kappa Theta
Kansas City, Missouri

VANILLA POPPY SEED BREAD

1 (2-layer) package white cake mix
4 eggs
1/2 cup vegetable oil
1 (6-ounce) package vanilla instant pudding mix
2 teaspoons almond extract
2 1/2 tablespoons poppy seeds
1 cup confectioners' sugar
2 tablespoons (or more) milk

Preheat oven to 350 degrees. Combine cake mix, eggs, oil, pudding mix, almond extract and poppy seeds in large mixer bowl. Beat at medium speed for 4 minutes. Pour into 2 greased and floured 5-by-9-inch loaf pans. Bake at 350 degrees for 45 minutes. Remove to serving plate. Pour mixture of confectioners' sugar and milk over hot loaves. Yield: 2 loaves.

Nancy Stauffer, Xi Eta Chi
Niles, Ohio

PUMPKIN CREAM CHEESE BREAD

This bread is a family favorite during the holiday season.

1 3/4 cups all-purpose flour
1 1/2 cups sugar
1 teaspoon baking soda
1/2 teaspoon salt
1 teaspoon cinnamon
1/4 teaspoon nutmeg
1 cup canned pumpkin
1/2 cup melted butter or margarine
1 egg, beaten
1/3 cup water
8 ounces cream cheese, softened
1/4 cup sugar
1 egg, beaten

Preheat oven to 350 degrees. Mix flour, 1 1/2 cups sugar, baking soda, salt and spices in large mixer bowl. Add mixture of pumpkin, butter, 1 egg and water; mix just until moistened. Pour half the pumpkin mixture into greased and floured 5-by-9-inch loaf pan. Top with beaten mixture of cream cheese, 1/4 cup sugar and 1 egg. Layer remaining pumpkin mixture over top. Pull knife through the batter for swirl effect. Bake at 350 degrees for 1 hour and 10 minutes. Yield: 1 loaf.

Tina Andrews, Nu Epsilon
Medicine Lodge, Kansas

HONEY PUMPKIN LOAF

1/2 cup margarine, softened
1 cup honey
2 eggs, beaten
2/3 cup pumpkin
2 cups all-purpose flour
3 teaspoons baking powder
1/4 teaspoon salt
1/4 teaspoon ground cloves
1 1/2 teaspoons cinnamon
1/2 teaspoon nutmeg
1/2 teaspoon ginger
1/2 cup milk

Preheat oven to 350 degrees. Cream margarine and honey in large mixer bowl until smooth. Add eggs and pumpkin; mix well. Add mixture of flour, baking powder, salt, cloves, cinnamon, nutmeg and ginger alternately with milk, mixing well after each addition. Pour into greased 5-by-9-inch loaf pan. Bake at 350 degrees for 30 to 40 minutes. Yield: 8 to 10 slices.

Maria Hedderson, Xi Gamma Tau
Mission, British Columbia, Canada

Mary Urton, Xi Lambda Pi, Quincy, Illinois, makes Cherry Bread that is easy enough for a child to make. She thaws a loaf of frozen bread until thawed but not yet risen, cuts the loaf lengthwise into 4 strips and each strip into 6 pieces. Arrange in greased 9-by-13-inch baking pan, make indentation in each with back of spoon and spoon cherry pie filling into indentations. Sprinkle with cinnamon-sugar, let rise to top of pan and bake in preheated 350-degree oven for 40 minutes.

PUMPKIN RAISIN BREAD

2/3 cup vegetable shortening
2 2/3 cups sugar
4 eggs
1 (16-ounce) can pumpkin
2/3 cup water
3 1/3 cups all-purpose flour
2 teaspoons baking soda
1 1/2 teaspoons salt
1/2 teaspoon baking powder
1 teaspoon each cinnamon and cloves
2/3 cup chopped walnuts
2/3 cup raisins

Preheat oven to 350 degrees. Cream shortening and sugar in large mixer bowl until light and fluffy. Add eggs, pumpkin and water; mix well. Add mixture of flour, baking soda, salt, baking powder, cinnamon and cloves; mix well. Stir in walnuts and raisins. Pour into 2 nonstick 5-by-9-inch loaf pans. Bake at 350 degrees for 65 to 75 minutes. May spread with your favorite cream cheese frosting. May bake in 6 miniature nonstick loaf pans for 35 to 40 minutes or bake 36 cupcakes for 20 minutes. Yield: 2 loaves.

Heather Cooper, Theta Iota
Roswell, Georgia

PUMPKIN SPICE BREAD

3 cups sugar
4 eggs
1 cup vegetable oil
2 cups canned pumpkin
3 1/3 cups all-purpose flour
1 teaspoon cinnamon
1 1/2 teaspoons salt
1 teaspoon nutmeg
1/2 teaspoon allspice or pumpkin pie spice
2 teaspoons baking soda
2/3 cup water
1 cup chopped walnuts

Preheat oven to 350 degrees. Cream sugar, eggs and oil together in large mixer bowl. Add pumpkin; mix well. Add mixture of flour, cinnamon, salt, nutmeg, allspice and baking soda alternately with water, mixing well after each addition. Stir in walnuts. Pour into 3 greased and floured 1-pound coffee cans, filling each half full. Bake at 350 degrees for 1 hour and 15 minutes. Yield: 3 loaves.

Georjeana Miller, Beta Rho
Panama City, Florida

PUMPKIN SWIRL BREAD

1 3/4 cups all-purpose flour
1 1/2 cups sugar
1 teaspoon baking soda
1 teaspoon cinnamon
1/2 teaspoon salt
1/4 teaspoon ground nutmeg
1 cup canned pumpkin
1/2 cup melted margarine
1 egg, beaten
1/3 cup water
8 ounces cream cheese, softened
1/4 cup sugar
1 egg, beaten

Preheat oven to 350 degrees. Combine flour, sugar, baking soda, cinnamon, salt and nutmeg in large mixer bowl; mix well. Add mixture of pumpkin, margarine, 1 egg and water, mixing just until moistened. Reserve 2 cups pumpkin mixture. Divide remaining mixture evenly, spooning into 2 greased and floured 5-by-9-inch loaf pans. Beat cream cheese, sugar and 1 egg in bowl. Spread half the cream cheese mixture over each loaf. Pour reserved pumpkin mixture over the top. Pull knife through batter several times for swirl effect. Bake at 350 degrees for 1 hour and 10 minutes or until wooden pick inserted in center comes out clean. Let cool in pans for 5 minutes. Remove to wire rack to cool completely. Yield: 2 loaves.

Nedra Murphy, Xi Phi Iota
Apple Valley, California

PUMPKIN WALNUT BREAD

3 eggs
3/4 cup vegetable oil
1/2 cup water
1 (16-ounce) can pumpkin
2 1/2 cups all-purpose flour
1 1/2 teaspoons baking soda
1 1/4 teaspoons salt
3/4 teaspoon nutmeg
3/4 teaspoon cinnamon
1 cup golden raisins
1/2 cup chopped walnuts
4 ounces cream cheese, softened
3 tablespoons butter or margarine, softened
1 teaspoon lemon juice
1/2 (1-pound) package confectioners' sugar
1/4 cup chopped walnuts

Preheat oven to 350 degrees. Beat eggs, oil, water and pumpkin together in large mixer bowl. Add mixture of flour, baking soda, salt, nutmeg and cinnamon; mix well. Stir in raisins and 1/2 cup walnuts. Pour batter into 3 buttered 1-pound coffee cans. Bake at 350 degrees for 1 hour and 10 minutes. Let stand until cool. Spread with mixture of cream cheese, butter, lemon juice and confectioners' sugar. Sprinkle with 1/4 cup chopped walnuts. Yield: 3 loaves.

George (Gerry) Hurd,
Jacksonville, Florida

STRAWBERRY BREAD

3 cups all-purpose flour
1 teaspoon baking soda
1/2 teaspoon salt
1 teaspoon cinnamon
2 cups sugar
3 eggs, beaten
1 cup vegetable oil
1 (10-ounce) package frozen strawberries or 1 quart fresh strawberries
1 cup chopped pecans

Combine flour, baking soda, salt, cinnamon and sugar in large mixer bowl; mix well. Add mixture of eggs and oil; mix well. Purée strawberries in blender. Add to flour mixture, stirring to combine. Stir in pecans. Pour into 2 nonstick 5-by-9-inch loaf pans. Bake at 350 degrees for 1 hour or until wooden pick inserted in center comes out clean. Let cool in pans. Yield: 2 loaves.

Judy Poland, Preceptor Alpha
Frostburg, Maryland

STRAWBERRY WALNUT BREAD

1 cup butter or margarine, softened
$1^1/2$ cups sugar
1 teaspoon vanilla extract
$^1/4$ teaspoon lemon extract
4 eggs
3 cups all-purpose flour
1 teaspoon salt
1 teaspoon cream of tartar
$^1/2$ teaspoon baking soda
1 cup strawberry jam
$^1/2$ cup sour cream
$^1/2$ cup chopped walnuts
3 ounces cream cheese, softened
2 tablespoons strawberry jam

Preheat oven to 350 degrees. Cream butter, sugar, vanilla and lemon extract in large mixer bowl until light and fluffy. Add eggs 1 at a time, beating well after each addition. Add mixture of flour, salt, cream of tartar and baking soda alternately with mixture of 1 cup jam and sour cream, mixing well after each addition. Stir in walnuts. Pour into 2 greased and floured 5-by-9-inch loaf pans. Bake at 350 degrees for 50 minutes or until wooden pick inserted in center comes out clean. Cool in pans fo 10 minutes. Remove to wire racks to cool completely. Combine cream cheese and 2 tablespoons strawberry jam in bowl; mix well. Serve strawberry cream cheese with thinly sliced strawberry bread. Yield: 2 loaves.

Brenda Staggenborg, Preceptor Zeta
Marysville, Kansas

SWEET POTATO BREAD

$1^1/2$ pounds sweet potatoes, peeled, cubed
$3^1/2$ cups all-purpose flour
2 teaspoons baking soda
1 teaspoon salt
$1^1/2$ teaspoons pumpkin pie spice
4 eggs, beaten
1 cup vegetable oil
3 cups sugar
1 cup chopped pecans
$^1/2$ cup raisins

Preheat oven to 350 degrees. Cook sweet potatoes, covered, in enough boiling water to cover until tender. Drain, reserving $^2/3$ cup of the cooking water. Mash sweet potatoes; set aside. Combine flour, baking soda, salt and pumpkin pie spice in large mixer bowl; mix well. Beat eggs with oil and sugar. Add to flour mixture; mix well. Add sweet potatoes and reserved cooking water; mix well. Stir in pecans and raisins. Pour into 3 nonstick 5-by-9-inch loaf pans. Bake at 350 degrees for 50 minutes. Cover with foil. Bake for 10 minutes longer. Cool in pans for 10 minutes. Remove to wire racks to cool completely. Wrap and store for 8 to 12 hours before serving.
Yield: 3 loaves.

Linda Robertson, Missouri Omega Nu
Gilman City, Missouri

ZUCCHINI CHERRY BREAD

4 eggs, beaten
1 cup vegetable oil
2 cups sugar
1 teaspoon vanilla extract
4 cups grated unpeeled zucchini
$2^1/2$ cups all-purpose flour
1 teaspoon salt
$1^1/2$ teaspoons baking soda
1 teaspoon baking powder
1 cup chopped pecans
1 cup maraschino cherries, drained
1 cup raisins, plumped
1 cup all-purpose flour

Preheat oven to 350 degrees. Combine eggs, oil, sugar and vanilla in large mixer bowl; mix well. Stir in zucchini. Add mixture of $2^1/2$ cups flour, salt, baking soda and baking powder; mix well. Coat pecans, cherries and raisins in 1 cup flour in small bowl. Add to zucchini mixture; mix well. Pour into 3 greased 5-by-9-inch loaf pans. Bake at 350 degrees for 50 to 60 minutes. Yield: 3 loaves.

Marleene Montague, Preceptor Pi
St. Catharines, Ontario, Canada

CHOCOLATE CHIP ZUCCHINI BREAD

3 eggs
1 cup vegetable oil
$1^1/2$ cups sugar
2 cups zucchini
1 tablespoon vanilla extract
3 cups all-purpose flour
1 tablespoon cinnamon
1 teaspoon baking soda
1 teaspoon baking powder
1 teaspoon salt
1 cup semisweet chocolate chips
1 cup chopped pecans

Preheat oven to 350 degrees. Mix eggs, oil, sugar, zucchini and vanilla in large mixer bowl. Add mixture of next 5 ingredients; mix well. Stir in chocolate chips and pecans. Pour into nonstick loaf pan. Bake at 350 degrees for 1 hour. Yield: 1 loaf.

Kim Bussey, Gamma Delta
Aurora, Colorado

EASY ZUCCHINI BREAD

2 cups sugar
3 eggs
1 cup vegetable oil
1 tablespoon vanilla extract
3 cups all-purpose flour
1 teaspoon baking soda
1 teaspoon salt
1 tablespoon cinnamon
2 cups grated zucchini
1 cup chopped pecans

Preheat oven to 350 degrees. Combine sugar, eggs, oil and vanilla in large mixer bowl. Add mixture of flour, baking soda, salt and cinnamon; mix well. Stir in zucchini and pecans. Pour into 1 large or 2 small greased loaf pans. Bake at 350 degrees for 1 to $1^1/2$ hours or until bread pulls away from sides of pan. Yield: 1 large or 2 small loaves.

Cindy Wagner, Chi Omicron
Naperville, Illinois

ZUCCHINI PINEAPPLE BREAD

3 eggs, beaten
1 1/2 to 2 cups sugar
1 cup vegetable oil
1 tablespoon vanilla extract
1 (18-ounce) can crushed pineapple
2 cups grated zucchini
3 cups all-purpose flour
1 teaspoon salt
1 teaspoon baking powder
1 teaspoon baking soda
1 teaspoon cinnamon
1 teaspoon allspice
1/2 teaspoon cloves

Preheat oven to 350 degrees. Combine eggs, sugar, oil, vanilla, pineapple and zucchini in large mixer bowl; mix lightly. Add mixture of flour, salt, baking powder, baking soda, cinnamon, allspice and cloves, stirring until blended. Pour into 2 greased 5-by-9-inch loaf pans. Bake at 350 degrees for 1 hour or until browned on top and wooden pick inserted in center comes out clean. Yield: 2 loaves.

Delores A. Shinn, Preceptor Alpha Psi
Kingman, Arizona

ZUCCHINI RAISIN NUT BREAD

3 eggs
1 cup vegetable oil
2 cups sugar
3 teaspoons vanilla extract
2 cups grated peeled zucchini
3 cups all-purpose flour
1 teaspoon salt
1 teaspoon baking soda
1/4 teaspoon nutmeg
2 to 3 teaspoons cinnamon
1 1/4 teaspoons baking powder
1/2 cup chopped pecans
1/2 cup raisins

Preheat oven to 350 degrees. Beat eggs in large mixer bowl. Add oil, sugar, vanilla and zucchini, mixing gently. Add sifted mixture of flour, salt, baking soda, nutmeg, cinnamon and baking powder, stirring to combine. Stir in pecans and raisins. Pour into 2 greased and floured 5-by-9-inch loaf pans. Bake at 350 degrees for 1 hour or until bread tests done. Yield: 2 loaves.

Carolyn Murphey, Preceptor Alpha Omicron
Mechanicsville, Virginia

ZUCCHINI ZIP LOAVES

This is the only way my family will eat zucchini.

3 eggs
1 cup vegetable oil
2 cups sugar
1 teaspoon vanilla extract
2 cups shredded unpeeled zucchini
1 cup whole wheat flour
1 1/2 cups bread flour, sifted
1/2 cup wheat germ
1 teaspoon salt
2 teaspoons nutmeg
1 teaspoon baking soda
1/2 teaspoon baking powder
1/2 cup chopped pecans

Preheat oven to 325 degrees. Beat eggs, oil, sugar, vanilla and zucchini together in large mixer bowl. Add mixture of whole wheat flour, sifted bread flour, wheat germ, salt, nutmeg, baking soda and baking powder; mix well. Stir in pecans. Pour into 2 greased 5-by-9-inch loaf pans. Bake at 325 degrees for 1 hour. May freeze, if desired. Yield: 2 loaves.

Margaret Gordon, Preceptor Alpha
Winnipeg, Manitoba, Canada

DOUBLE APPLE MUFFINS

1 1/3 cups all-purpose flour
1 cup rolled oats
1/3 cup packed light brown sugar
1 tablespoon baking powder
1 teaspoon cinnamon
1/2 teaspoon salt
1/3 cup apple juice
1 egg white, beaten
2/3 cup milk
1 tablespoon vegetable oil
3 tablespoons applesauce
3/4 cup peeled chopped apple

Preheat oven to 400 degrees. Mix flour, oats, brown sugar, baking powder, cinnamon and salt together in bowl. Add combination of apple juice, egg white, milk, oil and applesauce, mixing until just moistened. Fold in apple gently. Fill greased or paper-lined medium muffin cups 2/3 full. Bake at 400 degrees for 20 to 22 minutes or until golden brown on top. Yield: 12 servings.

Joellen Skonseng, Alpha
Fargo, North Dakota

FRESH APPLE OATMEAL MUFFINS

2 cups all-purpose flour
1 teaspoon salt
1 teaspoon baking soda
1 1/2 teaspoons cinnamon
1/4 teaspoon nutmeg
1/4 teaspoon cloves
1 egg white, beaten
1/2 cup applesauce
1 cup packed light brown sugar
1 teaspoon vanilla extract
1/2 cup rolled oats
1/2 cup raisins
1/2 cup pecan pieces
1 large apple, grated

Preheat oven to 400 degrees. Mix flour, salt, baking soda, cinnamon, nutmeg and cloves in bowl; make a well in the center. Mix egg white, applesauce, brown sugar and vanilla in bowl. Spoon into well; mix until moist. Add mixture of oats, raisins, pecans and apple, mixing until moistened. Fill greased large muffin cups 3/4 full. Bake at 400 degrees for 20 to 25 minutes or until muffins test done.
Yield: 12 large servings.

Shirley Dolan, Laureate Theta
Bentonville, Arkansas

HEALTHY APPLE MUFFINS

1 1/2 cups all-purpose flour
1 1/2 cups peeled chopped apples
1/2 cup whole wheat flour
1/2 cup packed light brown sugar
2 teaspoons baking powder
1/2 teaspoon salt
1/4 teaspoon cinnamon
1/2 cup milk
1/4 cup melted butter
1 egg, beaten
1/3 cup packed light brown sugar
1/3 cup chopped nuts
1/2 teaspoon cinnamon

Preheat oven to 400 degrees. Combine 1/2 cup all-purpose flour and apples in small bowl, tossing to coat. Mix remaining 1 cup flour, whole wheat flour, 1/2 cup brown sugar, baking powder, salt and 1/4 teaspoon cinnamon in large bowl. Stir in coated apple mixture, milk, butter and egg until just moistened. Fill greased or paper-lined medium muffin cups 2/3 full. Combine 1/3 cup brown sugar, nuts and 1/2 teaspoon cinnamon in small bowl; mix well. Sprinkle over muffins. Bake at 400 degrees for 20 to 25 minutes or until wooden pick inserted in center comes out clean. Serve warm. Yield: 12 servings.

Priscilla Eales, Preceptor Epsilon Rho
Tampa, Florida

BANANA MUFFINS

1 tablespoon hot water
1/2 teaspoon baking soda
1 teaspoon vanilla extract
1 egg
1 cup sugar
1/2 cup vegetable oil
2 to 3 bananas, mashed
1 1/2 cups all-purpose flour
1/2 cup walnuts (optional)

Preheat oven to 350 degrees. Mix together hot water, baking soda and vanilla in bowl; set aside. Beat egg, sugar and oil in mixer bowl until light and fluffy. Add bananas and flour; do not mix. Add baking soda mixture, stirring to combine. Stir in walnuts. Spoon into greased large or medium muffin cups. Bake at 350 degrees for 20 minutes.
Yield: 8 large or 12 medium muffins.

Terry Mitchell, Xi Zeta Rho
Orangeville, Ontario, Canada

BANANA BLUEBERRY OAT MUFFINS

1 cup all-purpose or whole wheat flour
1 cup rolled oats
1/2 cup sugar
1 1/2 teaspoons baking powder
1 teaspoon baking soda
1/4 cup wheat germ
1/4 teaspoon salt
2 egg whites
2 cups mashed ripe bananas
1/4 cup melted margarine
1 cup fresh or frozen blueberries

Preheat oven to 375 degrees. Combine first 7 ingredients in mixer bowl; mix well. Beat egg whites, bananas and margarine in mixer bowl until smooth. Stir into flour mixture, mixing until moistened. Fold in blueberries. Fill paper-lined large muffin cups 3/4 full. Bake at 375 degrees for 20 to 25 minutes or until tops spring back when lightly touched.
Yield: 12 servings.

Tamalea Meister, Beta Kappa
Atikokan, Ontario, Canada

BANANA CHOCOLATE CHIP MUFFINS

3 large bananas, mashed
3/4 cup sugar
Cinnamon to taste
1 egg
1/3 cup melted margarine
1 teaspoon baking soda
1 teaspoon baking powder
1/2 teaspoon salt
1 tablespoon wheat germ (optional)
1 1/2 cups all-purpose flour or mixture of 1 cup all-purpose and 1/2 cup whole wheat flour
1/2 cup semisweeet chocolate chips

Preheat oven to 375 degrees. Combine bananas, sugar and cinnamon in large mixer bowl; mix well. Add egg; mix well. Add margarine, baking soda, baking powder, salt, wheat germ and flour, mixing after each addition. Stir in chocolate chips. Spoon into paper-lined medium muffin cups. Bake at 375 degrees for 20 minutes. May substitute applesauce for 1 of the bananas. May decrease amount of margarine to 1/4 cup. Yield: 12 servings.

Laurie Stone, Iota Nu
Iroquois Falls, Ontario, Canada

BANANA NUT MUFFINS

2 medium ripe bananas, mashed
2 eggs
1/2 cup vegetable oil
2/3 cup milk
2 1/2 cups all-purpose flour
1 cup sugar
4 teaspoons baking powder
1 teaspoon salt
1 (4-ounce) package vanilla instant pudding mix
1 cup chopped nuts
2/3 cup sugar
2 teaspoons butter or margarine, softened
4 teaspoons all-purpose flour

Preheat oven to 400 degrees. Combine bananas and eggs in mixer bowl; beat until blended. Beat in oil and milk. Combine 2 1/2 cups flour, 1 cup sugar, baking powder, salt and pudding mix in bowl; mix well. Add banana mixture; mix thoroughly. Stir in nuts. Fill greased muffin cups almost full. Combine 2/3 cup sugar, butter and 4 teaspoons flour in bowl; mix until crumbly. Sprinkle over batter. Bake at 400 degrees for 20 to 25 minutes or until muffins test done.
Yield: 18 to 20 servings.

Alaura Scheuerman Lillie
Topeka, Kansas

BANANA POPPY SEED MUFFINS

3 ripe bananas, mashed
1 egg
1/3 cup dry artificial sweetener or 1/2 cup sugar
1/4 cup vegetable oil
1/2 cup skim milk
21/2 teaspoons poppy seeds
2 teaspoons baking powder
1/2 teaspoon baking soda
11/2 cups all-purpose flour
1/2 teaspoon vanilla or almond extract (optional)

Preheat oven to 350 degrees. Combine bananas and egg in bowl; mix well. Add sweetener, oil, milk, poppy seeds, baking powder, baking soda, flour and vanilla; mix until blended. Fill medium muffin cups sprayed with nonstick cooking spray 2/3 full. Bake at 350 degrees for 20 minutes. Yield: 12 servings.

Jolene Korb, Beta Delta
Havre, Montana

HEALTHY BRAN MUFFINS

1 (16-ounce) package raisin bran cereal
3 cups sugar
5 cups all-purpose flour
5 teaspoons baking soda
2 teaspoons salt
1 cup applesauce
Egg substitute equal to 4 eggs or 4 eggs
4 cups buttermilk

Preheat oven to 400 degrees. Mix cereal, sugar, flour, baking soda and salt in large bowl. Add applesauce, egg substitute and buttermilk; mix well. Store, tightly covered, in refrigerator for up to 6 weeks until ready to bake. Fill muffin cups sprayed with nonstick cooking spray 2/3 full. Bake at 400 degrees for 20 minutes. May bake in miniature muffin tins for 10 minutes. Yield: 5 dozen.

Leta L. Homan, Laureate Alpha Eta
Mt. Carmel, Illinois

BLUEBERRY MUFFINS

11/2 cups all-purpose flour
3/4 cup sugar
2 teaspoons baking powder
1 teaspoon baking soda
1/2 teaspoon salt
2/3 cup nonfat or low-fat plain yogurt
1 tablespoon flour
1/2 cup frozen blueberries

Preheat oven to 400 degrees. Combine 11/2 cups flour, sugar, baking powder, baking soda, salt and yogurt in bowl; mix well. Shake an additional 1 tablespoon flour over blueberries in bowl; toss to coat. Stir blueberries into yogurt mixture. Fill greased medium muffin cups 2/3 full. Bake at 400 degrees for 18 minutes. Yield: 12 servings.

Janet Kerschner, Xi Epsilon Delta
Topeka, Kansas

THE BEST BLUEBERRY MUFFINS

2 cups all-purpose flour
1 tablespoon baking powder
1/2 teaspoon salt
1/2 cup sugar
1 egg, lightly beaten
1 cup milk
1/4 cup melted butter or margarine
1/2 cup chopped pecans (optional)
11/2 cups fresh or frozen unsweetened blueberries

Preheat oven to 400 degrees. Combine flour, baking powder, salt and sugar in large bowl; mix well. Mix egg, milk and butter in bowl, stirring until blended. Make a well in center of flour mixture; spoon in egg mixture, mixing until just moistened and lumpy. Stir in pecans. Fold in blueberries gently. Fill greased medium muffin cups 3/4 full. Bake at 400 degrees in center of oven for 20 to 25 minutes or until light brown. Yield: 12 servings.

Brenda Bagwell, Xi Beta Iota
Chesapeake, Virginia

BIG BLUES

I brought these muffins to a Christmas brunch that included sorority sisters and husbands. They didn't leave a crumb!

2 cups all-purpose flour
2 teaspoons baking powder
1/2 teaspoon salt
1/2 cup butter or margarine
1 cup sugar
2 eggs
1/3 cup milk
2 cups fresh or frozen blueberries
Sugar to taste

Preheat oven to 450 degrees. Mix flour, baking powder and salt in bowl; set aside. Cream butter and sugar in mixer bowl until light and fluffy. Beat in eggs until smooth. Add flour mixture and milk alternately, beating until well blended. Stir in blueberries. Spoon into greased large or medium muffin cups. Sprinkle with sugar. Bake at 450 degrees for 5 minutes. Reduce heat and bake at 375 degrees for 30 to 35 minutes longer or until muffins spring back when lightly touched. Do not thaw frozen blueberries. Yield: 8 jumbo or 12 medium muffins.

Paula Grabinsky, Epsilon Omega
Abbotsford, British Columbia, Canada

EASY CINNAMON PUFFS

1 (8-count) can crescent rolls
8 large marshmallows
1/4 cup melted butter or margarine
Cinnamon and sugar to taste
Confectioners' sugar glaze

Preheat oven to 375 degrees. Unroll and separate crescent roll dough. Dip each marshmallow in butter, then in mixture of cinnamon and sugar. Place 1 marshmallow on narrow end of each roll. Roll toward wide end, covering marshmallows. Seal edges. Dip in butter and cinnamon-sugar mixture. Place in greased muffin cups. Bake at 375 degrees for 10 to 15 minutes or until light brown. Drizzle with confectioners' sugar glaze. Yield: 8 servings.

Susan Holste, Xi Eta Omicron
Great Bend, Kansas

FRENCH CINNAMON PUFFS

Several years ago, my family of 5 flew from Seattle to the Twin Cities for a family reunion. We took 6 dozen of these cinnamon puffs as our carry-on luggage. They were very much appreciated by the family.

1/3 cup butter-flavor shortening
1/2 cup sugar
1 egg
1 1/2 cups all-purpose flour
1 1/2 teaspoons baking powder
1/2 teaspoon salt
1/4 teaspoon nutmeg
1/2 cup milk
6 tablespoons melted butter or margarine
1/2 cup sugar
1 teaspoon cinnamon

Preheat oven to 350 degrees. Cream shortening and 1/2 cup sugar in mixer bowl until light and fluffy. Add egg; mix until smooth. Add mixture of flour, baking powder, salt and nutmeg alternately with milk; mix until blended. Fill greased muffin cups 2/3 full. Bake at 350 degrees for 20 minutes. Roll in melted butter and mixture of 1/2 cup sugar and cinnamon. Yield: 6 servings.

Sue-Ellen Parker, Delta Pi
Monroe, Washington

CITRUS MUFFINS

There is a special joy felt by a hostess when guests bite into these muffins and smile in surprise at the taste!

1 3/4 cups sifted all-purpose flour
3 tablespoons sugar
2 1/2 teaspoons baking powder
1/2 teaspoon salt
1 egg
3/4 cup milk
1/3 cup unsalted butter or margarine, melted
1 tablespoon grated orange rind
1 tablespoon grated lime rind

Preheat oven to 400 degrees. Combine flour, sugar, baking powder and salt in bowl. Combine egg, milk and butter in mixer bowl; beat until blended. Stir in orange and lime rinds. Add to flour mixture, mixing until just moistened. Fill greased medium muffin cups 2/3 full. Bake at 400 degrees for 20 minutes. Yield: 12 to 15 servings.

Kathy Herschberg, Laureate Zeta
Park City, Utah

CRANBERRY ORANGE MUFFINS

I found this recipe in the "Lighthearted Cookbook" put out by the Canadian Heart Foundation after my husband had heart bypass surgery.

3/4 cup natural bran powder
3/4 cup whole wheat flour
1/2 cup sugar
1 1/2 teaspoons cinnamon
1 teaspoon baking powder
1 teaspoon baking soda
1 1/3 cups cranberry sauce
1 egg
1/2 cup buttermilk or low-fat plain yogurt
1/4 cup vegetable oil
1 teaspoon grated orange rind

Preheat oven to 400 degrees. Combine bran, flour, sugar, cinnamon, baking powder and baking soda in bowl; mix well. Add cranberry sauce, egg, buttermilk, oil and orange rind; mix until just moistened. Spoon into paper-lined or nonstick medium muffin cups. Bake at 400 degrees for 25 minutes or until firm. Yield: 12 servings.

Donna Jones, Laureate Alpha Tau
Exeter, Ontario, Canada

MAKE-AHEAD MUFFIN MIX

This recipe makes hurried mornings easier by cutting down on breakfast preparation time.

2 cups all-purpose flour
1/4 cup sugar
1 tablespoon baking powder
1/2 teaspoon salt
1/3 cup powdered milk
1 egg, beaten
1 cup water
1/3 cup vegetable oil or melted shortening
3/4 cup mashed banana
1/2 cup chopped nuts (optional)

Preheat oven to 400 degrees. Sift together flour, sugar, baking powder, salt and powdered milk in bowl. Store, covered, for 8 hours or longer. Make a well in center. Add egg, water, oil, banana and nuts; mix until just moistened. Fill greased medium muffin cups 2/3 full. Bake at 400 degrees for 20 to 25 minutes or until muffins spring back when lightly touched. Serve with jam. May substitute 3/4 cup blueberries or raisins for banana. Yield: 12 servings.

Jeannie Gross, Xi Eta Psi
Junction City, Kansas

Kay Garrett, Xi Beta Kappa, Prattville, Alabama, makes Sourdough Cheese Bread by mixing 1 cup Sourdough starter with 6 cups bread flour, 1 teaspoon salt, 1 cup shredded Cheddar cheese and 1 1/2 cups warm water, letting dough rise for 8 hours and dividing among 3 greased loaf pans. Let rise for 8 hours and bake in preheated 350-degree oven for 30 minutes.

✣ SPICY MANDARIN MUFFINS

1 1/2 cups sifted all-purpose flour
1/2 cup sugar
1 3/4 teaspoons baking powder
1/2 teaspoon salt
1/2 teaspoon nutmeg
1/4 teaspoon allspice
1/3 cup butter or margarine
1/2 cup milk
1 egg, beaten
1 (11-ounce) can mandarin oranges, drained, chopped
1/4 cup sugar
1/4 teaspoon cinnamon
1/4 cup melted butter or margarine

Preheat oven to 400 degrees. Combine flour, 1/2 cup sugar, baking powder, salt, nutmeg and allspice in bowl; mix well. Cut in 1/3 cup butter until mixture is crumbly and resembles coarse meal. Add mixture of milk and egg; mix until blended. Stir in mandarin oranges. Fill greased medium muffin cups 2/3 full. Bake at 400 degrees for 15 to 20 minutes or until muffins test done. Remove immediately from pan. Dip tops in mixture of 1/4 cup sugar, cinnamon and 1/4 cup melted butter. Yield: 12 to 20 servings.

Shannon Robinson, Alpha Delta Lambda
Cameron, Missouri

MORNING GLORY MUFFINS

1 1/2 cups all-purpose flour
1 teaspoon baking powder
1 teaspoon baking soda
1/2 teaspoon salt
1/2 teaspoon cinnamon
1/4 teaspoon nutmeg
Ginger and allspice to taste
3/4 cup packed light brown sugar
1 egg
1/2 cup plain yogurt
1/4 cup vegetable oil
1/2 teaspoon vanilla extract
3/4 cup drained crushed pineapple
3/4 cup grated carrots
1/2 cup raisins
1/2 cup chopped walnuts

Preheat oven to 400 degrees. Mix flour, baking powder, baking soda, salt, cinnamon, nutmeg, ginger, allspice and brown sugar in large bowl. Whisk egg, yogurt, oil and vanilla in bowl until blended. Stir in pineapple. Add to flour mixture; mix well. Stir in carrots, raisins and walnuts. Spoon into greased or paper-lined medium muffin cups, filling 2/3 full. Bake at 400 degrees for 16 minutes. Yield: 12 servings.

Bonnie G. Munslow, Kappa Chi
Aurora, Ontario, Canada

Anne Scanlon, Xi Beta Kappa, Prattville, Alabama, makes Cheese Muffins by mixing 1 cup melted butter or margarine with 2 cups shredded Cheddar cheese, 2 tablespoons dried chives, 1 cup sour cream and 2 cups self-rising flour. Fill ungreased miniature muffin cups and bake in preheated 375-degree oven for 20 to 25 minutes.

OAT BRAN MUFFINS

This recipe cuts down on fats, sugar and cholesterol.

2 1/4 cups oat bran cereal
1 tablespoon baking powder
1/4 cup walnuts
1/4 cup raisins
1/4 cup sugar or honey
1 1/4 cups skim milk
2 egg whites
2 tablespoons vegetable oil

Preheat oven to 425 degrees. Combine cereal, baking powder, walnuts, raisins, sugar, milk, egg whites and oil in large bowl; mix until blended. Spoon into greased medium muffin cups. Bake at 425 degrees for 15 to 17 minutes or until muffins test done. Yield: 12 servings.

Beatrice Young, Laureate Xi
Trail, British Columbia, Canada

OATMEAL APPLE RAISIN MUFFINS

My mother adapted this recipe for my father, who is diabetic.

2 egg whites or 1 carton egg substitute
3/4 cup skim milk
1 cup raisins
1 apple, chopped
1/2 cup unsweetened applesauce
1 cup all-purpose flour
1 cup quick-cooking oats
1 tablespoon brown sugar substitute
1 tablespoon baking powder
1 teaspoon salt
2 teaspoons nutmeg
4 teaspoons cinnamon

Preheat oven to 400 degrees. Beat egg whites in mixer bowl until stiff peaks form. Add milk, raisins, apple, applesauce, flour, oats, brown sugar substitute, baking powder, salt, nutmeg and cinnamon; mix until just moistened. Spoon into medium muffin cups sprayed with nonstick cooking spray. Bake at 400 degrees for 15 to 20 minutes or until muffins test done. Yield: 12 servings.

Brenda C. Hill, Beta Eta
Hamlin, West Virginia

OATMEAL CARROT MUFFINS

1 cup buttermilk
1 cup quick-cooking oats
1/2 cup grated carrots
1/4 cup packed light brown sugar
1/4 cup melted margarine
1 egg, lightly beaten
1 teaspoon orange rind
1 cup all-purpose flour
1/4 cup sugar
1 teaspoon baking powder
1 teaspoon salt
1/2 teaspoon baking soda
3/4 cup raisins

Preheat oven to 400 degrees. Pour buttermilk over oats in large bowl; mix well. Let stand, covered, for at least 2 hours or chill for 8 hours. Combine carrots, brown sugar, margarine, egg and orange rind in bowl; mix well. Stir into oat mixture. Add sifted mixture of flour, sugar, baking powder, salt and baking soda. Stir in raisins, mixing until just moistened. Spoon into greased large muffin cups. Bake at 400 degrees for 20 to 25 minutes or until muffins test done. Yield: 12 servings.

Dorothy Leeder, Gamma Rho
Kemptville, Ontario, Canada

OATMEAL ORANGE MUFFINS

This recipe was given to me by a friend while my husband was stationed in Canada as a U.S. Coast Guard Exchange Pilot with the Canadian Armed Forces. Fresh from the oven with a cup of coffee, with snow falling outside and a roomful of friends inside—it's sheer ecstacy!

1 cup rolled oats
1/2 cup orange juice
1/2 cup boiling water
1/2 cup butter or margarine
1/2 cup sugar
1/2 cup light brown sugar
2 eggs
1 cup raisins
1 cup all-purpose flour
1 teaspoon baking powder
1 teaspoon baking soda
1 teaspoon salt
1 teaspoon vanilla extract

Preheat oven to 350 degrees. Soak oats in orange juice and boiling water in bowl for 15 minutes. Cream butter, sugar and brown sugar in mixer bowl until light and fluffy. Beat in eggs. Add oat mixture; mix well. Stir in raisins, flour, baking powder, baking soda, salt and vanilla; mix until blended. Spoon into greased medium muffin cups. Bake at 350 degrees for 20 minutes. May increase amount of orange juice and decrease amount of water if stronger orange flavor is desired. Yield: 12 to 18 servings.

Cathy Robb, Preceptor Alpha Beta
Harvey, Louisiana

ORANGE NUT MUFFINS

2 cups all-purpose flour
1 teaspoon baking powder
1/2 teaspoon baking soda
3/4 cup coarsely chopped walnuts
1 cup sugar
1/2 cup margarine, softened
2 eggs
1 cup lemon yogurt
2 tablespoons grated orange rind

Preheat oven to 400 degrees. Sift flour, baking powder and baking soda into bowl. Add walnuts; toss to coat. Cream sugar and margarine in mixer bowl until light and fluffy. Beat in eggs 1 at a time, beating after each addition. Add yogurt and orange rind; mix well. Stir in flour mixture. Spoon into nonstick medium muffin cups. Bake at 400 degrees for 18 to 20 minutes or until muffins test done. May substitute lemon rind for orange rind. Yield: 12 servings.

Rose A. Harris, Alpha Master
Nashville, Tennessee

PUMPKIN MUFFINS

3 cups sugar
2/3 cup vegetable oil
2/3 cup water
2 cups solid-pack pumpkin
4 eggs
3 1/2 cups all-purpose flour
2 teaspoons baking soda
1/2 teaspoon baking powder
1 1/2 teaspoons salt
1 teaspoon cinnamon
1/2 teaspoon ground cloves
1 cup chopped walnuts (optional)

Preheat oven to 350 degrees. Mix sugar, oil, water, pumpkin and eggs in bowl; mix well. Combine flour, baking soda, baking powder, salt, cinnamon and cloves in bowl. Stir into sugar mixture. Stir in walnuts. Spoon into nonstick medium muffin cups. Bake at 350 degrees for 20 to 25 minutes or until muffins test done. May substitute applesauce for vegetable oil. Yield: 4 dozen.

Mollie Biggs, Gamma Gamma
Duluth, Minnesota

✣ COCONUT PUMPKIN PRALINE MUFFINS

2 cups all-purpose flour
3/4 cup packed light brown sugar
1/2 cup shredded coconut
1/2 cup chopped pecans
2 1/4 teaspoons pumpkin pie spice
2 teaspoons baking powder
1 egg
1 cup solid-pack pumpkin
1/2 cup milk
1/3 cup vegetable oil
1/2 cup packed light brown sugar
1/2 cup shredded coconut
1/2 cup chopped pecans
3 tablespoons milk

Preheat oven to 400 degrees. Combine flour, 3/4 cup brown sugar, 1/2 cup coconut, 1/2 cup pecans, pumpkin pie spice and baking powder in large bowl; mix well. Combine egg, pumpkin, 1/2 cup milk and oil in medium bowl; mix until blended. Stir into flour mixture. Spoon into greased or paper-lined medium muffin cups, filling 3/4 full. Combine 1/2 cup brown sugar, 1/2 cup coconut, 1/2 cup pecans and 3 tablespoons milk in small bowl; mix well. Sprinkle over batter. Bake at 400 degrees for 18 to 20 minutes or until wooden pick inserted in center comes out clean. Cool in pan for 15 minutes. Remove to wire rack to cool completely. Yield: 12 servings.

Dorothy M. Broadwater, Preceptor Theta
Ormond Beach, Florida

Sherrie Ruyan, Mu Kappa, Ellinwood, Kansas, makes Crescent Coffee Cake by pressing 1 can crescent roll dough into greased 9-by-13-inch pan, spreading with a mixture of 8 ounces cream cheese, 3/4 cup sugar, 2 eggs and 1 teaspoon vanilla, topping with another layer of roll dough and sprinkling with cinnamon-sugar. Bake in preheated 350-degree oven for 25 to 30 minutes.

LOW-FAT PUMPKIN MUFFINS

1 cup all-purpose flour
1/2 cup packed light brown sugar
1/4 teaspoon baking soda
2 teaspoons baking powder
1 teaspoon pumpkin pie spice
1/2 teaspoon nutmeg
3/4 cup solid-pack pumpkin
1 egg, beaten
1/4 cup low-fat milk
1/4 cup vegetable oil
1/2 cup raisins (optional)
1 cup rolled oats

Preheat oven to 350 degrees. Sift flour, brown sugar, baking soda, baking powder, pumpkin pie spice and nutmeg into bowl. Add pumpkin; mix well. Add egg, milk and oil; mix until blended. Stir in raisins and oats. Spoon into nonstick medium muffin cups. Bake at 350 degrees for 18 to 20 minutes or until muffins test done. Yield: 8 to 10 servings.

Lois A. Pratt, Preceptor Lambda
Westbrook, Maine

MOM'S RISE AND RUN MUFFINS

11/2 cups low-fat buttermilk
3/4 cup apple juice concentrate, thawed
1/4 cup honey
2 cups all-bran cereal
1 cup raisins, soaked, drained
1/3 cup canola oil
2 teaspoons cinnamon
1 teaspoon vanilla extract
3 egg whites
1/2 cup shredded apple
2 cups unbleached all-purpose flour
1/2 cup wheat germ
11/2 teaspoons baking powder
11/2 teaspoons baking soda
1 teaspoon salt

Preheat oven to 350 degrees. Combine buttermilk, apple juice concentrate, honey and cereal in large bowl; mix well. Let stand for 30 minutes. Add raisins, oil, cinnamon, vanilla, egg whites and apple; mix until blended. Combine flour, wheat germ, baking powder, baking soda and salt in bowl; mix well. Stir into buttermilk mixture until just moistened. Fill medium muffin cups sprayed with nonstick cooking spray 3/4 full. Bake at 350 degrees for 20 to 25 minutes or until muffins test done. Do not use bran flakes for bran. Yield: 18 servings.

Mary Golden, Xi Delta Psi
Lake City, Pennsylvania

SUNSHINE MUFFINS

1 seedless orange, unpeeled, cut into 8 sections
1/2 cup orange juice
1 egg
1/4 cup vegetable oil
11/2 cups all-purpose flour
3/4 cup sugar
11/2 teaspoons baking powder
11/2 teaspoons baking soda
1 teaspoon salt
1/2 cup raisins (optional)
1/2 cup chopped nuts (optional)

Preheat oven to 375 degrees. Place orange sections, orange juice, egg and oil in blender container; process until smooth. Combine next 5 ingredients in bowl. Add orange mixture; mix until blended. Stir in raisins and nuts. Spoon into nonstick medium muffin cups. Bake at 375 degrees for 15 to 20 minutes or until muffins test done. Yield: 12 servings.

Gayle Havrot, Gamma Zeta
Sesekinika, Ontario, Canada

SWEET MUFFINS

1 egg
1/2 cup milk
1/4 cup vegetable oil
1/2 cup sugar
1/2 teaspoon salt
2 teaspoons baking powder
11/2 cups all-purpose flour

Preheat oven to 400 degrees. Beat egg in mixer bowl until frothy. Add milk and oil; mix well. Add sugar, salt, baking powder and flour, mixing until just moistened. Fill greased medium muffin cups 2/3 full. Bake at 400 degrees for 20 to 25 minutes or until muffins test done. Yield: 9 to 12 servings.

Mary Een Pence, Xi Epsilon Beta
Woodstock, Virginia

APPLE STICKY BUNS

2 to 3 apples, sliced
1 (10-count) can biscuits
1/2 cup packed light brown sugar
2 teaspoons cinnamon
1 teaspoon nutmeg
1/2 cup melted butter or margarine

Preheat oven to 350 degrees. Arrange apple slices in bottom of greased 8-by-8-inch baking dish. Separate biscuits. Coat with mixture of brown sugar, cinnamon and nutmeg. Arrange over apple slices. Drizzle with butter. Bake at 350 degrees for 20 to 30 minutes or until golden brown. Remove to serving plate immediately. Yield: 6 to 8 servings.

Joyce Keller, Preceptor Epsilon Theta
Pinellas Park, Florida

BEST ANYTIME BREAKFAST ROLLS

My youngest sister loves these rolls. Whenever we are going to be together and sometimes in the most unexpected places, it has become our shared joke for me to take one of these rolls from a bag, suitcase or purse.

3 cups all-purpose flour
1/4 teaspoon salt
31/2 teaspoons baking powder
1/2 cup sugar
1/2 cup milk
2 eggs, beaten
1/2 cup melted butter or margarine
1/2 cup sugar
1 teaspoon cinnamon
1/4 cup melted butter or margarine
1/2 cup packed light brown sugar
1/4 cup chopped walnuts
1/4 cup melted butter or margarine

Preheat oven to 375 degrees. Combine flour, salt, baking powder and 1/2 cup sugar in bowl. Add mixture of milk, eggs and 1/2 cup butter; mix well. Knead on lightly floured surface. Roll into 1/2-inch-thick rectangle. Combine 1/2 cup sugar, cinnamon and 1/4 cup butter in bowl; spread over dough and roll as for cinnamon buns. Cut into 16 pieces. Arrange in greased medium muffin cups over mixture of brown sugar, walnuts and 1/4 cup butter. Bake at 375 degrees for 25 to 30 minutes or until rolls test done.
Yield: 16 servings.

Linda Pilling, Beta Sigma Phi
Spiritwood, Saskatchewan, Canada

CINNAMON BISCUITS

1/2 cup butter or margarine
1 1/4 cups sugar
2 tablespoons cinnamon
2 (10-count) cans biscuits

Preheat oven to 450 degrees. Melt butter in 9-inch round baking pan. Add sugar and cinnamon; mix well. Dip dough rounds into mixture. Arrange in baking pan so that 17 fit standing on sides around outer edge and 3 fit on inside. Bake at 450 degrees for 10 minutes. Yield: 10 servings.

Margaret Ballard, Xi Tau Alpha
Electra, Texas

ONE'S NOT ENOUGH CINNAMON BUNS

18 small frozen buns
1/3 (6-ounce) package butterscotch pudding and pie filling mix
1/2 cup margarine
1/2 cup packed light brown sugar
1 teaspoon cinnamon

Preheat oven to 350 degrees. Arrange buns in greased bundt pan. Sprinkle with pudding mix. Melt margarine with brown sugar and cinnamon in saucepan over low heat; mix well. Drizzle over buns. Cover tightly with towel; set aside in warm room for 8 hours. Bake at 350 degrees for 25 minutes.
Yield: 6 servings.

Alice Lanes
Sherwood Park, Alberta, Canada

CINNAMON CRESCENT DELIGHT

I have made this for teachers at my school; they always rave about it and ask for the recipe.

1 (8-count) can crescent rolls
16 ounces cream cheese, softened
1 cup sugar
1 egg yolk
1 tablespoon vanilla extract
1 (8-count) can crescent rolls
1 egg white
Cinnamon and sugar to taste

Preheat oven to 350 degrees. Unroll 1 can crescent roll dough; press into bottom of greased 9-by-13-inch baking pan. Combine cream cheese, sugar, egg yolk and vanilla in bowl; beat until creamy. Spread in prepared pan. Top with remaining crescent rolls. Brush with egg white. Sprinkle with mixture of cinnamon and sugar. Bake at 350 degrees for 25 minutes.
Yield: 24 servings.

Kathleen Cole, Alpha Psi Delta
Odessa, Texas

QUICK AND EASY CINNAMON ROLLS

A very special friend made these for my children when we moved to another town away from our family and friends because of a job transfer.

1 (10-count) can biscuits
1/2 cup packed light brown sugar
1 cup sugar
1 tablespoon cinnamon
1/2 cup melted butter or margarine

Preheat oven to 450 degrees. Roll each biscuit round into 5-inch log. Combine brown sugar, sugar and cinnamon in bowl. Pour butter into shallow bowl. Dip each biscuit into butter, then into brown sugar mixture. Tie each log into a knot and arrange in greased 9-inch round baking pan. Bake at 450 degrees for 8 to 10 minutes or until golden brown. May drizzle with confectioner's sugar icing. May vary amounts of sugar, brown sugar and cinnamon to suit taste. Yield: 10 servings.

Judy Redel, Mu Epsilon
Jefferson City, Missouri

QUICK CINNAMON ROLLS

1 (2-layer) package yellow cake mix
2 envelopes rapid-rise dry yeast
5 cups all-purpose flour
2 1/2 cups hot water
Butter or margarine, sugar and cinnamon to taste

Preheat oven to 400 degrees. Combine cake mix, yeast and 4 cups flour in large bowl. Add hot water; mix well. Add remaining cup flour; mix until blended. Let rise. Punch down and knead dough. Spread with butter. Sprinkle with mixture of sugar and cinnamon. Roll as for jelly roll and cut into 24 slices. Arrange on baking sheet. Let stand until doubled in bulk. Bake at 400 degrees for 12 minutes or until rolls test done. May use nuts, raisins, prunes or other filling of choice. Frost, if desired.
Yield: 24 servings.

Virginia Leszczewicz, Beta Omega
Bourbonnais, Illinois

UBC CINNAMON SNAILS

3 cups all-purpose flour
1/2 cup sugar
5 teaspoons baking powder
1/2 teaspoon salt
3/4 cup margarine or butter
1 egg
1 cup milk
1 egg, beaten
6 tablespoons sugar
1 1/2 teaspoons cinnamon

Combine flour, 1/2 cup sugar, baking powder and salt in bowl. Cut in margarine until crumbly, resembling coarse meal. Beat 1 egg slightly. Add to milk in small bowl; beat until frothy. Stir into sugar mixture. Shape dough into ball. Knead 12 times on lightly floured surface. Roll into 9-by-18-inch rectangle. Brush beaten egg over dough. Sprinkle with mixture of 6 tablespoons sugar and cinnamon. Roll as for jelly roll, starting at long side. Cut into 18 slices. Place each in paper-lined medium muffin cups. Bake at 350 degrees for 25 to 30 minutes or until golden brown. Remove snails in paper liners; place on wire rack to cool or serve warm. Yield: 18 servings.

Lorraine Good, Laureate Alpha Zeta
Richmond, British Columbia, Canada

PENNSYLVANIA DUTCH FUNNY CAKE

When these cakes are done, the chocolate sauce poured on top will be on the bottoms of cakes—hence the name "Funny Cake." I am Pennsylvania Dutch. This is my all-time favorite breakfast time, tea time or anytime cake. The recipe comes from my 90-year-old aunt.

1 3/4 cups sugar
1/2 cup margarine
1 cup milk
2 1/2 cups all-purpose flour
2 eggs
2 teaspoons baking powder
1 teaspoon vanilla extract
2 unbaked (9-inch) pie shells
1 cup sugar
1/2 cup baking cocoa
3/4 cup boiling water
1 teaspoon vanilla extract

Preheat oven to 350 degrees. Combine 1 3/4 cups sugar, margarine, milk, flour, eggs, baking powder and 1 teaspoon vanilla in bowl; mix well. Divide mixture between pie shells. Spread evenly. Combine 1 cup sugar, cocoa, water and 1 teaspoon vanilla in bowl; mix well and pour over batter. Bake at 350 degrees for 40 minutes or until "cakes" test done. Yield: 12 to 16 servings.

Joanne K. Mohr, Preceptor Alpha Rho
Brunswick, Georgia

SCONES

3 cups all-purpose flour
1 cup packed light brown sugar
Salt to taste
1 tablespoon baking powder
1 teaspoon baking soda
1 cup vegetable shortening
1 cup raisins
1 cup milk
1 teaspoon vinegar
Sugar to taste

Preheat oven to 375 degrees. Mix flour, brown sugar, salt, baking powder and baking soda in bowl. Cut in shortening until crumbly. Stir in raisins. Mix milk and vinegar in bowl. Add to flour mixture; mix well. Pat into 2 circles on lightly floured surface. Cut into wedges. Arrange on ungreased baking sheet. Sprinkle with sugar. Bake at 375 degrees for 10 minutes. Yield: 16 servings.

Maureen Haddow, Xi Alpha Theta
Lively, Ontario, Canada

SWEET ROLLS

1/2 cup sugar
1 tablespoon salt
2 cups hot water
2 envelopes active dry yeast
2 eggs, lightly beaten
1/4 cup vegetable oil
6 to 6 1/2 cups all-purpose flour
3/4 cup butter or margarine, softened
3/4 cup sugar
2 tablespoons cinnamon
1/2 cup melted butter or margarine
1 1/2 cups packed light brown sugar
Pecans to taste

Preheat oven to 375 degrees. Combine 1/2 cup sugar and salt in hot water in bowl. Cool. Dissolve yeast in mixture. Add eggs, oil and 3 cups flour; mix well. Add 2 more cups flour 1 cup at a time, mixing well after each addition. Add remaining flour; mix until blended. Knead until smooth. Place in oiled bowl; turn once. Let rise, covered, in warm room for 2 hours or until doubled in bulk. Divide into 3 parts. Roll out each on lightly floured surface. Spread each with mixture of 3/4 cup butter, 3/4 cup sugar and cinnamon. Roll dough as for jelly roll. Divide mixture of 1/2 cup melted butter, brown sugar and pecans between two 10-by-15-inch baking pans. Slice dough and arrange in prepared pans. Let rise, covered, for 1 hour. Bake at 375 degrees for 15 minutes. Remove to foil-covered surface when done.
Yield: 36 servings.

Judy Horton, Xi Iota Tau
Pattonsburg, Missouri

Karen Searle, Preceptor Sigma, Penticton, British Columbia, Canada, makes Welsh Cakes by mixing 3 cups flour, 1 tablespoon baking powder, 1/2 teaspoon salt and 1 cup sugar, cutting in 1 cup shortening and adding 2 eggs, 1 cup raisins and milk to make stiff dough. Pat out, cut with biscuit cutter and bake on preheated 400-degree griddle until brown on both sides.

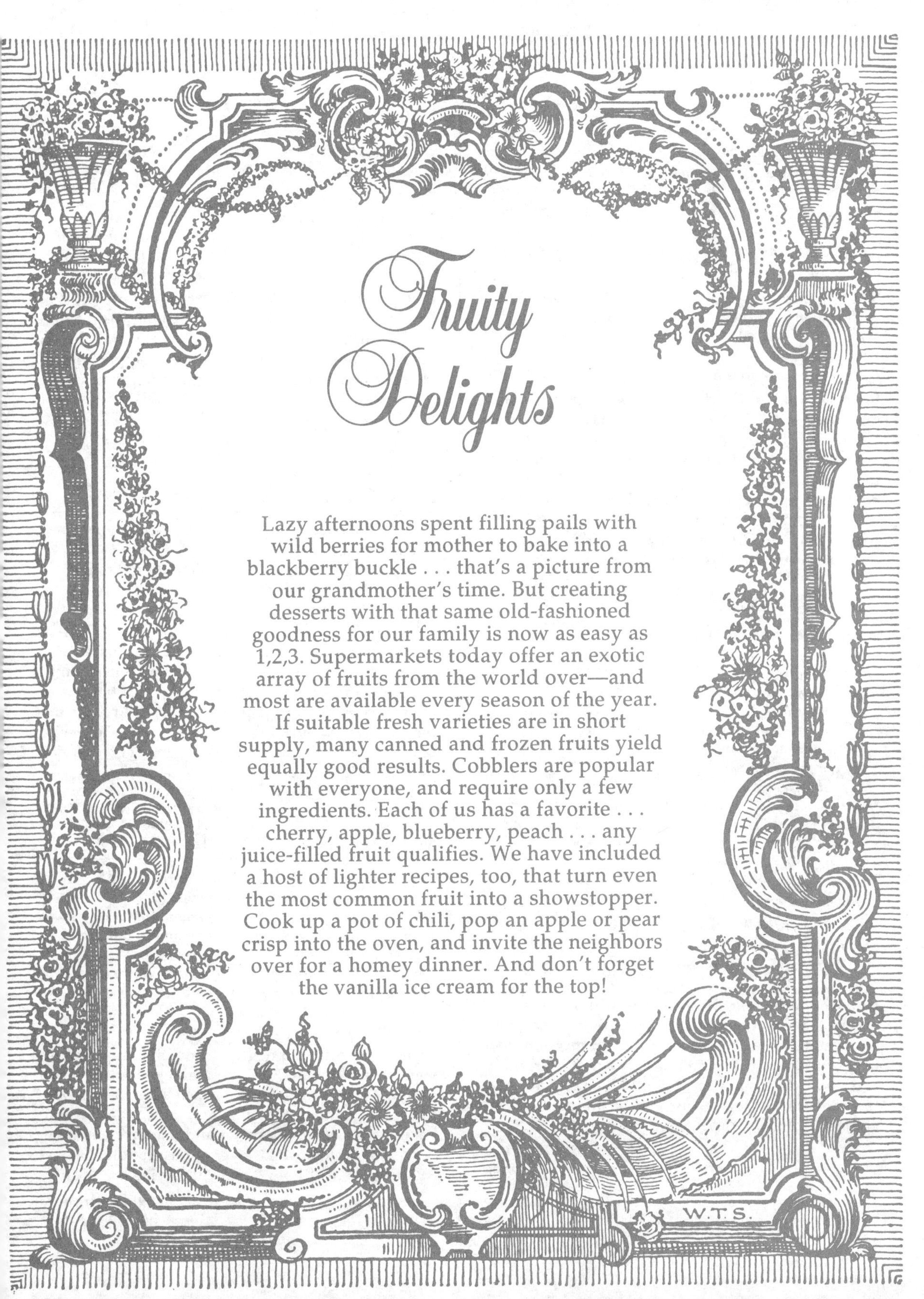

Fruity Delights

Lazy afternoons spent filling pails with wild berries for mother to bake into a blackberry buckle . . . that's a picture from our grandmother's time. But creating desserts with that same old-fashioned goodness for our family is now as easy as 1,2,3. Supermarkets today offer an exotic array of fruits from the world over—and most are available every season of the year. If suitable fresh varieties are in short supply, many canned and frozen fruits yield equally good results. Cobblers are popular with everyone, and require only a few ingredients. Each of us has a favorite . . . cherry, apple, blueberry, peach . . . any juice-filled fruit qualifies. We have included a host of lighter recipes, too, that turn even the most common fruit into a showstopper. Cook up a pot of chili, pop an apple or pear crisp into the oven, and invite the neighbors over for a homey dinner. And don't forget the vanilla ice cream for the top!

APPLE CRISP

This recipe has always been special to our family and friends, because it was made from the heart by my mother, who is now 102 years old. Since her ten children did not like brown sugar or oatmeal, Mom made this recipe for us with granulated sugar. It has been passed down through five generations of family and to lots of friends as well.

6 large apples, sliced
3 tablespoons orange juice
1/2 cup sugar
1/2 teaspoon cinnamon
3/4 cup all-purpose flour
1/2 cup sugar
1/2 teaspoon salt
6 tablespoons butter or margarine, softened

Preheat oven to 350 degrees; 325 degrees if using glass baking dish. Arrange apple slices in greased 8-by-8-inch baking pan. Drizzle juice over apples. Sprinkle mixture of 1/2 cup sugar and cinnamon on top. Combine flour, 1/2 cup sugar, salt and butter in bowl; mix until crumbly. Spread over top and pat until smooth. Bake at 350 degrees for 40 to 45 minutes or until golden brown. Use either Granny Smith or Rome Beauty apples. Yield: 6 servings.

Shirley Collingwood, Preceptor Iota
Springfield, Oregon

APPLE BLACKBERRY CRISP

1 pound apples, peeled, sliced
1 pound wild blackberries or 1 (16-ounce) package frozen unsweetened blackberries
1/2 cup sugar
3 teaspoons vanilla extract
1 1/2 teaspoons cinnamon
1 teaspoon ground nutmeg
3/4 cup all-purpose flour
3/4 cup packed dark brown sugar
1/2 cup coarsely chopped walnuts
1/4 cup rolled oats
1/4 teaspoon salt
1/2 cup cold margarine, cut into pieces

Preheat oven to 350 degrees. Combine apple slices, blackberries, sugar, 1 teaspoon vanilla, 1/2 teaspoon cinnamon and 1/2 teaspoon nutmeg in large bowl; mix well. Spoon into greased 8-by-8-inch baking pan. Combine flour, brown sugar, walnuts, oats, remaining 2 teaspoons vanilla, remaining 1 teaspoon cinnamon, remaining 1/2 teaspoon nutmeg and salt in bowl. Cut in margarine until mixture is crumbly and resembles coarse meal. Sprinkle over fruit mixture. Bake at 350 degrees for 45 to 50 minutes or until apples are tender. Yield: 6 to 8 servings.

Juanita Lunn, Preceptor Theta Rho
Eustis, Florida

MICHIGAN APPLE CRISP

This dish reminds me of Michigan in the fall—it gives the whole house a loving feeling.

5 to 6 cups sliced apples
1 cup all-purpose flour
1 teaspoon baking powder
1 egg
1/2 cup sugar
1/2 teaspoon salt
1/2 teaspoon cinnamon
1/3 cup melted butter or margarine, cooled

Preheat oven to 350 degrees. Arrange apple slices in bottom of greased 6-by-10-inch baking dish. Combine flour, baking powder, egg, sugar and salt in bowl; mix until crumbly. Sprinkle over apples. Sprinkle with cinnamon. Drizzle with butter. Bake at 350 degrees for 35 minutes. Serve with milk.
Yield: 8 to 10 servings.

Marge Hefty, Laureate Alpha Epsilon
Tucson, Arizona

MOM'S APPLE CRISP

1 cup rolled oats
1 cup packed light brown sugar
1/2 cup all-purpose flour
1/2 cup margarine or butter, softened
5 to 6 medium apples, peeled, sliced
Cinnamon to taste

Preheat oven to 350 degrees. Combine oats, brown sugar and flour in bowl. Cut in margarine until crumbly. Spread 1/2 of the mixture over bottom of greased 8-by-8-inch square baking pan. Arrange apples over top. Sprinkle with cinnamon. Top with remaining crumb mixture. Bake at 350 degrees for 50 minutes. Yield: 8 servings.

Nancy Evanson
Halifax, Nova Scotia, Canada

MOM'S OATMEAL APPLE CRISP

6 cups sliced peeled apples
1 1/2 cups sugar
1 tablespoon (heaping) all-purpose flour
2 teaspoons cinnamon
Salt to taste
3/4 cup packed light brown sugar
3/4 cup rolled oats
3/4 cup flour
1/4 teaspoon baking soda
1/4 teaspoon baking powder
1/3 cup melted margarine

Preheat oven to 350 degrees. Combine apples with sugar, 1 tablespoon flour, cinnamon and salt in bowl, tossing to coat. Arrange in greased 9-by-13-inch baking pan. Combine brown sugar, oats, 3/4 cup flour, baking soda, baking powder and margarine in large bowl; mix well. Sprinkle over apple mixture. Bake at 350 degrees for 1 hour. Yield: 20 servings.

Lori Thornburg, Phi Alpha Xi
Goodland, Kansas

✣ CARAMEL APPLE BARS

My family loves this dessert, warm from the oven and topped with double vanilla ice cream, after a day of winter sports.

1/2 cup butter or margarine, softened
1/4 cup shortening
1 cup packed light brown sugar
1 3/4 cups quick-cooking oats
1 teaspoon salt
1/2 cup chopped pecans
4 1/2 cups coarsely chopped apples
3 tablespoons all-purpose flour
1 (14-ounce) jar caramel topping
3 tablespoons butter or margarine

Preheat oven to 400 degrees. Cream 1/2 cup butter, shortening and brown sugar in mixer bowl until light and fluffy. Add oats, salt and pecans; mix well. Set aside 2 cups for topping. Press remaining mixture into ungreased 9-by-13-inch baking pan. Combine apples and flour in bowl, tossing to coat. Arrange over crust mixture. Melt caramel topping and 3 tablespoons butter in saucepan over low heat; mix well. Drizzle over apples. Sprinkle with reserved 2 cups crust mixture. Bake at 400 degrees for 25 to 30 minutes or until light brown. Yield: 12 servings.

JoAnne McBride, Theta Omega
Rifle, Colorado

APPLE DUMPLINGS

This family favorite was in a book left to me by my mother.

1 1/3 cups all-purpose flour
1 1/2 teaspoons baking powder
1/4 teaspoon salt
1/3 cup shortening
1/4 cup milk
4 apples, peeled, cored
4 tablespoons light brown sugar
Butter or margarine and cinnamon to taste
1 cup sugar
1/2 cup water
1/2 teaspoon cinnamon

Preheat oven to 400 degrees. Sift flour, baking powder and salt into bowl. Cut in shortening until crumbly. Add milk; mix until soft dough forms. Roll out into 12-inch square. Cut into 4 smaller squares. Place apple in center of each. Place 1 tablespoon brown sugar, butter and cinnamon to taste in centers of apples. Bring up dough over each and seal over tops. Combine sugar, water and 1/2 teaspoon cinnamon in saucepan. Bring to a boil. Cook for 5 minutes, stirring frequently. Arrange apple dumplings in greased 8-by-8-inch baking dish. Drizzle with sugar mixture. Bake at 400 degrees for 30 to 35 minutes or until bubbly. Yield: 4 servings.

Frances Popovics, Omega
Monroe, Louisiana

APPLE GOODIE

6 cups sliced apples
2 cups sugar
3 tablespoons (heaping) all-purpose flour
1/4 teaspoon salt
1 1/2 cups all-purpose flour
1 teaspoon baking soda
1 tablespoon baking powder
1 1/2 cups packed light brown sugar
1 1/2 teaspoons cinnamon
1 1/2 cups rolled oats
1 cup butter or margarine, softened

Preheat oven to 375 degrees. Combine apples, sugar, 3 tablespoons flour and salt in bowl; mix well. Arrange in greased 9-by-13-inch baking pan. Sift 1 1/2 cups flour, baking soda and baking powder into bowl. Add brown sugar, cinnamon, oats and butter; mix well. Spread over apples. Bake at 375 degrees for 40 minutes. Yield: 12 to 14 servings.

Marge Green, Nu Gamma
Abilene, Kansas

APPLE BATTER PUDDING

2 cups packed light brown sugar
3 tablespoons (heaping) all-purpose flour
2 cups water
2 tablespoons butter or margarine
1 teaspoon vanilla extract
8 medium apples, peeled, sliced
1/2 cup sugar
1 teaspoon cinnamon
1/2 cup butter or margarine
1 cup sugar
2 eggs, beaten
1 cup milk
3 1/2 teaspoons baking powder
1/4 teaspoon salt
2 cups all-purpose flour
1 teaspoon vanilla extract

Preheat oven to 350 degrees. Combine brown sugar and 3 tablespoons flour in saucepan. Add water and 2 tablespoons butter. Bring to a boil. Cook for 5 minutes or until sugar dissolves and liquid thickens, stirring constantly. Remove from heat. Stir in 1 teaspoon vanilla. Place apple slices in bowl. Sprinkle with mixture of 1/2 cup sugar and cinnamon. Cream 1/2 cup butter in mixer bowl; add 1 cup sugar gradually, beating until light and fluffy. Beat in eggs and milk alternately with mixture of baking powder, salt and 2 cups flour. Stir in 1 teaspoon vanilla. Place apple mixture in greased 9-by-13-inch baking dish. Spoon batter evenly over apples; spread flat with spatula. Spoon a small portion of brown sugar sauce over top, reserving remaining sauce to serve warm with pudding. Bake at 350 degrees for 40 minutes. Serve warm. Yield: 12 servings.

Bonnie Tidy, Delta Omicron
Campbell River, British Columbia, Canada

CHERRY CHEWBILEES

1 1/4 cups all-purpose flour
1/2 cup packed light brown sugar
1/2 cup butter-flavor shortening
1 cup chopped walnuts
1/2 cup flaked coconut
16 ounces cream cheese, softened
2/3 cup sugar
2 eggs
2 teaspoons vanilla extract
2 (21-ounce) cans cherry pie filling

Preheat oven to 350 degrees. Mix flour and brown sugar in bowl. Cut in shortening until crumbly. Stir in 1/2 cup walnuts and coconut. Press crumb mixture into greased 9-by-13-inch baking pan, reserving 1/2 cup. Bake at 350 degrees for 12 to 15 minutes or until light brown. Beat cream cheese, sugar, eggs and vanilla in mixer bowl until smooth. Spread over baked crust. Bake at 350 degrees for 15 minutes longer. Spread pie filling over top. Sprinkle with mixture of reserved crumbs and remaining 1/2 cup walnuts. Bake at 350 degrees for 15 minutes longer. Cool. Chill until ready to serve. Yield: 20 servings.

Melva J. Wilkie, Beta Pi
Lakeview, Oregon

CHERRY DUMP CAKE

2 (21-ounce) cans cherry pie filling
1 (2-layer) package yellow cake mix
1/2 cup melted butter or margarine
1/2 cup chopped walnuts

Preheat oven to 350 degrees. Spread pie filling over bottom of greased 9-by-13-inch baking pan. Sprinkle with dry cake mix. Pour melted butter on top. Sprinkle with walnuts. Bake at 350 degrees for 30 minutes. Yield: 12 to 15 servings.

Mary Katherine Cook, Xi Omega Nu
Needville, Texas

CHERRY NUT SQUARES

1 cup butter or margarine, softened
1 cup sugar
1 teaspoon vanilla extract
2 eggs
2 cups all-purpose flour
1 cup chopped nuts
1 (21-ounce) can cherry pie filling
Confectioners' sugar to taste

Preheat oven to 350 degrees. Cream butter and sugar in mixer bowl until light and fluffy. Add vanilla and eggs; mix well. Stir in flour and nuts. Spread 1/2 to 3/4 of the batter into ungreased 9-by-13-inch baking pan. Spoon pie filling over top. Spoon remaining batter over pie filling. Bake at 350 degrees for 40 to 45 minutes or until brown. Let stand until cool. Sprinkle with confectioners' sugar. Cut into squares. Yield: 12 to 15 servings.

Peg Crandall, Xi Epsilon Beta
Ft. Wayne, Indiana

CHERRY-PINEAPPLE DUMP CAKE

1 (20-ounce) can crushed pineapple
1 (21-ounce) can cherry or other fruit pie filling
1 (2-layer) package yellow cake mix
1 cup chopped pecans or walnuts
1/2 cup butter or margarine

Preheat oven to 350 degrees. Spread pineapple evenly in bottom of greased 9-by-13-inch baking pan. Spread pie filling evenly on top. Sprinkle with cake mix. Top with pecans. Dot with butter. Bake at 350 degrees for 45 to 50 minutes or until bubbly. Yield: 15 servings.

Carol L. McRae, Preceptor Alpha Theta
Horton, Michigan

"CHERRY JUNK" SQUARES

My sister-in-law usually brought this dessert to family gatherings. She could never remember the name of the recipe, so she just called it "Cherry Junk."

1 (21-ounce) can cherry pie filling
1 (2-layer) package yellow cake mix
1 cup melted butter or margarine
1 cup chopped pecans

Preheat oven to 350 degrees. Spoon pie filling into greased 9-by-13-inch baking dish. Sprinkle cake mix evenly on top, pressing gently into filling. Pour butter evenly over top. Sprinkle with pecans. Bake at 350 degrees for 25 to 30 minutes or until light brown. Yield: 12 to 15 servings.

Skipper Henderson, Xi Omicron Nu
Friendswood, Texas

CHERRY PUFF

1 (16-ounce) package soda crackers
1 (6-ounce) package light vanilla instant pudding mix, prepared
16 ounces light whipped topping
1 (21-ounce) can light cherry pie filling

Layer crackers, pudding mix and whipped topping 1/2 at a time in 9-by-13-inch pan. Spread pie filling evenly over top. Chill for 8 hours to overnight. Yield: 12 servings.

Sharon Guthrie, Laureate Beta Tau
Waterford, Ontario, Canada

Olga Clark, Satellite Beach, Florida, makes Versatile Cherry Stuff by mixing a 20-ounce can of drained pineapple chunks with a can of light cherry pie filling and 5 sliced bananas. She serves it chilled as a salad or adds whipped topping to serve as dessert.

QUICK MICROWAVE CHERRY CRISP

1 (21-ounce) can cherry pie filling
1/2 teaspoon almond extract
1/4 cup rolled or quick-cooking oats
1/4 cup toasted flaked coconut
2 tablespoons all-purpose flour
2 tablespoons light brown sugar
1/2 teaspoon ground cinnamon
2 tablespoons butter or margarine, softened

Spoon cherry pie filling into greased 8-inch round microwave-safe dish. Sprinkle with almond extract. Combine oats, coconut, flour, brown sugar and cinnamon in bowl; mix well. Cut in butter until crumbly. Sprinkle over filling. Microwave, uncovered, on High for 4 to 5 minutes or until bubbly. Yield: 4 to 6 servings.

Linda McKenzie, Theta Beta
Troy, Ohio

APPLE-CRANBERRY CASSEROLE

1 (16-ounce) can whole cranberries
1 cup sugar
1 cup chopped pecans
2 cups apple pie filling
1/2 cup butter or margarine, softened
1 cup packed light brown sugar
1/2 cup chopped pecans
1 cup instant oats

Preheat oven to 350 degrees. Combine cranberries, sugar, pecans and pie filling in bowl; mix well. Spoon into greased 9-by-13-inch baking dish. Combine butter, brown sugar, pecans and oats in bowl; mix well. Spread over filling. Bake at 350 degrees for 20 minutes. Yield: 8 to 10 servings.

Neta Laughlin, Preceptor Beta Zeta
Greensboro, North Carolina

CRANBERRY-APPLE CASSEROLE

3 cups chopped peeled apples
2 cups fresh cranberries
2 tablespoons all-purpose flour
1 cup sugar
1/2 cup all-purpose flour
3 packages cinnamon-spice instant oats
1/2 cup packed light brown sugar
3/4 cup chopped pecans
1/2 cup melted margarine

Combine apples, cranberries, 2 tablespoons flour and sugar in bowl; toss to mix. Spread in greased 2-quart casserole. Combine 1/2 cup flour, oats, brown sugar, pecans and margarine in bowl; mix until crumbly. Sprinkle over fruit mixture. Bake, uncovered, at 350 degrees for 45 minutes.
Yield: 12 servings.

Juanita Mason, Preceptor Delta Phi
Georgetown, Texas

CRANBERRY-APPLE CRISP

This family favorite is a great "light" Christmas dessert with ice cream or whipped cream.

1/2 cup sugar
1 teaspoon cornstarch
3 tablespoons cold water
1 cup fresh cranberries
4 apples, peeled, sliced
Almond extract to taste
1/2 cup rolled oats
1/2 cup packed light brown sugar
2 tablespoons all-purpose flour
1/4 teaspoon cinnamon
2 tablespoons butter or margarine, softened

Preheat oven to 350 degrees. Combine sugar and cornstarch in microwave-safe 8-by-8-inch square baking dish or 1-quart casserole. Mix in water and cranberries. Microwave, covered, on High for 3 minutes or until cranberries pop. Add apples and almond extract; mix well. Combine oats, brown sugar, flour, cinnamon and butter in bowl; mix until crumbly. Sprinkle over fruit mixture. Bake in oven at 350 degrees for 35 to 40 minutes or until light brown and bubbly. Yield: 4 to 6 servings.

Marjorie L. Coon, Laureate Alpha Zeta
Richmond, British Columbia, Canada

CRANBERRY SALAD

2 cups fresh cranberries
2 cups cubed winesap apples
1 cup sugar
1/2 cup melted butter or margarine
1/3 cup all-purpose flour

Preheat oven to 325 degrees. Combine cranberries, apples and sugar in greased 1-quart casserole. Crumble mixture of butter and flour on top. Bake at 325 degrees for 30 to 45 minutes or until light brown. Yield: 6 to 8 servings.

Virginia Driscoll, Preceptor Beta Zeta
Greensboro, North Carolina

CRANBERRY SQUARES

1 cup sifted all-purpose flour
1 cup packed light brown sugar
2 3/4 cups quick-cooking oats
1 cup shortening
1 (16-ounce) can jellied cranberry sauce, stirred
5 apples, peeled, chopped
Ice cream (optional)

Preheat oven to 400 degrees. Combine flour, brown sugar and oats in bowl. Cut in shortening until crumbly. Pat half the mixture into greased 8-by-8-inch square baking pan. Spread cranberry sauce on top. Top with apples. Sprinkle with remaining crumb mixture. Bake at 400 degrees for 40 minutes. Serve with ice cream. Yield: 8 servings.

Judy Miller, Kappa Theta
Kansas City, Missouri

FRUIT COBBLER

1/2 cup margarine
1 cup sugar
1 cup all-purpose flour
3/4 cup 1% milk
1/2 teaspoon salt
2 teaspoons baking powder
1 (21-ounce) can favorite fruit pie filling
1/2 cup sugar

Preheat oven to 350 degrees. Melt margarine in 9-by-13-inch baking pan. Add 1 cup sugar, flour, milk, salt and baking powder; mix well. Spread with pie filling. Sprinkle with 1/2 cup sugar. Bake at 350 degrees for 1 hour. Serve warm with vanilla ice cream or nonfat frozen yogurt. Yield: 12 servings.

Linda Hubert, Preceptor Beta Omega
Emporia, Kansas

FRUIT COCKTAIL COBBLER

1/4 cup butter or margarine
1 cup all-purpose flour
1 teaspoon baking powder
1/2 teaspoon baking soda
1 cup sugar
1/2 teaspoon salt
1 cup milk
1 (16-ounce) can fruit cocktail
2 tablespoons cornstarch

Preheat oven to 350 degrees. Melt butter in 9-by-13-inch baking pan; coat evenly. Combine flour, baking powder, baking soda, sugar and salt in bowl. Whisk in milk gently; beat until thick. Spoon into prepared pan. Heat fruit cocktail in saucepan. Add cornstarch. Cook until thickened, stirring constantly. Spoon fruit mixture in mounds on top of batter. Do not stir. Bake at 350 degrees for 35 to 40 minutes or until golden brown. Yield: 6 to 8 servings.

Brenda Dickinson, Preceptor Beta Pi
Lakeview, Oregon

FRUITY DANISH SQUARES

I make this dessert with apple pie filling and sprinkle with cinnamon and sugar. My sisters fight over the last slice every time.

1 cup margarine, softened
1 3/4 cups sugar
4 eggs
1 teaspoon vanilla extract
1 1/2 teaspoons baking powder
3 cups all-purpose flour
1/2 teaspoon salt
1 (21-ounce) can apple or cherry pie filling
Confectioners' sugar or mixture of cinnamon and sugar to taste

Preheat oven to 350 degrees. Cream margarine and sugar in mixer bowl until light and fluffy. Add eggs 1 at a time, beating well after each addition. Stir in vanilla. Combine baking powder, flour and salt. Add to egg mixture; mix well. Spread 1/2 to 2/3 of the mixture on greased 12-by-18-inch baking sheet. Spoon pie filling on top. Pipe remaining batter over top in crisscrossed diagonal strips. Sprinkle liberally with confectioners' sugar or mixture of cinnamon and sugar. Bake at 350 degrees for 35 to 45 minutes or until brown. Yield: 3 dozen.

Susan Phillips Tanner, Xi Alpha Delta Zeta
Live Oak, Texas

HOT SPICED FRUIT

1 (16-ounce) can sliced peaches
1 (16-ounce) can pear halves
1 (20-ounce) can pineapple chunks
1/2 cup orange marmalade
1 cinnamon stick
1/2 teaspoon ground nutmeg
1/4 teaspoon ground cloves

Combine peaches, pears, pineapple, marmalade, cinnamon stick, nutmeg and cloves in large saucepan. Bring to a boil. Reduce heat and simmer, covered, for up to 1 hour. Remove cinnamon stick.
Yield: 6 to 10 servings.

Jane Holtsclaw, Alpha Beta
Oolitic, Indiana

HUCKLEBERRY BUCKLE SQUARES

3/4 cup sugar
3 tablespoons butter or margarine, softened
1 cup all-purpose flour
1 teaspoon baking powder
1/4 teaspoon salt
4 cups huckleberries
1/2 cup milk
3/4 cup sugar
1 tablespoon confectioners' sugar
1 tablespoon cornstarch
1/4 teaspoon salt
1 cup boiling water

Preheat oven to 350 degrees. Combine 3/4 cup sugar, butter, flour, baking powder and 1/4 teaspoon salt in bowl; mix well. Stir in huckleberries. Spoon into greased 9-by-9-inch square baking pan. Combine milk, 3/4 cup sugar, confectioners' sugar, cornstarch and 1/4 teaspoon salt in bowl; mix until blended. Sprinkle over berry mixture. Pour boiling water over top. Bake at 350 degrees for 45 to 60 minutes or until brown. Yield: 9 servings.

Valerie Herriges, Preceptor Alpha Epsilon
The Dalles, Oregon

HUNGARIAN FRUIT SQUARES

3 cups all-purpose flour
1 cup sugar
1 teaspoon baking powder
1/2 teaspoon salt
1 cup margarine or butter, softened
2 eggs, beaten
2 teaspoons vanilla extract
2 to 3 tablespoons all-purpose flour
1/2 cup sugar
1 pound farmer cheese, mashed
1/2 teaspoon vanilla extract
1 egg, beaten
Apricot and raspberry jam to taste
1 egg, beaten

Preheat oven to 325 degrees. Combine 3 cups flour, 1 cup sugar, baking powder and salt in bowl. Cut in margarine with pastry blender until crumbly. Add 2 eggs and 2 teaspoons vanilla; mix well. Reserve 1/4 of the dough. Chill reserved dough for 20 minutes. Press remaining dough into bottom and halfway up sides of greased 9-by-13-inch baking pan. Add 2 to 3 tablespoons flour to chilled dough. Roll out and cut into strips; set aside. Combine 1/2 cup sugar, cheese, 1/2 teaspoon vanilla and 1 egg in bowl; mix until blended. Spread in prepared pan. Top with equal amounts of jam. Arrange dough strips on top. Brush strips with beaten egg. Bake at 325 degrees for 30 to 35 minutes or until brown. Yield: 15 servings.

Dolores Schultz, Xi Alpha Alpha
North Salem, New Hampshire

PEACHES AND CREAM

3/4 cup all-purpose flour
1 (4-ounce) package vanilla instant pudding mix
1/4 cup margarine, softened
1 egg
1/2 cup milk
1 (16-ounce) can sliced peaches
8 ounces cream cheese, softened
1/2 cup sugar

Preheat oven to 350 degrees. Combine flour, pudding mix, margarine, egg and milk in mixer bowl; beat until blended. Spoon into greased 9-inch round baking pan. Drain peaches, reserving 1/2 cup juice. Arrange peaches over batter, leaving spaces between slices. Combine cream cheese, sugar and reserved peach juice in mixer bowl; beat until smooth. Spread over peaches, leaving 1/2 inch around edge of pan. Bake at 350 degrees for 30 to 35 minutes or until firm. Let stand until cool. Yield: 8 to 10 servings.

Lois Kelle, Preceptor Alpha Pi
Beatrice, Nebraska

BROWN SUGAR PEACH COBBLER

2 pie pastries
2 (8-ounce) cans peaches, undrained
3/4 cup packed light brown sugar
1/4 cup sugar
Butter or margarine to taste
1 teaspoon cinnamon
1/2 teaspoon nutmeg
3 tablespoons all-purpose flour
2 tablespoons sugar

Preheat oven to 375 degrees. Cut 1 pie pastry into strips. Line bottom of greased 9-by-13-inch baking pan with dough strips. Combine peaches, brown sugar and sugar in bowl. Spoon over dough strips. Dot with butter. Sprinkle with mixture of cinnamon, nutmeg, and flour. Top with remaining pie pastry. Sprinkle with sugar. Bake at 375 degrees for 35 minutes. Yield: 6 servings.

Patricia Taylor
Garden Grove, California

EASY PEACH COBBLER

2 (16-ounce) cans peaches
Cinnamon to taste
1 (2-layer) package yellow cake mix
1/2 cup butter or margarine

Preheat oven to 350 degrees. Spoon peaches into greased 9-by-13-inch baking pan. Sprinkle with cinnamon. Sprinkle with cake mix. Dot with slices of butter. Bake at 350 degrees for 35 to 40 minutes or until golden brown. Serve warm or cold. Store in refrigerator. Yield: 6 to 8 servings.

Joni Siess, Beta Tau
Emporia, Kansas

TOO-EASY PEACH COBBLER

5 to 6 peaches, peeled, sliced
5 (or more) slices white bread
1 1/2 cups sugar
2 tablespoons all-purpose flour
1/2 cup margarine
1 egg

Preheat oven to 350 degrees. Arrange peaches in greased 9-by-13-inch baking dish. Remove crusts from bread; cut each slice into 5 strips. Cover peaches completely with bread strips. Combine sugar and flour in bowl. Melt margarine slightly in small saucepan over low heat. Beat in egg. Add flour mixture; mix well. Spoon over bread. Bake at 350 degrees for 35 to 45 minutes or until brown. May double recipe. May use drained canned sliced peaches.
Yield: 8 to 10 servings.

Conni Haynes
Troutdale, Oregon

MOTHER'S PEACH COBBLER

Mother used to make this cobbler for our family on winter evenings as a late-night treat.

1/2 cup all-purpose flour
1/2 cup sugar
1/2 cup evaporated milk
1 teaspoon baking powder
Salt to taste
1/8 teaspoon nutmeg
1/4 teaspoon cinnamon
1/4 cup melted butter or margarine
2 cups sliced peaches
1 cup peach juice

Preheat oven to 350 degrees. Combine flour, sugar, evaporated milk, baking powder, salt and spices in bowl. Whisk gently until batter forms. Coat 1-quart casserole with half the melted butter. Spoon in peaches and juice. Add remaining melted butter to batter; mix well. Pour into casserole. Bake at 350 degrees for 35 to 40 minutes or until golden brown. Serve warm with half-and-half or ice cream.
Yield: 6 servings.

Charla DeLeo, Phi Alpha Chi
Salida, Colorado

PEACH MERINGUE DESSERT

2 cups all-purpose flour
1 cup sugar
1 egg yolk
1 teaspoon vanilla extract
1 cup margarine
2 (21-ounce) cans peach pie filling
3 egg whites
1 1/4 teaspoons cream of tartar
3/4 cup sugar
1/2 cup finely chopped pecans

Preheat oven to 350 degrees. Combine flour, 1 cup sugar, egg yolk and vanilla in bowl. Cut in margarine until mixture is crumbly and resembles coarse meal. Press into bottom and up sides of greased 10-by-15-inch baking pan. Beat pie filling in mixer bowl until peaches are reduced to small chunks. Spread over crumb mixture. Combine egg whites, cream of tartar and 3/4 cup sugar in mixer bowl; beat until stiff peaks form. Spread over filling. Top with pecans. Bake at 350 degrees for 20 to 30 minutes or until golden brown. Yield: 12 to 15 servings.

Carol Panzer, Gamma Tau
Ellsworth, Kansas

HEAVENLY PEARS

2 (16-ounce) cans pears
2 egg yolks
1/4 cup sugar
1 tablespoon lemon juice
2 tablespoons all-purpose flour
1 tablespoon lemon juice
2/3 cup all-purpose flour
1/4 teaspoon salt
1/4 teaspoon baking soda
2/3 cup graham cracker crumbs
1/3 cup packed light brown sugar
1/2 teaspoon cinnamon
1/2 teaspoon vanilla extract
1/2 cup chopped pecans
1/2 cup melted butter or margarine
2 egg whites
1/4 cup sugar
1/2 teaspoon cinnamon

Preheat oven to 375 degrees. Drain pears, reserving 1 cup liquid. Combine reserved liquid with egg yolks, 1/4 cup sugar, 1 tablespoon lemon juice and 2 tablespoons flour in saucepan. Cook over medium heat until thickened, stirring constantly. Spoon into greased 2-quart casserole. Arrange pears on top. Combine 1 tablespoon lemon juice, 2/3 cup flour, salt, baking soda, graham cracker crumbs, brown sugar, 1/2 teaspoon cinnamon, vanilla, pecans and melted butter in small bowl; mix well. Sprinkle over pears. Bake at 375 degrees for 30 to 35 minutes or until light brown and bubbly. Beat egg whites in mixer bowl until soft peaks form. Add 1/4 cup sugar and 1/2 teaspoon cinnamon gradually; beat until stiff peaks form. Drop by spoonfuls onto pear mixture. Bake at 375 degrees for 5 minutes longer or until golden brown. Yield: 8 to 10 servings.

Christina Schuttinga, Preceptor Beta Kappa
Victoria, British Columbia, Canada

SCALLOPED PINEAPPLE

This is a wonderful dish to serve with holiday food.

8 slices bread, cubed
3/4 cup melted butter
3/4 cup (scant) milk
1 1/2 cups sugar
3 eggs, beaten
1 (20-ounce) can pineapple chunks or 1 (15-ounce) can pineapple tidbits, undrained

Preheat oven to 350 degrees. Combine bread cubes and melted butter in bowl; toss to coat. Add milk, sugar, eggs and pineapple; mix well. Spoon into greased 2-quart glass casserole. Bake at 350 degrees for 45 minutes or until golden brown and firm in center. Yield: 6 to 8 servings.

Elaine Hillan, Xi Theta Epsilon
Kettering, Ohio

PLUM PLATZ

3 cups all-purpose flour
1 cup margarine, softened
1 tablespoon baking powder
1 cup milk
Sugar to taste
2 cups plum halves
3/4 cup sugar
1 1/2 cups all-purpose flour
1 teaspoon baking powder
1/2 cup margarine, softened

Preheat oven to 350 degrees. Combine 3 cups flour, margarine and baking powder in bowl; mix until crumbly. Stir in milk. Press into greased 12-by-18-inch baking pan. Sprinkle with sugar to taste. Arrange plums on top. Combine 3/4 cup sugar, 1 1/2 cups flour, baking powder and margarine in bowl; mix until crumbly. Sprinkle over top. Bake at 350 degrees until light golden brown. May substitute another fruit for plums. Yield: 16 to 18 servings.

Mary Murkin, Preceptor Sigma
Penticton, British Columbia, Canada

RASPBERRY BISQUE

My children, their wives, 9 grandchildren and 5 great-grandchildren love this "just" dessert.

2 cups crushed graham crackers
1/2 cup melted margarine
1 (3-ounce) package raspberry or other fruit-flavor gelatin
1 cup boiling water
1 (12-ounce) can evaporated milk, chilled
8 ounces cream cheese, softened
1/2 cup sugar

Combine graham cracker crumbs with margarine in 9-by-13-inch baking pan. Reserve 1/4 cup crumbs. Pat remaining crumbs over bottom of pan. Dissolve gelatin in boiling water in bowl. Cool. Beat evaporated milk in bowl. Beat cream cheese and 1/2 cup sugar in large mixer bowl until light and fluffy. Beat in evaporated milk. Stir in gelatin mixture. Pour over crumb mixture in pan. Sprinkle with reserved crumbs. Chill until serving time. Yield: 12 to 14 servings.

Jeanne R. Patterson, Laureate Alpha Epsilon
Bloomsburg, Pennsylvania

RHUBARB CRISP

- *4 cups diced unpeeled rhubarb*
- *1 tablespoon all-purpose flour*
- *1/2 cup sugar*
- *1 teaspoon cinnamon*
- *1/8 teaspoon salt*
- *1 tablespoon water*
- *6 tablespoons butter or margarine*
- *6 tablespoons all-purpose flour*
- *1/2 cup packed light brown sugar*
- *1/2 cup quick-cooking oats*

Preheat oven to 350 degrees. Combine rhubarb, 1 tablespoon flour, 1/2 cup sugar, cinnamon, salt and water in greased 8-inch round baking dish; mix well. Cream butter, 6 tablespoons flour and brown sugar in mixer bowl until light and fluffy. Stir in oats. Sprinkle over rhubarb mixture. Bake at 350 degrees for 40 minutes or until rhubarb is tender and topping is golden brown. Serve warm. Yield: 6 servings.

Helen S. Beck, Preceptor Chi
Warren, New Jersey

RHUBARB CRUNCH

- *2 1/2 cups biscuit mix*
- *3 tablespoons sugar*
- *3 tablespoons margarine or butter, softened*
- *1 egg*
- *3 tablespoons milk*
- *4 cups chopped rhubarb*
- *1 (3-ounce) package strawberry or other red fruit gelatin*
- *1 1/4 cups sugar*
- *1/2 cup all-purpose flour*
- *1/3 cup margarine or butter, softened*
- *1/2 cup chopped pecans*

Preheat oven to 400 degrees. Combine biscuit mix, 3 tablespoons sugar, 3 tablespoons margarine, egg and milk in bowl; mix well. Pat into greased 9-by-13-inch baking pan. Spoon rhubarb evenly over crumbs. Sprinkle with gelatin. Combine 1 1/4 cups sugar, 1/2 cup flour and 1/3 cup margarine in bowl; mix until crumbly. Spread over rhubarb mixture. Top with pecans. Bake at 400 degrees for 25 to 30 minutes or until golden brown. Yield: 16 to 20 servings.

Jacquelynn L. Jensen, Laureate Beta Zeta
Port Orchard, Washington

RHUBARB-BROWN SUGAR CRUNCH

- *1 cup all-purpose flour*
- *3/4 cup rolled oats*
- *1 cup packed light brown sugar*
- *1/2 cup melted butter or margarine*
- *1 teaspoon cinnamon*
- *4 cups diced rhubarb*
- *1 cup sugar*
- *2 tablespoons cornstarch*
- *1 cup water*
- *1 teaspoon vanilla extract*

Preheat oven to 350 degrees. Combine flour, oats, brown sugar, butter and cinnamon in bowl; mix until crumbly. Press half the mixture into greased 9-by-9-inch square baking pan. Spread rhubarb on top. Combine sugar, cornstarch, water and vanilla in saucepan. Cook until clear and thick, stirring constantly. Spoon over rhubarb. Top with remaining crumb mixture. Bake at 350 degrees for 1 hour. Yield: 8 servings.

Jane Clark, Laureate Beta Eta
Clive, Iowa

APPLE TORTE

- *3/4 cup butter or margarine*
- *1/2 cup sugar*
- *1/2 teaspoon vanilla extract*
- *1 1/2 cups all-purpose flour*
- *2 eggs*
- *1/2 cup sugar*
- *1/2 teaspoon vanilla extract*
- *8 ounces cream cheese, softened*
- *3 apples, peeled, cubed*
- *1/2 cup sugar*
- *1 teaspoon cinnamon*
- *1 cup slivered blanched almonds*

Preheat oven to 350 degrees. Combine butter, 1/2 cup sugar, 1/2 teaspoon vanilla and flour in mixer bowl; mix until crumbly. Press into greased 9-by-13-inch baking pan. Beat eggs in mixer bowl until frothy. Add 1/2 cup sugar, 1/2 teaspoon vanilla and cream cheese; beat until smooth. Spread over crumb layer. Top with apple cubes and mixture of 1/2 cup sugar and cinnamon. Sprinkle with slivered almonds. Bake at 350 degrees for 50 minutes. Yield: 10 to 12 servings.

Diane Greschuk, Preceptor Eta
Yorkton, Saskatchewan, Canada

FROZEN BANANA SALAD

- *4 large bananas, mashed*
- *8 ounces whipped topping*
- *1 cup sour cream*
- *3/4 cup sugar*
- *2 tablespoons lemon juice*
- *1/2 cup (or more) maraschino cherries*
- *1 (8-ounce) can crushed pineapple, drained*

Combine bananas, whipped topping, sour cream, sugar, lemon juice, cherries and pineapple in bowl; mix gently. Spoon into paper-lined muffin cups. Freeze until firm. Remove from freezer 10 minutes before serving. Store tightly covered. Yield: 24 servings.

Natalie H. Todd, Laureate Alpha Alpha
Bryan, Texas

Mary J. Johnson, Preceptor Beta Mu, Prineville, Oregon makes Cool and Fruity by mixing 8 ounces whipped topping with 16 ounces cottage cheese, adding any flavor dry gelatin with 2 cups of drained complementary fruit and chilling for 15 minutes.

FROZEN FRUIT-MARSHMALLOW SALAD

3 1/2 cups miniature marshmallows
2 tablespoons fruit juice
2 cups ginger ale
1 cup finely chopped peaches
1 1/2 cups crushed pineapple, drained
1/2 cup maraschino cherries
8 ounces whipped topping
Mint leaves

Melt marshmallows in fruit juice in large saucepan. Remove from heat; mix in ginger ale. Fold in peaches, pineapple, cherries and whipped topping. Spoon into individual serving molds or 8-by-8-inch square dish. Freeze until firm. Remove from molds or cut into squares. Garnish with mint leaves and additional cherries. Yield: 6 to 8 servings.

Mary J. Raider, Mu Lambda
Tell City, Indiana

FROZEN FRUIT SALAD OR TROPICAL SLUSH

2 cups water
1 cup sugar
6 medium bananas, mashed
1 (8-ounce) can sliced peaches, cut into pieces
1 (20-ounce) can crushed pineapple
1 (12-ounce) can frozen orange juice concentrate, thawed
2 tablespoons lemon juice

Combine water and sugar in small saucepan. Bring to a boil. Cook for 1 minute, stirring constantly. Set aside until cool. Combine bananas, undrained peaches and pineapple, orange juice concentrate and lemon juice in large bowl; mix well. Stir in sugar mixture. Ladle into 9-by-13-inch dish, or use individual 4- to-8-ounce paper cups for ease in serving. May place cups in cardboard box and cover with plastic wrap to freeze. Freeze until firm. Thaw for 30 minutes or until slushy before serving. Use as a side dish with sandwiches, breakfast or brunch.
Yield: 24 (1/2-cup) servings.

Linda Reed, Preceptor Beta Alpha
Plainview, Texas

RASPBERRY CRUNCH

Make this crunchy treat a day ahead of serving.

1/2 cup butter or margarine
1/4 cup packed light brown sugar
1/2 cup chopped pecans
1 cup all-purpose flour
1 (10-ounce) package frozen raspberries, thawed
2 egg whites
3/4 cup sugar
1 envelope whipped topping mix

Preheat oven to 325 degrees. Melt butter in saucepan. Add brown sugar, pecans and flour; mix until crumbly. Press into greased 8-by-8-inch square baking pan. Bake at 325 degrees for 15 minutes or until crunchy, stirring once. Combine raspberries, egg whites and sugar in large mixer bowl; beat for 20 minutes; do not underbeat. Prepare whipped topping using package instructions. Fold into raspberry mixture. Sprinkle half the baked crumbs into 9-by-13-inch baking pan. Top with raspberry mixture. Sprinkle remaining baked crumbs on top. Freeze for 8 to 24 hours. Serve frozen. Store in freezer.
Yield: 6 to 8 servings.

Jeanne Gordon, Xi Zeta Omicron
Trenton, Ontario, Canada

BERRY-PINEAPPLE DESSERT (SINFUL PINK CLOUDS)

16 ounces whipped topping
1 (21-ounce) can favorite berry pie filling
1 (20-ounce) can crushed pineapple
1 (14-ounce) can sweetened condensed milk

Combine whipped topping, pie filling, pineapple and condensed milk in bowl; mix well. Spoon into 9-by-13-inch pan. Chill until firm. May freeze to make ice cream-like dessert. May use blackberry, blueberry, cherry or raspberry pie filling.
Yield: 8 to 12 servings.

Melissa McClure, Alpha Sigma
Elkins, West Virginia

STRAWBERRY FROZEN DESSERT

1 cup sifted all-purpose flour
1/4 cup packed light brown sugar
1/2 cup chopped walnuts
1/2 cup melted butter or margarine
2 egg whites
1 cup sugar
2 cups sliced fresh strawberries
2 tablespoons lemon juice
1 cup whipping cream, whipped
Fresh whole strawberries

Preheat oven to 350 degrees. Combine flour, brown sugar, walnuts and butter in bowl; mix until crumbly. Spread evenly on 12-by-18-inch baking sheet. Bake at 350 degrees for 20 minutes or until brown, stirring occasionally. Sprinkle 2/3 of the crumb mixture in 9-by-13-inch baking pan. Combine egg whites, sugar, strawberries and lemon juice in large mixer bowl; beat for 10 minutes or until stiff peaks form. Fold in whipped cream. Spoon over crumbs. Top with remaining crumbs. Freeze for 8 hours. Cut into squares. Garnish with whole strawberries. May substitute one 10-ounce package frozen strawberries, partially thawed, for fresh strawberries and reduce amount of sugar to 2/3 cup. Yield: 10 to 12 servings.

Colette Carrothers, Laureate Alpha Rho
Oakville, Ontario, Canada

AUTUMN APPLE SALAD

1 (20-ounce) can crushed pineapple
2/3 cup sugar
1 (6-ounce) package lemon gelatin
8 ounces cream cheese, softened
1 cup chopped unpeeled apples
1/2 to 1 cup chopped walnuts or pecans
1 cup chopped celery
1 cup whipped topping

Combine pineapple and sugar in saucepan. Bring to a boil. Cook for 3 minutes, stirring constantly. Remove from heat. Stir in gelatin until dissolved. Add cream cheese; mix until melted. Cool. Stir in apples, walnuts and celery. Fold in whipped topping. Spoon into 9-by-9-inch pan. Chill until firm. Cut into squares. Serve over lettuce leaves. Yield: 6 to 9 servings.

Patricia Thompson, Beta Master
Comox, British Columbia, Canada

APRICOT SALAD

2 (3-ounce) packages apricot gelatin
2 cups boiling water
8 ounces cream cheese, softened
1 cup milk
1 (20-ounce) can crushed pineapple
4 ounces whipped topping

Dissolve gelatin in boiling water in bowl; set aside. Beat cream cheese in mixer bowl until light and fluffy. Add milk; beat until smooth. Stir in gelatin mixture. Add pineapple; mix well. Fold in whipped topping as mixture starts to thicken. Spoon into 2 1/2-quart serving bowl. Chill for 2 hours or longer. Yield: 8 to 10 servings.

Florence Peschel, Xi Epsilon Nu
Westchester, Illinois

APRICOT GELATIN SALAD

1 (20-ounce) can crushed pineapple
2 (3-ounce) packages apricot gelatin
2 cups boiling water
2 cups cold water
1 cup miniature marshmallows
2 bananas, sliced
1 egg, beaten
1/2 cup sugar
2 tablespoons all-purpose flour
8 ounces cream cheese, softened
2 cups whipped topping

Drain pineapple, reserving juice. Dissolve gelatin in boiling water in bowl. Add cold water; mix well. Stir in pineapple, marshmallows and bananas. Spoon into 9-by-13-inch pan. Chill until firm. Combine egg, sugar and reserved pineapple juice in saucepan. Stir in flour. Cook until thickened, stirring constantly. Remove from heat. Let stand until cool. Beat cream cheese in mixer bowl until light and fluffy. Fold in egg mixture and whipped topping. Spread over gelatin. Yield: 8 to 10 servings.

Kay E. Hoffman, Xi Chi
Butler, Pennsylvania

BANANA SALAD

1 large package sugar-free lemon gelatin
1 1/2 cups boiling water
1 cup cold water
Ice cubes
1 large banana, sliced
1/2 cup low-fat sour cream or vanilla yogurt
1/4 cup diced celery
1/4 cup chopped walnuts
Banana slices

Dissolve gelatin in boiling water in bowl. Add cold water and enough ice cubes to measure 2 cups, stirring until slightly thickened. Remove ice cubes. Reserve 1 cup gelatin. Combine remaining gelatin and slices of 1 banana in 5-cup serving bowl. Combine reserved gelatin and sour cream in bowl. Stir in celery and walnuts. Spoon carefully over banana mixture. Chill for 3 hours or longer. May use additional sliced bananas to garnish. Yield: 8 servings.

Vikki Stevens, Preceptor Chi
Rockview, West Virginia

BLUEBERRY SALAD

1 (16-ounce) package frozen blueberries, thawed
1 (20-ounce) can crushed pineapple
1 (6-ounce) package raspberry gelatin
1/2 cup chopped pecans
1 envelope whipped topping mix
Whipped cream to taste

Drain blueberries and pineapple, reserving 3/4 cup blueberry juice and 1/4 cup pineapple juice. Combine reserved juices and gelatin in saucepan. Cook over low heat until gelatin is dissolved, stirring constantly. Stir in blueberries, pineapple and pecans. Cool slightly. Spoon into large bowl. Prepare whipped topping using package directions. Fold into gelatin mixture. Pour into dish. Chill for 8 hours. Garnish with whipped cream. Yield: 8 to 10 servings.

Barbara Ayres, Pi
Brunswick, Missouri

BLUEBERRY AND BLACKBERRY SALAD

2 (3-ounce) packages blackberry gelatin
2 cups hot water
1 (16-ounce) can blueberries
1 (8-ounce) can crushed pineapple
8 ounces cream cheese, softened
1/2 cup sugar
1 cup sour cream
1/2 teaspoon vanilla extract
1/2 cup chopped pecans

Dissolve gelatin in hot water in large bowl. Drain blueberries and pineapple, reserving 1/2 cup juice from each. Add to gelatin mixture. Stir in blueberries and pineapple. Pour into 2-quart casserole. Chill until firm. Beat cream cheese, sugar, sour cream and vanilla in mixer bowl until smooth. Spread over gelatin. Sprinkle with pecans. Yield: 10 to 12 servings.

Connie Rizer, Xi Zeta Iota
Winter Haven, Florida

BLUEBERRY AND GRAPE SALAD

2 (3-ounce) packages grape gelatin
2 cups boiling water
1 (21-ounce) can blueberry pie filling
1 (20-ounce) can crushed pineapple
8 ounces cream cheese, softened
1 teaspoon vanilla extract
1/2 cup confectioners' sugar
1/2 cup chopped pecans

Dissolve gelatin in boiling water in large bowl. Stir in pie filling and pineapple. Pour into 9-by-13-inch dish. Chill for 8 hours or longer. Beat cream cheese, vanilla and confectioners' sugar in mixer bowl until light and fluffy. Stir in pecans. Spread over gelatin. Yield: 12 to 15 servings.

Leta Hartgroves, Preceptor Zeta Alpha
Waco, Texas

BLUEBERRY GELATIN SALAD

2 (3-ounce) packages raspberry gelatin
2 cups boiling water
1 (8-ounce) can crushed pineapple
1 (21-ounce) can blueberry pie filling
1 cup sour cream
8 ounces cream cheese, softened
1/2 cup sugar

Dissolve gelatin in boiling water in large bowl. Stir in pineapple and pie filling. Pour into 9-by-13-inch pan. Chill until set. Combine sour cream, cream cheese and sugar in mixer bowl; beat until light and fluffy. Spread over gelatin. Yield: 24 servings.

Sandra Ewing-Reichardt, Preceptor Alpha Tau
Lawton, Oklahoma

BLUEBERRY MOLDED SALAD

2 (3-ounce) packages raspberry gelatin
1 cup boiling water
1 (20-ounce) can crushed pineapple
1 (21-ounce) can blueberry pie filling
1/2 cup crushed walnuts
8 ounces cream cheese, softened
1/3 cup sugar
Milk

Dissolve gelatin in boiling water in large bowl or 12-cup mold. Drain pineapple, reserving juice. Add enough cold water to pineapple juice to measure 1 1/2 cups. Stir into gelatin mixture. Fold in pineapple, pie filling and walnuts. Pour into 9-by-13-inch pan. Chill until set. Beat cream cheese and sugar in mixer bowl until light and fluffy. Add enough milk to make of spreadable consistency. Spread over gelatin. Yield: 12 servings.

Evelyn Lakeman, Preceptor Delta
East Millinocket, Maine

BUTTERMILK SALAD

This salad is easy to slice and looks beautiful arranged over lettuce leaves.

1 (6-ounce) package any flavor gelatin
1 (8-ounce) can crushed pineapple
2 cups buttermilk
8 ounces whipped topping

Combine gelatin and pineapple in saucepan. Bring to a boil. Cook for 2 minutes, stirring frequently. Let stand until cool. Add buttermilk; mix until blended. Spoon into 9-by-13-inch pan. Chill for 30 to 45 minutes or just until set. Stir in whipped topping. Chill until set. May use cherry, orange or other flavor gelatin. Yield: 12 servings.

Suzanne Willingham, Xi Beta Mu
Montgomery, Alabama

CHERRY AND PINEAPPLE GELATIN SALAD

2 (3-ounce) packages cherry gelatin
2 cups boiling water
1 (20-ounce) can crushed pineapple
1 (21-ounce) can cherry pie filling
8 ounces cream cheese, softened
1/2 cup sugar
1/2 cup sour cream
1/2 cup crushed pecans

Dissolve gelatin in boiling water in 9-by-9-inch pan. Add pineapple and pie filling; mix gently. Chill until set. Combine cream cheese, sugar and sour cream in mixer bowl. Beat until light and fluffy. Spread over gelatin. Sprinkle with pecans. Cut into squares. Yield: 8 to 12 servings.

Nancy DeRosier, Gamma Gamma
Duluth, Minnesota

CHERRY COLA SALAD

3/4 cup water
3/4 cup sugar
1 (21-ounce) can cherry pie filling
1 (6-ounce) package cherry gelatin
1 (20-ounce) can crushed pineapple
1 tablespoon lemon juice
1 cup cola
1/2 cup chopped pecans

Bring water to a boil in saucepan. Stir in sugar and pie filling. Add gelatin, undrained pineapple, lemon juice, cola and pecans; mix well. Spoon into greased 12-cup mold. Chill until set. Unmold onto serving plate. Cut into slices. Yield: 12 servings.

Judy Wittenberg, Laureate Alpha Epsilon
Strasburg, Illinois

CHERRY SALAD SUPREME

1 (3-ounce) package raspberry gelatin
1 cup boiling water
1 (21-ounce) can cherry pie filling
1 (3-ounce) package lemon gelatin
1 cup boiling water
3 ounces cream cheese, softened
1/3 cup mayonnaise or mayonnaise-type salad dressing
1 (8-ounce) can crushed pineapple
1/2 cup whipping cream, whipped
1 cup miniature marshmallows
2 tablespoons chopped pecans

Dissolve raspberry gelatin in 1 cup boiling water in bowl. Stir in pie filling. Spoon into 9-by-9-inch dish. Chill until partially set. Dissolve lemon gelatin in 1 cup boiling water in bowl. Combine cream cheese and mayonnaise in mixer bowl; beat until blended. Add lemon gelatin mixture gradually; mix well. Stir in pineapple. Fold in whipped cream and marshmallows. Spread over pie filling mixture. Top with pecans. Chill until set. Yield: 12 servings.

Dorothy Jones, Xi Upsilon
Wichita, Kansas

TART CHERRY SALAD

2 (16-ounce) cans tart red cherries
2 (8-ounce) cans crushed pineapple
1 cup sugar
4 (3-ounce) packages cherry gelatin
3 cups ginger ale
1 cup chopped pecans (optional)
3/4 cup shredded coconut

Drain cherries and pineapple, reserving juices. Add enough water to mixture of reserved juices to measure 3 1/4 cups. Pour into saucepan. Stir in sugar. Bring to a boil. Add gelatin; stir until dissolved. Stir in cherries and pineapple. Add ginger ale; mix well. Spoon into bowl. Chill until very thick but not set. Stir in pecans and coconut. Spoon into 2-quart mold. Chill until set. Unmold onto serving plate.
Yield: 12 to 14 servings.

Marilyn J. Schoenborn, Laureate Epsilon Kappa
Easton, Pennsylvania

COKE SALAD

1 (20-ounce) can crushed pineapple
1 (16-ounce) can dark sweet pitted cherries
1 (6-ounce) package black cherry gelatin
8 ounces cream cheese, softened
1 (12-ounce) can cola
1 cup broken walnuts

Drain pineapple and cherries, reserving juices. Heat juices in saucepan almost to boiling. Add gelatin; stir until dissolved. Remove from heat. Add cream cheese; break into small pieces with a fork. Stir in cola. Spoon into 9-by-13-inch dish. Chill until almost set. Stir in pineapple, cherries and walnuts. Chill until firm. Yield: 6 to 8 servings.

Kathy King, Theta Alpha
Gridley, California

CRANBERRY GELATIN SALAD

2 (3-ounce) packages raspberry gelatin
2 cups boiling water
1 (16-ounce) can whole cranberry sauce
1 (20-ounce) can crushed pineapple
3/4 cup burgundy
1/2 cup chopped pecans

Dissolve gelatin in boiling water in bowl. Stir in cranberry sauce and pineapple. Pour into 9-by-13-inch pan. Chill for 1 hour or until thickened. Stir in wine and pecans. Chill until set. Yield: 8 servings.

Hermagean Culbertson, Laureate Delta Delta
Fort Worth, Texas

CRANBERRY APPLE SALAD

Our church has served this salad at our annual Turkey Dinner for more than 20 years. Everyone in town loves it!

1 (6-ounce) package cherry gelatin
2 cups boiling water
1 pound fresh cranberries
1 whole unpeeled orange
1 2/3 cups sugar
1 cup chopped celery
1 cup chopped pecans
2 apples, chopped

Dissolve gelatin in boiling water. Pour into 9-by-13-inch dish; set aside. Force cranberries and orange through food chopper into large bowl. Add sugar; mix well. Stir in celery, pecans and apples. Stir into gelatin mixture. Chill until set. May freeze cranberries for easier grinding. Yield: 15 servings.

Judi Craig, Theta Nu
Batesville, Indiana

QUICK CRANBERRY ORANGE GELATIN

2 (3-ounce) packages orange gelatin
2 cups boiling water
2 (6-ounce) cans frozen cranberry juice concentrate
2 cups (or more) fresh cranberries
Grated rind of 1 orange

Dissolve gelatin in boiling water in saucepan. Stir in frozen juice. Pour into 12-cup mold. Stir in cranberries. Chill until set. Unmold onto serving plate. Garnish with additional cranberries and orange rind. Yield: 12 servings.

Joyce A. Grubb, Eta Alpha
Powell, Tennessee

CRAN-RASPBERRY SALAD

This is my neighbor's recipe; she modified it to use pineapple juice instead of the carbonated beverage used in original recipe.

1 (3-ounce) package raspberry gelatin
1 (3-ounce) package lemon gelatin
2 cups boiling water
1 (10-ounce) package frozen raspberries
1 (14-ounce) container cranberry-orange relish
1 cup lemon-lime soda
1 (15-ounce) can pineapple tidbits

Dissolve raspberry and lemon gelatins in boiling water. Stir in raspberries, mixing until thawed. Add relish and soda; mix well. Pour into 9-by-13-inch dish. Chill until cold but not set. Drain pineapple, reserving juice. Stir in pineapple. Chill until thickened. Add reserved juice; mix gently. Chill until firm. Yield: 8 to 10 servings.

Frances W. Ferraro, Zeta Master
Mesa, Arizona

FRUIT SALAD

1 (16-ounce) can fruit cocktail
1 (11-ounce) can mandarin oranges
1 (8-ounce) can crushed pineapple
1 cup creamed cottage cheese
1 (3-ounce) package raspberry gelatin
8 ounces whipped topping
1/2 cup chopped walnuts

Drain fruit cocktail, mandarin oranges and pineapple in colander over bowl for 8 hours or longer. Combine drained fruit with cottage cheese and gelatin in salad bowl; mix well. Fold in whipped topping and half the walnuts. Sprinkle remaining walnuts on top. Chill, covered, for 3 hours or longer.
Yield: 8 to 12 servings.

Linda Nungesser, Preceptor Alpha Gamma
Nampa, Idaho

LEMON-LIME MOLD

I got this recipe in 1963 from a lady whose house I cleaned when I was in high school. It is a great Christmas dessert.

1 (3-ounce) package lemon gelatin
1 (3-ounce) package lime gelatin
2 cups boiling water
1 cup milk
1 cup mayonnaise
8 ounces cottage cheese
1 cup chopped maraschino cherries
1 cup crushed pineapple, drained
1 cup chopped walnuts

Dissolve gelatins in boiling water in bowl. Let stand until cool. Add milk, mayonnaise and cottage cheese; mix well. Chill until syrupy. Add cherries, pineapple and walnuts; mix well. Spoon into 8-cup mold sprayed with nonstick cooking spray. Chill until set. Unmold onto serving plate. Yield: 12 to 16 servings.

Sharron DeMontigny, Xi Kappa
Corvallis, Oregon

LEMON-LIME GELATIN SALAD

1 small package sugar-free lemon gelatin
1 small package sugar-free lime gelatin
2 cups boiling water
1 cup cold water
1 cup crushed pineapple
1 cup low-calorie mayonnaise
1 (5-ounce) can evaporated milk
1/2 cup chopped pecans
1 teaspoon horseradish powder
16 ounces low-fat cottage cheese
Paprika to taste

Dissolve gelatins in boiling water in bowl. Stir in cold water. Let stand until partially set. Combine pineapple, mayonnaise, evaporated milk, pecans, horseradish powder, cottage cheese and paprika in bowl; mix well. Stir into gelatin mixture. Spoon into 2-quart mold. Chill for 24 hours. Unmold onto serving plate. Yield: 16 servings.

Josephine Knepp, Laureate Sigma
Harbor, Oregon

LIME GELATIN RING WITH STRAWBERRIES

This is my mother's recipe. Traditionally, we serve this decorative and delicious dessert at every Thanksgiving and Christmas dinner. Mom has been gone now for 12 years, but my teenage children still make certain this dish is served at our holiday meals.

1 (16-ounce) can pears
1 (3-ounce) package lime gelatin
6 ounces cream cheese, softened
1 cup whipping cream
Strawberries

Drain pears, reserving 1 cup juice. Pour juice into saucepan. Bring to a boil. Add gelatin; stir until dissolved. Remove from heat; let stand for 20 minutes. Mash pears in bowl, draining excess juice. Beat cream cheese with 2 tablespoons whipping cream in mixer bowl until smooth. Whip remaining cream in mixer bowl with cold beaters until soft peaks form. Add cream cheese mixture; mix well. Stir in pears. Add to gelatin mixture; mix gently. Spoon into 4-cup ring mold. Chill for 8 hours or longer. Unmold onto serving plate. Garnish with strawberries in center.
Yield: 8 servings.

Susan L. Young, Epsilon Gamma
Gallatin, Tennessee

LIME SUPREME

1 (3-ounce) package lime gelatin
1 cup boiling water
1 (20-ounce) can crushed pineapple
8 ounces cottage cheese
1/2 cup chopped celery
1/2 cup chopped walnuts
3 ounces cream cheese, softened
1 teaspoon lemon juice
Mayonnaise-type salad dressing
Lettuce leaves

Dissolve gelatin in boiling water in bowl. Add pineapple, cottage cheese, celery and walnuts; mix well. Spoon into 9-by-13-inch dish. Chill until set. Combine cream cheese and lemon juice in bowl; mix until blended. Stir in enough salad dressing to make of spreadable consistency. Spread over gelatin. Arrange on serving platter over lettuce leaves.
Yield: 8 servings.

Peggy Snyder, Preceptor Alpha
Frostburg, Maryland

ORANGE GELATIN MOLD

1 (3-ounce) package orange, orange-pineapple or lemon gelatin
3/4 cup boiling water
3/4 cup cold water
1 tablespoon lemon juice
1 cup orange sections, cut up

Dissolve gelatin in boiling water in bowl. Add cold water and lemon juice; mix well. Chill until very thick. Fold in orange pieces. Spoon into 1-quart mold. Chill until firm. Unmold onto serving plate. Serve alone or with cream. Yield: 4 to 6 servings.

Rosemary Ricken, Xi Alpha Delta
Eugene, Oregon

ORANGE GELATIN SALAD

1 (6-ounce) package orange gelatin
1 1/2 cups boiling water
10 to 20 ice cubes
12 ounces whipped topping
1 (8-ounce) can crushed pineapple
1 to 1 1/2 cups shredded American cheese
1 cup (or more) chopped pecans

Spray 2 1/2-quart gelatin mold with nonstick cooking spray. Dissolve gelatin in boiling water in bowl. Add ice cubes, stirring constantly until thickened. Remove unmelted cubes. Add whipped topping, pineapple, cheese and pecans; mix well. Spoon into prepared mold. Chill until set. Unmold onto serving plate. Garnish as desired. May use bundt pan instead of gelatin mold. Yield: 8 to 10 servings.

Bonnie Floyd, Laureate Nu
Moody, Alabama

MANDARIN ORANGE SALAD

My boys love this dessert. It is a "must" at Thanksgiving and Christmas!

8 ounces cottage cheese
12 ounces whipped topping
2 (11-ounce) cans mandarin oranges, drained, cut into pieces
1 (6-ounce) package orange gelatin
1 cup chopped walnuts
1 cup crushed pineapple, drained

Combine cottage cheese, whipped topping, mandarin orange pieces, gelatin, walnuts and pineapple in bowl; mix well. Spoon into 2 1/2-quart mold. Chill for 8 hours or longer. Unmold onto serving plate.
Yield: 8 to 10 servings.

Bebe Browning, Preceptor Alpha Rho
Brunswick, Georgia

ORANGE PINEAPPLE SALAD

1 (6-ounce) package strawberry or other red fruit-flavor gelatin
1 cup boiling water
1 container cran-orange relish
1 (20-ounce) can crushed pineapple
1 cup chopped walnuts
Whipped cream to taste

Dissolve gelatin in boiling water in bowl. Let stand until cool. Add relish, pineapple and walnuts; mix well. Fold in whipped cream. Spoon into 2 1/2-quart mold. Chill until set. Unmold onto serving plate.
Yield: 10 servings.

Karen Walcott, Xi Zeta Iota
Winter Haven, Florida

PEACHES AND CREAM SALAD

1 (3-ounce) package orange gelatin
1 cup boiling water
2/3 (8-ounce) container whipped topping
3 ounces cream cheese, softened
1/4 cup chopped pecans
1 (3-ounce) package peach gelatin
1 cup boiling water
1 (21-ounce) can peach pie filling

Dissolve orange gelatin in 1 cup boiling water in bowl. Chill until thick. Beat whipped topping and cream cheese in bowl until smooth. Add pecans; mix well. Stir into orange gelatin mixture. Spoon into 9-by-9-inch dish. Chill until firm. Dissolve peach gelatin in 1 cup boiling water in bowl. Chill until thick. Stir in pie filling. Spoon over orange gelatin mixture. Chill until firm. Cut into squares.
Yield: 8 to 12 servings.

Norma Bullerman, Preceptor Beta Delta
Calmar, Iowa

PINEAPPLE SALAD

1 (20-ounce) can crushed pineapple
1 (3-ounce) package lemon gelatin
1 cup whipped topping
1 cup Colby cheese, shredded
1/2 cup chopped pecans

Bring pineapple to a boil in saucepan. Add gelatin; stir until dissolved. Chill until partially set. Stir in whipped topping, cheese and pecans. Spoon into 9-by-13-inch dish. Chill until set.
Yield: 18 to 24 servings.

June Adams, Laureate Pi
Dallas, Texas

PINEAPPLE CHERRY CREAM CHEESE SWEETHEART SALAD

This is a holiday tradition in our family.

2 cups crushed pineapple
1/2 cup sugar
1 1/2 tablespoons unflavored gelatin
1/4 cup cold water
2 tablespoons lemon juice
2 tablespoons maraschino cherry juice
6 ounces cream cheese, softened
12 finely chopped maraschino cherries
1 cup whipping cream, whipped

Combine pineapple and sugar in saucepan. Heat just until warm. Soften gelatin in cold water. Stir into pineapple mixture. Add lemon and cherry juices; mix well. Combine cream cheese and cherries in bowl; mash until mixed. Mix pineapple gradually into cream cheese mixture. Fold in whipped cream. Spoon into 4-cup mold. Chill until set. Unmold onto serving plate. Yield: 6 to 8 servings.

June Wilson, Laureate Epsilon
Anchorage, Alaska

PINEAPPLE LIME SNOW

1 small package sugar-free lime gelatin
1 cup boiling water
3/4 cup nonfat dry milk
3/4 cup small curd cottage cheese
1 tablespoon lime juice
2 tablespoons confectioners' sugar
1 (8-ounce) can crushed pineapple, drained
Sliced stuffed green olives

Dissolve gelatin in boiling water in mixer bowl. Let stand until cooled. Add milk and cottage cheese; beat until blended. Chill until partially set. Remove from refrigerator; beat for 5 minutes or until frothy. Add lime juice and confectioners' sugar; beat until blended. Fold in pineapple and olives. Spoon into 4-cup mold. Chill until set. May use regular instead of sugar-free gelatin and omit cottage cheese and olives to make a dessert dish. Yield: 4 servings.

Bette J. Bragg, Theta Master
Albany, Oregon

PINEAPPLE WALNUT WHITE SALAD

1 envelope plus 1 teaspoon unflavored gelatin
1/2 cup cold water
1 (20-ounce) can crushed pineapple, drained
1/2 cup sugar
16 ounces cream cheese, softened
1 (7-ounce) jar marshmallow creme
2 envelopes whipped topping mix
1/2 cup chopped walnuts or pecans

Soften gelatin in 1/2 cup cold water. Combine pineapple and sugar in saucepan. Bring to a boil. Remove from heat. Add gelatin to pineapple mixture, stirring until dissolved. Combine cream cheese and marshmallow creme in mixer bowl; beat until smooth. Fold in pineapple mixture. Chill for 20 minutes. Prepare whipped topping using package directions. Fold into pineapple mixture. Spoon into 9-by-13-inch pan. Sprinkle with walnuts. Chill until serving time. Yield: 15 servings.

Mary Lou Settle, Delta Theta
Hendersonville, Tennessee

RASPBERRY APPLESAUCE GELATIN SALAD

1 cup low-fat sour cream
1 1/2 cups miniature marshmallows
2 (3-ounce) packages raspberry gelatin
1 1/2 cups boiling water
1 (10-ounce) package frozen raspberries
1 (16-ounce) can applesauce

Combine sour cream and marshmallows in mixer bowl; mix gently. Chill for 8 hours or longer. Dissolve gelatin in boiling water in large compote dish. Add raspberries and applesauce; mix well. Chill until firm. Beat sour cream mixture until smooth. Pour over gelatin mixture. Chill until set. Yield: 8 servings.

Julie Adams, Xi Zeta Zeta
Muskogee, Oklahoma

RASPBERRY DELIGHT

2 (3-ounce) packages raspberry gelatin
2 cups boiling water
2 cups applesauce
1 teaspoon lemon juice
1 (10-ounce) package frozen raspberries, thawed

Dissolve gelatin in boiling water in bowl. Let stand until cool. Stir in applesauce and lemon juice. Fold in raspberries. Spoon into 4-cup gelatin mold. Chill until firm. Unmold onto serving plate.
Yield: 8 servings.

Cathy Kreft, Gamma Gamma
Duluth, Minnesota

RASPBERRY DESSERT SALAD

4 (3-ounce) packages raspberry gelatin
3 cups boiling water
3 bananas, sliced
1 (20-ounce) can crushed pineapple
2 (10-ounce) packages frozen raspberries, thawed
2 cups sour cream
1/2 cup chopped pecans or walnuts (optional)
Lettuce leaves

Dissolve gelatin in boiling water in large bowl. Let stand until cool. Add bananas, pineapple and raspberries; mix well. Spoon half the mixture into 9-by-13-inch glass dish. Chill until set. Spread with sour cream. Spread remaining fruit mixture over top. Top with pecans. Chill until firm. Serve over lettuce leaves on serving plates. Yield: 12 to 24 servings.

Saundra K. Self, Preceptor Gamma Theta
Canton, Ohio

RASPBERRY SOUR CREAM SALAD

2 (3-ounce) packages raspberry gelatin
3 cups boiling water
1 carton fresh or 1 (10-ounce) package frozen raspberries
Juice of 1 lemon (optional)
2 cups applesauce
2 cups sour cream
2 cups miniature marshmallows

Dissolve gelatin in boiling water in bowl. Stir in raspberries. Let stand until cool. Add lemon juice; mix well. Stir in applesauce. Spoon into 9-by-13-inch pan. Chill until set. Combine sour cream and marshmallows in mixer bowl; mix well. Chill for 3 hours. Beat well. Spread over gelatin. Serve over lettuce leaves on serving plates. Yield: 12 servings.

Lucille Dempster, Preceptor Iota
Council Bluffs, Iowa

✣ RUBY RED RASPBERRY SALAD

This dessert was made by my youngest sister at our first shared Christmas dinner in 30 years; we have lived apart in different states for so many years that we never were able to be together at Christmas until December, 1994. It was a special celebration.

1 (3-ounce) package raspberry gelatin
1 cup boiling water
1 (10-ounce) package frozen raspberries
1 1/2 cups sour cream
1 (3-ounce) package cherry gelatin
1 cup boiling water
1 (20-ounce) can crushed pineapple, drained
1 (16-ounce) whole cranberry sauce
Mayonnaise or mayonnaise-type salad dressing (optional)

Dissolve raspberry gelatin in 1 cup boiling water in bowl. Add raspberries, stirring until thawed. Ladle into 9-by-13-inch pan. Chill until firm. Spread sour cream on top. Chill until set. Dissolve cherry gelatin in 1 cup boiling water in bowl. Stir in pineapple and cranberry sauce. Let stand until slightly thickened. Spoon over sour cream. Chill until set. Cut into squares. Serve over lettuce leaves on serving plates. Top with dollop of mayonnaise. Yield: 16 servings.

Frances J. Neidrauer, Laureate Beta Omicron
Fort Myers, Florida

RASPBERRY WHIP SWEETHEART SALAD

The first time I made this salad, I had requests for the recipe at our Square Dance Club.

1 (6-ounce) package raspberry gelatin
1 cup nonfat raspberry or boysenberry yogurt
1 tablespoon unflavored gelatin
12 ounces light whipped topping
1 (16-ounce) can favorite berries, drained
Red food coloring
Fresh berries

Prepare gelatin in bowl using package directions and decreasing cold water by 1/2 cup. Pour into 2-quart dish. Chill for 4 hours or until very firm. Combine yogurt and unflavored gelatin in bowl; mix well. Stir in 1 1/2 cups of the whipped topping, canned berries and food coloring. Spread half the yogurt mixture in thin layer on top of gelatin mixture. Spread with remaining whipped topping. Top with remaining yogurt mixture. Garnish with fresh berries. Chill for 4 hours or longer; do not freeze. May add more food coloring to yogurt mixture for brighter red color. May serve as salad or dessert. Yield: 15 servings.

Delores Bartholomew, Xi Phi Upsilon
Mariposa, California

SEVEN-UP SALAD

1 (6-ounce) package lemon gelatin
2 cups boiling water
2 cups lemon-lime soda
1 (20-ounce) can crushed pineapple
3 to 4 bananas, sliced
1/2 cup crushed walnuts or pecans
1/2 (10-ounce) package miniature marshmallows
1 cup sugar
3 tablespoons all-purpose flour
1 envelope whipped topping mix, prepared, or 2 cups whipped topping
Chopped walnuts and maraschino cherries to taste

Dissolve gelatin in boiling water in bowl; add soda. Pour into 9-by-13-inch pan. Chill until thickened but not set. Drain pineapple, reserving juice. Fold pineapple, bananas and crushed walnuts into gelatin. Cover with marshmallows. Chill until firm. Combine sugar, flour and reserved pineapple juice in saucepan. Cook until thick, stirring constantly. Chill. Fold into whipped topping. Spread over marshmallow layer. Sprinkle with walnuts and cherries.
Yield: 15 to 20 servings.

Roxanne Ritter, Theta
Moore, Oklahoma

STRAWBERRY GELATIN SALAD

1 1/3 cups coarsely ground pretzels
6 tablespoons margarine, softened
4 ounces cream cheese, softened
1/2 cup sugar
1/2 cup whipped cream
1 cup pineapple juice
1 (3-ounce) package strawberry gelatin
1 (10-ounce) package frozen strawberries, partially thawed

Preheat oven to 400 degrees. Combine pretzels and margarine in bowl; mix well. Press into greased 8-by-8-inch pan. Bake at 400 degrees for 10 minutes. Let stand until cool. Beat cream cheese and sugar in mixer bowl until light and fluffy. Fold in whipped cream. Spoon over prepared crust. Chill until set. Heat pineapple juice in saucepan. Add gelatin; stir until dissolved. Add strawberries; mix well. Let stand until partially set. Spoon over cream cheese layer. Chill until firm. Yield: 12 to 16 servings.

Margaret Stubbs, Laureate Beta Zeta
Port Orchard, Washington

STRAWBERRY PECAN SALAD

2 (3-ounce) packages strawberry gelatin
1 cup boiling water
2 (10-ounce) packages frozen sliced strawberries
1 (8-ounce) can crushed pineapple, drained
3 medium bananas, mashed
1 cup pecans or walnuts
2 cups sour cream

Dissolve gelatin in boiling water in large bowl. Fold in next 4 ingredients. Reserve half the mixture. Spoon remaining mixture into 4-by-6-inch dish. Chill for 1 1/2 hours or until firm. Spread sour cream evenly on top. Spoon reserved fruit mixture over top. Chill until firm. Yield: 12 servings.

Bonnie Ruth Fahey, Alpha Eta Master
Beaumont, Texas

STRAWBERRY PINEAPPLE PINK SALAD

1 (20-ounce) can crushed pineapple
1 (3-ounce) package strawberry gelatin
1 (16-ounce) package marshmallows
1/3 cup water
1 envelope whipped topping mix
8 ounces cream cheese, softened
1 cup chopped walnuts
1 cup shredded coconut

Combine first 4 ingredients in medium saucepan. Cook until marshmallows are melted, stirring constantly. Let stand until cool. Prepare whipped topping using package directions. Fold into pineapple mixture. Beat cream cheese in mixer bowl until light. Fold into pineapple mixture. Add walnuts and coconut; mix well. Spoon into 8-cup mold. Chill until set. Yield: 16 servings.

Kathy Gessel, Alpha Tau
Kennewick, Washington

LOW-FAT STRAWBERRY PRETZEL DESSERT

2 cups crushed fat-free pretzels
3/4 cup melted light margarine
3 tablespoons sugar
8 ounces fat-free cream cheese, softened
8 ounces light whipped topping
10 envelopes artificial sweetener
1 (6-ounce) package strawberry gelatin
2 cups boiling water
1 (16-ounce) package unsweetened frozen strawberries

Preheat oven to 400 degrees. Combine pretzels, margarine and sugar in bowl; mix well. Press into greased 9-by-13-inch pan. Bake at 400 degrees for 8 to 10 minutes or until light brown. Let stand until cool. Combine cream cheese, whipped topping and sweetener in bowl; mix until light and fluffy. Spread over crust. Dissolve gelatin in boiling water in large bowl. Add strawberries; mix well. Spoon over cream cheese layer. Chill until firm. Yield: 18 servings.

Betty Kaminski
Minde, Nevada

QUICK STRAWBERRY SURPRISE

1 (6-ounce) package strawberry, cherry, raspberry or peach gelatin
1 1/2 cups boiling water
1 (10-ounce) package frozen strawberries, cherries, raspberries or peaches

Dissolve gelatin in boiling water in mixer bowl. Add frozen fruit; mix until thawed. Beat for 1 minute. Spoon into 5-cup mold. Chill until set. Unmold onto serving plate. Yield: 10 servings.

Barbara M. Dawson, Alpha Eta
Nanton, Alberta, Canada

STRAWBERRY VELVET MOLD

1/2 cup mayonnaise
8 ounces cream cheese, softened
1/4 cup orange juice
1 (3-ounce) package strawberry gelatin
1 cup boiling water
1 (10-ounce) package frozen strawberries, thawed
Sprigs of mint

Preheat oven to 200 degrees. Combine mayonnaise and cream cheese in pan. Heat in oven at 200 degrees for 5 minutes. Remove and mix well. Add orange juice gradually; mix well. Dissolve gelatin in boiling water in bowl. Drain strawberries, reserving 1/2 cup juice. Add reserved juice to gelatin mixture; mix well. Stir in cream cheese mixture gradually. Spoon into lightly greased 4-cup mold. Fold in strawberries. Chill for 8 hours or longer. Garnish with mint. Yield: 6 to 8 servings.

Susan Cunningham, Epsilon Pi
Longmont, Colorado

WALDORF YOGURT SALAD

1 (3-ounce) package lemon gelatin
1 cup boiling water
1 cup nonfat plain yogurt
1 cup diced peeled apple
1 cup chopped celery

Dissolve gelatin in boiling water in bowl. Stir in yogurt. Chill until thickened. Stir in apple and celery. Chill until set. Yield: 6 servings.

Kay Hague, Laureate Zeta Zeta
Lancaster, California

BUTTERMILK SALAD

1 (4-ounce) package vanilla instant pudding mix
$1^1/_2$ cups buttermilk
8 ounces whipped topping
1 (8-ounce) can crushed pineapple, drained
1 (8-ounce) can mandarin oranges, drained
1 package fudge striped cookies

Combine pudding mix and buttermilk in large mixer bowl; beat until smooth. Fold in whipped topping. Stir in pineapple and mandarin oranges. Spoon into medium serving dish. Break cookies over top before serving. Yield: 6 to 8 servings.

Shelly Hutton, Zeta
Shawnee, Kansas

BEST-EVER FRUIT SALAD

1 (8-ounce) jar maraschino cherries
1 (16-ounce) can pineapple chunks
2 (8-ounce) cans mandarin oranges
2 to 4 bananas, sliced into rounds
1 (4-ounce) package vanilla pudding and pie filling mix

Drain cherries, pineapple and mandarin oranges, reserving juices. Combine fruit in large bowl; mix gently. Prepare pudding in small saucepan using package directions, substituting reserved juices for milk. Remove from heat. Let cool for 10 to 15 minutes. Add to fruit mixture; toss gently. Chill until serving time. Yield: 6 to 8 servings.

Lea Kope, Gamma Lambda
Annapolis, Maryland

ORANGE SALAD

1 (4-ounce) package tapioca pudding and pie filling mix
1 (4-ounce) package vanilla pudding and pie filling mix
1 (6-ounce) package orange gelatin
3 cups water
1 (11-ounce) can mandarin oranges
8 ounces whipped topping

Combine tapioca pudding mix, vanilla pudding mix, orange gelatin and water in medium saucepan. Cook over medium heat until thickened, stirring constantly. Let stand until cool. Pour into medium mixer bowl. Beat in undrained mandarin oranges and whipped topping. Chill until serving time.
Yield: 6 to 8 servings.

Julie Frank, Xi Beta Beta
Amherst, Ohio

MICROWAVE FRUIT SALAD

1 (4-ounce) package vanilla pudding and pie filling mix
1 (20-ounce) can juice-pack chunk pineapple
1 (11-ounce) can mandarin oranges, drained
2 medium bananas sliced into rounds
Maraschino cherries

Pour pudding mix into 4-cup measure. Drain pineapple, reserving juice. Combine pineapple juice and enough water to measure 1 cup liquid in glass measure. Microwave on High for $1^1/_2$ minutes; stir. Microwave 1 to 2 minutes longer or until mixture boils. Pour over pineapple and mandarin oranges in medium serving bowl. Chill until ready to serve. Stir in bananas and cherries just before serving.
Yield: 6 to 8 servings.

Ronda Liles, Alpha Kappa Rho
Yoakum, Texas

ORANGE TAPIOCA PUDDING SALAD

2 (8-ounce) cans mandarin oranges
1 (8-ounce) can crushed pineapple
1 (3-ounce) package orange gelatin
2 (4-ounce) packages tapioca pudding mix
12 ounces whipped topping
1 kiwifruit, sliced

Drain mandarin oranges and pineapple, reserving juice. Pour juice into 4-cup measure. Add enough water to reserved juices to measure $2^2/_3$ cups liquid. Combine juice mixture, gelatin and pudding mix in saucepan. Bring to a boil, stirring constantly. Remove from heat; let stand until cool. Stir in mandarin oranges and pineapple. Fold in whipped topping. Spoon into large serving bowl. Chill until ready to serve. Garnish with kiwifruit. Yield: 10 to 20 servings.

Micki McCray, Delta Gamma
Jamestown, New York

Carol Wicker, Eta Zeta, Port Dover, Ontario, Canada gets multiple uses from Orange Creme Dip. She blends a 17-ounce jar of marshmallow creme with 8 ounces cream cheese, 2 tablespoons orange juice and 1 tablespoon grated orange rind to serve with chilled bite-size fresh fruit. Sometimes she reduces the orange juice to 1 tablespoon to make icing for sweet breads or muffins.

PISTACHIO AND PINEAPPLE DESSERT

12 ounces whipped topping
1 (4-ounce) package pistachio instant pudding mix
1 (14-ounce) can crushed pineapple
1 cup miniature marshmallows

Combine whipped topping, pudding mix, pineapple and marshmallows in medium serving bowl; mix well. Chill in refrigerator until serving time.
Yield: 6 servings.

Barbara Kreics, Sigma
Lampman, Saskatchewan, Canada

PISTACHIO SALAD

1 (4-ounce) package pistachio pudding mix
8 ounces whipped topping
1 (16-ounce) can fruit cocktail, drained
1 cup miniature marshmallows
1/2 cup shredded coconut

Combine pudding mix and whipped topping in medium bowl. Stir in fruit cocktail, marshmallows and coconut. Spoon into medium serving dish. Chill until serving time. May substitute chunk or crushed pineapple for fruit cocktail. May add chopped pecans. Yield: 6 to 8 servings.

Elizabeth A. Margo, Beta Zeta Omicron
Rio Grande City, Texas

COOL FRUIT SALAD

8 ounces whipped topping
1 cup sour cream
1 small package sugar-free vanilla pudding mix
1 (20-ounce) can juice-pack chunk pineapple
1 cup sliced strawberries
1 cup blueberries
1 cup sliced peaches

Combine whipped topping, sour cream and pudding mix in large serving bowl; mix well. Add pineapple, strawberries, blueberries and peaches; mix gently. Chill until serving time. May add any additional fruits desired. Yield: 6 to 8 servings.

Barb Rockers, Theta Sigma
Hays, Kansas

QUICK AND EASY FRUIT SALAD

1 (20-ounce) can juice-pack pineapple chunks
1 (16-ounce) can chunky mixed fruit, drained
1 (4-ounce) package vanilla instant pudding mix
3 tablespoons orange instant breakfast drink mix
2 large bananas, sliced into rounds

Drain pineapple, reserving juice. Combine juice, pudding mix and orange breakfast drink mix in small bowl; mix well. Pour over pineapple, mixed fruit and bananas in medium serving bowl. Toss to coat. Chill until serving time. Yield: 4 servings.

Joyce Crede, Laureate Alpha Alpha
South Charleston, West Virginia

RASPBERRY TAPIOCA SALAD

1 cup sugar
1/3 cup quick-cooking tapioca
2 cups milk
1 cup whipping cream, whipped or 1 envelope whipped topping mix, prepared
1 (10-ounce) package frozen raspberries, thawed, drained

Combine sugar, tapioca and milk in small saucepan. Bring to a boil. Cook until thickened, stirring constantly. Remove from heat; let stand until cool. Combine whipped cream, tapioca mixture and raspberries in medium serving bowl. Chill until serving time. Yield: 6 servings.

Sandra Wenthe, Upsilon Omicron
Newton, Illinois

SPECIAL FRUIT SALAD

1 (20-ounce) can juice-pack chunk pineapple
1 (4-ounce) package vanilla instant pudding mix
1 (11-ounce) can mandarin oranges, drained
2 bananas, sliced into rounds
2 cups halved strawberries
1 1/2 cups halved green grapes
1 cup fresh or frozen blueberries

Drain pineapple, reserving juice. Combine pudding mix and reserved juice in small bowl, stirring until thickened. Combine pineapple, mandarin oranges, bananas, strawberries, grapes and blueberries in large serving bowl. Fold in pudding mixture.
Yield: 12 to 16 servings.

Bessie Stewart, Manitoba Chi
Shoal Lake, Manitoba, Canada

CELERY APPLE SALAD

1/2 cup light sour cream
1/2 cup light mayonnaise
2 cups chopped peeled apples
3/4 cup chopped celery
1 cup mandarin oranges, drained
3/4 cup miniature marshmallows
1/2 cup chopped pecans

Spoon mixture of sour cream and mayonnaise over remaining ingredients in medium serving bowl; toss gently to coat. Yield: 6 servings.

Ann Weimer, Theta Omega
Salisbury, Missouri

CINNAMON APPLE SALAD

This is beautiful to serve with Christmas or Valentine's Day dinners.

1 1/2 cups water
1/2 cup sugar
1/2 cup red cinnamon candies
6 whole cloves
6 apples
1 cup cottage cheese
4 tablespoons chopped pecans
1/3 cup mayonnaise
Lettuce leaves

Bring water, sugar, cinnamon candies and cloves to a boil in large saucepan, stirring until candies are dissolved. Peel and core apples, leaving a 1-inch hole in center of apple. Place apples in red candy mixture. Simmer until tender and well-colored; drain. Chill in refrigerator. Combine cottage cheese, pecans and mayonnaise in bowl. Fill apples with cottage cheese mixture. Arrange on lettuce on individual serving dishes. Chill until serving time. Yield: 6 servings.

Marilyn Harty, Preceptor Tau
Denver, Colorado

GRANDMA'S APPLE SALAD

1 tablespoon butter or margarine
1 cup sugar
2 tablespoons (scant) vinegar
1 tablespoon all-purpose flour
1 egg
1 teaspoon vanilla extract
4 cups chopped peeled apples
1 cup raisins
1 cup chopped pecans
2 cups sliced bananas

Combine butter, sugar, vinegar, flour, egg and vanilla in small saucepan. Cook over medium heat until thickened, stirring constantly. Remove from heat; let stand until cool. Pour over apples, raisins, pecans and bananas in large serving bowl. Toss before serving. Yield: 10 to 12 servings.

Debbie Bellis, Xi Iota Sigma
Archie, Missouri

PENNSYLVANIA DUTCH APPLE SALAD

This recipe has been passed down through my family for many generations. There is never any left in the bowl when I serve it at our sorority dinners.

2 tablespoons all-purpose flour
1 tablespoon sugar
1 egg, beaten
1 cup milk
4 large yellow apples, chopped
1/2 cup chopped walnuts

Cook flour, sugar, egg and milk in small saucepan over medium heat until thickened, stirring constantly. Remove from heat; cool completely. Pour over apples and walnuts in large serving bowl; toss to coat. Chill until ready to serve. Yield: 6 servings.

Barbara Brock, Laureate Lambda
Jensen Beach, Florida

SNICKERS AND APPLE SALAD

This is the most unusual salad I've ever made. It's worth the risk.

6 Snickers candy bars, chopped
6 red apples, chopped
8 ounces whipped topping

Combine candy, apples and whipped topping in medium serving bowl; mix well. Chill until serving time. Yield: 8 servings.

Lucy Eaton, Omicron Eta
Steeleville, Illinois

✣ TAFFY APPLE SALAD

1 tablespoon all-purpose flour
1/2 cup sugar
2 tablespoons vinegar
1 egg
1 (8-ounce) can crushed pineapple
8 ounces whipped topping
4 cups chopped apples
1 cup cashews

Combine flour, sugar, vinegar, egg and undrained pineapple in medium saucepan. Cook until thickened, stirring constantly. Pour into medium bowl. Chill, covered, 8 to 12 hours. Fold in whipped topping. Fold into mixture of apples and cashews in large serving bowl. Chill until serving time.
Yield: 8 to 10 servings.

Susan Rothmann, Xi Alpha Pi
Madison, Wisconsin

AUTUMN FRUIT SALAD

This recipe was served by my daughter on Thanksgiving Day.

1 cup vanilla yogurt
1 teaspoon cinnamon
1/4 teaspoon ground ginger
1/2 teaspoon nutmeg
1 tablespoon apple cider
2 Red Delicious apples, cut into 1-inch chunks
1 Granny Smith apple, cut into 1-inch chunks
1 banana, sliced into 1/2-inch rounds
2 Bartlett pears, cut into 1-inch chunks
1/2 pound red grapes, halved
1/2 cup toasted almond slivers

Combine yogurt, cinnamon, ginger, nutmeg and apple cider in bowl; mix well. Combine apples, banana, pears, grapes and almonds in large bowl. Pour yogurt mixture over fruit mixture. Toss to coat. Chill until ready to serve. May peel apples and pears if desired. Yield: 8 servings.

Mary Creekmore, Beta Chi
Ocala, Florida

BANANA SALAD

2 cups cold water
1/4 cup butter or margarine
2 tablespoons vinegar
1 cup sugar
2 eggs
4 tablespoons all-purpose flour
6 to 8 bananas, sliced into rounds
1/4 cup crushed peanuts

Bring water, butter and vinegar to a boil in small saucepan. Add sugar, eggs and flour; mix well. Cook until thickened, stirring constantly. Pour into medium bowl. Chill, covered, for 8 to 12 hours. Alternate layers of bananas and butter mixture in large serving bowl. Top with peanuts.
Yield: 6 to 8 servings.

Lois M. Zardinskas, Tau Delta
Tampa, Florida

CHERRIES IN THE SNOW

8 ounces cream cheese, softened
1 cup confectioners' sugar
8 ounces whipped topping
1 (21-ounce) can cherry pie filling

Beat cream cheese and confectioners' sugar in large mixer bowl until smooth. Fold in whipped topping. Spoon into serving dish. Make a well in center of cream cheese mixture. Pour pie filling in center. Chill until serving time. May prepare and pour into pie shell. Yield: 6 to 8 servings.

Marion Louise Craig, Omega Mu
Ridgeway, Missouri

CHERRY SALAD

1 (8-ounce) can pineapple chunks, drained
2 bananas, sliced into rounds
1 cup miniature marshmallows
1/2 cup chopped pecans
1 cup white grapes
3 ounces whipped topping
1 (21-ounce) can cherry pie filling

Combine pineapple, bananas, marshmallows, pecans and grapes in 1-quart serving bowl. Fold in whipped topping and pie filling. Chill for 8 to 12 hours before serving. Yield: 6 servings.

Sheryl Orr, Beta Upsilon
Warrensburg, Missouri

DARK CHERRY SALAD

8 ounces cream cheese, softened
1 cup sour cream
1 1/4 cups sugar
1/4 teaspoon salt
1 (16-ounce) can pitted dark sweet cherries, drained
1 (8-ounce) can crushed pineapple, drained
1 (11-ounce) can mandarin oranges, drained
1/2 cup chopped pecans
2 cups miniature marshmallows

Beat cream cheese in mixer bowl until light. Add sour cream, sugar and salt. Stir in cherries, pineapple, mandarin oranges, pecans and marshmallows. Spoon into 9-by-13-inch dish. Freeze, covered, for 6 to 12 hours. Yield: 10 servings.

Donna Coone, Preceptor Zeta Alpha
Hewitt, Texas

CREAMY FRUIT SALAD

1 (21-ounce) can cherry pie filling
1 (14-ounce) can sweetened condensed milk
1 (15-ounce) can crushed pineapple
8 ounces whipped topping
1/4 cup chopped pecans

Combine pie filling, condensed milk and pineapple in large bowl, stirring just until mixed. Fold in whipped topping. Spread into 9-by-13-inch dish. Sprinkle with pecans. Chill or freeze until ready to serve. Yield: 12 to 15 servings.

Fred (Jean) Rathburn, Alpha Beta Lambda
Lee's Summit, Missouri

EASY FRUIT SALAD

2 (11-ounce) cans mandarin oranges, drained
1 (16-ounce) can pineapple chunks, drained
1 (10-ounce) package sliced frozen strawberries
1 (21-ounce) can peach pie filling
4 bananas, sliced

Combine mandarin oranges, pineapple, strawberries and pie filling in large serving bowl. Chill until serving time. Stir in bananas just before serving.
Yield: 12 to 16 servings.

Jeff (Jan) Baldwin, Preceptor Zeta Alpha
Waco, Texas

OVERNIGHT FRUIT SALAD

1 (11-ounce) can mandarin oranges, drained
1 (20-ounce) can pineapple chunks, drained
1 (21-ounce) can peach pie filling
1/2 (16-ounce) package frozen strawberries with juice, thawed, drained
1/2 to 1 cup chopped pecans (optional)
2 medium bananas, sliced

Combine mandarin oranges, pineapple, pie filling, strawberries and pecans in large serving bowl. Chill, covered, for 8 to 12 hours. Stir in bananas just before serving. Yield: 15 servings.

Nanette Rancour, Alpha Rho Theta
Friendswood, Texas

FRUIT SALAD

5 navel oranges, peeled, sectioned
2 apples, cubed
2 bananas, sliced
1 (4-ounce) jar maraschino cherries with juice
1 cup chopped pecans
1 (7-ounce) can flaked coconut
1 pint whipping cream
Sugar to taste

Combine oranges, apples, bananas, cherries with juice, pecans and coconut in large serving bowl. Pour in whipping cream. Chill, covered, for 8 to 12 hours. Add sugar to desired sweetness before serving. Yield: 6 to 8 servings.

Ann Tomlinson, Preceptor Alpha Beta
Terrytown, Louisiana

FIVE-CUP FRUIT SALAD

1 (20-ounce) can pineapple chunks, drained
1 (11-ounce) can mandarin oranges, drained
1 cup sour cream or vanilla yogurt
1 cup miniature marshmallows
Coconut to taste (optional)

Combine pineapple, mandarin oranges and sour cream in medium serving bowl. Chill, covered, for 2 hours or until serving time. Stir in marshmallows and coconut. Yield: 6 to 8 servings.

Susan Stinchfield, Xi Alpha Xi
Bridgton, Maine

FROG EYE SALAD

1 cup sugar
1/2 teaspoon salt
2 tablespoons all-purpose flour
1 1/2 cups pineapple juice
2 eggs, beaten
1 tablespoon lemon juice
8 ounces acini di pepe
1 teaspoon vegetable oil
1 teaspoon salt
1 cup flaked coconut (optional)
3 (11-ounce) cans mandarin oranges, drained
1 (20-ounce) can crushed pineapple, drained
2 (20-ounce) cans pineapple chunks, drained
1 cup miniature marshmallows (optional)

Combine sugar, salt, flour, pineapple juice and eggs in 2-quart saucepan. Cook over medium heat until thickened, stirring constantly. Add lemon juice. Remove from heat; let stand until cool. Boil pasta with oil and salt in 1 1/2 quarts water in large saucepan until tender. Drain; let stand until cool. Combine pineapple juice mixture, pasta, coconut, mandarin oranges, crushed pineapple, pineapple chunks and marshmallows in large serving bowl. Chill until serving time. Yield: 20 servings.

Lauretta Philhower, Laureate Beta Kappa
Middletown, Ohio

ACINI DI PEPE SALAD

1 (8-ounce) can crushed pineapple
1 (11-ounce) can mandarin oranges
3/4 cup sugar
2 tablespoons all-purpose flour
2 eggs
8 ounces acini di pepe, cooked, drained
4 ounces whipped topping
Fresh cherries or blueberries

Drain pineapple and mandarin oranges, reserving juices. Cook mixture of sugar, flour, eggs and reserved juices in small saucepan over medium heat until thickened, stirring constantly. Pour over pasta in medium serving bowl; mix gently. Chill for 8 to 12 hours. Stir in pineapple, mandarin oranges and whipped topping; mix gently. Garnish with cherries or blueberries. Yield: 6 to 8 servings.

Barbara Koczent, Xi Theta
Wellsville, New York

MANDARIN SALAD

60 butter crackers, crushed
1/2 cup melted margarine
1/4 cup sugar
1 cup frozen orange juice concentrate
1 (14-ounce) can sweetened condensed milk
8 ounces whipped topping
2 (8-ounce) cans mandarin oranges

Press mixture of cracker crumbs, margarine and sugar into bottom of 9-by-13-inch dish. Combine orange juice concentrate, condensed milk, whipped topping and mandarin oranges in large bowl; mix well. Spoon over cracker mixture. Chill until serving time. Yield: 12 servings.

Debbie Helficecht, Preceptor Gamma Theta
Pendleton, Oregon

FRUIT SALAD WITH PINEAPPLE DRESSING

3/4 cup pineapple juice
3 tablespoons cornstarch
2 tablespoons vinegar
2 egg yolks
1/4 cup water
1/4 cup sugar or artificial sweetener
5 apples, sliced
2 (8-ounce) cans pineapple tidbits
1 cup chopped pecans or walnuts
1 cup shredded sharp Cheddar cheese
Grapes, coconut and raisins to taste

Combine pineapple juice, cornstarch, vinegar, egg yolks, water and sugar in medium saucepan. Cook until thickened, stirring constantly. Remove from heat. Cool. Pour over mixture of apples, pineapple, pecans, cheese, grapes, coconut and raisins in large serving bowl. Toss to coat. Yield: 10 to 12 servings.

Pam Childs, Xi Delta Gamma
Lee's Summit, Missouri

PINEAPPLE DELIGHT

1/2 cup butter or margarine, softened
1 1/2 cups confectioners' sugar
2 eggs
24 graham crackers, crushed
1 cup whipping cream, whipped
1 (20-ounce) can crushed pineapple, drained

Cream butter and confectioners' sugar in mixer bowl until light and fluffy. Add eggs 1 at a time, mixing well after each addition. Layer half the graham cracker crumbs, butter mixture, whipped cream, pineapple and remaining graham cracker crumbs in greased 9-by-13-inch dish. Chill for 12 hours. Yield: 10 to 12 servings.

June Walker, Xi Delta Lambda
Windsor, Ontario, Canada

PINEAPPLE DESSERT

1 1/2 cups graham cracker crumbs
1/2 cup melted butter or margarine
36 large marshmallows
1 cup milk
1 (20-ounce) can crushed pineapple
8 ounces whipped topping
1/2 cup graham cracker crumbs

Preheat oven to 350 degrees. Press mixture of 1 1/2 cups graham cracker crumbs and butter in bottom of 9-by-13-inch baking dish. Bake at 350 degrees for 8 minutes. Melt marshmallows in milk over low heat in medium saucepan, stirring constantly. Remove from heat. Let stand until cool. Add pineapple and whipped topping; mix well. Pour over baked layer. Sprinkle 1/2 cup graham cracker crumbs over top. Chill for 8 to 24 hours. Yield: 12 servings.

Inez Whaley, Laureate Beta Omega
Kankakee, Illinois

PINEAPPLE PRETZEL SALAD

1/2 cup melted margarine
1/2 cup sugar
1 cup broken pretzels
1/2 cup sugar
8 ounces cream cheese, softened
1 (20-ounce) can crushed pineapple, drained
8 ounces whipped topping

Preheat oven to 400 degrees. Bake mixture of margarine, 1/2 cup sugar and pretzels in 9-by-13-inch baking dish. Bake at 400 degrees for 7 to 10 minutes or until brown. Let stand until cool. Beat 1/2 cup sugar and cream cheese in medium mixer bowl until smooth. Add pineapple and whipped topping. Stir in crumbled pretzel mixture. Chill for 8 to 12 hours. Yield: 6 to 8 servings.

Jennifer Johnson, Nu Psi
Lexington, Missouri

RASPBERRY PRETZEL DESSERT

1/2 cup butter or margarine, softened
1/2 cup sugar
1 1/2 cups finely crushed pretzels
8 ounces cream cheese, softened
1 cup confectioners' sugar
8 ounces whipped topping
1 (6-ounce) package raspberry gelatin
2 cups boiling water
2 (10-ounce) packages frozen raspberries

Press mixture of butter, sugar and pretzels into buttered 9-by-13-inch dish. Beat cream cheese and confectioners' sugar in small mixer bowl until light and fluffy. Fold in whipped topping. Spread over pretzel mixture. Dissolve gelatin in boiling water in medium bowl. Stir in raspberries. Pour over cream cheese mixture. Chill until serving time. Yield: 12 to 15 servings.

Peggy Redfield, Preceptor Omega
Belmond, Iowa

RASPBERRY DESSERT

2 (10-ounce) packages frozen raspberries in syrup
1 cup water
1/2 cup sugar
2 teaspoons lemon juice
4 tablespoons cornstarch
1/4 cup cold water
50 large marshmallows
1 cup milk
2 cups whipping cream, whipped
1 1/4 cups graham cracker crumbs
1/4 cup chopped pecans
1/4 cup melted butter or margarine

Heat raspberries, water, sugar and lemon juice in large saucepan over low heat, stirring constantly. Dissolve cornstarch in cold water. Stir into raspberry mixture gradually. Cook until thickened and clear, stirring constantly. Remove from heat; let stand until cool. Melt marshmallows in milk in small saucepan over low heat, stirring constantly. Remove from heat to cool. Fold whipped cream into marshmallow mixture. Press mixture of graham cracker crumbs, pecans and butter into 9-by-13-inch pan. Layer marshmallow mixture and raspberries mixture over the top. Chill until firm. Yield: 12 servings.

Kandie LaMunyan, Xi Alpha
Bozeman, Montana

Teresa Groff, Zeta Kappa, Emerson, Iowa, prepares Make-Ahead Strawberry Cream Cheese Dressing by combining 3 ounces cream cheese, half a 10-ounce package frozen strawberries, 1 tablespoon sugar, 1 tablespoon lemon juice and a dash of salt and beating until smooth. She adds 1/2 cup vegetable oil in a fine stream, beating until thick, and stores in the refrigerator to serve with fresh fruit such as bananas, kiwifruit, melons, papayas, peaches and berries.

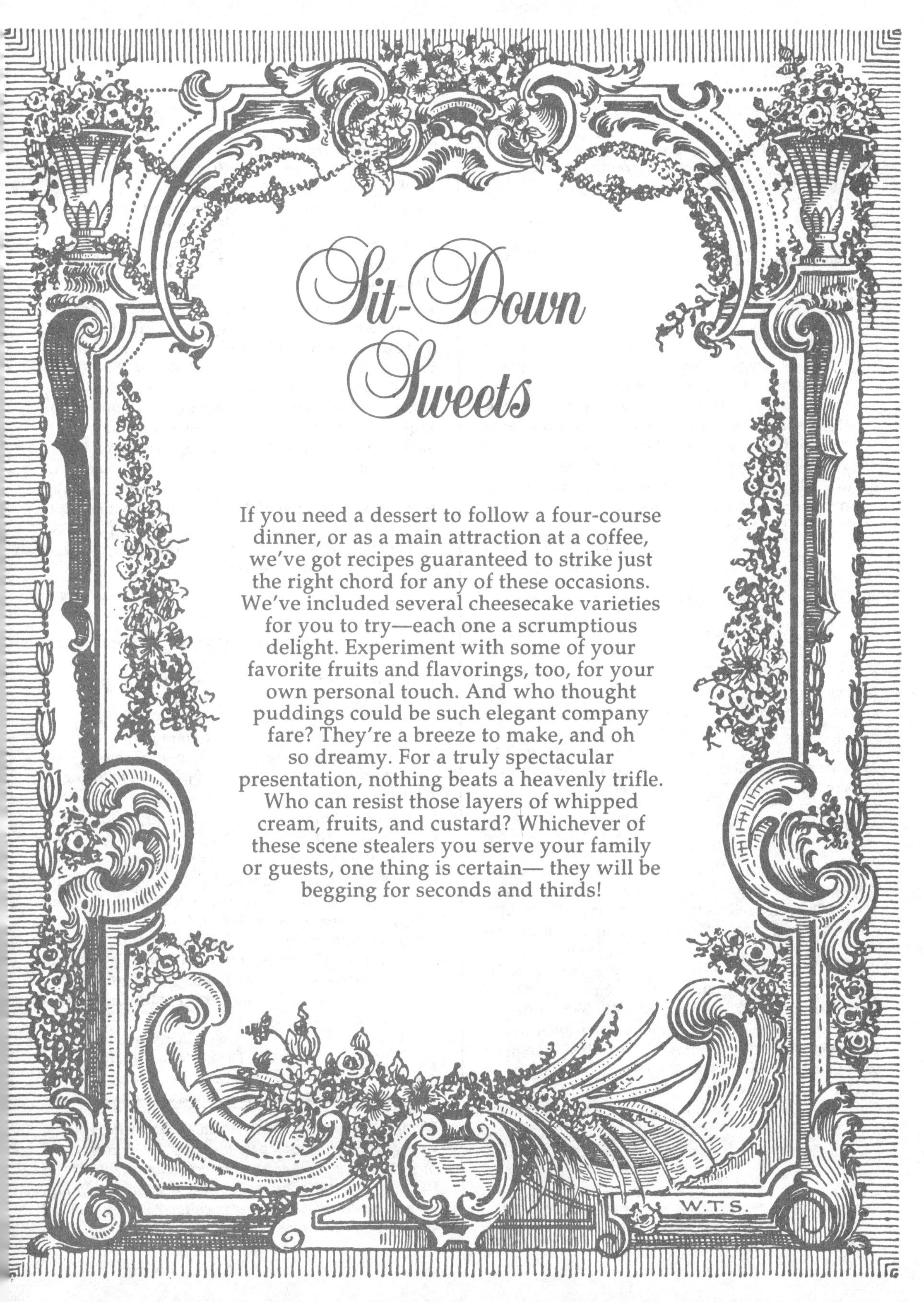

Sit-Down Sweets

If you need a dessert to follow a four-course dinner, or as a main attraction at a coffee, we've got recipes guaranteed to strike just the right chord for any of these occasions. We've included several cheesecake varieties for you to try—each one a scrumptious delight. Experiment with some of your favorite fruits and flavorings, too, for your own personal touch. And who thought puddings could be such elegant company fare? They're a breeze to make, and oh so dreamy. For a truly spectacular presentation, nothing beats a heavenly trifle. Who can resist those layers of whipped cream, fruits, and custard? Whichever of these scene stealers you serve your family or guests, one thing is certain— they will be begging for seconds and thirds!

ALMOND CHEESECAKE

1 cup graham cracker crumbs
40 ounces cream cheese, softened
1 cup sugar
2 eggs
1 teaspoon almond extract
1 teaspoon vanilla extract
2 cups sour cream
3/4 cup sugar
1 teaspoon almond extract

Preheat oven to 350 degrees. Spread crumbs over bottom of 9-inch springform pan sprayed with nonstick cooking spray. Combine cream cheese, 1 cup sugar, eggs, 1 teaspoon almond extract and vanilla in large mixer bowl; beat until smooth. Spread over crumb layer. Bake at 350 degrees for 40 minutes. Combine sour cream, 3/4 cup sugar and 1 teaspoon almond extract in mixer bowl; beat until just blended. Spread over top. Bake at 350 degrees for 15 minutes longer. Cool completely in pan before removing rim. Chill for 8 hours.
Yield: 10 to 12 servings.

Bev Gerke, Theta Chi
Jenison, Michigan

AMARETTO (ROMANTIC EVENING) CHEESECAKE

3/4 cup graham cracker crumbs
1 teaspoon cinnamon
2 1/2 tablespoons sugar
1/3 cup butter or margarine
24 ounces cream cheese, softened
1 1/4 cups sugar
4 eggs, at room temperature
1/4 cup amaretto or 2 teaspoons vanilla extract
1 1/2 cups sour cream
1/4 cup sugar
3 tablespoons amaretto or 1 teaspoon vanilla extract

Preheat oven to 375 degrees. Combine graham cracker crumbs, cinnamon, 2 1/2 tablespoons sugar and butter in bowl; mix until crumbly. Press into greased 9-inch springform pan. Beat cream cheese and 1 1/4 cups sugar in mixer bowl until light and fluffy. Add eggs 1 at a time, beating after each addition. Beat in 1/4 cup amaretto. Spread over crumb mixture. Bake at 375 degrees for 45 to 55 minutes or until firm. Combine sour cream, 1/4 cup sugar and 3 tablespoons amaretto in bowl; mix well. Spoon over top of cheesecake. Bake at 375 degrees for 10 minutes longer. Cool completely in pan before removing rim. Chill for 8 hours for optimum taste. Yield: 8 servings.

Susan M. Baxley, Xi Kappa
Rawlins, Wyoming

APPLE HARVEST CHEESECAKE

1 cup graham cracker crumbs
3 tablespoons sugar
1/2 teaspoon cinnamon
1/4 cup melted margarine
16 ounces cream cheese, softened
1/2 cup sugar
2 eggs
1/2 teaspoon vanilla extract
4 cups thin apple slices
1/3 cup sugar
1/2 teaspoon cinnamon
1/4 cup chopped pecans

Preheat oven to 350 degrees. Combine crumbs, 3 tablespoons sugar, 1/2 teaspoon cinnamon and margarine in bowl; mix until crumbly. Press into bottom of 9-inch springform pan. Bake at 350 degrees for 10 minutes. Combine cream cheese and 1/2 cup sugar in mixer bowl; beat until light and fluffy. Add eggs 1 at a time, beating after each addition. Stir in vanilla. Spread over prepared crust. Toss apple slices with combination of 1/3 cup sugar and 1/2 teaspoon cinnamon. Arrange over cream cheese layer. Sprinkle with pecans. Bake at 350 degrees for 1 hour and 10 minutes. Loosen cheesecake from side of pan. Cool in pan before removing rim. Chill until ready to serve. Yield: 10 to 12 servings.

Ann Knaack, Xi Theta Pi
Grinnell, Iowa

BLUEBERRY CREAM CHEESE SQUARES

1 (16-ounce) package graham crackers, crushed
3/4 cup melted margarine
16 ounces cream cheese, softened
1 1/2 cups sugar
2 teaspoons vanilla extract
16 ounces whipped topping
1 (21-ounce) can blueberry pie filling

Combine graham cracker crumbs and margarine in bowl; mix until crumbly. Press 1/2 of mixture into greased 9-by-13-inch baking pan. Beat cream cheese in mixer bowl until light and fluffy. Add sugar and vanilla gradually; beat until blended. Fold in whipped topping. Spread 1/2 of cream cheese mixture over crumbs. Spoon pie filling on top. Top with remaining cream cheese mixture. Sprinkle with remaining crumbs. Chill or freeze for 8 hours. May substitute apple, lemon or cherry pie filling for blueberry. Yield: 15 servings.

Barbara Jones, Xi Mu
Londonderry, New Hampshire

Elaine Newman, Xi Alpha Alpha, Jacksonville, Florida, makes Mini Cheesecakes by blending 24 ounces cream cheese, 1 cup sugar, 3 eggs, 1 teaspoon vanilla extract and 1/4 teaspoon nutmeg. Fill paper-lined muffin cups 3/4 full. Bake in preheated 350-degree oven for 25 minutes. Cool and top with fresh or canned fruit.

CHERRY CHEESECAKE

2 envelopes dry whipped topping mix
8 ounces cream cheese, softened
3/4 cup sugar
1/3 cup butter or margarine, melted
2 1/3 cups graham cracker crumbs
1 (21-ounce) can cherry pie filling

Preheat oven to 350 degrees. Prepare whipped topping using package directions. Beat cream cheese and sugar in mixer bowl until light and fluffy. Fold in whipped topping; set aside. Mix melted butter and graham cracker crumbs in a bowl. Reserve a small amount for topping. Press the remaining mixture into greased 9-by-13-inch glass baking dish. Bake at 350 degrees for 10 minutes. Let stand until cool. Spread with cream cheese mixture. Top with pie filling. Sprinkle with reserved crumb mixture. Chill for 8 hours. Yield: 12 servings.

Anita Stade, Sigma
Estevan, Saskatchewan, Canada

CHERRY-PECAN CHEESECAKE

12 saltine crackers, crumbled
1 cup sugar
1/2 cup chopped pecans
1 teaspoon baking powder
3 egg whites, stiffly beaten
1 teaspoon vanilla extract
1 teaspoon white vinegar
8 ounces cream cheese, softened
8 ounces whipped topping
1 (21-ounce) can cherry pie filling

Preheat oven to 325 degrees. Combine first 4 ingredients in bowl; set aside. Mix egg whites, vanilla and vinegar in bowl. Fold in pecan mixture. Spoon into greased 8-by-8-inch square baking pan. Bake at 325 degrees for 30 minutes or until golden brown. Cool on wire rack. Combine cream cheese and whipped topping in bowl; mix until smooth and creamy. Spread over baked layer. Top with pie filling. Chill until ready to serve. Yield: 8 servings.

Sharon K. Crisjohn, Xi Delta Pi
Yale, Oklahoma

CREAMY CHERRY CHEESECAKE

20 graham crackers, crushed
1/4 cup margarine
1/4 cup sugar
8 ounces cream cheese, softened
2 tablespoons milk
1 cup sugar
2 cups whipped topping
1 (21-ounce) can cherry pie filling

Preheat oven to 375 degrees. Combine graham cracker crumbs, margarine and 1/4 cup sugar in bowl; mix until crumbly. Press into greased 9-by-13-inch pan. Bake at 375 degrees for 8 minutes. Cool. Beat cream cheese, milk and 1 cup sugar in mixer bowl until light and fluffy. Fold in whipped topping gently. Spread over crust. Top with pie filling. Chill until ready to serve. Yield: 12 servings.

Shirley A. Aversman, Delta Sigma Preceptor
Waverly, Missouri

MINI CHERRY CHEESECAKES

1 cup vanilla wafer crumbs
3 tablespoons melted margarine
8 ounces cream cheese, softened
1 1/2 teaspoons vanilla extract
2 teaspoons lemon juice
1/3 cup sugar
1 egg
1 (16-ounce) can pitted tart red or 1 (16-ounce) package frozen dark sweet cherries
1/2 cup sugar
2 tablespoons cornstarch
Red food coloring (optional)

Preheat oven to 375 degrees. Combine crumbs and margarine in bowl; mix until crumbly. Press gently into bottom of paper-lined muffin cups. Combine cream cheese, vanilla, lemon juice, 1/3 cup sugar and egg in mixer bowl; beat until smooth. Spoon into prepared muffin cups. Bake at 375 degrees for 12 to 15 minutes. Cool completely in muffin cups. Remove to serving plate. Drain cherries, reserving 1/2 cup juice. Combine reserved juice, cherries, 1/2 cup sugar, cornstarch and food coloring in saucepan; mix well. Bring to a boil. Cook for 1 minute, stirring constantly. Cool completely. Spoon over cheesecakes. Chill for 2 hours or longer. Yield: 12 servings.

JoAnn Lippolt, Xi Zeta Omega
Hardy, Iowa

DREAMY CHOCOLATE CHEESECAKE

1 cup crushed salted or unsalted pretzels
1 tablespoon sugar
1/2 cup melted margarine
16 ounces cream cheese, softened
1 cup sugar
1/3 cup baking cocoa
2 eggs
1 cup sour cream
2 teaspoons vanilla extract

Preheat oven to 350 degrees. Combine pretzels and 1 tablespoon sugar in bowl. Cut in margarine until crumbly. Press into greased 9-inch springform pan. Bake at 350 degrees for 8 minutes. Cool slightly. Beat cream cheese in large mixer bowl until smooth and fluffy. Beat in 1 cup sugar and cocoa. Add eggs 1 at a time, beating well after each addition. Stir in sour cream and vanilla. Spoon into prepared pan. Bake at 350 degrees for 35 minutes. Turn off oven, leaving cheesecake inside for 20 minutes. Remove from oven. Loosen from side of pan. Cool completely in pan before removing rim. Chill, covered, until ready to serve. Garnish as desired. Yield: 12 to 16 servings.

Melba S. King, Xi Beta Kappa
Millbrook, Alabama

CHOCOLATE FESTIVAL CHEESECAKE

1 1/2 cups vanilla wafer crumbs
1/3 cup confectioners' sugar
1/3 cup baking cocoa
1/4 cup melted butter or margarine
24 ounces cream cheese, softened
1 1/4 cups sugar
1/4 cup baking cocoa
1/2 cup sour cream
2 teaspoons vanilla extract
2 tablespoons all-purpose flour
3 eggs
Chocolate curls
Whipped cream

Preheat oven to 450 degrees. Mix vanilla wafer crumbs, confectioners' sugar and 1/3 cup baking cocoa in bowl. Cut in butter until crumbly. Press into bottom and 1/2-inch up sides of greased 9-inch springform pan. Bake at 450 degrees for 8 to 10 minutes or until brown. Cool in pan. Combine cream cheese, sugar, 1/4 cup baking cocoa, sour cream and vanilla in large mixer bowl; beat until smooth. Beat in flour and eggs. Spoon into prepared crust. Bake at 450 degrees for 10 minutes. Reduce heat to 250 degrees. Bake for 30 minutes longer. Turn off oven, leaving cheesecake inside for 30 minutes. Remove from oven. Loosen side from pan. Cool to room temperature. Remove sides of pan. Chill for 8 hours or longer. Garnish with chocolate curls and whipped cream. Refrigerate, covered. Yield: 10 to 12 servings.

Anne Chamberlain, Nu
Hampton, New Brunswick, Canada

✣ CHOCOLATE FUDGE PRALINE CHEESECAKE

1 cup graham cracker crumbs
1/4 cup ground pecans
1/4 cup melted margarine
3 tablespoons light brown sugar
1/2 teaspoon cinnamon
24 ounces cream cheese, softened
1/2 cup packed light brown sugar
1/2 cup sugar
2 tablespoons all-purpose flour
3 eggs
1 cup sour cream
2 ounces unsweetened chocolate, melted
1/4 cup packed light brown sugar
1 tablespoon melted margarine
1/2 cup chopped pecans

Preheat oven to 350 degrees. Combine crumbs, 1/4 cup pecans, 1/4 cup margarine, 3 tablespoons brown sugar and cinnamon in bowl; mix until crumbly. Press into bottom and sides of greased 9-inch springform pan. Bake at 350 degrees for 10 minutes. Cool completely. Combine cream cheese, 1/2 cup brown sugar, sugar and flour in mixer bowl; beat until smooth. Add eggs 1 at a time, mixing well after each addition. Add sour cream and chocolate; mix until blended. Spread over prepared crust. Bake at 425 degrees for 10 minutes. Reduce heat to 250 degrees. Sprinkle with mixture of 1/4 cup brown sugar, 1 tablespoon margarine and pecans on top. Bake at 250 degrees for 45 minutes longer. Loosen from side of pan. Cool completely in pan before removing rim. Store in refrigerator. Yield: 10 to 12 servings.

Patricia McKelvy, Preceptor Theta Sigma
Brackettville, Texas

CHOCOLATE SOUR CREAM CHEESECAKE

1 cup semisweet chocolate chips
1/4 cup sugar
1/4 cup chocolate sandwich cookie crumbs
16 ounces cream cheese, softened
3/4 cup sugar
1/2 cup sour cream
1 teaspoon vanilla extract
4 eggs

Preheat oven to 325 degrees. Combine chocolate chips and 1/4 cup sugar in microwave-safe bowl. Microwave on High until chips are melted. Pat cookie crumbs over bottom and halfway up sides of greased 9-inch springform pan. Beat cream cheese in large mixer bowl until light. Add sugar, sour cream and vanilla gradually. Beat in eggs 1 at a time. Fold in chocolate mixture. Spoon into prepared pan. Bake at 325 degrees for 50 to 60 minutes or until 2- to 3-inch circle in center shakes. Loosen from side of pan before removing rim. Cool to room temperature. Chill. Yield: 10 to 12 servings.

Susan Taylor, Xi Alpha Sigma
Kankakee, Illinois

DOUBLE CHOCOLATE DECADENT CHEESECAKE

1 cup chocolate wafer crumbs
3 tablespoons melted butter or margarine
24 ounces cream cheese, softened
3/4 cup sugar
3 eggs
12 ounces white chocolate
6 ounces bittersweet chocolate
3 tablespoons confectioners' sugar
3 tablespoons shortening

Preheat oven to 425 degrees. Mix crumbs and butter in bowl until crumbly. Press into bottom of greased 9-inch springform pan. Beat cream cheese and sugar in mixer bowl until light and fluffy. Add eggs 1 at a time, beating well after each addition. Remove half the mixture to separate bowl. Melt 3 ounces white chocolate in saucepan over low heat. Stir into 1/2 of cream cheese mixture. Melt 3 ounces bittersweet chocolate in saucepan over low heat. Stir into remaining 1/2 of cream cheese mixture. Spread white chocolate mixture evenly into prepared springform pan. Top with bittersweet chocolate mixture. Bake at 425 degrees for 10 minutes. Reduce heat to 250 degrees. Bake for 30 minutes longer or until center is barely firm. Loosen from side of pan. Invert cooled cake onto serving plate. Melt 9 ounces white chocolate with confectioners' sugar and shortening in saucepan over low heat; mix until smooth. Cool for 5 minutes. Spread over top and side of cooled cheesecake. Melt 3 ounces bittersweet chocolate in saucepan over low heat. Drizzle over top. Swirl with knife. Yield: 12 servings.

Heather Gunderson, Xi Gamma
Winnipeg, Manitoba, Canada

HEAVENLY RICH CHEESECAKE

1 1/4 cups graham cracker crumbs
1/2 cup packed light brown sugar
1/4 cup butter or margarine, softened
16 ounces cream cheese, softened
1 teaspoon heavy sweet cream
3 eggs
3/4 cup sugar
1 1/2 teaspoons vanilla extract
2 tablespoons fresh lemon juice, strained
16 ounces sour cream
1/2 cup sugar
1 teaspoon vanilla extract

Preheat oven to 350 degrees. Combine crumbs, brown sugar and butter in bowl; mix until crumbly. Press into greased 8-inch springform pan. Combine cream cheese, cream, eggs, 3/4 cup sugar, 1 1/2 teaspoons vanilla and lemon juice in mixer bowl; beat until very smooth and creamy. Spoon into prepared shell. Bake at 350 degrees for 10 minutes. Reduce heat to 300 degrees and bake for 35 minutes longer. Turn off oven; open door and let stand for 5 minutes. Remove from oven. Cool completely in pan before removing rim. Preheat oven to 400 degrees. Combine sour cream, 1/2 cup sugar and 1 teaspoon vanilla in mixer bowl; beat until smooth. Spread over cheesecake. Bake at 400 degrees for 7 minutes. Chill for 4 hours or longer. Yield: 8 servings.

Susan Vetter, Preceptor Beta Zeta
Greensboro, North Carolina

HEAVENLY RICOTTA CHEESECAKE

3/4 cup crushed graham crackers
2 tablespoons melted margarine
8 ounces light cream cheese or Neufchâtel cheese, softened
15 ounces nonfat or low-fat ricotta cheese
1 cup plain nonfat yogurt
1 cup sugar
2 tablespoons all-purpose flour
2 tablespoons lemon juice
1 tablespoon vanilla extract
6 or 7 egg whites or 3/4 cup egg substitute
2 sliced peeled kiwifruit
1/2 cup sliced strawberries
1/4 cup blueberries

Preheat oven to 325 degrees. Mix graham cracker crumbs and margarine in bowl until crumbly. Press into greased 9-inch springform pan. Bake at 325 degrees for 5 minutes. Cool completely. Combine cream cheese and ricotta cheese in mixer bowl; beat until smooth. Add yogurt, sugar, flour, lemon juice and vanilla; mix well. Add egg whites; beat until just mixed. Spoon into prepared crust. Place springform pan on 12-by-18-inch baking sheet in oven. Bake at 325 degrees for 55 to 65 minutes or until center appears almost set when gently shaken. Cool for 15 minutes. Loosen from side of pan. Cool in pan for 30 minutes longer before removing rim. Remove to wire rack to cool completely. Chill, covered, for 4 to 24 hours. Top with fruit. Yield: 12 servings.

Sue Watson, Xi Beta Beta
Lincoln, Nebraska

LEMON CHEESECAKE

1 (3-ounce) package lemon gelatin
1 cup boiling water
Juice of 1 lemon
8 ounces cream cheese, softened
1 cup sugar
1 teaspoon vanilla extract
1 (12-ounce) can evaporated milk, chilled
1 (16-ounce) package graham crackers, crushed
1/2 cup melted butter or margarine
Whipped topping

Dissolve gelatin in boiling water in bowl. Add lemon juice; cool. Cream next 3 ingredients in mixer bowl until light and fluffy. Beat in gelatin mixture. Whip evaporated milk in bowl; fold into cream cheese mixture. Mix graham cracker crumbs and butter in bowl until crumbly. Press into greased 9-by-13-inch pan. Spread cream cheese mixture evenly on top. Chill for 4 hours or longer. Cut into squares. Top each square with whipped topping. Yield: 12 servings.

Gloria J. Feddersen, Xi Pi Epsilon
Big Spring, Texas

MILNOT LEMON CHEESECAKE

1 (16-ounce) package graham crackers, crushed
1/2 cup melted butter or margarine
2 tablespoons confectioners' sugar
1 (3-ounce) package lemon gelatin
1 cup boiling water
8 to 9 ounces cream cheese, softened
1/2 cup sugar
1 teaspoon vanilla extract
1 can Milnot

Combine graham cracker crumbs, butter and confectioners' sugar in bowl; mix until crumbly. Press 2/3 of mixture firmly into bottom and up sides of greased 9-by-13-inch dish. Dissolve gelatin in boiling water in bowl. Cool completely. Beat cream cheese, sugar and vanilla in mixer bowl until light and fluffy. Stir in gelatin mixture. Fold in Milnot. Pour into prepared crust. Top with remaining crumb mixture. Chill until set. Yield: 12 servings.

Jean Baker, Alpha Beta
Bedford, Indiana

RICH LEMON CHEESECAKE

I first ate this fast, easy and refreshing treat at a shower. It has been a family favorite ever since. My husband likes to keep a pan in the freezer during the summer to eat whenever he wants.

1 1/2 cups graham cracker crumbs
3 tablespoons sugar
1/3 cup melted butter or margarine
1 (3-ounce) package lemon gelatin
1 cup hot water
3 tablespoons lemon juice
1 (12-ounce) can evaporated milk, chilled
8 ounces cream cheese, softened
2/3 cup sugar
1 teaspoon vanilla extract
Additional graham cracker crumbs

Preheat oven to 350 degrees. Chill mixer bowl and beaters in freezer for 30 to 45 minutes or until very cold. Combine crumbs, 3 tablespoons sugar and butter in bowl; mix until crumbly. Press into greased 9-by-13-inch pan. Bake at 350 degrees for 10 minutes. Cool completely. Dissolve gelatin in hot water in bowl; stir in lemon juice. Chill until firm but not set. Whip evaporated milk in cold mixer bowl with chilled beaters until light and fluffy; set aside. Beat cream cheese, 2/3 cup sugar and vanilla in mixer bowl until light and fluffy. Add gelatin mixture and whipped evaporated milk; mix well. Spread over prepared crust. Sprinkle with additional crumbs. Freeze, covered, until set. Cut into squares. Serve frozen or at room temperature. May refreeze.
Yield: 12 to 15 servings.

Pat Scharch, Beta Epsilon
Madison, Wisconsin

✣ REFRESHING KEY LIME CHEESECAKE

1 cup graham cracker crumbs
1/4 cup sugar
1/3 cup melted butter or margarine
1 cup lime juice
1/4 cup water
2 envelopes unflavored gelatin
1 1/2 cups sugar
1 tablespoon grated lime rind
5 eggs, slightly beaten
1/2 cup butter or margarine, softened
16 ounces cream cheese, softened
1/2 cup whipping cream, chilled
5 to 6 drops green food coloring (optional)
Sweetened whipped cream to taste
Lime slices

Combine crumbs, 1/4 cup sugar and 1/3 cup butter in medium bowl; mix until crumbly. Press into greased 9-inch springform pan; set aside. Mix lime juice, water and gelatin in 2-quart saucepan. Let stand for 5 minutes or until gelatin is softened. Stir in 1 1/2 cups sugar, lemon rind and eggs. Cook over medium heat for 6 to 7 minutes or until mixture is just at boiling point, stirring constantly. Do not boil. Combine 1/2 cup butter and cream cheese in mixer bowl; beat until smooth. Beat in lime mixture gradually. Chill for 1 hour, stirring occasionally. Beat whipping cream in small mixer bowl until stiff peaks form, scraping side often. Fold into lime mixture. Stir in food coloring. Spread over prepared crust. Chill, covered, for 1 1/2 to 3 hours or until firm. Loosen from side of pan. Remove rim. Garnish with sweetened whipped cream and lime slices. Yield: 12 servings.

Jana Gammel, Theta
Moose Jaw, Saskatchewan, Canada

"LOWER-CALORIE" CHEESECAKE

I usually slice the cake first and then add the topping, or serve several different toppings on the side.

16 ounces cottage cheese
16 ounces cream cheese, softened
2 cups sour cream
3 tablespoons all-purpose flour
3 tablespoons cornstarch
1 1/2 cups sugar
4 eggs
1 tablespoon vanilla extract
1/2 cup melted butter or margarine
1 tablespoon lemon juice

Preheat oven to 350 degrees. Process cottage cheese in blender container until smooth. Combine cottage cheese, cream cheese, sour cream, flour, cornstarch, sugar, eggs, vanilla, butter and lemon juice 1 at a time in order listed in large mixer bowl, beating after each addition. Beat until smooth. Spoon into greased 10-inch springform pan. Bake at 350 degrees for 1 hour. Turn off oven. Leave in closed oven for 2 hours. May use dental floss or fishing line for easier slicing.
Yield: 12 to 16 servings.

Barbara A. McMullen, Iota Iota
Blairsville, Georgia

MOCHA MELT CHEESECAKE

1 1/3 cups vanilla wafer crumbs
1/3 cup melted butter or margarine
24 ounces cream cheese, softened
1 1/3 cups sugar
4 eggs
1/2 cup Kahlúa
12 ounces bittersweet chocolate
Andes Mints (optional)
Mint extract (optional)

Preheat oven to 325 degrees. Combine wafer crumbs and butter in small bowl; mix until crumbly. Press evenly into greased 10-inch springform pan. Beat cream cheese in mixer bowl until light and fluffy. Add sugar; beat until smooth. Beat eggs in small mixer bowl until frothy. Add to cream cheese mixture gradually; mix well. Beat in Kahlúa. Melt 8 ounces bittersweet chocolate in small saucepan over low heat, stirring constantly. Fold into cream cheese mixture. Spoon mixture into prepared pan. Bake at 325 degrees for 65 minutes or until top springs back when lightly touched. Loosen from side of pan before removing rim. Chill for 8 hours or longer. Melt remaining 4 ounces chocolate in saucepan over low heat. Add Andes Mints and mint extract; mix well. Drizzle over top of cheesecake. Yield: 16 servings.

Glenda Bull, Phi
Moscow, Idaho

NEW YORK CHEESECAKE

1 cup graham cracker crumbs
3 tablespoons sugar
3 tablespoons melted margarine
32 ounces cream cheese, softened
1 cup sugar
3 tablespoons all-purpose flour
1 tablespoon vanilla extract
4 eggs
1 cup sour cream
1 (21-ounce) can cherry pie filling or 3 cups fresh whole strawberries (optional)

Preheat oven to 325 degrees. Combine crumbs, 3 tablespoons sugar and margarine in bowl; mix until crumbly. Press into greased 9-inch springform pan. Bake at 325 degrees for 10 minutes. Set aside to cool. Beat cream cheese, 1 cup sugar, flour and vanilla in large mixer bowl until light and fluffy. Add eggs 1 at a time, beating after each addition until just blended. Beat in sour cream. Spoon into prepared pan. Bake at 325 degrees for 1 hour and 5 minutes or until center is almost set. Loosen from side of pan with knife. Cool completely before removing rim. Spoon pie filling over top. Chill for 4 to 8 hours or longer. Yield: 12 servings.

Kay Berry, Beta Zeta Mu
Kerens, Texas

PEACHES AND CREAM CHEESECAKE

3/4 cup all-purpose flour
1 (4-ounce) package vanilla instant pudding mix
1 teaspoon baking powder
1/8 teaspoon salt
1 egg, beaten
1/2 cup milk
3 tablespoons butter or margarine, softened
1 (16-ounce) can sliced peaches
8 ounces cream cheese, softened
1/2 cup sugar
1 tablespoon sugar
1/2 teaspoon cinnamon

Preheat oven to 350 degrees. Combine flour, pudding mix, baking powder, salt, egg, milk and butter in large mixer bowl; beat until smooth. Pour into greased 10-inch deep-dish pie plate. Drain peaches, reserving 3 tablespoons juice. Arrange peaches over batter. Combine reserved juice, cream cheese and 1/2 cup sugar in medium mixer bowl; beat until smooth. Spread over peaches to within 1 inch of edge of plate. Sprinkle with mixture of 1 tablespoon sugar and 1/2 teaspoon cinnamon. Bake at 350 degrees for 35 to 40 minutes or until almost set. Cool. Serve warm or chilled. Yield: 8 to 10 servings.

Cheri Christensen, Gamma Epsilon
Willmar, Minnesota

PEACHES AND CREAM VANILLA CHEESECAKE

3/4 cup all-purpose flour
1 teaspoon baking powder
1/2 teaspoon salt
1 (4-ounce) package vanilla pudding and pie filling mix
1 egg
1/2 cup milk
1 (16-ounce) can sliced peaches
8 ounces cream cheese, softened
1/2 cup sugar
1 tablespoon sugar
1 teaspoon cinnamon

Preheat oven to 350 degrees. Combine flour, baking powder, salt, pudding mix, egg and milk in mixer bowl; beat until smooth. Spoon into greased 9-inch pie pan. Drain peaches, reserving 3 tablespoons juice. Arrange peach slices on top. Combine reserved peach juice, cream cheese and 1/2 cup sugar in mixer bowl; beat until smooth. Spoon over peach slices to within 1 inch of edge of pan. Sprinkle with mixture of 1 tablespoon sugar and cinnamon. Bake at 350 degrees for 30 minutes. Cool in pan. Store in refrigerator. Yield: 6 servings.

Marilyn Bieter, Gamma Gamma
Duluth, Minnesota

PEANUT BUTTER AND CHOCOLATE CHEESECAKES

3/4 cup crushed chocolate graham crackers
11 ounces cream cheese, softened
1/2 cup sugar
1 teaspoon vanilla extract
1/2 cup milk
2 eggs
1/2 cup semisweet chocolate chips, melted, cooled
1/3 cup peanut butter

Preheat oven to 325 degrees. Sprinkle 1 tablespoon graham cracker crumbs in each of 12 paper-lined muffin cups; set aside. Beat cream cheese in mixer bowl until smooth. Add sugar and vanilla; mix well. Add milk and eggs; beat until just blended. Do not overbeat. Remove half the mixture to separate bowl. Stir melted chocolate into half of mixture. Stir peanut butter into remaining half. Spoon 2 tablespoons each chocolate and peanut butter mixtures into prepared muffin cups. Bake at 325 degrees for 20 to 25 minutes or until set. Let stand until cool. Invert onto serving plate; remove liners. Store in refrigerator.
Yield: 12 servings.

Helen Kress, Zeta Epsilon
Wheeling, West Virginia

PEPPERMINT CHOCOLATE CHEESECAKE

1 cup chocolate wafer crumbs
3 tablespoons melted margarine
1 envelope unflavored gelatin
1/4 cup cold water
16 ounces cream cheese, softened
1/2 cup sugar
1/2 cup milk
1/4 cup crushed peppermint candy
1 cup whipping cream, whipped
2 (16-ounce) milk chocolate candy bars, finely chopped
Additional whipped cream and peppermint candy

Preheat oven to 350 degrees. Combine crumbs and margarine in bowl; mix until crumbly. Press into greased 9-inch springform pan. Bake at 350 degrees for 10 minutes. Cool completely. Soften gelatin in cold water in saucepan. Cook over low heat until dissolved. Combine cream cheese and sugar in mixer bowl; beat until light and fluffy. Add gelatin mixture, milk and peppermint candy gradually; beat until blended. Chill until thickened but not set. Fold in whipped cream and chocolate candy. Spoon into prepared crust. Chill until firm. Loosen from side of pan. Remove rim. Garnish with additional whipped cream and peppermint candy.
Yield: 10 to 12 servings.

Patricia K. Lyons, Xi Xi
Portland, Oregon

PINEAPPLE CHEESECAKE

1 (12-ounce) can evaporated milk
1 (3-ounce) package lemon gelatin
2/3 cup boiling water
2 (16-ounce) packages graham crackers, crushed
2/3 cup melted butter or margarine
8 ounces cream cheese, softened
1/2 cup sugar
1 teaspoon vanilla extract
1 (20-ounce) can crushed pineapple, drained

Place evaporated milk, mixer bowl and beaters in freezer; chill until very cold. Dissolve gelatin in boiling water in bowl; set aside to cool. Combine graham cracker crumbs and butter in bowl; mix until crumbly. Press 1/2 of mixture into greased 9-by-13-inch pan. Combine cream cheese, sugar and vanilla in mixer bowl; beat until light and fluffy. Stir in pineapple and gelatin mixture. Whip evaporated milk in chilled mixer bowl until thick and foamy. Fold into cream cheese mixture. Spread over crust mixture. Sprinkle with remaining crumbs. Chill for 8 hours or longer. Yield: 20 or more servings.

Peg Glaeser, Preceptor Gamma Kappa
Lewiston, Michigan

DELIGHTFUL PINEAPPLE CHEESECAKE

This dessert is one my diabetic husband can eat. It doesn't taste sugar-free and may be varied by using different fruits to garnish.

2 envelopes unflavored gelatin
1/2 cup cold water
1 (20-ounce) can unsweetened crushed pineapple
11/2 cups cottage cheese, creamed
3 egg yolks
1 tablespoon liquid artificial sweetener
2 tablespoons lemon juice
1 teaspoon vanilla extract
1/4 teaspoon salt
3 egg whites
1 (9-inch) graham cracker pie shell
Sliced pineapple, strawberries or other fresh fruit

Soften gelatin in cold water in bowl. Drain pineapple, reserving 3/4 cup juice. Bring reserved juice to a boil in saucepan. Add gelatin mixture; mix well. Remove from heat. Beat cottage cheese in mixer bowl until smooth. Add egg yolks; mix until blended. Add sweetener, lemon juice, vanilla and salt; mix until blended. Stir in pineapple juice mixture. Chill for 1 hour or until slightly thickened but not set, stirring occasionally. Beat egg whites in small mixer bowl until soft peaks form. Fold gently into cream cheese mixture. Spoon into pie shell. Top with pineapple, strawberries or other fresh fruit. Chill until ready to serve. Yield: 8 servings.

Clara Steendahl, Xi Delta
Royal City, Washington

TANGY PINEAPPLE CHEESECAKE

3 cups graham cracker crumbs
3/4 cup melted margarine
5 tablespoons sugar
16 ounces cream cheese, softened
11/2 cups sugar
2 eggs
2/3 cup pineapple juice
1 (20-ounce) can crushed pineapple
1/4 cup all-purpose flour
1/4 cup sugar
1/2 cup whipped topping
Maraschino cherries

Combine crumbs, margarine and 5 tablespoons sugar in bowl; mix until crumbly. Reserve 1/2 cup crumb mixture. Press remaining crumb mixture into greased 9-by-13-inch pan. Beat cream cheese in mixer bowl until smooth. Add 11/2 cups sugar and eggs; beat until light and fluffy. Add pineapple juice; beat until blended. Spoon over crumb mixture. Bake at 350 degrees for 20 to 30 minutes or until center is set. Cool completely in pan. Drain pineapple, reserving 1 cup juice. Combine reserved juice, flour and 1/4 cup sugar in saucepan. Bring to a boil over low heat. Cook for 1 minute, stirring constantly. Remove from heat. Stir in pineapple. Freeze for 30 minutes. Fold in whipped topping. Spread over cheesecake. Sprinkle with reserved crumbs. Chill, loosely covered, for 4 hours or until firm. Garnish with maraschino cherries if desired. Yield: 12 to 15 servings.

Kathy Chapman, Xi Gamma Eta
Wyoming, Michigan

PRALINE AND PUMPKIN HARVEST CHEESECAKE

3/4 cup graham cracker crumbs
1/2 cup finely chopped pecans
1/4 cup packed light brown sugar
5 tablespoons melted butter or margarine
9 ounces cream cheese, softened
1/2 cup packed light brown sugar
1/2 cup sugar
3 eggs
1 1/2 cups canned pumpkin
1 1/2 teaspoons cinnamon
1/2 teaspoon each nutmeg and ginger
2 tablespoons milk
1 tablespoon cornstarch
1 tablespoon bourbon (optional)

Combine crumbs, pecans, 1/4 cup brown sugar and butter in bowl; mix until crumbly. Press firmly into bottom and 1/2 inch up side of greased 9-inch springform pan. Chill until firm. Preheat oven to 350 degrees. Beat cream cheese, 1/2 cup brown sugar and sugar in mixer bowl until very smooth. Beat in eggs 1 at a time, beating until just blended. Add pumpkin, spices, milk, cornstarch and bourbon; beat until blended. Spread over prepared crust mixture. Bake at 350 degrees for 50 to 55 minutes or until center is just set. Yield: 12 servings.

Maude McNamara, Preceptor Beta
Fredericton, New Brunswick, Canada

PUMPKIN CHEESECAKE

1/3 cup margarine or butter, softened
1/3 cup sugar
1 egg
1 1/4 cups all-purpose flour
16 ounces cream cheese, softened
3/4 cup sugar
1 (16-ounce) can pumpkin
Salt to taste
1 teaspoon ginger
1 teaspoon cinnamon
1/4 teaspoon nutmeg
2 eggs
Whipped cream

Preheat oven to 400 degrees. Cream margarine and 1/3 cup sugar in mixer bowl until light and fluffy. Mix in 1 egg and flour until crumbly. Press into bottom and 2 inches up side of greased 9-inch springform pan. Bake at 400 degrees for 5 minutes. Set aside to cool. Reduce heat to 350 degrees. Combine cream cheese and 3/4 cup sugar in mixer bowl; beat until smooth. Add pumpkin, salt, spices and 2 eggs; mix well. Spoon into prepared crust. Bake at 350 degrees for 50 minutes. Loosen from side of pan. Cool completely; remove rim. Chill until ready to serve. Garnish with whipped cream. Yield: 12 servings.

Doris Bartlett, Laureate
Chadron, Nebraska

PUMPKIN GINGER CHEESECAKE

1 1/2 cups graham cracker crumbs
1 teaspoon cinnamon
1 teaspoon ginger
1 tablespoon sugar
1/2 cup melted butter or margarine
24 ounces cream cheese, softened
1 1/2 cups sugar
5 eggs
1 (16-ounce) can pumpkin
1 tablespoon vanilla extract
2 tablespoons dark rum
2 tablespoons ginger
2 teaspoons cinnamon
1/2 teaspoon nutmeg
1 1/2 cups sour cream
1/2 cup sugar
1/2 teaspoon cinnamon
2 tablespoons dark rum

Combine crumbs, 1 teaspoon cinnamon, 1 teaspoon ginger, 1 tablespoon sugar and butter in bowl; mix until crumbly. Press into bottom and 1/3 up side of greased 10-inch springform pan. Chill for 30 minutes. Preheat oven to 325 degrees. Beat cream cheese and 1 1/2 cups sugar in mixer bowl until light and fluffy. Add eggs 1 at a time, beating well after each addition. Combine pumpkin, vanilla, 2 tablespoons rum, 2 tablespoons ginger, 2 teaspoons cinnamon and nutmeg in separate mixer bowl; beat until smooth. Stir into cream cheese mixture. Spread over crust mixture. Bake at 325 degrees for 1 1/2 hours or until set. Whisk sour cream, 1/2 cup sugar, 1/2 teaspoon cinnamon and 2 tablespoons rum in bowl until blended. Spread over hot cheesecake. Loosen from side of pan. Cool completely in pan before removing rim. Chill for 5 hours or longer.
Yield: 10 to 12 servings.

Sharon Cummins
Harleysville, Pennsylvania

SPICY PUMPKIN CHEESECAKE

1 egg yolk
1 (9-inch) graham cracker pie shell
16 ounces cream cheese, softened
3/4 cup sugar
2 eggs
1 (16-ounce) can pumpkin
1 1/2 teaspoons cinnamon
1/2 teaspoon ginger
1/4 teaspoon cloves
Whipped cream to taste
Toasted pecan halves to taste

Preheat oven to 350 degrees. Beat egg yolk in bowl until frothy. Brush over pie shell. Bake at 350 degrees for 5 minutes. Set aside to cool. Beat cream cheese, sugar and eggs in large mixer bowl until smooth. Add pumpkin and spices; beat until blended. Spoon into prepared pie crust. Bake at 350 degrees for 40 to 45 minutes or until set. Cool in pan. Chill for 8 hours or longer. Garnish with whipped cream and pecan halves. Yield: 8 to 12 servings.

Dianne L. Berry, Epsilon Beta
Truman, Minnesota

PUMPKIN SOUR CREAM CHEESECAKE

1 cup graham cracker crumbs
1 tablespoon sugar
1/4 cup melted butter or margarine
16 ounces cream cheese, softened
3/4 cup sugar
1 (16-ounce) can pumpkin
1 1/4 teaspoons cinnamon
1/2 teaspoon ginger
1/2 teaspoon nutmeg
1/4 teaspoon salt
2 eggs
2 cups sour cream
2 tablespoons sugar
1 teaspoon vanilla extract
12 to 16 pecans halves

Preheat oven to 350 degrees. Combine crumbs, 1 tablespoon sugar and butter in bowl; mix until crumbly. Press into greased 9-inch springform pan. Chill until firm. Beat cream cheese and 3/4 cup sugar in large mixer bowl until light and fluffy. Add pumpkin, cinnamon, ginger, nutmeg and salt; mix until blended. Add eggs 1 at a time, beating well after each addition. Spread over prepared crust mixture. Bake at 350 degrees for 50 minutes or until firm. Combine sour cream, 2 tablespoons sugar and vanilla in bowl; mix well. Spread over baked mixture. Bake for 5 minutes longer. Place on wire rack to cool completely. Place on serving plate; remove side of pan. Chill, covered, for 8 hours or longer. Cut into squares. Garnish each slice with pecan halves. Yield: 12 to 16 servings.

Barbara Grabski, Alpha
Minden, Nevada

CHEESECAKE TART

6 to 8 (3-inch) oatmeal cookies
2 tablespoons margarine, softened
2 cups part-skim ricotta or low-fat cottage cheese
2 egg whites
1 teaspoon vanilla extract
1/4 teaspoon almond extract
3 tablespoons light honey
Fresh tangerine sections, kiwifruit slices or fresh berries

Preheat oven to 325 degrees. Combine cookies and margarine in food processor container or blender container. Process until crumbly. Press over bottom and up side of greased 9-inch tart pan. Chill until firm. Combine ricotta cheese, egg whites, vanilla, almond extract and honey in food processor container; process until smooth. Spoon into prepared tart pan. Bake at 325 degrees for 30 minutes or until firm. Let stand until cool. Chill until serving time. Garnish with tangerine slices, kiwifruit sections or berries. Yield: 8 servings.

Marjorie Engle, Preceptor Epsilon Gamma
Warren, Ohio

ANGEL FOOD DESSERT

1 angel food cake
1 cup sugar
16 ounces light cream cheese, softened
1 (5-ounce) can evaporated milk
1 (21-ounce) can cherry pie filling
1 cup coconut
1 cup chopped pecans
12 ounces whipped topping

Break up cake into bite-size pieces in 9-by-13-inch pan. Combine sugar, cream cheese and evaporated milk in bowl; mix well. Spread over cake. Top with pie filling. Spread with mixture of coconut, pecans and whipped topping. Chill until ready to serve. Yield: 15 servings.

Joan Summers, Xi Delta Omega
Smyrna, Georgia

ANGEL FOOD FLUFF

My Beta sisters love this dessert.

1 angel food cake, broken into bite-size pieces
1 (6-ounce) package vanilla instant pudding mix, prepared
2 bananas, sliced
2 kiwifruit, sliced
12 ounces whipped topping
4 slices kiwifruit

Layer cake, alternating with pudding, bananas, kiwifruit and whipped topping, ending with whipped topping, in large glass dessert bowl. Garnish with 4 additional slices kiwifruit. Yield: 15 servings.

Kathryn S. McNary, Xi Beta Beta
Amherst, Ohio

BANANA SPLIT CAKE

This dessert is a crowd pleaser. I am asked to bring it to many parties and family get-togethers. It is best when made a day ahead of serving.

1 angel food cake, broken into bite-size pieces
1 (21-ounce) can cherry pie filling
1 (20-ounce) can crushed pineapple, undrained
2 (4-ounce) packages vanilla instant pudding mix, prepared
3 to 4 bananas, sliced into 1/4-inch pieces
16 ounces whipped topping

Layer cake, pie filling, undrained pineapple, pudding, bananas and whipped topping 1/2 at a time in large serving bowl. May use light pie filling, pineapple in its own juice, sugar-free pudding and light whipped topping for a lower-calorie dessert. Yield: 20 to 30 servings.

Mary Crochet, Preceptor Mu Pi
Missouri City, Texas

BROWNIE TRIFLE DELIGHT

1 (22-ounce) package brownie mix
2 (4-ounce) packages chocolate instant pudding mix
6 to 8 Heath candy bars, crumbled
16 ounces whipped topping

Prepare brownies using package directions; set aside. Prepare pudding using package directions. Chill until partially set. Crumble brownies. Layer crumbled brownies, pudding mix, candy crumbs and whipped topping 1/2 at a time in clear, deep trifle bowl. Yield: 12 to 16 servings.

Denise K. Cressman, Member-at-Large
Danville, Pennsylvania

CHERRY ANGEL CREAM CAKE TRIFLE

1 angel food cake
1 (14-ounce) can sweetened condensed milk
1 cup cold water
1 teaspoon almond extract
1 (4-ounce) package vanilla instant pudding mix
2 cups whipping cream, whipped
2 (21-ounce) cans cherry pie filling

Cut cake into 1/4-inch slices. Arrange in single layer in 9-by-13-inch dish, reserving remaining slices. Combine condensed milk, water and almond extract in large mixer bowl; beat until blended. Add pudding mix; mix well. Chill for 5 minutes. Fold in whipped cream. Layer half the pudding mixture, half the pie filling, reserved cake slices, remaining pudding mixture and remaining pie filling in prepared dish. Chill for 4 hours or until set.
Yield: 18 to 20 servings.

Jane M. Brackett, Upsilon Omicron
Newton, Illinois

CHOCOLATE BROWNIE TRIFLE

This dessert is a big hit with my chocoholic sorority sisters!

1 (22-ounce) package fudge brownie mix
1/4 cup Kahlúa
1 (4-ounce) package chocolate fudge instant pudding mix
1 package fun-size Heath bars, crushed
12 ounces whipped topping

Prepare and bake brownies using package directions. Prick top of warm brownies at 1-inch intervals. Brush with Kahlúa. Cool. Crumble into bite-size pieces. Prepare pudding, using package directions. Layer brownies pieces, pudding, crushed candy and whipped topping 1/2 at a time in 3-quart trifle bowl. Chill for 8 hours or longer. Yield: 16 servings.

Cindy Trahan, Xi Alpha Delta Alpha
Highland Village, Texas

CHOCOLATE CHIP ANGEL FOOD TRIFLE

12 ounces chocolate chips
4 egg yolks, beaten
1/4 cup warm water
4 egg whites
1/2 cup confectioners' sugar
1/2 teaspoon salt
1 teaspoon vanilla extract
2 cups whipping cream, whipped
1 angel food cake, broken into bite-size pieces
Whipped cream
Maraschino cherries

Melt chocolate chips in top of double boiler over low heat. Add egg yolks and warm water; mix well. Cook until thickened, stirring constantly. Beat egg whites in mixer bowl until frothy. Add confectioners' sugar gradually, beating until stiff peaks form. Beat in salt and vanilla. Fold in chocolate mixture gently. Fold in whipped cream. Layer cake pieces and chocolate mixture 1/2 at a time in 2-quart serving bowl. Chill for 8 hours or longer. Top with whipped cream and cherries. Yield: 12 to 16 servings.

Linda Ervin, Xi Upsilon Omicron
Altaville, California

ANGEL FRUIT TRIFLE

1 angel food cake, broken into bite-size pieces
1 (11-ounce) can mandarin oranges, drained
1 (16-ounce) can sliced peaches, drained, chopped
1 (21-ounce) can cherry pie filling
2 bananas, sliced
1 (16-ounce) can prepared vanilla pudding
1 quart fresh strawberries or 1 (16-ounce) package frozen raspberries or blueberries
1/2 cup sugar
8 ounces whipped topping

Layer 1/3 of the cake pieces, half the mandarin oranges, half the peaches and all the pie filling, half the remaining cake pieces, remaining mandarin oranges and peaches, bananas, vanilla pudding and cake pieces in large trifle bowl. Reserve several whole strawberries. Crush remaining strawberries with sugar in bowl. Spoon strawberry mixture over cake pieces. Spread whipped topping over layers. Chill, covered, for 3 hours. Garnish with reserved strawberries just before serving.
Yield: 16 to 24 servings.

Rose Mary Coakes, Laureate Alpha Rho
Marshall, Michigan

CHOCOLATE TRIFLE

1 (2-layer) package chocolate cake mix
3 cups whipped topping
2 (6-ounce) packages chocolate instant pudding mix, prepared
Chocolate syrup, sliced bananas and maraschino cherries to taste

Prepare and bake cake using package directions for 8-inch layer cake. Cut into pieces. Layer 1/2 of the cake pieces, 1/2 of whipped topping, 1/2 of pudding, chocolate syrup, bananas and cherries in large trifle bowl. Repeat, ending with cherries.
Yield: 12 to 16 servings.

Gloria Chapman, Sigma
Estevan, Saskatchewan, Canada

DEATH BY CHOCOLATE TRIFLE

1 (22-ounce) package fudge brownie mix
1/4 to 1/2 cup coffee liqueur
3 (4-ounce) packages chocolate instant mousse mix
8 Heath or Skor candy bars, broken into bite-size pieces
12 ounces whipped topping

Prepare and bake brownies using package directions. Cool in pan. Cut into squares. Prick holes in brownies. Pour coffee liqueur over top. Let stand for several minutes. Prepare mousse using package directions. Place 1/2 of brownies in large trifle bowl. Layer with 1/2 of mousse, 1/2 of candy pieces and 1/2 of whipped topping. Repeat layers, ending with whipped topping. May substitute mixture of 1 teaspoon sugar and 1/4 cup coffee for coffee liqueur. Yield: 12 to 16 servings.

Linda Grow, Beta Upsilon
Warrensburg, Missouri

CHOCOLATE DIVINE "LOW-FAT" TRIFLE

2 large packages fat-free, sugar-free chocolate instant pudding mix
2 cups skim milk
1 angel food cake, torn into 1-inch pieces
16 ounces light whipped topping
Strawberries (optional)

Prepare pudding mix with skim milk using package directions. Layer cake pieces, pudding and whipped topping alternately in clear glass trifle bowl until all ingredients are used, ending with whipped topping. Garnish with strawberries. Yield: 12 to 16 servings.

Marilyn Sebby, Eta Alpha
Powell, Tennessee

ENGLISH TRIFLE

1 (3-ounce) package raspberry or strawberry gelatin
1/2 plain pound cake
1/4 cup sherry or Scotch whiskey (optional)
1 (16-ounce) can fruit cocktail, drained
1 (4-ounce) package lemon or vanilla instant pudding mix
12 ounces whipped topping

Prepare gelatin using package directions. Chill until partially set. Punch holes in cake with fork. Pour sherry over top. Crumble cake in large serving bowl. Top with gelatin mixture. Spread with fruit cocktail. Prepare pudding using package directions. Spread over fruit cocktail. Chill until set. Add whipped topping. Yield: 12 to 16 servings.

Jean Frink, Laureate Zeta Zeta
Palmdale, California

ENGLISH TRIFLE PUDDING

1/2 pound cake, sliced, or 6 ladyfingers
1 (6-ounce) package strawberry gelatin mix
1 firm banana, sliced
1 (4-ounce) package vanilla instant pudding mix

Line bottom and sides of large glass bowl with cake slices. Prepare gelatin using package directions. Pour over cake. Chill until set. Arrange 1/2 of banana slices over gelatin. Prepare pudding using package directions. Spread over top. Chill until firm. Garnish with remaining banana slices just before serving.
Yield: 12 servings.

Barbara Danner, Laureate Alpha Kappa Phi
Phoenix, Arizona

OLDE ENGLISH RASPBERRY TRIFLE

4 trifle sponge cakes or 1 pound cake, sliced
Jam
1/2 cup sherry
2 cups raspberries
1 1/2 cups milk
3 eggs
1/4 cup sugar
1/2 cup plus 2 tablespoons fresh cream, whipped
1/8 cup chopped nuts

Spread cake slices with jam. Place 2 slices together, sandwich fashion. Repeat until all slices are used. Arrange in glass serving bowl. Sprinkle with sherry. Reserve 1/2 cup raspberries. Top with remaining raspberries. Heat milk in saucepan almost to boiling. Whisk together eggs and sugar in bowl. Stir into hot milk. Cook until custard is thickened and coats back of wooden spoon, stirring constantly. Set aside to cool. Spoon over raspberries. Chill until set. Pipe whipped cream over custard. Garnish with nuts and reserved raspberries. Yield: 6 to 8 servings.

Ann Leonard, Laureate Sigma
Brookings, Oregon

"LEGAL" GELATIN PUDDING TRIFLE

I prepare this dessert for my mother, who is diabetic. She says it is "legal" and really enjoys it.

1 angel food cake, broken into chunks
1 (16-ounce) can fruit cocktail, undrained
1 (3-ounce) package light raspberry or strawberry gelatin
1 (4-ounce) package light vanilla instant pudding mix
1 cup 1% milk
Low-fat whipped topping

Arrange cake chunks in large glass bowl. Spread fruit cocktail and juice on top. Prepare gelatin using package directions. Spoon over fruit cocktail. Prepare pudding using package directions using one-percent milk. Spoon over gelatin. Top with whipped topping. Yield: 12 to 16 servings.

Kathie Geekie, Chi
Strathclair, Manitoba, Canada

JELLY ROLL TRIFLE

1 large jelly roll or sponge cake, cut into 1/2-inch squares
1/3 cup dry sherry (optional)
1 (16-ounce) can fruit cocktail
1 (6-ounce) package strawberry gelatin
Custard mix or 1 (4-ounce) package vanilla instant pudding mix
1 cup whipping cream
1 tablespoon sugar
1 teaspoon vanilla extract

Arrange cake in bottom of glass serving bowl. Sprinkle with sherry. Drain fruit cocktail, reserving juice. Prepare gelatin using package directions, using reserved juice from fruit cocktail for part of water requirement. Spread fruit cocktail over cake. Top with gelatin. Chill until partially set. Prepare custard or pudding using package directions. Cool completely. Spoon over fruit cocktail. Chill until set. Combine whipping cream with sugar and vanilla in mixer bowl; beat until soft peaks form. Spread over custard layer. Chill. Yield: 12 servings.

Barbara Simpson, Eta Sigma
Kamloops, British Columbia, Canada

LEMON CUSTARD CAKE

1 angel food cake, torn into bite-size pieces
1 (4-ounce) package lemon instant pudding mix
1 1/2 cups cold milk
1 cup sour cream
1 (21-ounce) can cherry pie filling

Arrange cake pieces in 9-by-13-inch pan. Combine next 3 ingredients in mixer bowl; beat until thickened. Spread over cake. Top with pie filling. Chill until ready to serve. Yield: 12 to 16 servings.

Gloria Wagstaff, Laureate Zeta Zeta
Palmdale, California

PINEAPPLE PUNCH BOWL CAKE

1 (2-layer) package yellow cake mix
1 (20-ounce) can crushed pineapple
1 (6-ounce) package vanilla instant pudding mix, prepared
1 (21-ounce) can cherry pie filling
16 ounces (or more) whipped topping
1 cup chopped nuts
1/2 cup flaked coconut

Prepare and bake cake using package directions. Cool. Break into chunks. Arrange in large punch bowl. Spread pineapple over cake. Spread pudding over pineapple. Add pie filling. Spread with whipped topping. Sprinkle with nuts and coconut. Chill, tightly covered, for 8 hours. Yield: 16 to 24 servings.

Roberta Waters, Xi Lambda Mu
Camdenton, Missouri

"JUST A TRIFLE" PUDDING CAKE

1 angel food cake, broken into pieces
2 (4-ounce) packages favorite flavor instant pudding mix
2 cups milk
1 teaspoon bourbon or other liqueur flavoring
16 ounces whipped topping
Cherries to taste

Arrange cake pieces in large serving bowl. Prepare pudding using package directions, using 2 cups milk. Add flavoring; mix well. Spoon over cake. Top with whipped topping and cherries. Chill until ready to serve. Yield: 6 to 8 servings.

Maureen Humphreys, Preceptor Theta
Virginia Beach, Virginia

STRAWBERRY PUNCH BOWL TRIFLE

1 (2-layer) package yellow cake mix
2 (10-ounce) packages frozen strawberries with juice, thawed
2 (20-ounce) cans crushed pineapple
4 bananas, sliced
1 (3-ounce) can flaked coconut (optional)
1/4 cup chopped pecans
1 (6-ounce) package vanilla instant pudding mix
1 cup sour cream
32 ounces whipped topping
1 cup (or more) chopped pecans
Strawberries and blueberries

Prepare cake mix using package directions; cool. Break into pieces. Layer cake pieces, strawberries, pineapple, bananas, coconut and 1/4 cup pecans in large punch bowl until all ingredients are used. Prepare pudding using package directions. Add sour cream; mix until blended. Spread over pecans. Top with whipped topping. Garnish with 1 cup pecans, additional strawberries and blueberries. Chill for 8 hours or longer. Serve cold. Yield: 25 to 30 servings.

Sharon Ingram, Preceptor Epsilon Theta
St. Petersburg, Florida

PUNCH BOWL VANILLA TRIFLE

1 (2-layer) package yellow pudding-recipe cake mix
2 (10-ounce) packages frozen sliced strawberries
1 (6-ounce) package vanilla instant pudding mix, prepared
1 (20-ounce) can crushed pineapple, drained
2 bananas, sliced
16 ounces whipped topping

Bake cake using package directions. Cool completely. Break into pieces. Layer cake, strawberries, pudding, pineapple, bananas and whipped topping 1/2 at a time in large punch bowl. Chill for 8 hours or longer. Yield: 15 servings.

Veda M. Kraich, Preceptor Beta Psi
Akron, Colorado

"SINLESS" PINEAPPLE VANILLA TRIFLE

1 (15-ounce) can pineapple tidbits
2 large packages sugar-free vanilla instant pudding mix
5 cups low-fat milk
1 cup fat-free sour cream
1 angel food cake, cut into 1-inch squares
Strawberries to taste
Low-fat whipped topping

Drain pineapple, reserving 1 cup juice. Mix pudding mix and milk in bowl until thick. Add 1/2 cup of the reserved juice and sour cream; mix well. Stir in pineapple. Layer cake and pudding 1/3 at a time in a trifle dish, sprinkling remaining reserved juice over cake. Arrange sliced strawberries over layers. Top with whipped topping. Chill until set.
Yield: 10 to 12 servings.

Laura Key, Preceptor Beta Phi
Bryan, Texas

STRAWBERRY ANGEL TRIFLE

2 (3-ounce) packages strawberry gelatin
2 1/2 cups boiling water
1 (16-ounce) package frozen strawberries
1 tablespoon sugar
1/8 teaspoon salt
2 envelopes dry whipped topping mix
1 large angel food cake, broken into chunks

Dissolve gelatin in boiling water in bowl. Stir in frozen strawberries until thawed. Add sugar and salt; mix well. Chill until thickened. Prepare whipped topping using package directions. Stir in 1/2 of whipped topping. Layer cake and strawberry mixture in bundt pan. Chill until firm. Invert onto serving plate. Spread with remaining whipped topping over top and side. Yield: 24 servings.

Melinda Tindel, Eta Mu
Bay City, Texas

STRAWBERRY CHEESECAKE TRIFLE

16 ounces cream cheese, softened
2 cups confectioners' sugar
1 cup sour cream
1/2 teaspoon vanilla extract
12 ounces whipped topping
1 angel food cake, torn into pieces
2 quarts sweetened strawberries

Beat cream cheese and confectioners' sugar in mixer bowl until light and fluffy. Stir in sour cream and vanilla. Fold in whipped topping. Stir in cake pieces gently. Spread 1/2 of strawberries in bottom of punch bowl. Layer with cream cheese mixture and remaining strawberries. Chill until set. Yield: 16 servings.

Marcia R. Smith, Alpha Delta Lambda
Cameron, Missouri

STRAWBERRY DESSERT TRIFLE

1 angel food cake, broken into pieces
1 (4-ounce) package vanilla instant pudding mix
1 cup milk
2 cups vanilla ice cream
1 (3-ounce) package strawberry gelatin
1 cup boiling water
1 (10-ounce) package frozen strawberries

Arrange cake pieces in 9-by-13-inch pan. Prepare pudding using package directions, using 1 cup milk. Fold in softened ice cream. Spread over cake. Dissolve gelatin in boiling water in bowl. Stir in strawberries. Spoon over pudding mixture. Chill until firm. Yield: 15 servings.

Jody Boone, Alpha Chi
Chanute, Kansas

STRAWBERRY TRIFLE

1 (6-ounce) package coconut cream pudding and pie filling mix
2 cups whipping cream
1/4 cup sugar
1 teaspoon vanilla extract
1 cup sour cream
1 sponge cake, broken into small pieces
1 quart fresh strawberries, sliced

Prepare pudding using package directions for the microwave. Beat whipping cream in mixer bowl until soft peaks form. Add sugar and vanilla; beat until stiff peaks form. Fold in pudding mixture and sour cream. Arrange half the cake pieces in bottom of large serving bowl. Alternate layers of whipped cream mixture, strawberries and remaining cake pieces until all ingredients are used, ending with strawberries. Chill for 2 hours. Yield: 12 servings.

Cheryl Davis, Laureate Alpha Alpha
Kingston, Ontario, Canada

"TRUFFLE" TRIFLE

1 (10-ounce) package vanilla wafers
1 (8-ounce) jar raspberry jam
1 (6-ounce) package vanilla pudding and pie filling mix, prepared
1 cup chopped walnuts
1 (16-ounce) can fruit cocktail
1 large envelope dry whipped topping mix, prepared
1/3 cup maraschino cherries
Additional walnuts

Spread flat sides of wafers with jam. Layer wafers, hot pudding, walnuts and fruit cocktail 1/3 at a time in 2-quart glass bowl. Top with whipped topping, cherries and additional walnuts. Yield: 20 servings.

Carole Beadnell-Tucker, Xi Beta Beta
Lincoln, Nebraska

APPLE BUTTERSCOTCH PUDDING

1 1/4 cups dried apples
1 cup packed light brown sugar
1 1/2 cups all-purpose flour
2 1/2 teaspoons baking powder
1/2 teaspoon salt
1/4 cup butter or margarine, softened
1/2 cup milk
1 cup packed light brown sugar
1/4 cup butter or margarine
2 cups water

Preheat oven to 400 degrees. Sprinkle apples with 1/3 cup brown sugar in small bowl. Combine sifted mixture of flour, baking powder and salt with 2/3 cup brown sugar in large mixer bowl; mix well. Add 1/4 cup butter and milk, stirring just until moistened. Stir in apple mixture. Bring 1 cup brown sugar, 1/4 cup butter and water to a boil in large saucepan. Boil for 2 minutes. Add apple mixture; mix well. Pour into 8-inch baking dish. Bake at 400 degrees for 30 minutes. Yield: 6 to 8 servings.

Barbara Huggard, Preceptor Beta
Fredericton, New Brunswick, Canada

BEST-EVER APPLE PUDDING

1/4 cup butter or margarine, softened
1 cup sugar
1 egg, beaten
1 cup sifted all-purpose flour
1 teaspoon baking soda
1 teaspoon cinnamon
1/2 teaspoon nutmeg
1/4 teaspoon salt
2 large apples, peeled, grated
1/2 cup chopped pecans
1/2 cup butter or margarine
1 cup sugar
1/2 cup half-and-half
Nutmeg to taste
1/2 teaspoon vanilla extract

Preheat oven to 350 degrees. Cream 1/4 cup butter and 1 cup sugar in large mixer bowl. Add egg; mix well. Add mixture of sifted flour, baking soda, cinnamon, 1/2 teaspoon nutmeg and salt; mix well. Stir in apples and pecans. Spread in 8-inch square baking pan. Bake at 350 degrees for 35 to 45 minutes. Combine 1/2 cup butter, 1 cup sugar, half-and-half and nutmeg in small saucepan; mix well. Cook over low heat for 10 to 15 minutes, stirring occasionally. Stir in vanilla. Cut baked layer into 12 squares. Spoon sauce over each individual serving on serving plates. Serve warm. Yield: 12 servings.

Evelyn Willis, Texas Preceptor Laureate
Longview, Texas

OLD-TIME APPLE PUDDING

2 eggs
2 cups sugar
1/3 cup all-purpose flour
2 1/2 teaspoons baking powder
1/4 teaspoon salt
2 teaspoons vanilla extract
3 1/2 to 4 cups chopped peeled tart apples
1 cup chopped walnuts or pecans
1/2 cup raisins
Ice cream, whipped cream or whipped topping

Preheat oven to 350 degrees. Beat eggs, adding sugar gradually, until light and creamy. Add sifted mixture of flour, baking powder and salt; mix well. Stir in vanilla, apples, walnuts and raisins. Spread in greased 9-by-13-inch baking pan. Bake at 350 degrees for 30 minutes or until light brown and apples are tender. Serve warm or cold with ice cream, whipped cream or whipped topping. Yield: 12 servings.

Nancy H. McCreary, Xi Epsilon Beta
Maurertown, Virginia

SWEDISH APPLE PUDDING

1 package Zwieback crackers, crushed
1/2 cup sugar
1/2 cup melted butter or margarine
1 (16-ounce) can applesauce
Whipped topping

Combine cracker crumbs, sugar and butter in small bowl; mix well. Press 1/2 cracker mixture into bottom of 9-by-9-inch baking pan. Layer applesauce and remaining cracker crumbs over the top. Press down lightly. Chill, covered, for 2 to 4 hours or bake in preheated 350-degree oven for 15 minutes. Serve warm or chilled with whipped topping.
Yield: 6 to 8 servings.

Sue Nelson, Preceptor Mu Kappa
Fresno, California

Glenda Clark, Alpha Delta Lambda, Cameron, Missouri, makes Sugar-Free Banana Pudding by layering vanilla wafers, 2 sliced bananas, prepared sugar-free banana instant pudding and a few crushed vanilla wafers in a bowl. Chill until set.

CREAMY BANANA PUDDING

1 (14-ounce) can sweetened condensed milk
1 1/2 cups cold water
1 (4-ounce) package vanilla instant pudding mix
2 cups whipping cream, whipped
36 vanilla wafers
3 medium bananas, sliced into rounds, dipped in lemon juice

Beat condensed milk, water and pudding mix in large mixer bowl. Chill, covered, for 5 minutes. Fold in whipped cream. Reserve a small amount of pudding mixture. Alternate layers of remaining pudding mixture, vanilla wafers and bananas in 2 1/2-quart glass dish until all ingredients are used. Top with reserved pudding mixture. Store in refrigerator. Yield: 8 to 10 servings.

Phyllis Lauer, Alpha Kappa Rho
Yoakum, Texas

BANANA PUDDING

1 (6-ounce) package vanilla instant pudding mix
2 1/2 cups milk
1/2 cup sour cream
8 ounces whipped topping
Vanilla wafers
3 (or more) bananas, sliced into rounds

Whisk pudding mix and milk in large bowl. Add sour cream and one heaping spoonful of whipped topping; mix well. Alternate layers of vanilla wafers, bananas and pudding mixture in 2-quart serving dish until all ingredients are used, ending with pudding mixture. Spread remaining whipped topping over the top. Store in refrigerator. Yield: 8 to 10 servings.

Margie Akelewicz, Preceptor Tau
Merritt Island, Florida

BERRY CUSTARD CUPS

2 cups fresh berries of choice
2 teaspoons cornstarch
2 tablespoons sugar
1 egg, lightly beaten
1 cup skim milk
2 tablespoons low-fat or fat-free sour cream
1/2 teaspoon vanilla extract
4 teaspoons light brown sugar

Preheat broiler. Place 1/2 cup berries in each of 4 custard cups. Mix cornstarch and sugar in small saucepan. Add egg; mix well. Add milk gradually; mix well. Cook over low heat until thickened, stirring constantly. Let cool slightly. Stir in sour cream and vanilla. Spoon over berries. Sprinkle with brown sugar. Broil 4 to 5 inches from heat source until sugar melts. Serve warm. Yield: 4 servings.

Natasha N. Nobbe, Indiana Beta Gamma
Batesville, Indiana

OLD-FASHIONED BLUEBERRY PUDDING

2 cups fresh or frozen blueberries
Juice and grated rind of 1 lemon
1/2 teaspoon cinnamon
3 tablespoons butter or margarine, softened
1/2 cup sugar
1/2 cup milk
1 cup all-purpose flour
1 teaspoon baking powder
1/4 teaspoon salt
1/2 cup sugar
1 tablespoon cornstarch
Salt to taste
1 cup boiling water

Preheat oven to 375 degrees. Mix blueberries, lemon juice, lemon rind and cinnamon in medium bowl. Spoon into greased 8-inch baking pan. Cream butter and 1/2 cup sugar in large mixer bowl until smooth. Add milk alternately with mixture of flour, baking powder and salt, mixing well after each addition. Spread over blueberries. Blend 1/2 cup sugar, cornstarch and salt in small bowl. Sprinkle over the top. Pour boiling water over cornstarch mixture; do not stir. Bake at 375 degrees for 1 hour. Yield: 6 to 8 servings.

Olga Tombs, Preceptor Delta Rho
Orangeville, Ontario, Canada

BLUEBERRY PUDDING

2 cups fresh blueberries
1 cup all-purpose flour
3/4 cup sugar
1 teaspoon baking powder
1/2 teaspoon salt
1/2 cup milk
3 tablespoons melted butter or corn oil
3/4 cup sugar
1 tablespoon cornstarch
1 cup boiling water

Preheat oven to 350 degrees. Place blueberries in bottom of 8-by-8-inch baking pan. Mix flour, 3/4 cup sugar, baking powder and salt in large mixer bowl. Add milk and butter; mix well. Drop by spoonfuls over blueberries. Sprinkle with mixture of 3/4 cup sugar and cornstarch. Pour boiling water over the top. Bake at 350 degrees for 45 minutes. Serve warm or cold with ice cream or whipped topping. May substitute 2 cups raspberries or 2 1/2 cups rhubarb for blueberries. Yield: 6 servings.

Phyllis Lodge, Laureate Alpha Alpha
Amherstview, Ontario, Canada

BREAD PUDDING

3 cups torn bread
2 cups milk
1 cup sugar
Nutmeg or vanilla extract to taste
2 eggs
1 cup sugar
2 eggs
1 teaspoon vanilla extract
1/2 cup butter or margarine

Preheat oven to 350 degrees. Soak bread in 1 cup of milk in medium bowl. Add mixture of 1 cup sugar, nutmeg, 2 eggs and remaining 1 cup milk; mix well.

Spoon into 5-by-9-inch nonstick loaf pan. Bake at 350 degrees for 1 hour. Beat 1 cup sugar, 2 eggs and vanilla in small mixer bowl. Pour into top of double boiler. Stir in butter. Cook over low heat until smooth. Spoon over baked layer before serving. Yield: 6 servings.

Barbara Dudek, Xi Theta Psi
Anaheim, California

GOLDEN BREAD PUDDING

1 1/2 teaspoons unflavored gelatin
2 tablespoons cold water
1 cup sugar
3/4 teaspoon nutmeg
3/4 teaspoon salt
6 eggs
4 cups milk
3/4 teaspoon vanilla extract
2 to 3 drops yellow food coloring
2 to 3 slices bread, torn
1 cup raisins (optional)

Preheat oven to 350 degrees. Soften gelatin in cold water. Mix gelatin, sugar, nutmeg and salt in medium mixer bowl. Add eggs 1 at a time, mixing well after each addition. Add milk and vanilla; mix well. Stir in food coloring. Pour over bread and raisins in 8-by-8-inch baking pan. Bake at 350 degrees for 30 to 40 minutes or until firm and golden. Yield: 10 servings.

Vonda Cederlof, Eta Upsilon
Fresno, California

BREAD PUDDING WITH LEMON SAUCE

2 eggs, slightly beaten
2 cups one-percent milk
1/3 cup packed light brown sugar
1 teaspoon vanilla extract
1/4 teaspoon cinnamon
1/4 teaspoon nutmeg
6 slices raisin bread, torn
1/2 cup sugar
1 tablespoon all-purpose flour
1 cup water
Salt to taste
2 tablespoons margarine
2 tablespoons lemon juice

Preheat oven to 350 degrees. Combine eggs, milk, brown sugar, vanilla, cinnamon and nutmeg in large bowl; mix well. Stir in bread. Spoon into 8-by-8-inch baking dish sprayed with nonstick cooking spray. Place dish in larger baking pan containing 1-inch water. Bake at 350 degrees for 35 to 40 minutes or until knife inserted in center comes out clean. Microwave mixture of sugar, flour, water and salt in small microwave-safe dish on High for 2 to 3 minutes or until thickened, stirring twice. Stir in margarine and lemon juice. Pour over baked layer before serving. Yield: 9 to 12 servings.

Judy Gieselman, Laureate Gamma Kappa
Columbia, Missouri

CAPIROTADA (BREAD PUDDING)

12 slices of raisin bread, crusts removed, toasted
2 cups shredded longhorn cheese
1 cup packed light brown sugar
1 cup sugar
2 cups hot water
2 teaspoons cinnamon
1/4 teaspoon ginger
Salt to taste
Whipped cream

Layer bread and cheese 1/2 at a time in 9-by-9-inch nonstick baking pan. Cook brown sugar and sugar in heavy skillet over low heat until melted. Add 2 cups hot water in a stream, stirring constantly. Add cinnamon, ginger and salt. Simmer 5 to 7 minutes or until smooth. Pour over bread and cheese layers; do not press down. Let stand, covered, for 1 hour. Serve warm with whipped cream. Yield: 6 to 8 servings.

Wanda E. Dudley, Laureate Alpha
Albuquerque, New Mexico

BREAD AND BUTTER PUDDING

1/2 cup butter or margine, softened
7 slices white bread
4 cups milk
3 eggs, lightly beaten
1/2 cup sugar
1/4 teaspoon salt
1/2 cup raisins
1 teaspoon vanilla extract
1/2 teaspoon cinnamon

Preheat oven to 325 degrees. Spread a generous amount of butter on 1 side of each bread slice. Line bottom and sides of 2-quart buttered baking dish with bread slices. Combine milk, eggs, sugar, salt, raisins, vanilla and cinnamon in small bowl; mix well. Pour over bread. Press down to soak bread. Let stand for 10 minutes. Bake, covered, at 325 degrees for 30 minutes. Uncover and bake 30 minutes longer. Yield: 6 to 8 servings.

Wilma (Jean) Bachelor, Xi Beta Kappa
Prattville, Alabama

BREAD CUSTARD PUDDING

4 eggs
1 cup sugar
2 cups milk
1/2 cup melted butter or margarine, cooled
1 teaspoon vanilla extract
5 slices bread, each torn into eight pieces
1/4 cup sugar
1/2 teaspoon cinnamon

Preheat oven to 350 degrees. Mix eggs, 1 cup sugar and milk in medium mixer bowl. Add melted butter and vanilla; mix well. Stir in bread pieces. Spoon into 9-by-13-inch nonstick baking dish. Sprinkle with mixture of 1/4 cup sugar and cinnamon. Bake at 350 degrees for 35 to 45 minutes or until golden brown. Yield: 10 servings.

Diane F. Howell, Xi Epsilon Phi
Port O'Connor, Texas

LOW-FAT BREAD PUDDING

1 cup bread crumbs or stale bread
1 1/2 cups skim milk
2 eggs, lightly beaten
1 teaspoon vanilla extract
1/2 teaspoon cinnamon
8 envelopes artificial sweetener
1/2 cup raisins

Preheat oven to 325 degrees. Soak bread crumbs in milk in large bowl for 5 minutes. Add eggs, vanilla, cinnamon, artificial sweetener and raisins, mixing well after each addition. Pour into 9-by-9-inch glass baking dish. Bake at 325 degrees for 50 minutes or until browned and firm. Yield: 4 servings.

Becky Wallroff, Beta #120
Lincoln, Nebraska

LEMON BREAD PUDDING

2 cups milk
4 or 5 slices fresh white bread, crusts trimmed, torn into pieces
2 eggs, beaten
2/3 cup sugar
1/4 teaspoon salt
2 teaspoons grated lemon zest
1/2 teaspoon lemon extract
Sweetened whipped cream or whipped topping and orange marmalade

Preheat oven to 350 degrees. Pour milk over bread in large bowl. Let stand for 5 minutes. Add eggs, sugar, salt, lemon zest and lemon extract; mix well. Pour into 1 1/2-quart baking dish. Set dish in larger pan of hot water. Bake at 350 degrees for 1 hour or until knife inserted in center comes out clean. Serve with sweetened whipped cream or mixture of whipped topping and orange marmalade. Serve hot or cold. Yield: 4 servings.

Frances Sudduth, Laureate Epsilon Sigma
Santa Rosa, California

BREAD PUDDING WITH GLAZED TOPPING

1/4 cup butter or margarine, softened
4 eggs
2 cups sugar
2 tablespoons all-purpose flour
1/2 cup light corn syrup
1 tablespoon vanilla bean marinade
4 cups hot milk
1/2 cup raisins
1/2 cup crushed pineapple
1/2 loaf stale French bread, cut into 1-inch slices
1/2 cup whipping cream
1/3 cup sugar
1/4 cup butter or margarine

Preheat oven to 375 degrees. Spread 1/4 cup butter in 9-by-13-inch glass baking dish. Mix eggs, 2 cups sugar, flour, corn syrup, vanilla marinade and hot milk in large mixer bowl. Add raisins and pineapple; mix well. Stir in bread. Let stand for 20 minutes. Pour into prepared dish. Bake at 375 degrees for 40 minutes. Remove from oven. Let cool in dish for 10 minutes. Increase oven temperature to 425 degrees. Pour whipping cream over top of baked layer. Sprinkle with 1/3 cup sugar. Dot with 1/4 cup butter. Bake at 425 degrees for 10 to 15 minutes or until whipping cream is set. Yield: 12 servings.

Kitty Schuler, Laureate Delta Alpha
Silsbee, Texas

RAISIN BREAD PUDDING

4 slices buttered bread
4 eggs, beaten
2/3 cup sugar
3/4 cup raisins
1/4 teaspoon nutmeg
2 cups scalded milk
1 teaspoon salt
1 teaspoon vanilla extract

Preheat oven to 350 degrees. Line 1-quart baking dish with bread. Combine eggs, sugar, raisins, nutmeg, milk, salt and vanilla in medium bowl; mix well. Pour over bread. Place dish in larger pan of water. Bake at 350 degrees for 30 minutes.
Yield: 4 to 5 servings.

Ellen L. Wheeler, Alpha Omicron Master
Findlay, Ohio

RUM BREAD PUDDING

4 cups milk
4 eggs
2 cups sugar
1 cup melted butter or margarine
1 teaspoon cinnamon
1 teaspoon nutmeg
2 teaspoons vanilla extract
2 tablespoons rum
4 cups bread cubes

Preheat oven to 350 degrees. Combine milk, eggs, sugar, butter, cinnamon, nutmeg, vanilla and rum in medium bowl; mix well. Pour over bread cubes in 9-by-13-inch baking dish. Bake at 350 degrees for 1 1/4 hours. Yield: 8 to 10 servings.

Peggy Spitzner, Laureate Rho
North Wales, Pennsylvania

CARROT PUDDING

1 cup packed light brown sugar
1/4 cup vegetable shortening
1 egg
1 1/2 cups all-purpose flour
1 teaspoon baking soda
1/2 teaspoon cinnamon
1 teaspoon nutmeg
1/4 teaspoon cloves
Salt to taste
1 cup grated carrots
1 cup currants
1 cup packed light brown sugar
1 tablespoon butter or margarine
1/2 cup water
1/2 cup milk
1 tablespoon all-purpose flour
1/2 teaspoon vanilla extract

Preheat oven to 350 degrees. Beat 1 cup brown sugar and shortening in large mixer bowl until light and fluffy. Add egg; mix well. Add sifted mixture of 1 1/2 cups flour, baking soda, cinnamon, nutmeg, cloves and salt; mix well. Stir in carrots and currants. Spoon into nonstick 5-by-9-inch loaf pan. Bake at 350 degrees for 1 hour or until knife inserted in center comes out clean. Cook 1 cup brown sugar and butter in small saucepan over low heat until caramelized, stirring constantly. Add water. Bring to a boil, stirring constantly. Blend milk with 1 tablespoon flour. Stir into caramel mixture. Cook until thickened, stirring constantly. Stir in vanilla. Pour caramel sauce over slices of pudding. Yield: 6 to 8 servings.

Patricia Thorpe, Xi Sigma Rho
Crescent City, California

CHERRY PUDDING

1 1/2 cups milk, heated
2/3 cup graham cracker crumbs
1 cup cherries, pitted
1/4 cup sugar
1 tablespoon vanilla extract
1 teaspoon white rum
2 tablespoons chopped lemon rind
3 eggs, beaten
Ice cream

Combine milk and graham cracker crumbs in bowl; mix well. Let stand 15 minutes. Preheat oven to 350 degrees. Combine cherries, sugar, vanilla, rum, lemon rind and eggs in medium bowl; mix well. Add to graham cracker mixture; mix well. Pour into greased and floured 8-inch round baking dish. Bake at 350 degrees for 40 to 50 minutes. Serve warm with ice cream. Yield: 4 servings.

Lilian McCollum, Xi Kappa Omega
Pickersnigton, Ohio

BROWNIE PUDDING

2 cups sifted all-purpose flour
1 1/2 cups sugar
1/4 cup baking cocoa
4 teaspoons baking powder
1 teaspoon salt
1/4 cup vegetable oil
1 cup milk
2 teaspoons vanilla extract
1/4 cup chopped pecans
1 1/2 cups packed light brown sugar
1/2 cup baking cocoa
3 1/2 cups hot water
Whipped topping

Preheat oven to 350 degrees. Combine sifted mixture of flour, sugar, 1/4 cup baking cocoa, baking powder and salt with oil, milk and vanilla in large mixer bowl; mix well. Stir in pecans. Pour into greased 9-by-13-inch baking pan. Combine brown sugar, 1/2 cup baking cocoa and hot water in small bowl; mix well. Pour over batter. Bake at 350 degrees for 45 minutes. Invert onto serving plate. Spoon syrup over cake. Serve with whipped topping.
Yield: 10 to 12 servings.

Cathy Jones, Delta Sigma
Summerville, South Carolina

WALNUT BROWNIE PUDDING

1 cup all-purpose flour
3/4 cup sugar
2 tablespoons baking cocoa
2 teaspoons baking powder
1/2 teaspoon salt
1/2 cup milk
2 tablespoons melted vegetable shortening
1 teaspoon vanilla extract
3/4 to 1 cup chopped walnuts
3/4 cup packed light brown sugar
1/4 cup baking cocoa
1 3/4 cups hot water

Preheat oven to 350 degrees. Sift flour, sugar, 2 tablespoons baking cocoa, baking powder and salt into large mixer bowl. Add milk, shortening and vanilla; mix until smooth. Stir in walnuts. Pour into greased 8-by-8-inch baking pan. Combine brown sugar and 1/4 cup baking cocoa in small bowl; mix well. Sprinkle over batter. Pour hot water over the top. Bake at 350 degrees for 45 minutes. Yield: 6 to 8 servings.

Judith Hovan, Nevada Preceptor Tau
Elko, Nevada

CHOCOLATE PUDDING CAKE WITH COFFEE SAUCE

1 cup all-purpose flour
1/3 cup sugar
1/4 cup baking cocoa
2 teaspoons baking powder
1/2 teaspoon salt
1 egg, lightly beaten
1/2 cup skim milk
2 tablespoons canola oil
2 teaspoons vanilla extract
3/4 cup packed light brown sugar
1 1/3 cups hot brewed coffee or 1 1/2 tablespoons instant coffee dissolved in 1 1/3 cups boiling water
2 tablespoons chopped pecans or walnuts, toasted
Confectioners' sugar to taste

Preheat oven to 375 degrees. Mix flour, sugar, baking cocoa, baking powder and salt in large mixer bowl. Beat egg with skim milk, canola oil and vanilla in small bowl. Add to cocoa mixture; stir just until melted. Spoon batter into 6 custard cups sprayed lightly with nonstick cooking spray. Dissolve brown sugar in coffee; drizzle over batter. Sprinkle with pecans. Bake at 375 degrees for 15 to 20 minutes or until top springs back when lightly touched. Let cool for 5 minutes. Sprinkle with confectioners' sugar. Serve hot or warm. Yield: 6 servings.

Pamela Richards, Xi Alpha Eta
Bangor, Maine

CHOCOLATE PUDDING

3/4 cup sugar
1 cup all-purpose flour
2 teaspoons baking powder
1/8 teaspoon salt
3 tablespoons baking cocoa
3/4 cup milk
1/2 teaspoon vanilla extract
1/2 cup packed light brown sugar
1/2 cup sugar
2 to 3 tablespoons baking cocoa
1 1/2 cups cold water or coffee or mixture of both

Preheat oven to 350 degrees. Combine 3/4 cup sugar, flour, baking powder, salt and 3 tablespoons baking cocoa in medium bowl; mix well. Stir in milk and vanilla. Pour into 9-by-13-inch baking dish. Sprinkle with mixture of brown sugar, 1/2 cup sugar and 2 to 3 tablespoons baking cocoa. Pour cold water over the top. Bake at 350 degrees for 40 minutes.
Yield: 10 servings.

Anita Irwin, Gamma
Riverview, New Brunswick, Canada

BAKED EGG CUSTARD

1/2 cup melted margarine
2 cups sugar
8 eggs, beaten
1/4 cup all-purpose flour
1 teaspoon vanilla extract
3 cups milk
2 unbaked (10-inch) deep-dish pie shells

Preheat oven to 325 degrees. Mix margarine, sugar, eggs and flour in medium mixer bowl. Add vanilla and milk; mix well. Pour into 2 pie shells. Bake at 325 degrees for 45 minutes. Yield: 12 servings.

Mary S. Ballard, Preceptor Alpha Nu
Dublin, Georgia

DATE PUDDING

1 (8-ounce) package dates, cut in small pieces
1 teaspoon baking soda
1 cup boiling water
1 tablespoon melted butter or margarine
1 cup sugar
1 egg, beaten
1 1/2 cups all-purpose flour
1 teaspoon baking powder
1/2 cup pecans
1/2 cup sugar
3/4 cup boiling water

Preheat oven to 325 degrees. Combine 1/2 package dates and baking soda in 1 cup boiling water in large mixer bowl. Let stand until cool. Add butter, 1 cup sugar and egg; mix well. Stir in flour, baking powder and pecans. Pour into nonstick 5-by-9-inch loaf pan. Bake at 325 degrees for 45 minutes. Stir 1/2 cup sugar and remaining 1/2 package dates into 3/4 cup boiling water in small saucepan. Cook over medium heat for 15 minutes, stirring constantly. Pour over hot baked layer. Yield: 6 to 8 servings.

Velma Parker
Lawton, Oklahoma

✣ FANTASY PUDDING

1 1/2 cups graham cracker crumbs
1 teaspoon cinnamon
2/3 cup sugar
1/2 cup melted margarine
4 egg yolks
2/3 cup sugar
3 tablespoons all-purpose flour
2 1/2 cups milk
1 teaspoon vanilla extract
4 egg whites
1/4 cup sugar

Preheat oven to 325 degrees. Reserve 1/4 cup graham cracker crumbs. Cover bottom of greased 9-by-13-inch pan with remaining crumbs. Add cinnamon, 2/3 cup sugar and margarine; mix until crumbly. Press firmly into pan. Combine egg yolks, 2/3 cup sugar, flour and milk in double boiler over hot water. Cook until thickened. Stir in vanilla. Spread over prepared crust mixture. Combine egg whites and 1/4 cup sugar in mixer bowl; beat until stiff peaks form. Spread over custard mixture. Sprinkle with reserved crumbs. Bake at 325 degrees for 30 minutes. Cool completely. Store, covered, in refrigerator.
Yield: 12 servings.

Martha Laughlin, Xi Iota Sigma
Archie, Missouri

FRUIT COCKTAIL PUDDING

1 cup sifted all-purpose flour
1 cup sugar
1 teaspoon baking soda
1/2 teaspoon salt
1 (16-ounce) can fruit cocktail, undrained
1 egg, lightly beaten
1 teaspoon vanilla extract
1/2 cup packed light brown sugar
1/2 cup pecans
Whipped topping

Preheat oven to 350 degrees. Combine flour, sugar, baking soda, salt, undrained fruit cocktail, egg and vanilla in bowl; mix until blended. Pour into greased 5-by-9-inch loaf pan. Sprinkle with mixture of brown sugar and pecans. Bake at 350 degrees for 40 to 45 minutes or until firm. Serve warm with whipped topping. Yield: 8 servings.

Lennie Bates, Preceptor Mu
Neosho, Missouri

Glenda Deatherage, Preceptor Gamma Gamma, Broken Arrow, Oklahoma, makes an Easy Mousse by dissolving a 3-ounce package of any flavor gelatin in 1 cup boiling water, adding 1 cup vanilla ice cream, mixing until smooth and pouring into a pretty bowl or individual dessert dishes. Chill until firm.

OLD-FASHIONED INDIAN PUDDING

4 cups milk
1/4 cup butter or margarine
2/3 cup molasses
3 tablespoons honey
2/3 cup cornmeal
3/4 teaspoon cinnamon
3/4 teaspoon nutmeg

Preheat oven to 300 degrees. Heat 3 cups of milk in saucepan over low heat. Add butter, molasses and honey; mix well. Mix cornmeal, cinnamon and nutmeg in bowl. Whisk into milk mixture gradually. Cook over low heat for 10 minutes or until thickened, stirring constantly. Spoon into greased 1-quart casserole. Pour remaining 1 cup milk on top. Bake at 300 degrees for 3 hours. Yield: 8 servings.

Frances Kucera, Laureate Omicron
Eugene, Oregon

POOR MAN'S PUDDING

1/2 cup sugar
2 tablespoons butter or shortening
1/2 cup milk
1 cup all-purpose flour
1 teaspoon baking powder
Salt to taste
1 cup coconut or 1/2 cup semisweet chocolate chips
1/2 cup packed light brown sugar
1 cup hot water

Preheat oven to 350 degrees. Combine sugar, butter, milk, flour, baking powder and salt in bowl; mix until of doughy consistency. Spread into greased 8-by-8-inch baking pan. Sprinkle with mixture of coconut and brown sugar. Pour hot water over top. Bake at 350 degrees for 25 minutes or until golden brown. Yield: 8 to 12 servings.

Marlene Matiation
Shoal Lake, Manitoba, Canada

MAGIC MOCHA PUDDING

2/3 cup baking cocoa
21/2 teaspoons margarine
11/2 tablespoons cornstarch
2 teaspoons instant coffee granules
11/2 cups milk
6 tablespoons margarine, softened
11/2 cups sugar
1 egg
1/3 cup milk
1/2 teaspoon vanilla extract
11/2 cups all-purpose flour
21/2 teaspoons baking powder

Preheat oven to 350 degrees. Combine baking cocoa, margarine, cornstarch and coffee granules in top of double boiler. Bring to a boil over low heat, stirring constantly. Keep warm, covered, over hot water. Cream margarine in mixer bowl until light and fluffy. Add sugar; mix well. Beat in egg. Combine milk and vanilla in bowl; mix until blended. Sift flour and baking powder together. Add to creamed mixture 1/3 at a time, alternately with milk mixture. Spoon into greased 1-quart casserole. Drizzle 2 cups cocoa mixture over top. Reserve remaining cocoa mixture to top individual servings. Bake at 350 degrees for 50 minutes. Yield: 16 servings.

Niki Scallon, Eta Sigma
Kamloops, British Columbia, Canada

PERSIMMON PUDDING

11/3 cups all-purpose flour
12/3 cups sugar
1 teaspoon cinnamon
11/2 teaspoons baking powder
2 cups persimmon pulp
2 eggs, lightly beaten
1 (12-ounce) can evaporated milk
1 teaspoon baking soda
1 teaspoon vanilla extract
1/8 cup melted margarine
Whipped cream

Preheat oven to 350 degrees. Combine flour, sugar, cinnamon and baking powder in bowl; mix well. Stir in persimmon pulp and eggs. Add enough water to evaporated milk to equal 2 cups liquid. Combine with baking soda in bowl; mix well. Stir into flour mixture. Add vanilla and margarine; mix until blended. Pour into greased 9-by-13-inch baking pan. Bake at 350 degrees for 40 minutes or until knife inserted in center comes out clean. Serve with whipped cream if desired. Yield: 12 servings.

Joyce A. Sons, Alpha Beta
Bedford, Indiana

RICH PERSIMMON PUDDING

This is a 100-year-old recipe that my mother gave me 40 years ago.

11/2 cups sugar
1 cup all-purpose flour
1 teaspoon baking soda
1 teaspoon baking powder
1/2 teaspoon salt
2 tablespoons butter or margarine, softened
2 eggs, beaten
2 cups persimmon pulp
4 cups milk
Whipped topping

Preheat oven to 325 degrees. Combine sugar, flour, baking soda, baking powder and salt in bowl. Stir in butter and eggs. Add persimmon pulp and milk; mix until blended. Pour into greased 9-by-13-inch pan. Bake at 325 degrees for 2 hours, stirring occasionally. Remove from oven. Cool and cut into pieces. Serve with whipped topping. Yield: 16 servings.

Marilyn M. Charles, Xi Delta Mu
Riverside, California

Margaret Murdoch, Xi Zeta Rho, Orangeville, Ontario, Canada, makes Raspberry Bavarian by dissolving a small package of raspberry gelatin in 1 cup boiling water, draining a package of frozen raspberries and reserving the juice. Add juice with enough water to measure 1 cup. Chill gelatin until partially set and fold in 2 cups whipped cream and raspberries. Chill until set.

MY MOM'S HALF-HOUR PUDDING

1 cup all-purpose flour
1/8 teaspoon salt
2 teaspoons baking soda
1 tablespoon sugar
3/4 cup raisins
Nutmeg to taste
1 cup packed light brown sugar
1 tablespoon butter or margarine
Salt to taste
2 cups boiling water
1 teaspoon vanilla extract
Whipped cream

Preheat oven to 350 degrees. Combine flour, salt, baking soda, sugar, raisins and nutmeg in bowl; mix well. Place in greased 1-quart casserole. Combine brown sugar, butter, salt, boiling water and vanilla in large bowl; mix until blended. Pour over flour mixture. Bake at 350 degrees for 30 to 40 minutes or until firm. Serve with whipped cream.
Yield: 6 servings.

Dorothy (Dede) Connolly
Merritt, British Columbia, Canada

OLD-FASHIONED RICE PUDDING

1 cup uncooked rice
8 cups milk
1 teaspoon vanilla extract
4 egg yolks
2/3 cup sugar
1 cup raisins (optional)
4 egg whites
2 tablespoons sugar
1 teaspoon cream of tartar
Salt to taste

Cook rice and milk in saucepan for 1 hour. Add vanilla, egg yolks, 2/3 cup sugar and raisins; mix well. Spoon into greased 2-quart casserole. Preheat broiler. Beat egg whites in mixer bowl until soft peaks form. Add 2 tablespoons sugar, cream of tartar and salt; beat until stiff peaks form. Spread over pudding. Brown under broiler until firm and golden.
Yield: 6 to 8 servings.

Doris Lee, Preceptor Alpha Mu
San Jose, California

EASY RICE PUDDING

2 eggs
2 1/4 cups milk
1/4 teaspoon nutmeg
1/3 cup sugar
1/2 teaspoon salt
1/4 cup raisins
1 teaspoon vanilla extract
2/3 cup quick-cooking rice, uncooked

Preheat oven to 350 degrees. Combine eggs, milk, nutmeg, sugar, salt, raisins, vanilla and rice in nonstick 2-quart casserole; mix until blended. Set dish in 9-by-13-inch pan filled with hot water. Bake at 350 degrees for 40 minutes or until set around edges.
Yield: 5 servings.

Ann Margeson, Xi Theta
Wellsville, New York

RICH RICE PUDDING

4 cups milk
Salt to taste
3/4 cup uncooked short grain rice
2 eggs, beaten
1/2 cup sugar
1 teaspoon vanilla extract
1 (12-ounce) can evaporated milk
Cinnamon to taste

Combine milk, salt and rice in saucepan. Bring to a boil over low heat. Cook, covered, for 30 minutes, stirring occasionally. Combine eggs, sugar, vanilla and evaporated milk. Beat in mixer bowl until blended. Stir into rice mixture. Bring to a boil. Spoon into large serving bowl. Sprinkle with cinnamon.
Yield: 6 servings.

Patricia Ragan, Xi Alpha Delta
Eugene, Oregon

SOUTHERN RICE CUSTARD

3/4 cup uncooked long grain rice
1/2 cup sugar
1 teaspoon (scant) salt
4 cups milk
2 tablespoons butter or margarine, softened

Combine rice, sugar, salt, milk and butter in greased 2-quart casserole; mix well. Bake at 300 degrees for 2 1/2 hours. Serve hot or cold. Yield: 8 servings.

Betty Scholl Windle, Laureate Beta Delta
Reynoldsburg, Ohio

CORNSTARCH PUDDING

2 cups milk
2 egg yolks, beaten
Salt to taste
1/3 cup sugar
2 tablespoons cornstarch
1/4 cup cold milk
1 teaspoon vanilla extract
2 egg whites, stiffly beaten

Combine milk, egg yolks, salt and sugar in saucepan. Bring to a boil, stirring constantly. Add mixture of cornstarch and milk; mix until thickened. Stir in vanilla. Fold into egg whites in bowl. Spoon into serving bowl. Chill until ready to serve.
Yield: 6 servings.

Sue Trowbridge, Preceptor Beta Omega
Emporia, Kansas

CORNSTARCH VANILLA PUDDING

1 1/2 cups milk
2 eggs, beaten
2 tablespoons cornstarch
1/3 cup sugar
1 teaspoon vanilla extract

Combine milk, eggs, cornstarch, sugar and vanilla in saucepan. Bring to a boil over low heat. Cook for 1 minute, stirring constantly. Spoon into individual dessert dishes. Yield: 2 servings.

Elaine Penner, Preceptor Epsilon Theta
St. Petersburg, Florida

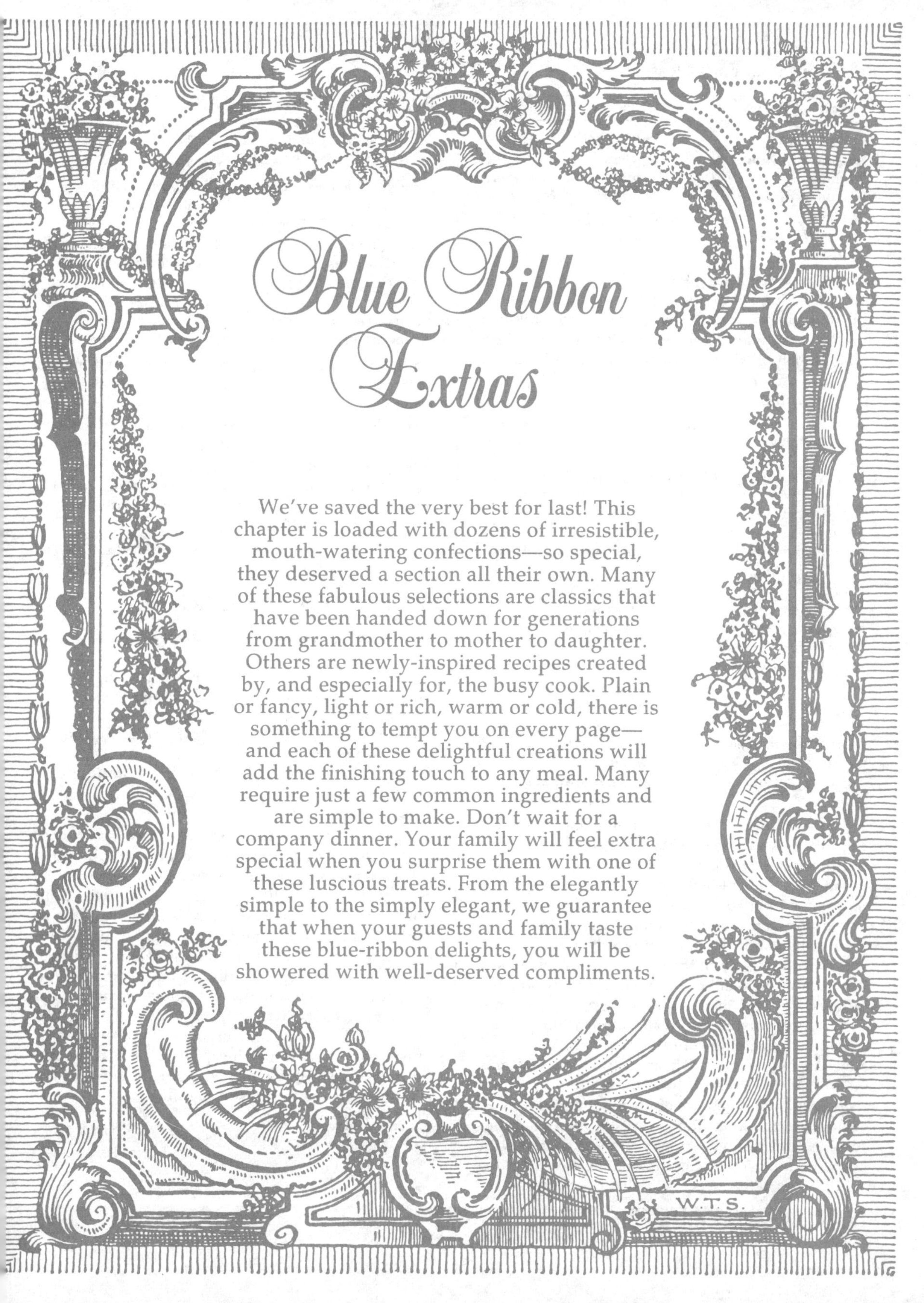

Blue Ribbon Extras

We've saved the very best for last! This chapter is loaded with dozens of irresistible, mouth-watering confections—so special, they deserved a section all their own. Many of these fabulous selections are classics that have been handed down for generations from grandmother to mother to daughter. Others are newly-inspired recipes created by, and especially for, the busy cook. Plain or fancy, light or rich, warm or cold, there is something to tempt you on every page—and each of these delightful creations will add the finishing touch to any meal. Many require just a few common ingredients and are simple to make. Don't wait for a company dinner. Your family will feel extra special when you surprise them with one of these luscious treats. From the elegantly simple to the simply elegant, we guarantee that when your guests and family taste these blue-ribbon delights, you will be showered with well-deserved compliments.

ANGEL HEART PIE

1/2 cup sugar
1 teaspoon baking powder
1 teaspoon almond extract
3 egg whites, stiffly beaten
2 cups crushed vanilla wafers
1/3 cup melted margarine
1 cup whipped topping
1/2 cup chopped pecans

Preheat oven to 325 degrees. Mix first 3 ingredients into egg whites in medium mixer bowl. Press mixture of vanilla wafers and margarine into 8- or 9-inch square baking pan. Spoon egg white mixture into prepared pan. Bake at 325 degrees for 15 minutes or until light brown. Cool. Top with whipped topping. Sprinkle with pecans. Yield: 8 servings.

Joanne S. Cain, Preceptor Theta
Augusta, Georgia

BANANA SPLIT CAKE DESSERT

1 cup sifted all-purpose flour
1 (4-ounce) package vanilla instant pudding mix
1/2 cup butter or margarine, softened
1/2 cup chopped pecans
2 large bananas, cut into 1/4-inch slices
2 tablespoons lemon juice
8 ounces cream cheese, softened
2 cups confectioners' sugar
1/2 cup butter or margarine, softened
1 (8-ounce) can crushed pineapple
1 cup miniature marshmallows
1 1/2 cups evaporated milk
1/4 cup butter or margarine
4 ounces whipped topping
1 cup semisweet chocolate chips
1/4 cup chopped pecans
10 maraschino cherries

Preheat oven to 375 degrees. Combine flour and pudding mix in small bowl. Cut in 1/2 cup butter until mixture resembles coarse meal. Stir in 1/2 cup pecans. Spread into 9-by-13-inch baking pan. Bake at 375 degrees for 15 to 20 minutes. Scrape off and reserve 1 tablespoon crumbs from crust after baking. Dip bananas in lemon juice. Arrange over crust. Beat cream cheese, 1/2 cup of the confectioners' sugar and 1/2 cup butter in small mixer bowl until smooth. Stir in pineapple and marshmallows. Spread over bananas. Cook mixture of evaporated milk, 1/4 cup butter and remaining confectioners' sugar in small saucepan over medium heat until thickened and smooth, stirring constantly. Remove from heat. Let stand until cool. Spoon over cream cheese mixture. Chill in refrigerator. Top with whipped topping. Sprinkle with reserved crust crumbs. Garnish with chocolate chips, 1/4 cup pecans and cherries. Chill for 8 to 12 hours before serving. Yield: 12 servings.

Bobbie McCandless, Preceptor Xi Epsilon
San Diego, California

BANANA SPLIT DESSERT

My sons, Matt and Shawn, love this dessert and always want it for their birthday.

2 cups crushed graham crackers
1/2 cup melted butter or margarine
1 (1-pound) package confectioners' sugar
2 eggs
1 cup butter or margarine, softened
1 (20-ounce) can crushed pineapple, drained
4 to 5 bananas, sliced
12 ounces whipped topping
1 cup chopped pecans
1 (12-ounce) can chocolate syrup

Press mixture of graham cracker crumbs and melted butter into bottom of 9-by-13-inch dish. Beat confectioners' sugar, eggs and softened butter in medium mixer bowl for 15 minutes. Spread over graham cracker mixture. Let stand for 30 minutes. Layer pineapple, bananas and whipped topping over confectioners' sugar mixture. Sprinkle with pecans. Drizzle with chocolate syrup. Chill until serving time. Yield: 12 to 36 servings.

Marie B. Lettic, Xi Alpha
Seattle, Washington

BROKEN GLASS DESSERT

5 (3-ounce) packages flavored gelatin
5 cups boiling water
2 1/2 cups cold water
25 graham crackers, crushed
1/2 cup sugar
1/2 cup melted butter or margarine
1 cup pineapple juice
1 envelope unflavored gelatin
1/4 cup cold water
2 1/2 cups whipping cream
1/2 cup confectioners' sugar
1 teaspoon vanilla extract

Select 5 gelatins of differing flavors and colors for most interesting and attractive presentation. Dissolve each flavor gelatin in 1 cup boiling water in separate bowl. Add 1/2 cup cold water to each. Chill until firm. Cut into small squares. Press mixture of graham cracker crumbs, sugar and butter into buttered springform pan. Boil pineapple juice in small saucepan. Add mixture of unflavored gelatin softened in 1/4 cup cold water. Remove from heat. Let stand until cool. Beat whipping cream in medium mixer bowl, adding confectioners' sugar gradually. Stir in vanilla. Fold in pineapple juice mixture and gelatin squares. Spoon over graham cracker mixture. Chill for 1 hour or until serving time.
Yield: 8 to 10 servings.

Diane L. Rafferty, Delta Sigma
Louisville, Colorado

BUTTER BRICKLE DESSERT

1 angel food cake
2 (4-ounce) packages butter pecan or butterscotch instant pudding mix
1¾ cups milk
1 quart butter brickle ice cream, softened
8 ounces whipped topping
1 Heath candy bar, crushed
1 Butterfinger candy bar, crushed

Tear cake into pieces and arrange in bottom of 9-by-13-inch baking pan. Beat pudding mix and milk in large mixer bowl until blended. Beat in ice cream until smooth. Pour over cake pieces. Top with whipped topping. Sprinkle with crushed candy bars. Chill until serving time. Yield: 10 servings.

Stephanie Kaul, Beta Tau
Albany, Oregon

CALEDONIAN CREAM

This recipe is from Scotland and was a family favorite when I grew up there.

16 ounces cottage cheese
2 tablespoons marmalade
2 tablespoons castor sugar
1 tablespoon lemon juice
2 tablespoons malt whiskey

Whisk cottage cheese, marmalade, sugar, lemon juice and whiskey together in large bowl. Pour into 4 or 5 individual serving cups or dishes. Chill until serving time. Yield: 4 to 5 servings.

Elizabeth Perry, Preceptor Eta
Lewisporte, Newfoundland, Canada

COCONUT PUDDING SALAD

60 butter crackers, crushed
½ cup melted margarine
½ gallon vanilla ice cream, softened
1½ cups milk
2 (4-ounce) packages coconut cream instant pudding mix
8 ounces whipped topping

Reserve ½ cup crushed crackers. Press mixture of remaining crushed crackers and margarine in bottom of 9-by-13-inch baking dish. Beat ice cream, milk and pudding mix in large mixer bowl for 2 minutes or until smooth. Spread over cracker mixture. Chill for 10 minutes. Top with whipped topping. Sprinkle with ½ cup reserved cracker crumbs. Store in refrigerator. Yield: 10 servings.

Sue Warner
Foley, Alabama

CHOCOLATE HEATH BAR DESSERT

1 (22-ounce) package brownie mix, prepared
8 ounces cream cheese, softened
2 cups whipped topping
1 cup confectioners' sugar
1 (4-ounce) package chocolate instant pudding mix
1½ cups milk
¼ cup Kahlúa
4 Heath candy bars, crushed

Crumble brownies in bottom of 3-quart dish. Top with beaten mixture of cream cheese, 1 cup whipped topping and confectioners' sugar. Layer beaten mixture of pudding mix, milk and Kahlúa over the top. Sprinkle with crushed candy bars. Top with remaining 1 cup whipped topping. Yield: 10 servings.

Jean Walzak
Holly Hill, Florida

CHOCOLATE DELIGHT

1 cup all-purpose flour
½ cup melted butter or margarine
½ cup chopped pecans
8 ounces cream cheese, softened
1 cup confectioners' sugar
16 ounces whipped topping
1 (4-ounce) package chocolate instant pudding mix
1 (4-ounce) package butterscotch instant pudding mix
2½ cups milk

Preheat oven to 350 degrees. Press mixture of flour, butter and pecans into bottom of 9-by-13-inch baking dish. Bake at 350 degrees for 25 minutes. Layer beaten mixture of cream cheese, confectioners' sugar and 8 ounces of the whipped topping over cooled baked layer. Beat pudding mixes and milk in medium mixer bowl until thickened. Spoon over cream cheese mixture. Top with remaining whipped topping. Yield: 12 to 15 servings.

Rita Carlisle, Xi Epsilon Omega
Laverne, Oklahoma

CHOCOLATE DESSERT

2 eggs
1 cup sugar
½ cup melted butter or margarine
1 teaspoon vanilla extract
2 tablespoons all-purpose flour
1 tablespoon baking cocoa
3 tablespoons hot water
1 cup chopped pecans

Preheat oven to 300 degrees. Mix eggs, sugar, butter, vanilla and flour in large mixer bowl. Dissolve cocoa in hot water. Add to eggs mixture; mix well. Stir in pecans. Pour into 9-by-13-inch baking pan. Set baking pan in larger pan of water. Bake at 300 degrees for 45 minutes. Yield: 15 servings.

Kenna Ashpaugh, Xi Gamma Lambda
Shattuck, Oklahoma

CHOCOLATE BANANA PUDDING TREAT

4 (1-ounce) squares semisweet chocolate
2 tablespoons milk
1 tablespoon margarine or butter
1 1/2 cups graham cracker crumbs
1/4 cup sugar
1/3 cup melted margarine or butter
3 bananas, sliced
3 cups milk
2 envelopes whipped topping mix
2 (4-ounce) packages banana cream instant pudding mix
8 ounces whipped topping

Microwave chocolate, 2 tablespoons milk and 1 tablespoon margarine on High in microwave-safe bowl for 1 to 1 1/2 minutes, stirring every 30 seconds. Press mixture of cracker crumbs, sugar and 1/3 cup margarine into 9-by-13-inch pan. Spread with chocolate mixture. Chill for 30 minutes. Arrange banana slices over chocolate mixture. Beat 3 cups milk, whipped topping mix and pudding mix in mixer bowl until blended. Spread over bananas. Top with whipped topping. Chill for 8 to 12 hours. Yield: 15 servings.

Bonnie Walls, Xi Omicron Sigma
Lakehead, California

LIGHT CHOCOLATE DELIGHT

1 (6-ounce) package chocolate pudding and pie filling mix
2 1/2 cups skim milk
8 ounces light whipped topping
1/2 teaspoon almond extract
1 package fat-free devil's food cookies, crumbled
Additional light whipped topping

Whisk pudding mix and milk in medium microwave-safe bowl. Microwave on High for 5 minutes. Whisk mixture again. Microwave for 3 to 4 minutes longer or until thickened. Let stand until cool. Whisk in whipped topping and almond extract. Reserve 1 tablespoon cookie crumbs. Arrange remaining cookie crumbs in bottom of trifle dish. Spread pudding mixture over crumbs. Top with additional whipped topping. Sprinkle with reserved crumbs. Yield: 6 to 8 servings.

Betty Jo Tucker, Laureate Theta
Floyds Knobs, Indiana

LIGHT CHOCOLATE LAYER DESSERT

1 pint whipping cream
1/2 cup sugar
1 to 2 teaspoons vanilla extract
1 (10-ounce) package chocolate wafers
1/4 cup slivered almonds
3 tablespoons butter or margarine
1 1/2 tablespoons sugar
Grated rind of 1 orange

Beat whipping cream with 1/2 cup sugar and vanilla in mixer bowl until stiff peaks form. Alternate layers of wafers and whipping cream mixture in 9-by-13-inch dish, ending with whipping cream mixture. Brown almonds in mixture of butter and 1 1/2 tablespoons sugar in skillet. Sprinkle almond mixture and orange rind over top of whipped cream mixture. Yield: 12 servings.

Margie Yellowega, Alpha Rho
Estevan, Saskatchewan, Canada

CHOCOLATI

1 envelope unflavored gelatin
1/4 cup cold water
3/4 cup nonfat dry milk powder
1/3 cup baking cocoa
1/4 cup sugar
2 cups skim milk
1/4 cup crème de cacao
1/4 cup crème de menthe (optional)

Soften gelatin in cold water in bowl. Cook milk powder, baking cocoa, sugar, gelatin and milk in heavy medium saucepan over medium-low heat for 5 minutes, stirring constantly. Remove from heat. Stir in crème de cacao and crème de menthe. Pour into large freezer container. Freeze for 4 hours or until partially frozen. Beat at high speed until smooth, scraping bowl with rubber spatula. Spoon into eight 6-ounce freezer-safe dessert glasses. Freeze until firm. Let stand at room temperature for 10 minutes before serving. Yield: 8 servings.

Angela Wilson, Delta Alpha
Harrison, Idaho

POT DE CREME CHOCOLAT (INDIVIDUAL CHOCOLATE MOUSSE)

1 1/4 cups semisweet chocolate chips
5 tablespoons cold water
1 tablespoon instant coffee
2 tablespoons light rum
5 egg yolks
5 egg whites
1/2 cup whipping cream
2 teaspoons sugar
2 teaspoons ground almonds
2 tablespoons coffee liqueur

Combine chocolate chips, water and instant coffee in top of double boiler; mix well. Cook over medium heat, until chocolate melts. Stir in rum; let cool slightly. Beat egg yolks into chocolate mixture. Beat egg whites in small mixer bowl until soft peaks form. Fold into chocolate mixture. Pour into 8 pot de crème cups with lids or any small cups with covers. Chill until serving time. Beat whipping cream in small mixer bowl until soft peaks form. Add sugar, beat until stiff peaks form. Stir in almonds and coffee liqueur. Serve with pot de crème. Yield: 8 servings.

Gayle Lacy Crawford, Preceptor Iota Psi
Covina, California

EASY CHOCOLATE MOUSSE

6 tablespoons strong coffee
4 tablespoons Cognac
8 ounces semisweet chocolate chips
1/4 cup sugar
1/4 teaspoon vanilla extract
2 cups whipping cream, whipped
1 tablespoon sugar

Heat coffee and Cognac in top of double boiler over hot water. Add chocolate chips and 1/4 cup sugar, stirring until glossy. Stir in vanilla. Remove from heat. Let stand until cool. Beat whipping cream in large mixer bowl until soft peaks form. Add 1 tablespoon sugar; beat until stiff peaks form. Fold chocolate mixture into whipped cream mixture. Chill until serving time. Yield: 8 servings.

Margie Wentz, Laureate Gamma
Great Falls, Montana

✣ CHOCOLATE MOUSSE SURPRISE

1 1/2 cups crushed cornflakes
3 tablespoons honey
8 ounces light cream cheese, softened
1 cup confectioners' sugar
16 ounces light whipped topping
3 cups skim milk
2 (4-ounce) packages sugar-free, fat-free chocolate fudge instant pudding mix
1/2 cup fat-free fudge topping
Semisweet chocolate chips to taste

Preheat oven to 350 degrees. Press mixture of cornflakes and honey into bottom of 9-by-13-inch glass baking dish sprayed with nonstick cooking spray. Bake at 350 degrees for 10 minutes. Let stand until cool. Beat cream cheese and confectioners' sugar in mixer bowl until smooth. Fold in 8 ounces whipped topping. Beat skim milk and pudding mix in medium mixer bowl until thickened. Fold into cream cheese mixture. Spoon over baked layer. Spoon dollops of fudge topping over the top. Spread with remaining 8 ounces whipped topping. Sprinkle with chocolate chips. Chill 2 to 4 hours before serving. Yield: 12 servings.

Joan L. Collins, Xi Alpha Xi
Mt. Airy, Maryland

MILLE FILLE

30 whole graham crackers
1 (6-ounce) package vanilla pudding mix
2 cups whipping cream, whipped
1 cup confectioners' sugar
2 to 3 tablespoons butter or margarine
1/2 teaspoon vanilla extract
3 to 4 ounces unsweetened chocolate, melted

Layer 15 graham crackers in bottom of 9-by-13-inch baking pan. Prepare pudding using package directions. Layer pudding, whipped cream and remaining graham crackers over the top. Spread beaten mixture of confectioners' sugar, butter and vanilla over crackers. Drizzle with melted chocolate.
Yield: 12 to 18 servings.

Susan Hevesy, Preceptor Alpha Sigma
Kitchener, Ontario, Canada

CHOCOLATE ECLAIR TORTES

1/2 cup butter
1 cup water
1 cup all-purpose flour
4 eggs
2 (4-ounce) packages vanilla instant pudding mix
2 1/4 cups milk
8 ounces whipped topping
1/4 cup semisweet chocolate chips
2 tablespoons margarine
2 tablespoons milk
1 cup confectioners' sugar
1 teaspooon vanilla extract

Preheat oven to 400 degrees. Bring butter and water to a boil in small saucepan. Stir in flour. Beat for 1 minute over low heat. Beat in eggs 1 at a time until smooth. Drop by 2 tablespoonful-size portions onto nonstick baking sheets. Bake at 400 degrees for 35 minutes. Let stand until cool. Split horizontally and fill with beaten mixture of pudding mix, 2 1/4 cups milk and whipped topping. Combine chocolate chips, margarine, 2 tablespoons milk, confectioners' sugar and vanilla in small saucepan. Heat until smooth and well blended. Drizzle over top of tortes. Chill until serving time. Yield: 8 to 10 servings.

Suzie Locke, Xi Alpha Iota
Sioux City, Iowa

✣ KAHLUA FUDGE SAUCE

This recipe was given to me by a friend who worked in a local popular restaurant.

2 1/2 pounds chocolate, chopped
2 cups sugar
4 cups cream
2 cups unsalted butter or margarine, softened
1 cup light corn syrup
1/2 cup Kahlúa

Melt chocolate in top of double boiler. Add sugar and cream, blending well. Stir in butter, corn syrup and Kahlúa; mix well. Store in refrigerator.
Yield: 50 servings.

Vicki Whitt, Laureate Beta Omega
Bremerton, Washington

Nancy L. Barclay, Preceptor Gamma Nu, Pittsburgh, Pennsylvania, makes Banana Mousse by marinating 2 or 3 sliced bananas in 2 tablespoons dark rum and 1 teaspoon lemon juice for 1 hour, puréeing and folding in 1/2 cup whipped topping.

HOT FUDGE

1/3 cup baking cocoa
3/4 cup sugar
2/3 cup evaporated milk
1/3 cup light corn syrup
1/3 cup butter or margarine
1 teaspoon vanilla extract

Combine cocoa, sugar, evaporated milk and corn syrup in small saucepan. Cook over medium-high heat until boiling, stirring constantly. Boil for 1 minute. Remove from heat. Add butter and vanilla; mix well. Store in airtight container in refrigerator. Yield: 1 pint.

Barb Kaiser, Mu Sigma
Mt. Pleasant, Michigan

BUNUELOS (MEXICAN PUFF PASTRY)

2 cups all-purpose flour
1 teaspoon baking powder
1/2 teaspoon cinnamon
1 teaspoon butter or margarine, softened
1 egg
2 tablespoons sugar
1/2 cup milk
Vegetable oil for frying
Sugar and cinnamon to taste

Sift flour, baking powder and cinnamon into large mixer bowl. Add mixture of butter and egg. Add sugar dissolved in milk. Knead for 5 minutes. Let stand, covered, for 2 hours. Preheat oil in deep-fat fryer. Knead dough again. Shape dough into 1-inch balls. Place balls separately on cloth, stretching them as thin as possible. Fry in oil at 325 degrees 1 at a time until light brown on both sides; drain. Sprinkle with mixture of sugar and cinnamon while hot. Serve with vanilla ice cream, coffee, hot chocolate or tea. Yield: 3 dozen.

Sylvia M. Breitenbach, Preceptor Mu Tau
Austin, Texas

CREAM PUFFS

1/2 cup margarine
1 cup water
1 cup all-purpose flour
4 eggs
2 tablespoons melted margarine
1/4 cup cornstarch
3/4 cup sugar
1/2 teaspoon salt
2 cups milk
2 egg yolks, beaten
1 teaspoon vanilla extract

Preheat oven to 350 degrees. Bring 1/2 cup margarine and water to a boil in small saucepan. Add flour. Cook until thickened, stirring constantly. Remove from heat. Pour into large mixer bowl. Add eggs 1 at a time, mixing well after each addition. Drop 12 mounds of batter 1 1/2 inches apart onto greased baking sheet. Bake at 350 degrees for 35 to 45 minutes. Turn off oven. Let stand in oven 5 minutes. Remove to wire rack immediately. Cut slit in base of puffs to permit steam to escape. Combine melted margarine, cornstarch, sugar and salt in saucepan. Add milk gradually. Bring to a boil, stirring constantly. Stir a small amount of hot mixture into egg yolks. Stir egg yolks and vanilla into hot mixture. Cook for 2 minutes, stirring constantly. Remove from heat. Let stand until cool. Fill puffs with vanilla filling. Can use filling for pies or as pudding dessert. Yield: 12 servings.

Terry Branick, Omicron Psi
Russell, Kansas

CREAM PUFF PUDDING DESSERT

1/2 cup butter or margarine
1 cup boiling water
1 cup all-purpose flour
4 eggs
3 cups milk
16 ounces cream cheese, softened
3 (4-ounce) packages vanilla instant pudding mix
8 ounces whipped topping
1/4 cup chocolate syrup

Preheat oven to 350 degrees. Melt butter in boiling water in small saucepan. Add flour all at once. Cook for 1 minute or until mixture forms ball, stirring constantly. Remove from heat. Cool for 5 minutes. Add eggs 1 at a time, mixing well after each addition. Spread in greased 9-by-13-inch baking pan. Bake at 350 degrees for 35 minutes or until golden brown. Let stand until cool. Beat 1/2 cup milk and cream cheese in large mixer bowl for 2 minutes. Add pudding mix and remaining 2 1/2 cups milk. Beat on low speed for 2 minutes. Fold in whipped topping. Spread over baked layer. Drizzle with chocolate syrup. Yield: 20 servings.

Lauri Ann Kraft, Xi Alpha Omega
Story, Wyoming

CREAM PUFF DESSERT

1 cup all-purpose flour
1/2 cup low-fat margarine, softened
1 1/4 cups water
1/2 cup margarine
1 cup all-purpose flour
3 eggs
1 teaspoon almond extract

Preheat oven to 350 degrees. Combine 1 cup flour, 1/2 cup margarine and 1/4 cup water in bowl. Divide into 2 portions. Press each portion into 5x15-inch rectangle in baking pan. Combine remaining 1 cup water, 1/2 cup margarine and 1 cup flour in saucepan. Cook until mixture leaves side of pan, stirring constantly. Let stand to cool. Add eggs 1 at a time, beating well after each addition. Stir in almond extract. Spread on rectangles. Bake at 350 degrees for 1 hour. May drizzle with confectioners' sugar icing and pecans or serve plain with ice cream on top. Yield: 10 to 15 servings.

Jackie Rohrke, Xi Epsilon Delta
Topeka, Kansas

CREAM PUFF TREAT

1/2 cup margarine
1 cup water
1 cup all-purpose flour
4 eggs
1 (6-ounce) package vanilla instant pudding mix
3 cups milk
8 ounces cream cheese, softened
8 ounces whipped topping
Chocolate syrup to taste

Preheat oven to 400 degrees. Bring margarine and water to a boil in small saucepan. Add flour; mix well. Remove from heat; cool slightly. Add eggs 1 at a time, mixing well after each addition. Spread into greased 9-by-13-inch baking pan. Bake at 400 degrees for 30 minutes. Cool. Beat pudding mix, milk and cream cheese in large mixer bowl until smooth. Spoon over baked layer. Top with whipped topping. Drizzle with chocolate syrup. Chill until serving time. Store in refrigerator. Yield: 12 to 15 servings.

Diane Allred, Eta Omega
Colorado Springs, Colorado

EASY CREAM PUFFS

1 cup water
1/2 cup butter or margarine
1/4 teaspoon salt
1 cup all-purpose flour
4 eggs
1 (4-ounce) package vanilla instant pudding mix, prepared
1 cup chocolate frosting

Preheat oven to 400 degrees. Bring water, butter and salt to a boil in medium saucepan. Add flour; mix well. Reduce heat to medium. Add eggs 1 at a time, mixing well after each addition. Drop in 12 portions onto greased baking sheet. Bake at 400 degrees for 30 minutes. Reduce oven temperature to 350 degrees. Bake for 25 minutes. Remove to wire rack to cool completely. Cut off tops using serrated knife. Remove centers. Fill each with vanilla pudding. Replace tops. Spread with chocolate frosting. Yield: 12 servings.

Nancy L. East, Xi Kappa
Harrisonburg, Virginia

DESPERATION DESSERT

8 ounces cream cheese, softened
1 1/2 cups milk
1 (4-ounce) package vanilla instant pudding mix
1 baked (9-inch) pie shell
1 (21-ounce) can apple pie filling
Whipped cream to taste

Beat cream cheese in medium mixer bowl until smooth. Add milk gradually, beating until blended. Add pudding mix; mix well. Spoon into pie shell. Chill until slightly set. Spread pie filling over the top. Chill until serving time. Serve with whipped cream. Yield: 6 to 8 servings.

Virginia Miles, Laureate Gamma Theta
Rowland Heights, California

DIRT CAKE

8 ounces cream cheese, softened
1/2 cup margarine, softened
1 cup confectioners' sugar
2 (4-ounce) packages vanilla instant pudding mix
3 1/2 cups milk
8 ounces whipped topping
1 (20-ounce) package chocolate sandwich cookies, crushed

Beat cream cheese, margarine and confectioners' sugar in small mixer bowl until smooth; set aside. Mix pudding mix, milk and whipped topping in medium mixer bowl until smooth. Alternate layers of cookie crumbs, cream cheese mixture and pudding mixture in medium plastic flower pot, ending with cookie crumbs. Add flowers, gummy worms and plastic frog on top. Yield: 10 to 12 servings.

Denise Weaver, Mu Epsilon
Jefferson City, Missouri

HAZELNUT MERINGUE

4 egg whites
1 1/2 cups superfine sugar
2 to 3 drops vanilla extract
1 teaspoon vinegar
1 1/4 cups ground roasted hazelnuts
1 (8-ounce) package raspberries
1 cup whipping cream, whipped
1 tablespoon superfine sugar
Sifted confectioners' sugar to taste

Preheat oven to 350 degrees. Whisk egg whites in medium mixer bowl until soft peaks form. Add 1 1/2 cups sugar, 1 tablespoon at a time, beating until stiff peaks form. Add the vanilla, vinegar and hazelnuts, stirring gently. Spoon into 2 greased 8-inch round baking pans, spreading evenly. Bake at 350 degrees for 40 to 45 minutes or until firm. Loosen from edge of pans with sharp knife. Invert onto wire rack to cool. Reserve a few raspberries for garnish. Spread mixture of 2/3 of whipped cream, 1 tablespoon sugar and remaining raspberries between baked layers. Sprinkle confectioners' sugar over the top. Garnish with rosettes made with remaining whipped cream and reserved raspberries. Yield: 6 servings.

Katrina Sheppard, Lambda
Lincoln, Nebraska

Susan Edwardson, Preceptor Upsilon, Red Oak, Iowa, makes Molded Piña Colada by softening 1 envelope unflavored gelatin in 1/2 cup pineapple juice and heating until dissolved. Beat 8 ounces cream cheese until fluffy, beat in gelatin and 1 cup cream of coconut. Chill until thickened, fold in 2 cups whipped cream and spoon into mold. Chill until firm.

NONFAT FROZEN DELIGHT

1 cup chunky applesauce
1 (10-ounce) package frozen strawberries, thawed
1 (10-ounce) package frozen raspberries, thawed
1 (11-ounce) can mandarin oranges, drained
1 cup seedless grapes
2 tablespoons frozen orange juice concentrate, thawed

Combine applesauce, strawberries, raspberries, mandarin oranges, grapes and orange juice concentrate in large bowl; mix well. Spoon into eight individual 1/2-cup freezer containers. Freeze until firm. Let stand at room temperature 30 minutes before serving. Yield: 8 servings.

Mindy Wise, Delta Alpha
Lima, Ohio

BAKED FUDGE AND ICE CREAM

4 eggs
2 cups sugar
1 cup melted margarine
1/2 cup all-purpose flour
1/2 cup baking cocoa
2 teaspoons vanilla extract
1 cup chopped pecans

Preheat oven to 325 degrees. Cream eggs and sugar in large mixer bowl. Add margarine; mix well. Add sifted mixture of flour and baking cocoa. Stir in vanilla and pecans; mix well. Pour into greased 9-by-13-inch baking pan. Place baking pan in larger pan of water. Bake at 325 degrees for 1 hour. Spoon into serving bowls while warm. Top with ice cream. Yield: 20 servings.

Jeannette Reynolds, Zeta Gamma
Delhi, Louisiana

ECLAIR BARS

1/2 cup butter or margarine
1 cup water
1 cup all-purpose flour
4 eggs
1 (6-ounce) package vanilla instant pudding mix
8 ounces cream cheese, softened
3 cups milk
8 ounces whipped topping
1/4 cup chocolate syrup

Preheat oven to 425 degrees. Bring butter and water to a boil in small saucepan. Remove from heat. Add flour, stirring until dough forms a ball. Let stand until cool. Add eggs 1 at a time, mixing well after each addition. Spread in 10-by-15-inch pan. Bake at 425 degrees for 15 minutes. Reduce oven temperature to 350 degrees. Bake at 350 degrees for 20 minutes. Let stand until cool. Spread beaten mixture of pudding mix, cream cheese and milk over baked layer. Top with whipped topping. Drizzle with chocolate syrup. Yield: 8 to 12 servings.

Karen Preble, Beta Lambda
Hampden, Maine

ECLAIR RING

1 cup water
1/2 cup margarine
1/4 teaspoon salt
1 cup all-purpose flour
4 eggs
2 (4-ounce) packages vanilla instant pudding mix
2 1/2 cups milk
8 ounces whipped topping
2 teaspoons light corn syrup
2 packages Nestlé Choco Bake unsweetened baking chocolate
1 teaspoon vanilla extract
3 tablespoons butter or margarine, softened
1 1/2 cups confectioners' sugar
3 tablespoons milk

Preheat oven to 400 degrees. Bring water, margarine and salt to a boil in small saucepan. Remove from heat. Add flour and eggs 1 at a time, mixing well after each addition. Spread in a circle on round nonstick pizza pan. Bake at 400 degrees for 20 to 25 minutes. Let stand until cool. Split into 2 layers horizontally. Beat pudding mix and 2 1/2 cups milk in medium mixer bowl. Fold in whipped topping. Spread between baked layers. Combine corn syrup, unsweetened chocolate, vanilla, butter, confectioners' sugar and 3 tablespoons milk in bowl; beat well. Spread over top. Yield: 12 servings.

Jean E. Saveraid
Huxley, Iowa

EASY DELIGHT

1 (16-ounce) package chocolate cookies
1 cup 2% milk
16 ounces whipped topping
Chocolate shavings, cherries or strawberries to taste

Layer chocolate cookies dunked in milk alternately with whipped topping in 9-by-13-inch baking dish, ending with whipped topping. Chill for 12 hours before serving. Garnish with chocolate shavings, cherries or strawberries before serving.
Yield: 8 to 12 servings.

Norris J. King, Preceptor Alpha Phi
Kinston, North Carolina

LEMON LUSH

1/2 cup margarine, softened
1 cup all-purpose flour
3/4 cup chopped pecans
1 cup confectioners' sugar
8 ounces cream cheese, softened
12 ounces whipped topping
2 (4-ounce) packages lemon instant pudding mix
3 cups milk

Preheat oven to 350 degrees. Press mixture of margarine, flour and 1/2 cup pecans in bottom of 9-by-13-inch baking pan. Bake at 350 degrees for 15 minutes. Let stand until cool. Beat confectioners' sugar, cream cheese and 8 ounces whipped topping in large mixer bowl until smooth. Add mixture of pudding mix and milk; mix well. Spread over baked layer. Top with remaining 4 ounces whipped topping and 1/4 cup pecans. Yield: 10 to 15 servings.

Kathy Hedrick, Xi Epsilon Beta
Mt. Jackson, Virginia

✣ LEMON MERINGUE DESSERT

1/2 cup melted margarine
1 (2-layer) package yellow cake mix
1 egg
1 1/3 cups sugar
1/2 cup cornstarch
Salt to taste
1 3/4 cups water
4 egg yolks, lightly beaten
2 tablespoons margarine
2 tablespoons grated lemon rind
1/2 cup lemon juice
4 egg whites
1/4 teaspoon cream of tartar
1/2 cup sugar

Preheat oven to 350 degrees. Press mixture of 1/2 cup margarine, cake mix and 1 egg into bottom of greased 9-by-13-inch baking pan. Combine 1 1/3 cups sugar, cornstarch and salt in medium saucepan. Add water gradually, stirring until smooth. Bring mixture to a boil over medium heat, stirring constantly. Remove from heat. Mix half of hot mixture into egg yolks in small bowl. Return egg mixture to saucepan. Cook until bubbly and thick. Remove from heat. Stir in 2 tablespoons margarine, lemon rind and lemon juice. Pour over cake mix mixture. Beat egg whites and cream of tartar in small mixer bowl until soft peaks form. Add 1/2 cup sugar, beating until stiff peaks form. Spread over lemon mixture. Bake at 350 degrees for 25 to 30 minutes. Let stand to cool for 1 hour. Chill, covered, for 1 hour before serving.
Yield: 10 to 12 servings.

Marlene Sharp, Xi Master
Coos Bay, Oregon

NO-BAKE LEMON SOUFFLE

2 envelopes unflavored gelatin
1/2 cup water
6 eggs, at room temperature
1 cup (about) sugar
1 1/2 tablespoons grated lemon rind
2/3 cup fresh lemon juice
2 cups whipping cream, whipped, chilled
Lemon wedges to taste

Soften gelatin in water for 10 minutes in small saucepan. Heat over very low heat until mixture becomes clear. Remove from heat. Let stand until cool. Beat eggs and enough sugar to sweeten to your taste in large mixer bowl for 10 to 15 minutes or until thickened. Add lemon rind, lemon juice and gelatin mixture to egg mixture, beating until well blended. Chill in refrigerator for 5 minutes, stirring every 1 minute to check for thickness. Fold in 1 1/2 cups whipped cream with rubber spatula just until blended. Pour into 4-cup soufflé dish. Chill, covered, for 8 to 12 hours. Garnish with remaining 1/2 cup whipped cream and lemon wedges. Editors Note: Because these eggs are not cooked, the editor recommends that, for safety, cooks should substitute pasteurized egg substitute for fresh eggs.
Yield: 10 to 12 servings.

Lisa J. Kurth, Mu Eta
San Antonio, Texas

LEMON FLUFF

1 (14-ounce) can sweetened condensed milk
1 (3-ounce) package lemon gelatin
1 3/4 cups hot water
1/4 cup lemon juice
1 cup sugar
2 1/2 cups vanilla wafer crumbs
12 maraschino cherries

Chill unopened can of condensed milk in refrigerator for 4 hours. Dissolve lemon gelatin in hot water in large mixer bowl. Chill until partially set. Whip until light and fluffy. Add lemon juice and sugar gradually; mix well. Whip chilled condensed milk in small mixer bowl. Fold into gelatin mixture. Line bottom of 9-by-13-inch dish with 2 cups of vanilla wafer crumbs. Spoon gelatin mixture over the top. Sprinkle with remaining 1/2 cup vanilla wafer crumbs. Chill in refrigerator until firm. Cut into squares. Garnish each square with 1 maraschino cherry.
Yield: 12 servings.

Mary Ann Mietty, Xi Lambda Sigma
Painesville, Ohio

LEMON SWIRL

1 (3-ounce) package lemon gelatin
1/2 cup boiling water
1 teaspoon grated lemon rind
1 cup sugar
1/4 cup lemon juice
1 (14-ounce) can evaporated milk, chilled
1/2 cup sugar
3 tablespoons melted butter or margarine
14 graham crackers, crushed

Dissolve gelatin in boiling water in large bowl. Add lemon rind, 1 cup sugar and lemon juice; mix well. Whip evaporated milk in small mixer bowl. Fold into lemon mixture. Press mixture of 1/2 cup sugar, butter and graham cracker crumbs into buttered 9-inch pie pan, reserving 2 teaspoons of crumb mixture. Spoon lemon mixture over graham cracker crumb mixture. Sprinkle with reserved crumbs. Chill 8 to 12 hours before serving. Yield: 6 to 8 servings.

Mary Kane, Preceptor Xi
Baxter Springs, Kansas

REFRIGERATOR MISSISSIPPI MUD PIE

3/4 cup melted margarine
1 1/2 cups all-purpose flour
1 cup chopped pecans
12 ounces whipped topping
8 ounces light cream cheese, softened
1 cup confectioners' sugar
1 (4-ounce) package vanilla instant pudding mix
1 (4-ounce) package chocolate instant pudding mix
1 teaspoon vanilla extract
2 1/2 cups skim milk

Preheat oven to 350 degrees. Press mixture of margarine, flour and 1/2 cup pecans in 9-by-13-inch baking dish. Bake at 350 degrees for 20 minutes. Let stand until cool. Beat 6 ounces whipped topping, cream cheese and confectioners' sugar in small mixer bowl at medium speed until blended. Spread over baked layer. Chill in refrigerator for 15 minutes. Beat pudding mixes, vanilla and milk in medium mixer bowl at low speed. Spread over cream cheese mixture. Whip remaining whipped topping with wire whisk. Spread over pudding mixture. Sprinkle with remaining 1/2 cup pecans. May garnish with semisweet chocolate chips or chocolate shavings.
Yield: 10 to 12 servings.

Kathleen Tafelski, Preceptor Epsilon Theta
Pinellas Park, Florida

MACAROON DESSERT

8 ounces macaroon cookies
1 envelope unflavored gelatin
1/4 cup cold water
4 cups milk
1 1/2 cups sugar
6 egg yolks
1 teaspoon vanilla extract
6 egg whites, beaten
Whipped cream to taste

Preheat oven to 350 degrees. Crumble cookies into 9-by-13-inch baking dish. Bake at 350 degrees until browned. Soften gelatin in water in small bowl. Bring milk to a boil in medium saucepan. Add sugar, egg yolks, vanilla and gelatin mixture. Cook over low heat for 3 minutes. Fold in beaten egg whites. Pour over cookie crumbs. Top with whipped cream. Chill for 8 to 12 hours before serving.
Yield: 10 servings.

Emma Irene Powell
Grants Pass, Oregon

MOON CAKE

1 cup water
1/2 cup margarine
1 cup all-purpose flour
4 eggs
2 (4-ounce) packages French vanilla instant pudding mix, prepared
8 ounces cream cheese, softened
12 ounces whipped topping
1/4 cup chocolate syrup
1/2 cup slivered almonds

Preheat oven to 400 degrees. Bring water and margarine to a boil in small saucepan. Add flour, stirring until mixture forms a ball. Remove from heat. Add eggs 1 at a time, mixing well after each addition. Spread in 11-by-15-inch nonstick jelly roll pan. Bake at 400 degrees for 30 minutes. Let stand until cool. Combine prepared pudding and cream cheese in small mixer bowl. Spread over baked layer. Top with whipped topping. Drizzle with chocolate syrup. Sprinkle with almonds. Yield: 12 to 15 servings.

Diane Uken, Preceptor Alpha Chi
Harvard, Nebraska

NEOPOLITAN SLICE

20 graham crackers, crushed
1 tablespoon all-purpose flour
1/2 cup packed light brown sugar
1/2 cup melted margarine
1 (14-ounce) can sweetened condensed milk
2 cups finely grated coconut

Preheat oven to 350 degrees. Press mixture of graham cracker crumbs, flour, brown sugar and margarine into greased 8-by-8-inch baking pan. Bake at 350 degrees for 10 minutes. Spread mixture of condensed milk and coconut over baked layer. Bake at 350 degrees for 18 to 20 minutes. Spread with favorite butter icing. Chill for 12 to 24 hours before serving.
Yield: 16 servings.

Ruth Kahler, Preceptor Omicron
Calgary, Alberta, Canada

CREAM-FILLED CHOCOLATE COOKIE DESSERT

30 cream-filled chocolate cookies, crushed
1/4 cup melted butter or margarine
3/4 cup creamy peanut butter
2 cups confectioners' sugar
1 cup milk
8 ounces cream cheese, softened
16 ounces whipped topping

Mix 1/2 of the cookie crumbs and butter in bowl. Press in bottom of 9-by-13-inch baking pan. Combine peanut butter, confectioners' sugar, milk, cream cheese and whipped topping in medium mixer bowl until smooth. Spread in prepared pan. Top with remaining half of cookie crumbs. Freeze, covered, until firm. Yield: 15 servings.

Becky Moorman, Xi Gamma Omega
Lima, Ohio

JIMMY CARTER CAKE

2/3 cup chopped peanuts
1 cup all-purpose flour
1/4 cup melted butter or margarine
1/3 cup peanut butter
1 cup confectioners' sugar
8 ounces cream cheese, softened
12 ounces whipped topping
1 (4-ounce) package vanilla instant pudding mix
1 (4-ounce) package chocolate instant pudding mix
1 chocolate candy bar, grated

Preheat oven to 325 degrees. Press mixture of peanuts, flour and butter in 9-by-13-inch baking pan. Bake at 325 degrees for 15 minutes. Let stand until cool. Beat peanut butter, confectioners' sugar, cream cheese and 8 ounces of the whipped topping in medium mixer bowl until smooth. Spread over baked layer. Prepare puddings in separate small mixer bowls using package directions. Layer vanilla pudding and chocolate pudding over cream cheese mixture. Top with remaining whipped topping. Garnish with grated chocolate. Yield: 8 servings.

Rod (Crystal) Carle
Westbank, British Columbia, Canada

ONE-TWO-THREE DELIGHT

1 cup all-purpose flour
1/2 cup melted butter
1 1/4 cups chopped pecans
8 ounces cream cheese, softened
1 cup confectioners' sugar
12 ounces whipped topping
2 (4-ounce) packages any flavor instant pudding mix
3 cups milk

Preheat oven to 325 degrees. Press mixture of flour, butter and 1 cup of the pecans into 9-by-13-inch baking dish. Bake at 325 degrees for 20 minutes. Let stand until cool. Beat cream cheese, confectioners' sugar and 8 ounces of the whipped topping in small mixer bowl. Spread over baked layer. Spread beaten mixture of pudding mix and milk over cream cheese layer. Top with remaining whipped topping. Sprinkle with remaining pecans. Yield: 15 servings.

Kristy Mankel, Beta Zeta Ometa
Euless, Texas

PEACHES AND CREAM SUPREME

1 cup unbleached all-purpose flour
1/2 cup unsalted butter, softened
3 tablespoons confectioners' sugar
8 ounces sour cream
2 ounces cream cheese, softened
1 egg yolk
3 tablespoons sugar
1 cup whipping cream, whipped
1 (16-ounce) can sliced peaches in heavy syrup
2 envelopes unflavored gelatin
Additional sliced peaches
Maraschino cherries

Preheat oven to 350 degrees. Blend flour, butter and confectioners' sugar in small bowl. Shape into a ball. Spread in bottom of medium-size springform pan. Bake at 350 degrees for 30 minutes. Let stand until cool. Beat sour cream, cream cheese, egg yolk and sugar in small mixer bowl until smooth. Fold whipped cream into sour cream mixture. Drain peaches, reserving syrup. Chop peaches. Soften gelatin in 1/2 cup cold water. Heat reserved syrup and gelatin in small saucepan until gelatin dissolves. Add to sour cream mixture; mix well. Stir in peaches. Pour over baked layer. Chill in refrigerator until set. Garnish with additional peach slices or maraschino cherries. Yield: 8 to 12 servings.

Betty Ozark, Xi Zeta Epsilon
Kalamazoo, Michigan

HAWAIIAN DREAM DESSERT

1 (2-layer) package yellow cake mix
16 ounces cream cheese, softened
3 tablespoons sugar
1 cup milk
2 (4-ounce) packages vanilla instant pudding mix
3 cups milk
1 (20-ounce) can crushed pineapple, drained
12 ounces whipped topping
1/2 cup chopped pecans or 3/4 cup toasted coconut

Prepare and bake cake mix using package directions for 12-by-18-inch baking pan. Beat cream cheese and sugar in mixer bowl until creamy. Beat in 1 cup milk until smooth. Beat pudding mix with 3 cups milk until thick and smooth. Stir in cream cheese mixture. Spread over baked layer. Layer pineapple and whipped topping over the top. Sprinkle with pecans. Chill for several hours before serving.
Yield: 24 servings.

Marjorie Teter, Beta Upsilon
Warrensburg, Missouri

DELICIOUS ANGEL FOOD DESSERT

1 angel food cake, torn into pieces
2 (4-ounce) packages vanilla or chocolate pudding and pie filling, prepared, cooled
1 (8-ounce) can crushed pineapple, drained
12 ounces whipped topping
1/2 cup chopped nuts (optional)

Arrange cake pieces in bottom of 9-by-13-inch dish. Spread pudding on top. Combine pineapple and whipped topping in bowl; mix well. Spoon over top. Chill until set. Sprinkle with nuts. Yield: 15 servings.

Evelyn Davis, Laureate Gamma Mu
Jacksonville, Florida

POPPY SEED TORTE

2 cups graham cracker crumbs
1/2 cup melted butter or margarine
2 tablespoons sugar
1/3 cup sugar
3 tablespoons cornstarch
2 cups milk
8 egg yolks
1/2 cup poppy seeds
2 envelopes unflavored gelatin
1/2 cup cold water
8 egg whites
1 1/2 teaspoons cream of tartar
1/2 cup sugar
2 cups whipped cream (optional)
1/2 cup flaked coconut (optional)

Combine crumbs, butter and 2 tablespoons sugar in bowl; mix until crumbly. Press into 9-by-13-inch dish. Combine 1/3 cup sugar and cornstarch in double boiler over hot water. Add milk and egg yolks; mix well. Cook until thickened and of custard consistency or until mixture coats back of spoon. Remove from heat. Stir in poppy seeds. Soften gelatin in cold water in bowl; stir into milk mixture. Spoon over crumb layer. Chill for 4 to 6 hours or until thick around edges. Beat egg whites and cream of tartar in mixer bowl until soft peaks form. Add 1/2 cup sugar gradually; beat until stiff peaks form. Spread over custard layer. Chill for 4 hours or longer. Top with whipped cream and sprinkle with coconut before serving. Yield: 12 to 15 servings.

Mary Bartkowiak, Epsilon Beta
Brookfield, Wisconsin

PUMPKIN CHIFFON

1 3/4 cups graham cracker crumbs
1/4 cup sugar
1/2 cup melted butter or margarine
8 ounces cream cheese, softened
2 eggs, beaten
3/4 cup sugar
2 (4-ounce) packages French vanilla instant pudding
1 3/4 cups milk
1 (21-ounce) can pumpkin
1/4 teaspoon cinnamon
8 ounces whipped topping
1/2 cup chopped pecans

Preheat oven to 350 degrees. Combine crumbs, 1/4 cup sugar and butter in bowl; mix until crumbly. Press into greased 9-by-13-inch baking dish; set aside. Combine cream cheese, eggs and 3/4 cup sugar in mixer bowl; beat until light and fluffy. Spread over crumb layer. Bake at 350 degrees for 20 minutes. Cool completely. Combine pudding mix and milk in mixer bowl; beat until thick. Add pumpkin and cinnamon; mix well. Reserve 1/4 cup of the whipped topping. Fold in remaining whipped topping. Spread over baked layer. Spread with reserved whipped topping. Sprinkle with pecans. Yield: 15 servings.

Patty Bruce, Laureate Alpha Alpha
Charleston, West Virginia

PUMPKIN CRUNCH

1 (21-ounce) can pumpkin
4 eggs
1 cup sugar
1 (12-ounce) can evaporated milk
2 teaspoons pumpkin pie spice
1 (2-layer) package yellow cake mix
1 1/2 cups chopped walnuts
1 cup melted butter or margarine
8 ounces cream cheese, softened
1/2 cup confectioners' sugar
1 cup whipped topping
1 1/2 teaspoons vanilla extract
Whole walnut pieces
Nutmeg

Preheat oven to 350 degrees. Combine pumpkin, eggs, sugar, evaporated milk and pumpkin pie spice in large mixer bowl; beat until blended. Spoon into waxed paper-lined 9-by-13-inch baking pan. Sprinkle with cake mix and walnuts. Drizzle melted butter over top. Bake at 350 degrees for 1 hour. Cool for 20 to 30 minutes or until almost completely cool. Invert onto serving platter; remove waxed paper. Cool completely. Combine cream cheese, confectioners' sugar, whipped topping and vanilla in bowl; mix until blended. Spread evenly over top of baked layer. Chill for 4 hours or longer; flavor is enhanced when chilled for at least 8 hours. Garnish with whole walnuts and nutmeg. Yield: 10 to 12 servings.

Katherine Furey, Xi Phi Chi
Yorba Linda, California

PUMPKIN PIE SQUARES

1 cup sifted all-purpose flour
1/2 cup quick-cooking oats
1/2 cup packed light brown sugar
1/2 cup butter or margarine, softened
2 cups pumpkin
1 (12-ounce) can evaporated milk
2 eggs
3/4 cup packed light brown sugar
1/2 teaspoon salt
1 teaspoon pumpkin pie spice
1/2 cup packed light brown sugar
2 tablespoons butter or margarine
1/2 cup chopped pecans

Preheat oven to 350 degrees. Combine flour, oats, 1/2 cup brown sugar and 1/2 cup butter in mixer bowl; beat until crumbly. Press into ungreased 9-by-13-inch baking dish. Bake at 350 degrees for 15 minutes. Combine pumpkin, evaporated milk, eggs, 3/4 cup brown sugar, salt and pumpkin pie spice in bowl; beat until blended. Spread over hot crust. Bake for 20 minutes. Sprinkle with mixture of 1/2 cup brown sugar, 2 tablespoons butter and pecans. Bake for 15 to 20 minutes longer. Cool completely. Cut into squares. Serve with whipped cream. Yield: 15 servings.

Pat Riach, Epsilon Xi
Page, Arizona

PUMPKIN SUPREME

1 3/4 cups graham cracker crumbs
1 cup sugar
1/2 cup melted margarine
2 eggs, beaten
3/4 cup sugar
8 ounces cream cheese, softened
3/4 cup milk
2 (4-ounce) packages vanilla instant pudding mix
2 cups canned pumpkin
Cinnamon and nutmeg to taste
12 ounces whipped topping
Chopped pecans

Preheat oven to 350 degrees. Combine crumbs, 1 cup sugar and margarine in bowl; mix until crumbly. Press into greased 9-by-13-inch baking dish. Combine eggs, 3/4 cup sugar and cream cheese in mixer bowl; beat until light and fluffy. Spread over crumb layer. Bake at 350 degrees for 20 minutes. Cool completely. Combine milk and pudding mix in bowl; mix well. Add pumpkin and spices; mix until blended. Fold in 1 cup whipped topping. Spread over cream cheese layer. Cover with remaining whipped topping. Garnish with pecans. Yield: 24 servings.

Beth Roberson, Beta Kappa
Meeteetse, Wyoming

SPECIAL-OCCASION TORTE

This dessert is present at all christenings, confirmations and birthdays in our family.

3 cups milk
8 tablespoons cream of wheat
1 cup butter or margarine, softened
1 1/4 cups sugar
1 teaspoon vanilla extract
Food colorings
1 (16-ounce) package graham cracker squares
3 egg whites
3/4 cup confectioners' sugar
3/4 cup butter or margarine, softened
3/4 cup confectioners' sugar
1/3 cup baking cocoa
1 teaspoon vanilla extract

Combine milk and cream of wheat in saucepan. Bring to a boil. Cook until thickened, stirring frequently. Cool completely. Beat 1 cup butter in mixer bowl until light and fluffy. Add sugar; mix well. Fold in cream of wheat mixture a little at a time. Add 1 teaspoon vanilla; mix until blended. Divide batter into equal portions in 4 bowls. Add red food color to one portion, green to another, blue to a third and yellow to remaining bowl; mix well. Layer graham crackers and tinted fillings alternately in 9-by-13-inch dish until, all ingredients are used. Beat egg whites in small mixer bowl until soft peaks form. Add 3/4 cup confectioners' sugar gradually; mix until stiff peaks form. Beat 3/4 cup butter in separate bowl until creamy. Mix in 3/4 cup confectioners' sugar and baking cocoa. Stir in 1 teaspoon vanilla. Fold in egg white mixture. Frost tops of graham cracker squares. Yield: 24 servings.

Judy Suke, Delta Kappa
Mississauga, Ontario, Canada

TERRIFIC CREAM CHEESE TRIANGLES

This recipe was given to me by a special friend as a newcomer to Canada.

2 egg whites
16 ounces cream cheese, softened
1 cup confectioners' sugar
2 egg yolks
Butter or margarine to taste
1 teaspoon vanilla extract
1 tablespoon rum (optional)
42 tea cookies
2 tablespoons baking cocoa
Chocolate icing

Beat egg whites in mixer bowl until foamy. Chill until thickened. Cream cream cheese and confectioners' sugar in mixer bowl. Add egg yolks, butter and vanilla. Beat until light and fluffy. Beat in egg whites. Stir in rum. Divide batter into 2 equal portions. Arrange 21 tea cookies on foil in rows 3 across and 7 down. Top with cream cheese mixture using 1/2 of mixture. Sprinkle baking cocoa into remaining mixture; mix well. Layer 21 cookies on top. Top with chocolate cream cheese mixture. Fold each side of cookies on foil to meet in center, forming tent. Chill for 8 hours or longer. Remove to serving plate. Spread with chocolate icing. Slice and serve. Yield: 42 servings.

Elaine Goving, Xi Beta Tau
London, Ontario, Canada

TIRAMISU

3 egg yolks
1/2 cup sugar
1 cup espresso or strong coffee
2 tablespoons Cognac or brandy
1 cup shredded mascarpone cheese
3 egg whites
Sugar to taste
20 ladyfingers, toasted
2 tablespoons baking cocoa

Combine egg yolks, 1/2 cup sugar, 1 tablespoon expresso and cognac in large mixer bowl; beat until thickened and frothy. Add cheese; beat for 3 to 5 minutes longer or until smooth. Combine egg whites and sugar to taste in small mixer bowl; beat until stiff peaks form. Fold into cheese mixture gently. Dip ladyfingers into remaining espresso in flat dish. Alternate layers of ladyfingers, cheese mixture and baking cocoa in 8-by-8-inch serving dish until all ingredients are used. Top with additional sprinkling of baking cocoa. Chill for 1 hour before serving. Yield: 9 servings.

Vera Bacon, Preceptor Alpha Rho
Rochester, New York

BRICKLE BRACKEL ICE CREAM CRUMBLE

This dessert can be made ahead of time and kept for unexpected company.

2 cups all-purpose flour
1/2 cup rolled oats
1 cup chopped pecans
2 cups butter or margarine
1 (12-ounce) jar caramel ice cream topping
1 quart vanilla or brickle brackel ice cream

Preheat oven to 400 degrees. Combine flour, oats and pecans in bowl; toss to mix. Melt butter in saucepan over low heat. Stir into flour mixture. Pat onto greased 12-by-18-inch baking sheet. Bake at 400 degrees for 10 minutes. Crumble while hot. Pat 1/2 of the crumb mixture into 9-by-13-inch pan. Drizzle 1/2 of the caramel sauce on top. Slice ice cream. Arrange over crumb mixture in prepared pan. Sprinkle with remaining crumb mixture. Drizzle with remaining caramel sauce. Freeze until set. Remove from freezer a few minutes before serving.
Yield: 12 to 15 servings.

Betty Byatt, Master Tau
Stratford, Ontario, Canada

BUSTER BAR DESSERT

1 (16-ounce) package Oreo cookies, finely crushed
1/2 cup melted margarine
1/2 gallon vanilla ice cream, softened
1 to 1 1/2 cups salted peanuts
1 1/2 cups evaporated milk
2/3 cup melted semisweet chocolate chips
1/2 cup margarine
2 cups confectioners' sugar
1 teaspoon vanilla extract

Combine cookies and 1/2 cup melted margarine in bowl; mix until crumbly. Pat into greased 9-by-13-inch pan. Chill for 1 hour. Spoon ice cream over cookie mixture, covering completely. Sprinkle with peanuts. Freeze until set. Combine evaporated milk, chocolate chips and 1/2 cup margarine in saucepan. Bring to a boil. Reduce heat. Cook for 12 minutes over low heat, stirring frequently. Add confectioners' sugar and vanilla; mix until smooth. Remove from heat. Cool completely. Spread over ice cream layer. Sprinkle with additional peanuts. Freeze until ready to serve. Yield: 12 to 18 servings.

Jan Davis, Pi Iota
Shawnee, Kansas

Nikki Maloy, Phi, Moscow, Idaho, makes Instant Summer Treats by placing an ice cream sandwich on a dessert plate, adding sweetened sliced strawberries and a dollop of whipped topping.

BUTTERFINGER ICE CREAM

4 eggs
1 1/2 cups sugar
16 ounces whipped topping
3 cups whipping cream
2 cups half-and-half
2 tablespoons vanilla extract
1 (6-ounce) package vanilla instant pudding mix
6 large Butterfinger candy bars, crushed
Milk to taste

Beat eggs and sugar in mixer bowl until frothy. Add whipped topping, whipping cream and half-and-half; beat until thick and creamy. Beat in vanilla and pudding mix. Stir in crushed candy. Pour into 4-quart ice cream freezer container. Add milk to fill line. Freeze using manufacturer's directions. Let ripen for several hours or until set. Yield: 16 to 20 servings.

Gayla McAtee, Xi Epsilon Omega
Laverne, Oklahoma

CARAMEL ICE CREAM DESSERT

2 cups all-purpose flour
1/2 cup rolled oats
1/2 cup packed light brown sugar
1 cup melted margarine
1 cup chopped pecans
1 (12-ounce) jar caramel sauce or caramel ice cream topping
1/2 gallon vanilla ice cream

Preheat oven to 400 degrees. Combine flour, oats, brown sugar, margarine and pecans in bowl; mix until crumbly. Crumble onto greased 12-by-18-inch baking sheet. Bake at 400 degrees for 15 to 20 minutes or until golden brown. Press 1/2 of the crumb mixture into 9-by-13-inch pan. Reserve a small amount of caramel sauce for topping. Layer remaining caramel sauce and ice cream over top. Sprinkle with remaining crumbs. Freeze until ready to serve. Cut into squares. Top with additional caramel sauce. Yield: 24 to 36 servings.

Barbara Homer, Alpha Mu Xi
Groom, Texas

CREME DE MENTHE DESSERT

1 (16-ounce) package Oreo cookies, finely crushed
1/2 cup margarine
1/2 gallon vanilla ice cream, softened
1/2 cup crème de menthe liqueur

Combine cookie crumbs and margarine in bowl; mix until crumbly. Reserve a small amount of crumb mixture for topping. Pat remaining crumb mixture into greased 9-by-13-inch pan. Combine ice cream and crème de menthe in bowl; mix until blended. Spread over prepared crumb mixture. Sprinkle with reserved crumb mixture. Serve immediately or freeze. Yield: 15 servings.

Pat Skatlum, Preceptor Delta Delta
Olathe, Kansas

CHOCOLATE ICE CREAM BROWNIES

1 (22-ounce) package fudge brownie mix
1/2 gallon vanilla ice cream, softened
2 cups confectioners' sugar
2/3 cup semisweet chocolate chips
1 1/2 cups evaporated milk
1/2 cup margarine
1 teaspoon vanilla extract
1 1/2 cups chopped pecans or walnuts (optional)

Prepare and bake brownies using package directions for 9-by-13-inch baking pan. Cool in pan. Spread ice cream over brownies. Freeze until firm. Combine next 4 ingredients in saucepan. Bring to a boil over high heat. Reduce heat to medium. Cook for 8 minutes, stirring constantly. Remove from heat. Stir in vanilla and pecans; mix well. Cool in pan. Spread over ice cream. Freeze until firm. Remove from freezer 5 to 10 minutes before serving. Cut into squares. Yield: 12 to 15 servings.

Teresa Lewis, Xi Alpha Lambda
Whitesburg, Kentucky

DEEP-DISH BROWNIE SUNDAES

We often have guests for dessert nights. This is one of those favorites that becomes a great conversation piece and helps people become better acquainted.

3/4 cup margarine, softened
1 1/2 cups sugar
1 1/2 teaspoons vanilla extract
3 eggs
2/3 cup baking cocoa
3/4 cup plus 2 tablespoons all-purpose flour
1/2 teaspoon baking powder
1/2 teaspoon salt
1 1/2 cups semisweeet chocolate chips
Vanilla ice cream
Chocolate syrup
Peanuts

Preheat oven to 350 degrees. Combine margarine, sugar and vanilla in mixer bowl; beat until light and fluffy. Add eggs; mix until blended. Add mixture of next 4 ingredients; mix well. Stir in chocolate chips. Spoon into greased and floured 9-by-9-inch baking pan. Bake at 350 degrees for 40 to 45 minutes or until brownies test done. Do not overbake. Remove from oven. Top with vanilla ice cream. Drizzle with chocolate syrup. Sprinkle with peanuts. Yield: 16 servings.

Michelle Smith, Iota Tau
Buena Vista, California

Stephany Harper, Laureate Gamma Theta, Fullerton, California, makes Raspberry Applesauce Delight by mixing a small package of dry raspberry gelatin with 2 cups applesauce and alternating layers of the mixture with graham crackers. Frost with whipped topping and refrigerate for several hours to overnight.

DELICIOUS DRIZZLY DESSERT

1 1/2 cups butter or margarine
1 1/3 cups packed light brown sugar
3 1/2 cups crumbled Rice Chex cereal
1 1/3 cups flaked coconut
1 1/2 cups chopped pecans
1/2 gallon favorite flavor ice cream, softened
1 cup semisweet chocolate chips
1/2 cup butter or margarine
1 1/2 cups evaporated milk
2 cups confectioners' sugar
1 teaspoon vanilla extract

Combine 1 1/2 cups butter and brown sugar in saucepan. Cook over low heat until butter melts, stirring constantly. Add cereal, coconut and pecans; mix well. Press 1/2 of the cereal mixture into greased 9-by-13-inch dish. Freeze until firm. Spread with ice cream. Sprinkle remaining cereal mixture on top. Freeze until set. Melt chocolate chips with 1/2 cup butter in saucepan, stirring constantly. Add evaporated milk and confectioners' sugar; mix well. Bring to a boil. Cook for 8 minutes, stirring constantly. Stir in vanilla. Cut ice cream mixture into squares. Drizzle with hot chocolate syrup. Yield: 15 servings.

Verna Robertson, Xi Iota
Weatherford, Texas

PEANUT BUTTER ICE CREAM DRUMSTICK

1 1/2 cups graham cracker crumbs
1/2 cup crushed unsalted peanuts
1/4 cup melted butter or margarine
2 tablespoons peanut butter
8 ounces cream cheese, softened
1/2 cup sugar
1/2 cup peanut butter
1 teaspoon vanilla extract
3 eggs
16 ounces whipped topping
2 tablespoons plus 2 teaspoons chocolate sauce or fudge sundae sauce

Combine crumbs, peanuts, butter and 2 tablespoons peanut butter in bowl; mix until crumbly. Reserve 1/4 cup of the crumb mixture. Press remaining crumb mixture into greased 9-by-13-inch pan. Cream cream cheese, sugar and 1/2 cup peanut butter in mixer bowl until light. Add vanilla; mix well. Add eggs 1 at a time, beating after each addition. Add whipped topping; mix well. Spread over prepared crumb layer. Drizzle with chocolate sauce. Swirl with knife to marbleize. Sprinkle with reserved crumbs. Freeze until set. Thaw before serving. Yield: 15 servings.

Tracey Fieber, Sigma
Estevan, Saskatchewan, Canada

CHOCOLATE LAYERED DESSERT

I brought this recipe to a friend's party. She liked it so well that she took it to another party and also to a family get-together. Her mom liked it so much that she made it for a school party. This dessert has made its rounds in our town!

1 (16-ounce) package vanilla wafers, crushed
1/2 cup melted butter or margarine
1/2 cup ground pecans
1/4 cup sugar
2 cups confectioners' sugar
1 cup butter or margarine, softened
1/2 teaspoon vanilla extract
6 egg yolks
3 ounces unsweetened chocolate, melted
6 egg whites, beaten
1/2 gallon vanilla ice cream, softened

Preheat oven to 400 degrees. Combine crumbs, 1/2 cup melted butter, pecans and sugar in bowl. Press 1/2 of the mixture into greased 9-by-13-inch baking pan. Bake at 400 degrees for 15 minutes. Cool completely. Cream confectioners' sugar, 1 cup butter and vanilla in mixer bowl until light and fluffy. Add egg yolks and chocolate; mix well. Fold in egg whites. Spread 1/2 of the chocolate mixture over crumb layer. Chill until firm. Spread ice cream over chocolate layer. Freeze until set. Drizzle remaining chocolate and sprinkle remaining crumb mixture over top. May make 1/2 of recipe and use 9-by-9-inch pan. Yield: 10 to 12 servings.

Beth Chamberlain, Lambda Alpha
Tuscola, Illinois

FROZEN CREAM CUPS WITH FRUIT

8 ounces cream cheese, softened
1 cup confectioners' sugar
1 cup light cream
1/2 teaspoon vanilla extract
Strawberry juice
2 cups fresh or frozen strawberries

Beat cream cheese in mixer bowl until smooth. Add confectioners' sugar gradually; mix until light and fluffy. Beat in cream and vanilla. Will make thin mixture. Fill fluted paper-lined muffin cups to top. Freeze for 2 hours or until firm. Remove paper liners. Arrange on serving dishes. Let stand until softened. Spoon strawberry juice on top. Top with strawberries. Spoon strawberries around base. May substitute raspberries, blueberries, peaches or mixed fruit for strawberries. Yield: 8 to 10 servings.

Marilyn R. Mulhall, Alpha Master
Nashville, Tennessee

ICE CREAM CAKE

2 to 2 1/2 cups crushed butter crackers
1/2 cup melted butter or margarine
2 (4-ounce) packages butter pecan instant pudding mix
1 cup milk
1/2 gallon butter pecan ice cream, softened
16 ounces whipped topping

Combine cracker crumbs and butter in bowl; mix until crumbly. Press into 9-by-13-inch pan. Freeze for 10 minutes. Prepare pudding in large bowl using package directions, using milk. Add ice cream; mix until blended. Spread ice cream mixture evenly over top of crumb layer. Freeze for 4 to 8 hours. Top with whipped topping before serving. Yield: 15 servings.

Kim Craft, Beta Kappa
Whitesburg, Kentucky

ICE CREAM ROLL

1/2 cup all-purpose flour
1 teaspoon baking powder
1/4 teaspoon salt
4 egg yolks
1/2 teaspoon vanilla extract
1/3 cup sugar
4 egg whites
Confectioners' sugar to taste
Peppermint ice cream to taste, softened
12 ounces whipped topping
1 peppermint candy cane, crushed
Chocolate syrup to taste

Preheat oven to 375 degrees. Combine flour, baking powder and salt in bowl; mix well. Beat egg yolks and vanilla in mixer bowl until thick. Add sugar; beat until sugar dissolves. Beat egg whites in mixer bowl until stiff peaks form. Fold egg yolk mixture into egg whites. Fold in flour mixture gently. Spoon into greased and floured jelly roll pan. Bake at 375 degrees for 12 to 15 minutes or until firm. Loosen from sides of pan. Remove to towel sprinkled with confectioners' sugar. Roll up with towel as for jelly roll. Let stand until cool. Unroll cake layer. Remove towel. Spread with ice cream. Re-roll cake. Freeze until ready to serve. Combine whipped topping and candy in bowl. Spread over top of cake roll and garnish with additional crushed candy and chocolate syrup before serving. Yield: 12 to 15 servings.

Tonya Mills, Alpha
Solomon, Kansas

Beth-Ann Jarvis, Alpha Iota, Sunrise, Florida, makes Frozen Banana Pops by melting a package of semisweet chocolate chips with 1 teaspoon vegetable oil, cutting peeled bananas in half crosswise, inserting popsicle sticks or wooden skewers in one end and dipping in the chocolate to cover. Place on waxed paper and freeze until firm.

LEMON DELIGHT

This is a tart, very light dessert.

Vanilla wafers
2 eggs
3 egg yolks
3/4 cup lemon juice
1 cup sugar
2 cups whipping cream, whipped
3 egg whites
Cream of tartar
1/4 cup confectioners' sugar

Line springform pan on bottom and side with vanilla wafers. Beat eggs and egg yolks in mixer bowl until frothy. Add lemon juice and sugar; mix well. Transfer to double boiler. Cook over hot water until thick, stirring constantly. Cool completely. Fold in whipped cream. Spoon into prepared pan. Preheat broiler. Beat egg whites until foamy. Add cream of tartar and confectioners' sugar. Beat until stiff peaks form. Spread over lemon layer. Brown until light brown. Freeze for 8 hours or longer. Remove from freezer 1 1/2 hours before serving. Yield: 6 servings.

Eugenia Richardson, Preceptor Laureate
Medicine Hat, Alberta, Canada

FROZEN LEMON DESSERT

1 1/2 cups graham cracker crumbs
4 egg whites
3/4 cup sugar
4 egg yolks
2 envelopes dry whipped topping mix
1 1/2 teaspoons grated lemon rind
1/2 cup (or more) lemon juice
Lemon twist

Reserve a small amount of crumbs for topping. Sprinkle remaining crumbs over bottom of greased 9-by-13-inch pan. Beat egg whites in mixer bowl until soft peaks form. Add sugar gradually, beating until stiff glossy peaks form. Beat egg yolks in small mixer bowl until frothy. Fold into egg white mixture. Prepare whipped topping using package directions. Fold into egg mixture. Add lemon rind and lemon juice; mix well. Spoon into prepared pan. Sprinkle with reserved crumbs. Freeze for 8 hours or longer. Garnish with lemon twist. Yield: 15 servings.

Pat Novak, Preceptor Beta Delta
Waukon, Iowa

PINK LEMONADE SQUARES

1/2 cup melted margarine
1/4 cup confectioners' sugar
60 butter crackers, crushed
2 envelopes dry whipped topping mix
1 (12-ounce) can frozen pink lemonade, thawed
1 (14-ounce) can sweetened condensed milk

Combine margarine and confectioners' sugar in bowl; mix well. Add crackers; mix until crumbly. Reserve 1/4 cup of crumb mixture. Press remaining crumb mixture into greased 9-by-13-inch pan. Prepare whipped topping in large mixer bowl using package directions. Add lemonade and condensed milk; beat until blended. Spread over crumb layer. Sprinkle with reserved crumbs. Freeze until firm. Cut into squares. Serve frozen. Yield: 24 servings.

Margie Nichol, Pi
Killarney, Manitoba, Canada

NEAPOLITAN FROZEN DESSERT

1 envelope dry whipped topping mix
1/2 cup cold milk
Red food coloring
2 tablespoons light rum
1 (6-ounce) package chocolate instant pudding mix
3/4 cup cold milk
1/3 cup sliced almonds
Green food coloring
2 tablespoons crème de menthe flavoring
2 cups vanilla ice cream, softened
1 envelope dry whipped topping mix
1/2 cup cold milk
Maraschino cherries or crushed candy to taste

Prepare 1 envelope whipped topping mix in bowl using package directions, using 1/2 cup milk. Mix in red food coloring until of desired color. Add rum; mix well. Spoon into 8-cup mold, leaving hollowed ring in center. Freeze until firm. Prepare pudding in bowl using package directions, using 3/4 cup milk. Stir in almonds. Spread inside pink layer, leaving center hollow. Freeze until firm. Combine green food coloring, crème de menthe flavoring and ice cream in bowl; mix well. Spoon into center of mold. Freeze, covered with plastic wrap, for 4 hours or longer. Unmold onto serving plate. Prepare 1 envelope whipped topping mix using package directions, using 1/2 cup milk. Spread over frozen dessert. Garnish with additional almonds, maraschino cherries or crushed candy. Yield: 8 to 10 servings.

Roberta Renvelle, Beta Omega
Kankakee, Illinois

OREO COOKIE DESSERT

1 (16-ounce) package Oreo cookies crumbled
1/4 cup melted butter or margarine
1/2 gallon vanilla ice cream
1 (5-ounce) jar fudge topping, heated
8 ounces whipped topping

Reserve 1/4 cup cookie crumbs for topping. Combine remaining crumb mixture and butter in bowl; mix until crumbly. Press into 9-by-13-inch dish. Layer with ice cream, hot fudge topping and whipped topping. Top with reserved crumbs. Freeze for 8 hours or longer. Yield: 15 servings.

Becky Castellari, Preceptor Delta
Centralia, Illinois

SPICED WALNUT BRITTLE

2 cups sugar
1/2 cup light corn syrup
1/4 cup water
2 tablespoons butter
1/2 teaspoon vanilla extract
1 teaspoon baking soda
1 teaspoon ground cinnamon
2 cups chopped walnuts

Combine sugar, corn syrup and water in 2-quart microwave-safe bowl. Microwave on High for 5 to 6 minutes or until boiling. Microwave for 6 to 10 minutes longer to 290 degrees on candy thermometer (hard-crack stage). Let bubbling stop. Stir in butter, vanilla, baking soda, cinnamon and walnuts. Pour onto buttered baking sheet; spread thinly immediately. Let stand until hard. Break into pieces.
Yield: 1 1/2 pounds.

Photograph for this recipe on cover.

CRANBERRY JEWEL BARS

2 cups all-purpose flour
1 1/2 cups rolled oats
3/4 cup packed light brown sugar
1 cup cold butter or margarine
1 (14-ounce) can sweetened condensed milk
1 cup ricotta cheese
2 eggs
1 1/2 teaspoons vanilla extract
1 teaspoon freshly grated orange rind
1 tablespoon light brown sugar
2 tablespoons cornstarch
1 (16-ounce) can whole cranberry sauce

Preheat oven to 350 degrees. Combine flour, oats and 3/4 cup brown sugar in bowl. Cut in butter until crumbly. Reserve 2 cups of the mixture. Press remaining mixture over bottom of 9-by-13-inch baking pan. Bake at 350 degrees for 15 minutes. Combine condensed milk, ricotta cheese, eggs, vanilla and orange rind in mixer bowl; beat until smooth. Spread evenly over baked layer. Combine remaining tablespoon brown sugar, cornstarch and cranberry sauce in bowl; mix well. Spoon over cheese layer. Sprinkle with reserved crumb mixture. Bake at 350 degrees for 40 minutes or until light brown. Let stand until cool. Cut into bars. Store, covered, in the refrigerator.
Yield: 36 to 40 bars.

Photograph for this recipe on cover.

FUDGE WALNUT WEDGES

1/2 cup butter or margarine
1 cup graham cracker crumbs
1 (14-ounce) can sweetened condensed milk
1 egg
1/2 cup baking cocoa
1 tablespoon all-purpose flour
1 cup chopped walnuts

Microwave butter in 9-inch microwave-safe pie plate on High for 1 minute or until butter is melted. Add crumbs; mix well. Press evenly over bottom of pie plate. Combine condensed milk, egg, cocoa and flour in bowl; mix well. Stir in half the walnuts. Pour over crumb layer. Sprinkle with remaining walnuts. Microwave on High for 4 1/2 minutes, turning 1/4 turn after each minute. Let stand until cool. Cut into small wedges. Serve with ice cream if desired.
Yield: 12 servings.

Photograph for this recipe on cover.

CHOCOLATE RIBBON CHEESECAKE

1 cup finely chopped walnuts
1 cup graham cracker crumbs
1/4 cup sugar
1/4 cup melted butter or margarine
1/3 cup baking cocoa
1/4 cup melted butter or margarine
24 ounces cream cheese, softened
1 (14-ounce) can sweetened condensed milk
3 eggs
1 tablespoon vanilla extract

Preheat oven to 300 degrees. Combine walnuts, crumbs, sugar and 1/4 cup melted butter in bowl; mix well. Press over bottom and 2 inches up side of 9-inch springform pan. Blend cocoa with 1/4 cup melted butter in small bowl; set aside. Beat cream cheese in mixer bowl until fluffy. Add condensed milk gradually, beating until smooth. Beat in eggs and vanilla. Reserve 1 1/2 cups of the mixture. Add chocolate mixture to the remaining mixture; beat well. Alternate layers of chocolate and vanilla mixture 1/2 at a time in prepared pan, ending with vanilla mixture. Cut through layers to marbleize. Bake at 300 degrees for 65 minutes or until set. Cool for 30 minutes. Loosen from side of pan with knife. Let stand until completely cool. Chill, covered, for several hours. Remove side of pan.
Yield: 10 to 12 servings.

Photograph for this recipe on cover.

CHOCOLATE WALNUT PIE

6 tablespoons butter or margarine
1/3 cup baking cocoa
1 (14-ounce) can sweetened condensed milk
1/2 cup water
2 eggs, beaten
1/2 teaspoon vanilla extract
1/2 teaspoon maple flavoring
1 cup coarsely chopped walnuts
1 unbaked (9-inch) pie shell

Preheat oven to 350 degrees. Melt butter in medium saucepan over low heat. Add cocoa; blend well. Stir in condensed milk, water and eggs; beat with wire whisk until well blended. Remove from heat; stir in vanilla, maple flavoring and walnuts. Pour into pie shell. Bake at 350 degrees for 40 to 45 minutes or until set. Serve warm or chilled. Refrigerate leftovers. Yield: 8 servings.

Photograph for this recipe on cover.

CHOCOLATE RASPBERRY POUND CAKE

1 (10-ounce) package frozen raspberries in light syrup, thawed
8 ounces whipped topping
2 tablespoons raspberry liqueur
3/4 cup seedless black raspberry preserves
2 cups all-purpose flour
1 1/2 cups sugar
3/4 cup baking cocoa
1 1/2 teaspoons baking soda
1 teaspoon salt
2/3 cup butter or margarine, softened
2 cups sour cream
2 eggs
1 teaspoon vanilla extract
1/4 cup seedless black raspberry preserves
Confectioners' sugar

Purée raspberries in blender or food processor; strain into bowl. Blend in whipped topping and liqueur. Chill raspberry cream until serving time. Preheat oven to 350 degrees. Grease and flour 12-cup fluted tube pan. Melt 3/4 cup preserves; cool. Combine flour, sugar, cocoa, baking soda and salt in large mixer bowl. Add butter, sour cream, eggs, vanilla and melted preserves. Beat at medium speed for 3 to 4 minutes or until well blended. Pour into prepared pan. Bake at 350 degrees for 50 to 60 minutes or until cake tests done. Cool in pan for 10 minutes. Remove to wire rack. Melt remaining 1/4 cup preserves. Brush over warm cake. Cool completely. Place on serving plate. Sprinkle with confectioners sugar just before serving. Fill cavity with raspberry cream.
Yield: 12 servings.

Photograph for this recipe on cover.

EASY PEANUT BUTTER COOKIES

1 (14-ounce) can sweetened condensed milk
3/4 cup peanut butter
2 cups baking mix
1 teaspoon vanilla extract
Sugar

Preheat oven to 375 degrees. Combine condensed milk and peanut butter in mixer bowl; beat until smooth. Add baking mix and vanilla; mix well. Shape into 1-inch balls; roll in sugar. Place 2 inches apart on ungreased cookie sheet; flatten with fork. Bake at 375 degrees for 6 to 8 minutes or until light brown; do not overbake. Cool on wire rack. Store, tightly covered, at room temperature. Yield: 5 dozen.

VARIATIONS

Peanut Blossoms: Prepare and shape as above but do not flatten. Press milk chocolate kiss into center of each cookie immediately after baking.

Peanut Butter and Jelly Gems: Prepare and shape as above but do not flatten. Press thumb into center of each ball; fill with jelly, jam or preserves. Bake as above.

Any-Way-You-Like'm Cookies: Add 1 cup semi-sweet chocolate chips or chopped peanuts or raisins or flaked coconut into dough. Shape and bake as above.

Photograph for this recipe on page 1.

SORBET AND CREAM FRUIT SALAD

1 cantaloupe
1 honeydew melon
1 Crenshaw melon
1 kiwifruit
1 head Bibb lettuce
1 cup blueberries
2 peaches, sliced
12 large strawberries
1 pint lime and cream sorbet
1 pint orange and cream sorbet

Peel and slice melons and kiwifruit. Arrange slices on Bibb lettuce-lined plates. Add blueberries and peach slices. Slice strawberries from tip to cap and open to form blossoms. Place small scoop of lime sorbet in center of each strawberry; arrange on plates. Add large scoop of orange sorbet to each plate. Yield: 4 servings.

Photograph for this recipe on page 2.

SORBET MARGARITA

1 pint lime and cream sorbet
3 tablespoons tequila (optional)
1 tablespoon triple sec (optional)
2 tablespoons lime juice
Lime slices

Combine sorbet, tequila, triple sec and lime juice in blender container. Process until smooth. Rub rims of 4 glasses with lime slices; pour in sorbet mixture. Garnish with additional lime slices. Yield: 4 servings.

Photograph for this recipe on page 2.

RASPBERRY FLOATING ISLAND

1/3 cup apricot nectar
1 tablespoon amaretto (optional)
1 1/2 pounds fresh apricots
1 pound cake
1 pint raspberry and cream sorbet
1 pint fresh raspberries
Mint leaves

Blend apricot nectar and amaretto. Peel apricots; discard pits. Combine apricots and 1/4 cup apricot nectar mixture in blender container; purée. Spoon 1/4 cup purée onto each of 4 dessert plates. Trim crust from cake; cut into 12 slices. Cut each slice into diamond; arrange 3 diamonds on each plate. Brush with remaining apricot mixture. Place large scoop sorbet on each plate. Garnish with raspberries and mint leaves. Yield: 4 servings.

Photograph for this recipe on page 2.

Metric Equivalents

Although the United States has opted to postpone converting to metric measurements, most other countries, including England and Canada, use the metric system. The following chart provides convenient approximate equivalents for allowing use of regular kitchen measures when cooking from foreign recipes.

Volume

These metric measures are approximate benchmarks for purposes of home food preparation.
1 milliliter = 1 cubic centimeter = 1 gram

Liquid		Dry	
1 teaspoon	= 5 milliliters	1 quart	= 1 liter
1 tablespoon	= 15 milliliters	1 ounce	= 30 grams
1 fluid ounce	= 30 milliliters	1 pound	= 450 grams
1 cup	= 250 milliliters	2.2 pounds	= 1 kilogram
1 pint	= 500 milliliters		

Weight

1 ounce	= 28 grams
1 pound	= 450 grams

Length

1 inch	= 2½ centimeters
1/16 inch	= 1 millimeter

Formulas Using Conversion Factors

When approximate conversions are not accurate enough, use these formulas to convert measures from one system to another.

Measurements	Formulas
ounces to grams:	# ounces x 28.3 = # grams
grams to ounces:	# grams x 0.035 = # ounces
pounds to grams:	# pounds x 453.6 = # grams
pounds to kilograms:	# pounds x 0.45 = # kilograms
ounces to milliliters:	# ounces x 30 = # milliliters
cups to liters:	# cups x 0.24 = # liters
inches to centimeters:	# inches x 2.54 = # centimeters
centimeters to inches:	# centimeters x 0.39 = # inches

Approximate Weight to Volume

Some ingredients which we commonly measure by volume are measured by weight in foreign recipes. Here are a few examples for easy reference.

flour, all-purpose, unsifted	1 pound = 450 grams = 3½ cups
flour, all-purpose, sifted	1 pound = 450 grams = 4 cups
sugar, granulated	1 pound = 450 grams = 2 cups
sugar, brown, packed	1 pound = 450 grams = 2¼ cups
sugar, confectioners'	1 pound = 450 grams = 4 cups
sugar, confectioners', sifted	1 pound = 450 grams = 4½ cups
butter	1 pound = 450 grams = 2 cups

Temperature

Remember that foreign recipes frequently express temperatures in Centigrade rather than Fahrenheit.

Temperatures	Fahrenheit	Centigrade
room temperature	68°	20°
water boils	212°	100°
baking temperature	350°	177°
baking temperature	375°	190.5°
baking temperature	400°	204.4°
baking temperature	425°	218.3°
baking temperature	450°	232°

Use the following formulas when temperature conversions are necessary.

Centigrade degrees x 9/5 + 32 = Fahrenheit degrees
Fahrenheit degrees - 32 x 5/9 = Centigrade degrees

American Measurement Equivalents

1 tablespoon = 3 teaspoons	12 tablespoons = ¾ cup
2 tablespoons = 1 ounce	16 tablespoons = 1 cup
4 tablespoons = ¼ cup	1 cup = 8 ounces
5 tablespoons + 1 teaspoon =⅓ cup	2 cups = 1 pint
8 tablespoons = ½ cup	4 cups = 1 quart
	4 quarts = 1 gallon

Merit Winners

BAKER'S PLEASURES
First Prize
Hackbarth, Sharon K., page 19
Second Prize
Voss, Katherine, page 37
Third Prize
Miller, Mary, page 46
QUICK PICK-ME-UPS
First Prize
Carey-Spark, Faith, page 68
Second Prize
Fitch, Marilyn, page 71
Third Prize
Wolfe, Phyllis, page 63
THE PIE'S THE LIMIT
First Prize
Hobson, Esther, page 106
Second Prize
Graybeal, Michelle, page 110
Third Prize
Swingley, Nancy, page 105
TEA TIME
First Prize
Lundy, Donna, page 135
Second Prize
Robinson, Shannon, page 144
Third Prize
Broadwater, Dorothy M., page 145
FRUITY DELIGHTS
First Prize
Rothmann, Susan, page 169
Second Prize
McBride, JoAnne, page 151
Third Prize
Neidrauer, Frances J., page 165
SIT-DOWN SWEETS
First Prize
McKelvy, Patricia, page 176
Second Prize
Gammel, Jana, page 178
Third Prize
Laughlin, Martha, page 192
BLUE RIBBON EXTRAS
First Prize
Collins, Joan L., page 199
Second Prize
Whitt, Vicki, page 199
Third Prize
Sharp, Marlene, page 203
HONORABLE MENTION
Adams, Julie, page 164
Amedee, Dorothy, page 86
Anand, Susie, page 31
Andrews, Tina, page 137
Atkinson, Donna, page 17
Ayers, Virginia, page 80
Bacon, Merilee, page 36
Bacon, Vera, page 207
Badstibner, Suzanne M., page 63
Balfour, Donita, page 98
Bartkowiak, Mary, page 206
Barton, Judy, page 8
Baxley, Susan M., page 174
Beauchamp, Kathy, page 30
Beaver, Coeta, page 126
Beaver, Vickie L., page 21
Beddinger, Diane, page 106
Bentlage, Cindy, page 117
Bicking, Jennifer, page 113
Bixenman, Colleen, page 104
Black, Angela, page 46
Bland, Harriette S., page 17
Blue, Amy Beth, page 82
Boling, Sharon L., page 112
Bolt, Wilburn (Kathleen), page 108
Bond, Marianna, page 42
Boone, Jody, page 186
Boone, Patti, page 96
Bowen, Patsy, page 107
Boyd, Hrefna Valdis, page 92
Bradley, Becky, page 19
Brailey, Bette, page 22
Brantley, Sharlene, page 40
Brazeal, Carol, page 116
Brennan, Amie, page 135
Bressler, Margaret W.S., page 101
Brewer, Sheri, page 22
Brondel, Karen, page 117
Brown, Marilyn, page 23
Brushaber, Lucy, page 95
Bull, Glenda, page 179
Bullerman, Norma, page 163
Burrus, Billie, page 124
Byatt, Betty, page 208
Byerly, Sarah, page 103
Callihan, Johnny (Robbi), page 135
Carr, Ralph (Mildred), page 123
Chamberlain, Beth, page 210
Charles, Marilyn M., page 193
Christensen, Florence, page 61
Christiansen, Mary, page 118
Clapton, Donna, page 20
Collins, Lisa, page 35
Comer, Marnell, page 111
Conne, Donna, page 170
Connor, Joan, page 94
Crager, Claudia, page 58
Cram, Marina, page 122
Creekmore, Mary, page 169
Crosby, Dolores, page 35
Cunningham, Roberta, page 45
Cunningham, Susan, page 166
Cyphery, Carol, page 124
Dalpiaz, Kristen, page 38
Darst, Theresa, page 85
Davis-Sweat, Shiela, page 30
Dawson, Barbara M., page 166
DeLauriea, Lucille, page 73
DeVore, Eleanor, page 114
Dickinson, Brenda, page 154
Dighero, Tammy, page 26
Dingess, Margaret A., page 115
Dudley, Wanda E., page 189
Duke, Lisa, page 101
Eads, Nancy, page 102
Eaton, Lucy, page 169
Eek, Joanne, page 91
Elling, JoAnne, page 105
Faulhaber, Marie, page 59
Feebeck, Jo, page 109
Ferraro, Frances W., page 162
Fieber, Tracey, page 209
Finleyson, Cynthia K., page 89
Fleming, Anne, page 90
Forbes, Audrey, page 128
Freese, Stacy, page 50
Furey, Katherine, page 206
Gatzke, Shirley, page 26
Gawley, S. Marlene, page 28
Gebhardt, Margaret, page 114
Gelhaus, E. Fay, page 106
Gholston, Marlyce, page 50
Gieselman, Judy, page 189
Gilks, Colleen, page 19
Godfrey, Terrye, page 109
Golden, Mary, page 146
Gordon, Jeanne, page 158
Goving, Elaine, page 207
Grim, Myrtle D., page 111
Gross, Jeannie, page 143
Grubb, Joyce A., page 161
Gumfory, Darlene M., page 13
Gunderson, Heather, page 177
Guthrie, Sharon, page 152
Hague, Kay, page 167
Hannan, Laura, page 36
Hansen, Janet, page 37
Harper, Ruth A., page 34
Hasson, Joyce E., page 125
Hathaway, Nancy, page 65
Hayes, Lori, page 93
Head, Danielle, page 48
Hedderson, Maria, page 137
Hendrick, Carolyn, page 132
Hill, Brenda C., page 144
Hillmann, Dorothy, page 60
Hoad, Bert (Catherine), page 14
Hoendorf, Kimberly Ann, page 137

Holliday, Belinda, page 116
Holst, Cordelia M., page 33
Holste, Susan, page 143
Holtsclaw, Jane, page 154
Huggard, Barbara, page 187
Hughey, Mickey, page 43
Hutton, Shelly, page 167
Jensen, Jacquelynn L., page 157
Johnson, Jennifer, page 172
Jones, Cathy, page 191
Jones, Robin, page 47
Kahler, Ruth, page 204
Kaiser, Dorothy, page 74
Kaufman, Mary, page 51
Kaul, Stephanie, page 197
Keele, Teresa, page 82
Kelle, Lois, page 155
Keller, Joyce, page 146
Kellestine, Diann, page 129
Kimbro, Kari, page 136
King, Melba S., page 175
Kirk, Barbara, page 130
Kirkhart, Nena, page 51
Knox, Linda, page 81
Koczent, Barbara, page 171
Korb, Jolene, page 142
Kraft, Lauri Ann, page 200
Kreklewich, Lynda, page 118
Kress, Helen, page 179
Kruse, Patti, page 66
Lakeman, Evelyn, page 160
LaMunyan, Kandie, page 172
Lannholm, Darlene K., page 51
Lauer, Phyllis, page 188
Laughlin, Neta, page 153
Leclair, Virginia, page 84
Lee, Doris, page 194
Leeder, Dorothy, page 145
Leetsch, Connie, page 45
Leonard, Ann, page 184
Leoty, Margaret, page 68
Lepine, Juliette, page 133
Lester, Lynn, page 56
Leszczewicz, Virginia, page 147
Lewis, Teresa, page 209
Lotz, Carolyn, page 24
Lowe, Billie K., page 70
Loyd, Kathy, page 114
Lunn, Juanita, page 150
Lyons, Patricia K., page 180
Manuel, Diana, page 66
Marker, Crystal, page 28
Mason, Jeannie, page 52
Massey, Lyn, page 15
Massingham, Karen, page 71
Mather, Patricia, page 132
Maulsby, Catherine, page 30
McAtee, Gayla, page 208
McBride, Alice, page 67
McCandless, Bobbie, page 196
McCray, Micki, page 167
McKenzie, Linda, page 153
McLemore, Charlotte, page 59
McNeeley, Myrna, page 35
Meister, Tamalea, page 141
Middleton, Nancy J., page 16
Miles, Virginia, page 201
Miller, Dolores, page 126
Miller, Judy, page 153
Moorman, Becky, page 204
Morris, Louise, page 11
Morris, Tanya, page 78
Nelson, Doreen, page 61
Nelson, Sue, page 187
Nichol, Margie, page 211
Nichols, Alice, page 55
Nobbe, Natasha N., page 188
Nye, Myrtle, page 92
Oian, Irene, page 62
Olson, Marion, page 113
Ousey, Kirsten, page 27
Ozark, Betty, page 205
Panzer, Carol, page 156
Paris, Marsha, page 88
Patterson, Molly A., page 15
Patterson, Norma, page 32
Peterson, Joan M., page 89
Petrunak, Elizabeth, page 32
Pilling, Linda, page 147
Pointer, Denise M., page 16
Pollak, Bobbe, page 31
Potyka, Pat, page 29
Powell, Emma Irene, page 204
Prevost, Lynne, page 25
Rafferty, Diane L., page 196
Rand, Kathy, page 117
Randolph, Tatia D., page 105
Rankin, Valerie, page 104
Rawlings, Geneva, page 35
Reiter, Phyllis, page 108
Renvelle, Roberta, page 211
Reynolds, Jeannette, page 202
Rhodes, Val, page 94
Richards, Mary, page 111
Richards, Pamela, page 191
Rine-Steagal, Sue, page 74
Robertson, Linda, page 139
Robinson, Marie, page 96
Rockers, Barb, page 168
Rose, Elisa F., page 107
Ross, Charlie E., page 93
Rundlett, Susan, page 84
Ruppel-Rada, Joyce, page 52
Saveraid, Jean E., page 202
Scharch, Pat, page 178
Schenck, Jo, page 33
Schoenborn, Marilyn J., page 161
Scholes, Rebecca A., page 98
Schroder, Myrna, page 75
Schuler, Kitty, page 190
Seachrist, Estelle D., page 107
Seger, Joyce, page 21
Seipel, Lucille (Becky), page 111
Sherstone, Barb, page 107
Shipston, Julie, page 77
Shorey, Mary Patricia, page 75
Short, Cheryl, page 23
Shrum, Becki, page 135
Shwaluk, Bonnie, page 112
Simpson, Barbara, page 185
Singley, Karen, page 24
Sjogren, Donna, page 42
Skatlum, Pat, page 208
Skonseng, Joellen, page 140
Smirl, Jane, page 133
Smith, Carolyn, page 60
Smith, Evelyn, page 53
Smith, Michelle, page 209
Sowadzki, Betty, page 83
Sparks, Joyce, page 41
Sproule, Marie, page 64
Stahl, Lynne, page 29
Staller, Maureen B., page 92
Starring, Becky, page 41
Steely, Joy, page 40
Steendahl, Clara, page 180
Stevens, Vikki, page 159
Stockebrand, Janet, page 9
Stoltenberg, Barbara, page 27
Stombock, Barbie, page 89
Stone, Laurie, page 141
Stricklin, Nikki, page 56
Sudduth, Frances, page 190
Summers, Roberta, page 87
Summers, Sally, page 61
Theodore, Susan, page 97
Thompson, Patricia, page 159
Throm, Robin, page 44
Todd, Natalie H., page 157
Trahan, Cindy, page 183
Tucker, Betty Jo, page 198
Van Stolk, Teddy, page 18
Vieregge, Debbie, page 104
Vokart, Dayla, page 127
Waldner, Janine, page 20
Walls, Bonnie, page 198
Wantiez, Wanda, page 72
Warner, Sue, page 197
Waryk, Janice, page 79
Watson, Sue, page 177
Weakland, Kay, page 77
Weber, Kayce L., page 14
Weir, Irene, page 43
Wells, Shirley J., page 65
Wenthe, Sandra, page 168
Wheeler, Ellen L., page 190
Whidden, Sandy, page 12
Whitacre, Julie, page 57
White, Kim, page 79
Whitworth, Ida M., page 121
Whitworth, Pat, page 122
Wilkie, Melva J., page 152
Williams, Janet, page 110
Wilson, Jeannette, page 96
Wilson, June, page 164
Windle, Betty Scholl, page 194
Wylie, Caryl, page 38
Yates, Debbie, page 133
Young, Susan L., page 162

Index

Beta Sigma Phi Cookbooks

available from *Favorite Recipes® Press* are chock-full of home-tested recipes from Beta Sigma Phi members that earn you the best compliment of all... "More Please!"

Every cookbook includes:

- ✩ color photos or black-and-white photos
- ✩ delicious, family-pleasing recipes
- ✩ lay-flat binding
- ✩ wipe-clean color covers
- ✩ easy-to-read format
- ✩ comprehensive index

To place your order, call our **toll free** number **1-800-251-1520** or clip and mail the convenient form below.

BETA SIGMA PHI COOKBOOKS	Item #	Qty.	U.S. Retail Price	Canadian Retail Price	Total
The Best of Beta Sigma Phi Cookbook	88285		$9.95	$12.95	
Home Sweet Home Cooking: Company's Coming	01260		$9.95	$12.95	
Home Sweet Home Cooking: Family Favorites	01252		$9.95	$12.95	
Food In The Fast Lane	94323		$9.95	$12.95	
Shipping and Handling		1	$1.95	$2.95	
TOTAL AMOUNT					

☐ Payment Enclosed
☐ Please Charge My ☐ MasterCard ☐ Visa ☐ Discover

Canadian orders: Visa or checks only

Signature ____________________

Account Number ____________________

Name ____________________

Address ____________________

City ____________ State ____ Zip ______

No COD orders please.
Call our toll free number for faster ordering.
Prices subject to change.
Books offered subject to availability.
Please allow 30 days for delivery.

Mail completed order form to:

Favorite Recipes® Press
P.O. Box 305141
Nashville, TN 37230